W9-BYZ-942

The Beer Lover's Guide to the USA

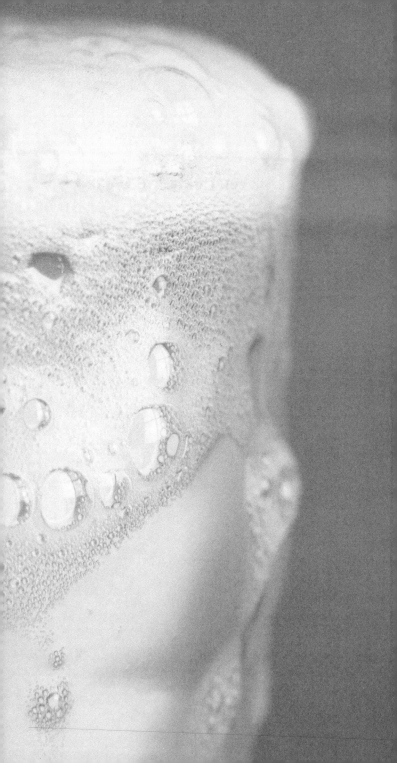

The
BEER
LOVER'S
GUIDE
to the USA

Brewpubs, Taverns, and Good Beer Bars

Stan Hieronymous and Daria Labinsky

St. Martin's Griffin
New York

Book design by Judith Stagnitto Abbate/ABBATE DESIGN

ISBN 0-312-24664-1

First Edition: March 2000

10   9   8   7   6   5   4   3   2   1

Contents

Acknowledgments

To thank all the people who made this book a reality and made it better simply is not possible. We are in debt to every editor who has encouraged our writing; to every writer whose work has helped us; to all the brewers and publicans who put making and serving quality beers ahead of making money; and to all our fellow beer drinkers.

Once in Gillette, Wyoming, a perfect stranger got into his pickup truck and led us across town to Humphrey's Bar & Grill, pointed to it as we arrived, then drove off before we could even buy him a beer.

We thank him and all the others to whom we still owe a beer.

Foreword:
Staying out of the Gloop

----

by Michael Jackson

Where in the world would you find the most diverse range of beers? Germany? Belgium? Britain? None of the above. The various states of Germany scarcely recognize each other's beers, let alone those of Belgium or Britain. Those latter countries are less parochial, but not nearly as cosmopolitan in their beer selections as the United States.

Almost every style of beer made in the great brewing nations is imported to the U.S. Better still, most styles are also made by American breweries, whether national or regional, micro or brewpub.

Nowhere in the world are so many beers available as in the U.S. In some states—but by no means all—supermarkets offer huge selections. The snag is that you can't normally sit down for a beer with your partner, or lean against a bar with your buddies, in a supermarket. It is not always easy to find a bar, pub, or restaurant with a good selection of beers, and even more difficult to find one that combines that virtue with your every other requirement.

You want to turn off the interstate for a good meal washed down with something characterful? You fancy a flavorsome beer in a restful corner bar in a strange town? You could handle an evening of brews and barbecue (and perhaps blues)? Whether you are staying at a Motel 6 or in the Ritz Carlton, you cannot rely on the hotel to know the locale of a convenient Kölsch, abbey brew, or India pale ale.

Inquire locally and you may be greeted by blank looks, or directed to the place in town with the "world famous" polystyrene-and-gloop dinner, biggest television screens, or brashest sign. Some people, unaccountably, do not drink beer or know a good bar from a contrived "leisure experience;" their advice is highly suspect. Millions of people do regularly enjoy a brew, but fewer of us demand that it taste of malt and hops. For discerning folk like you and me, that can be a desperate requirement.

Some of life's frustrations are hard to take, such as having been directed to a bland, bloating brewski in a charming town like High Krausen, Minnesota, then learning a week later that we missed a delicious, distinctive, new beer on tap on the rehabbed riverside.

Such distress can be avoid by consulting the pages that follow. So let us offer a prayer of thanks to Saint Arnold for the diligent research of Stan Hieronymus and Daria Labinsky.

MICHAEL JACKSON *is the world's leading writer on beer. His books include* Ultimate Beer, Michael Jackson's Beer Companion, *and the* Simon & Schuster Pocket Guide to Beer. *His work is also available at Michael Jackson's Beer Hunter on the Internet (www.beerhunter.com).*

Introduction

In the early 1990s, when we began to keep track of interesting places where we could drink interesting beer, we never envisioned that the number of spots we'd find would fill 340 pages. At the outset, we used Pat Baker's *Beer and Bar Atlas,* a booklet he put together in 1988 with the help of friends around the country. It listed fewer than 300 beer joints in the United States, included places with often modest beer lists, and was the only thing like it around.

We started our own journey with a few hundred places in our database. When we completed the *Beer Travelers Guide* in 1995, we were able to include all 1,700 spots we had found by then. Now, even though our standards have become stricter, our database has grown past 4,000.

Plenty of other statistics document the explosion of interest in beer with flavor. The numbers, however, don't capture the pure delight of sitting out back at Humphrey's Bar & Grill in Gillette, Wyoming, sipping a Kessler Doppelbock and watching regulars pitch horseshoes. Or the literally eye-opening experience of washing down Belgian waffles with Delirium Tremens—served in a Delirium Tremens glass—during brunch at the Bistrot Belgique Gourmande in Occoquan, Virginia. We don't care that there are now more than 1,000 brewpubs in the United States, or more than sixty bars that offer more than fifty beers on tap, when we are enjoying a single glass of Stoudt's Honey Double Mai-Bock at the Old Bay in New Brunswick, New Jersey, and talking to a person who just minutes before was a total stranger about which of singer-songwriter Robert Earl Keen's CDs is his "signature" work.

While it's moments like these that we treasure, we took readers' interests into account in deciding which places to include in this book and which ones to write about in more detail. We know that many people want to drink beer only where it is brewed, so the brewpub list is particularly extensive. We know how popular both Irish and British pubs are, and how dependable German restaurants are, so we included many of them, although they may not offer the range of beers you'll find elsewhere.

We had to make some hard decisions to keep this book from being twice as thick. In order to provide geographic diversity, in beer-rich areas we limited the number of places that receive complete portraits. The fact is, there might be one hundred taverns in Seattle that would be considered beer Meccas if they moved to other parts of the country, but we only wrote about thirty.

This book is intended for all those who want to find interesting places to enjoy specialty beer. It's meant not only for those driving on Interstate 80 from New York to San Francisco, but also for locals in St. Louis, Athens, Georgia, and Santa Fe, New Mexico, who are looking for new beer spots.

How to Use the Book

The listings are pretty straightforward. States are in alphabetical order, and cities are listed alphabetically within the states. Pubs described in detail are listed first in a city, followed by other interesting spots. At the end of each state is another list of interesting places in cities not previously listed.

We generally include a place that is a member of a chain just once. There are thirty-nine Old Chicagos, for instance. You'll find the charter member listed under Boulder, Colorado; we run only the addresses and phone numbers of the others, but you can assume they are all two-star spots. In some cases, where a chain is confined to a smaller region—like the Winking Lizard bars in the Cleveland area—we only describe one and mention that there are others. We have not listed members of the Bennigan's or bw-3 chains (with one exception), although both usually offer at least ten draft choices at any location. Bennigan's seriously upgraded the beer selection at each of its 300 or so outlets a few years ago, and even did some in-pub training to teach the staff about beer. Some offer a few regional beers, but a Bennigan's in Dallas doesn't differ a whole lot from one in Bloomington, Illinois.

Next to the name of some establishments you'll see this icon ⓑ, which denotes places that are brewpubs; microbreweries with restaurants and/or tasting rooms—places where you can buy a glass of beer brewed on-site. Some may also offer $25 entrees, while others sell only potato chips. You'll also see a rating (more about that later) and information about when the place is open. Some pubs have varying hours; while we've tried to give you a good time frame in a small amount of space, call for details if you are going particularly early or after 10:30 P.M. on a weeknight.

Food is described in general terms. British pub fare, Irish pub fare, German restaurant, Belgian cuisine, and similar descriptions are pretty specific. However, we also use the terms "tavern fare" and "brewpub fare," and often owners will note, "We don't just serve bar food," or, "We are a restaurant, not just a brewpub." Granted, many of the first brewpubs featured basic "pub grub"— burgers, fried foods, hot wings, and the like—but that was in the mid-1980s. Today, brewpubs serve everything from tapas to steak to goat cheese and sun-dried tomatoes, and we expect brewpub fare to be more diverse than Applebee's. Many brewpub menus now offer dishes designed to be served with beer or that include beer as one of the ingredients; and while tavern fare may be as basic as hamburgers and warm sandwiches, many taverns put food right out on the bar that is as innovative and well-made as you'd expect to find in a full-service restaurant.

We've also included smoking rules, for obvious reasons. Quite honestly, in some one-room places with separate smoking sections, the smoke is not particularly separate. Meanwhile, a few bars that permit smoking throughout put in ventilation systems that make them seem almost smoke-free. Some states have mandated smoking rules for restaurants and/or bars and expect establishments to enforce the rules, which they may or may not do; you may find yourself in a brewpub in California and see the bartender hand a patron a book of matches while telling him or her that smoking in the pub is against state law.

The descriptions are intended to indicate what sets a place apart, with beer the most important criterion. We may write about the food or the ambience, then other amenities such as a large number of single-malt whiskies or an outstanding wine selection. We're more likely to describe what's available on tap rather than in bottles, except where the bottle selection is overwhelming. We may also note whether a place serves beer via a beer engine (also know as a handpump)—it may or may not be cask-conditioned ale like you would expect in England, but it's definitely not mainstream.

If you discover a place you really want to try and start planning an evening around a visit, we suggest you call first. Brewpubs, restaurants, and bars go out of business every day, even great ones.

About the Ratings

Rating places is fun when it's just between the two of us, but not so easy when it's for public consumption. We wish every bar or brewpub was a four-star stop, but they're not. We wish that readers wouldn't assume that a four-star bar is four times better than one with one star, but we know they will. The fact is, the difference between the ninety-nine–plus percent of the bars in this country that aren't in this book and the ones in this book that receive no stars is far greater than the difference between those with no stars and four.

Were we to assign words, one star would equal Very Good, two Excellent, three Superior, four Extraordinary.

The ratings start with beer selection, but how it is cared for and presented is nearly as important. We set a somewhat arbitrary rule that no place with more than sixty taps would receive four stars. It wasn't easy, because many of these bars are run by owners who are at the forefront in promoting flavorful beer. However, we decided we had to draw a line somewhere, and while places with bunches of taps are fun, there is a greater danger that beer won't be presented at its peak. Even though some multi-taps go to great lengths to avoid this, they simply can't guarantee the beer quality as well as a properly-run establishment with twenty or thirty handles can.

We also tend to visit places at all hours—to review a dozen bars in a day, you have to start pretty early, sometimes drawing curious looks from barkeeps. We've been to a lot of joints that seemed much friendlier at four in the afternoon than at ten-thirty on a Friday night when we revisited. Food critics at large newspapers may test a restaurant several times and sample most of the menu before making their rating. We don't have that luxury, and that's one of the reasons we know not to take ourselves too seriously.

While beer is most important, food and ambience earn places

additional stars. For instance, Embudo Station gets an extra star because it sits in a canyon alongside the Rio Grande in Northern New Mexico. Blue Moon in Seattle gets one because of its character, even though that includes a lot of dust and old Grateful Dead posters that patrons familiar with sparkling-new brewpubs might find unappealing.

Just as you would not expect Greek and Italian restaurants receiving two-star ratings to be alike, brewpubs with equal ratings may be equally different. For instance, Vino's Brewpub and River-Rock Brewery, both in Little Rock, Arkansas, are excellent places. However, RiverRock offers a broader menu and range of house beers, while Vino's is a grittier bar. "We're a little too laid back, a little too weird for a lot of people," owner Henry Lee points out.

We think beer should be inclusive. Many of our friends and relatives prefer mainstream beers. If they will humor us by picking a place where we can drink beer we like, it seems only fair that when we go to a bar or restaurant, they can enjoy their favorites. Remember, the book is about the places that serve the beer drinker as well as the beer itself. The two are closely connected. Booming interest in flavorful beer certainly increased the number of choices in the 1990s, but rightfully raised expectations. Now it's not enough to serve any old beer brewed on-premise. It should be well-made. It's not enough to offer Spaten, Samuel Adams, Sierra Nevada, and a locally brewed beer on tap. The lines should be clean, the beer should be fresh, and it shouldn't be served ice cold.

There was a bit of a gold rush mentality in the mid-1990s. Brewpubs opened without much concern about the quality of their beer (or even the quality of food and service). Bars added taps, sometimes dozens of taps, just so they could advertise that novelty.

The fact is, beer in the United States is primarily a commodity, consumed mostly in the home. Because taste is not a major consideration for most drinkers, major brewers who dominate the market can focus on things other than taste. They can pasteurize and filter the heck out of beer to extend its shelf life and protect it against poor handling before and after it reaches the consumer.

They do their best to ship a commodity that's equally foolproof for bar owners. Where legal, beer distributors (often working in partnership with major breweries) may take care of virtually everything for the bars, not only delivering kegs of beer but hooking them up to the taps, paying to have those taps cleaned, and—of course—plastering advertising all over the bar.

Craft beer is more delicate. It may have to be babied on its way to being dispensed and is more likely to thrive in a friendly environment. So are we all.

Finally, we don't claim to have visited every place listed here, though we've certainly tried. It's a big country, and there are places that too many people whose opinions we value have recommended too strongly for us to leave out. They're at the top of our list to visit next. Hope to see you there.

—Stan & Daria
June 1999

Don't Drink and Drive

There are good reasons this book isn't called *Two for the Road* or *Drink Your Way Across America*. There is nothing funny about drinking and driving. A growing number of states have toughened their drinking and driving laws, with many of them declaring drivers with a blood-alcohol level of .08 percent legally drunk.

How many beers is that? In theory, a 160-pound person can consume four twelve-ounce bottles of "average strength" beer in an hour before his or her blood-alcohol level reaches .08 percent and five before it gets to .10 percent. Of course, most brewpubs and interesting bars serve beer in fourteen-, sixteen- or even twenty-ounce glasses.

There are many variables beyond weight that determine how you may be affected by alcohol, such as whether you are drinking on a full or empty stomach, the altitude at which you are drinking, whether you are a man or a woman, your mood, the strength of the beer, etc.

Although some customers complain, the Vermont Pub & Brewery in Burlington, Vermont, limits customers to two pints an hour, knowing full well alcohol has a cumulative effect. After forty-eight ounces in the first hour, the "average" 160-pound person need drink only twelve more ounces in the next hour to have a blood-alcohol level of .09 percent.

At Vermont Pub and a sibling brewery in West Lebanon, New Hampshire, Ben Franklin's saying, "all things in moderation," is beautifully displayed in etched glass. It is worth remembering whenever and wherever you drink.

The Beer Lover's Guide to the USA

STATE-BY-STATE

LISTINGS

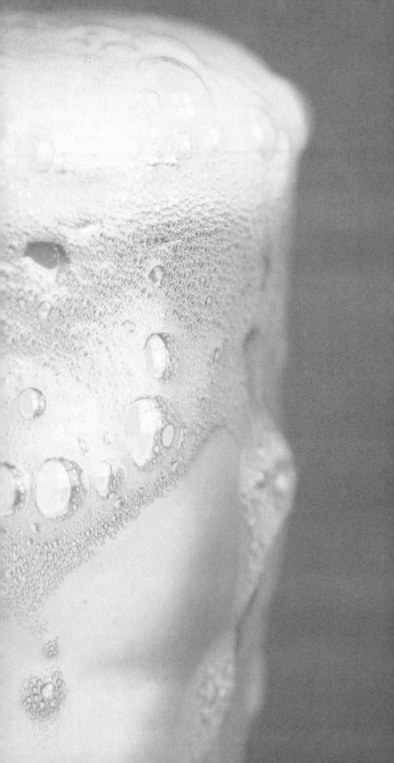

ALABAMA

Regional beers to look for: Vulcan Brewery/Birmingham products, particularly Red Mountain Red Ale.
Just for fun: Zydeco, in Birmingham. Signed pictures of Martin Milner and Casey Kasem, excellent live music.
Best city for a pub crawl: Birmingham.

BIRMINGHAM

Dave's Pub
20th St. & 12th Ave. S., 205-933-4030
★☆☆☆   3 P.M.–4 A.M.
Food: No kitchen   *Smoking:* Throughout

Eighteen beers on draft, solid bottle selection. Draft choices focus on imports, with rotating selection of local beers. Voted Birmingham's best bar by readers of the local paper.

Dugan's
2011 Highland Ave. S., 205-933-9020
☆☆☆☆   Lunch–late
Food: Tavern fare   *Smoking:* Throughout

A lively fixture in Five Points for more than twenty-five years. Irish-influenced pub, but cross-section of craft and imports available from nine taps.

Magic City Brewery Ⓑ
420 21st St. S., 205-328-2739
★☆☆☆   Lunch–late
Food: Brewpub fare   *Smoking:* Separate sections

Immaculate, with a beautiful three-sided bar wrapping around the brewery, which is behind glass in the center of the pub. Drinkable beers, some pushing the Alabama alcohol limits.

Zydeco
2001 15th Ave. S., 205-933-1032
★☆☆☆   Dinner–late (closed Sundays)
Food: Cajun/creole   *Smoking:* Throughout

Seventeen taps include a little of everything. Live music (an eclectic mix) on the large outdoor patio. Decorated in New Orleans funk (Elvis bust, Santa hat, Mardi Gras beads on the back bar).

Also in Birmingham
Mill Brewery, Bakery & Eatery, 1035 20th St. S., 205-939-3001.
   The pub's beer is actually made at a microbrewery next door.
Taco Mac, 1914 11th Ave. S., 205-322-0088. Twenty-five taps
   and, like Taco Macs in Atlanta, specializing in sports and hot
   wings.

DOTHAN

Poplar Head Mule Co. Ⓑ
155 S. St. Andrew St., 334-794-7991
  ☆☆☆☆ 11 A.M.–late
Food: Tavern fare *Smoking:* Throughout

Located in an old storefront, with a beautiful back bar. Good
food, well-made though not particularly adventurous beer.

MONTGOMERY

Montgomery Brewing Ⓑ
12 W. Jefferson St., 334-834-2739
  ★☆☆☆ Lunch–late (opens at 3 P.M. weekends)
Food: Brewpub fare *Smoking:* Separate sections

Located in a former railroad equipment storage warehouse, and
one of Montgomery's most popular restaurants. The lightest
beers are best-sellers.

Also in Alabama
Auburn: Little Ireland Pub, 122-B Magnolia, 334-821-5634.
   Irish pub.
Huntsville: Finnegan's, 3310 Memorial Parkway SW, 256-881-
   9732. Irish pub.
Mobile: Port City Brewery, 225 Dauphin St., 334-438-2739.
   Brewpub.

Regional beers to look for: Alaskan Brewing's beers, including the classic Smoked Porter. Also, many Northwest craft beers are available in Alaska.

Essential stops: Humpy's in Anchorage. They print a new beer menu every night that includes a list of kegs that will go on if one kicks.

Just for fun: The Hangar on the Wharf in Juneau. Watch the planes come and go.

Best city for a pub crawl: Anchorage.

ANCHORAGE

Chilkoot Charlie's
2435 Spenard Road, 907-272-1010

★☆☆☆   Before noon–late

Food: Tavern fare   *Smoking:* Separate sections

A rambling, rustic Alaskan saloon with six bars, three stages, and seating on padded tree stumps and kegs. Mainstream beers, imports, and micros all available. Set national records for one-night sales of everything from St. Pauli Girl (198 cases) to Coors Extra Gold to Stoli.

Glacier Brewhouse ⓑ
737 W. 5th Ave., 907-274-2739

★☆☆☆   11 A.M.–11 P.M. (opens at 4 P.M. Sundays)

Food: Brewpub fare   *Smoking:* Separate sections

An upscale restaurant stylishly decorated with wood and stone, sporting a hunting lodge motif. Specializing in Alaskan seafood.

Humpy's Great Alaskan Ale House
610 W. 6th Ave., 907-276-2337

★★★⯪   Lunch–very late

Food: Tavern fare plus   *Smoking:* Throughout

The best micros from the West are available, forty-plus on tap plus two handpumps, and the lineup changes nightly. Solid selection of import beers in bottles, single malts, and single-batch bourbons. Excellent food specials, particularly fish.

Snow Goose Restaurant Ⓑ
717 W. 3rd Ave., 907-277-7727
★★☆☆   11:30 A.M.–closing (call for winter hours)
Food: Full menu   *Smoking:* Separate sections

The pub, and its patio in the summer, offer a lovely view of Cook Inlet that's perfect for watching whales. Plenty of full-bodied beers, several of them award winners.

Also in Anchorage
Cusak's Brewpub, 589 N. Northern Lights, 907-278-2739. Brewpub.

Harry's Bar & Grill, 101 W. Benson Blvd., 907-561-5317. Restaurant with twenty-four taps.

Moose's Tooth Pub & Pizzeria, 3300 Old Seward Highway, 907-258-2537. Brewpub.

EAGLE RIVER

Regal Eagle Brewery Ⓑ
11501 Old Glenn Highway, 907-694-9120
★☆☆☆   6 A.M.–10 P.M.
Food: Full menu   *Smoking:* Separate sections

Alaska's first brewpub welcomes locals and tourists with both hunting trophies and antiques. Serves a full range of beer styles.

FAIRBANKS

Gold Rush Saloon
3399 Peger Road, 907-456-6410
★☆☆☆   10 A.M.–2 A.M.
Food: Tavern fare   *Smoking:* Throughout

The state's largest darts bar (sixteen lanes) features a taproom with twenty-four Alaskan and Northwest craft beers on tap.

Also in Fairbanks
Chena Pump House, 796 Chena Pump Road, 907-479-8452. Tavern.

Fairbanks Princess Hotel, 4477 Pikes Landing Road, 907-455-4477. Hotel/bar.

JUNEAU

The Hangar on the Wharf
2 Market Way, 907-586-5018

★★☆☆   11 A.M.–10 P.M.

Food: Tavern fare   *Smoking:* Separate sections

Set on a wharf and formerly a hangar for seaplanes. The wharf-side wall is glass, so patrons can watch seaplanes take off and land. Twenty-six taps offer imports, domestics, and micro-brews, including Alaskan beers.

Also in Juneau
Alaskan Hotel Bar, 167 S. Franklin St., 907-586-1000. Bar.

Armadillo Tex-Mex Cafe, 431 S. Franklin St., 907-586-1880. Brewpub.

Red Dog Saloon, 159 S. Franklin St., 907-586-9954. Bar.

Also in Alaska
Skagway: Skagway Brewing, 3rd and Broadway, 907-983-2451. Brewpub.

ARIZONA

Regional beers to look for: Those from Nimbus Brewing, Four Peaks Brewing, Sonora Brewing, and Oak Creek Brewing.

Essential stops: Cougan's Brewery & Grill in Glendale; Four Peaks in Tempe; Timberwolf Pub in Tempe.

Just for fun: Bandersnatch Brewpub in Tempe. Join the "Beer in the Face Club."

Best city for a pub crawl: Tempe.

CAVE CREEK

The Satisfied Frog/Cave Creek Brewing ⓑ
6245 E. Cave Creek Road, 602-488-3317
★☆☆☆   11 A.M.–closing
Food: Brewpub fare   *Smoking:* Separate sections

Across the street from the Horny Toad, hence the name. House beers are more interesting than the Crazy Ed's chili beers sold nationally.

FLAGSTAFF

Beaver Street Brewery ⓑ
11 S. Beaver St., 520-779-0079
★☆☆☆   11:30 A.M.–midnight
Food: Brewpub fare   *Smoking:* Separate sections

Operates in a renovated grocery store, with a classic bar on the tavern side and an excellent mountain view from the patio. Innovative comfort food, solid beer.

Flagstaff Brewing ⓑ
16 E. Route 66, 520-773-1442
★☆☆☆   11 A.M.–1 A.M.
Food: Limited menu   *Smoking:* Separate sections

Two-room pub in old brick building on Route 66, with music in side room. Laid-back bar area, Deadhead friendly, serving house beers (one on handpump) and fine guest products.

Mogollon Brewing Co. Ⓑ
15 N. Agassiz, 520-773-8950
    ★☆☆☆   1 P.M.–1 A.M.
    Food: No kitchen (order in)   *Smoking:* Throughout

No division between tasting room and microbrewery in this stone building. Chainsaw above the pool table, stage for live music, easy chairs.

Uptown Billiards
114 N. Leroux St., 520-773-0551
    ★★⯪☆   1 P.M.–1 A.M.
    Food: No kitchen   *Smoking:* None indoors

Upscale pool hall with thirty-eight beers—mostly micros and imports—on tap, plus an excellent wine list. Beer meticulously cared for. Large humidor, though smoking is only allowed on patio.

GLENDALE

Cougan's Brewery & Grill Ⓑ
7640 W. Bell Road, 602-878-8822
    ★★★☆   11:30 A.M.–11 P.M. (10:30 A.M.–midnight Fridays and Saturdays)
    Food: Upscale brewpub fare   *Smoking:* Separate sections

Beautifully appointed, quiet enough for conversation, yet loud enough that children don't seem out of place. Excellent, nicely presented food and assertive beer.

PHOENIX

Coyote Springs Ⓑ
4883 N. 20th St., 602-468-0403
    ★★☆☆   11 A.M.–1 A.M.
    Food: Brewpub fare   *Smoking:* Separate sections

Down-to-earth beer place, from the hundred-year-old bar to the brewing specs posted on a board beside the entrance to the inviting patio. Coyote Springs also has a pub at 122 E. Washington that serves its beer and other craft products.

Felsen Haus
1008 E. Camelback, 602-277-1119
    ☆☆☆☆   11:30 A.M.–9 P.M. (10 P.M. Fridays and Saturdays)
Food: German fare   *Smoking:* Throughout

German to the core, with wood beams, German travel posters on the wall, and a polka band on weekends. Authentic German dishes, solid selection of German beers on tap, German cocktails.

George & Dragon
4240 N. Central Ave., 602-241-0018
    ★☆☆☆   11 A.M.–1 A.M.
Food: British pub fare   *Smoking:* Separate sections

State's first British pub. Most of the twenty-one draft selections are UK products. British menu, music, European soccer on the big-screen TV.

Lagerfields
12601 N. Paradise Village Parkway, 602-765-0059
    ★☆☆☆   3 P.M.–late (opens 11 A.M. weekends)
Food: Tavern fare   *Smoking:* Separate sections

Subdued sports bar, with plenty of televisions but not the other trappings. The fifteen draft choices include a nice selection of regional products.

Leinenkugel's Ballyard Brewery   Ⓑ
201 S. Fourth St., 602-462-3800
    ★★☆☆   11 A.M.–closing (open Sundays for home games only)
Food: Brewpub fare   *Smoking:* Separate sections

Gigantic brewpub at the Bank One Ballpark. Hall-of-Famer Robin Yount is a partner, the bar is 60 feet, six inches long, and the stools are topped with bases. Serves a thirst-quenching traditional hefeweizen.

McCraffey's Irish Pub
18 W. Monroe, 602-253-6081
    ★☆☆☆   10:30 A.M.–1 A.M. (9 A.M. Sundays)
Food: Irish pub fare plus   *Smoking:* Throughout

Downtown hideaway. Dublin native Seamus McCraffey, who was the first bar owner in Arizona to offer Guinness on tap (elsewhere, in 1986), has decorated the place with plenty from home.

PRESCOTT

Moctezuma's
144 S. Montezuma, 520-445-1244
★☆☆☆ Noon–1 A.M.
Food: No kitchen   *Smoking:* Throughout

When a fire ravaged the Palace Bar and most of Whiskey Row in 1900, patrons carried the Palace's ornately carved Brunswick bar to safety across the street, where they allegedly resumed drinking. The Palace, a few doors down, has been beautifully restored but has a limited beer selection. This basic tavern with two pool tables offers a surprisingly wide variety of choices from thirteen taps.

Prescott Brewing Co. Ⓑ
30 W. Gurley St., 520-771-2795
★★★☆ 11 A.M.–1 A.M.
Food: Brewpub fare   *Smoking:* Separate sections

Excellent food and excellent beer on the historic town square. Breweriana sets tone in bar, while two other dining areas are more family-oriented.

Also in Prescott
Gurley St. Grill, 230 W. Gurley, 520-445-3388. Thirteen beers on tap.
Murphy's, 102 N. Cortez, 520-445-4044. Restaurant.

SCOTTSDALE

Hops! Bistro and Brewery Ⓑ
7000 E. Camelback Road, 602-945-4677
★★☆☆ 11:30 A.M.–1 A.M.
Food: Bistro fare   *Smoking:* Separate sections

Upscale dining in an upscale setting, offering wood-smoked pizzas and Southwestern cuisine as well as food-friendly beer.

Pinnacle Peak Brewery Ⓑ
10426 E. Jomax Road, 602-585-1599
★☆☆☆ 4 P.M.–after dinner (opens at noon Sundays)
Food: Steakhouse   *Smoking:* Separate sections

Gigantic western steakhouse serving mesquite-broiled steaks and chicken. They've been cutting off patrons' ties for forty years and hanging them on the ceiling. Began brewing beer in 1997.

Also in Scottsdale

Olde English Inn, 7111 E. Thomas Road, 602-941-4915. British pub.

Uptown Brewery No. 2, 6910 E. Shea Blvd., 602-905-5200. Brewpub; offspring of the Uptown in Tempe.

TEMPE

Arizona Roadhouse & Brewery Ⓑ

1120 Apache Blvd., 602-929-9940

★☆☆☆   11 A.M.–1 A.M.

Food: Brewpub fare   *Smoking:* Separate sections

Far too tidy to be a roadhouse, with an attractive bar at the door and the regulars' bar further back. Serves Crazy Fingers, a beef version of chicken fingers, and other, more healthy fare.

Bandersnatch Brewpub Ⓑ

125 E. 5th Ave., 602-966-4438

★☆☆☆   Lunch–late

Food: Tavern fare   *Smoking:* Separate sections

Home of the "Beer in the Face Club," where customers pay $20 to have beer tossed in their face. Pubby, even a little dark, inside, with a sprawling tree-covered patio.

Four Peaks Brewing Co. Ⓑ

1340 E. 8th St., 602-303-9967

★★⯪☆   11 A.M.–late (opens at 1 P.M. Sundays)

Food: Brewpub fare   *Smoking:* Separate sections

A laid-back pub in a spacious former Bordens Creamery building, with a living-room area, complete with couch and armchairs, and an Elvis shrine. Award-winning beers.

Mill Avenue Beer Co.

605 S. Mill Ave., 602-829-6775

★★☆☆   11 A.M.–1 A.M.

Food: Tavern fare   *Smoking:* Separate sections

A storefront bar, long from front to back, with thirty-two draft choices—more imports and well-known micros than Arizona beers.

Timberwolf Pub
740 E. Apache Blvd., 602-517-9383

★★★⯪   4 P.M.–1 A.M.

Food: Tavern fare   *Smoking:* Throughout

A church of beer, with 150 taps bathed by spotlights along the back wall. First in the region to serve many new beers. Like the first Timberwolf in Houston, built to look like a Yukon lodge.

Uptown Brewery by the Streets of New York Ⓑ
1470 E. Southern, 602-777-9600

★★⯪☆   11 A.M.–after dinner

Food: Brewpub fare   *Smoking:* Separate sections

A luxurious pub where the waitstaff dresses in classy black and white. Well-made beer, plus other spirits and cigars. Excellent signature pizzas, sandwiches, and pasta on the upscale side.

Also in Tempe

Alcatraz Brewing Co., Gate 5, Arizona Mills Circle, 602-491-0000. Brewpub; see Indianapolis, Indiana.

Club Rio, 430 N. Scottsdale, 602-894-0533. Dance club with large tap selection.

Gordon Biersch Brewing Co., 420 S. Mill, 602-736-0033. Brewpub; see San Francisco, California.

Murphy's Irish Pub, 1810 E. Apache, 602-894-0103. Irish pub.

Old Chicago, 530 W. Broadway, 602-921-9431. See Boulder, Colorado.

Tombstone Brewing Co., 710 E. Gilbert, 602-967-2337. Brewpub and brew-on-premise.

TUCSON

Gentle Ben's Ⓑ
865 E. University Blvd., 520-624-4177

★☆☆☆   11 A.M.–1 A.M. (closed Sundays)

Food: Brewpub fare   *Smoking:* Separate sections

Once a bar called Dirtbags West, Gentle Ben's was Tucson's original brewpub. Forced to move, and closed for nearly two years in the 1990s, it reopened a little bigger and cleaner. Keeps a wide range of sometimes adventurous house beers available.

Pusch Ridge Brewing Ⓑ

5861 N. Oracle Road, 520-888-7547

★★☆☆ 11:30 A.M.–late (3 P.M.–11 P.M. Mondays)

Food: Pizza, sandwiches   *Smoking:* Separate sections

Family-run and family-friendly, bargain food and beer. Well-executed house ales plus a nice lineup of guest beers on tap.

The Shanty

401 E. 9th St., 520-622-9210

★☆☆☆ Noon–1 A.M.

Food: Limited   *Smoking:* Throughout

Arizona's oldest continuously licensed bar, in business since 1938. More than 200 bottle choices. Lovely patio and gardens. Ask if you don't want your beer served in a chilled glass.

Zachary's Pizza

1019 E. 6th St., 520-623-6323

★★☆☆ Lunch–late

Food: Pizza   *Smoking:* Separate sections

No bar area here, but a nice cross-section of twenty-five draft beers available with meals. Top-flight deep-dish pizza.

Also in Tucson

Breckenridge Brewery & Pub, 1890 E. River Road, 520-577-0800. Brewpub; no longer owned by the Colorado chain.

Old Chicago, 2960 N. Campbell, 520-327-6200. See Boulder, Colorado.

Thunder Canyon Brewery, Restaurant & Pub, 7401 N. LaCholla Blvd., 520-797-2652. Offspring of Prescott Brewing in Prescott.

Also in Arizona

Bisbee: Bisbee Grand Hotel, 61 Main St., 602-432-5900. Hotel bar with twelve taps.

Chandler: Copper Canyon Brewing & Alehouse, 5945 W. Ray Road, 602-705-9700. Brewpub.

Globe: Globe Brewery & Barbecue Co., 190 N. Broad St., 520-425-8227. Brewpub.

Jerome: Jerome Brewery, Deli, Pizza & Cafe, 111 Main St., 520-639-8477. Brewpub in former ghost town.

Lake Havasu City: Barley Brothers Brewery & Grill, 1425 Mc-Culloch Blvd., 520-505-7837. Brewpub.

London Bridge Brewery, 422 English Village, 520-855-8782. Brewpub.

Mudshark Brewing Co., 210 Swanson Ave., 520-453-2981. Brewpub.

Mesa: Bavarian Point Restaurant, 4815 E. Main St., 602-830-0999. German restaurant.

Cellar Pub, 235 N. Country Club, 602-834-5050. Small bar in basement of Mesa Liquors.

North Scottsdale: Hops! Bistro and Brewery, 8668 Shea Blvd., 602-998-7777. Brewpub; see Scottsdale.

Sedona: Oak Creek Brewing Co., 2050 Yavapai Drive, 520-204-1300. Microbrewery with tasting room, limited hours, in beautiful mountain town.

ARKANSAS

Regional beers to look for: Weidman's Brewing.
Just for fun: Vino's in Little Rock. The music room.
Best city for a pub crawl: Little Rock (the only one, really).

ALTUS

Kelt's
106 E. Main St., 501-468-2413
    ★☆☆☆   11 A.M.–after dinner
Food: Full menu   *Smoking:* Throughout

A vaguely Irish pub with eight beers on tap, all imports. Spoken menu includes a full range of offerings, and specials really are.

LITTLE ROCK

RiverRock Brewery Ⓑ
500 E. Markham, 501-376-2337
    ★★☆☆   11 A.M.–late (closes at 10 P.M. Sundays)
Food: Brewpub fare   *Smoking:* Separate sections

Spacious brewpub in former newspaper building, with large deck overlooking the Arkansas River and a neon river flowing along the bar top. Variety of well-made beers available on tap. Beer movies on Saturday mornings.

Vino's Brewpub Ⓑ
923 W. 7th, 501-375-8466
    ★★☆☆   Lunch–late
Food: Tavern fare   *Smoking:* Separate sections

Brewpub draws suits and ties for lunch and happy hour, the tattooed and pierced crowd for live music later in the night. Great calzones, beer much improved since the early days.

Also in Little Rock
Flying Saucer Draught Emporium, 323 E. Markham St., 501-372-8032. Seventy-five draft selections; see Fort Worth, Texas.

Also in Arkansas
Eureka Springs: Bavarian Inn Restaurant, U.S. 62 West, 501-253-7734. German restaurant in a triple-A four-diamond lodge.

Fayetteville: Ozark Brewing Co., 430 W. Dickson, 501-521-2739. Brewpub.
Wet Mountain Brewing Co., 21 W. Mountain, 501-442-9090. Brewpub.

CALIFORNIA

Regional beers to look for: Too many to list, so start with Anchor Brewing, Sierra Nevada Brewing, Anderson Valley Brewing, Stone Brewing (in San Diego), Lind Brewing, Sudwerk/Hubsch, Russian River Brewing, and Moonlight Brewing. Many of the microbrewery/restaurants and brewpubs listed here distribute excellent beer beyond their doors.

Essential stops: Again, too many to list. Just five: Toronado in San Francisco, Mendocino Brewing in Hopland, the White Cockade near Boulder Creek, Goat Hill Tavern in Costa Mesa, and Jupiter in Berkeley.

Just for fun: Barney's Beanery in Hollywood. Janis Joplin may have beaned Jim Morrison with a Southern Comfort bottle here, and even if it was elsewhere, they were among the celebrities who imbibed here.

Best city for a pub crawl: San Francisco, specifically the area near Toronado.

Worth noting: California law prohibits smoking inside bars and restaurants, although not every place is diligent about enforcing the law. Also, smoking is still permitted outdoors in patios, on decks and in beer gardens.

ANAHEIM

JT Schmid's Brewhouse & Eatery Ⓑ
2610 E. Katella Blvd., 714-634-9200
★☆☆☆   Lunch–late (closes at 10 P.M. Sundays)
Food: Brewpub fare   *Smoking:* None

California cuisine and ales served in spacious, modern setting. Inviting enclosed beer garden. Weekly cigar dinners. Can be crowded when Mighty Ducks are at home.

ARCATA

Humboldt Brewery Ⓑ
856 10th St., 707-826-2739
★★☆☆   Lunch–late
Food: Brewpub fare   *Smoking:* None

The brewpub for the microbrewery that distributes popular Red Nectar Ale to most of the West Coast. Casual (laminated plastic table tops) and a fine popular music venue.

BELMONT

Marvin Gardens
1160 Old County Road, 650-592-6154
★☆☆☆   11:30 A.M.–closing
Food: Tavern fare   *Smoking:* None

Look for the sign that says "Eat Here." Bright, clean roadhouse with sixteen beers on tap, plenty of regional craft selections, and a wall of beer containers.

BERKELEY

Albatross Pub
1822 San Pablo, 510-843-2473
★☆☆☆   Hours: 4:30 P.M.–2 A.M.
Food: Limited, no kitchen   *Smoking:* None

"Meet me at the 'bird'" took on a new meaning (after thirty years) when this former dive became a civilized pub. Only jazz and classical music in the background, board games available (and the six darts lanes remain). Small but solid selection of craft beers.

Bison Brewing Ⓑ
2598 Telegraph Ave., 510-841-7734
★☆☆☆   7 A.M.–1 A.M. (opens at 11 A.M. Saturdays, closed Sundays)
Food: Brewpub fare   *Smoking:* None

Draws an eclectic crowd for always-interesting beer and pretty good food. Very inviting, with floor-to-ceiling windows and a small balcony on the second floor.

Henry's Publick House and Grille
2600 Durant Ave., 510-845-8981
★★☆☆   11 A.M.–1 A.M.
Food: Full menu   *Smoking:* None

Luxurious pub in the restaurant for the Hotel Durant. Beautifully appointed, and offering a full range from fifty-one taps. Gets crowded before UC football games and many nights.

Jupiter Ⓑ
2181 Shattuck Ave., 510-843-8277
★★★★   Lunch–late
Food: Brewpub fare   *Smoking:* None

"Beer Gothic": Bronze-colored pressed tin in a Gothic design panels the walls, large Gothic church lights hang from the ceiling, and you can sit on old church pews. Vintage games upstairs, excellent food, California craft beers supplemented by choices from its own small brewhouse. In 1999, Jupiter opened a brewpub with a full-sized brewery in Walnut Creek.

Triple Rock Ale House Ⓑ
1920 Shattuck Ave., 510-843-2739
★★☆☆   Lunch–late
Food: Brewpub fare   *Smoking:* None

The nation's fifth brewpub, located in a yellow brick building that dates back to the turn of the century, stocked with breweriana and a regulation shuffleboard table. Same ownership as Jupiter and Twenty Tank (San Francisco).

Also in Berkeley
Pyramid Brewery & Alehouse, 901 Gilman St., 510-527-9090. Restaurant attached to massive microbrewery. See Seattle, Washington.

Raleighs, 2438 Telegraph, 510-848-8652. Pub/restaurant across from People's Park.

Skates on the Bay, 100 Seawall Drive, 510-549-1900. Restaurant.

Starry Plough, 3101 Shattuck, 510-841-2082. Irish pub.

BOONVILLE

Buckhorn Saloon/Anderson Valley Brewing Co. Ⓑ
14081 Highway 128, 707-895-2337
★★★★   11 A.M.–10 P.M.
Food: Brewpub fare   *Smoking:* None

Three-story cedar-and-glass pub with surrounding redwood decks, beer T-shirts on the ceiling, and bar stools made from tractor seats. The views of the surrounding hillside are like those on the beer's bottles. Great beer, some from the nationally distributing micro just up the road.

BOULDER CREEK

Boulder Creek Grill & Cafe Ⓑ
13040 Highway 9, 408-338-7882
> ★☆☆☆ Lunch–late
> *Food:* Tavern fare *Smoking:* None

Small, casual pub in an older building, with brewing equipment tucked right behind the bar. Pool table in back, basic food and solid beer.

White Cockade
18025 Highway 9, 408-338-4148
> ★★☆☆ 3:30 A.M.–midnight (closed Mondays)
> *Food:* British pub fare *Smoking:* None

Scottish pub set in a log building with low ceilings, knotty pine paneling and a wood-burning fireplace. Tucked into the redwood forests northeast of Santa Cruz, offers mostly UK beers in a WWII setting. Menu is supplemented by fresh fish landed by the landlord from his own fishing boat.

BREA

BJ's Brewery Ⓑ
600 Brea Mall Drive, 714-990-2095
> ★★½☆ 11 A.M.–late
> *Food:* Pizza, pasta *Smoking:* None

This chain has pubs in California, Colorado and Oregon, but doesn't brew in all locations. Solid beer and interesting range of choices. Some locations serve handpumped beer.

CALISTOGA

Calistoga Inn Ⓑ
1250 Lincoln Ave., 707-942-4101
> ★☆☆☆ 11:30 A.M.–closing
> *Food:* Full menu *Smoking:* None

The nation's original bed and breakfast brewpub, located in a ninety-year-old inn. Excellent food, particularly the fresh fish, and beer from Napa Valley Brewing in the same building.

Also in Calistoga
Lord Derby Arms, 1923 Lake St., 707-942-9155. British pub.

CHICO

Sierra Nevada Taproom 🅑
1075 E. 20th, 530-893-3520
★★★☆   11 A.M.–11 P.M.
Food: Brewpub fare   *Smoking:* None

Well-appointed taproom next to Sierra Nevada's brewery. Beautiful stained-glass and mirrored back bar and open, airy dining, but the chief attraction remains the great beer.

CONCORD

Concord Depot
1839 Colfax, 925-825-7665
★★★☆   Noon-midnight
Food: Tavern fare   *Smoking:* None

A showcase for West Coast craft beers, with the twenty-eight draft choices changing so often that you could drink here every day for a year and not repeat a beer. Neon-lit wood-finished bar, murals. Bargain food.

COSTA MESA

Goat Hill Tavern
1380 Newport Blvd., 949-548-8428
★★★☆   9 A.M.–closing
Food: Tavern fare   *Smoking:* None

One part dive, one part garage sale, two parts sports bar, and three parts local bar. Funky stuff hangs all over, and there are 141 taps, usually pouring ninety to a hundred different beers. One customer may be ordering a pitcher of Pabst while another asks for a pint of Sierra Nevada Pale Ale. Giant single-malt whisky menu.

Also in Costa Mesa
The Harp Inn, 130 E. 17th St., 949-548-8428. Irish pub.
Skewer's Brewpub, 298 E. 17th St., 949-645-6459. Brewpub.

DANVILLE

Pete's Brass Rail & Car Wash
331 Hartz Ave., 925-820-8281
　　★★☆☆　　11 A.M.–11 P.M. (11:30 A.M.–8:30 P.M. Sundays)
Food: Tavern fare　　*Smoking:* None

The disclaimer is that there is no brass rail, no car wash and no Pete. Only draft beer, twenty choices, mostly West Coast craft beer. The walls are covered with cartoons of "Pete" and names of customers who have consumed at least 100 different beers.

DAVIS

Cantina del Cabo
139 G St., 530-756-2226
　　★★⯪☆　　10 A.M.–2 A.M.
Food: Mexican　　*Smoking:* None

Mexican restaurant offering a full range of beer choices, but primarily California craft products, from sixty-nine well-cared-for taps.

Sudwerk Privatbrauerei Hubsch ⓑ
2001 2ⁿᵈ St., 530-756-2739
　　★★⯪☆　　Lunch–late
Food: German fare　　*Smoking:* None

Virtually everything is traditionally German at this large brewpub, including the food and excellent beer. Live music nightly, both Bavarian and jazz. Also operates a brewpub in Sacramento and a brewery that distributes beer throughout the region.

DUBLIN

Hooligan's
7924 San Ramon Road, 925-829-9071
　　★★★☆　　Noon–late
Food: Tavern fare　　*Smoking:* None

Tavern built around its beer cooler by well-known publican Judy Ashworth, since retired. The forty-plus taps favor craft beers. Comfortable bar, excellent music venue.

ELK GROVE

Elk Grove Brewing Co. Ⓑ
9085 Elk Grove Blvd., 916-685-2537
★★☆☆   11:30 A.M.–midnight (closes at 10 P.M. Sundays)
Food: Brewpub fare   *Smoking:* None

Located in the old General Store, a classic hundred-year-old building on the National Register. Family friendly. Usually a wide range of well-made ales on tap, interesting seasonals.

EUREKA

Lost Coast Brewery & Pub Ⓑ
617 4th St., 707-445-4480
★★☆☆   11 A.M.–closing
Food: Brewpub fare   *Smoking:* None

Pub for the first micro in the country founded by women. A meticulously decorated old saloon set in a neighborhood of Victorian houses. The malty Lost Coast beers are widely distributed.

FORT BRAGG

North Coast Brewing Ⓑ
444 N. Main St., 707-964-2739
★★★★   2–11 P.M.
Food: Brewpub fare   *Smoking:* None

Pub attached to an outstanding microbrewery in an inviting eighty-five-year-old brick building. Old Rasputin, Red Seal Pale Ale and Pranqster are three of several outstanding beers, and the food is just as good.

FRESNO

Butterfield Brewing, Bar & Grill Ⓑ
777 E. Olive, 559-264-5521
★★☆☆   11 A.M.–late
Food: Tavern fare   *Smoking:* None

Upscale pub in the Tower District, named for the stagecoach run by the founder's great-great-grandfather. Excellent food and full-bodied ales.

Also in Fresno
Bullfrog Brewing Co., 706 W. Shaw Ave., 559-224-5100. Brewpub; a division of Steelhead Brewing; see Eugene, Oregon.

FULLERTON

Heroes Bar & Grill
305 N. Harbor, 714-738-4356
★★★☆   11 A.M.–late
Food: Full menu   *Smoking:* None

Welcoming pub decorated with black-and-white photos, antiques. Each of 102 taps pours a different beer, covering the spectrum. Gourmet hamburgers during the day, steaks at night. Also has a pub in Claremont with forty-plus taps.

The Olde Ship Inn
709 N. Harbor Blvd., 714-871-7447
★☆☆☆   11 A.M.–11 P.M.
Food: British pub fare   *Smoking:* None

Nineteen beers, all from the UK, and Blackthorn Cider on tap. Decorated in British nautical theme with plenty of black timber. No television. Pub sing-along each Tuesday. Selection of English teas.

GUERNEVILLE

Russian River Brewing Co. Ⓑ
13250 River Road, 707-887-2294
★★☆☆   Tasting room closes at 5 P.M.
Food: Deli   *Smoking:* None

Deli and tasting room, not a bar, but offering the very well-made Russian River beers in a lovely setting. The brewery is owned by Korbel Winery and Champagne Cellars, and its beers are worth seeking out.

HAYWARD

Buffalo Bill's Ⓑ
1082 B St., 510-886-9823
★☆☆☆   Lunch–late
Food: Brewpub fare   *Smoking:* None

California's second brewpub, a reminder of how basic the concept was in the 1980s. Oak bar, exposed brick, limited menu and a few house beers. Founder Bill Owens no longer owns the pub, and Buffalo Bill beers distributed nationally are brewed elsewhere.

Vintage Cellar Bistro
1001 B St., 510-886-8525
★☆☆☆   11 A.M.–late
Food: Bistro fare   *Smoking:* None

Housed in a concrete structure built in 1921, complete with leaded glass. Bar is made of Honduran mahogany, and the back bar from cherry and bird's-eye maple. Twelve-tap lineup features West Coast craft breweries exclusively.

HEALDSBURG

Bear Republic Brewing Co. Ⓑ
345 Healdsburg Ave., 707-433-2337
★★★☆   Lunch–late
Food: Brewpub fare   *Smoking:* None

Family-run pub with award-winning beers that are sold throughout the region. Distinctive, fairly priced food. Decorated in cycling motif. Patio sits beside a grass field and stream in the heart of wine country.

HOLLISTER

San Andreas Brewing Ⓑ
737 San Benito St., 408-637-7074
★☆☆☆   11 A.M.–late
Food: Brewpub fare   *Smoking:* None

Brewery and pub located in old creamery building, retaining beautiful tile walls. Serving a wide range of ales whose names reflect the fact this town sits on the faultline.

HOLLYWOOD

Barney's Beanery
8447 Santa Monica Blvd., 323-654-2287
★★⯪☆   10 A.M.–2 A.M.
Food: Tavern fare plus   *Smoking:* None

A Hollywood staple since the 1920s and still a popular place for well-known musicians and film personalities. Dozens of draft choices in a roadhouse setting, where the menu includes forty chili dishes and 140 versions of hamburgers.

HOPLAND

Mendocino Brewing Co. Ⓑ
13351 Highway 101, 707-744-1015
★★½☆   11 A.M.–late
Food: Brewpub fare   *Smoking:* None

California's first brewpub, now selling its distinctive Red Tail Ale across much of the country. Set in an inviting brick building with a lovely shaded beer garden, its real draw is the beer. Live music.

LARKSPUR

Marin Brewing Co. Ⓑ
1809 Larkspur Landing Circle, 415-461-4677
★★★☆   11:30 A.M.–late
Food: Brewpub fare   *Smoking:* None

Casual brewpub with award-winning beers and good food, a ferry ride across the bay from San Francisco. A mixture of sports bar, English pub, and Deadhead bar. Can be jammed on weekend evenings.

LONG BEACH

The Yard House
401 Shoreline Drive, 562-628-0455
★★☆☆   10 A.M.–late
Food: Full menu   *Smoking:* None

Two hundred and fifty taps, offering 180–200 different beers. The beer cooler alone is bigger than most corner bars. Upscale dining, martini lounge, large wine menu.

Also in Long Beach
Pacific Coast Brewery & Restaurant, 6272 E. Pacific Coast Highway, 562-431-8211. Brewpub.
Rock Bottom Brewery & Restaurant, 1 Pine Ave., 562-308-2255. Brewpub; see Denver, Colorado.

LOS ANGELES

Otto's Grill & Beer Bar
135 N. Grand Ave., 213-972-7322
★☆☆☆   11:30 A.M.–midnight
Food: Continental & grill   *Smoking:* None

Upscale restaurant pairing menu items with an excellent beer selection (twelve draft choices). Known for outstanding special beer dinners.

Also in Los Angeles
Bonaventure Brewing Co., 404 S. Figuero St., 213-236-0802. Brewpub.

MODESTO

St. Stan's Brewery & Restaurant Ⓑ
821 L St., 209-524-2337
★★⯪☆   11 A.M.–midnight
Food: Brewpub fare   *Smoking:* None

Restaurant attached to brewery distributing its beers nationally, offering those beers and draft-only products. Replica of "St. Stan in the Forest" sculpture above the bar (ask about the legend). Excellent selection of traditional German alt-style as well as hoppy West Coast beers.

MONTEREY

Blue Fin Cafe & Billiards
685 Cannery Row, 408-375-7000
★☆☆☆   11 A.M.–1:30 A.M. (opens at noon in winter)
Food: Tavern fare   *Smoking:* None

Casual pool room, with 18 billiards tables and other games. Broad lineup of twenty-two beers on tap. Patio offers an excellent view of the bay.

Also in Monterey
The Bulldog, 611 Lighthouse Ave., 408-372-5565. British pub.
The Mucky Duck, 479 Alvarado St., 408-655-3031. Irish pub.
O'Kane's Irish Pub, 97 Prescott, 408-375-7564. Irish pub.
Peter B's Brewpub, 2 Portola Plaza, 408-649-4511. Brewpub.

MOUNTAIN VIEW

Tied House Cafe & Brewery Ⓑ
954 Villa St., 650-965-2739
★★☆☆   11:30 A.M.–late
Food: Brewpub fare   *Smoking:* None

The original Tied House—there are now others in Alameda and San Jose. Extensive menus features items made on-premise, including smoked barbecue ribs, and beers have won more than a dozen Great American Beer Festival medals.

Also in Mountain View
Fibbar Magees Mountain View, 223 Castro St., 650-964-9151. Irish pub.

NAPA

Billco's Billiards & Darts
1234 3rd Ave., 707-226-7506
★★☆☆   11:30 A.M.–late
Food: Tavern fare   *Smoking:* None

Looks a little like an auto parts store outside, but an upscale pool hall inside with fifty-five beers on tap. Weekly tournaments.

Harry O's Yard of Ale
304 Lincoln Ave., 707-253-0432
★☆☆☆   11 A.M.–closing (opens at 9 A.M. weekends)
Food: Irish pub fare   *Smoking:* None

Locals hangout with Irish bent and forty-plus beers on tap, mostly craft products. Fine view of river seventy feet below.

NEVADA CITY

Mad Dogs & Englishmen
211 Spring St., 530-265-8173
★☆☆☆   Noon–closing
Food: British pub fare   *Smoking:* None

English pub that fits right in with a city of Victorian homes, offering both imports and craft beers on twenty-four taps, one of them a beer engine.

Also in Nevada City
Stonehouse Brewery & Restaurant, 107 Sacramento St., 530-265-3960. Brewpub.

NEWPORT BEACH

D.P.'s Pub & Grill
3110 Newport Blvd., 949-723-0293
★★☆☆   11 A.M.–2 A.M.
Food: Tavern fare   *Smoking:* None

A sports bar/pool hall that experimented with a hundred-plus taps, then cut back to thirty because the beer wasn't moving quickly enough. Favors American craft beers.

Newport Beach Brewing Co. Ⓑ
2930 Newport Beach, 949-675-8449
★★☆☆   11:30 A.M.–late
Food: Brewpub fare   *Smoking:* None

Large gabled pub with a beer garden, serving distinctive food and supplementing its regular beer lineup with some excellent experiments. Often a line on weekend nights.

Also in Newport Beach
Shamrock Bar & Grill, 2633 W. Coast Highway, 949-631-5633. Irish pub.

NOVATO

Moylan's Brewery & Restaurant Ⓑ
11 Roland Way, 415-898-4677
★★★☆   11:30 A.M.–midnight
Food: Brewpub fare   *Smoking:* None

Founded by Brendan Moylan of Marin Brewing (see Larkspur) and shows its heritage. Woody, with a beautiful white birch bar, solid food, and excellent beer across the board.

OAKLAND

Barclay's
5940 College Ave., 510-654-1650
★★★☆   11 A.M.–midnight
Food: Bistro fare   *Smoking:* None

Thirty taps (two handpumps) offer an always-changing choice of West Coast craft beers. Casually nice, family friendly, with overhead fans and wooden tables and benches. Interesting food specials daily.

Cato's Alehouse
3891 Piedmont Ave., 510-655-3349
★★☆☆   11:30 A.M.–midnight
Food: Tavern fare   *Smoking:* None

Located in an old house with a hardwood floor and a fine glass-enclosed front porch. Fine light menu (order at bar, delivered to table). Twenty-two taps, mostly West Coast products, some imports.

Heinhold's 1ˢᵗ & Last Chance Saloon
56 Jack London Square, 510-839-6761
☆☆☆☆   None–closing
Food: No kitchen   *Smoking:* None

Built from the timbers of old whaling ships, this tiny place was twenty-three years old when the 1906 earthquake destroyed San Francisco, leaving the floor, and everything else, severely tilted. Jack London was a regular and used the tales he heard here in his books. Limited beer selection.

Pacific Coast Brewing   Ⓑ
906 Washington St., 510-836-2739
★★☆☆   11:30 A.M.–closing
Food: Brewpub fare   *Smoking:* None

Parts of the bar in this restored Victorian building actually came out of a museum. Offers several guest beers as well as its own excellent ales.

Also in Oakland
Ben 'n' Nick's, 5612 College Ave., 510-923-0327. Tavern.

ORANGE

Hollingshead's Delicatessen
368 S. Main St., 714-978-9467
★★☆☆   10 A.M.–7 P.M. (closes at 4 P.M. Saturdays, closed Sundays)
Food: Deli   *Smoking:* None

A basic deli/beer store with a bar along the back wall. Offers fifteen West Coast beers on tap, 300 in bottles. Sells beer to go by the bottle or case.

Also in Orange

Gordon Biersch Brewing Co., 1623 W. Katella Ave., 714-288-0115. Brewpub; see San Francisco.

Old Towne Brewing Co., 186 N. Atchison St., 714-744-4181. Brewpub.

PALO ALTO

Empire Tap Room

651 Emerson, 415-321-3030

★☆☆☆   Lunch–late

Food: Full menu   *Smoking:* None

Upscale in clientele and decor, with a mahogany bar that is the longest on the Peninsula. Solid sixteen-beer draft lineup. Popular spot for cocktails and wine.

Also in Palo Alto

Gordon Biersch, 640 Emerson St., 415-323-7723. Brewpub; this is where it all started for the chain. See San Francisco.

PASADENA

Crown City Brewery 🅑

300 S. Raymond Ave., 626-577-5548

★★☆☆   11 A.M.–midnight

Food: Brewpub fare   *Smoking:* None

Brewpub since 1988, serving both its own beer and an extensive list of guest beers available from five five-tap towers. Decorated with breweriana.

Lucky Baldwin's

17 S. Raymond Ave., 626-795-0652

★★½☆   10 A.M.–11 P.M.

Food: British pub fare   *Smoking:* None

Part English pub, part alehouse. The thirty-eight draft choices include plenty of UK beers, there are two handpumps, and fish and chips are a specialty. Also plenty of West Coast micros and Belgian beers, frequent special beer events.

Also in Pasadena

Gordon Biersch, 41 Hugus Alley, 626-449-0052. Brewpub. See San Francisco.

John Bull English Pub, 958 S. Fair Oaks, 626-441-4353. English pub.

PETALUMA

Dempsey's Ale House 🅱

50 E. Washington St., 707-765-9694
★★☆☆   11 A.M.–closing
Food: Bistro fare   *Smoking:* None

Solid beers and outstanding food, with many items prepared using Thai and Indian spices. In the historic downtown with a patio that overlooks the Petaluma River.

PLEASANTON

Hop Yard American Ale House

3015 Hopyard Road, 925-426-9600
★★★☆   11 A.M.–midnight
Food: Tavern fare   *Smoking:* None

Well-cared-for beer from thirty-one taps, handpump. Lovely thirty-foot oak bar. Beer decorations offset strip-mall setting. On the site of what was once the largest hop farm in the world. A second Hop Yard in San Ramon has thirty beers on tap and an excellent patio.

Sunshine Saloon

1807 Santa Rita Road, 925-846-6108
★★☆☆   10 A.M.–2 A.M.
Food: Tavern fare   *Smoking:* None

Sports bar with thirty-two beers (craft and imports) on tap, plenty of TVs, and live comedy and dancing seven nights a week.

Also in Pleasanton
Main Street Brewery, 830 Main St., 925-462-8218. Brewpub.

PORTA COSTA

Warehouse Cafe

5 Canyon Lake Drive, 510-787-1827
★★⯪☆   10 A.M.–closing (noon–8 P.M. Mondays and Tuesdays)
Food: Bar snacks   *Smoking:* None

A former grain warehouse, decorated with a ten-foot stuffed polar bear, rustic wooden tables, and a Christmas tree that stays up all year. One beer on tap, Pilsner Urquell, and a 450-bottle menu that spans the globe. Full menu served Friday and Saturday for dinner.

REDONDO BEACH

Naja's Place
154 International Boardwalk, 310-376-9951
★★★☆   11 A.M.–closing
Food: Middle Eastern   *Smoking:* None

Disguised as just another joint along the marina, this board-walk spot's beer menu includes seventy tap and 700 bottle choices. Food ranges from Middle Eastern fare to pub grub.

Also in Redondo Beach
Redondo Beach Brewing Co., 1814 S. Catalina Ave., 310-316-8477. Brewpub.

REDWOOD CITY

City Pub
2620 Broadway St., 650-363-2620
★☆☆☆   11 A.M.–closing
Food: Tavern fare   *Smoking:* None

The twenty-four draft choices include no mainstream lagers, mostly craft beers. Has both an espresso bar and a dessert bar. Games available include liar's dice.

RESEDA

Weber's Place
19321 Vanowen St., 818-345-9800
★★☆☆   11:30 A.M.–1 A.M.
Food: Tavern fare   *Smoking:* None

Local homebrewers helped choose the beers when this place ex-panded to twenty-seven taps. Pick the right hermit crab in the Thursday night crab races and you might win a trip to Las Vegas.

RIVERSIDE

Riverside Brewing Co. ℬ
3397 7th St., 909-682-5465
    ★★☆☆   11 A.M.–midnight
Food: Brewpub fare   *Smoking:* None

Comfortable restaurant for microbrewery that has won awards for its wide range of beers. The ceiling is covered with T-shirts from microbreweries across the country, while the dining room points to more local heritage with orange-crate labels.

ROSEVILLE

Owl Club
109 Church St., 916-773-1919
    ★☆☆☆   4 P.M.–late (opens at 7:30 P.M. Saturdays, closed Sundays and Mondays)
Food: Tavern fare   *Smoking:* None

Great owl and neon sign outside, outstanding selection of neon inside. A friendly local spot that has been around for more than 60 years.

SACRAMENTO

Hopstreet Bistro & Brewery ℬ
6300 Folsom, 916-451-4677
    ★☆☆☆   Hours: 11 A.M.–late
Food: Brewpub fare   *Smoking:* None

Located in warehouse space where Sutter Brewing (also a brewpub) failed. Totally redone, including trees planted out front, to create a bistro feel. Solid beer, excellent food, with beer used in some dishes.

River City Brewing ℬ
545 Downtown Plaza, #1115, 916-447-2739
    ★★✫☆   Lunch–late
Food: Bistro fare   *Smoking:* None

This spacious, industrial pub with several dining rooms and a separate bar area that can get crowded, is a dining destination. Food runs from European to Southwestern, with some dishes better suited for wine. Solid house beers.

River's End Brewpub Ⓑ
3535 Fair Oaks Blvd., 916-978-8080
    ★★⯪☆   11:30 A.M.–late
Food: Brewpub fare   *Smoking:* None

Located inside Fountain Plaza, not actually a brewpub but a multi-tap with fifty draft beers, including plenty of West Coast micros.

Sacramento Brewing Co. Ⓑ
2713 El Paseo, 916-485-4677
    ★★☆☆   11 A.M.–11 P.M. (closes at midnight Fridays and Saturdays, 10 A.M.–10 P.M. Sundays)
Food: Brewpub fare   *Smoking:* None

Excellent food in the lovely dining area with rosewood trim and terra-cotta–colored walls, plus comfortable open pub and solid beers.

Also in Sacramento
Bonn Lair, 3651 J St., 916-455-7155. Irish pub.
Fox & Goose Public House, 1001 R St., 916-443-8825. British pub.
Hogshead Brewpub, 114 J St., 916-443-2739. Brewpub.
Rubicon Brewing, 2004 Capitol Ave., 916-448-7032. Brewpub.
Sudwerk Privatbrauerei Hubsch, 1375 Exposition Blvd., 916-925-6623. Brewpub; see Davis.

SAN DIEGO

Blue Collar Grill
4015 Avati Drive, 619-483-0763
    ★☆☆☆   11 A.M.–10 P.M. (closes at 9 P.M. Sundays)
Food: Full menu   *Smoking:* None

Family-friendly place in a rec-room setting with unpretentious trappings. Basic bar food with a twist, fair prices. Nice mix of beer from fourteen taps. TVs and pool.

Cass Street Bar & Grill
4612 Cass St., 619-270-1320
    ★☆☆☆   10 A.M.–2 A.M.
Food: Tavern fare   *Smoking:* None

A great beach bar, with sixteen tap choices and excellent burgers and fresh fish. The pictures here are of regulars taken during fishing trips, the game is tabletop shuffleboard.

Hang Ten Brewery Ⓑ
310 5th Ave., 619-232-6336

☆☆☆☆ Lunch–late

Food: Brewpub fare   *Smoking:* None

The latest operation here (the place has had several owners and several names) has a surfer theme, which extends to the names of the beers. On the ground floor of a building full of artisans' lofts.

Karl Strauss' Old Columbia Ⓑ
1157 Columbia, 619-587-2739

★★☆☆ 11:30 A.M.–closing

Food: Brewpub fare   *Smoking:* None

Karl Strauss, formerly of Pabst Brewing, has helped scores of brewpubs open their doors. Although he's not actually involved with running them, four pubs in the San Diego area carry his name, and a brewery distributes Karl Strauss beer. This downtown location was the first, offering a step up from casual dining and a solid lineup of beers. The brewpub on the north side of town is worth visiting for the Oriental gardens alone.

Moondoggie's
832 Garnet Ave., 619-483-6550

★☆☆☆ 11 A.M.–2 A.M.

Food: Tavern fare   *Smoking:* None

A wall of TVs was replaced, but Moondoggie's still is pretty much a beach sports bar with a fine patio. Twenty-plus taps offer mainstream beers, imports and craft products. Also a Moondoggie's in La Jolla.

Newport Ave. Bar & Grill
4935 Newport Ave., 619-222-0168

★★☆☆ 11 A.M.–closing (open for breakfast weekends)

Food: Tavern fare   *Smoking:* None

A surfer bar in the Ocean Beach area. The former storefront lunch counter café still has vinyl booths and serves an excellent mix of West Coast craft beers, including local products.

O'Brien's Microbrew Pub
4646 Convoy St., 619-278-9908
    ★★☆☆   Hours: 11 A.M.–9 P.M.
Food: Tavern fare   *Smoking:* None

Not fancy. Set in a shopping center and catering to a lunch/after-work crowd, offering an excellent beer menu. One tap goes to Guinness, the other twenty to microbrewed beers, many from the Northwest.

Princess Pub & Grille
1665 India St., 619-238-1266
    ★☆☆☆   Hours: 11 A.M.–1 A.M.
Food: British pub fare   *Smoking:* None

A surprising spot in the middle of Little Italy. Twenty-one beers on tap (mostly from the UK), pub grub, a long single-malt menu, real darts, and kid friendly.

San Diego Brewing Co. Ⓑ
10450 Friars Road, 619-284-2739
    ★★⯪☆   Hours: 11 A.M.–late
Food: Brewpub fare   *Smoking:* None

Strip-mall brewpub with fifty taps, usually offering a wide range of forty-plus guest beers plus four or so of its own beers.

Also in San Diego
Brewer's Union, 5553 Kearny Villa Road, 619-278-2739. Brewpub.

Callahan's Pub & Brewery, 8280A Mira Mesa Blvd., 619-578-7892. Brewpub.

Del Mar Stuft Pizza & Brewing Co., 12840 Carmel Country Road, 619-592-7883. Brewpub.

Dino & Luigi's Stuft Pizza, 10155 Rancho Carmel Drive, 619-592-7883. Brewpub.

Gordon Biersch, 5050 Mission Center Road, 619-618-1120. Brewpub; see San Francisco.

Karl Strauss' Brewery Gardens, 9675 Scranton Road, 619-587-2739. Brewpub.

Shakespeare's Pub, 3701 India St., 619-299-0230. British pub.

SAN FRANCISCO

Beach Chalet Brewery & Restaurant Ⓑ
100 Great Highway, 415-386-8439
★★⯪☆   9 A.M.–late
Food: Brewpub fare   *Smoking:* None

The last four digits of the phone number spell VIEW, and the view of the Pacific coastline is spectacular. It was built in 1925 as a restaurant and bath house, and in the 1930s the WPA commissioned an artist to paint frescoes—now restored—depicting San Francisco life.

Betelnut
2030 Union St., 415-929-9955
★★☆☆   11:30 A.M.–12:30 A.M.
Food: Asian   *Smoking:* None

Excellent Asian food made from fresh local ingredients seasoned with regional spices, often hot. Wide range of Asian beers, plus contract-brewed house beers. Sidewalk dining. Inviting Dragonfly Lounge has broad swaying fans and serves exotic drinks.

Connecticut Yankee
100 Connecticut St., 415-552-4440
★☆☆☆   Lunch–late
Food: Tavern fare   *Smoking:* None

Once a well-known Barbary Coast bar called Hilda's Saloon, now a Potrero Hill hangout and New England sports bar, specializing in seafood (check the chalkboard for daily specials). Nice cross-section of beer from twelve taps.

E&O Trading Co. Ⓑ
314 Sutter St., 415-693-0303
★★☆☆   Lunch–late (opens at 4 P.M. Sundays)
Food: Southeast Asian   *Smoking:* None

Fully re-created Asian trading post. Dozens of antique Chinese birdcages and pierced tin lizard lights hang about, and a dragon guards the bar. Food that *Gourmet* magazine has written about often paired with West Coast-style beers.

Edinburgh Castle

950 Geary St., 415-885-4074

★★☆☆   5 p.m.–2 a.m.

Food: No kitchen   *Smoking:* None

Home to the Scottish Cultural & Arts Foundation. Good fish 'n' chips (they come from around the corner), nineteen beers on tap, a lovely Tudor multi-room pub with frequent live music.

Gordon Biersch   Ⓑ

2 Harrison St., 415-243-8246

★★★☆   11 a.m.–late

Food: Upscale brewpub fare   *Smoking:* None

Wonderful food that's almost too pretty to eat paired with classic German-style beer. Located in an old Hills Brothers Coffee building on the Embarcadero, with great views, particularly of the Bay Bridge. Large display brewery, excellent service.

Great Water Bar & Cafe

373 Broadway, 415-956-5158

★★☆☆   Lunch–late (closed Sundays)

Food: Tavern fare   *Smoking:* None

Formerly known as Bierhaus on Broadway. Well-appointed pub—shiny brass taps across a granite-like bar top—with thirty draft choices and wide bottle range. Excellent selection of West Coast craft beers.

Hamburger Mary's

1582 Folsom, 415-626-1985

★☆☆☆   Lunch–late

Food: Tavern fare   *Smoking:* None

A fixture in the SOMA nightclub district for more than twenty years, and apparently accumulating flea market goods since day one. Plenty of comfort food and burgers—though a bit pricey—plus thirteen draft choices in the Backside Bar.

Jacks Elixir

3200 16th St., 415-522-1633

★★⯨☆   2 p.m.–2 a.m.

Food: No kitchen   *Smoking:* None

Jacks bars are all over town, each a bit different and with draft choices ranging from the teens into the eighties. There are sixty-one taps jammed in here, leaving just enough room for patrons to get to know each other well.

Lucky 13
2140 Market, 415-487-1313
★★★☆   4 P.M.–2 A.M.
Food: No kitchen   *Smoking:* None

Dark, hip, black-cat place with the longest bar in the city, a snake mural on the walls, a cool women's room, and a deer head with plastic breasts. Serious about beer and spirits. Twenty-eight taps, imports and craft beers, and wide bottle selection. There's also a Lucky 13 in Alameda.

Mad Dog in the Fog
530 Haight, 415-626-7279
★★☆☆   11:30 A.M.–2 A.M.
Food: British pub fare   *Smoking:* None

Across from the venerable Toronado, with a green pub front and a pub feeling. Bright front room with tall windows, pubby with comfy leather chairs in back. Both imports and craft beers from twenty taps. Trivia competition Monday and Thursday nights.

Magnolia Pub & Brewery 🅑
1398 Haight St., 415-864-7168
★★☆☆   Hours: 11 A.M.–11 P.M. (opens earlier weekends)
Food: Brewpub fare   *Smoking:* None

The Haight meets the McMenamins (founders of the popular Oregon-based pub chain), with a mural that covers two walls and a laid-back beer drinkin' atmosphere. Pharmacy decor remains from when this was a drugstore. Adventurous house beers, some cask-conditioned, and well-chosen guest beers.

Pig & Whistle
2801 Geary Blvd., 415-885-4779
★★☆☆   11:30 A.M.–2 A.M.
Food: British pub fare   *Smoking:* None

Plenty of patrons speaking with English accents, plus dart supplies for sale. Emphasis on European imports among the twenty-two draft choices. Try Drake's Best Bitter (Lind Brewing) on handpump.

Rat & Raven

4054 24th St., 415-285-0674

★★☆☆   1 P.M.–closing

Food: No kitchen   *Smoking:* None

Down to earth, casual spot with pool, darts, and pinball, but not a lot of folks watching sports on TV. The thirty-two tap choices include a nice mix of imports and craft beers.

San Francisco Brewing Co. Ⓑ

155 Columbus Ave., 415-434-3344

☆☆☆☆   Lunch–late

Food: Tavern fare   *Smoking:* None

The old Barbary Coast's last remaining bar, with a plank of solid mahogany running the length of the bar and exquisite mahogany columns supporting the back bar.

Suppenkuche

601 Hayes St., 415-252-9289

★☆☆☆   5–10 P.M. (brunch Sundays)

Food: German fare   *Smoking:* None

Traditional German restaurant where virtually all the taps go to German beers (with an occasional British or Belgian beer available). Cozy bar area.

Thirsty Bear Brewing Co. Ⓑ

661 Howard St., 415-974-0905

★★☆☆   Lunch–late (opens at 2:30 P.M. weekends)

Food: Spanish tapas   *Smoking:* None

A popular Financial District spot serving tasty traditional tapas in a warehouse setting. The tapas and a wide range of beers—usually seven available—make for some fascinating pairings.

Tommy's Joynt

Geary at Van Ness, 415-775-4216

★★☆☆   11 A.M.–2 A.M.

Food: Full menu   *Smoking:* None

Traditional, historic saloon that gives you an idea of what bars must have been like before the 1906 earthquake. Order freshly-made, hearty fare from a buffet line and check out the eclectic, beer-friendly decor.

Toronado

547 Haight, 415-863-2276
★★★★   11:30 A.M.–2 A.M.
Food: Limited   *Smoking:* None

Draws a mixed crowd of locals—it's Haight-Ashbury, after all—and beer geeks. The beer menu (forty-six taps, two hand-pumps, great bottle lineup) is as good as it gets. Chalkboard with the day's selections hangs high, like a toteboard in a bookie parlor. Hosts world-class barleywine festival each February.

Twenty Tank Brewing Ⓑ

316 11ᵗʰ St., 415-255-9455
★★★☆   11:30 A.M.–1:30 A.M.
Food: Brewpub fare   *Smoking:* None

Beautifully appointed with a five-foot neon beer mug out front and plenty of warm wood inside. Shuffleboard, excellent hand-tossed pizza, and a full range of award-winning beers, some on handpump. Gets crowded with the SOMA district set.

Union St. Alehouse

1980 Union, 415-921-0300
★★☆☆   3:30 P.M.–2 A.M. (opens at 11:30 A.M. Fridays through Sundays)
Food: Tavern fare   *Smoking:* None

Decorated to look like the interior of a ship, serving an excellent cross-section of West Coast beers and imports from twenty taps (one handpump). Draws a young crowd, popular TV sports spot.

Zeitgeist: Bar and Guest Haus

199 Valencia St., 415-255-7505
★☆☆☆   9 A.M.–2 A.M.
Food: Tavern fare   *Smoking:* None

A biker bar with a motorcycle shop next door. Hodgepodge inside with picnic-type seating in back and basic rooms for rent upstairs. A lovely selection of West Coast beers, plus a few imports, from twenty-five taps.

Also in San Francisco

An Bodhran, 668 Haight St., 415-431-4724. Irish pub.
Armadillo's, 200 Fillmore, 415-641-1416. Club.
Café du Nord, 2170 Market, 415-861-5016. Restaurant/bar.
Durty Nelly's, 2328 Irving St., 415-664-2555. Irish pub.
Ireland's, 32 Geary Street, 415-386-6173. Irish pub.

Pat O'Shea's Mad Hatter, 3848 Geary Blvd., 415-752-3148. Irish pub.

Plough & Stars, 116 Clement, 415-751-1122. Irish pub.

Potrero Brewing Co., 535 Florida St., 415-552-1967. Brewpub.

The Royal Exchange, 301 Sacramento, 415-956-1710, Multi-tap.

Steelhead Brewery at Fisherman's Wharf, 353 Jefferson, 415-775-1795. Brewpub; see Eugene, Oregon.

SAN GABRIEL

Stuffed Sandwich
413 W. Las Tunas Drive, 818-576-9554
    ★★★☆   11 A.M.–8 P.M. (closed Sundays and Mondays)
Food: Tavern fare   *Smoking:* None

Restaurant serving enormous portions of food and offering an enormous beer list—800 in bottles, often several vintages of the same beers. No bar area.

SAN JOSE

Britannia Arms
1087 Sunnyvale Road, 408-252-7262
    ★☆☆☆   11 A.M.–2 A.M.
Food: British pub fare   *Smoking:* None

Fifteen draft choices, both imports and craft beers, with televised NFL games on Sundays and soccer the rest of the time. There is another Britannia Arms at 5027 Almaden Expressway and also one in Aptos.

Mission Ale House
97 E. Santa Clara, 408-292-4058
    ★☆☆☆   11 A.M.–2 A.M. (opens at 1 P.M. weekends)
Food: Tavern fare   *Smoking:* None

Retro-style bar, with twenty-eight-foot-long mahogany bar, open since the 1940s, now offering a trendy drink lineup (twenty-four taps, mostly micros) that includes single malts and martinis. Order food at the bar. Jammed on hockey nights.

Also in San Jose

Gordon Biersch, 33 E. Fernando St., 408-294-6785. Brewpub; see San Francisco.

The Olde Fox, 69 N. San Pedro, 408-298-6969. British pub.

Tied House #2, 65 N. San Pedro, 408-295-2739. Brewpub; see Mountain View.

SAN LEANDRO

Englander Sports Pub
101 Parrott St., 510-357-3571
★★½☆   11 A.M.–closing
Food: Tavern fare   *Smoking:* None

A little English and a lot sports bar, with two big-screen TVs and smaller monitors everywhere. Seventy-three taps include plenty of UK beers but also a wide range of West Coast beers.

SAN LUIS OBISPO

Frog & Peach Pub
728 Higuera St., 805-595-3764
★☆☆☆   Lunch–late
Food: Tavern fare   *Smoking:* None

Fifteen taps offer a mix of British ales and American craft beers. Woody and dark, with a fine long bar. Quiet Celtic jams some nights, rowdy Morris dancing others.

Original Spike's Restaurant
570 Higuera, 805-544-7157
★★☆☆   11 A.M.–closing
Food: Tavern fare   *Smoking:* None

Small plaques list the thousands who completed a forty-beer tour here decorate the walls. An early bastion for flavorful beer, with an excellent twenty-five-tap lineup. Intimate.

Also in San Luis Obispo
SLO Brewing, 1119 Garden St., 805-543-1843. Brewpub.

SAN MATEO

Prince of Wales Pub
106 E. 25th Ave., 650-574-9723
★★½☆   11 A.M.–late (usually closed Sundays)
Food: Tavern fare   *Smoking:* None

Darts, beer and lots of regulars in this fifty-seat pub that Jack Curry—a former U.S. darts champion and award-winning chili chef—has run for more than twenty years. Local craft beers and UK products on tap.

Also in San Mateo
Chalkers Redbird Brewing Co., 201 S. B St., 650-579-0209. Brewpub.

SANTA BARBARA

Santa Barbara Brewing Co. Ⓑ
501 State St., 650-730-1040
    ★★☆☆   11:30 A.M.–midnight
Food: Brewpub fare   *Smoking:* None

Located in a stately brick building on State Street, where other bars frequently come and go. Solid food, a wider range of beers than when it opened, late-night dining, glistening tanks right behind the copper-topped bar.

SANTA CRUZ

Front Street Pub/Santa Cruz Brewing Ⓑ
516 Front St., 831-429-8838
    ★★½☆   11:30 A.M.–late
Food: Brewpub fare   *Smoking:* None

A lighthouse lamp blinks above the shake-roofed bar, and historic photographs of West Coast lighthouses decorate the walls. Conversation-friendly, always a wide range of well-made house beers available, both ales and lagers.

Poet & Patriot
320 E. Cedar St., 831-426-8620
    ★★☆☆   Noon–late
Food: Tavern fare   *Smoking:* None

A blue-collar local Irish bar that fits right into laid-back Santa Cruz. Three rooms—including one for serious darts and another for music—with Guinness and Murphy's stouts on tap, as well as California favorites Sierra Nevada and Anchor Steam.

Seabright Brewery Ⓑ
519 Seabright, 831-426-2739
    ★★★☆   11:30 A.M.–late
Food: Brewpub fare   *Smoking:* None

Excellent house beers, particularly the oatmeal stout, on tap and handpump. Has a real beach feel, open and airy, with light wood, pastel colors outside and in, overhead fans.

Also in Santa Cruz
99 Bottles of Beer on the Wall, 110 Walnut Ave., 831-459-9999. Multi-tap.

SANTA MONICA

Father's Office
1018 Montana, 310-393-2337
★★½☆   4 P.M.–late (opens at noon Fridays through Sundays)
Food: No kitchen   *Smoking:* None

Long-established beer bar (first in the area to feature the full line of Anchor beers), serving only draft beer and only West Coast craft beers. Acoustic jazz and classical music plays in the background.

Library Ale House
2911 Main St., 310-314-4855
★★☆☆   11:30 A.M.–midnight
Food: Tavern fare   *Smoking:* None

Restaurant with a fine patio and serious emphasis on beer. The twenty-eight taps favor beers from Northern California, Washington, and Oregon; the bound beer menu is informative; and tasters are available in flights of five.

Also in Santa Monica
McGinty's Irish Pub, 2615 Wilshire Blvd., 310-828-9839. Irish pub.
Ye Olde King's Head, 116 Santa Monica Blvd., 310-451-1402. British pub.

SANTA ROSA

Third Street Aleworks 🅱
610 Third St., 707-523-3060
★★☆☆   Lunch–late
Food: Brewpub fare   *Smoking:* None

Two-level pub—one industrial with glass and metal, the other woody and lodge-like—with pool and darts upstairs. Well-designed beers.

SEAL BEACH

The Abbey
306 Main St., 562-799-4246
  ★☆☆☆   11 A.M.–late
Food: California fusion   *Smoking:* None

A storefront restaurant that emphasizes beer-food pairings. Twelve tap choices, micros and Belgian beers. Received national attention in 1998 when baseball slugger Mark McGwire began wearing the pub's hat. McGwire, pub insiders say, sticks to soda.

SEBASTOPOL

Powerhouse Brewing Co. Ⓑ
268 Petaluma Ave., 707-209-2739
  ★★☆☆   Noon–midnight (closed Mondays; evening-only Tuesdays)
Food: Brewpub fare   *Smoking:* None

Located in a former railroad powerhouse, decorated with folk art and New Orleans-inspired items. Regular New Orleans-style live music, also blues and folk. Food focuses on fresh ingredients and menu changes seasonally. Well-made ales. No television.

SOLANA BEACH

Pizza Port Ⓑ
135 N. U.S. Highway 101, 760-481-7332
  ★★☆☆   11 A.M.–midnight
Food: Pizza, pasta   *Smoking:* None

Caters to surfers, plays skiing and surfing videotapes when there are no live sporting events on television. As well as its own well-done beers, serves interesting guest beers.

SUNNYVALE

Stoddard's Brewhouse & Eatery Ⓑ
111 S. Murphy Ave., 408-733-7824
★★★☆   Lunch–late
Food: Brewpub fare plus   *Smoking:* None

Terrific food, including wood-fried pizzas, but expect to spend more than in the average brewpub. Stylish setting. Wonderful, award-winning ales. Live music draws crowds Friday nights, Sunday afternoons.

Also in Sunnyvale
Faultline Brewing, 1235 Oakmead Parkway, 408-736-2739. Brewpub; another in Walnut Creek.

Also in California
Arnold: Snowshoe Brewing, 2050 Highway 4, 530-795-2272. Brewpub.
Belmont Shores: Belmont Brewing Co., 25 39th Place, 562-433-3891. Brewpub.
Burbank: Gordon Biersch Brewing Co., 145 S. San Fernando Blvd., 818-592-5240. Brewpub; see San Francisco.
Burlingame: Dicey Riley's, 221 Park Road, 650-347-7656. Irish pub.
Burlingame: Steelhead Brewing Co. at Burlingame Station, 333 California Drive, 650-344-6050. Brewpub.
Campbell: Rock Bottom Restaurant & Brewery, 1875 S. Bascom Ave., 408-377-0707. Brewpub; see Denver, Colorado.
Carlsbad: Carlsbad Pizza Port, 571 Carlsbad Village Drive, 760-720-7007. Brewpub; see Solana Beach.
Columbia: Parrotts Ferry Brewing Co., 22265 Parrotts Ferry Road, 209-532-3089. Brewpub.
Corona: Main Street Brewery, 300 N. Main St., 909-371-1471. Brewpub.
Coronado: Coronado Brewing Co., 170 Orange Ave., 619-437-4452. Brewpub.
Cupertino: Duke of Edinburgh, 10801 N. Wolfe Road, 408-446-3853. British pub.
Escondido: Bubba's, 201 W. Mission, 760-745-9005. Multi-tap.
Fairfax: Ross Valley Brewing Co., 765 Center Blvd., 415-485-1005. Brewpub.
Fortuna: Eel River Brewing Co., 1777 Alamar Way, 707-725-2739. Brewpub.
Hermosa Beach: Brewski's Brewing Co., 73 Pier Ave., 310-273-9754. Brewpub.

Ein Stein's Restaurant & Brewery, 1301 Manhattan Ave., 310-379-3943. Brewpub.

Huntington Beach: Huntington Beach Beer Co., 201 Main St., 714-960-5343. Brewpub.

Irvine: Backstreet Brewery/Lampost Pizza, 14450 Culver, 949-857-0160. Brewpub.

McCormick & Schmick's/Bayhawk Ales, 2000 Main St., 949-442-7565. Brewpub.

Rock Bottom Restaurant & Brewery, 71 Fortune Drive, 949-453-0777. Brewpub; see Denver, Colorado.

Steelhead Brewery & Cafe, 4175 Campus Drive, 949-856-2227. Brewpub; see Eugene, Oregon.

Kensington: Kensington Circus, 389 Colusa, 510-524-8814. British pub.

La Jolla: Hops! Bistro & Brewery, 4353 La Jolla Village Drive, 619-587-6677. Brewpub.

Karl Strauss' Brewery & Grill, 1044 Wall St., 619-551-2739. Brewpub; see San Diego.

La Jolla Brewing, 7536 Fay Ave., 619-456-2739. Brewpub.

Laguna Beach: Laguna Beach Brewing, 422 S. Coast Highway, 949-499-2337. Brewpub.

Ocean Brewing Co., 237 Ocean Ave., 949-497-3381. Brewpub.

Laguna Hills: Gordon Biersch, Brewery Restaurant, 24032 El Toro Road, 949-770-0123. Brewpub.

Lancaster: Antelope Brewing Co., 44599 Valley Central Way, 805-940-7390. Brewpub.

McKinleyville: Six Rivers Brewing Co., 1300 Central Ave., 707-839-7580. Brewpub.

Manhattan Beach: Manhattan Beach Brewing, 124 Manhattan Beach Blvd., 310-798-2744. Brewpub.

Middletown: Mount St. Helens Brewing Co., 21167 Calistoga St., 707-987-3361. Brewpub.

Millbrae: Fiddler's Green, 333 El Camino Real, 650-697-4319. Irish pub.

Morro Bay: Morro Bay Brewing Co., 280 Harbor St., 805-772-3534. Brew-on-premise, brewpub.

Northridge: Country Club Brewery & Restaurant, 19530 Nordhoff St., 818-773-4677. Brewpub.

Oakdale: Oakdale Brewing Co., 160 N. Third Ave., 209-845-2739. Brewpub.

Pacific Beach: Terrific Pacific, 721 Grand Ave., 619-270-3596. Brewpub.

Pinole: Atlas Alehouse, 2361 San Pablo Ave., 510-724-2537. Alehouse.

Rancho Cucamonga: Compass Creek Restaurant & Brewery, 11837 Foothill Blvd., 909-483-1140. Brewpub.

Redlands: Brickhouse Brewery & Restaurant, 19 E. Citrus Ave., 909-798-7172. Brewpub.

Salinas: Penny Farthing Tavern, 9 E. San Luis St., 408-424-5652. British pub.

San Bernardino: Pig's Eye Pub, 1987 Diners Court, 909-889-1442. Restaurant/pub.

San Marcos: San Marcos Brewery & Grill, 1080 W. San Marcos Blvd., 760-471-0050. Brewpub.

San Rafael: Broken Drum Brewery & Wood Grill, 1132 4th St., 415-456-4677. Brewpub.

Willow Street Pizza & Brewery, 812 4th St., 415-453-4200. Brewpub.

Santa Fe Springs: Maggie's Pub, 11900 Telegraph Road, 562-944-5399. British pub.

Santa Fe Hops Brewhouse, 12120 Telegraph Road, 562-941-1065. Brewpub.

Sonoma: Sienna Red Brewery, 529 1st St. W., 707-938-1313. Brewpub.

South Lake Tahoe: Brewery at Lake Tahoe, 3542 S. Lake Tahoe Blvd., 916-544-2739. Brewpub.

Stinson Beach: Stinson Beach Grill, 3465 Shoreline, 415-868-2002. Restaurant/pub.

Stockton: Valley Brewing Co., 157 W. Adams St., 209-948-2537. Brewpub.

Suisun City: Grizzly Bear Brewing Co., 325 Main St., 707-434-8033. Brewpub.

Tustin: Tustin Brewpub, 13011 Newport Ave., 714-665-2337. Brewpub.

Upland: British Bulldog Pub & Restaurant, 1667 N. Mountain Ave., 909-946-6614. British pub.

Old Baldy Brewing, 271 2nd Ave., 909-946-1750. Brewpub.

Valencia: Maltzee's Stuft Pizza & Brewery, 18810 Soledad Canyon Blvd., 661-252-7883. Brewpub.

Wolf Creek Brewing, 277746 McBean Parkway, 661-263-9653. Brewpub.

Van Nuys: Robin Hood Inn, 13640 Burbank Blvd., 818-994-6045. British pub.

Walnut Creek: Black Diamond Brewing, 2330 N. Main St., 925-943-2330. Brewpub.

Faultline Brewing Co., 1563 Cypress St., 925-938-2739. Brewpub.

Westwood: Westwood Brewing Co., 1097 Glendon, 310-209-2739. Brewpub.

Woodland Hills: BJ's Pizza, Grill & Brewery, 6424 Canoga Ave., 818-340-1748. Brewpub; see Brea.

Regional beers to look for: Again, too many to list; so, keeping to five, we suggest: New Belgium Brewing (don't stop with Fat Tire); Lefthand/Tabernash Brewing; Great Divide; Odell Brewing; and Avery Brewing.

Essential stops: Wynkoop and Falling Rock in Denver; Phantom Canyon in Colorado Springs.

Just for fun: You can visit the original New Belgium brewhouse at Wolf Tongue Brewery in Nederland.

Best city for a pub crawl: Denver; start at Wynkoop and head for Coors Field.

ASPEN

Howling Wolf Ⓑ
424 E. Cooper, 970-920-7771
★★☆☆   11:30 A.M.–late
Food: Brewpub fare   *Smoking:* Separate sections

The Flying Dog Brewpub became the Howling Wolf in 1999, all the dog stuff came off the walls, a hardwood floor went in and this became a brewpub/nightclub. However, brewer Don Wolfe remained in charge of the beer.

BOULDER

Mountain Sun Pub & Brewery Ⓑ
1535 Pearl St., 303-546-0866
★★★☆   11 A.M.–late
Food: Brewpub fare   *Smoking:* None

Feels like it's related to the McMenamins pubs in Oregon, with a sun painted on the wall, a laid-back atmosphere, and food that's a value. An airy, comfortable storefront. Supplements its own interesting beers with other Colorado craft beers.

Oasis Brewery Ⓑ
1095 Canyon Blvd., 303-449-0363
★★⯪☆   11:30 A.M.–late
Food: Brewpub fare   *Smoking:* None

Egyptian decor from the pyramids on top of the building to the mural behind the bar. Patio has nice view of the Rockies. Tasty higher-gravity ales, but remember you're drinking at altitude.

Old Chicago
1102 Pearl St., 303-443-5031
★★☆☆   11 A.M.–2 A.M.
Food: Pizza, calzones   *Smoking:* None

This was the first restaurant in the Old Chicago chain, which stood at thirty-nine in mid-1999. It opened on the Pearl Street Mall in the early 1970s, named after a pinball machine. Each location has thirty or more beers on tap, an extensive bottle selection, and offers a "beer tour."

Redfish Brewing Co. Ⓑ
2027 13th St., 303-440-5858
★★☆☆   11 A.M.–2 A.M. (opens at 10 A.M. weekends)
Food: Bistro fare   *Smoking:* None

Excellent New Orleans-style cuisine with focus on fish in a stylish setting. More casual bar in back, with a wide range of styles, including several Belgian ales brewed here.

Walnut Brewery Ⓑ
1123 Walnut, 303-447-1345
★★☆☆   11 A.M.–late
Food: Brewpub fare   *Smoking:* None

The first brewpub in Boulder. A former warehouse, with thirty-foot ceilings, lots of exposed brick, and a nifty perch for the piano. Part of the Rock Bottom chain, very good food.

Wilderness Pub Ⓑ
2880 Wilderness Place, 303-444-8448
★★☆☆   11 A.M.–late (closed Sundays)
Food: Brewpub fare   *Smoking:* None

Rockies Brewing (maker of Boulder beers) started in a goat-shed in Longmont, then moved here. The pub overlooks the brewery.

BRECKENRIDGE

Breckenridge Brewery & Pub Ⓑ
600 S. Main, 970-453-1550
★★☆☆   11 A.M.–late
Food: Brewpub fare   *Smoking:* Separate sections

Breckenridge beers were first brewed here within view of the ski slopes. The owners then built pubs in several states before retreating to Colorado, where they still run several pubs, including a nearby barbecue restaurant that features many guest beers.

CARBONDALE

Lone Wolfe Brew Pub Ⓑ
403 Main St., 970-963-9757

★★☆☆   3:30 P.M.–2 A.M. (opens at noon weekends)
Food: Sandwiches   *Smoking:* Throughout

Has the western feel of a place that was previously called the Old Nugget Pub. Nothing fancy, a couple of pool tables, bar food and interesting beer, particularly the IPA.

COLORADO SPRINGS

Jack Quinn's Irish Ale House & Pub
21 S. Tejon, 719-385-0766

★☆☆☆   11 A.M.–2 A.M.
Food: Irish pub fare   *Smoking:* Separate sections

Elegant, urban Irish pub with wood-paneled booths, long communal tables, and dim lighting. Large single-malt menu complements mostly British and Irish beers on tap. Vintage advertising bedecks the walls, with other antiques in glass cases. Offspring of Jack Quinn's in Covington, Kentucky; more may be coming.

Phantom Canyon Brewing Ⓑ
2 E. Pikes Peak Ave., 719-635-2800

★★★☆   11 A.M.–2 A.M.
Food: Brewpub fare   *Smoking:* Separate sections

In a building that first housed railroad offices one hundred years ago. A nicely-appointed, open restaurant with a pool hall upstairs. Food packs 'em in at lunch, families come here for dinner, and the crowd gets younger at night. Excellent beers, including two on handpump.

Also in Colorado Springs

Hops Grill & Bar, 975 N. Academy Blvd., 719-380-7100. Brewpub; part of Florida-based chain.

Il Vicino, 11 S. Tejon, 719-475-9224. Brewpub; see Albuquerque, New Mexico.

Judge Baldwin's Brewing Co., Doubletree Hotel, 4 S. Cascade, 719-473-5600. Brewpub.

Old Chicago, 7115 Commerce Center Drive, 719-593-7678. See Boulder.

Old Chicago, 4110 N. Academy Blvd., 719-536-0633.

Old Chicago, 118 N. Tejon, 719-634-8812.

Warehouse Restaurant/Palmer Lake Brewing, 25 W. Cimarron St., 719-475-8880. Brewpub.

CRESTED BUTTE

The Idlespur/Crested Butte Brewing ⓑ
226 Elk Ave., 970-349-5026
★★☆☆   2 P.M.–2 A.M.
Food: Brewpub fare   *Smoking:* Separate sections

A ski pub with rough-hewn beams and a river-rock fireplace. Actor Tom Skerritt is one of the owners and collected the medal the brewery won at the 1998 Great American Beer Festival.

Also in Crested Butte

The Eldo Brewery & Taproom, 215 Elk Ave., 970-349-6125. Brewpub.

DENVER

Brendan's
1624 Market St., 303-595-0609
★☆☆☆   4 P.M.–late (opens at 7 P.M. weekends)
Food: Tavern fare   *Smoking:* Throughout

A spare downstairs blues bar, often featuring national acts. Nineteen beers on tap, mostly craft products.

Broadway Pub & Tasting Room ⓑ
2441 Broadway, 303-292-5027
★★☆☆   11 A.M.–2 A.M. (opens at 5 P.M. Sundays)
Food: Tavern fare   *Smoking:* Separate sections

Lively pub-restaurant attached to the brewery owned by Flying Dog, which brews Flying Dog and other Colorado-labeled beers here. Those beers plus other Colorado products available.

Bull & Bush Pub & Brewery ⓑ
4700 Cherry Creek Drive S., 303-759-0333
★★½☆   11 A.M.–2 A.M. (opens at 10 A.M. weekends)
Food: British pub fare   *Smoking:* Separate sections

A British pub for nearly thirty years, with classic fixtures and a menu that also includes American dishes. Added its own brewery a few years ago, making excellent British-style ales.

Champion Brewing Co. Ⓑ
Larimer Square, 303-534-5444
　　★☆☆☆　　　11 A.M.–2 A.M.
　　Food: Brewpub fare　　*Smoking:* Separate sections

Expansive brewery-restaurant in Larimer Square, where crowds gather in the basement to watch sports on TV. Inviting outdoor patio.

Cherry Cricket
2641 E. 2nd Ave., 303-322-7666
　　★★☆☆　　　11 A.M.–2 A.M.
　　Food: Tavern fare　　*Smoking:* Throughout

Draws a mixed but youngish crowd in upscale Cherry Creek; great burgers and comfortable dining. Full spirits menu, eighteen beers on tap, mostly craft products.

Denver Chop House & Brewery Ⓑ
1735 19th St., 303-296-0800
　　★★☆☆　　　11 A.M.–closing
　　Food: Steakhouse　　*Smoking:* Separate sections

Part of the Rock Bottom family, offering food two cuts above many brewpubs. Something—spirits, wines, house beers for the beginner—for everybody. Although Rock Bottom and related pubs are part of a chain, brewers at each location are free to produce some special beers, and the ones here are quite interesting.

Falling Rock Tap House
1919 Blake St., 303-293-8338
　　★★★↓　　　11 A.M.–1 A.M.
　　Food: Tavern fare　　*Smoking:* Throughout

The T-shirts here advertise "No Crap on Tap." Sixty-nine taps offer the widest selection of beer available in Colorado, both local products and excellent beer from afar; also a full menu of upscale spirits. Comfortable brick setting, knowledgeable staff.

Goosetown Tavern

3242 E. Colfax Ave., 303-399-9703

★★☆☆   11 A.M.–late

Food: Tavern fare   *Smoking:* Separate sections

The state's oldest bar. Operated as Goosetown Tavern and then Sam's Land since 1873 in Golden, before Coors Brewing bought it and ticketed the tavern for demolition. Many of the parts were saved and moved here. Twelve draft choices, mostly local craft beers.

My Brother's Bar

2376 15th St., 303-455-9991

★★☆☆   11 A.M.–1:30 A.M.

Food: Tavern fare   *Smoking:* Separate sections

This place has been around with one name or another for a hundred-plus years. Brick walls, a tin ceiling, theater posters on the walls, and classical music in the background mix well with unpretentious food and a solid draft lineup.

Pint's Pub 🅑

221 W. 13th Ave., 303-534-7543

★★⯪☆   11 A.M.–11 P.M. (closes at 8 P.M. Sundays)

Food: British pub fare   *Smoking:* Separate sections

A British pub that added its own small brewhouse in 1997. Still offers a wide range of imports and Colorado beers on tap, delivers food orders on beer trays and has an astonishing selection (a hundred-plus) of single-malt whiskies.

Rock Bottom Brewery & Restaurant 🅑

1001 16th St., 303-534-7616

★★☆☆   11 A.M.–late

Food: Brewpub fare   *Smoking:* Separate sections

The cornerstone pub in the national chain that includes Old Chicago, Chop House, and Walnut Brewery. Huge, airy and always busy. Like all Rock Bottoms, offers well-made food, pool.

SandLot Brewery at Coors Field 🅑

Coors Field, 2145 Blake St., 303-298-1587

★★☆☆   11 A.M.–7 P.M. (opens two hours before games)

Food: Tavern fare   *Smoking:* Separate sections

An adventurous lineup of in-house beers. As you would expect, crowded on game days, when you need a ticket even to get in. Visit when the Rockies aren't playing.

Skyline Café
777 W. 29th Ave., 303-296-3232

☆☆☆☆ 11 A.M.–2 A.M.

Food: Tavern fare *Smoking:* Throughout

Comfortable, though smoky, roadhouse with live music and a wide range of beer from twenty taps. Popular spot for live music.

Wynkoop Brewing Co. Ⓑ
1634 18th St., 303-297-2700

★★★☆ 11 A.M.–late

Food: Brewpub fare *Smoking:* Separate sections

The first brewpub in the Rockies, in a neighborhood that has grown trendy. Regionally inspired food, beer, service, ambience. Large pool hall upstairs.

Also in Denver

Breckenridge Brewery and Pub, 2220 Blake St., 303-297-3644. Brewpub.

Café Berlin, 2005 E. 17th Ave., 303-377-5896. Restaurant.

Dixon's Downtown Grill, 16th & Wazee, 303-573-6100. Brewpub.

Fadó Irish Pub, 1735 19th St., 303-297-0066. Irish pub.

Great Northern Tavern, 8101 E. Belleview Ave., Unit C, 303-770-4741. Taproom for Keystone Brewery.

Heavenly Daze Warehouse, Brewery and Bar, 208 S. Kalamath St., 303-744-8000. Brewpub.

Hops Grill & Bar, 149 Steele St., 303-377-0909. Brewpub.

Nallen's Irish Pub & Grill,1429 Market St., 303-572-0667. Irish bar.

Old Chicago, 1415 Market St., 303-893-1806. See Boulder.

Old Chicago, 1280 S. Colorado Blvd., 303-753-0824.

Pearl Street Grill, 1477 Pearl St., 303-778-6475. Restaurant.

Zang Brewing Co., 2301 7th St., 303-455-2500. Sports bar located in Colorado's first brewery.

DURANGO

Carver's Bakery Café Brewery Ⓑ
1022 Main St., 970-259-2545

★★☆☆ 6 A.M.–10 P.M. (closed Sundays)

Food: Café fare *Smoking:* Separate sections

Comfortable spot to hang out for coffee in the morning (the bakery is outstanding), beer at night. Wide range of beers, some on handpump.

Lady Falconburgh's Barley Exchange
640 Main St., 970-382-9664
★★★☆   11:30 A.M.–2:30 A.M.
Food: Bistro fare   *Smoking:* Separate sections

A beer and food venue, offering twenty imports and craft beers on tap, large bottle menu. Located in the basement of a historic building, decorated with murals, beer ads, and hopvines.

Also in Durango
Steamworks Brewing Co., 801 E. 2nd Ave., 970-259-9200. Brewpub.

ESTES PARK

Estes Park Brewery Ⓑ
470 Prospect Village Drive, 970-586-5421
★☆☆☆   Noon–closing
Food: Brewpub fare   *Smoking:* Separate sections

Slightly off the beaten path in this tourist town at the entrance to Rocky Mountain National Park. Beer isn't as interesting as when the pub opened.

FORT COLLINS

CooperSmith's Pub and Brewing Ⓑ
No. 5 Old Town Square, 970-498-0483
★★★☆   11 A.M.–2 A.M.
Food: Brewpub fare   *Smoking:* Separate sections

Excellent beer—usually one on handpump—solid food, and always interesting seasonals. Outdoor seating is on the Old Town Plaza, and there's a second bar and pool room. Large single-malt menu.

Crown Pub
134 S. College Ave., 970-484-5929
★☆☆☆   11:30 A.M.–2:30 A.M.
Food: Tavern fare   *Smoking:* Throughout

A cigar-friendly bar with twenty-five single-malt whiskies and a rotating selection of imports and regional craft beers available from eight taps.

Washington's
132 LaPorte Ave., 970-493-1603
   ★☆☆☆   11:30 A.M.–closing
Food: Tavern fare   *Smoking:* Separate sections

Rambling tavern that's been around for twenty years. Dark and comfortable with walls covered with "stuff." Seven bars in the place, the longest offering twenty-seven taps, both mainstream beers and imports.

Also in Fort Collins
C.B. & Potts/Big Horn Brewing, 1427 W. Elizabeth St., 970-221-5954. Brewpub.
Linden's Brewing Co., 214 Linden St., 970-982-9191. Brewpub.
Moot House, 2626 S. College Ave., 970-226-2121. Restaurant.
Old Chicago, 147 S. College, 970-482-8599. See Boulder.

FRISCO

Backcountry Brewery & Restaurant Ⓑ
720 Main St., 970-468-6488
   ★☆☆☆   11 A.M.–midnight
Food: Brewpub fare   *Smoking:* Separate sections

Spacious, airy brewpub with a vaulted ceiling and large windows overlooking downtown Frisco, mountains, and lake. Salad bar includes excellent soups.

IDAHO SPRINGS

Tommyknocker Brewery & Pub Ⓑ
1401 E. Miner St., 303-567-2688
   ★★⯪☆   11 A.M.–2 A.M.
Food: Brewpub fare   *Smoking:* Separate sections

First pub in chain that has spread to other states and also distributes bottled beers. As Victorian as the rest of the buildings in town. Tommyknockers are elflike creatures who protected the miners who settled here in the 1860s. Distinctive beers.

KEYSTONE

Great Northern Tavern & Brewery Ⓑ
91 River Run Road, 970-262-2202
   ★★☆☆   11:30 A.M.–midnight
Food: Brewpub fare   *Smoking:* Separate sections

A large, shiny ski pub, with plenty of dark wood and prices a bit above average. Solid beer and outstanding food.

LONGMONT

Mike O'Shay's Restaurant
512 Main St., 303-772-0252
★☆☆☆   11 A.M.–late (closed Sundays)
Food: Tavern fare   *Smoking:* Separate sections

Locals hangout in popular stretch of Main Street. Solid grub, full bar. Gathering spot for both Bud and craft beer drinkers.

Pumphouse Brewery & Restaurant Ⓑ
540 Main St., 303-702-0881
★★☆☆   11 A.M.–late (opens at 11:30 A.M. weekends)
Food: Brewpub fare   *Smoking:* Separate sections

Family-friendly restaurant decorated in firehouse motif (mini-hydrants on the tap handles). Interesting house ales, plus Colorado guest beers.

Also in Longmont
Left Hand Taproom, 562 Main St., 303-772-6500. Sells beer from
    Left Hand/Tabernash Brewing.
Old Chicago, 1805 Industrial Circle, 303-651-7000. See Boulder.

NEDERLAND

Wolf Tongue Brewery Ⓑ
35 E. 1st St., 303-258-7001
★★☆☆   Lunch–closing
Food: Tavern fare   *Smoking:* Throughout

A rustic tavern with a potbellied stove, a fine moosehead, lots of wood, and locals who still order Bud. Beers brewed here are award winners, made in New Belgium Brewing's original four-barrel brewhouse.

STEAMBOAT SPRINGS

Heavenly Daze Brewery Ⓑ
1860 Ski Times Square, 970-879-8080
★★☆☆   11 A.M.–10 P.M.
Food: Brewpub fare   *Smoking:* Separate sections

A multi-level pub with great views of the slopes and beer good enough to distribute throughout Colorado.

Steamboat Brewery & Tavern Ⓑ
435 Lincoln Ave., 970-879-2233
   ★★☆☆   11:30 A.M.–1 A.M.
Food: Brewpub fare   *Smoking:* Separate sections

Very much a tavern, with plenty of breweriana on the walls. Solid lineup of ales with some excellent seasonals.

VAIL

Hubcap Brewery and Kitchen Ⓑ
143 E. Meadow Drive, 970-476-5757
   ★★☆☆   11 A.M.–2 A.M.
Food: Brewpub fare   *Smoking:* Separate sections

Comfortable, friendly pub, an escape of sorts from the usual in upscale Vail. Intimate pub area, with wide range of beers usually available. Ozone Barley Wine is an award winner and perfect for a cold night.

Kaltenberg Castle Royal Bavarian Brewhouse Ⓑ
600 Lionshead Mall, 970-479-1050
   ★★☆☆   Lunch–late (more limited out of season)
Food: German fare   *Smoking:* Separate sections

Once a ski lift gondola house, now a German chalet. The brewing system and much of the decor come from Germany, the food is German, and the beers are brewed true to German styles.

Also in Colorado
Arvada: Old Chicago, 8711 Wadsworth, 303-431-7707. See Boulder.
Aurora: Old Chicago, 16990 E. Iliff Ave., 303-338-0144.
Cortez: Main Street Brewery, 21 E. Main St., 970-564-9112. Brewpub.
Dillon: Dillon Dam Brewery, 100 Little Dam Road, 970-262-7777. Brewpub.
    Pug Ryan's Brew Pub, 104 Village Place, 970-468-2145. Brewpub.
Englewood: Walnut Brewery, 9627 E. County Line Road, 303-792-9090. Brewpub; see Boulder.
Glenwood Springs: Glenwood Canyon Brewpub, 402 7th St., 970-945-1276. Brewpub.
Grand Junction: Old Chicago, 120 North Ave., 970-244-8383.
    Rock Slide Brewery, 401 Main St., 970-245-2111. Brewpub.
Greeley: Old Chicago, 2349 W. 29th St., 970-330-1116.
    Smiling Moose, 25011 11th Ave., 970-356-7010. Brewpub.

Union Colony Brewery, 1412 8th Ave., 970-356-4116. Brewpub.

Lakewood: Old Chicago, 3550 S. Wadsworth, 303-988-3414.

Littleton: Alcatraz Brewing Co., 8405 Park Meadows Center Drive, 303-649-1144. Brewpub.

5280 Roadhouse & Brewery, 5498 S. Rapp St., 303-798-5280. Brewpub.

Old Chicago, 7961 S. Broadway, 303-794-5959.

Louisville: Majestic Brewing Co., 270 S. Taylor Ave., 303-666-5914. Microbrewery tasting room.

Old Louisville Inn, 740 Front St., 303-666-9982.

Loveland: Namaqua Brewing Co., 437 N. Garfield, 970-635-9288. Brewpub.

Lyons: Oskar Blues Grill & Brew, 303 Main St., 303-823-6685. Brewpub.

Pueblo: Irish Brewpub, 108 W. 3rd St., 719-543-7272. Brewpub.

Salida: Il Vicino, 135 E. 2nd St., 719-539-5219. Brewpub; see Albuquerque, New Mexico.

Silverthorne: Old Chicago, 560 Silverthorne Lane, 970-468-2882.

Telluride: Smuggler's Brewpub, 225 S. Pine, 970-728-0919. Brewpub.

Thornton: Old Chicago, 3909 E. 120th Ave., 303-252-1113.

Westminster: C.B. & Potts/Big Horn Brewing Co., 1257 W. 120th Ave., 303-280-5008. Brewpub.

Old Chicago, 8711 Wadsworth Blvd., 303-431-7707.

CONNECTICUT

Regional beers to look for: New England Brewing and Hammer
  & Nail Brewery.
Essential stops: Eli Cannon's in Middletown; Main Street Café in
  Willimantic; BrüRm at BAR in New Haven. The latter is
  across the street from the venerable Louis Lunch, which claims
  to have invented the hamburger.
Just for fun: The Griswold Inn in Essex. Afternoons beside the
  piano in the Tap Room.
Best city for a pub crawl: Hartford.

BETHEL

Greenwood's
186 Greenwood Ave., 203-748-3900
  ★☆☆☆   Lunch–late
  Food: Full menu   *Smoking:* Separate sections

An English-style pub in an old Victorian opera house, with
four imports and a rotating fifth selection on tap, large bottle
menu. Frequently hosts beer tastings.

DANBURY

Hat City Ale House
253 Main St., 203-790-4287
  ★★☆☆   7 P.M.–late (opens at 4 P.M. Thursdays through
  Saturdays)
  Food: No kitchen   *Smoking:* Throughout

Twenty beers on tap in 125-year-old building with classic tin
ceiling, long dark bar. Decorated with photos that celebrate
city's hat-making tradition. Sells cigars, rents humidors.

Also in Danbury
Classic Rock Brewpub, 1 Wiebling Road, 203-792-4430. Brewpub.

ESSEX

Griswold Inn
36 Main St., 860-767-2633
★☆☆☆   11 A.M.–1 A.M.
Food: Full menu   *Smoking:* Separate sections

The oldest inn in continuous operation in the United States, once a stagecoach and steamboat stop. You may find someone playing the piano in the Tap Room, described by historian Lucius Beebe as "the most handsome barroom in America." Eight taps, favoring imports.

HARTFORD

Hartford Brewery Ⓑ
35 Pearl St., 860-246-2337
★★☆☆   Lunch–late
Food: Brewpub fare   *Smoking:* Separate sections

Upscale restaurant featuring New England specialties, with pub menu for bar area. Brewhouse used first in England, popular ales show British influence.

Trout Brook Brewery & Restaurant Ⓑ
45 Bartholomew Ave., 860-951-1680
★★☆☆   Lunch–late
Food: Brewpub fare   *Smoking:* Separate sections

Restaurant/sports bar/cigar bar with wide range of beers, barbecue and more on the menu. Also has a restaurant in Wallingford and its beer is on tap at more than one hundred locations.

Also in Hartford
City Steam Brasserie & Brewery Café, 942 Main St., 860-525-1600. Brewpub.
Lord Jim's Pub, 100 Pratt St., 860-522-7623. Restaurant/pub.

MIDDLETOWN

Eli Cannon's Tap Room
695 Main St., 860-347-3547
★★☆☆   Opening hours vary; closes late
Food: Tavern fare plus   *Smoking:* Throughout

Jammed with flea market finds, serving a wide-ranging menu with plenty of hot and spicy choices, thirty-six beers on tap, cigars, and single malts. Draft menu on a blackboard that includes the date a keg was tapped. Beer garden, twelve dartboards.

MYSTIC

Sam Adams Pub
105 Greenmanville Ave., 203-536-9649
★☆☆☆   Lunch–after dinner
Food: Full menu   *Smoking:* Separate sections

An upscale restaurant located in the Seamen's Inne, a replica of a sea captain's home overlooking Mystic Seaport Museum. Licenses the Sam Adams name and serves that beer among others.

NEW HAVEN

BrüRm at BAR Ⓑ
254 Crown St., 203-495-8924
★★½☆   Dinner–late (opens for lunch Tuesdays through Fridays)
Food: Brewpub fare, pizza   *Smoking:* Separate sections

Post-industrial modern in former garage with several cozy nooks. Innovative, well-done house beers. Thin, crispy, giant pizzas cooked in an oven that looks like it belongs in a foundry.

Also in New Haven
Naples Pizza, 90 Wall St., 203-776-9021. Brewpub.
Richter's, 900 Chapel St., 203-777-8400. Tavern.

SOUTH NORWALK

Brewhouse Restaurant Ⓑ
13 Marshall St., 203-866-1339
★★★☆   11 A.M.–late (closes early Sundays)
Food: Brewpub fare   *Smoking:* Only in the bar

New England Brewing's gleaming copper brewhouse sits in the middle of the restaurant in a restored warehouse. Excellent beer and food designed to go together in a wonderful setting—from the breweriana to the sixty-five-foot clock tower at the entrance (its Westminster chimes still work).

STAMFORD

Bank Street Brewing Co. Ⓑ
65 Bank St., 203-975-8728

★★☆☆　　11:30 A.M.–not particularly late

Food: Brewpub fare　　*Smoking:* Separate sections

Stunning brewpub in eighty-five-year-old restored bank building with beautiful arched windows and the bar where bank tellers once stood. Private parties are held in the old boardroom, which has a fireplace. Well-made British-style ales.

WILLIMANTIC

Willimantic Brewing Co./Main Street Café Ⓑ
967 Main St., 860-423-6777

★★⯪☆　　11:30 A.M.–late (opens 4 P.M. Sundays and Mondays)

Food: Brewpub fare　　*Smoking:* Separate sections

Restaurant-pub housed in the beautifully restored former post office at this old mill town, retaining many of the trappings and adding a sixty-foot mahogany bar. Serves a solid lineup of house beers with several outstanding guest products also on tap.

Also in Connecticut

Chester: The Pattaconk 1850 Bar, 33 Main St., 860-526-8134. Tavern.

Glastonbury: The Union, 2935 Main St., 860-633-0880. Brewpub.

Manchester: John Harvard's Brew House, 1487 Pleasant Valley Road, 860-644-2739. Brewpub; see Cambridge, Massachusetts.

Montville: Racebook Brewpub at the Mohegan Sun Casino, 860-204-8000. Brewpub.

Southport: Southport Brewing Co., 2600 Post Road, 203-256-2337. Brewpub.

Westport: John Harvard's Brew House, 540 Riverside Ave., 203-454-2337. Brewpub.

DELAWARE

Regional beers to look for: Dogfish Head Brewing.
Essential stops: Iron Hill Brewery & Restaurant.
Just for fun: The Deer Park Inn in Newark. Rumor has it that an old Mason and Dixon Line marker was once in the Deer Park's basement.
Best city for a pub crawl: Newark.

BEAR

Stewart's Brewing Co. Ⓑ
219 Governor's Square, 302-836-2739
★★☆☆   11 A.M.–1 A.M.
Food: Brewpub fare   *Smoking:* Separate sections

Comfortable pub that offers buffalo and ostrich on the menu and caters to a broad clientele. Plenty of TVs and nice horse-shoe-shaped bar. Usually a half dozen well-made beers available, mostly British-inspired ales.

GREENVILLE

Brandywine Restaurant & Brewpub Ⓑ
3901 Kennett Pike, 302-655-8000
★☆☆☆   11:30 A.M.–1 A.M.
Food: Brewpub fare   *Smoking:* Separate sections

Popular gathering spot upstairs in the back of an upscale out-door mall. Lovely back bar stacked with spirits, comfortable dining, fireplace.

NEWARK

Deer Park Inn
108 W. Main St., 302-731-5315
★☆☆☆   11 A.M.–1 A.M.
Food: Tex-Mex, more   *Smoking:* Separate sections

Rambling historic inn with a comfortable main barroom. Craft beers on tap and wide range in bottles. Victorian-style porch for dining.

Iron Hill Brewery & Restaurant Ⓑ
147 E. Main St., 302-888-2739
★★½☆   11:30 A.M.–late
Food: Brewpub fare   *Smoking:* Separate sections

A fine family stop with good food. Named for a local landmark that dates to the Revolutionary War, with beer names that draw on local heritage. Solid beer, and its Pig Iron Porter keeps winning the "Philly's Favorite Beer" blind tasting. Opened a second brewpub in West Chester, Pennsylvania.

Also in Newark
The Crab Trap, 57 Elkton Road, 302-366-8447. Restaurant with solid draft lineup.

REHOBOTH BEACH

Dogfish Head Brewery Ⓑ
320 Rehoboth Ave., 302-226-2739
★★★☆   4 P.M.–late (opens at noon Saturdays and Sundays, closed Mondays and Tuesdays)
Food: Brewpub fare   *Smoking:* Separate sections

Comfortable tavern, decorated with beer stuff and serving distinctive beers (shipped throughout the region from a separate microbrewery). Good food, much of it cooked with beer. Excellent live music on weekends.

WILMINGTON

Buckley's Tavern
15812 Kennett Pike, 302-656-9776
★☆☆☆   Lunch–late
Food: Full menu   *Smoking:* Separate sections

A popular dining spot for nearly fifty years, set in a colonial-style building. Eight draft selections, large bottle list, with limited seating at bar. Rooftop seating.

Also in Wilmington
John Harvard's Restaurant & Brewhouse, 303 Rocky Run Parkway, 302-477-6965. Brewpub; see Cambridge, Massachusetts.

Also in Delaware
Lewes: Rose & Crown Restaurant & Pub, 108 2nd St., 302-645-2373. Restaurant/pub.

DISTRICT OF COLUMBIA

Regional beers to look for: No microbreweries operate in Washington, D.C., but because of unique laws, more imports have generally been available here than in most places. Several retail stores offer massive selections of beer.

Essential stop: The Brickskeller.

Just for fun: Kramerbooks/Afterwords. Sip a craft beer at the bar and watch singles pretend to look for books while shopping for other singles. Remember, Monica Lewinsky shopped here.

The Big Hunt

1345 Connecticut Ave. NW, 202-785-2333

★★✫☆   11:30 A.M.–late (opens later weekends)

Food: Tavern fare   *Smoking:* Throughout

A small, narrow tavern with twenty-eight beers on tap, featuring Mid-Atlantic micros and imports. Funky stuff, like a mural with an alligator. Draws a large post-work crowd.

Brickskeller

1523 22nd St. NW, 202-293-1885

★★★★   11:30 A.M.–closing (opens at 6 P.M. weekends)

Food: Tavern fare   *Smoking:* Separate sections

Legendary for its enormous selection of beers, its auctions of "vintage" bottles, and visits from beer luminaries. It really is in a huge brick cellar, there are more than 600 bottle choices at any time, and every member of the staff has passed a 140-question beer exam.

Capitol City Brewing   🅑

1100 New York Ave. NW, 202-628-2222

★☆☆☆   11 A.M.–2 A.M.

Food: Brewpub fare   *Smoking:* Separate sections

The flagship pub for a chain that now operates inside and outside the Beltway. These are large pubs, meant to cater to crowds, and several of the house beers are aimed at the mainstream. Look for the one-off specials.

Kelly's Irish Times
14 F St. NW, 202-543-5433
★☆☆☆   10 A.M.–late
Food: Tavern fare   *Smoking:* Throughout

The welcome sign reads, "Give me your thirsty, your famished, your befuddled masses." There's a large picture of Richard Nixon shaking hands with Elvis over the bar. Popular bar for politicians, Irish and otherwise. Was a St. Patrick's Day favorite of President Ronald Reagan.

Kramerbooks/Afterwords
1517 Connecticut Ave. NW, 202-387-1400
★☆☆☆   11 A.M.–closing
Food: Bistro fare   *Smoking:* Separate sections

Afterwords, a café with a small bar area, is connected to Kramerbooks, a great and popular bookstore in Dupont Circle. Excellent food, nice patio, and the bar has a dozen taps with imports and craft beers.

My Brother's Place
237 2nd St. NW, 202-347-1350
★★½☆   11 A.M.–closing
Food: Tavern fare   *Smoking:* Separate sections

A sports bar and locals spot with late-night dancing. The most taps inside the Beltway, thirty-one handles covering the spectrum from mainstream to esoteric. Plenty of specials keep beer moving and fresh.

The Tombs
1226 36th St. NW, 202-337-6668
★☆☆☆   11 A.M.–late
Food: Tavern fare   *Smoking:* Separate sections

Located downstairs from the upscale 1789 restaurant, the Tombs is dark and woody, attracting a college and post-college crowd. Six taps, both mainstream and micros offered, and solid bottle selection.

Also in D.C.
Café Berlin, 322 Massachusetts Ave. NE, 202-543-7656. Restaurant.

Capitol City Brewing Co., 2 Massachusetts Ave. NE, 202-842-2337. Brewpub.

Colonel Brooks' Tavern NE, 901 Monroe St., 202-529-4002. Restaurant.

District Chophouse & Brewery, 509 7th St. NW, 202-347-3434. Brewpub; see Denver Chophouse, Denver, Colorado.

The Dubliner, 520 N. Capitol NW, 202-737-3772. Irish pub.

Fadó, 808 7th St., 202-789-0066. Irish pub.

Four Provinces, 3421 Connecticut Ave NW, 202-244-0860. Irish pub.

John Harvard's Brew House, 1299 Pennsylvania Ave. NW, 202-783-2739. Brewpub; see Cambridge, Massachusetts.

Murphy's Irish Pub, 2609 24th St. NW, 202-462-7171. Irish pub.

Regional beers to look for: Ybor City Brewing.
Essential stops: Paradise Alley in Jacksonville Beach, McGuire's Irish Pub in Pensacola.
Just for fun: McGuire's Irish Pub in Pensacola. Kiss the moose.
Best city for a pub crawl: Fort Lauderdale.

ATLANTIC BEACH

Ragtime Tavern & Grill ⓑ
207 Atlantic Blvd., 904-241-7877
★☆☆☆   11 A.M.–closing
Food: Brewpub fare   *Smoking:* Throughout

Housed in the oldest commercial building in the area and just a block from the ocean. Seating on two levels, with three bars. Seafood and Louisiana cuisine a specialty, quaffable ales.

BOCA RATON

Boca Ale House & Raw Bar
9244 Glades Road, 561-487-2989
★☆☆☆   11 A.M.–late
Food: Tavern fare   *Smoking:* Separate sections

This Ale House chain has more than a dozen locations in Boca, Jensen Beach, and Orlando-Kissimmee. Each offers about twenty beers on tap, a mixture of imports, mainstream beers, and better-known micros.

Gatsby's Boca
5970 SW 18th St., 561-393-3900
★☆☆☆   4 P.M.–late
Food: Tavern fare plus   *Smoking:* Throughout

Upscale billiards parlor with twenty beers on tap, plus carpeting, lots of mahogany, separate cigar/martini lounge.

Wilt Chamberlain's
8903 Glades Road, 561-488-8881
★☆☆☆   11:30 A.M.–late
Food: Full menu   *Smoking:* Separate sections

Multi-tap with wide selection of beer, sports bar, family spot. Arcade games for the kids, and even a small basketball court.

Also in Boca Raton
Brewzzi, 2222 Glades Road, 561-392-2739. Brewpub.
Lion and Eagle, 2410 N. Federal Highway, 561-394-3190.
  British pub.

DAYTONA BEACH

Bernkastel Festhaus
100 N. Atlantic Ave., 904-255-8300
  ★★⯪☆   10 A.M.–late
Food: Tavern fare   *Smoking:* Separate sections

A German bier hall with palm trees, separated from the Atlantic Ocean only by a beach. Forty-plus taps, mostly imports but some microbrewery beers.

FERN PARK

Hubb's
6557 Highway 17-92, 407-834-2337
  ★★☆☆   Lunch–late
Food: Tavern fare   *Smoking:* Separate sections

The first Hubb's opened nearly twenty years ago, and franchised versions operate in Florida and elsewhere. Each has thirty-nine beers on tap, 250-plus in bottles, and "colossal sandwiches."

FORT LAUDERDALE

Bier Brunnen
427-431 S. Atlantic Blvd., 954-462-1008
  ★☆☆☆   Lunch–2 A.M.
Food: German fare   *Smoking:* Throughout

German to the core, with six German beers on tap—each served in its own distinctive glass—and more in the bottle. Excellent red cabbage.

Shakespeare's Pub & Grill
1015 NE 26th St., 954-563-7833
  ★☆☆☆   Noon–late
Food: British pub fare   *Smoking:* Throughout

More than a dozen draft choices, mostly UK beers, with some keg beer served via handpump. Sunday roast with Yorkshire pudding.

Also in Fort Lauderdale
Brady's Irish Pub, 986 S. State Road 7, 954-973-1390. Irish pub.
Independence Restaurant & Brewery, 111 SW 2ⁿᵈ Ave., 954-524-2111. Brewpub.
Maguire's Hill 16, 535 N. Andrews Ave., 954-764-4453. Irish pub.
Rose & Crown Pub, 3660-80 W. Commercial Blvd., 954-731-6245. British pub.

FORT MYERS BEACH

Dusseldorf on the Beach
1113 Estero Blvd., 941-463-5251
★☆☆☆   Lunch–late
Food: Tavern fare   *Smoking:* Throughout

Bar in a two-story pink building across from the beach, offering mostly British ales and German lagers on tap and 125-plus bottled beers, including craft products and excellent imports. Friendly, knowledgeable service.

GAINESVILLE

Market Street Pub   Ⓑ
120 SW 1ˢᵗ Ave., 352-433-6789
★☆☆☆   11 A.M.–late (1–9 P.M. Sundays)
Food: British pub fare   *Smoking:* Separate sections

Old grocery store turned into a country British pub, with lots of wood, a separate room for darts. British-inspired pub fare (gourmet sausage) and ales.

JACKSONVILLE

Blue Anchor Pub
10550-2 Old St. Augustine Road, 904-262-1592
★★☆☆   11:30 A.M.–2 A.M.
Food: Tavern fare   *Smoking:* Throughout

Strip mall tavern, not fancy but very beery. Mostly imports and craft beers from twenty-five taps. Well-stocked humidor.

River City Brewing Co. Ⓑ
835 Museum Circle, 904-399-2299
★☆☆☆   11 A.M.–1 A.M.
Food: Brewpub fare   *Smoking:* Separate sections

Very large restaurant with equally expansive deck areas on the St. Johns River. A happy hour so popular patrons line up and pay for the buffet. Tasty ales, though served cold.

Also in Jacksonville
Bombay Bicycle Club, 8909 Baymeadows, 904-737-9555. Brewpub.
Hops Grill & Bar, 9826 San Jose Blvd., 904-886-0296. Brewpub.
Renaissance Brewing Co., 9810 Baymeadows Road, 904-642-6310. Taproom.
Seven Bridge Grille & Brewery, 9735 Gate Parkway N., 904-997-1999. Brewpub.

JACKSONVILLE BEACH

Paradise Alley
831 N. 1st St., 904-246-2837
★★★½   8:30 A.M.–closing
Food: Full menu   *Smoking:* Separate sections

Fifty-plus beers on tap (with plans to expand) and about 1,000 in bottles. If a beer is available in Florida it's here, and mixed six-packs are sold to go. Home cooking (meats from Pennsylvania, for instance). Friendly, knowledgeable service.

Also in Jacksonville Beach
Lynch's Irish Pub, 514 N. 1st St., 904-249-5181. Irish pub.

KEY WEST

Kelly's Caribbean Bar & Grill Ⓑ
301 Whitehead St., 305-293-8484
★☆☆☆   11 A.M.–late
Food: Brewpub fare   *Smoking:* Throughout

Actress Kelly McGillis and her husband own this brewpub. The menu is Caribbean inspired. One of the downstairs dining rooms is decorated with airline memorabilia. The other, the Crash Room, has a full bar fashioned after airplane wings.

LAKE BUENA VISTA

Big River Grille & Brewing Works 🅱
Disney's BoardWalk, 407-560-0253
★★☆☆   11:30 A.M.–late
Food: Brewpub fare   *Smoking:* Separate sections

Long and narrow brewpub located on Disney's BoardWalk. Busy all the time. Good beer, although not the range served at other Big River pubs.

MELBOURNE

Charlie & Jakes B-B-Q & Brewery 🅱
6300 N. Wickham Road, 407-752-7675
★☆☆☆   11 A.M.–after dinner (noon–9 P.M. Sundays)
Food: Barbecue   *Smoking:* Separate sections

A shopping center brewpub, family- and sports fan-friendly. Excellent barbecue, pleasant long bar. Award-winning beer.

Also in Melbourne
Coaster's Pub, 971-A Eau Gallie Blvd., 407-779-2739. Brewpub.

MIAMI

Churchill's Hideaway
5501 NE 2nd Ave., 305-757-1807
★☆☆☆   11:30 A.M.–3 A.M.
Food: Tavern fare   *Smoking:* Throughout

A British pub since 1937, with six British ales and Rolling Rock on tap. Known for its nightly music from national and local rock bands.

Also in Miami
Duffy's Tavern, 2100 SW 57th Ave., 305-264-6580. Tavern.
Thai Orchid, 965 SW 72nd St., 305-279-8583. Former brewpub, still serves craft beer.
Tobacco Road, 626 S. Miami Ave., 305-374-1198. Music club.

NAPLES

The English Pub
2408 Linwood, 941-774-2408

★☆☆☆   11 A.M.–midnight (call about Sundays)

Food: English pub fare   *Smoking:* Separate sections

An authentic British pub, nearly twenty years old. Mostly UK beers on tap, some (keg versions) on handpump. Darts.

Also in Naples

Old Florida Pub & Brewery, 1948 9th St. N., 941-403-3536. Brewpub.

ORLANDO

Shipyard Brew Pub Ⓑ
Main Terminal, Orlando Airport, 407-825-6474

★★☆☆   8 A.M.–8 P.M.

Food: Brewpub fare   *Smoking:* Separate sections.

The only airport "brewpub" in the U.S. that actually makes beer in the airport. Serving the excellent Shipyard beers in a pubby setting, with darts, checkers, and backgammon available. Decorated in a nautical theme.

Also in Orlando

Bull & Bush, 2408 E. Robinson St., 407-896-7546. British pub.

Cricketers Arms, 8445 International Drive, 407-354-0686. British pub.

Go Lounge, 5 Wall St., 407-422-1669. Tavern.

Hops Grill & Bar, 848 Sand Lake Road, 407-851-3131. Brewpub.

Mill Brewery, Eatery & Bakery, 5905 S. Kirkman Road, 407-345-4833. Brewpub.

Mulvaney's Irish Pub, 7220 International Drive, 407-352-7031. Irish pub.

Mulvaney's Irish Pub, 27 W. Church, 407-872-3296. Irish pub.

Orlando Ale House, 5573 S. Kirkman Road, 407-248-0000. Tavern.

Seven Red Roses English Tavern, 9472 S. Orange Blossom Trace, 407-240-9216. British pub.

PALM BAY

Tapp's Pub & Bistro
4711 Babcock St. NE, 407-952-2337
★★☆☆   11 A.M.–late
Food: Tavern fare   *Smoking:* Separate sections

A sports and darts bar (four leagues) that offers thirty-nine beers on tap and 200-plus in bottles. Most of the draft choices are imports and mainstream lagers, while the bottle selection includes craft beer.

PALM HARBOR

Brooker Creek Grille & Taproom Ⓑ
36221 E. Lake Road, 813-786-2966
★★☆☆   Lunch–late
Food: Brewpub fare   *Smoking:* Separate sections

Multi-tap (forty handles) with its own small brewhouse. Plenty of TVs usually turned to sports, excellent breweriana.

Also in Palm Harbor
Hoppers Pub & Grille, 3438 E. Lake Road, 813-786-3882. Restaurant/pub.
Hops Grill & Bar, 33086 U.S. 19 N., 813-789-5678. Brewpub.

PENSACOLA

McGuire's Irish Pub & Brewery Ⓑ
600 E. Gregory St., 850-433-6789
★★★☆   11 A.M.–late
Food: Full menu   *Smoking:* Separate sections

Repeat winner of *Florida Trend* magazine's Golden Spoon Award. Eclectic decorations include a giant moosehead, a Notre Dame room, and more than 150,000 signed dollar bills fluttering from the walls and ceiling. Among the beers brewed on the premises is a creamy stout.

Also in Pensacola
Brews Brothers, 830 N. Navy Blvd., 850-456-2534. Tavern.

ST. AUGUSTINE

A1A Taproom & Grille ⓑ
1 King St., 904-829-2977

★☆☆☆   Lunch–late

Food: Brewpub fare   *Smoking:* Separate sections

Two-level restaurant/pub, with copper-topped bar on first level, balcony seating on the second with a fine view of the marina. Nice seafood dishes, solid house beers.

Kings Head British Pub
6460 U.S. 1 N, 904-823-9787

★☆☆☆   11 A.M.–after dinner

Food: British pub fare   *Smoking:* Separate sections

A British pub housed in a Tudor-style building with a red double-decker bus and red telephone booth out front. Six beers on tap, mostly British. In the country six miles north of St. Augustine.

Also in St. Augustine
Sampson Brewery & Grill, 72 Spanish St., 904-829-0906. Brewpub.

SANIBEL

Sanibel Brew Pub ⓑ
1547 Periwinkle Way, 941-395-2030

★★☆☆   11:30 A.M.–10 P.M.

Food: Brewpub fare   *Smoking:* Separate sections

Well-made, true-to-style beers across the board, from a quaffable hefeweizen to the award-winning Hammerhead Sweet Stout.

SARASOTA

Sarasota Brewing Co. ⓑ
6607 Gateway Ave., 813-925-2337

★☆☆☆   11 A.M.–late (opens at noon Sundays)

Food: Tavern fare   *Smoking:* Separate sections

A woody lodge and sports bar catering to both locals and tourists. Investors were allowed to pick the names of some of the ales brewed here (but not the recipes).

SEMINOLE

London Bus
5667 Seminole Blvd., 727-399-1122
★☆☆☆   11:30 A.M.–late (opens at 5 P.M. Sundays)
Food: British pub fare   *Smoking:* Separate sections

Friendly pub with a bus out front, and the bar and darts area right inside the front door (dining in back). Mostly UK beers available from ten taps.

Also in Seminole
Rose & Crown, 11002 Seminole Blvd., 727-393-2867. British pub.

SOUTH PASADENA

Horse & Jockey
1155 Pasadena Ave. S., 727-345-4995
★☆☆☆   11:30 A.M.–10:30 P.M.
Food: British pub fare   *Smoking:* Separate sections

More than 2,000 antique plates and horse brasses decorate this pub, which serves as an English-style carvery on Sundays. Nine UK beers on tap, two (keg versions) served by handpump.

TAMPA

Four Green Fields
205 W. Platt St., 813-573-1623
★★☆☆   11 A.M.–2 A.M.
Food: Irish pub fare   *Smoking:* Separate sections

The only authentic thatched-roof pub in the United States. Thoroughly Irish in food, decorations, beer (four Guinness taps), and music. Music five times a week, often including international Irish performers.

Also in Tampa
Cobblestone Grille & Alehouse, 6902 Hanley Road, 813-249-5119. Restaurant/pub.
Hops Grill & Bar, 327 N. Dale Mabry Highway, 813-871-3600. Brewpub.
Hops Grill & Bar, 14303 N. Dale Mabry Highway, 813-264-0522. Brewpub.
Hops Grill & Bar, 1241 Fowler, 813-632-0717. Brewpub.
Hubb's, 13150 N. Dale Mabry Highway, 813-961-2337. Multitap.

New World Brewery, 1313 8ᵗʰ Ave. E., 813-248-4969. Multi-tap.
Tampa Bay Brewing Co., 1812 N. 15ᵗʰ St., 813-247-1422. Brew-pub.

WEST PALM BEACH

Lost Weekend
115 S. Olive Ave., 561-832-3452
★☆☆☆   4:30 P.M.–late
Food: No kitchen   *Smoking:* Throughout

College-type bar with thirteen beers on tap, imports and main-stream choices. Excellent 150-bottle menu and staff that knows about beer.

Also in West Palm Beach
John Bull English Pub, 801 Village Blvd., 561-697-2855. British pub.

Also in Florida
Boynton Beach: Boynton Beach Ale House & Raw Bar, 2212 W. Congress Ave., 561-735-0591. Restaurant/pub.
Hops Grill & Bar, 545 N. Congress Ave., 561-731-3313. Brewpub.
Red Lion Pub, 10114 S. Military Trail, 561-737-0434. British pub.
Bradenton: Crown & Anchor, 4921 Cortez Road W., 941-795-4575. British pub.
Hops Grill & Bar, 4502 14ᵗʰ St. W., 941-756-1069. Brewpub.
Brandon: Fox & Hounds, 229 E. Brandon Blvd., 813-685-8151. British pub.
Clearwater: Bombay Bicycle Club/Wildcat Brewing Co., 2721 Gulf to Bay Blvd., 727-799-1841. Brewpub.
Hops Grill & Bar, 1451 U.S. 19 S., 727-531-5300. Brewpub.
Tucson's Restaurant & Brewery, 13563 Icot Blvd., 727-530-0637. Brewpub.
Cocoa Beach: Pig & Whistle English Pub, 801 N. Atlantic Ave., 407-799-0724. British pub.
Coral Gables: The Crown & Garter, 270 Catalonia Ave., 305-441-0204. British pub.
Coral Springs: Big Bear Brewing Co., 1800 University Drive, 954-341-5545. Brewpub.
Delray Beach: Blue Anchor Pub, 804 E. Atlantic Ave., 561-272-7272. British pub.
Destin: McGuire's Irish Pub & Brewery of Destin, 33 Highway 98 E., 850-654-0567. Brewpub; see Pensacola.

Morgan's Sports Bar & Brewery, 14051 Emerald Coast Parkway, 850-650-2337. Brewpub.

Dunedin: Flanagan's Hunt Irish Pub, 465 Main St., 727-736-4994. Irish pub.

Fort Walton Beach: Santa Rosa Bay Brewery, 54 Miracle Strip Parkway, 850-664-2739. Brewpub.

Indian Rocks Beach: The Red Lion, 14-7 Gulf Blvd., 727-596-5411. British pub.

Jensen Beach: Jensen Ale House & Raw Bar, 3611 NW Federal Highway, 561-692-3293. Restaurant/pub.

Kissimmee: British Castle Tavern, I-92 in Kissimmee, 407-390-0504. British pub.

Fox & Hound Pub, 3514 W. Vine St., 407-847-9927. British pub.

Lady Lake: Spanish Springs Brewing Co., 1100 Main St., 352-750-4466. Brewpub.

Lakeland: Hops Grill & Bar, 4820 S. Florida Ave., 941-471-6200. Brewpub.

Ocala: Hops Grill & Bar, 2505 W. College Road, 352-237-8182. Brewpub.

Orange Park: Hops Grill & Bar, 1780 Wells Road, 904-278-7273. Brewpub.

Panama City: Panama City Brewery & Café, 11040 Hutchinson, 850-230-2739. Brewpub.

Pembroke Park: Billabong Pub, 3000 Country Club Lane, 954-985-1050. Australian pub.

Port Richey: Hops Grill & Bar, 10042 U.S. 19, 727-862-5913. Brewpub.

St. Petersburg Beach: Der Eisenhut, 357 Corey Ave., 727-367-6495. German.

Sebring: The Highlands Brewery, 623 Highway 27 S., 941-471-6280. Brewpub.

Tallahassee: Buckhead Brewery & Grill, 1900 Capital Circle NE, 850-942-4947. Brewpub.

Weston: The Sporting Brews, 2460 Weston Road, 954-385-8080. Brewpub.

Winter Park: Mulvaney's, 544 W. Fairbanks, 407-645-1117. Irish pub.

Orlando Ale House & Raw Bar, 101 University Park Drive, 407-671-1011. Restaurant/pub.

Ybor City: Irish Pub, 1721 7th Ave. E., 813-248-2099. Irish pub.

GEORGIA

Regional beers to look for: Atlanta Brewing's Red Brick beers; Sweetwater Brewing; Blind Man Ales.

Essential stops: Taco Mac in Cumming, Sandy Springs, or Snellville; The Globe in Athens.

Just for fun: Churchill Arms in Atlanta. Piano sing-alongs that defy the Buckhead "scene."

Best city for a pub crawl: Atlanta (and sneak up to Sandy Springs).

ALPHARETTA

Taco Mac
4305 State Bridge Road, 770-754-9290

★★☆☆   11 A.M.–late (opens at noon weekends)

Food: Tavern fare   *Smoking:* Separate sections

Taco Mac operates throughout the Atlanta area, serving Buffalo-style chicken wings and always a variety of beer. This location has ninety taps, much more than average (except for those run by Andy Klubock; see Cumming).

U.S. Border Brewery Cantina   Ⓑ
12460 Crabapple Road, 770-772-4400

★★☆☆   Lunch–late

Food: Tex-Mex   *Smoking:* Separate sections

Suburban brewpub that supplements regular house beers with outstanding special brews, some of them served on handpump.

ATHENS

Athens Brewing Co.   Ⓑ
312 E. Washington, 706-549-0027

★☆☆☆   11 A.M.–2 A.M. (closes earlier Sundays)

Food: Brewpub fare   *Smoking:* Separate sections

Two-story pub with more casual beer-hall seating, darts upstairs. Many house brews are styles less common in Georgia, supplemented with excellent menu of guest beers (some draft, mostly bottles). Beer books, magazines for in-house use. Good food.

The Globe
199 N. Lumpkin St., 706-353-4721
★★♪☆   4 P.M.–closing
Food: No kitchen   *Smoking:* Throughout

Downtown spot catering to an older (than student) crowd, with a nice bar area and stuffed chairs that offer a view of the street. Thirteen well-chosen taps, long bottle menu, more than sixty single-malts. No TV here (not even during the Olympics).

Also in Athens
Burnstone Brewhouse, 140 E. Washington, 706-549-5999. Brewpub.
Engine Room, 235 W. Washington, 706-353-3800. Neighborhood bar with solid tap section.
Mellow Mushroom, 259 E. Broad St., 706-613-0892. Multi-tap; see Atlanta.

ATLANTA

Atkins Park Restaurant
794 N. Highland Ave. NE, 404-876-7249
★☆☆☆   11 A.M.–4 A.M.
Food: Tavern   *Smoking:* Separate sections

The oldest bar in Atlanta. Dark and woody, a lovely neighborhood pub in the lovely Virginia-Highland neighborhood. Nine taps, mostly imports.

Churchill Arms
3223 Cains Hill Place, 404-233-5633
★☆☆☆   4 P.M.–2 A.M.
Food: No kitchen   *Smoking:* Throughout

Buckhead's neighborhood pub, with a piano right beside the bar for sing-alongs.

Fadó

3035 Peachtree Road, 404-841-0066

★☆☆☆   11:30 A.M.–late

Food: Irish pub fare   *Smoking:* Separate sections

The Irish Pub Co. has built scores of pubs in the United States and hundreds around the world, shipping the parts from Ireland. This was the first. The offspring are known as Fadó in many places, but also by other names. This one has five theme areas—Dublin Victorian, Country Cottage, Pub Store, Gaelic, and Brewery—which are common in other company pubs, although not usually all in the same one.

Max Lager's American Grill & Brewery **ⓑ**

320 Peachtree St., 404-525-4400

★☆☆☆   11:30 A.M.–late (opens 1 P.M. weekends)

Food: Brewpub fare   *Smoking:* Separate sections

Large downtown brewpub with fusion fare from a wood-fired grill. Solid house beers include a range of styles, both ales and lagers.

Mellow Mushroom

30 Pharr Road NW, 404-233-3443

★☆☆☆   Lunch–late

Food: Pizza   *Smoking:* Separate sections

This member of the pizza chain offers thirty-four draft selections and one hundred bottle choices. Included are many imports and several craft beers. Very casual dining.

Percy's Fish House **ⓑ**

3227 Roswell Road, 404-237-3227

★☆☆☆   5 P.M.–late

Food: Brewpub fare   *Smoking:* Separate sections

One of four brewpubs within walking distance in Buckhead, and the second to operate in this location. Solid ales, excellent fish, fine raw bar.

Prince of Wales

1144 Piedmont Ave. NE, 404-876-0227

★☆☆☆   Lunch–late

Food: British pub fare   *Smoking:* Throughout

A well-appointed, properly British pub in a lovely setting across from Piedmont Park. Twelve taps, most UK beers, and more than thirty single-malt whiskies. Under the same ownership as the Fox & Hounds and the Rose & Crown, which have a similar feel, but not Piedmont Park.

Taco Mac

1006 N. Highland Ave. NE, 404-873-6529
★☆☆☆   11 A.M.–2 A.M.
Food: Tavern fare   *Smoking:* Throughout

This is the site of the original Taco Mac, and representative of what to expect in beer—nine taps and more than 300 bottle choices—at most of the others.

The Vortex Bar & Grill

878 Peachtree St., 404-875-1667
★★☆☆   11:30 A.M.–late
Food: Tavern fare   *Smoking:* Separate sections

Moved from smaller quarters to here, but still didn't have room to accommodate a massive flea market-type collection. Solid draft selection, long bottle list, massive spirits menu. Good food, killer hamburgers, all served with an attitude that works. Also has a spot on Moreland Avenue.

Also in Atlanta

Atlanta BeerGarten, 3013 Peachtree Road, 404-261-9898. Brewpub.

Basta, 659 Peachtree St. NE, #1000, 404-874-8980. Bar.

Everybody's Pizza, 1040 N. Highland Ave., 404-873-4545. Pizza/beer.

Fox & Hounds, 1193 Collier Road NW, 404-352-1007. See Prince of Wales.

John Harvard's Brew House, 3041 Peachtree Ave., 404-816-2739. Brewpub; see Cambridge, Massachusetts.

Limerick Junction, 822 N. Highland Ave., 404-874-7147. Irish pub.

Manuel's Tavern, 602 N. Highland NE, 404-525-3447. Vintage tavern.

Mill Brewery, Eatery & Bakery, 500 10th St., 404-249-0001. Brewpub.

Rathskeller, 590 W. Peachtree St. NW, 404-881-6000. German.

Reggie's British Pub, 100 Techwood Drive, 404-525-1437. British pub.

Rock Bottom Brewery, 3242 Peachtree Road NE, 404-264-0253. Brewpub.

Rose & Crown, 288 E. Paces Ferry Road NE, 404-233-8168. See Prince of Wales.

CUMMING

Taco Mac
525 Lake Center Parkway, 770-886-4374
★★★☆   11 A.M.–late
Food: Tavern fare   *Smoking:* Separate sections

The third Taco Mac operated by Andy Klubock opened in early 1999 with 224 taps, giving it the largest draft selection in the world. It's a little more upscale than the other locations. Sports jerseys hang in Sandy Springs and Snellville; here the foyer is lined with 13,000 hand-glued stamps, and there's a hand-crafted eighteen-bell glockenspiel clock. With so many taps, offerings from a brewery tend to be very complete—for instance, up to seventeen beers from Rogue Ales in Newport, Oregon, have been on at one time.

DECATUR

Melton's App & Tap
2500 N. Decatur Road, 404-634-9112
★☆☆☆   Lunch–late
Food: Tavern fare   *Smoking:* Throughout

More restaurant than bar, with food made from scratch, but a well-chosen thirteen-tap lineup of beers includes both imports and craft products. Also many craft beers available by the bottle.

Also in Decatur
The Brick Store Pub, 125 E. Court Square, 404-687-0990. Restaurant/pub.
Twain's Billiards, 211 E. Trinity Place, 404-373-0063. Pool hall.

MARIETTA

Wild Wing Café
2145 Roswell Road, 770-509-9464
★★☆☆   Noon–late (opens at 4 P.M. Mondays)
Food: Tavern fare   *Smoking:* Separate sections

Very beer friendly, with frequent special events and tastings (such as single firkins of British ales). Fine twenty-five-tap lineup, excellent breweriana collection on display.

SANDY SPRINGS

Taco Mac
5830 Roswell Road, 404-257-0735
★★★☆   11 A.M.–closing
Food: Tavern fare   *Smoking:* Throughout

A showcase, with more than a hundred taps across the back wall and around the bar, plus coolers jammed with bottles. Island of spirits in the middle of the bar. See Cumming.

SNELLVILLE

Taco Mac
3334 U.S. 78, 770-736-1333
★★★☆   11 A.M.–closing
Food: Tavern fare   *Smoking:* Throughout

This Taco Mac has about 150 taps, most along a side wall, so you can stroll up and down to make your choice. See Cumming.

Also in Georgia
Augusta: King George Restaurant & Pub, Riverwalk at 8th St., 706-724-4755. Brewpub.
Kennesaw: Hops Grill & Bar, 745 Ernest Barrett Parkway, 770-919-0434. Brewpub.
Water Tower Brewing Co., 775 Cobb Place Blvd., 770-427-7679. Brewpub; see Eden Prairie, Minnesota.
Macon: Texas Cattle Co., Border Grille & Brewery, 2480 Riverside Drive, 912-741-1389. Brewpub.
Roswell: John Harvard's Brew House, 1574 Holcomb Bridge Road, 770-645-2739. Brewpub; see Cambridge, Massachusetts.
St. Simon's Island: St. Simon's Brewing Co., 100 Marina Drive, 912-638-0011. Brewpub.
Savannah: Moon River Brewing Co., 21 W. Bay St., 912-232-0933. Brewpub.
Warner Robins: Texas Cattle Co., Border Grille & Brewery, 2067 Watson Blvd., 912-929-7070. Brewpub.

HAWAII

Regional beers to look for: Kona Brewing; many West Coast products, including Deschutes Brewing.
Essential stops: Gordon Biersch.
Just for fun: Sam Choy's in Honolulu. Reserve the table in the small boat inside the restaurant—you may have to call well in advance.
Best city for a pub crawl: Honolulu.

HONOLULU

Gordon Biersch Ⓑ
101 Ala Moana Blvd., #1123, 808-599-4877
   ★★★☆   11:30 A.M.–late (opens at 10:30 A.M. Sundays)
Food: Upscale brewpub fare   *Smoking:* Separate sections

It feels timeless here, beneath the giant clock at Aloha Tower (once the tallest structure in Honolulu). Sit in the outdoor beer garden and get a sense of Honolulu's role as a major port. Ocean liners are tied up across the harbor, and smaller ships almost right next to you. The usual outstanding GB food and beer.

Murphy's Bar & Restaurant
2 Merchant St., 808-531-0422
   ★☆☆☆   11:30 A.M.–2 A.M.
Food: Tavern fare   *Smoking:* Separate sections

A two-room restaurant/pub with thirteen beers on tap, a few imports and mostly West Coast craft products, very well handled.

Ryan's Parkplace Bar & Grill
1200 Ala Moana Blvd., 808-523-9132
   ★☆☆☆   Lunch–late (opens at 5 P.M. Sundays)
Food: Tavern fare plus   *Smoking:* Separate sections

Twenty beers on tap, plenty from West Coast micros; award-winning pupus (appetizers) and other island food. Plenty of fruit drinks and a nice single-malt menu.

Sam Choy's Breakfast Lunch & Crab Shack
580 Nimitz Highway, 808-545-7979
    ★★☆☆   Breakfast–late
Food: Hawaiian   *Smoking:* Separate sections

Giant pub from a Hawaiian cooking legend. Large chalkboards hang above the display kitchen: one lists oysters available that day, another crab, another lobster, and another, appropriately enough, five fresh beers. Opened a second brewpub in Lahaina on Maui.

Also in Honolulu
brew moon, 1200 Ala Moana Blvd., 808-593-0088. Brewpub; see Boston, Massachusetts.

LIHUE (KAUAI)

Whalers Brewpub ⓑ
3132 Ninini Point St., 808-245-2000
    ★☆☆☆   11 A.M.–11 P.M.
Food: Regional fare   *Smoking:* Separate sections

Set atop the cliffs at Kalapaki Bay on Kauai. Commanding view of the Pacific and the Hoary Head Mountain Range of southern Kauai. Hawaiian dining, wide range of ales.

WAHIAWA (OAHU)

Old English Pub
1718 Wilikina Drive, 808-621-1835
    ★☆☆☆   11 A.M.–2 A.M.
Food: No kitchen   *Smoking:* Throughout

The novel *From Here to Eternity* starts here, scenes from the movie were shot here, and the cast drank here. Has scars from the Japanese attack on Pearl Harbor and a liquor license dating from 1933. Solid draft selection, plus 120 bottle choices.

Also in Hawaii
Kihei (Maui): Hapa's Brewhaus, 41 E. Lipoa St., 808-879-9001. Brewpub.
Waimea (Kauai): Waimea Brewing Co., 9400 Kaumauali Highway, 808-338-9733. Brewpub.

Regional beers to look for: This is the beginning of the Northwest, so many of those products are available here.
Essential stops: Moon Time Alehouse in Coeur D'Alene.
Just for fun: The Abbey in Boise: horseshoes.
Best city for a pub crawl: Boise.

BOISE

The Abbey
650 Vista Ave., 208-331-1415
★★⯪☆   11 A.M.–late
Food: Tavern fare   *Smoking:* Throughout

Woody ale house showcasing both Northwest beers and imports, with twenty-five taps (and a handpump) and a large bottle selection long on Belgian beers. Patios front and back, with a horseshoe pit in back.

Bittercreek Ale House
246 N. 8th St., 208-345-1813
★★⯪☆   11 A.M.–late
Food: Tavern fare   *Smoking:* Throughout

Downtown alehouse specializing in Northwest ales (twenty-nine taps, one mainstream lager, two imports, the rest micros). Long wooden bar in an open space, but can get crowded and smoky.

Brews Brothers
6928 W. State, 208-853-0526
★☆☆☆   11:30 A.M.–midnight
Food: Tavern fare   *Smoking:* Throughout

A contemporary strip mall bar with twenty-three taps offering Northwest craft beers, imports, and mainstream choices.

Harrison Hollow Brewhouse Ⓑ
2455 Harrison Hollow Blvd., 208-343-6820
★☆☆☆   11 A.M.–1 A.M.
Food: Brewpub fare   *Smoking:* Separate sections

Round fireplace in the middle adds to the ski lodge feel, while old *Guitar* magazines and vintage 78s are scattered about the walls.

TableRock Brewpub and Grill ⓑ
705 Fulton St., 208-342-0944
★☆☆☆   Lunch–late
Food: Brewpub fare   *Smoking:* Separate sections

Regularly keeps five ales on tap, plus one to three seasonals. Skylights and windows give the place an open, spacious feeling. Try the Basque chorizo sausage.

Also in Boise
Big Horn Brewing Co., 709 E. Park Blvd., 208-584-3191. Brewpub.

Old Chicago, 350 N. Milwaukee, 208-321-0033. See Boulder, Colorado.

Old Chicago, 730 W. Idaho St., 208-363-0037.

COEUR D'ALENE

Capone's
751 N. 4th St., 208-667-4843
★☆☆☆   11 A.M.–late
Food: Pizza   *Smoking:* Separate sections

More taps than tables in this small corner bar. Most of the nineteen taps go to Northwest craft beers. Excellent East Coast-style grinders and pizza.

Moon Time Alehouse
1602 Sherman Ave., 208-667-2331
★★★☆   11 A.M.–late
Food: Tavern fare   *Smoking:* Throughout

Classic Pacific Northwest alehouse, woody and intimate, with eighteen taps pouring plenty of craft beers. A large blackboard notes what's on tap. Creative menu offerings, such as Italian bread salad.

TW Fisher's ⓑ
204 N. 2nd St., 208-664-2739
★☆☆☆   11 A.M.–2 A.M.
Food: Brewpub fare   *Smoking:* Throughout

Look for the six-foot beer mug being filled from a tap out front. Decorated with breweriana, its popular beers are available throughout the region.

MOSCOW

Treaty Grounds Brewpub   🅱

W. 2124 Pullman Road, 208-882-3807

    ★☆☆☆   Lunch–closing (not late)

Food: Brewpub fare   *Smoking:* Separate sections

Mall brewpub serving its own ales plus beer from Washington, Canada, and America's largest breweries. Common ground for sports fans of the University of Idaho and Washington State University.

TWIN FALLS

Dunken's Draught House

102 Main Ave. N., 208-733-8114

    ★★☆☆   11 A.M.–closing

Food: Tavern fare, pizza   *Smoking:* Throughout

Dunken's has been serving Northwest craft beers and imports for more than ten years, offering twenty on tap plus a hand-pump. Often listed as a brewpub, but no brewery here (and no TVs, either).

Also in Twin Falls

Mugger's Brewpub/Twin Falls Brewing, 516 2nd St., 208-733-8159. Brewpub.

Also in Idaho

Caldwell: Gem State Brewing, 704 Arthur, 208-454-9944. Brewpub.

Driggs: Knight's British Rail, 65 Depot St., 208-345-8365. Restaurant/pub.

Hailey: Sun Valley Brewing, 202 N. Main, 208-788-5777. Brewpub.

Idaho Falls: Brownstone Restaurant & Brewery, 455 River Parkway, 208-535-0310. Brewpub.

Lewiston: MJ Barleyhoppers Brewery & Sports Pub, 621 21st St., 208-746-5300. Brewpub.

McCall: McCall Brewing Co., 807 N. 3rd St., 208-634-2333. Brewpub.

Post Falls: Falls Brewing Co./Casey's Pub, 315 N. Ross Point Road, 208-777-7047. Brewpub.

Salmon: Bertram's Salmon Valley Brewery, 101 S. Andrews, 208-756-3391. Brewpub.

Sandpoint: Pend Orielle Brewing Co., 220 Cedar St., 208-263-7873. Brewpub.

Victor: Otto Brothers Brewing, 430 Old Jackson Highway, 208-787-9000. Brewpub.

ILLINOIS

Regional beers to look for: Goose Island Brewing; Three Brothers Brewing; many of the best beers from small brewers in Wisconsin, Indiana, Michigan, and Minnesota.

Essential stops: Map Room, Goose Island, and Village Tap in Chicago.

Just for fun: Southport Lanes in Chicago. Four hand-set lanes, and a sign that reads, "Remember, if you see legs—DON'T BOWL."

Best city for a pub crawl: Chicago, obviously.

AURORA

America's Brewpub Ⓑ
205 N. Broadway, 630-264-2739
    ★☆☆☆   Lunch–late
Food: Brewpub fare   *Smoking:* Separate sections

Large pub in Walter Payton's Roundhouse Complex, a castle-like limestone building that housed the Chicago, Burlington & Quincy Car Works and now houses a Payton Hall of Fame. Expansive menu, wide range of beers.

BLUE ISLAND

Maple Tree Inn
13301 S. Olde Western, 708-388-3461
    ★★☆☆   4 P.M.–closing (closed Mondays)
Food: Full menu   *Smoking:* Separate sections

Two-story New Orleans-style restaurant with excellent food. Carved wood bar, imposing back bar downstairs, and a stay-a-while pub.

BROOKFIELD

Brixie's
9526 Ogden, 708-387-0050
    ★☆☆☆   7 P.M.–late
Food: Tavern fare   *Smoking:* Throughout

Tavern/music venue/pool hall with twenty-two taps, some mainstream choices but mainly microbrewed beers and imports.

Irish Times

8869 Burlington Ave., 708-485-8787

★☆☆☆   Lunch–late

Food: Irish pub fare   *Smoking:* Separate sections

Enticing Irish pub jammed with antiques. Offers twenty-four beers—Irish and UK products and American craft beers—on tap. All-you-can-eat fish every Friday.

CHICAGO

Benedict's Barroom

3937 N. Lincoln, 773-549-5599

★★★☆   4 P.M.–late

Food: Tavern fare   *Smoking:* Separate sections

A relative newcomer with the largest draft selection in Chicago, the fifty taps pouring both imports and micros. Biker bar, rock saloon in previous lives. Fresh fish, seafood available most days.

Berghoff Restaurant

17 W. Adams St., 312-787-7313

★☆☆☆   Lunch–after dinner

Food: Full menu   *Smoking:* Separate sections

Granted liquor license No. 1 in Chicago after Prohibition and fought mightily to keep the bar men-only, until women fought back in the early '70s. Classic standup long bar. Excellent German restaurant.

Chicago Brauhaus

4732 N. Lincoln, 773-784-4444

★★☆☆   11 A.M.–2 A.M. (closed Tuesdays)

Food: German fare   *Smoking:* Separate sections

Its 1960s furnishings are immaculately well-kept, and the soothing, dim lighting makes everything look rosy even before you start drinking. Live music six nights a week and on weekend afternoons. Tasty traditional German dishes and four German beers on tap.

Clark Street Ale House

742 N. Clark, 312-642-9253

★★★☆   4 P.M.–2 A.M.

Food: No kitchen   *Smoking:* Throughout

The "Stop 'n' Drink" neon still hangs above what has become a classy beer joint just north of downtown. A lovely lineup of twenty-four taps, usually something special on handpump, and a wide range of single-malt whiskies and single-barrel bourbons. Beer garden in back.

Cody's Public House

1658 W. Barry, 773-528-4050

★☆☆☆   2:30 P.M.–late (opens at 11 A.M. weekends)

Food: No kitchen   *Smoking:* Throughout

Fine neighborhood tavern named after owner's dog (other dogs welcome). Six beers on tap, solid bottle selection. Excellent beer garden with regulation bocce ball court.

Cork and Kerry

10614 S. Western, 773-445-2675

★☆☆☆   2 P.M.–2 A.M. (opens at noon weekends)

Food: No kitchen   *Smoking:* Throughout

Warm and cozy pub with ten taps. Amazing decorations—many of them mechanized—for the Christmas season. Terrific beer garden.

Duke of Perth

2913 N. Clark, 773-477-1741

★☆☆☆   Lunch–late (opens at 5 P.M. Mondays)

Food: Scottish fare   *Smoking:* Separate sections

A Scottish bar with a good draft selection of imports on tap, seventy-plus single-malt whiskies, bartenders who know about both, and a fine beer garden.

Fireside Restaurant

5739 N. Ravenswood, 773-561-7433

★☆☆☆   11 A.M.–late

Food: Full menu   *Smoking:* Separate sections

An outstanding restaurant with a solid beer lineup, featuring ten on tap. The outdoor patio has seven levels. Hosts very nice beer dinners.

Ginger Man

3740 N. Clark, 773-549-2040

★☆☆☆   3 P.M.–late (opens earlier Fridays through Sundays)

Food: Tavern fare   *Smoking:* Throughout

When the Cubs game ends, John Lee Hooker comes off the music system and Wagner comes booming on. Many Cubs fans stream by, but regulars know to drop in. Wood, exposed brick, and pool table are paired with fifteen draft choices.

Goose Island Brewing Co. 🅑

1800 N. Clybourn, 773-915-0071

★★★★   Lunch–late

Food: Brewpub fare   *Smoking:* Separate sections

Always interesting beers on tap here, available in a bar decorated with eye-catching breweriana, an atrium/beer garden, a pool hall, and a dining area. Yummy homemade chips. Goose Island beers are on tap throughout the region, and bottled beers are brewed at a separate brewery a few miles away. Opened a second pub, Goose Island Wrigleyville, in April 1999, where another pub had failed.

Great Beer Palace

4128 N. Lincoln, 773-525-4906

★☆☆☆   Lunch–late

Food: Pizza   *Smoking:* Throughout

It still looks like a German restaurant, but now it's really a place to drink beer and eat pizza. The twenty-four-tap lineup favors imports, with a few craft beers thrown in. Beer by the boot available.

Heartland Café

7000 N. Greenview, 773-465-8005

★☆☆☆   Breakfast–late

Food: Café fare   *Smoking:* Separate sections

Just like the '60s, except the beer is better—with nine taps offering imports and craft products. Counterculture hangout with attached bookstore in Rogers Park. Excellent vegetarian offerings. The place to go after a protest march.

Hopleaf Bar
5148 N. Clark, 773-334-9851
★★☆☆   Noon–2 A.M.
Food: No kitchen   *Smoking:* Throughout

Good beer choices from eight taps, an outstanding bottle menu (including Belgians), and one fine place to hang out, whether you choose from the board games or lean on the jukebox jammed with amazing 45s. Can get crowded.

House of Beer
16 W. Division, 773-646-2345
★☆☆☆   4 P.M.–late (opens at 11 A.M. weekends)
Food: Tavern fare   *Smoking:* Separate sections

Rush Street-area bar that's jammed on weekends. Full of games, including an indoor basketball court. Solid twenty-one-tap lineup and plenty to choose from in bottles.

Jaks Tap
901 W. Jackson, 312-666-3001
★★★☆   11 A.M.–2 A.M.
Food: Tavern fare   *Smoking:* Throughout

Site of the Tap & Growler, Chicago's first brewpub to go belly-up, now under the same ownership as the Village Tap. Solid comfort food and an excellent mix of imports, faraway micros, and local beers from forty taps.

John Barleycorn
658 W. Belden, 773-348-8899
★★½☆   11 A.M.–late
Food: Full menu   *Smoking:* Separate sections

Reputedly a front for bootleggers in the 1920s, this was a favorite of John Dillinger. Thirty-two taps offer a full range of beers. Classical music always plays in the background, with more than 5,000 art slides showing continuously on three screens. Separate darts room, fireplace in the rear dining room, and a splendid patio.

The Map Room
1949 N. Hoyne, 773-252-7636
★★★★ Very early–late
Food: No kitchen   *Smoking:* Throughout

Travelers' bar with travel books on shelves, maps on the wall, and postcards regulars send the bar from trips. Twenty-plus taps and one handpump offer a solid mix of quality imports plus microbrewed beers from near and far. International Night every Tuesday, with a buffet. Beer school once a month. Open in the morning for coffee.

Puffer's
3356 S. Halsted, 773-927-6073
★☆☆☆ Early afternoon–late
Food: No kitchen   *Smoking:* Throughout

Neighborhood spot not far from Comiskey Park, with windows that open onto the street and customers who help older customers up the steps. Fine selection of imports and craft beer on tap, augmented by changing bottle selection.

Quencher's Saloon
2401 N. Western, 773-276-9730
★★⯪☆ 11 A.M.–2 A.M.
Food: Tavern fare   *Smoking:* Throughout

Good selection from fifteen taps, fine choices from 200-plus bottle menu, excellent prices. Working-class tavern with fine breweriana and excellent chili for lunch.

Resi's Bierstube
2034 W. Irving Park Road, 773-472-1749
★★☆☆ 3 P.M.–late
Food: German fare   *Smoking:* Separate sections

A small German bar with good food, an outstanding beer garden, and a very good selection of well-cared-for German beer on tap.

Schuba's
3159 N. Southport, 773-525-2508
★☆☆☆ 8 A.M.–late (opens at noon Mondays)
Food: Tavern fare   *Smoking:* Separate sections

Don't overlook the terra-cotta Schlitz globes on the side of the building, which once was a Schlitz tied house. First-class music venue, where acoustic musicians play in a former school auditorium. Small, solid draft lineup.

Sheffield's

3258 N. Sheffield, 773-281-4989

★★⯨☆ 2 P.M.–late (opens at noon weekends)

Food: No kitchen   *Smoking:* Throughout

Terrific corner tavern that suffers only from its popularity (and proximity to Wrigley Field). Two dozen fine taps, well-chosen bottle menu. Or go with the Bad Beer of the Month. Historic cottonwood tree in outstanding beer garden.

Silver Cloud

1700 N. Damen Ave., 773-489-6212

★☆☆☆ Lunch–late

Food: Tavern fare   *Smoking:* Throughout

Restaurant-diner with excellent food. Ten taps, mostly featuring regional craft beers and West Coast products. Menu is posted on a blackboard that's a map of the United States.

Southport Lanes

3325 N. Southport, 773-472-1601

★☆☆☆ 4 P.M.–late (opens at noon weekends)

Food: Tavern fare   *Smoking:* Separate sections

The last four hand-set bowling lanes in Chicago are here, so it gets crowded on weekends. The tavern is in a former Schlitz bar and still has a classic terra-cotta Schlitz ball on the side of the building. Eleven-tap lineup includes craft beers and imports. Same owners run Lucky Strike (2747 N. Lincoln), which has eight lanes and an early-generation automatic pin setter. Thirteen beers on tap there.

Twisted Spoke

501 N. Ogden, 312-666-1500

★☆☆☆ 11 A.M.–2 A.M.

Food: Tavern fare   *Smoking:* Throughout

A friendly motorcycle-theme bar that draws lots of bikers for huge portions of good food. Their bikes outside and the motorcycle high above make the place easy to spot. Excellent twelve-tap lineup. Biker brunch on weekends.

U.S. Beer Co.

1801 N. Clybourn, 773-871-7799

★☆☆☆   11 A.M.–late

Food: Tavern fare   *Smoking:* Throughout

Was the Triangle Tavern, which in its prime sold more than a hundred cases of bottled Bud per week and more on tap. Took down the "25-cent draft" sign and went to twenty-four taps, still serving mainstream lagers but also micros.

Village Tap

2055 W. Roscoe, 773-883-0817

★★★↟   5 P.M.–late (opens earlier Fridays through Sundays)

Food: Tavern fare   *Smoking:* Throughout

The Baskin-Robbins of beer in Chicago, with thirty-one taps, most of them pouring craft beers, many regional. A true neighborhood tavern and a vital part of Roscoe Village's revival. Local art on the walls and regulars on the bar stools. Crowded on weekends when a more suburban crowd arrives. Excellent food, vegetarian-friendly.

Zum Deutschen Eck

2924 N. Southport, 773-525-8121

★☆☆☆   Lunch–late

Food: German fare   *Smoking:* Separate sections

"The corner bar" has long since grown into a large Bavarian chalet that occupies almost a whole block. Plenty of German beers on tap and live *oom-pah-pah* music Friday through Sunday evenings.

Also in Chicago

Abbey Pub, 3420 W. Grace, 773-478-4408. Irish pub.

Beverly Fireside, 10730 S. Western Ave., 773-779-3606. Southside offspring of Fireside.

Bricks, 1909 N. Lincoln Ave., 773-255-0851. Pizza and plenty of Sierra Nevada beers.

Celtic Crossings, 751 N. Clark St., 312-337-1005. Irish pub.

The Charleston, 2076 N. Hoyne, 773-489-4757. Corner bar.

Claddagh Ring, 2306 W. Foster, 773-271-5551. Irish pub.

Delilah's, 2771 N. Lincoln Ave., 773-472-2771. Giant spirits menu.

Fadó Irish Pub, 100 W. Grand, 312-836-0066. Irish pub.

Fireside Restaurant, 773-561-7433. Sprawling restaurant, great patio, popular beer dinners.

Griffin's Public House, 2170 Halsted St., 773-525-7313.

Gunther Murphy's, 1638 W. Belmont, 773-472-5139. Semi-Irish, nighttime music spot.

Guthries, 1300 W. Addison, 773-477-2900. Restaurant/pub.

Hidden Shamrock, 2723 N. Halsted, 773-883-0304. Irish pub with four Guinness handles.

Irish Oak Pub & Restaurant, 3511 N. Clark, 773-935-6669. Irish pub.

JT Collins, 3358 N. Paulina Ave., 773-327-7467. Neighborhood tavern.

Laschet's, 2119 W. Irving Park Road, 773-478-7915. German restaurant.

Lemming's, 1850 N. Damen, 773-862-1688. Tavern.

Lucky Strike, 2747 N. Lincoln, 773-549-2695. See Southport Lanes.

Mirabell, 3443 W. Addison, 773-463-1962. German.

O'Malley's Schoolyard Tavern, 3258 N. Southport, 773-528-8226. Neighborhood hangout.

Red Lion, 2446 N. Lincoln, 773-348-2695. British pub.

River West Brewing Co., 925 W. Chicago, 773-226-3200. Brewpub; offspring of suburban Weinkeller.

Rock Bottom Brewery & Restaurant, 1 W. Grand Ave., 312-755-9339. Brewpub; see Denver, Colorado. Outstanding rooftop beer garden.

Sedgwick's, 1935 N. Sedgwick, 773-337-7900. Tavern.

DOWNERS GROVE

Founders Hill Brewing Co. Ⓑ
5200 Main St., 630-963-2739
    ★★☆☆   Lunch–late
Food: Brewpub fare   *Smoking:* Separate sections

Solid, sometimes complex beers plus excellent food. In refurbished hundred-year-old building. Takes its name from nearby historic cemetery.

ELGIN

Prairie Rock Brewing Co.
127 S. Grove, 847-622-8888
    ★★☆☆   4 P.M.–late
Food: Brewpub fare   *Smoking:* Separate sections

Deserted theater turned into spacious restaurant, with a four-sided fireplace and white tablecloths. More casual dining in the pub area, which has a wonderful stone bar. Solid lineup of ales.

EVANSTON

Tommy Nevin's Pub
1450 Sherman Ave., 847-869-0450
★☆☆☆   Lunch–late
Food: Full menu   *Smoking:* Separate sections

Guinness is the attraction here. A classic, slow, two-part pour from two taps—the bartender will ask you if you want another while you're still working on the first.

FLOSSMOOR

Flossmoor Station Ⓑ
1035 Sterling Ave., 708-957-2739
★★⯪☆   Lunch–late
Food: Brewpub fare   *Smoking:* Separate sections

Housed in a lovely old train station that sits handily by a modern commuter stop. Solid lineup of regular beers, with truly wonderful seasonals.

FOREST PARK

Healy's West Side
7217 W. Madison St., 708-366-4277
★☆☆☆   11 A.M.–late
Food: Tavern fare   *Smoking:* Throughout

Owner Mike Healy's dad once ran a Chicago Irish bar where new immigrants would go first to get a green card and a job. Irish influence remains, with twenty-two taps favoring imports.

FRANKFURT

Die Bierstube
42 Kansas St., 815-469-6660
★★☆☆   11 A.M.–after dinner
Food: German fare   *Smoking:* Separate sections

A German restaurant for twenty-five years, offering German food and three German beers on tap. Excellent Oktoberfest celebration. Prime seating in booths that are like small rooms.

GARDNER

Gardner Haus Inn
120 Depot St., 815-237-8602

★★☆☆   10 A.M.–11:30 P.M. (1–9 P.M. Sundays, closed Mondays)

Food: German fare   *Smoking:* Separate sections

Excellent German food (killer red cabbage), plus four fresh German beers on tap. Cooler full of bottled beer includes both imports and craft beers. They understand Gemutlichkeit here.

GIBSON CITY

Bayern Stube
209 N. Sangamon, 217-784-8304

★☆☆☆   Hours vary; call

Food: German fare   *Smoking:* Separate sections

Traditional German restaurant with German beer that draws from a wide area. Barroom has working fireplace and impressive collection of mounted animals.

GLEN ELLYN

Glen Ellyn Brewing Co. 🅱
433 N. Main St., 630-942-1140

★★☆☆   Lunch–late (closed Mondays)

Food: Brewpub fare   *Smoking:* None while food is served

Intimate pub, with brewery's glass doors literally opening into the dining room. Small separate bar area. Solid beers, excellent food, often designed to go together.

LIBERTYVILLE

Mickey Finn's Brewery 🅱
412 N. Milwaukee Ave., 847-362-2739

★★½☆   11 A.M.–1 A.M.

Food: Brewpub fare   *Smoking:* Separate sections

A popular saloon that made the successful transition to brewpub. Usually seven beers available, including two seasonals. Two operating model trains add to the decor.

Also in Libertyville

Edelweiss Inn, 411 E. Park, 847-367-9696. German.

Tavern-in-the-Town, 519 N. Milwaukee, 847-367-5755. Fine restaurant with wide beer selection.

LINCOLNSHIRE

Flatlander's Chophouse & Brewery Ⓑ
200 Village Green, 847-821-1234
★★☆☆   11 A.M.–midnight
Food: Upscale brewpub fare   *Smoking:* In bar area only

It cost $6 million to develop the land and build this palatial, freestanding, prairie-style restaurant, and it shows. Fine range of beers, adventurous menu with more high-end items than the average brewpub.

PEORIA

Crooked Waters Brewery & Pub Ⓑ
330 SW Constitution Ave., 309-673-2739
☆☆☆☆   Lunch–late
Food: Brewpub fare   *Smoking:* Separate sections

Refurbished electric switching station has a deck that literally hangs over the Illinois River. Worth the wait to sit there. Intimate pub area.

Peoria Hofbrau
2210 NE Jefferson, 309-686-9739
★☆☆☆   Lunch–after dinner
Food: German fare   *Smoking:* Throughout

A small German tavern with good German food and sandwiches. Taps pour mostly German beer but the bottle selection is large and varied.

Also in Peoria
John S. Rhodell Brewery, 619A Constitution, 309-674-7267. Brew-on-premise with tap room.

Sully's Pub & Cafe, 121 SW Adams, 309-674-0238. Wide tap selection, sports bar.

ROCK ISLAND

Blue Cat Brewpub Ⓑ
                    113 18th St., 309-788-8247
★★☆☆   11 A.M.–late
Food: Brewpub fare   *Smoking:* Separate sections

A brewpub in the happening part of Rock Island, just off the Mississippi River. Casual bar, pool area upstairs, and excellent dining downstairs. Dependable lineup of ales.

SOUTH BARRINGTON

Mill Rose Brewing Ⓑ
45 S. Barrington Road, 847-382-7673
★★☆☆   11 A.M.–late
Food: Upscale brewpub fare   *Smoking:* Separate sections

A fine restaurant housed in two barns and known for its pork and beef dishes; expect a wait. Woody decor inside, built-in fireplaces on patio.

SPRINGFIELD

Brewhaus
617 E. Washington, 217-525-6399
★★☆☆   7 A.M.–closing (opens at 5 P.M. Sundays)
Food: Tavern fare   *Smoking:* Throughout

A long, narrow, dimly-lit bar in the heart of downtown. A few imports on draft and tons of imports and craft beers in bottles, including Belgians. Outstanding tin ceiling, historic back bar.

WESTMONT

Weinkeller Ⓑ
651 Westmont Drive, 630-789-2236
★★☆☆   11:30 A.M.–late (opens later Sundays)
Food: Full menu   *Smoking:* Separate sections

The Weinkeller in Berwyn was one of the region's first beer bars and then brewpubs. It closed in 1999 because of a fire, leaving its future uncertain. This offspring in a newer suburban setting turns out a fine range of beers.

WINFIELD

John's Buffet
27 W. 474 Jewell Road, 630-752-2000
★☆☆☆   11 A.M.–1 A.M.
Food: Full menu   *Smoking:* Separate sections

There's no buffet here, but a fine selection of twenty beers on tap in two bar areas. John's sold bootleg beer in the 1920s and moved to this spot in 1947, opening the area's most modern bar at the time, featuring European beers on tap.

Also in Illinois

Arlington Heights: O'Grady's Brewery & Pub, 372 E. Golf Road, 847-640-0600. Brewpub.

Bloomington: Lucca Grill, 116 E. Market, 309-828-7521. Great pizza, usually something outstanding on tap.
Rosie's, 106 E. Front St., 309-827-0785. Restaurant/pub.

Carbondale: Pinch Penny Pub, 700 E. Grand Ave., 618-549-3348. Brewpub.

LaGrange: Palmers Place Restaurant & Beer Garden, 56 S. La-Grange Road, 708-482-7127. Multi-tap.

Lyons: Lyons Brewing Co., 7905 Ogden Ave., 708-447-4106. Multi-tap.

Moline: Bent River Brewing Co., 1413 5th Ave., 309-797-2722. Brewpub.

Mundelein: Irish Mill Pub, 26592 N. Illinois Route 83, 847-566-7044. Irish pub.

Orland Park: Harrison's Brewing Co., 15845 S. LaGrange Road, 708-226-0100. Brewpub.

Palatine: Durty Nelly's, 55 N. Bothwell, 708-358-9150. Tavern.

Richmond: JW Platek's Restaurant & Brewery, 8609 Highway 12, 815-678-4078. Restaurant with small brewhouse.

Rockford: Old Chicago, 6280 E. State St., 815-277-4040. See Boulder, Colorado.

Villa Park: Lunar Brewing Co., 54 E. St. Charles Road, 630-530-2077. Brewpub.

Warrenville: Rock Bottom Brewery & Restaurant, 28256 Diehl Road, 630-836-1380. Brewpub; see Denver, Colorado.

Washington: The Rat'skeller, 103 Washington Square, 309-444-4620. German bar.

Wheeling: Hans Bavarian Lodge, 931 N. Milwaukee Ave., 847-537-4141. German restaurant.

Regional beers to look for: Three Floyds Brewing; Oaken Barrel Brewing; Circle V Brewing; Upland Brewing.

Essential stops: Broad Ripple Brewing and Chalkie's in Indianapolis; Rich O's in New Albany.

Just for fun: Rich O's in New Albany. A bottle of Bud costs $6.50—they don't sell many.

Best city for a pub crawl: Indianapolis.

BLOOMINGTON

Bloomington Brewing Co. Ⓑ
1795 E. 10th St., 812-339-2256
★☆☆☆   Lunch–late
Food: Pizza, calzones   *Smoking:* None

Set in a mall near the IU campus, but not a college bar. Nice English-inspired ales available. Bar made of Hoosier limestone. Dining room has a country-diner feeling.

Crazy Horse
214 W. Kirkwood, 812-336-8877
★☆☆☆   11 A.M.–late
Food: Tavern fare   *Smoking:* Throughout

Comfortable bar with a tin ceiling and exposed brick. Solid selection from sixteen taps, including beers from Indiana brewpubs you usually only see at those pubs.

Also in Bloomington
Irish Lion, 212 W. Kirkwood Ave., 812-336-9076. Irish pub with excellent soda bread.
Upland Brewing Co., 350 W. 11th St., 812-330-7425. Brewpub.

GREENWOOD

Oaken Barrel Brewing Co. Ⓑ
50 N. Airport Parkway, 317-887-2287
★★★☆   Lunch–late (limited hours Sundays)
Food: Brewpub fare   *Smoking:* Separate sections

Well-made beer includes fascinating seasonals like a plum stout. Generous food portions and unique dishes (Thai coconut fried chicken). Family friendly, nice beer garden.

INDIANAPOLIS

Alcatraz Brewing Co. Ⓑ
49 W. Maryland, 317-488-1230
★☆☆☆   11 A.M.–late
Food: Brewpub fare   *Smoking:* Separate sections

Prison theme throughout, from the decorations to the names of
menu items and beers. First member in a chain, where the
theme plays out even bigger—and in some places includes an
eighty-foot replica of the Golden Gate Bridge within the pub.
Well-made though not always adventurous ales.

Ale Emporium
8617 Allisonville Road, 317-842-1333
★☆☆☆   11 A.M.–late
Food: Tavern fare   *Smoking:* Separate sections

Despite the strip mall setting, has a classic long bar and back
bar, offers a nice lineup of micros and imports from thirteen
taps, and serves excellent pizza. Another Ale Emporium at
86th & Townline Road is much the same.

Broad Ripple Brewpub Ⓑ
842 E. 65th St., 317-253-2739
★★★☆   11 A.M.–late
Food: Pub fare   *Smoking:* Separate sections

Publican John Hill turned a former auto parts store into a cozy
English pub with a Victorian dining area. Ales—some on
handpump—are designed to take you to Yorkshire. The nearby
Corner Wine Bar/Wellington Pub (6331 N. Guilford Ave.) is
under the same ownership. Slightly more upscale dining, good
beer menu, and nice separate pub room.

bw-3
15 E. Maryland St., 317-916-9464
★★⯪☆   11 A.M.–closing
Food: Tavern fare   *Smoking:* Separate sections

The beer lineup here is way above average for a bw-3 (Buffalo
wild wings and weck, which is a sandwich on a kaiser roll).
Many franchises in the chain offer many draft choices but not
necessarily interesting ones. However, here forty draft choices
include microbrewed beers and excellent imports.

Chalkies
560 E. 82nd St., 317-578-2221
    ★★★☆   3 P.M.–late (opens at 11:30 A.M. Fridays)
Food: Full menu   *Smoking:* None

An upscale pool hall with innovative cuisine and an excellent beer selection. The seventeen draft choices include beer hand-pumped from firkins, a three-tower tap devoted to LaTrappe beers, and a fine mix of excellent micros and imports.

Rathskeller
401 E. Michigan Ave., 317-636-0396
    ★☆☆☆   11 A.M.–not always late; closes afternoons, some evenings
Food: German fare   *Smoking:* Separate sections

The city's oldest restaurant (since 1894) is in the massive brick Athenaeum Building, which was known as the German House until the onset of World War One. Six German beers on tap, many more in bottles as well as other European beers, available in a separate two-story bar area that is open to the top.

Shallo's Antique Restaurant & Bar
8811 Hartigan, Unit 1-B, 317-882-7997
    ★☆☆☆   11 A.M.–1 A.M.
Food: Tavern fare   *Smoking:* Throughout

You can actually sit at the bar and watch people shop inside the Target store next door. The choices from thirty-six taps cover the spectrum, and the bottle menu has 200-plus offerings. Woody and full of breweriana.

Union Jack
924 Broad Ripple Ave., 317-257-4343
    ★☆☆☆   11 A.M.–late
Food: British pub fare   *Smoking:* Separate sections

Pub in Broad Ripple neighborhood offers mostly imports from its eighteen taps. Well-worn floor with antiques throughout. A second Union Jack Pub is located in Speedway.

Also in Indianapolis
Elbow Room Pub, 605 N. Pennsylvania, 317-635-3354. Pub.
Henry Grattan, 745 Broad Ripple Ave., 317-257-6030. Irish pub.
Rock Bottom Brewery & Restaurant, 10 W. Washington St., 317-681-8180. Brewpub; see Denver, Colorado.
Slippery Noodle Inn, 372 S. Meridian, 317-631-6974. Historic blues bar.
Wildcat Brewing Co., 9111 N. Michigan Road, 317-872-3446. Brewpub.

LAFAYETTE

Lafayette Brewing Ⓑ
622 Main St., 317-742-2591
★☆☆☆   11 A.M.–late (closed Sundays)
Food: Brewpub fare   *Smoking:* Separate sections

Ale brewery set in a three-story brick building built in 1892. Expansive restaurant with a copper-topped bar and large carved wooden figures, interesting mural.

Knickerbocker Saloon
113 N. 5th St., 317-423-2234
☆☆☆☆   3 P.M.–3 A.M. (opens at 7 P.M. Saturdays, closed Sundays)
Food: No kitchen   *Smoking:* Throughout

Indiana's oldest bar, with a history stretching back to 1835. Conversation-friendly, growing beer list, jazz and blues.

MISHAWAKA

Mishawaka Brewing Ⓑ
3703 N. Main St., 219-256-9993
★★☆☆   11:30 A.M.–late
Food: Brewpub fare   *Smoking:* Separate sections

Once a fitness center, now a faithful re-creation of a British pub. A solid lineup of British-style ales, including the very nice Founders Stout.

MUNCIE

Scotty's Brewhouse
1700 W. University Ave., 765-747-5151
★☆☆☆   11 A.M.–late
Food: Tavern fare   *Smoking:* Throughout

No brewing here, but thirty beers on tap, including a solid selection of micros and imports. Close to the Ball State campus and attracts a student crowd.

NEW ALBANY

Rich O's Public House
3312 Plaza Drive, 812-949-2804

★★★⯨   11 A.M.–closing (opens at 1 P.M. Saturdays, closed Sundays)

Food: Tavern fare   *Smoking:* Separate sections

The beer menu—twenty taps, always changing—offers an intelligently balanced selection of styles, be they micros or imports. Most important, a place for conversation, about beer and equally important subjects. Attached to Sports Time Pizza, where you can order the same beers or mainstream lagers.

TERRE HAUTE

Sonka Irish Pub & Café
1366 Wabash, 812-234-8802

★☆☆☆   Lunch–late

Food: Tavern fare   *Smoking:* Throughout

Established as a bar by a Romanian in 1933, but long ago became an Irish pub with UK products on tap and a wide range of bottled beer. The building dates to 1899, and the original back bar remains.

Also in Indiana
Evansville: Firkin Brewpub, 329 Main St., 812-422-9700. Brewpub.

Turoni's-North Main, 408 N. Main, 812-424-9873. Brewpub.

Fort Wayne: Mad Anthony Brewing Co., 1109 Taylor St., 219-426-2537. Brewpub.

Michigan City: Duneland Brewing, 5718 S. Franklin, 219-762-9180. Brewpub.

IOWA

Regional beers to look for: Stone City Brewing.
Essential stops: The Sanctuary in Iowa City; Raccoon River in
Des Moines.
Just for fun: Stone City Brewing. Tour a homemade brewery.
Best city for a pub crawl: Iowa City.

CEDAR RAPIDS

Cedar Brewing Co. Ⓑ
500 Blairs Ferry Road NE, 319-378-9090
★☆☆☆   11 A.M.–late (10 A.M.–10 P.M. Sundays)
Food: Brewpub fare   *Smoking:* Separate sections

Casual brewpub and also the best sports bar (seventeen TVs,
one big screen in a modest-sized pub) in Cedar Rapids. Serious
about NTN (interactive trivia) and its Monday Night Football
counterpart.

DAVENPORT

Front Street Brewery Ⓑ
208 E. River Drive, 319-332-1569
☆☆☆☆   Lunch–late
Food: Brewpub fare   *Smoking:* Separate sections

Smallish, brick-walled brewpub near the river (it was closed for
months during the Great Flood of '93).

DES MOINES

Court Avenue Brewery Ⓑ
309 Court Ave., 515-282-2739
★★☆☆   Lunch–late
Food: Brewpub fare   *Smoking:* Separate sections

Multi-room brewpub in older historic Saddlery Building, decorated with plenty of breweriana. Excellent weekday lunch
buffet. Wide range of ales, some on handpump.

Raccoon River Brewing Co. Ⓑ
200 10th St., 515-283-1941
    ★★⯪☆   11 A.M.–late
Food: Brewpub fare   *Smoking:* Separate sections

Part of the Wynkoop group, so in a beautifully restored historic building, offering pool upstairs and a solid beer and food experience. Substantial front doors come from a local Victorian mansion.

EMMETSBURG

Dublin's Food & Spirits
3639 450th Ave., 712-852-2214
    ☆☆☆☆   4 P.M.–late (closed Sundays)
Food: Tavern fare   *Smoking:* Separate sections

Disposed to be Irish in a town where half the residents are Irish-American. Five pretty standard taps but a solid bottle lineup.

IOWA CITY

Dublin Underground
5 S. Dubuque St., 319-337-7660
    ☆☆☆☆   3 P.M.–2 A.M. (opens later Sundays)
Food: No kitchen   *Smoking:* Throughout

Downtown retreat in an area of campus bars, decorated Irish but serving microbrewery beers as well as imports and mainstream lagers.

The Sanctuary
405 S. Gilbert St., 319-351-5692
    ★★⯪☆   4 P.M.–late
Food: Tavern fare   *Smoking:* Separate sections

Aptly named and the best bar in the state. The first in Iowa to serve just about any of the products it offers on tap. Eight taps, a hundred-plus bottle choices. No TV, church pews for seating, an excellent music venue. Beautiful Mission oak back bar with stained-glass fixtures.

Also in Iowa City
Fitzpatrick's Brewing Co., 525 S. Gilbert, 319-356-6900. Brewpub.

SIOUX CITY

Buffalo Alice
1022 4th St., 712-255-4822
> ★☆☆☆   3:30 P.M.–2 A.M. (opens at noon Saturdays, closed Sundays)
> *Food:* Pizza, wings   *Smoking:* Throughout

Located in an old warehouse building on historic Fourth Street. Serves a range of beer unusual for the area. Twelve taps, 120 bottles, both micros and imports.

Also in Sioux City
Fourth Street Brewery, 1104 4th St., 712-234-1120. Brewpub.

SOLON

Stone City Brewing Co. Ⓑ
220 S. Dubuque St., 319-644-1360
> ★☆☆☆   Open afternoon–early evening
> *Food:* No kitchen   *Smoking:* None

Small tasting room for small microbrewery, but feels like a bar on a Friday evening. Call first.

Also in Iowa
Bettendorf: Old Chicago, 3030 Utica Ridge Road, 319-355-9494. See Boulder, Colorado.
Urbandale: Saint's Brewing Co., 3828 100th St., 515-278-4383. Brewpub.
West Des Moines: Rock Bottom Brewery & Restaurant, 4508 University Ave., 515-267-8900. Brewpub; see Denver, Colorado.

KANSAS

Regional beers to look for: Pony Express Brewing; Boulevard Brewing.
Essential stops: Free State in Lawrence.
Best city for a pub crawl: Lawrence.

LAWRENCE

Free State Brewing 🅱

636 Massachusetts, 785-843-4555

    ★★½☆   Lunch–late

Food: Brewpub fare   *Smoking:* Separate sections

Brewpub in a former trolley depot in the heart of downtown. Fine walled-in outdoor beer garden. Equal attention given to good beer and food.

Also in Lawrence

Bottleneck, 737 New Hampshire, 785-841-5483. Good bottle selection.

Brown Bear Brewery, 729 Massachusetts, 785-843-7487. Brewpub.

Old Chicago, 2329 Iowa St., 785-841-4124. See Boulder, Colorado.

Sports Page Brewery, 3512 Clinton Parkway, 785-832-9600. Brewpub.

LEAVENWORTH

High Noon Saloon & Brewery 🅱

206 Choctaw St., 913-682-4876

    ★☆☆☆   11 A.M.–late

Food: Tavern fare   *Smoking:* Throughout

Brewpub/Western saloon that occupies a building constructed just after the Civil War. Serves Kansas City-style barbecue and smoked meats.

LEAWOOD

Paddy O'Quigley's
11851 Roe Blvd., 913-345-1119
★☆☆☆   Lunch–late
Food: Irish pub fare   *Smoking:* Throughout

Opened in 1990 and claimed the first Guinness handle in the state. Now twenty beers on tap, including five from Boulevard Brewing in Kansas City. Fine cherry-red sculpted mahogany bar.

OVERLAND PARK

Barley's Brewhaus & Restaurant
11924 W. 119th St., 913-663-4099
★★☆☆   11 A.M.–2 A.M.
Food: Tavern fare   *Smoking:* Separate sections

Ninety-nine taps, so plenty of imports and micros, with local breweries getting multiple handles. A second Barley's in Shawnee also has ninety-nine taps.

Also in Overland Park
Dave's Brewpub, 10635 Floyd, 913-385-0003. Brewpub.
Sports Page Brewery, 9083 Metcalf, 913-385-2739. Brewpub.

TOPEKA

Blind Tiger Brewery Ⓑ
417 W. 37th St., 785-267-2739
★☆☆☆   11 A.M.–midnight
Food: Brewpub fare   *Smoking:* Separate sections

A spacious multi-level pub named after the Prohibition-era custom of displaying stuffed tigers to alert patrons to speakeasies or the availability of alcohol. Wide variety of beers usually available, and also distributed elsewhere.

WICHITA

River City Brewing ⓑ
150 N. Mosley, 316-263-2739

★☆☆☆   11 A.M.–late

Food: Brewpub fare   *Smoking:* Separate sections

Comfortable setting with exposed beams and cobblestones in a 1905 building. Food menu focuses on Kansas ingredients, such as Kansas-raised buffalo steak. Outstanding mural of historic Wichita.

Also in Wichita

Old Chicago, 7700 E. Kellogg, 316-685-3111. See Boulder, Colorado.

Also in Kansas

Lenexa: Old Chicago, 9720 Quivira, 913-894-2739. See Boulder, Colorado.

Manhattan: Little Apple Brewing, 1110 W. Loop Center, 913-539-5500. Brewpub.

KENTUCKY

Regional beers to look for: Lexington Brewing; Oldenberg Brewing; Bluegrass Brewing.

Essential stops: Baxter Station and Bluegrass Brewing in Louisville.

Just for fun: Marikkas German Restaurant. Play a little volleyball.

Best city for a pub crawl: Louisville.

BARDSTOWN

Beall's Row Coffee & Ale House
114 N. 3rd St., 502-348-9594

★☆☆☆   11 A.M.–9 P.M.

Food: Tavern fare   *Smoking:* None

Set in a circa 1810 building, offering six beers on tap and Bosnian food as well as the expected sandwiches and steaks. Popular stop during fall Bourbon Festival.

LEXINGTON

Marikkas German Restaurant
411 Southland Drive, 606-275-1925

★☆☆☆   4 P.M.–1 A.M. (opens at noon Sundays)

Food: German fare   *Smoking:* Separate sections

A German restaurant offering fourteen beers on tap, most of them German. Nearly 500 bottle choices, pretty much whatever is available in the state.

Also in Lexington

Lexington City Brewery, 1050 S. Broadway, 606-259-2739. Brewpub.

Lynagh's Irish Pub & Grill, University Plaza, 606-255-6614. Irish pub, also at other locations around town.

LOUISVILLE

Baxter Station Bar & Grill
1201 Payne St., 502-584-1635
★★★☆   11:30 A.M.–late (closed Sundays)
Food: Bistro fare   *Smoking:* Separate sections

Neighborhood pub with a model train running inside and passenger train seats at some of the tables. Twenty-plus taps offer beers only recently available in Kentucky, including imports and micros, plus local products.

Bluegrass Brewing Co. Ⓑ
3929 Shelbyville Road, 502-899-7070
★★★☆   Lunch–late
Food: Brewpub fare   *Smoking:* Separate sections

Solid food, but the real reason to visit is the beer. Both standard and unusual offerings (such as a mead) are outstanding, and the barleywine won back-to-back gold medals at the Great American Beer Festival.

Dundee Tavern
2222 Dundee Road, 502-473-1923
★☆☆☆   4 P.M.–closing (opens at 1 P.M. weekends)
Food: Tavern fare   *Smoking:* Throughout

A neighborhood bar, serving a wide-ranging clientele and beers (nineteen taps) that cover the spectrum. Large single-malt, single-batch bourbon menus.

The Irish Rover
2319 Frankfort Ave., 502-899-3544
★☆☆☆   11 A.M.–late
Food: Irish pub fare   *Smoking:* Separate sections

Irish pub that also serves UK stalwarts on tap. Hosts Irish dinners, whiskey dinners, and cigar and port dinners. House beer from Bluegrass Brewing.

Also in Louisville

Bristol Bar & Grill, 1321 Bardstown Road, 502-456-1702. One of three locations around town.

Buckhead Grill & Bar, 215 Hurstbourne Parkway, 502-429-6650. Another location on Bardstown Road.

O'Shea's Traditional, 956 Baxter Ave., 502-589-7373. Inviting Irish pub.

Oldenberg Grill, 6201 Dutchman Lane, 502-893-2244. Brewpub.

PADUCAH

Jeremiah's Froghead Brewery Ⓑ
225 Broadway, 502-443-3991

★☆☆☆   3 P.M.–late

Food: Full menu   *Smoking:* Separate sections

Downtown restaurant where you can cook your own steaks, also know for its frog's legs. Solid house beers from tiny upstairs brewhouse.

Also in Kentucky

Bowling Green: Hops of Bowling Green, 2945 Scottsville Road, 502-781-1101. Brewpub.

Covington: Jack Quinn's Irish Alehouse & Pub, 112 E. 4th St., 606-491-6699. Irish pub; see Colorado Springs, Colorado. Strasse Haus, 630 Main St., 606-261-1199. German. Wertheim's Gasthaus Zur Linde, 514 W. 6th St., 606-261-1233. German.

Regional beers to look for: Acadian Brewing; Abita Brewing; Dixie Brewing; Rikenjaks Brewing.
Essential stops: Cooter Brown's and Acadian Brewing in New Orleans; The Rivershack Tavern in Jefferson.
Just for fun: The Rivershack Tavern. Trade a properly tacky ashtray for a beer.
Best city for a pub crawl: New Orleans; you can almost do a streetcar crawl.

ABITA SPRINGS

Abita Springs Brewpub Ⓑ
72011 Holly St., 504-893-3143
★★☆☆   11 A.M.–2 A.M.
Food: Regional fare   *Smoking:* Separate sections

Brewpub for well-known microbrewery (located down the road) that distributes around the U.S., usually offering beers available only at the pub. Excellent regional fare, including seafood.

BATON ROUGE

Chimes Restaurant & Oyster House
3357 Highland Road, 225-383-1754
★★☆☆   Lunch–late
Food: Regional fare   *Smoking:* Throughout

Restaurant serving Louisiana cuisine with twenty beers on tap, both imports and craft beers at bargain prices. More than 120 bottled beers. Varsity Theater (music venue) next door.

COVINGTON

Columbia Street Tap Room
434 N. Columbia St., 504-898-0899
★★☆☆   11 A.M.–late (closed Sundays)
Food: Tavern fare   *Smoking:* Throughout

A restaurant by day, a bar at night, in the historic downtown. Inviting wood and brick, with Louisiana dishes and thirty taps, plenty of micros.

JEFFERSON

The Rivershack Tavern
3449 River Road, 504-835-6933
★★★☆   11 A.M.–closing
Food: Tavern fare   *Smoking:* Throughout

The outside is covered with original advertising from when this was a country store. Inside, it's the "Home of the Tacky Ashtray" and also has barstool bases sculpted to look like human legs. Fine seafood po-boys, twenty beers on tap, and live music.

METAIRIE

Lager's
3501 Veterans Blvd., 504-887-9923
★★☆☆   11 A.M.–3 A.M.
Food: Tavern fare   *Smoking:* Throughout

Decorated in green and dark wood with plenty of beer signs and mirrors, though set in a newish suburban building. Seventy-five beers on tap.

NEW ORLEANS

Acadian Brewing Co. Ⓑ
201 N. Carrollton, 504-483-9003
★★★☆   2 P.M.–late (opens at 1 P.M. Saturdays, 5 P.M. Sundays)
Food: No kitchen   *Smoking:* Throughout

Offers its own fine lagers in the casual bar beside the brewery, plus several other Louisiana microbrewed beers. Bring your own food; many good choices nearby. Live music regularly.

The Balcony Bar
3201 Magazine St., 504-895-1600
★★☆☆   5 P.M.–4 A.M.
Food: Tavern fare   *Smoking:* Throughout

Lovely long bar downstairs backed with seventy taps, more dining and excellent balcony seating looking down on revived stretch of Magazine Street.

The Bulldog
3236 Magazine St., 504-891-1516
★★☆☆   3 P.M.–closing (opens earlier Fridays and Saturdays)
Food: Sandwiches   *Smoking:* Throughout

A long and narrow neighborhood pub with fifty draft choices—half imports, most of the rest American craft beers. Just down the street from the Balcony.

Carrollton Station
8140 Willow St., 504-866-9104
★★☆☆   3 P.M.–late
Food: No kitchen   *Smoking:* Throughout

A rockin' music venue, as intimate as an English pub when the music isn't playing. The sixteen draft choices include beer from local and faraway microbreweries. Darts, ping-pong on Monday nights, an antique bowling machine, and a "Shoot the Bear" game.

Cooter Brown's
509 S. Carrollton, 504-866-9104
★★★☆   11 A.M.–closing
Food: Regional fare   *Smoking:* Throughout

A New Orleans oyster house with forty-plus beers on tap. Home of "Beer Heaven," a collection of sculptures that have oversized heads and undersized bodies. Each is a famous celebrity holding a bottle of beer, such as Alfred Hitchcock with Rogue's Dead Guy Ale.

Crescent City Brewhouse Ⓑ
527 Decatur St., 504-522-0571
★☆☆☆   11 A.M.–closing
Food: Brewpub fare   *Smoking:* Separate sections

Gleaming copper kettles sit right behind the bar, so if they're brewing, you'll get to watch. Lager brewery, menu emphasizes seafood. Second story has balcony overlooking street, Jax Brewery mall, and Mississippi River. To-go cups available. Live jazz.

O'Flaherty's Irish Channel Pub

514 Toulouse St., 504-529-1317

★☆☆☆   11 A.M.–closing

Food: Irish pub fare   ***Smoking:*** Separate section

Actually in the French Quarter, rather than in New Orleans' historic Irish Channel neighborhood. Irish music every night in the music room, great courtyard, separate poetry room. Celebrates Celtic Christmas in high style.

Ryan's Irish Pub

241 Decatur St., 504-523-3500

★☆☆☆   11 A.M.–3 A.M.

Food: No kitchen   ***Smoking:*** Throughout

The beautifully carved back bar is nearly 200 years old and has been here for a hundred years. Large windows open onto Decatur and Bienville streets in this happening part of the French Quarter. Fifteen taps favor imports, but include micros.

Also in Louisiana

Lake Charles: Rikenjaks Brewery, 333 Broad St., 318-433-4881. Microbrewery tasting room (open late, live music).

MAINE

Regional beers to look for: Maine is full of wonderful small
breweries, so the short list has Geary's Brewing; Allagash
Brewing; Sunday River Brewing; Shipyard Brewing; and Sea
Dog Brewing.
Essential stops: The Great Lost Bear and Gritty McDuff's in
Portland.
Just for fun: The Lompoc Café in Bangor. Bocce ball.
Best city for a pub crawl: Portland.

BANGOR

Lompoc Café & Brewpub Ⓑ
34-36 Rodick St., 207-288-9392
★★½☆   11:30 A.M.–1 A.M. (open May through November)
Food: Brewpub fare   *Smoking:* Separate sections

Serving the excellent Atlantic Brewing beers (including Coal
Porter) at the mahogany and Italian marble bar or outside by
the bocce bowling area. Seafood and vegetarian dishes, served
"world fusion" style.

Maine Coast Brewing Taproom Ⓑ
21A Cottage St., 207-288-4914
★★☆☆   11 A.M.–1 A.M.
Food: Brewpub fare   *Smoking:* None

A nice lineup of ales are served in the small taproom, some on
handpump. Jack Russell's Brewpub & Beer Garden on Eden
Street also serves the Maine Coast beers and a slightly broader
menu, and has an outdoor beer garden.

Also in Bangor
Sea Dog Brewing Co., 26 Front St., 207-947-8004. Brewpub; see
Camden.

BETHEL

The Moose's Tail/Sunday River Brewing Co. Ⓑ
1 Sunday River Road, 207-824-3541
★★☆☆   11:30 A.M.–1 A.M. (closed Mondays and Tuesdays)
Food: Brewpub fare   *Smoking:* Separate sections

A large pub that packs 'em in during ski season. Solid ales, and don't leave without trying the Black Bear Porter. Also operates Stone Coast Brewing in Portland and in Laconia, New Hampshire.

CAMDEN

Sea Dog Brewing Co. Ⓑ
43 Mechanic St., 207-236-6863
★★★☆   11:30 A.M.–1 A.M.
Food: Brewpub fare   *Smoking:* Separate sections

Brewpub with a woody interior that belies its office complex exterior. Nautical decor and seafaring menu. Some of its excellent ales served by handpump.

FARMINGTON

Granary Brew Pub & Coffeehouse Ⓑ
23 Pleasant St., 207-779-0710
☆☆☆☆   11 A.M.–10 P.M.
Food: Brewpub fare   *Smoking:* Separate sections

Located in a refurbished granary, while the beer names reflect that it's at the home base of a narrow-gauge railroad. Nice extras include a large fireplace, real darts, and a tableside magician some nights.

KENNEBUNK

Federal Jack's Brew Pub Ⓑ
8 Western Ave., 207-967-4322
★★★☆   Noon-1 A.M.
Food: Brewpub fare   *Smoking:* Separate sections

A nautical pub with windows that open onto Kennebunkport Harbor and a deck with great views of the river. The very nice Shipyard beers were born and are still brewed here. Excellent food.

PORTLAND

The Great Lost Bear
540 Forest Ave., 207-772-0300
    ★★★★   Lunch–late
Food: Tavern fare   *Smoking:* Separate sections

Virtually all fifty-three taps go to microbrewery beers, most of them Maine beers, four of them on handpump (try Geary's Hampshire Special Ale that way). Fine Maine memorabilia and advertising on the walls, hopvines in the beer garden. Celebrated its twentieth AnniBEARsary in 1999.

Gritty McDuff's Ⓑ
396 Fore St., 207-772-2739
    ★★★☆   Lunch–late
Food: Brewpub fare   *Smoking:* Throughout

It's gritty enough, with exposed brick and well-worn tables. The pub fare is hearty, the ales are excellent. Two beers served through beer engines—few bitters in American taste better than Gritty's does here. The bar is copper-topped, with "tap boxes" at each end. There's a second Gritty's in Freeport.

Three Dollar Dewey's
241 Commercial St., 207-772-3310
    ★★☆☆   11:30 A.M.–1 A.M.
Food: Tavern fare   *Smoking:* Separate sections

One of the East Coast's original beer bars, operating around the corner from its original location. Took many of the benches and tables from the old place. Serving thirty-four beers on tap, about half of them from regional craft breweries. Large bottle selection.

Also in Portland
Brian Boru Irish Pub, 57 Center St., 207-708-1506. Irish pub.
Stone Coast Brewing, 2 York St., 207-773-2337. Brewpub; see Bethel.

Also in Maine
Carrabassett Valley: Theo's Pub, Sugarloaf Mountain, 207-237-2211. Brewpub.
Naples: Bray's Brewpub and Eatery, Route 302 & Route 35, 207-693-6806. Brewpub.
Old Orchard Beach: Whale Tale Brewing Co., 213 Saco Ave., 207-934-7370. Brewpub.
Orono: Bear Brewpub, 36 Main St., 207-866-2739. Brewpub.
South Portland: Sebago Brewing Co., 150 Philbrook Ave., 207-879-2537. Brewpub.

MARYLAND

Regional beers to look for: DeGroen's (Baltimore Brewing); Clipper City Brewing; Frederick Brewing (Blue Ridge, Hempen Ale, Wild Goose and more).

Essential stops: Wharf Rat and Baltimore Brewing in Baltimore; Ram's Head Tavern in Annapolis.

Just for fun: Blob's Park in Jessup. Polka until you drop. The first Oktoberfest in the United States allegedly took place here in 1947.

Best city for a pub crawl: Baltimore, specifically Fells Point.

ANNAPOLIS

Griffin's Restaurant
22 Market Space, 410-268-2567

★☆☆☆   11 A.M.–2 A.M.

Food: Full menu   *Smoking:* Separate sections

A fixture on a historic downtown corner, offering eighteen beers on tap—just a few imports, mostly regional craft beers.

Middleton Tavern
2 Market Space, 410-263-3323

★☆☆☆   Lunch–late

Food: Tavern fare   *Smoking:* Separate sections

Historic spot dating to 1750 at the City Dock. House beer from Wild Goose/Frederick, and there are four others on tap.

Ram's Head Tavern   🅱
33 West St., 410-268-4545

★★★☆   11 A.M.–2 A.M.

Food: Brewpub fare   *Smoking:* Separate sections

Multi-tap brewpub (nice lagers from Fordham Brewery) serving guest beers, and an excellent music venue. The downstairs is a small thirty-seat tavern with 300 years of history. The upstairs pub used to be a hardware store.

Riordan's Saloon
26 Market Space, 410-263-5449
★★⯪☆   11 A.M.–late (opens at 10 A.M. Sundays)
Food: Tavern fare   *Smoking:* Throughout

Also at City Dock, serving mainstream lagers, imports, and micros from near and far from twenty taps, plus a handpump for cask beer. Somewhat Irish, particularly in the woody bar area.

Also in Annapolis
Castlebay Irish Pub, 193A Main St., 410-626-0165. Brewpub.

BALTIMORE

Baltimore Brewing Co. Ⓑ
104 Albemarle St., 410-837-5000
★★★⯪   Lunch–late (closed Sundays)
Food: German, brewpub fare   *Smoking:* Separate sections

A former food warehouse, now something of a German beer hall with a pleasant biergarten. Great German-style beers—distributed under the DeGroen label—and German food as well as American regional cuisine.

Bertha's
734 S. Broadway, 410-327-5795
★☆☆☆   11:30 A.M.–closing
Food: Tavern fare   *Smoking:* Separate sections

You've probably seen the "Eat Bertha's Mussels" bumper sticker somewhere. The tavern side wanders, yet remains intimate. The bar is long and narrow, with six taps and a handpump.

Brewer's Art
1106 N. Charles St., 410-547-6925
★★⯪☆   4 P.M.–late (opens at 5 P.M. Sundays)
Food: Full menu   *Smoking:* Separate sections

Quiet dining upstairs with European-style country cuisine, rowdier bar downstairs. Plenty of Belgian-style beers brewed in-house and a very impressive list of imports.

Café Tatoo
4825 Belair Road, 410-325-7427
★☆☆☆   4 P.M.–2 A.M.
Food: Barbecue   *Smoking:* Throughout

Five rotating taps offer imports and craft beers, and there are more than 300 bottled beers to choose from. Excellent ribs, with sauces that have won ribbons in international contests. Horseshoe pits out back.

Cat's Eye Pub
1730 Thames St., 410-276-9085
★★☆☆   Noon-2 A.M.
Food: No kitchen   *Smoking:* Throughout

Terrific venue for roots music, from Irish to zydeco. Twenty-eight beers at classic wooden bar and Baltimore's best bar mural.

Duda's
1600 Thames St., 410-276-9719
★☆☆☆   11 A.M.–1 A.M.
Food: Tavern fare   *Smoking:* Throughout

An intimate Fells Point corner bar often packed with locals, has been around since 1949. Nice cross-section of beers, fifteen taps and 200 bottles.

Hightopps Bar & Grill
1700 Thames, 410-563-1008
★☆☆☆   11 A.M.–2 A.M.
Food: Tavern fare   *Smoking:* Separate sections

A three-level pub with an English-style pub on the second level and a deck with fine views on the third. Pool, TVs, and microbrewed beer on tap.

John Steven, Ltd.
1800 Thames St., 410-276-9497
★★☆☆   11 A.M.–late
Food: Full menu   *Smoking:* Separate sections

Innovative Fells Point restaurant, properly dark and intimate in the bar area. Also has a sushi bar and inviting courtyard seating. Both imports and craft beers on tap.

Max's on Broadway

737 S. Broadway, 410-675-6297

★★★⯪ Noon–2 A.M.

Food: Tavern fare *Smoking:* Throughout

A tad trendy, with a cigar and martini bar upstairs and a web-cam behind the bar, but offers sixty-seven beers on tap and more than 200 in bottles. The draft selection is long on micros and loyal to regional beers. Special beer tastings every Tuesday. Operates smaller pub at Camden Yards.

Sisson's

36 E. Cross St., 410-539-2093

★★⯪☆ 11:30 A.M.–2 A.M. (opens at 4 P.M. Sundays)

Food: Brewpub fare *Smoking:* Separate sections

Brewpub in an old space next to Cross Street Market. Intimate downstairs; open, more expensive dining room upstairs. Excellent beer, goes well with innovative Cajun/Creole cuisine.

Wharf Rat Bar

801 S. Ann St., 410-276-9034

★★★⯪ 11 A.M.–2 A.M.

Food: Tavern fare *Smoking:* Throughout

A bar for maybe 200 years, properly grungy with an ancient-looking wooden floor that slants, bottle caps embedded in the tables, nautical memorabilia, a gigantic fireplace, and a small pool room. Lovely thirty-six-tap lineup, handpumped ale and three drafts for $3 before 7 P.M.

Wharf Rat Camden Yards Ⓑ

206 W. Pratt St., 410-244-8900

★★★☆ 11 A.M.–2 A.M.

Food: Brewpub fare *Smoking:* Separate sections

The Wharf Rat bar isn't big enough to hold a brewery, so owner Bill Oliver built the brewpub in a circa 1860 building that survived the fire of 1904. Jammed with breweriana and nautical antiques, with a set of five handpumps right at the bar. Fine house beers, also guest products.

Wild Mushroom

641 S. Montford, 410-675-4225

★☆☆☆ 11 A.M.–1 A.M.

Food: Full menu *Smoking:* Separate sections

A small corner restaurant offering an ever-changing selection from nine taps and emphasizing craft beer from across the nation. Wild mushroom dishes a specialty.

Also in Baltimore

Birds of a Feather, 1712 Aliceanna, 410-675-8466. Fells Point fixture with a hundred-plus single malts.

Capitol City Brewing, 301 S. Light St., 410-539-7468. Brewpub; see District of Columbia.

The Claddagh Pub, 2918 O'Donnell St., 410-522-4220. Irish pub.

Dougherty's Irish Pub, 223 W. Chase St., 410-752-4059. Irish pub.

The Horse You Came in On, 1626 Thames St., 410-327-8111. Historic bar, good bottle selection.

Leadbetter's, 1639 Thames St., 410-233-4009. Blues bar.

PJ's Pub, 3333 N. Charles St., 410-243-8844. College pub.

BETHESDA

Montgomery Grille

7200 Wisconsin Ave., 301-654-3595

★★☆☆   Lunch–late

Food: Full menu   *Smoking:* Separate sections

Large restaurant with a strong lineup of twenty-seven beers on tap, mostly craft beers with quality imports thrown in.

Also in Bethesda

Capitol City Brewing, 7735 Old Georgetown Road, 301-652-2282. Brewpub; see District of Columbia.

Rock Bottom Restaurant & Brewery, 7900 Norfolk Ave., 301-652-1311. Brewpub; see Denver, Colorado.

COLUMBIA

Last Chance Saloon

5888-A Robert Oliver Place, 410-730-5656

★★★☆   11:30 A.M.–closing (opens later weekends)

Food: Tavern fare   *Smoking:* Separate sections

A little bit of everything: dancing on weekend nights, comedy nights, a family-friendly menu, and we've seen a man plop a young child right on the bartop while he had a beer. Fifty-two draft choices, both craft beers and imports.

Also in Columbia

Rocky Run Tap & Grill, 6480 Dobbins Center Way, 410-730-6581. Brewpub; also operates two taprooms by the same name in the Baltimore area.

ELLICOTT CITY

Ellicott Mills Brewing Co. Ⓑ
8308 Main St., 410-313-8141
★★⯨☆   11:30 A.M.–late
Food: Brewpub fare   *Smoking:* Separate sections

Located in a nineteenth-century lumber mill, with a roomy dining room and stone-walled basement bar. Well-brewed German-style lagers served under Alpenhof name. Wide-ranging menu.

Also in Ellicott City
Bare Bones Grill & Brewery, 9150 Baltimore National Pike, 410-461-0770. Brewpub.

FREDERICK

Brewer's Alley Ⓑ
124 N. Market, 301-631-0039
★★★☆   11:30 A.M.–late
Food: Brewpub fare   *Smoking:* Only in the bar

Set in the former city hall in a historic village turned bedroom community, with excellent food and a wide range of delightfully complex ales.

GAITHERSBURG

Summit Station Restaurant & Brewery Ⓑ
227 E. Diamond Ave., 301-519-9400
★★☆☆   11 A.M.–1 A.M.
Food: Brewpub fare   *Smoking:* Separate sections

A busy three-level pub that still gets crowded. Recently taken over by owners of Brewer's Alley. Dependable ales and excellent burgers, plus a more extensive menu.

HAGERSTOWN

Washington Spy Restaurant
33 E. Antietam St., 301-745-5400

★★⯪☆   11:30 A.M.–9:30 P.M. (closes at 11 P.M. Fridays and Saturdays)

Food: Tavern fare   *Smoking:* Separate sections

Former Greyhound Bus Station, now a three-room pub with eighteenth-century, nineteenth-century and 1940s decors. No draft beer, but 400 bottle choices, 130 Belgian beers.

JESSUP

Blob's Park
8024 Blob's Road, 301-799-0155

★☆☆☆   Friday and Saturday evenings, Sunday afternoons

Food: German fare   *Smoking:* Separate sections

Began as small-frame bowling alley on a farm in 1933, now a German beer hall with beer, food, and dancing on weekends. Eight draft choices.

OCEAN CITY

Ollie's Pub
106 21st St., 410-289-6317

★☆☆☆   10 A.M.–midnight in season

Food: No kitchen   *Smoking:* None

A tiny bar cleverly disguised as a package store. Just 600 square feet for retail store and bar, so no place to sit. More than 700 bottled beers to choose from, plus a rotating selection of mostly craft beers from nine taps.

Also in Ocean City

Worcester Brewing Co., 102 Worcester St., 410-289-3707. Multi-tap, not brewpub.

PARKVILLE

Racers' Café
7732 Harford Road, 410-882-5212
   ★★★☆   10 A.M.–late
Food: No kitchen   *Smoking:* Throughout

The motif is auto racing, and everything else is beer, well cared for and well-handled. The fifteen draft choices change constantly, featuring micros and quality imports, usually one on handpump.

WHITE MARSH

White Marsh Brewing/Red Brick Station ⓑ
8149 Honeygo Blvd., 410-931-7827
   ★☆☆☆   Lunch–late
Food: Brewpub fare   *Smoking:* Separate sections

Large, stylish brewpub along the Avenue at White Marsh. Firehouse theme even extends to the kids' menu. Beer-battered crab cake is made with the house stout.

Also in Maryland

Bel Air: Du Claw Brewing Co., 16-A Bel Air South Station Parkway, 410-515-3222. Brewpub.

Clinton: Margellina, 9009 Stuart Lane, 301-868-0400. Restaurant.

Olney: Olney Ale House, 2000 Olney-Sandy Spring Road, 301-774-6708. Restaurant/pub.

Rockville: Shelly's Woodroast, 1699 Rockville Pike, 301-984-3300. Restaurant.

Silver Spring: Quarry House Tavern, Georgia Ave. & Bonifant St., 301-587-9406. Restaurant.

Towson: Champion Billiards Café, 1969 E. Joppa Road, 410-665-7500. Brewpub.

Westminster: Johansson's Dining Room, 4 W. Main St., 410-876-0101. Brewpub.

Regional beers to look for: The Boston Beer Co. has a pilot brewery in Jamaica Plain but most of the Samuel Adams beers are contract-brewed elsewhere. Nonetheless, it's a beer to look for. Also, Tremont Ale (from Atlantic Coast Brewing); Ipswich Brewing; and Mass. Bay Brewing (Harpoon).

Essential stops: Doyle's in Jamaica Plain; Boston Beer Works, Sunset Grill & Tap, and Big City in Boston (actually Allston); Redbones in Somerville.

Just for fun: Redbones in Somerville. Can't decide what to order? They'll spin the big wheel and let it pick the tap for you.

Best city for a pub crawl: Boston.

BOSTON

B.B. Wolf
109 Brookline Ave., 617-247-2227
    ★★☆☆   5 P.M.–late (opens at 2 P.M. weekends)
Food: Barbecue   *Smoking:* Separate sections

A barbecue spot from the folks at Boston Beer Works and just down the street. Twelve beers on tap, about half of them Beer Works products.

Back Bay Brewing Co. 🅑
755 Boylston St., 617-424-8300
    ★★⯪☆   Lunch–late
Food: Brewpub fare   *Smoking:* Separate sections

Excellent English-inspired ales, and Boylston Bitter on handpump is a particular delight. Wide-ranging menu, though hamburgers are still the standout.

Big City
138 Brighton Ave., 617-782-2020
    ★★★☆   11:30 A.M.–1 A.M.
Food: Tavern fare   *Smoking:* Separate sections

Spinoff of Sunset Grill (see page 141), right next door and with eighty-two taps. The theme is "metro retro" with decorations that include parking meters. Taps are on upstairs bar that's next to a stylish billiards room.

Black Rose
160 State St., 617-742-2286
★☆☆☆   11:30 A.M.–2 A.M.
Food: Full menu   *Smoking:* Throughout

Near Faneuil Hall, popular tourist spot because of its Irish link. As well as Irish beers, has a wide range of micros and imports on tap, equally diverse food menu. Nightly music.

Boston Beer Works Ⓑ
61 Brookline Ave., 617-536-2337
★★★☆   11:30 A.M.–1 A.M.
Food: Brewpub fare   *Smoking:* Separate sections

Massive brewpub across from Fenway Park that still can't accommodate the crowds on game days. Large food portions from an interesting menu, excellent and diverse selection of house beers.

Brendan Behan's Pub
378A Centre St., 617-522-5386
★★☆☆   11 A.M.–late (opens at noon Sundays)
Food: No kitchen   *Smoking:* Throughout

Exactly what you expect an Irish pub to be—too small to be a tourist trap, rather dark, with a low ceiling and walls covered with tattered theater posters, black-and-white photos of County Kerry, and portraits of the bar's namesake poet. The Guinness is always fresh.

brew moon Ⓑ
115 Stuart St., 617-523-6467
★☆☆☆   Lunch–late
Food: Brewpub fare   *Smoking:* Separate sections

Flagship pub in a growing chain that emphasizes each spot is a microbrewery-restaurant with a capital R. Each is comfortable, has jazz brunch, and serves technically fine if not always inspiring beer.

Commonwealth Brewing Co.
138 Portland St., 617-523-8383
★★☆☆   Lunch–late
Food: Brewpub fare   *Smoking:* Separate sections

A pioneer, opening in 1986 and serving cellar-temperature beers through handpumps. Specializing in tasty barbecue. Pubbier downstairs, and you can check out the old Burton Union casks, a reminder of a brewing procedure that's seldom used anymore.

Cornwall's
510 Commonwealth Ave., 617-262-3749
★★☆☆   Lunch–late (opens at 5 P.M. Sundays)
Food: British pub fare, raw bar   *Smoking:* Throughout

Very much a British pub, seventeen beers, mostly UK products but local Tremont Ale on cask. The pub is below street level in Kenmore Square near Fenway Park, and a sign at the entrance sets the tone: "Attention all Yankees fans: You can't wear your hat and we don't serve Budweiser."

Doyle's Café
3484 Washington St., 617-524-2343
★★★★   9 A.M.–1:30 A.M.
Food: Full menu   *Smoking:* Separate sections

Doyle's has been around since 1882. Murals, World War Two posters, photographs, newspaper clippings, a dining room dedicated to Irish freedom fighter Michael Collins, another room that pays tribute to John "Honey Fitz" Fitzgerald (JFK's grandfather)—they're all here. There's a story that a customer rode in on horseback one St. Patrick's Day, ordered a drink, rode around the inside of the bar and left. Actually located in Jamaica Plain.

Hill Tavern
228 Cambridge St., 617-742-6192
★☆☆☆   11:30 A.M.–1 A.M.
Food: Tavern fare   *Smoking:* Throughout

Popular gathering spot draws a young crowd primarily for the crowd. The wood grill turns out good pizza and the draft lineup is solid, featuring Tremont Ale on handpump.

Jacob Wirth
31 Stuart St., 617-338-8586
★★☆☆   Lunch–late (closes earlier Sundays)
Food: Full menu   *Smoking:* Separate sections

A Boston fixture since 1868, and still has the original mahogany-and-brass bar with the Wirth motto, "Suum Cuique" (To Each His Own), above it. The restaurant serves more than twenty tons of red cabbage and sauerkraut every year. Eighteen draft choices, German beers and regional craft products.

New England Brew Pub
19 Union St., 617-723-8080
★☆☆☆   11:30 A.M.–2 A.M.
Food: Tavern fare   *Smoking:* Separate sections

Tourist spot near Faneuil Hall, not a brewpub but offers a solid cross-section of local craft beers on tap.

North East Brewing Co. Ⓑ
1314 Commonwealth Ave., 617-566-6699
★★☆☆   Lunch–late
Food: Brewpub fare   *Smoking:* Separate sections

Casual friendly pub that keeps a wide selection of house beers on tap. Several menu items cooked with beer. Regular live music.

Sam Adams Brewhouse
710 Boylston St., 617-421-4961
★☆☆☆   11 A.M.–closing
Food: No kitchen   *Smoking:* Throughout

Despite the name, no brewery here. Licenses the use of Sam Adams from Boston Beer Co., serves only Samuel Adams beers on tap and promises freshly tapped kegs.

The Sevens Alehouse
77 Charles St., 617-523-9074
★☆☆☆   11:30 A.M.–late
Food: Sandwiches   *Smoking:* Throughout

Pub established right after Prohibition on Beacon Hill. Locals like to refer to it as the "real" Cheers (the Bull & Finch, whose front was used in the TV show, is virtually around the corner). Dark and smoky with a limited tap selection.

Sunset Grill & Tap
130 Brighton Ave., 617-254-1331
★★★⯪   11:30 A.M.–1 A.M.
Food: Tavern fare   *Smoking:* Separate sections

A place to loosen your belt. More than 110 draft beers to choose from, at least a couple more on handpump, and 400 by the bottle. To guarantee freshness, the house promises no keg will be tapped for more than thirteen days. Interesting though simple menu, with immense portions. Crowded enough to warrant opening Big City (see page 138) next door.

Also in Boston

Boodles, Back Bay Hilton, 14 Copley St., 617-266-3537. Hotel bar.

Boston Beer Garden, 732-734 E. Broadway, 617-269-0990. Locals' spot.

Cross Roads, 495 Beacon St., 617-262-7371. Irish pub.

The Grand Canal, 57 Canal St., 617-523-1112. Irish pub.

Hibernia, 25 Kingston St., 617-292-2333. Irish pub.

The Irish Embassy, 234 Friend St., 617-742-6618. Irish pub.

Michael Sherlock's, 99 Broad St., 617-350-7077. Irish pub.

The Original Sports Saloon, 47 Huntington Ave., 617-536-1908. Sports bar.

The Shanakee, 428 Washington St., 617-331-5648. Irish pub.

BOURNE

Trowbridge Tavern

100 Trowbridge Road, 508-759-1776

    ★☆☆☆   11:30 A.M.–late (opens at 3 P.M. Mondays and Tuesdays)

Food: British pub fare   *Smoking:* Separate sections

Just over the Bourne Bridge, very British. The twenty draft selections are primarily UK products, but also include regional craft beers brewed to British styles.

BRIGHTON

Roggie's Brew & Grille

356 Chestnut Hill Ave., 617-566-1880

    ★★☆☆   11 A.M.–closing

Food: Bistro fare   *Smoking:* Throughout

A barracuda hangs over the back bar, which is shiny metal with taps sprouting everywhere. Mostly craft beers on twenty taps, and excellent food.

BROOKLINE

Coolidge Corner Clubhouse
307A-309 Harvard St., 617-566-4948
★☆☆☆   11 A.M.–1:30 A.M.
Food: Tavern fare   *Smoking:* None

A crowded sports bar with seventeen televisions and sandwiches named after sports stars. The thirty-five draft choices include regional craft beers, West Coast choices, and excellent imports.

CAMBRIDGE

Cambridge Brewing Co. Ⓑ
1 Kendall Square, Bldg. 100, 617-494-1994
★★☆☆   Lunch–late
Food: Brewpub fare   *Smoking:* Separate sections

Tucked into an urban outdoor mall, with exposed brick and light wood. Draws both post-work and evening crowds, primarily for the well-made ales.

John Harvard's Brew House Ⓑ
33 Dunster St., 617-868-3585
★★☆☆   Lunch–late
Food: Brewpub fare   *Smoking:* Separate sections

Flagship of the East Coast chain. Woody, stained-glass, upscale student pub drawing an international crowd. Well-made British-inspired ales, some on handpump.

Also in Cambridge
brew moon, 50 Church St., 617-523-6467. Brewpub; see Boston.
Christopher's, 1920 Massachusetts Ave., 617-876-9180. Pub.
The Druid, 1357 Cambridge St., 617-497-0965. Irish pub.
Plough & Stars, 912 Massachusetts Ave., 617-492-9653. Irish pub.

GREENFIELD

The People's Pint Ⓑ
24 Federal St., 413-773-0333
★★☆☆   4 P.M.–closing
Food: Brewpub fare   *Smoking:* None

A friendly local, keeps about nine of its own ales on, with a cask-conditioned ale that changes twice a week. No TV, real darts, and board games. No credit cards.

HUDSON

Horseshoe Pub & Eatery
29 South St., 508-568-1265

 ★★⯪☆ 11:30 A.M.–midnight (closed Sundays)

Food: Tavern fare *Smoking:* Separate sections

Located in a 150-year-old building in the delightful country west of Boston. Fifty tap selections include imports and national micros, but also a wonderful lineup of regional choices. Handpump.

LOWELL

Brewhouse Cafe & Grill/Lowell Brewing Ⓑ
199 Cabot St., 978-937-2690

 ★★☆☆ 11:30 A.M.–2 A.M.

Food: Brewpub fare *Smoking:* Separate sections

Large pub in an old textile mill, serving the lovely Mill City beers brewed here for distribution. Dining on first floor, night-club on second, and game room on third.

Smithwick's
92 Middle St., #104, 978-937-2111

 ★★☆☆ 11 A.M.–2 A.M.

Food: British pub fare *Smoking:* Throughout

Beamed ceiling, dark wood, dimly lit, truly pubby. An excellent lineup of UK beers and regional standouts available on twenty-two taps and in a hundred-plus bottles. Fine single-malt menu.

NORFOLK

Eagle Brook Saloon
Route 1A, 508-384-7312

 ★☆☆☆ Lunch–late (closed Sundays)

Food: Tavern fare *Smoking:* Separate sections

Thirteen beers, all house beers custom-brewed for the tavern. Décor includes classic three-piece back bar.

NORTHAMPTON

Northampton Brewery Ⓑ
11 Brewster Court, 413-584-9903
★★☆☆   11:30 A.M.–1 A.M. (opens later Sundays)
Food: Brewpub fare   *Smoking:* Separate sections

One of the first breweries in the Northeast, opening in 1987 in a renovated nineteenth-century brick carriage house. Well-made ales. Excellent rooftop seating. Under the same leadership as Smuttynose Brewing Co. and Portsmouth Brewing.

OAK BLUFFS

Offshore Ale Co. Ⓑ
30 Kennebec Ave., 508-693-2626
★☆☆☆   Depends on season; call first
Food: Brewpub fare   *Smoking:* None

The first and only brewpub on Martha's Vineyard can get crowded. The sturdy interior sports exposed beams, a stone fireplace, high-back wooden booths and two small boats hanging from the ceiling. Nothing timid about the beers, some served from handpumps.

PLYMOUTH

The British Beer Co.
6 Middle St., 508-747-1776
★☆☆☆   11:30 A.M.–12:30 A.M.
Food: British pub fare   *Smoking:* Separate sections

Intended to re-create a British pub, with mostly UK beers on tap but also local micros, including a cask-conditioned beer on handpump. Upstairs room with leatherback chairs, fireplace, and darts.

Also in Plymouth
Plymouth Bay Brewing Co., 56 Main St., 508-746-7222. Brewpub.

SOMERVILLE

Redbones
55 Chester St., 617-628-2200
 ★★★★ Lunch–late
Food: Barbecue *Smoking:* Separate sections

While the small bar seems mostly like a holding area for this terrific barbecue restaurant, some customers come only for the beer. Outstanding lineup of twenty-four draft beers, with two handpumps. Regional beers favored, but also special offerings from overseas and special events that may showcase beer from anywhere.

Also in Somerville
The Burren, 247 Elm St., 617-776-6896. Irish pub.
Tír na nÓg, 366A Somerville Ave., 617-628-4300. Irish pub.

SOUTH EASTON

Blackthorn Tavern
402 Turnpike St., 508-238-9017
 ★☆☆☆ Lunch–late (opens at 3 P.M. Sundays)
Food: Full menu *Smoking:* Separate sections

Both restaurant and publike music venue, with a large fireplace and bookshelves. Eclectic music five nights a week. Eight taps offer primarily imports.

SPRINGFIELD

Student Prince/The Fort
8 Fort St., 413-734-7475
 ★☆☆☆ 11 A.M.–midnight
Food: German fare *Smoking:* Separate sections

The stein collection here numbers in the thousands. German fare and four German beers on tap, plus a full complement of German cordials and wines. Woody, old-world setting.

STOCKBRIDGE

The Red Lion
30 Main St., 413-298-5545
★☆☆☆   11 A.M.–1 A.M.
Food: Full menu   *Smoking:* Separate sections

Pub for a 110-room inn/restaurant that has a history dating to 1773. Seven drafts include both imports and craft beers.

WORCESTER

Plantation Club Draft House
151 Plantation St., 508-752-4666
★★☆☆   Hours vary; call first
Food: Tavern fare   *Smoking:* Throughout

A fine music venue on one side, pub/restaurant on the other. Twenty-seven draft choices, many craft beers, bargain prices. Inviting atrium seating.

Also in Worcester
Brew City Grill & Brew House, 104 Shrewsbury St., 508-752-3862. No brewery, but thirty draft choices.

Also in Massachusetts
Amherst: Amherst Brewing Co., 36 N. Pleasant St., 413-253-4400. Brewpub.
Beverly: Wild Horse Cafe, 392 Cabot St., 508-922-6868. Tavern.
Braintree: brew moon, 250 Granite St., 781-941-2739. Brewpub; see Boston.
Charlestown: Warren Tavern Restaurant, 2 Pleasant St. 617-241-8142. Historic tavern, solid draft selection.
Danvers: Brutole Brick Oven Brewery, 65 Newbury St., 978-777-6633. Brewpub.
Framingham: John Harvard's Brew House, Shopper's World-1 Wooster Road, 508-875-2337. Brewpub; see Cambridge.
Great Barrington: Barrington Brewery & Restaurant, 420 Stockbridge Road, 413-528-8282. Brewpub.
Haverhill: Riverside House of Brews, 100 Washington St., 508-469-0400. Tavern.
Wee Bit O'Blarney Pub & Grill, 105 Washington St., 978-521-5277. Irish pub.
Hyannis: Hyannisport Brewing Co., 720 Main St., 508-775-8289. Brewpub.
Natick: Owen O'Leary's, 319 Speen St., 508-650-0972. Brewpub.

Pittsfield: The Brewery at 34 Depot St., 34 Depot St., 413-442-2072. Brewpub.

Plainville: The Chieftain Pub, Route 1, 508-643-903. Irish.

Salem: Salem Beer Works, 278 Derby St., 978-774-0004. Brewpub.

Sturbridge: Ebenezer's Tavern, On the Common, Route 31, 800-782-5425. Part of the Publick House Historic Resort.

Waltham: Watch City Brewing, 256 Moody St., 617-647-4000. Brewpub.

West Harwich: Claddagh Tavern, 77 Main St., 508-430-2440. Irish pub.

Regional beers to look for: Bell's from Kalamazoo Brewing; Roffey Brewing.
Essential stops: The Eccentric Cafe and Corner Bar in Kalamazoo; Cadieux Cafe in Detroit.
Just for fun: Gusoline Alley in Royal Oak. The two televisions
here are usually turned to cartoons, and the story is that during
the Super Bowl, a customer had to ask for one to be turned to
the game so he could catch the score.
Best city for a pub crawl: Kalamazoo.

ANN ARBOR

Arbor Brewing ⓑ
114 E. Washington, 734-213-1993
   ★☆☆☆   Lunch–late
Food: Brewpub fare   *Smoking:* Separate sections

Brick walls, a hardwood floor, an inviting bar area, and a nice
lineup of classic beer styles. Also a shuffleboard table and real
darts. Extensive menu, ranging from brewpub fare to Southwestern entrees.

Ashley's Restaurant & Pub
335 S. State, 734-996-9191
   ★★⯪☆   Lunch–late
Food: Tavern fare   *Smoking:* Separate sections

Across from the University of Michigan campus, but no Bud
taps here. Sixty-four beers on tap, both imports and microbrewed beers, one handpump. More than fifty single-malt
whiskies.

Grizzly Peak Brewing Co. ⓑ
120 W. Washington, 734-741-7325
   ★☆☆☆   Lunch–late
Food: Brewpub fare   *Smoking:* Separate sections

Spacious pub that attracts a good crowd, sometimes loud. Solid
lineup of regular beers and some noteworthy seasonals. Wood-
fired pizza.

Also in Ann Arbor
Conor O'Neills Traditional Irish Pub, 318 S. Main St., 734-665-
2968. Irish pub.
Del Rio, 122 W. Washington, 734-761-2530. Friendly bistro.
One-Eyed Moose, 207 S. Main, 734-994-8484. Tavern.

BERKLEY

Berkley Front
3087 W. 12 Mile Road, 810-547-3331
★★⯪☆   Lunch–late (limited hours Sundays)
Food: Tavern fare   *Smoking:* None

Fifty taps with accent on American craft beers. "Eclectic garage sale meets beer garden" decor, with most seating at communal tables.

Also in Berkley
O'Mara's Restaurant, 2555 W. 12 Mile Road, 810-399-6750. Brewpub.

BOYNE CITY

Boyne City Brewing Co. Ⓑ
419 E. Main St., 616-582-5588
★☆☆☆   Lunch–late
Food: Tavern fare   *Smoking:* None

Home of the "Laid Back Ales" brewed in the distributing microbrewery in the back half of a building made of corrugated siding. Handmade tables, mismatched chairs, and walls covered with garage sale stuff. Beers have a solid following as far away as Detroit.

CHESTERFIELD

North Channel Brewing Co. Ⓑ
30400 23 Mile Road, 810-948-2739
★★☆☆   Lunch–late
Food: Brewpub fare   *Smoking:* Separate sections

Outdoors-oriented and built on the model of a Northern Michigan lodge, complete with fieldstone fireplace. Animals native to Michigan are mounted on the walls (personal trophies of the owners or friends). High marks for both the food and beer.

CLARKSTON

Clarkston Union
54 S. Main St., 248-620-9910
★★⯪☆   11 A.M.–late (9 A.M.–9 P.M. Sundays)
Food: Tavern fare   *Smoking:* Separate sections

Resurrected 1840s church has been turned into a pub, serving comfort food and offering a combination of imports and micros from thirty-five taps.

CROSS VILLAGE

Legs Inn
On M119, 616-526-2281
★☆☆☆   Noon–after dinner
Food: Full menu   *Smoking:* Separate sections

A sprawling fieldstone and timber structure built over several decades, best described as "Poland meets Native America." Warm, inviting, and woodsy, with knotty-pine-lined walls, huge stone fireplaces. Decorated with sculpted driftwood. Polish cuisine, wide range of bottled beers.

DETROIT

Atwater Block Brewing Co. Ⓑ
237 Joseph Campau, 313-393-2337
★★☆☆   11 A.M.–late (opens at noon weekends, closes early Sundays)
Food: Brewpub fare   *Smoking:* Separate sections

In the heart of Detroit's rivertown district, offering a wide-ranging menu and excellent German-style beers. Many of the beers are served in their own special glasses. Popular and loud. Has a sitting room (may be in private use) with a couch-ensconced fireplace and an area for darts.

Cadieux Café
4300 Cadieux, 313-882-8560
★★☆☆   4 P.M.–2:30 A.M. (opens early Thursdays through Saturdays)
Food: Belgian fare   *Smoking:* Separate sections

Home to the only two Belgian feather bowling lanes in the country, serving Belgian food (try the Mussels Creole) in a family-friendly setting. Wide choice of bottled Belgian beer. The eight draft selections also include local craft beer.

Dakota Inn Rathskeller
17324 John R St., 313-867-9722

★☆☆☆ Lunch only Mondays and Tuesdays; Lunch–late Thursdays and Fridays; opens at 5 P.M. Saturdays

Food: German fare *Smoking:* Separate sections

Barely changed since it was converted from a laundromat into a restaurant in 1933, and now run by a third generation. They carefully refurbish one room a year, so it looks new and old at the same time. Beautiful murals, traditional German fare and beer.

Tom's Oyster House
15402 Mack Ave., 313-884-6030

★☆☆☆ 11 A.M.–2 A.M. (limited hours Sundays)

Food: Full menu *Smoking:* Separate sections

Both a popular restaurant and a raw bar with a fine old bar area. Imports and craft beers among the nine on tap, plus solid bottle menu. One of three Tom's Oyster Houses in the Detroit area.

Ye Olde Taproom
14915 Charlevoix, 313-331-9154

★☆☆☆ 4:30 P.M.–2 A.M. (opens at 6 P.M. weekends)

Food: No kitchen *Smoking:* Throughout

Casual, European-style pub built in 1916 by Detroit's Kling Brewery, also once housed a brothel. Nice mix of imports and micros from eleven taps, plus serious bottle menu of 200-plus. More than thirty single-malt whiskies.

Also in Detroit
Nancy Whiskey's, 2644 Harrison, 313-962-4247. Irish pub.

O'Halloran's Tipperary Pub, 8287 Southfield, 313-271-5870. Irish pub.

The Old Shillelagh, 349 Monroe, 313-964-0007. Irish pub.

Traffic Jam and Snug, 511 W. Canfield, 313-831-9470. Brewpub.

DOWAGIAC

Zeke's
109 S. Front St., 616-782-5070
★☆☆☆   Breakfast–late evening
Food: Full menu   *Smoking:* Separate sections

Country restaurant meets bar in this downtown establishment.
More than 250 imports and American craft beers available by
the bottle.

ESCANABA

Hereford & Hops Brewing Co. Ⓑ
624 Ludington St., 906-789-1945
☆☆☆☆   11 A.M.–late
Food: Steakhouse   *Smoking:* Separate sections

Large brewpub with several dining rooms, a cozy bar. Communal grilling pits where customers cook their own steaks (you
can also let the chef do it).

GAYLORD

Big Buck Brewery Ⓑ
550 S. Wisconsin, 517-732-5781
★★☆☆   11:30 A.M.–late
Food: Brewpub fare   *Smoking:* Separate sections

Flagship pub for a growing chain. Each is good-sized and decorated like a lodge, with plenty of mounted game on the walls
and game on the menu. Both boring and interesting beers.

GRAND MARAIS

Lake Superior Brewing Co. at Dunes Saloon Ⓑ
N-14283 Lake Ave., 906-494-2337
★☆☆☆   Noon–2:30 A.M.
Food: Tavern fare   *Smoking:* Throughout

Located right across the street from Lake Superior. A long and
narrow locals' place, with hunting mounts up on the walls. Tables in the back room are glass-topped barrels with geodes under the glass, and the tap handles are made out of rocks, too.

HOLLAND

Butch's Dry Dock
44 E. 8th St., 616-396-8227

★☆☆☆   10 A.M.–late (closed Sundays)

Food: Deli   *Smoking:* None

Butch ran a carry-out liquor store for ten years before opening this spanking-clean, airy deli. Massive sandwich list, 200 beers by the bottle and seven on tap—mostly craft beers with two imports.

Also in Holland
Back Street Brewing Co., 13 W. 7th St., 616-394-4200. Brewpub.
New Holland Brewing Co., 205 Fairbanks, 616-355-6422. Brewpub.

ISHPEMING

Jasper Ridge Brewery
1075 Country Lane, 906-485-6017

★☆☆☆   11 A.M.–11 P.M. or midnight

Food: Tavern fare   *Smoking:* Separate sections

Sports bar in a mall of prefab buildings. Sleek, retro look inside, with windows between the dining and bar areas that reveal the brewing equipment. Solid beers.

KALAMAZOO

The Corner Bar
1030 E. Vine St., 616-385-2028

★★★⯪   10 A.M.–10:30 P.M. (last call); closed Sundays

Food: Tavern fare   *Smoking:* Separate sections

A museum of breweriana, with chalk statues, and cardboard, paper, tin and porcelain beer ads covering the walls. Eighteen draft choices, with a superb cross-section of well-known micros, imports, and Michigan beers such as Bell's and Roffey's, all at terrific prices. Excellent food, great lunch specials.

Eccentric Café Ⓑ
315 E. Kalamazoo, 616-383-2338
    ★★★⯨   10 A.M.–late (limited hours Sundays)
Food: No kitchen   *Smoking:* None

Communal bar in the midst of the truly eccentric Kalamazoo Brewing plant. Smoke-free and conversation-friendly, with a ping-pong area, a stage for live music, and a lovely beer garden in back. Most important are the excellent Bell's beers.

Also in Kalamazoo
Kraftbrau Brewery, 402 E. Kalamazoo, 616-384-0288. Brewpub.
Olde Peninsula Brewpub, 200 E. Michigan, 616-343-2739. Brewpub.

MARQUETTE

Vierling & Marquette Lower Harbor Brewery Ⓑ
119 S. Front St., 906-228-3533
    ★☆☆☆   11 A.M.–late (closed Sundays)
Food: Brewpub fare   *Smoking:* Separate sections

A longtime restaurant in a historic building that added brewing equipment and makes pretty good beer. Decor calls Victorian days to mind, with hunting prints and beer- and Marquette-related memorabilia on the walls.

NOVI

Local Color Brewing Co. Ⓑ
42705 Grand River Ave., 248-349-2600
    ★★☆☆   11:30 A.M.–late
Food: Brewpub fare   *Smoking:* Separate sections

Expansive restaurant attached to microbrewery. Brews a wide range of beers, including some very well-made German-style products.

OKEMOS

Travelers Club & Tuba Museum Ⓑ
2138 Hamilton Road, 517-349-1701
   ★☆☆☆   8 A.M.–after dinner
Food: International   *Smoking:* Separate sections

Really is a tuba museum, with horns on display. International/travel theme extends to the food (menu features different countries during the year) and the beer, mostly in bottles. Kid-friendly, with vintage soda fountain. Began brewing in fall of 1999.

PLYMOUTH

Box Bar
777 W. Ann Arbor Trail, 313-459-7390
   ★★☆☆   10:30 A.M.–1 A.M.
Food: Tavern fare   *Smoking:* Throughout

A locals' gathering spot for fifty years, with 240 bottled beers. 1999 expansion plans were for fifty taps, maybe 1,000 bottled beers. Framed jigsaw puzzles hang on the walls. Owner Chip Falcusan says the bar belongs to the people of Plymouth, and he's just a caretaker.

ROYAL OAK

Gusoline Alley
309 S. Center, 248-545-2235
   ★☆☆☆   10 A.M.–2 A.M. (noon–2 A.M. Sundays)
Food: No kitchen   *Smoking:* Throughout

A tiny place (capacity fifty-six) and gets crowded early. Annually voted "best dive" and "best jukebox" in the Detroit area. Good bottle list, three taps—usually Guinness, a Fuller's beer (from London), and a Michigan craft beer. Gas station decor with the front end of a 1976 Cadillac El Dorado jutting out from the wall near the rear. Its flashing headlights and booming horn signal last call.

Also in Royal Oak
The Four Green Fields, 3333 N. Woodward, 248-280-2902. Irish pub.
Memphis Smoke, 100 S. Main St., 248-543-4300 Restaurant/club.
Royal Oak Brewery, 215 E. 4th St., 248-544-1141. Brewpub.

UPPER TAHQUAMENON FALLS STATE PARK

Tahquamenon Brewing Co. Ⓑ
At Camp 33, 906-492-3300
☆☆☆☆   9:30 A.M.–11 P.M.
Food: Brewpub fare   *Smoking:* Separate sections

Located in the state park lodge, sixteen miles from the nearest town. Draws snowmobilers in winter, visitors to the falls in summer.

WILLIAMSTON

Michigan Brewing Co. Ⓑ
2582 M 52, 517-521-3600
★☆☆☆   Noon–9 P.M. (closes later Fridays and Saturdays, closed Sundays)
Food: Peanuts, chips   *Smoking:* None at the bar, separate room

A bar/tasting room serving an excellent lineup of house beers. Plans to add a restaurant in 2000.

Also in Michigan
Auburn Hills: Alcatraz Brewing Co., Great Lakes Crossing, 248-745-3400. Brewpub; see Indianapolis, Indiana.
  Big Buck Brewery & Steakhouse, 2550 Takata, 248-276-2337. Brewpub; see Gaylord.
Battle Creek: Arcadia Brewing Co., 103 W. Michigan Ave., 616-963-9690. Brewpub.
Birmingham: Big Rock Chop House, 245 S. Eton St., 248-647-7774. Brewpub.
  Dick O'Dows Public House, 160 W. Maple, 810-642-1135. Irish pub.
Clinton Township: Great Baraboo Brewing Co., 35905 Utica Road, 810-792-7397. Brewpub.
Commerce Township: CJ's Brewing Co., 8115 Richardson Road, 248-366-7979. Brewpub.
East Lansing: Evergreen Grill, 327 Abbott Road, 517-337-1200. Tavern.
  Harper's Brewing Co., 131 Albert Ave., 517-333-4040. Brewpub.
Eastpointe: Detroit Brew Factory, 18605 E. 8 Mile Road, 810-776-8848. BOP/pub.
Ferndale: Matt Brady's, 1820 9 Mile Road, 810-584-4242. Irish pub.
  Woodward Avenue Brewers, 22646 Woodward Ave., 248-546-3696. Brewpub.

Flint: The Redwood Lodge, 5304 Gateway Center, 810-233-8000. Tavern.

Grand Rapids: Big Buck Brewery, 2500 28th St. SE, 616-954-9635. Brewpub.

Bob's House of Brews, 20 Monroe Ave., 616-356-2000. Brewpub.

Canal Street Brewing Co., 648 Monroe NW, 616-776-1195. Brewpub.

Grand Rapids Brewing, 3689 28th St., 616-285-5970. Brewpub.

Grosse Pointe Park: O'Flaherty's Pub, 15119 Charlois, 313-824-1140. Irish pub.

Houghton: Library Bar & Restaurant, 62 Isle Royale St., 906-482-6211. Brewpub.

Jackson: Jackson Brewing Co., 6020 Ann Arbor Road, 517-764-5010. Brewpub.

Lansing: Blue Coyote, 113 Pere Marquette, 517-485-2583. Brewpub.

Lawton: Big T, 155 Main St., 616-624-1200. See Zeke's, Dowagiac.

Old Hat Bar, 114 N. Main St., 616-624-3771. Brewpub, owned by Kalamazoo Brewing.

Marshall: Dark Horse Brewing Co., 826 W. Michigan Ave., 616-781-7797. Brewpub.

Mount Pleasant: Mountain Town Station, 506 W. Broadway, 517-775-2337. Brewpub.

Northville: Bonfire Bistro & Brewery, 7 Mile and Haggerty, 248-735-4570. Brewpub.

Oscoda: Wiltse's Brew Pub & Family Restaurant, 5606 F-41, 517-739-2231. Brewpub.

Pontiac: Bo's Brewery & Bistro, 51 N. Saginaw, 810-338-6200. Brewpub.

Port Huron: Quay Street Brewery, 33 Quay St., 810-982-4100. Brewpub.

Rivertown: Franklin St. Brewing Co., 1560 Franklin St., 313-568-0390. Restaurant/bar.

Rochester: Rochester Mills Beer Co., 310 Water St., 248-650-5080. Brewpub.

Sanford: Sanford Lake Bar & Grill, 3770 Baily Road, 517-687-5620. Brewpub.

St. Clair Shores: Pat O'Brien's Tavern, 22385 10 Mile Road, 810-771-5715. Irish pub.

St. Joseph: Lighthouse Depot Restaurant & Brewpub, 1 Lighthouse Lane, 616-982-7397. Brewpub.

Southfield: Copper Canyon Brewery, 27522 Northwestern, 248-223-1700. Brewpub.

Spring Lake: Old Boys' Brewhouse, 971 W. Savidge St., 616-847-4287. Brewpub.

Traverse City: Mackinaw Brewing Co., 161 E. Front St., 616-933-1100. Brewpub.
North Peak Brewing Co., 400 W. Front St., 616-941-5984. Brewpub.

Westland: Fire Academy Brewery & Grill, 6677 N. Wayne Road, 734-595-1988. Brewpub.

Wyandotte: Sports Bar & Grill, 166 Maple St., 734-285-5060. Sports bar with craft beer on tap.

Regional beers to look for: Summit Brewing; August Schell Brewing.

Essential stops: Sherlock's Home in Minnetonka; The Black Forest in Minneapolis.

Just for fun: Bryant Lake Bowl in Minneapolis. Bowling on old-fashioned '60s bowling lanes, performance art in the small attached theater, and a bohemian dining room.

Best city for a pub crawl: Minneapolis.

EDEN PRAIRIE

Water Tower Brewing Co. ⓑ
12200 Singletree Lane, 612-941-8773

★☆☆☆   11 A.M.–late

Food: Brewpub fare   *Smoking:* Separate sections

Brunswick's first brewpub/bowling alley in a chain, featuring Northeast-style beers. Also home of Cosmic Bowling, which features pulsating music, laser lights, fog machines, and glow-in-the-dark sunglasses.

MINNEAPOLIS

The Black Forest
1 E. 26th St., 612-872-0812

★★☆☆   Lunch–late

Food: German fare   *Smoking:* Separate sections

Traditional German food and the best beer garden in Minneapolis draw big crowds nightly. Sixteen draft choices with an excellent range of German imports and regional favorites. Huge Richard Avedon photo and Frank Lloyd Wright–designed windows in bar area.

Brit's Pub and Eating Establishment
1110 Nichollet Mall, 612-332-3908

★☆☆☆   10 A.M.–late

Food: British pub fare   *Smoking:* Separate sections

A British pub with three fireplaces and a hundred-year-old bar that was retrieved from Wall Street in the main pub. A rambling place with plenty of antique furniture and couches. The seventeen tap choices include three lagers, three stouts, a cider, and ten ales, mostly British imports.

Bryant Lake Bowl
810 W. Lake St., 612-825-7109
★★★☆   8 A.M.–1 A.M.
Food: Full menu   *Smoking:* Separate sections

Eight bowling lanes, a popular (though small) theater, and a café area that opens for breakfast (organic oatmeal). Solid selection of draft and bottled beer, fine wine menu, beautiful twenty-five-foot-long Art Deco bar.

Gasthaus zur Gemutlichkeit
2300 University Ave. NE, 612-781-3860
★★☆☆   4 P.M.–1 A.M. (opens at 10:30 A.M. Sundays)
Food: German fare   *Smoking:* Separate sections

Different German theme in each of several rooms, plenty of German food, and twelve German beers on tap. Giant combo platters serve two or more.

Glueks Restaurant
16 N. 16th St., 612-338-6621
★☆☆☆   10 A.M.–1 A.M.
Food: Full menu   *Smoking:* Separate sections

Restaurant built by Gluek Brewing Co. in 1902, restored to its brick-oak-brass splendor after a devastating fire. Microbrewed, imported, and mainstream beers served from twenty-six taps.

MacKenzie Scotch Pub
918 Hennepin Ave., 612-333-7268
★☆☆☆   11 A.M.–1 A.M.
Food: Tavern fare   *Smoking:* Throughout

The focus is on imports, but the fifteen taps also offer a few craft beers (no mainstream products). Separate bar for deck, where you can chat with performers as they enter the back of the Orpheum Theater next door.

Minneapolis Town Hall Brewery 🅑
1430 Washington Ave. S., 612-339-8696
★★☆☆   11 A.M.–late
Food: Brewpub fare   *Smoking:* Separate sections

Set in an early working-class commercial district, woody and green with pictures of old Minneapolis throughout. Food a fusion of many cultures, fine beers.

New French Café
128 N. 4th St., 612-338-3790

★★⯪☆ Lunch–late in bar (opens later weekends)

Food: French   *Smoking:* Separate sections

This excellent French restaurant serves a less expensive (but not cheap) menu in the bar. Six well-chosen draft choices and international bottle selection.

Pracna on Main
117 SE Main, 612-379-3200

★☆☆☆ 11:30 A.M.–1 A.M.

Food: Full menu   *Smoking:* Separate sections

Minneapolis' oldest restaurant in a vintage stone building along the river, serving twenty beers on tap, including American craft beers and imports. Tap handles are mounted on old kegs.

William's Uptown
2911 Hennepin Ave., 612-823-6271

★★⯪☆ 4 P.M.–1 A.M.

Food: Tavern fare   *Smoking:* Throughout

Minneapolis institution, refurbished in 1995, putting seventy beers on tap with the kegs on display behind glass. Also has 300-plus bottled beers. Pool in upstairs pub, free peanuts in peanut bar.

Also in Minneapolis
District Warehouse Brewing Co., 430 1st Ave. N., 612-333-2739. Brewpub.

Kieran's Irish Pub & Restaurant, 330 2nd Ave. S., 612-339-4499. Irish pub.

Old Chicago, 2841 Hennepin, 612-870-1918. See Boulder, Colorado.

Old Chicago, 508 1st Ave. N., 612-338-8686.

Rock Bottom Brewery & Restaurant, 800 LaSalle Plaza, 612-332-2739. Brewpub; see Denver, Colorado.

MINNETONKA

Sherlock's Home 🅑
11000 Red Circle, 612-931-0203
> ★★★☆   11 A.M.–1 A.M. (opens at 4 P.M. Sundays)
> *Food:* Upscale British fare   *Smoking:* Separate sections

All the furnishings in this authentic, upscale English pub come from Britain. The beer is conditioned in traditional wooden firkins and kilderkins and served as "real ale" from handpumps. The single-malt whisky menu offers more than seventy choices. It doesn't get much more authentic than this.

Also in Minnetonka
Old Chicago, 17790 Highway 7, 612-401-0030.

RED WING

Staghead Restaurant
219 Bush St., 651-388-6581
> ★☆☆☆   10 A.M.–10 P.M. (10 A.M.–2:30 P.M. Mondays, closed Sundays)
> *Food:* Bistro fare   *Smoking:* None

A rivertown gathering spot, woody with oil paintings on the walls. Ten draft choices include regional beers. Excellent food from a menu that changes often.

ST. LOUIS PARK

Shelly's Woodroast
6501 Wayzata Blvd., 612-593-5050
> ★★☆☆   11 A.M.–late
> *Food:* Full menu   *Smoking:* Separate sections

Shelly's moved from downtown in 1989 to this rustic lodge setting, offering wood-roasted poultry and beef and a well-chosen draft beer menu. Included are several regional and West Coast craft beers.

ST. PAUL

The Great Waters Brew Pub ⓑ
426 St. Peter St., 651-224-2739

   ★★☆☆   11 A.M.–1 A.M. (opens at noon Sundays)

Food: Brewpub fare   *Smoking:* Separate sections

In the restored 1919 Hamm Building, brewing with water drawn from a 1,400-foot well beneath it. Lovely range of beers, several of them served on handpump and at cellar temperature.

Johnny's
2251 University Ave. W., 651-645-4116

   ★☆☆☆   11 A.M.–1 A.M.

Food: Tavern fare   *Smoking:* Throughout

A former "shots and mainstream lagers" bar that was across the street from the Summit Brewery before the brewery moved to bigger quarters. Comfortable blue-collar hangout with seventeen taps serving imports and micros, with Summit still the house favorite.

Sweany's Saloon
96 N. Dale St., 651-221-9157

   ★☆☆☆   11 A.M.–1 A.M. (closed Sundays)

Food: Tavern fare   *Smoking:* Throughout

Annually voted St. Paul's best neighborhood bar, offering the full spectrum from fourteen taps, including both national and regional craft beers. The Saloon label beer is made by August Schell.

Also in St. Paul
Lyon's, 788 Grand Ave., 651-224-1787. Sports bar, eighteen taps.

Mill Street Brewing Co., 57 S. Hamline, 651-698-0353. Brewpub.

STILLWATER

Gasthaus Bavarian Hunter Restaurant
8390 Lofton Ave., 651-439-7128

   ★★☆☆   Lunch–late (closes earlier Sundays)

Food: German fare   *Smoking:* Separate section

A rambling Bavarian restaurant with three dining rooms and outdoor dining in the woods. German-Bavarian food and German beer from all seven taps. Accordion music on weekends and polka music once a month.

Mad Capper Saloon & Eatery
224 S. Main, 651-430-3710

★☆☆☆   11 A.M.–1 A.M.

Food: Tavern fare   *Smoking:* Separate sections

Long and narrow with a bar running nearly the length of a historic Victorian building. Six beers on tap, generous portions of food.

Also in Minnesota
Apple Valley: Old Chicago, 14998 Glazier, 612-891-4600. See Boulder, Colorado.

Duluth: Fitger's Brewhouse, 600 E. Superior St., 218-726-1392. Brewpub.
Old Chicago, 327 Lake Ave. S., 218-720-2966.
Sir Benedict's Pub, 805 E. Superior St., 218-728-1192. British pub.

Eagan: Old Chicago, 1312 Town Centre Drive, 612-688-0882.

Maple Grove: Hops Grill & Bar, 7855 Elm Creek Blvd., 612-416-1754. Brewpub.

Moorhead: Trader & Trapper Brewing Co., 617 Center Ave., 218-236-0202. Brewpub.

Roseville: Old Chicago, 2100 N. Shelling Ave., 612-639-0303.

Shakopee: The Brew Station Brewery, 1128 Vierling Court, 612-403-9950. Brewpub.

St. Cloud: O'Hara's Brewpub & Restaurant, 3308 N. 3rd St., 320-251-9877. Brewpub.

Winona: Wellington's Back Water Brewing, 1429 W. Service Drive, 507-452-2103. Brewpub.

Essential stops: Hal & Mal's in Jackson. Long a great blues venue, now serving beer made on-premise.

Best city for a pub crawl: Jackson.

Worth noting: Mississippi was the last state to legalize brewery/restaurants, with the first opening in 1999. A limited number of imports, and even fewer microbrewed beers, are available in Mississippi.

BILOXI

Coast Brewing Co. Ⓑ
916 Beach Blvd., 228-386-7353

★☆☆☆　　11 A.M.–late

Food: Brewpub fare　　*Smoking:* Separate sections

Mississippi's first brewpub, located inside the Beau Rivage casino, so there are poker machines at both bars. Large dining area, but also with a "snug" fireplace.

HATTIESBURG

Mahogany Bar
3810 Hardy St., 601-264-0657

★☆☆☆　　11 A.M.–2 A.M. (closes at 10 P.M. Sundays)

Food: Tavern fare　　*Smoking:* Throughout

Moderately upscale pub attached to Crescent City Grill, offering eight beers on tap and a large bottle menu. Mostly imports.

JACKSON

Hal & Mal's Ⓑ
200 Commerce, 601-948-0888

★☆☆☆　　11 A.M.–late (opens at 5 P.M. Saturdays; closed Sundays; 11 A.M.–3 P.M. Mondays)

Food: Regional fare　　*Smoking:* Separate at lunch only

A venerable blues club whose owner fought for years to get brewpubs legalized. Added a brewhouse in the summer of 1999. Excellent Southern cuisine with a New Orleans slant.

Also in Jackson

Fenian's Pub, 901 E. Fortification, 601-948-0055. Irish pub.

Poets, 1855 Lakeland Drive, 601-981-2511. Pub.

OXFORD

City Grocery
152 Courthouse Square, 601-232-8080
 ★☆☆☆ 4 P.M.–late (closed Sundays)
Food: Full menu *Smoking:* Throughout

Housed in a nineteenth-century livery stable on the Oxford Square, the first-floor restaurant offers outstanding Deep Southern cuisine. Casual upstairs bar attracts grad students and older people for nice balcony seating, plus craft beers and mostly imports in bottles.

Regional beers to look for: Boulevard Brewing; Schlafly (from St. Louis Brewery).

Essential stops: Cicero's, King Louie, and St. Louis Brewery in St. Louis.

Just for fun: McCoys in Kansas City. Play chess or checkers for a chance to win a free beer.

Best city for a pub crawl: St. Louis.

COLUMBIA

Flat Branch Pub & Brewing Ⓑ
115 S. 5th St., 573-499-0400
★★☆☆   11 A.M.–late
Food: Brewpub fare   *Smoking:* Separate sections

Modern American pub with a nice dining area. Splendid wood bar with perfect elbow rests. Nice range of house beers, some on handpump.

Also in Columbia
Old Chicago, 1710 I-70 Drive SW, 573-445-0220. See Boulder, Colorado.

JOPLIN

Iron Horse Restaurant & Brewpub Ⓑ
2850 S. Rangeline, 417-624-7900
★☆☆☆   11 A.M.–after dinner (closed Sundays)
Food: Brewpub fare   *Smoking:* Separate sections

Built from the original stones of the Missouri/Pacific Depot that was located on Main Street in Joplin. Inviting small bar in front of the brewhouse, friendly service, solid beer and food.

KANSAS CITY

Charlie Hooper's Brookside Bar
12 W. 63rd St., 816-361-8841
★★☆☆   11 A.M.–3 A.M.
Food: Tavern fare   *Smoking:* Separate sections

A beer-comfortable sports bar, with plenty of breweriana. The thirty-plus beers on tap cover the spectrum, and coolers are jammed with bottles for the adventurous. Kid-friendly in afternoon, early evening.

McCoys Public House & Brewkitchen Ⓑ
4057 Pennsylvania, 816-960-0866

★★☆☆   11 A.M.–late (closed Sundays)

Food: Brewpub fare   *Smoking:* Separate sections

One of the house rules: "No one leaves our house without finishing their beer." Nicely presented food and beer. Plenty of extras, like live jazz and a cigar room, plus you can challenge staff members to a game of chess or checkers with a chance to win a free ale.

75th Street Brewery Ⓑ
520 W. 75th St., 816-523-4677

★★☆☆   Lunch–late (opens at 4 P.M. Sundays)

Food: Brewpub fare   *Smoking:* Separate sections

Kansas City's first brewpub, with dining virtually in the brewery and bags of malt on the back bar. Consistently solid beer, knowledgeable staff.

Also in Kansas City
Hofbrau Haus at Station Casino, 8201 NE Birmingham Road, 816-414-7000.

Mill Creek Brewing, 4050 Pennsylvania Ave., 816-931-4499. Brewpub.

O'Dowd's Little Dublin, 4742 Pennsylvania, 816-561-2700. Irish pub.

River Market Brewing, 500 Walnut, 816-471-6300. Brewpub.

Westport Flea Market Bar & Grill, 817 Westport Road, 816-931-1986. Tavern.

ST. CHARLES

Growlers Pub
1600 Heritage Landings, 314-939-9900

★★☆☆   11 A.M.–1 A.M.

Food: Tavern fare   *Smoking:* Separate sections

Growlers has three locations, two in St. Louis plus this spot. Each offers thirty-two draft beers, ninety-nine in bottles, thirty-plus single malts, and cigars, and is decorated with breweriana.

Rick's Taproom at BJ's

416 S. 5th St., 314-946-9990

★★☆☆   2 P.M.–1 A.M. (opens at 10 A.M. Saturdays, closed Sundays)

Food: No kitchen   *Smoking:* Throughout

Small taproom attached to liquor store, offering ten beers on tap and more than 200 bottles. Nine of the taps are imports, with Paulaner Hefeweizen usually the top seller.

Trailhead Brewery Ⓑ

921 S. Riverside Drive, 314-946-2739

★★☆☆   11 A.M.–10 P.M. (closes at 11 P.M. Fridays and Saturdays)

Food: Brewpub fare   *Smoking:* Separate sections

Set in a renovated brick building in St. Charles' historic district. Smoked meats are a specialty and pair well with the beer. Two beer gardens.

ST. LOUIS

Bevo Mill

4749 Gravois, 314-481-2626

★★☆☆   11 A.M.–10 P.M. (Sunday brunch 9:30 A.M.–2 P.M., closed until 4 P.M.)

Food: German fare   *Smoking:* Separate sections

Unsuccessfully trying to fend off Prohibition, August A. Busch built Bevo Mill in 1916 as an alternative to wicked saloons. Now fully restored, it's a replica of a Dutch mill with a large dining hall, plus a private dining room that has groined arches which end in carved-stone gnomes, each of them holding a mug. Excellent German food and beer.

Blueberry Hill

6504 Delmar Ave., 314-727-0880

★★½☆   11 A.M.–closing

Food: Tavern fare   *Smoking:* Separate sections

What Hard Rock Cafés would be like if they were cool. Nice draft lineup of imports and U.S. craft beers. A major darts bar where the jukebox has 2,000 songs, hamburgers are classic, and shelves and display cases are jammed with thousands of collectibles. Elvis room.

Cicero's
6691 Delmar Ave., 314-862-0009
★★★☆ 11 A.M.–12:45 A.M. (closes at 11 P.M. Sundays)
Food: Full menu   *Smoking:* Separate sections

Italian bistro and a pool hall with the largest draft selection for miles. The forty-seven handles include regional favorites and quality imports as well as top-flight micros.

Dressel's
419 N. Euclid Ave., 314-361-3003
★☆☆☆ Lunch–late (closed afternoons)
Food: British pub fare   *Smoking:* Separate sections

Only classical music or opera play in the background of this Welsh pub. The walls are covered with pictures of people from the music and literary worlds. Welsh ales and other UK ales served by the Imperial pint. Outstanding food, particularly the homemade potato chips.

King Louie's
3800 Chouteau, 314-865-3662
★★⯪☆ 11 A.M.–late (closed Sundays)
Food: Tavern fare   *Smoking:* Throughout

Once the hospitality room for the Stifel Brewery, now a tavern with thirty-three excellent taps, decorated with classic beer poster art. Coasters from the local microbrewery are shoved under the table legs to keep them from wobbling. Shaded beer garden.

Morgan Street Brewery Ⓑ
721 N. 2nd St., 314-231-9970
★☆☆☆ 11 A.M.–3 A.M.
Food: Brewpub fare   *Smoking:* Separate sections

Located in the oldest building in popular Laclede's Landing, lots of exposed brick. Cobblestone streets outside, shiny bars upstairs and down. Tasty food and better beer than when the pub first opened.

Riddles Penultimate Café
6307 Delmar Ave., 314-725-6985
★☆☆☆ 11 A.M.–midnight
Food: Full menu   *Smoking:* Separate sections

The front room's a classic storefront bar, the back room's a European wine café. Outstanding food and ten wines on tap, plus a wine list that runs forever. The beer list is more modest but is well-chosen and cared for.

St. Louis Brewery Tap Room Ⓑ

2100 Locust St., 314-241-2337

    ★★★☆   Lunch–late

Food: Brewpub fare   *Smoking:* Separate sections

The Schlafly beers are available around town, but here you'll frequently find a crowd drinking the full lineup, including excellent seasonals and cask beer served from a firkin. Multi-room pub housed in large turn-of-the-century brick buildings. Excellent food.

Schneithorst's Hofamberg Inn

Lindbergh & Clayton, 314-993-5600

    ★★⯪☆   11 A.M.–10 P.M. (until 11 P.M. Fridays and Saturdays, 10 A.M.–8 P.M. Sundays)

Food: German fare   *Smoking:* Separate sections

A rambling German chalet that seats nearly 800 including the biergarten deck. Excellent German food, thirty-two beers on tap. Decorated with antiques, wood carvings, an old cheese press, fireplaces, carved wood breakfronts, leaded glass scenes, paintings, European artwork, and steins.

Soulard Ale House

1732 S. 9ᵗʰ St., 314-436-7849

    ★★☆☆   11 A.M.–1:30 A.M. (noon–midnight Sundays)

Food: Tavern fare   *Smoking:* Throughout

Basic one-room tavern with thirty-four taps, divided equally between imports and micros. Patio, live music on weekends.

Also in St. Louis

Bacchus Brewery, Union Station, 314-421-2739. Brewpub.

Cheshire Pub in the Cheshire Inn, 6306 Clayton Road, 314-647-7300. Thirty-plus taps.

John D. McGurks, 1200 Russell Road, 314-776-8305. Irish pub.

McNulty's Irish Pub, 620 West Port Plaza, 314-878-6619. Irish pub.

Old 66 Brewery & Restaurant, 9846 Watson Road, 314-965-8866. Brewpub.

Trainwreck Saloon, 720 N. 1ˢᵗ St., 314-436-1006. Tavern, one of several by this name in the area.

SPRINGFIELD

Ebbets Field Ⓑ
1027 E. Walnut, 417-865-5050
★☆☆☆   11 A.M.–closing
Food: Italian plus   *Smoking:* Separate sections

Ebbets Field, the restaurant, was forced from its original home by university expansion, and landed in a turn-of-the century house that was built for the town's mayor. A brewpub had failed here but the equipment remained, and the result is a place that serves Italian food, excellent hamburgers, and fresh beer.

Also in Springfield
Springfield Brewing Co., 305 S. Market Ave., 417-832-8277. Brewpub.

Also in Missouri
Aurora: Bootleggers Restaurant & Brewery, 101 S. Madison, 417-678-2888. Brewpub.
Clayton: Il Vicino, 41 N. Central, 314-727-1333. See Albuquerque, New Mexico. St. Louis Brewery makes the beer for this location.
Parkville: The Power Plant Restaurant Brewery, 2 Main St., 816-746-5051. Brewpub.
St. Joseph: The Belt Brewing Co., 2317 N. Belt, 816-676-2739. Brewpub.

Regional beers to look for: Kessler Brewing; Lang Creek Brewery; Spanish Peaks Brewing; Black Star Brewing.

Esssential stops: The Rhinoceros. Plastered above the fifty taps are posters from Missoula's annual "kegger." The charity event used to draw massive crowds and was guaranteed to have a hundred kegs tapped all the time. "All Oly," a bartender explained, smiling.

Just for fun: Montana Bar in Miles City, when the cattle drive comes to town.

Best city for a pub crawl: Missoula.

BIGFORK

The Raven Pub & Grill Ⓑ
25999 Highway 35 S., 406-837-2836
★☆☆☆   11 A.M.–midnight in summer, 4–10 P.M. otherwise
Food: Limited   *Smoking:* Throughout

On the east shore of Flathead Lake outside Bigfork, offering a wide range of beers depending on the season. Deck on two sides of the building, and windows in bar look onto lake.

BILLINGS

Montana Brewing Co. Ⓑ
113 N. Broadway Ave., 406-252-9200
★☆☆☆   11 A.M.–2 A.M.
Food: Brewpub fare   *Smoking:* Separate sections

Bright, airy pub attached to the brewery, serving Italian and American dishes. Sharptail Pale Ale won gold in the very competitive pale ale category at the 1998 Great American Beer Festival.

BOZEMAN

Cat's Paw Casino
721 N. 7th, 406-586-3542
   ★☆☆☆   8 A.M.–2 A.M.
Food: Tavern fare   *Smoking:* Throughout

All twenty draft beers—plenty of imports and Northwest craft products—are $2 a pint (and 2-for-1 during happy hour from 8 A.M.–8 P.M.). Nothing fancy: pool and gambling machines with an attached restaurant.

Spanish Peaks Brewing Co. Ⓑ
120 N. 19th Ave., 406-585-2296
   ★☆☆☆   11:30 A.M.–11 P.M.
Food: Brewpub fare   *Smoking:* Separate sections

Modern setting with flashy marble-topped bar, usually offering six beers brewed here. The nationally distributed Spanish Peaks beers are contract-brewed elsewhere.

MILES CITY

Montana Bar
612 Main, 406-232-5809
   ★☆☆☆   11 A.M.–2 A.M.
Food: No kitchen   *Smoking:* Throughout

During the bucking horse sale in May and the cattle drive in September, they rope off the streets and sell beer outside. The rest of the time, a classic bar (dating to 1903), with animal heads and an old-fashioned jukebox. Draft choices limited, but include Milestown Brewing products.

Also in Miles City
Golden Spur/Milestown Brewing, 1014 S. Hanes Ave., 406-232-3544. Microbrewery/restaurant.

MISSOULA

Iron Horse Brewpub Ⓑ
100 Railroad St., 406-721-8705
   ★☆☆☆   Lunch–late
Food: Brewpub fare   *Smoking:* Separate sections

Pub/restaurant set in an old train station, serving the German-style beers of Bayern Brewing in the same building. Seating in back has view of still active railyard.

The Rhinoceros
158 Ryman St., 406-721-6061
 ★★★☆ 11 A.M.–2 A.M.
Food: Tavern fare *Smoking:* Throughout

A bit rough-and-tumble (the metal bar stools next to the high-tops are screwed to the floor), with fifty draft choices. Forty of those go to craft beers, mostly Northwest products. Drink fifty beers and earn a "Fifty Ways to Love Your Liver" T-shirt.

Also in Missoula
Paradise Falls, 3621 Brooks St., 406-728-3228. Sports bar/casino.
Squire's Pub, Fairway Shopping Center, 406-549-5059. Sports bar/casino.

Also in Montana
Belt: Harvest Moon Brewery, 57 Castner St., 406-277-3200. Brewpub.
Butte: Irish Times Pub, 2 E. Galena, 406-782-8142. Irish pub.
Helena: The Brewhouse at Sleeping Giant Brewery, 939½ Getchell St., 406-442-5960.

NEBRASKA

Regional beers to look for: Boulevard Brewing.
Essential stops: Crescent Moon Ale House in Omaha; Crane River Brewpub in Lincoln.
Just for fun: Ole's Big Game Lounge in Paxton. This is not really a beer stop, nor for the weak of heart. It opened the minute Prohibition ended and they began putting mounted game on the walls shortly thereafter. This place is not about being politically correct.
Best city for a pub crawl: Omaha.

LINCOLN

Crane River Brewpub & Café Ⓑ
200 N. 11ᵗʰ St., 402-476-7766
    ★★☆☆   11 A.M.–1 A.M. (noon–midnight Sundays)
Food: Brewpub fare   *Smoking:* Separate sections

Handmade quilts hang on the wall, and the island bar is made of concrete and river rocks, giving this brewpub a warm feeling despite its downtown setting. Usually seven beers—both ales and lagers—are on tap, and the menu is both well-conceived and well-executed.

Also in Lincoln
Lazlo's Brewery & Grill, 710 P St., 434-5636. Brewpub.
Old Chicago, 826 P St., 402-477-2277. See Boulder, Colorado.

OMAHA

Crescent Moon Ale House
3578 Farnam St., 402-345-1708
    ★★½☆   11 A.M.–1 A.M. (closed Sundays)
Food: Tavern fare, pizza   *Smoking:* Throughout

Comfortable neighborhood pub with thirty-two beers on tap (all American craft beers) and Nebraska breweriana on the walls. Located in older urban section known as Omaha's Gold Coast, surrounded by turn-of-the-century mansions.

Dubliner Pub

1205 Harney, 402-342-5887

★☆☆☆   11 A.M.–1 A.M.

Food: Irish pub fare   *Smoking:* Throughout

Basement Irish pub with twenty-five taps, mostly imports but also microbrewery beer. Popular music venue.

Jaipur Restaurant & Brew Pub Ⓑ

10922 Elm St., 402-392-7331

★☆☆☆   Lunch–after dinner (dinner only Sundays)

Food: Northern Indian   *Smoking:* Separate sections

Named after a city in India and serving tandoori cooking and Northern Indian cuisine, clearly a restaurant first and small brewery second. Nonetheless, brewing an interesting assortment of ales.

Upstream Brewing Co. Ⓑ

514 S. 11th St., 402-344-0200

★★½☆   Lunch–late

Food: Brewpub fare   *Smoking:* Separate sections

One of the Wynkoop clan (see Denver, Colorado), in a beautifully restored building. Good food, with dining in interior courtyard setting. Full range of well-brewed ales. Billiards upstairs.

Also in Omaha

Brazen Head, 78th & Dodge, 402-393-3731. Irish pub.

Old Chicago, 13110 Birch Drive, #180, 402-445-9393. See Boulder, Colorado.

Old Chicago, 1111 Harney St., 402-341-1616.

Also in Nebraska

Columbus: Gottberg Brew Pub, 2804 13th St., 402-562-6488. Brewpub.

Hastings: Murphy's Wagon Wheel, 107 N. Lincoln Ave., 402-463-3011. Brewpub.

Regional beers to look for: Gordon Biersch.
Essential stops: Triple 7 Brewpub and Holy Cow!
Just for fun: Holy Cow! You must know somebody who would look good in those bovine boxer shorts.
Best city for a pub crawl: Las Vegas.

HENDERSON

Barley's Casino & Brewing Co. Ⓑ
4500 E. Sunset Road, 702-458-2739
    ★☆☆☆   Lunch–after dinner or later
Food: Brewpub fare   *Smoking:* Separate sections

Originally a Gordon Biersch, but sold to the Sunset Station ownership shortly after opening. Like GB, makes only traditional German styles.

Sunset Station Hotel & Casino Ⓑ
1303 W. Sunset Road, 702-547-7777
    ★☆☆☆   4 P.M.–midnight (opens at noon Fridays through Sundays)
Food: Brewpub fare   *Smoking:* Separate sections

The beer is brewed at Barley's and fermented here, so it will seem familiar. Like Barley's, all the beers are brewed to traditional German styles.

LAS VEGAS

Holy Cow! Casino & Brewery Ⓑ
2423 Las Vegas Blvd. S., 702-732-2697
    ★☆☆☆   Open 24 hours
Food: Midwestern fare   *Smoking:* Throughout

Bovine motif gives it the look of a Gateway Computers ad. Robust food, with lots of Midwestern dishes. More than a hundred video poker and slot machines that clatter loudly. Good beer, which is sold by other members of the Big Dog chain in the area, all pubs with "dog" names.

Monte Carlo Pub & Brewery Ⓑ
3770 Las Vegas Blvd. S., 702-730-7777
★☆☆☆   11 A.M.–late
Food: Brewpub fare   *Smoking:* Separate sections

The first brewpub to open in a mega-resort, huge itself. Its beers are available throughout the Monte Carlo Hotel and Casino and in bottles.

Schuler's Roadhouse
4755 Spring Mountain Road, 702-252-7427
★☆☆☆   10 A.M.–late
Food: Ribs, chili, barbecue   *Smoking:* Separate sections

A locals' spot formerly known as Mad Dogs & Englishmen. Still sells a mixture of mainstream beers and imports from twenty-one taps, but now the food leans toward ribs and barbecue.

Triple 7 Brewpub Ⓑ
200 N. Main St., 702-387-1896
★★☆☆   11 A.M.–7 A.M.
Food: Brewpub fare   *Smoking:* Separate sections

Located in Main Street Station Casino and the only brewpub in the downtown area. Black Cherry Stout won a Great American Beer Festival medal, and the seasonals are excellent.

Also in Las Vegas
Ellis Island Brewery, 4178 Koval Lane, 702-733-8901. Brewpub.
Gordon Biersch at Hughes Center, 3987 Paradise Road, 702-312-5247. Brewpub; see San Francisco, California.

LAUGHLIN

Boiler Room Brew Pub Ⓑ
2100 Casino Drive, 702-298-4000
★☆☆☆   11 A.M.–2 A.M.
Food: Brewpub fare   *Smoking:* Throughout

One of six theme restaurants on the Colorado Belle, a replica of a Mississippi paddlewheeler. Wood-fired pizzas, mesquite-grilled food, and twenty-four TVs in a glistening setting.

Also in Nevada
Reno: Brew Brothers, 345 N. Virginia St., 702-786-5700. Brewpub.
Sparks: Great Basin Brewing Co., 846 Victorian Ave., 702-355-7711. Brewpub.

Regional beers to look for: Smuttynose Brewing; Nutfield Brewing; the Lucknow beers from Castle Springs Brewing.

Essential stops: Martha's Exchange and Skyview Café & Brewery in Nashua.

Just for fun: Woodstock Inn & Brewing Co. in North Woodstock. Spend a Brewers Weekend in the Victorian inn, making and drinking beer.

Best city for a pub crawl: Keene.

GLEN

Red Parka Pub

U.S. 302, 603-383-4344

★☆☆☆   4:30 P.M.–closing (opens earlier weekends)

Food: Tavern fare   *Smoking:* Separate sections

The eighteen draft choices offer a little of everything, including some excellent local beers. A ski pub with a dance floor and live bands several nights a week. Known for its steaks and ribs.

KEENE

Elm City Brewing Co. 🅑

Colony Mill Marketplace, 603-355-3335

★☆☆☆   Lunch–late

Food: Brewpub fare   *Smoking:* Separate sections

Located in a mall that's a former brick woolen mill. Outdoor seating in a screened-in beer hall. Food-friendly beers.

176 Main

176 Main St., 603-357-3100

★☆☆☆   Lunch–late evening

Food: Tavern fare   *Smoking:* Separate sections

A classic tavern on the National Register, with low ceilings and solid wood tables. Fifteen draft choices, including imports and craft beers.

Penuche's Ale House
91 Marlborough St., 603-352-9839
   ★☆☆☆   1 P.M.–1 A.M.
Food: No kitchen   *Smoking:* Throughout

Intimate, woody, dog-friendly pub that's been around for fifty years. Eleven taps mix mainstream beers and micros. A second Penuche's operates in Nashua.

LITTLETON

Italian Oasis & Brewery 🅱
127 Main St., 603-444-6995
   ☆☆☆☆   11 A.M.–midnight
Food: Italian   *Smoking:* Separate sections

A full Italian restaurant with a small two-barrel brewhouse, known primarily for the food and atmosphere. Walls covered with skiing paraphernalia.

MANCHESTER

Stark Mill Brewery & Restaurant 🅱
500 Commercial St., 603-622-0000
   ★☆☆☆   11 A.M.–1 A.M.
Food: Brewpub fare   *Smoking:* Separate sections

Spacious restaurant that also offers a Mongolian grill (customers pick the ingredients but don't cook the food). Its flagship beer is the porter, while the cream ale won a Great American Beer Festival medal.

Also in Manchester
Wild Rover, 21 Kosciuszko St., 603-669-7722. Irish pub.

NASHUA

Martha's Exchange 🅱
185 Main St., 603-883-8781
   ★★⯪☆   7 A.M.–late
Food: Brewpub fare   *Smoking:* Separate sections

Brewpub in a brick building from the 1870s that feels like a speakeasy museum, including a bar that is said to have come from one of Al Capone's pubs. Excellent beers include Al Capone IPA, a solid British version of the style.

Skyview Café & Brewery Ⓑ
385 E. Dunstable Road, 603-897-0005
★★☆☆   11:30 A.M.–late
Food: Brewpub fare   *Smoking:* Bar only

Free-standing pub built from the ground up has a newish feel, serving wood-fired fare and sometimes offering a raw bar. No punches pulled with a solid lineup of beers.

NORTH WOODSTOCK

Woodstock Inn & Brewing Co. Ⓑ
135 Main St., 603-745-3951
★★☆☆   3 P.M.–1 A.M. (opens at noon Sundays)
Food: Brewpub fare   *Smoking:* Separate

Delightful stop in the White Mountains, offering Brewers Weekends for those who want to stay in the Victorian-era inn and work as "apprentice brewers." The pub itself is in an old train depot that was moved from nearby Lincoln.

PORTSMOUTH

Coat of Arms
174 Fleet St., 603-431-0407
★☆☆☆   11:30 A.M.–late (opens at 4 P.M. Mondays)
Food: British fare   *Smoking:* Throughout

A modest-sized English pub, decorated in British fashion and serving primarily UK imports from fourteen taps. Two cask-conditioned ales on handpumps are U.S. products, usually a Shipyard beer, perhaps Old Thumper.

Portsmouth Brewery
56 Market St., 603-431-1115
★★☆☆   11:30 A.M.–1 A.M.
Food: Brewpub fare   *Smoking:* Separate sections

Excellent beer and food from the same owners as Northampton Brewery. Older building in the historic district with a restaurant upstairs and tavern downstairs. Brewing both ales and lagers.

Also in Portsmouth
Redhook Brewery/Cataqua Brewpub, 605 Spaulding Turnpike, 603-430-8600. Brewery tasting room.

WEST LEBANON

Seven Barrel Brewery Ⓑ
Route 12A, Plainfield Road, 603-298-5566
★★⯨☆   11:30 A.M.–1:30 A.M.
Food: Brewpub fare   *Smoking:* Separate sections

Woody pub in a brewhouse you can spot from Interstate 89.
Relaxed, *après*-ski feeling, with excellent food and beers beyond
the ordinary.

Also in New Hampshire
Laconia: Stone Coast on Winnipesaukee, 546 N. Main St., 603-
528-4188. Brewpub; see Maine.
New London: Flying Goose Brewpub, 115 Route 11, 603-526-
6899. Brewpub.
Wolfsboro: Wolf's Tavern, 44 Main St., 603-569-3016. Historic
tavern.

Beers to look for: Flying Fish Brewing; High Point (Ramstein) Brewing; Climax Brewing.

Essential stops: The Ship Inn in Milford, which made *The Beer & Bar Atlas* before it was a brewpub; The Old Bay in New Brunswick; Andy's Corner Bar in Bogota; Antone's in Cranford.

Just for fun: Quietly matching wits with the regulars playing NTN (interactive trivia) at Antone's.

Best city for a pub crawl: Hoboken.

BERKELEY HEIGHTS

Trap Rock Restaurant & Brewery Ⓑ
279 Springfield Ave., 908-665-1755

★☆☆☆   5:30 P.M.–late (opens at 4:30 P.M. Sundays)

Food: Upscale brewpub fare   *Smoking:* Separate sections

Upscale dining and prices to match. Beautifully appointed with nice outdoor dining. Beers are hit or miss.

BERNARDSVILLE

Stone Tavern & Brewery Ⓑ
1 Mill St., 908-766-6575

★★☆☆   11 A.M.–late (opens at 11:30 A.M. weekends)

Food: Full menu   *Smoking:* Separate sections

Longtime popular dining spot and stone-walled, old-fashioned tavern with booths and tables. Small separate bar, nice lineup of house beers, also guest products.

BOGOTA

Andy's Corner Bar
265 Queen Anne Road, 973-342-9887

★★⯪☆   2 P.M.–2 A.M. (opens at noon Sundays)

Food: No kitchen   *Smoking:* Throughout

A classic, intimate neighborhood bar that has been around for fifty years. Twelve taps include mainstream beers, imports, and micros from near and far. Coolers on the back wall jammed with interesting bottles.

CALDWELL

Cloverleaf Tavern
395 Bloomfield Ave., 973-226-9812
★★☆☆   10:30 A.M.–late
Food: Tavern fare   *Smoking:* Separate sections

Holds the first license issued in New Jersey after the end of Prohibition. A good-sized, casual tavern with a comfortable bar and sixteen taps offering imports and craft beers that include several N.J. products.

CRANFORD

Antone's Grill and Pub
112 South Ave., 908-276-3414
★★½☆   11:30 A.M.–2 A.M.
Food: Tavern fare   *Smoking:* Throughout

A locals' spot where regulars play NTN and you may spot a couple sitting in a booth choosing wedding invitations. Thirty-plus beers on tap and usually something special.

GARFIELD

Sidewinders Grille & Alehouse
279 Passaic St., 973-778-7500
★☆☆☆   Lunch–late (opens at 3 P.M. Sundays)
Food: Tavern fare   *Smoking:* Separate sections

Classic corner bar that serves a popular Southwestern menu in the small dining room. Rotating selection from ten taps, a solid selection of micros plus two mainstream beers. Knowledgeable service.

HAWTHORNE

Front Porch
217 Wagaraw Road, 973-427-4331
★★½☆   Lunch–late (opens at 1 P.M. Sundays)
Food: Tavern fare   *Smoking:* Throughout

Family-run bar that offers homemade food specials daily and feels like you're eating on somebody's front porch. Solid draft selection and large bottle menu.

HILLSBOROUGH

Jersey Jim's Brewing Co. Ⓑ
150 U.S. 206 S., 908-526-5584
★★☆☆   11:30 A.M.–late (opens at 10:30 A.M. Sundays, 4 P.M. Tuesdays and Wednesdays)
Food: Brewpub fare   *Smoking:* Separate sections

Longtime popular restaurant (Jasper's) that added a brewery, which is spread out behind the bar. Comfortable, with a fireplace in the dining room. Still known for its food, serves a nice Sunday brunch.

Also in Hillsborough
Petrock's, 419 Amwell Road, 908-359-2344. Tavern attached to liquor store.

HOBOKEN

Helmers'
1036 Washington St., 201-963-3333
★★☆☆   Noon–10 P.M. (11 A.M.–11 P.M. Fridays and Saturdays, closed Sundays)
Food: German fare   *Smoking:* Throughout

A bar in front with dark booths, German dining in back with tablecloth-covered tables. German beers on tap, but also some of the best craft selections of the region.

Also in Hoboken
Hennessy's Public House, 32 Newark St., 201-216-1766. Irish pub.
Mile Square Bar & Grill, 221 Washington St., 201-420-0222. Multi-tap.

LAMBERTVILLE

Inn of the Hawke
74 S. Union, 609-397-9555
★☆☆☆   Noon–late (opens at 11 A.M. Sundays for brunch)
Food: Full menu   *Smoking:* Separate sections

Working inn with an excellent restaurant that has a frequently changing menu, twelve beers on tap. Accommodations include seven rooms, four with private bath.

LONG VALLEY

Long Valley Pub & Brewery 🅑
1 Fairmont Road, 908-876-1122
    ★★☆☆   11:30 A.M.–late (opens at noon Sundays)
    Food: Brewpub fare   *Smoking:* Separate sections

Set in a 200-year-old fieldstone barn in a country village. Hand-hewn beams and a lofted wooden ceiling. Bold menu, interesting beers.

MILFORD

The Ship Inn 🅑
61 Bridge St., 908-995-7007
    ★★½☆   Lunch–closing
    Food: British pub fare   *Smoking:* Separate sections

Creekside British pub a few blocks from the Delaware River that brews lovely British-style ales. Some offered on handpump. More than fifty single-malt whiskies available.

NEW BRUNSWICK

Harvest Moon Brewery Café 🅑
392 George St., 732-249-6666
    ★☆☆☆   11:30 A.M.–late
    Food: Brewpub fare   *Smoking:* Separate sections

Inviting floor-to-ceiling French doors, beautiful wood paneling, and the original tin ceiling give the place a bistro feel. Interesting food, sometimes interesting beer.

Old Bay Restaurant
62-64 Church St., 732-246-3111
    ★★★☆   11:30 A.M.–late (opens at 4 P.M. Sundays)
    Food: New Orleans cuisine   *Smoking:* Separate sections

Former bar manager Chris Demetri built the small bar area in this New Orleans-style restaurant into one of the top pubs in the country. Always interesting selection from twenty-two taps, one handpump. Great food in the restaurant upstairs, excellent music club.

PRINCETON

Triumph Brewing Co. Ⓑ
138 Nassau St., 609-924-7855
★★☆☆   11:30 A.M.–late
Food: Brewpub fare   *Smoking:* Separate sections

Post-industrial-style brewpub with soaring ceiling, brewery on display, several dining areas. Upscale menu, solid beer lineup.

RED BANK

Basil T's Brew Pub and Italian Grill Ⓑ
183 Riverside Ave., 732-842-5990
★★☆☆   11:30 A.M.–1:30 A.M.
Food: Italian, pizza   *Smoking:* Separate sections

Established Italian eatery that added a brewhouse. Things went so well that it opened another brewpub in Toms River. Substantial menu includes classic thin-crust pizza. Well-made beers.

Also in Red Bank
Dubliner House, 30 Monmouth St., 732-747-6699. Irish pub.

SPARTA

Krogh's Restaurants & Brew Pub
23 White Deer Plaza, 973-729-8428
★★★☆   Noon–late
Food: Full menu   *Smoking:* Separate sections

This rustic, log cabin-style restaurant has been around since 1927. Recently added a brewery, supplementing its own well-made beers with choice guest selections. Freshly made soups, sandwiches, full dinners and yummy desserts. Kid-friendly, eclectic live music regularly. On the shores of beautiful Lake Mohawk, well worth a drive.

SUMMIT

Office Beer Bar & Grill
61 Union Place, 908-522-0550
　　★☆☆☆　　11:30 A.M.–1:30 A.M.
Food: Full menu　　*Smoking:* Separate sections

Chain of popular watering holes grew to six locations emphasizing beer in the nineties. Each has fifteen beers on tap, more in the bottle. Included are mainstream choices, imports, and micros, with some regional beers.

Also in New Jersey

Atlantic City: Black Forest Restaurant, Boardwalk at Arkansas, 609-348-0700. German restaurant.
　　Tun Tavern, 2000 Kirkman Blvd., 609-347-7800. Brewpub.

Egg Harbor City: Cedar Creek Brewery, 236 Philadelphia Ave., 609-965-6367. Brewpub.

Haledon: The Shepherd and the Knucklehead Pub, 529 Belmont Ave., 973-790-9657. Pub with twenty taps.

Metuchen: Pizzeria Uno/Chicago Grill & Brewery, 61 U.S. 1, 732-548-7979. Brewpub.

Point Pleasant: Ark Pub & Eatery, 401 Sea Ave., 732-295-1122. Tavern/pub.

Rutherford: Railroad Cafe, 170 Union Ave., 201-939-0644. Restaurant.

Secaucus: Phil McConkey's Big City Grill, 300 Plaza Drive, 201-271-1313. Bar.

South Orange: Gaslight Brewery, 15 S. Orange Ave., 973-762-7077.

Stirling: Stirling Hotel, 227 Main Ave., 908-647-6919. Hotel bar.

Toms River: Joshua Huddy's, 1250 Hooper Ave., 732-240-3640. Brewpub.

Trenton: Joe's Mill Hill Saloon, 300 Broad St., 609-394-7222. Brewpub.
　　Tir na nÓg, 1324 Hamilton Ave., 609-392-2554. Irish pub.

Wallington: The Green Onion, 15 Wallington Ave., 973-473-3677. Restaurant.

Wayne: Casey O'Toole's Tavern, 862 Hamburg Turnpike, 973-696-7737. Tavern.

Wildwood: Kokomo's Restaurant & Brewpub, 448 W. Rio Grande Ave., 732-523-1800. Brewpub, open seasonally.

Woodbridge: J.J. Bitting Brewing Co., 33 Main St., 908-634-2929. Brewpub.

NEW MEXICO

Regional beers to look for: Rio Grande Brewing; Santa Fe Brewing; Cabezon Brewing; Sierra Blanca Brewing.

Essential stops: Wolf Canyon in Santa Fe; Embudo Station in Embudo on the Rio Grande; Il Vicino in Albuquerque; Eske's in Taos.

Just for fun: Mine Shaft Tavern in Madrid. On a busy Sunday afternoon, bikers will drift in. Most order a Bud (available only in bottles), but every once in a while one will pick a Breckenridge Oatmeal Stout.

Best city for a pub crawl: Santa Fe.

ALBUQUERQUE

Assets Grill & Brewing ⓑ
6910 Montgomery NE, 505-889-6400
★★☆☆   Lunch–late
Food: Brewpub fare   *Smoking:* Separate sections

Popular dining spot with regional fare, California-style pizza. Full range of house beers, some of them bottled under the Southwest Brewing label.

Billy's Long Bar
4800 San Mateo NE, 505-889-0573
★★⯪☆   11 A.M.–2 A.M.
Food: Tavern fare   *Smoking:* Throughout

Jammed with singles in the evening, but quieter and more publike at other times. Impressive selection across fifty-one taps, although short on regional offerings. Large single-malt selection.

Brewster's Pub
312 Central Ave. SW, 505-247-2533
★★☆☆   11 A.M.–2 A.M.
Food: Tavern fare   *Smoking:* Throughout

In the restored stretch of downtown, with twenty-eight taps—both American craft beers and imports are well-represented—and live music nightly. Long and narrow, with dim lighting and a woody interior. By the way, Central is old Route 66.

Il Vicino Pizzeria Ⓑ

3403 Central Ave. NE, 505-266-7855

    ★★★☆   11:30 A.M.–closing

    Food: Pizza, calzones   *Smoking:* Separate sections

Excellent beer, particularly the Wet Mountain IPA, and wonderful pizza and calzones in a comfortable setting. Order when you enter, and beer and food are delivered to the table. The concept works so well that Il Vicino now operates in five states, though it does not brew at every location. Kid-friendly, with a fine small pizza and pizza dough available to play with while the pie is made.

Kelly's Brewery

3200 Central Ave. NE, 505-262-2739

    ★☆☆☆   11 A.M.–2 A.M. (noon–midnight Sundays)

    Food: Tavern fare   *Smoking:* Separate sections

A brew-on-premise that also makes beer for the public. Very popular patio looks onto Central/Route 66, and $2 pints are a major attraction.

O'Niell's Pub

3211 Central Ave. NE, 505-256-0564

    ★☆☆☆   11:30 A.M.–late

    Food: Tavern/bistro fare   *Smoking:* Throughout

Comfortable restaurant with sixteen taps, regular live music, and solid food. Beautiful handcrafted woodwork throughout.

The Quarters

801 Yale Blvd. SE, 505-843-7505

    ★☆☆☆   11 A.M.–after dinner

    Food: Barbecue   *Smoking:* Separate sections

Quarters serves up outstanding barbecue at two locations. Both are connected to liquor stores and have large bottle selections with plenty of micros. Each also has twenty-plus beers on tap and a stand-alone bar. The second Quarters is on Wyoming Boulevard.

Also in Albuquerque

Baker Street Pub, 5809 Juan Tabo NE, 505-299-0225. Wide selection.

Downtown Distillery, 406 Central SW, 505-765-1534. Restaurant/bar.

Stone Face Tavern, 8200 San Pedro, 505-822-8855. Wide selection.

EMBUDO

Embudo Station Ⓑ
US Highway 68, 505-852-4707
★★☆☆   Call; depends on season
Food: Full menu   *Smoking:* Separate sections

The setting doesn't get any better than this. In an old train depot along the fast road from Santa Fe to Taos, underneath a stand of cottonwoods right beside the Rio Grande. Makes a variety of ales, including both red and green chile beers.

FARMINGTON

Three Rivers Eatery & Brewery Ⓑ
101 E. Main, 505-324-2187
★☆☆☆   11 A.M.–10 P.M. (noon–9 P.M. Sundays)
Food: Brewpub fare   *Smoking:* None

Brewpub near the Four Corners, so popular it expanded into a second building. Indoor and outdoor seating, increasingly aggressive beers. Offers gourmet coffee.

LAS CRUCES

High Desert Brewing Co. Ⓑ
1201 W. Hadley Ave., 505-525-6752
★★☆☆   11 A.M.–late (noon–10 P.M. Sundays)
Food: Tavern fare   *Smoking:* None inside

A small pub with a small brewhouse that turns out an amazing variety of beers, all good and some outstanding. Knowledgeable bartenders and plenty of beer periodicals in the bar area.

O'Ryan's Brewery & Tavern Ⓑ
700 S. Telshor Blvd., 505-522-8191
★☆☆☆   Lunch–closing
Food: Tavern fare   *Smoking:* Separate sections

Spacious mall brewpub decorated Irish, but offering New Mexican fare as well as pub dishes. Interesting beer lineup includes the intense Dog Spit Stout.

Also in Las Cruces
Way Out West Restaurant, 1720 Avenida de Mesilla, 505-524-2408. Brewpub.

MADRID

Mine Shaft Tavern
2946 State Highway 14, 505-473-0743
★☆☆☆   11 A.M.–about 11 P.M.
Food: Tavern fare   *Smoking:* Throughout

A fifty-year-old roadhouse with a forty-foot lodgepole pine bar and most of the original furnishings. A dozen taps, including Dead Canary Ale, a golden ale brewed for Mine Shaft by Santa Fe Brewing. Popular Sunday spot for both motorcyclists and those shopping the town's art galleries. Live music.

RIO RANCHO

O'Hare's Grille & Pub
4100 Southern Blvd., 505-896-0123
★★☆☆   11 A.M.–late (closed some Sundays)
Food: Tavern fare plus   *Smoking:* Separate

Restaurant with indoor and outdoor seating in booths and at tables. Known for its soups, has a variety of sandwiches and burgers. Comfortable atmosphere; kids' menu comes with crayons. Sixteen beers on tap include imports and micros.

Turtle Mountain Brewing Co. Ⓑ
3775 Southern Blvd., 505-994-9497
★★☆☆   11 A.M.–late (noon–10 P.M. Sundays)
Food: Pizza, calzones   *Smoking:* Separate sections

Our local brewpub, opened in 1999. Beer off to a good start and good wood-fired pizzas and calzones. Located in a small strip mall with cigars allowed on patio. Kid-friendly.

SANTA FE

Blue Corn Café & Brewery Ⓑ
4056 Cerrillos Road, 505-438-1800
★★☆☆   11 A.M.–10 or 11 P.M.
Food: Brewpub fare   *Smoking:* Separate sections

Pueblo Revival-style building across the street from the Villa Linda Mall houses this leaning-toward-upscale brewpub. The corn and chipotle soup is to die for, while the brewers keep cleaning up at statewide beer competitions. Second brewpub in Albuquerque (4939 Pan American Parkway, NE).

Second Street Brewery Ⓑ
1884 2ⁿᵈ St., 505-982-3030
    ★★⯪☆   11 A.M.–late (noon–10 P.M. Sundays)
    Food: Brewpub fare   *Smoking:* None indoors

A Western take on an Irish or British pub, with photos and artwork on the walls, cozy indoor seating, and a beer garden. Bitters and stouts are favorites here. Superior french fries. Picked by local media as a place where women can feel comfortable dining alone, and also kid-friendly.

Wolf Canyon Brewing Co.
9885 Cerrillos Road, 505-438-7000
    ★★★☆   11 A.M.–late
    Food: Brewpub fare   *Smoking:* Bar only

Sit outside in the large beer garden or inside at one of the copper-topped tables and enjoy the Southwestern ambience. Award-winning ales, usually two on cask. Food includes New Mexican favorites, pastas, and traditional pub offerings. Wood-burning fireplaces in the winter, live music sometimes.

Also in Santa Fe
Cowgirl Hall of Fame, 319 S. Guadalupe St., 505-982-2565. Restaurant, twelve taps.

Evangelo's, 200 W. San Francisco St., 505-982-9014. Historic bar.

Il Vicino, 321 W. San Francisco St., 505-986-8700. See Albuquerque. No beer brewed here.

Santa Fe Brewing Co., 18 State Road 14, 505-424-3333. Inviting tasting room for a very micro brewery.

TAOS

Eske's Brewpub & Eatery
106 DeGeorges Lane, 505-758-1517
    ★★☆☆   Noon–closing
    Food: New Mexican fare   *Smoking:* Separate sections

Cozy adobe brewpub just over from the plaza, with a little indoor seating and lots of outdoor seating. Excellent English-style ales, many seasonals. Small, health-conscious menu.

Also in New Mexico
Alamogordo: Compass Rose Brewpub, 2203 E. 1ˢᵗ, 505-434-9633. Not brewing in mid-1999.
    Kegs Brewery & Fine Dining, 817 Scenic Drive, 505-434-4156. Not brewing in mid-1999.

Las Vegas: Ringside Sports & Spirits, 405 S. Grand, 505-425-7252. Roadhouse.

Red River: Lonesome Pine Pub, 500 W. Main, 505-754-2488. Several regional beers on tap.

Regional beers to look for: Brooklyn Brewery; Middle Ages Brewing; the products of the Brewery Ommegang.

Essential stops: Clark's Ale House and Blue Tusk in Syracuse; d.b.a. in Manhattan; Waterfront Ale House in Brooklyn; the Old Toad in Rochester.

Just for fun: North Star Pub in Manhattan. Boxing Day. An amazing party.

Best city for a pub crawl: Syracuse, specifically Armory Square.

ALBANY

The Lionheart
258 Lark St., 518-436-9530

★☆☆☆   5 P.M.–closing (opens at noon Fridays and Saturdays)

Food: Tavern fare   *Smoking:* None

Small second-floor blues bar with sixteen taps always rotating, serving imports and craft beers. Walls of the bar area plastered with coasters from craft breweries.

Mahar's Public Bar
1110 Madison Ave., 518-459-7868

★★★☆   Noon–midnight (closed Sundays)

Food: Tavern fare   *Smoking:* Throughout

A small place, but over time 15,000 members have broadened their beer horizons through the beer tour club. Experimented with fifty taps, then cut back to twenty-seven, and kept 300-400 bottles. Both imports and micros, including many you seldom see elsewhere.

Also in Albany
Big House Brewing Co., 90 N. Pearl St., 518-445-2739. Brewpub.

Justin's, 300 Lark St., 518-436-7008. Restaurant/bar.

AMHERST

Alternative Brews
3488 Sheridan Drive, 716-446-0424
★☆☆☆   4 P.M.–late (opens at 12:30 P.M. Sundays)
Food: Tavern fare   *Smoking:* Throughout

Bar set in a suburban mall, imports and craft beers on tap and large bottle selection. Regular Thursday-night tasting. Puts a cask of Middle Ages beer on top of the bar the first Friday of every month and serves it until it's gone.

Buffalo Tap Room & Grill
1009 Niagara Falls Blvd., 716-832-6052
★★☆☆   4 P.M.–late
Food: Tavern fare   *Smoking:* Separate sections

Excellent pub food on the dining side, comfortable peninsula bar. The twenty-one taps include mainstream beers and micros, with four special house beers and a handpumped ale from Middle Ages.

Also in Amherst
Shannon Pub, 505 Main St., 716-839-0002. Irish pub.

BEDFORD HILLS

Tap House Café
13 Adams St., 914-244-8591
★★☆☆   5:30 P.M.–2 A.M.
Food: Full menu   *Smoking:* Separate sections

Well-executed, though not cheap, food. Forty beers on tap, plenty of single-malt whiskies. Both a kid-friendly restaurant and a slightly upscale neighborhood watering hole.

BUFFALO

Colter Bay Grill
561-565 Delaware, 716-882-1330
★☆☆☆   11:30 A.M.–late
Food: Tavern fare   *Smoking:* Separate sections

Primarily craft beers available from twenty-one taps, with seating at a large, U-shaped bar or in the back dining room.

Cozumel Grill & Tequila Bar

153 Elmwood, 716-884-3866

★☆☆☆   11 A.M.–late (noon–midnight Sundays)

Food: Full menu   *Smoking:* Bar only

Southwestern/Mexican restaurant in motif, serving excellent food. Sixteen draft choices, imports, micros, and some regional beers.

Pearl Street Grill & Brewing Co.   🅑

76 Pearl St., 716-856-2337

★★⯪☆   11 A.M.–late

Food: Brewpub fare   *Smoking:* Separate sections

Like other brewpubs opened in partnership with Wynkoop (see Denver, Colorado), set in a carefully restored historic building. Offers excellent regional food, well-made beers, and an excellent billiards room.

Also in Buffalo

Mr. Goodbar, 1110 Elmwood Ave., 716-975-3363. Singles nightclub with thirty-two taps.

Shannon Pub, 5050 Main St., 716-839-0002. Brewpub/Irish pub. Many guest beers.

COBLESKILL

Bull's Head Inn   🅑

2 Park Place, 518-234-3591

★☆☆☆   Hours: 11 A.M.–closing

Food: Tavern fare   *Smoking:* Throughout

Inn and stagecoach stop with a history that dates to 1802. Previously served micros on tap, then added its own brewhouse in 1999 (beers too new to rate).

FRANKLIN SQUARE

Croxley Ales

129 New Hyde Park, 516-326-9542

★★★☆   11 A.M.–4 A.M. (opens at noon Sundays)

Food: British pub fare   *Smoking:* Separate sections

Named for a London subway stop. Has a pub look outside and a pub feel inside, although it's clearly an American ale house, with craft beers sharing the menu with imports. A second Croxley Ales offers a wide draft selection in Rockville Center.

FREDONIA

Barker Brew Co.
34 W. Main St., 716-679-3435

★☆☆☆   11:30 A.M.–2 A.M.

Food: Tavern fare   *Smoking:* Separate sections

Well-chosen lineup of sixteen craft beers on tap, in two-story feed mill that dates to the mid-1800s. A national historic landmark that has been everything from butcher shop to bicycle shop.

GARDEN CITY

Waterzooi
850 Franklin Ave., 516-877-2177

★★★☆   11:30 A.M.–late (opens at noon Saturdays, 4–10 P.M. Sundays)

Food: Belgian fare   *Smoking:* Separate sections

Named for the famous seafood stew of Belgium. Wide range—twenty-three taps and a hundred-plus bottles—of Belgian and/or Trappist beers, each served in its own special glass. Belgian menu, with moules (mussels) prepared ten different ways.

GLENS FALLS

Davidson Brothers Brewpub ⓑ
184 Glen, 518-743-9026

★★☆☆   11:30 A.M.–not particularly late (opens at noon Sundays)

Food: Brewpub fare   *Smoking:* Separate sections

Family-friendly pub in a nineteenth-century building, with fine outdoor seating. Keeps a wide range of solid beers on tap, some of them available elsewhere in the region.

HOOSICK FALLS

Man of Kent
Route 7, 518-686-9917

★★☆☆   11 A.M.–midnight (closed Tuesdays and Wednesdays)

Food: Tavern fare   *Smoking:* Throughout

An intimate pub (dining for twenty-four, fourteen seats at the bar) run by a popular and friendly English national. A dozen imports on taps from the UK and Germany. Very much a locals' spot.

HUNTINGTON

Canterbury Ales
314 New York Ave., 516-549-4404
★★☆☆   Lunch–late
Food: Full menu   *Smoking:* Separate sections

A seafood restaurant for going on twenty years, with interesting nightly specials and a cozy pub. The sixteen draft choices include imports and micros. Large bottle selection.

HYDE PARK

Hyde Park Brewing Co.
514 Albany Post Road, 914-229-8277
★☆☆☆   11 A.M.–midnight
Food: Brewpub fare   *Smoking:* Separate sections.

Located in a former Howard Johnson's, decorated with excellent breweriana (great neon for Ruppert Knickerbocker beer), and offering seating directly under fermentation vessels. Solid if not spectacular beer goes well with excellent food.

ITHACA

Chapter House Brewpub
400 Stewart Ave., 607-277-9782
★★½☆   4 P.M.–1 A.M.
Food: Tavern fare   *Smoking:* Throughout

A Cornell University hangout that has been a bar since 1939 and shows the years in a friendly way. Was a brewpub for ten years, but added a full liquor license in 1999 and converted to a multi-tap serving fifty-one draft beers.

KRUMVILLE

Country Inn
1380 County Route 2, 914-657-8956
★★★☆   4 P.M.–midnight (opens at noon weekends)
Food: Tavern fare   *Smoking:* Throughout

Larry Erenburg, the owner and guy behind the bar, has been building the beer menu in this Catskill Mountains outpost since 1975. Offers seven beers on tap and 400-plus in bottles. No TV, but darts, a fish tank, puzzles, chess, and a fireplace.

NEW YORK CITY–BROOKLYN

The Gate
321 5th Ave., 718-768-4329
★★⯪☆   4 P.M.–4 A.M.
Food: No kitchen   *Smoking:* Throughout

From the same owners as the Blind Tiger in Manhattan, offering an eclectic selection from twenty-six taps and weekend barbecues on the deck.

Mugs Ale House
125 Bedford Ave., 718-384-8494
★★⯪☆   2 P.M.–4 A.M.
Food: Tavern fare   *Smoking:* Throughout

A Williamsburg neighborhood bar that takes beer seriously, offering thirty-plus choices, two handpumps.

Sparky's Ale House
481 Court St., 718-624-5516
★★☆☆   4 P.M.–late (opens earlier Fridays through Sundays)
Food: No kitchen   *Smoking:* Throughout

A late-night spot with twenty-eight draft choices, mostly micros and imports (some on handpump), at reasonable prices. Welcomes dogs and cigar smokers.

Waterfront Ale House
155 Atlantic Ave., 718-522-3794
★★★⯪   11:30 A.M.–4 A.M.
Food: Tavern fare plus   *Smoking:* Separate sections

A terrific neighborhood bar, a fine neighborhood, wonderful food, and an excellent beer lineup. Specialties are barbecue and smoked foods, prepared with beer pairings in mind. Beers favor microbrewed products, but include imports.

Also in Brooklyn
Eamon Doran, 174 Montague St., 718-596-4969. Irish pub.
Teddy's Bar, 96 Berry St., 718-384-9787. Tavern.

NEW YORK CITY–MANHATTAN

Belgo Nieuw York
415 Lafayette St., 212-253-2828

★★☆☆   Noon–late

Food: Belgian   *Smoking:* Separate sections

Imported directly from London, where the Belgo chain is wildly popular. It's big, the waitstaff is dressed in monks' attire, and there are more than a hundred Belgian beers (six on tap). Plenty of mussels and frites, of course, served at communal tables.

Blind Tiger Ale House
518 Hudson, 212-675-3848

★★★☆   Noon–4 A.M. (opens at 1 P.M. weekends)

Food: No kitchen   *Smoking:* Throughout

Great beer lineup on twenty-four taps and two handpumps, fine spirits menu. Has somehow remained more of a locals' spot than a trendy Greenwich Village stop. Plenty of pine, tin ceiling, and beer trays on the walls. Free bagels on weekends, Wednesday night beer-cheese pairings.

Brewsky's
43 E. 7th St., 212-420-0671

★★★☆   5 P.M.–late (opens at 4 P.M. Saturdays, 3 P.M. Sundays)

Food: No kitchen   *Smoking:* Throughout

Next door to Burp Castle, but the only theme here is beer—a dozen taps and usually about 600 bottle choices. Friendly place, customers welcome to order in or bring food.

Burp Castle
41 E. 7th St., 212-982-4567

★★☆☆   4 P.M.–late

Food: No kitchen   *Smoking:* Throughout

Before there was Belgo, there was Burp Castle, considerably smaller and without the frites. "Brewist Monks" armed with walkie-talkies make sure the small place doesn't get too crowded. Medieval-scene murals on the walls, nine taps, and voluminous bottle menu—favoring Belgian beers and often pricey.

Café de Bruxelles

118 Greenwich Ave., 212-206-1830

★★☆☆   Noon–midnight (closed Mondays)

Food: Belgian   *Smoking:* Separate sections

This restaurant was pairing Belgian food and beers before it became trendy and continues to do it well. It's also OK to drop in for a Belgian beer, order outstanding pommes frites, and linger at the zinc-covered bar.

Chelsea Brewing Co. Ⓑ

Pier 59, Chelsea Piers, 212-336-6440

★☆☆☆   Lunch–late evening

Food: Brewpub fare   *Smoking:* Separate sections

Beautifully appointed pub with brick floors, wooden tables, and lots of shiny brass. A fine view of the Hudson River, not to mention the golf driving range. Award-winning beers.

Chumley's

86 Bedford St., 212-675-4449

★★☆☆   5 P.M.–late

Food: Tavern fare   *Smoking:* Separate sections

The original booths, fireplace, and false entrance are still intact at this former speakeasy. There's no sign to mark this place, but crowds find it on weekends, anyway. Sawdust on the floors, literariana on the walls, and twenty-two beers on tap.

Commonwealth Brewing Ⓑ

10 Rockefeller Plaza, 212-977-2269

★★☆☆   Lunch–after dinner

Food: Brewpub fare   *Smoking:* Separate sections

Glass walls offer nice views of Rockefeller Center. Solid lineup of beers, good food including excellent appetizers.

d.b.a. 41 1ˢᵗ avenue

41 1ˢᵗ Ave., 212-475-5097

★★★★   1 P.M.–4 A.M.

Food: No kitchen   *Smoking:* Throughout

The fourteen taps and one handpump may seem modest, but the excellent selection is always changing and the beer is always well cared for. It can get crowded—like when *The New York Times* ran a story about its ninety single-malt whiskies—but generally it belongs to neighborhood types and beer lovers. Nice bottle menu and outstanding spirits selections in addition to the single malts.

East Side Ale House

961 2nd Ave., 212-752-3615

★★☆☆ Noon–late

Food: No kitchen   *Smoking:* Throughout

A small upstairs bar (food comes from the pizza place below) with seventeen well-chosen taps. Large single-malt whisky and specialty bourbon menus. Cigar-friendly.

The Ginger Man

11 E. 36th St., 212-532-3740

★★★☆ Lunch–late (opens at 3 P.M. Sundays)

Food: Light tavern fare   *Smoking:* Throughout

The Texas multi-tap chain comes to Manhattan, with a slightly more upscale pub (nice lantern chandeliers) and sixty-six draft choices. Jammed after work, when cigar smoking is encouraged.

Heartland Brewery Ⓑ

35 Union Square W., 212-645-3400

★★☆☆ 11:30 A.M.–late

Food: Brewpub fare   *Smoking:* Separate sections

Decorated to evoke America's heartland with murals in the style of Thomas Hart Benton and regional cuisine comfort food on the menu. Lovely forty-foot mahogany bar, solid ales, some innovative. Also a Heartland Brewery in Midtown.

Jake's Dilemma

430 Amsterdam Ave., 212-580-0556

★☆☆☆ 5 P.M.–late (opens earlier weekends)

Food: No kitchen   *Smoking:* Throughout

A brick-and-pine tavern with fourteen draft choices and eighty-five bottles, both imports and micros. The back room in the three-room pub has couches and library shelves.

Jimmy Armstrong's Saloon

875 10th Ave., 212-581-0606

★☆☆☆ 11 A.M.–2 A.M.

Food: Tavern fare   *Smoking:* Separate sections

A well-appointed, intimate pub with lots of carved wood and leaded glass, offering a very good lineup of imports and craft beers on tap.

John Street Bar and Grill

17 John St., 212-349-3278

★☆☆☆　　11 A.M.–2 A.M.

Food: Tavern fare　　*Smoking:* Separate sections

Attractive post-work pub with fourteen taps, three hand-pumps. Full lineup of single malts and other spirits. Excellent jukebox, darts room.

Kinsale Tavern

1679 3rd Ave., 212-348-4370

★★☆☆　　8 A.M.–late

Food: Tavern fare　　*Smoking:* Throughout

A blue-collar bar/Irish pub that begins serving beer at eight in the morning and offers soccer and rugby on twelve TVs. Twenty-five beers on tap, well-chosen bottle menu.

Knitting Factory

74 Leonard St., 212-219-3055

★☆☆☆　　Noon–4 A.M.

Food: No kitchen　　*Smoking:* Throughout

A rambling top-flight jazz club and performance space, with music seeming to sprout up from here and there, a coffeehouse at the entrance, and a bar with beer one level down. Most of the eighteen taps pour craft beers, and there are sofas off to the side.

North Star Pub

South Street Seaport, 212-509-6757

★★★☆　　Lunch–midnight

Food: British pub fare　　*Smoking:* Separate sections

The British-American Chamber of Commerce once labeled the North Star the best pub anywhere. Good, fresh beer; excellent food; friendly; massive single-malt menu.

Peculier Pub

145 Bleecker St., 212-353-1327

★★★☆　　5 P.M.–2 A.M.

Food: Tavern fare　　*Smoking:* Throughout

New York's first beer pub has about 400 bottled beers to choose from and a fine cross-section from eleven tap handles. Both sexes share the bathroom here, and it's apparently OK to carve your initials into the wooden tables.

Riverrun
176 Franklin St., 212-966-3894
    ★★☆☆   Lunch–3 A.M.
Food: Full menu   *Smoking:* Separate sections

The first restaurant in Tribeca, which is now jammed with trendy spots. Good food, nice choices on fifteen taps, and a men's room with pull-chain urinals that Al Pacino is said to love.

Ruby's Taphouse
1754 2ⁿᵈ Ave., 212-987-8179
    ★★☆☆   Late afternoon–late (opens earlier weekends)
Food: Tavern fare   *Smoking:* Separate sections

A fine wood-and-brick tavern that's at its best when the big window that looks onto Second Avenue is open. Devoted to beer, with a well-chosen beer menu served from twenty-six taps and two beer engines.

Silver Swan
41 W. 20ᵗʰ St., 212-254-3611
    ★☆☆☆   Noon–late
Food: German fare   *Smoking:* Separate sections

Intimate German restaurant with a fine list of German beers as well as other European standouts described in the twelve-page beer menu. Surprisingly kid-friendly.

Swift Hibernian Lounge
34 E. 4ᵗʰ St., 212-260-3600
    ★★☆☆   Noon–4 A.M.
Food: Irish pub fare   *Smoking:* Throughout

More than a little Irish, with Irish murals, Tuesday night sessions, and UK beers on tap. Newish and a popular singles place, drawing a young crowd for European DJs most nights.

Tap Room Ⓑ
3 W. 18ᵗʰ St., 212-691-7666
    ☆☆☆☆   Noon–midnight (closes at 10 P.M. Sundays)
Food: Brewpub fare   *Smoking:* Separate sections

Opened on the site of the defunct Zip City brewpub, using the equipment to make Austrian and Czech lagers.

Telephone Bar and Grill
149 2nd Ave., 212-529-5000

★☆☆☆ 11:30 A.M.–late

Food: Tavern fare *Smoking:* Separate sections

Red telephone booths in front, a lounge with a fireplace in back, inviting bar in between with a dozen solid taps and more interest in cider than most bars. Makes "beer cocktails" and serves tea on weekday afternoons.

Times Square Brewery Restaurant ℬ
160 W. 42nd St., 212-398-1234

★☆☆☆ 11 A.M.–late

Food: Brewpub fare *Smoking:* Separate sections

Large pub takes up an entire blockfront at the south end of the "new" Times Square, offering spectacular views through glass walls. Routine food, beer.

Typhoon Brewery ℬ
22 E. 54th St., 212-754-9006

★★⯪☆ Noon–late (closed Sundays)

Food: Thai cuisine *Smoking:* Separate sections

A destination restaurant for Thai food lovers that serves award-winning beer. Some dishes and beers designed to be served together. Downstairs bar jammed early most evenings.

Wall Street Kitchen & Bar
70 Broad St., 212-797-7070

★★☆☆ 11:30 A.M.–11:30 P.M. (closed weekends)

Food: Full menu *Smoking:* Separate sections

Located in a former bank originally built in 1908, less than two blocks from the New York Stock Exchange, and spectacular inside and out. Fifty draft choices cover the spectrum.

Waterfront Ale House
540 2nd Ave., 212-696-4104

★★★☆ 11:30 A.M.-4 A.M.

Food: Tavern fare *Smoking:* Throughout

Branch of bar by the same name in Brooklyn, offering twenty draft choices as well as single-malts and special-batch bourbons. As in Brooklyn, excellent barbecued meats smoked on premises.

Also in Manhattan

Bar Six, 502 6th Ave., 212-691-1363. Bar.

British Open, 320 E. 59th St., 212-355-8467. British pub, golf theme.

Carnegie Hill Brewing Co., 1000 3rd Ave., 212-369-0808. Brewpub.

The Collins Bar, 735 8th Ave., 212-541-4206. Bar.

Fitzgerald's Pub , 336 3rd Ave., 212-679-6931. Irish pub.

Fraunces Tavern, 54 Pearl St., 212-269-0144. Historic tavern.

Gramercy Tavern, 42 E. 20th St., 212-477-0777. Upscale restaurant, separate tavern.

Greenwich Brewing Co., 418 6th Ave., 212-477-8744. House beers, but no house brewery.

Heidelberg Restaurant, 1648 2nd Ave., 212-628-2332. German.

Irish Eyes, 5008 Broadway, 212-567-9072. Irish pub.

Jameson's Pub, 975 2nd Ave., 212-980-4465. Irish pub.

Kennedy's, 327 W. 57th St., 212-759-4242. Irish pub.

McSorley's Ale House, 15 E. 7th St., 212-473-9148. One of America's best known bars, limited beer selection.

Maggie's Place, 21 E. 47th St., 212-473-5757. Irish pub.

Manchester, 920 2nd Ave., 212-223-7484. Sports bar, British.

Markt, 401 W. 14th St., 212-727-3314. Belgian.

Mars 2112, 1633 Broadway, 212-582-2112. Space-themed bar with brewing equipment.

Moran's, 145 10th Ave., 212-989-5689. Tavern.

Paddy Reilly's Music Bar, 519 2nd Ave., 212-686-1210. Guinness products-only Irish pub.

Puffy's Tavern, 81 Hudson St., 212-766-9159. Tavern.

Pugsley's Café, Washington & Albany, 212-385-4900. Small bar.

St. Marks Ale House, 2 St. Marks Place, 212-260-9762. 24 taps.

SoHo Kitchen & Bar, 103 Green St., 212-925-1866. 20-plus taps.

Tribeca Brewing Co., 247 W. Broadway, 212-965-0141. Multitap, not a brewery.

Virgil's Barbecue, 152 W. 44th St., 212-921-9494. Great food, good bottle selection.

West Side Brewing Co., 340 Amsterdam Ave., 212-721-2161. Brewpub.

NEW YORK CITY–STATEN ISLAND

Adobe Blues
63 Lafayette Ave., 718-720-2583
★★⯪☆   11 A.M.–late
Food: Southwestern fare   *Smoking:* Separate sections

The food is Southwestern, the bar Old West with swinging saloon doors, and the beer international. The bottle list tops 300. The same owners operate Killmeyer's Old Bavarian Inn, a comfortable German-oriented restaurant with breweriana on the walls and a large beer selection, on Arthur Kill Road.

NYACK

O'Donohue's Tavern
66 Main St., 914-358-0180
★☆☆☆   11 A.M.–closing
Food: Tavern fare   *Smoking:* Separate sections

Neighborhood bar in an area gone upscale, offering ten draft choices. One year, when Sierra Nevada announced it wouldn't ship its popular Celebration Ale east of the Rockies, regulars here made a videotape pleading for the beer and sent it to the California brewery. The tavern ended up with a fresh keg.

ORANGEBURG

Company B's
206 Route 303, 914-365-6060
★★☆☆   11:30 A.M.–4 A.M.
Food: Full menu   *Smoking:* Separate sections

This large and often loud restaurant offers fifty-two draft choices. Tasting flights for those intent on sampling.

POUGHKEEPSIE

Gentleman Jim's Bistro-Brewery 🅑
522 Dutchess Turnpike, 914-485-5467
★☆☆☆   3 P.M.–1 A.M.
Food: Full menu   *Smoking:* Separate sections

Gentleman Jim's has been serving good-value food for more than twenty years. In 1996 it began making the first commercially brewed beer in Dutchess County since the Matthew Vassar Brewery closed in 1896. More than thirty single-malts.

ROCHESTER

MacGregor's Grill & Tap Room
381 Gregory St., 716-271-3592
★★★☆   11 A.M.–2 A.M.
Food: Tavern fare   *Smoking:* Throughout

The first of what have become three MacGregor's, a corner spot with a black-and-white tile floor and great light. Terrific mixture of imports and craft beers on sixty-plus taps. Other MacGregor's are in Perinton and Syracuse.

Monty's Korner
East & Alexander, 716-263-7650
★★☆☆   4 P.M.–late (opens at 3 P.M. Fridays, 6 P.M. Sundays)
Food: No kitchen   *Smoking:* Throughout

European beer and wine bar with a well-chosen selection of primarily Belgian and German beers available from seventeen taps; also offers ports and other wines.

The Old Toad
271 Alexander St., 716-232-2626
★★⯪☆   11:30 A.M.–2 A.M. (opens at 1 P.M. Saturdays, 6 P.M. Sundays)
Food: British pub fare   *Smoking:* Throughout

Everything from the ceiling down comes from Great Britain, including most of the waitstaff (exchange students from England). Two beers cask-conditioned, cellared, and served as "real ale" and several other British kegged beers on tap.

Rohrbach Brewing Ⓑ
315 Gregory St., 716-244-5680
★☆☆☆   Lunch–late
Food: Brewpub fare   *Smoking:* Separate sections

Downstairs in a turn-of-the-century brick building. The bar area is domed, creating a feeling a little like being inside a barrel. Solid lineup of ales on tap. A second pub, also brewing its own beer, operates on Buffalo Road.

Rose & Crown
873 Monroe Ave., 716-271-7050

★★⯪☆　　　11:30 A.M.–2 A.M. (opens later weekends)
Food: British pub fare　　*Smoking:* Separate sections

The pub is a dues-paying member of Britain's Campaign for Real Ale (CAMRA) and serves two beers via handpump as well as a dozen imports on tap. Modeled after a "backstreet boozer" and has chess tournaments as well as darts.

Also in Rochester
The Distillery, 1142 Mt. Hope Ave., 716-271-4105. Brewpub/multi-tap, sports bar.
Empire Brewing Co., 300 State St., 716-454-2337. Brewpub; see Syracuse.

SARATOGA SPRINGS

The Parting Glass
4042 Lake Ave., 518-583-1916

★★☆☆　　　11 A.M.–2 A.M.
Food: Full menu　　*Smoking:* Separate sections

The dart hall is a separate room with fourteen boards. Excellent music room, with Irish folk music one of the mainstays. "Breakfast & Backgammon" on Sunday mornings features a very large Irish breakfast. Twenty-two taps, nice range in bottles.

Also in Saratoga Springs
Saratoga Springs Brewing Co., 14 Phila St., 518-583-3209. Brewpub.

SCHENECTADY

Van Dyck Restaurant & Brewery Ⓑ
237 Union St., 518-381-1111

★☆☆☆　　　4:30 P.M.–late
Food: Full menu　　*Smoking:* Throughout

An upscale Victorian restaurant with a jazz room that attracts national acts and a more casual pub. A wide range of house beers are available in the immaculate pub. Seventy-five-foot mahogany bar is held up by seven half-naked, carved wooden maidens.

SETAUKET

The Tavern
Nicols Road & Route 25A, 516-751-0615
 ★☆☆☆ 3 P.M.–closing
 Food: Tavern fare *Smoking:* Throughout

 A golfer-friendly tavern (putting green outside) with twenty-five draft choices, mostly imports and craft beer.

SOUTHAMPTON

Southampton Publick House ⓑ
40 Bowden Square, 516-283-2800
 ★★★☆ Noon–late
 Food: Brewpub fare *Smoking:* Separate sections

 Upscale dining in a historic setting. Excellent core beers, but it's the seasonals and innovative "one-offs" that set brewer Phil Markowski's beers apart.

SUFFERN

Mountain Valley Brew Pub ⓑ
122 Orange Ave., 914-357-0101
 ★★☆☆ 11:30 A.M.–1:30 A.M.
 Food: Brewpub fare *Smoking:* Separate sections

 Fine lineup of beers, which you can watch bottled here for sale elsewhere. Dining specialty Brew B/Que, a slow-cooking process that uses one of the house beers as a tenderizing agent. Three fireplaces.

SYRACUSE

Blue Tusk
165 Walton St., 315-479-1934
 ★★★☆ 10 A.M.–2 A.M. (open for breakfast weekdays)
 Food: Deli *Smoking:* Separate sections

 Deli with a bar area with four taps that grew into a bar with more than sixty. A terrific lineup of both imports and micro-brewed beers.

Clark's Ale House
122 W. Jefferson St., 315-479-9859
   ★★★★   11 A.M.–2 A.M.
Food: Sandwich   *Smoking:* Throughout

Bar for regular folks, with thirty-two taps including those that serve cider. One of the first bars anywhere to offer handpumped ales. A roast turkey sandwich has been added to the menu for the lunch crowd, but at night a killer roast beef sandwich is the only menu item (aside from a New York cheese plate). Perfectly attended-to beer, no TV, blacksmith's puzzles, board games, and reading matter.

Coleman's Irish Pub
100 S. Lowell, 315-476-1933
   ★☆☆☆   Lunch–late
Food: Irish pub fare   *Smoking:* Separate sections

Located in Tipperary Hill, Syracuse's Irish enclave, since 1933. Has a separate leprechaun's door. A tanker full of green beer is delivered the first Sunday of March, and at noon everybody in the place gets one free green beer. Opens for breakfast on St. Patrick's Day and shuts the door once the place is full. Then you've got to wait for somebody to leave before you may enter.

Empire Brewing Co. Ⓑ
120 Walton St., 315-475-2337
   ★★☆☆   Lunch–late (closes at 9 P.M. Sundays)
Food: Brewpub fare   *Smoking:* Separate sections

A large basement pub with brick walls and arched doorways that create a rathskeller feeling. Excellent food, award-winning beer.

Also in Syracuse
MacGregor's Grill & Tap, 253 E. Water St., 315-425-7740. See Rochester; sixty taps here.
Syracuse Suds, 210-216 W. Water St., 315-471-2253. Brewpub.

TROY

Troy Pub & Brewery Ⓑ
417-419 River St., 518-273-2337
   ★★☆☆   Lunch–late
Food: Brewpub fare   *Smoking:* Separate sections

Long, dark, comfortable pub, with beautiful outdoor deck on the Hudson River. Good food, large selection of solid house beers on tap.

VESTAL

Ale House
3744 Vestal Parkway E., 607-729-9053
★★☆☆   3 P.M.–late (opens at 7 P.M. Saturdays, closed Sundays)
Food: Limited tavern fare   *Smoking:* Throughout

Thirty-year-old tavern, modeled after British pubs, long and narrow with just nine tables. Wide range of micros and imports from thirty-six taps.

WHITE PLAINS

Lazy Boy Saloon
154 Mamaroneck Ave., 914-761-0272
★★☆☆   11:30 A.M.–4 A.M.
Food: Tavern fare   *Smoking:* Throughout

Storefront spot with thirty-five beers on tap, a handpump, and a bottle menu deep with Belgians. Drafts include mainstream lagers, micros, and imports.

Also in White Plains
Fireworks Brewery, 25 S. Broadway, 914-448-2337. Brewpub.

Also in New York
Auburn: Spirits Tavern & Café, 20 State St., 315-252-9702. Tavern.
Avon: Avon Inn, 55 E. Main St., 716-226-8181. Tavern.
Bellmore: McDougalls Ale House, 213 Bedford Ave., 516-221-1303. Wide selection.
Corning: Market Street Brewing Co. & Restaurant, 63-65 W. Market St., 607-936-2337. Brewpub.
DeWitt: R.J. O'Toole's, Nottingham Plaza, 315-445-1813. Restaurant/bar.
Ellicottville: Ellicottville Brewing, 28 Monroe St., 716-699-2537. Brewpub.
Endwell: O's Place, 2906 E. Main St., 607-785-9025. Tavern.
Farmingdale: Black Forest Brew Haus, 2015 New Highway, 516-391-9500. Brewpub.
Henrietta: Rochester Brewpub, 800 Jefferson Road, 716-272-1550. Brewpub.
Hicksville: Gourmet Pizza & Things, Broadway Mall, 516-681-8710. Restaurant/bar.
Lake Grove: John Harvard's Brew House, 2093 Smithaven Plaza, 576-979-2739. Brewpub; see Cambridge, Massachusetts.

Lake Placid: Lake Placid Pub & Brewery, 14 Shore Drive, 518-523-3813. Brewpub.

Latham: Malt River Brewing Co., Latham Circle Mall, 518-786-6258. Brewpub.

Little Neck: Patrick's Pub & Café, 252-12 Northern Blvd., 718-423-7800. Brewpub.

New Paltz: Gilded Otter, 3 Main St., 914-256-1700.

Oswego: Buckhout Brewing Co., 7 W. Bridge St., 315-343-1112. Brewpub.

Oyster Bay: Canterbury Ales Oyster Bar & Grill, 46 Audrey Ave. Restaurant/bar.

Patchogue: Brickhouse Brewery & Restaurant, 67 W. Main St., 516-447-2337. Brewpub.

Plattsburgh: Bootleggers Pub & Brewery, 495 Upper Cornelia St., 518-561-6222. Brewpub.

Sackets Harbor: Sackets Harbor Brewing Co., 212 W. Main, 315-646-2739. Brewpub.

Williamsville: Buffalo Brewpub, 6861 Main St., 716-632-0552. Brewpub.

   Pizza Plant, 5110 Main St., 716-626-5566. Restaurant/bar.

Williston Park: Fox & Fiddle, 71 Hillside Ave., 516-747-7975. Restaurant/pub.

NORTH CAROLINA

Regional beers to look for: Highland Brewing.
Essential stops: Barley's in Asheville; Cottonwood Grille &
  Brewery in Boone.
Just for fun: Olde Hickory Brewing in Hickory. Daria literally
  screamed when we drove up and she saw the giant wine barrels
  that serve as booths. "You didn't tell me we got to sit in bar-
  rels," she said.
Best city for a pub crawl: Chapel Hill.

ASHEVILLE

Barley's
42 Biltmore Ave., 828-255-0504
   ★★★☆   Lunch–late
Food: Pizza plus   *Smoking:* Throughout

Good pizza, good live music and a killer jukebox. More than
forty taps behind the fifty-eight-foot-long bar with imports
and American craft beers, including those from Highland
Brewing Co., which is located directly below.

Jack of the Wood Ⓑ
40 Wall St., 828-252-3445
   ★★☆☆   4 P.M.–late (opens at noon weekends)
Food: Tavern fare   *Smoking:* None

Brewpub modeled after a country pub, serving four of its own
beers and filling out ten taps with offerings such as Guinness,
Beamish, and a beer from Cottonwood Brewery in Boone. Regular live Celtic music.

The Bier Garden
46 Hayward St., 828-285-0002
   ★☆☆☆   Lunch–late (closed Sundays)
Food: Tavern fare   *Smoking:* Separate sections

If a beer is available in western North Carolina, the Bier Garden tries to carry it. Large bottle selection (six-packs sold to go)
and thirteen taps.

Also in Asheville
Asheville Pizza & Brewing Co., 675 Merrimon Ave., 828-236-
2774. Brewpub.

BOONE

Cottonwood Grille & Brewery 🅱

179 Howard St., 828-264-7111

★★⯪☆   11 A.M.–2 A.M.

Food: Brewpub fare   *Smoking:* Separate sections

Started as a small Mexican restaurant with a tiny brewery in back before moving to more spacious quarters. The first batch of beer out of the new brewery won a medal at the Great American Beer Festival, and more have since.

Also in Boone

Caribbean Café, 489B W. King St., 828-265-2233. Restaurant/pub.

CARRBORO

Tyler's Restaurant & Taproom

102 E. Main St., 919-929-6881

★★☆☆   Lunch–late (closed Mondays)

Food: Tavern fare   *Smoking:* None

Brightly colored, airy tavern with seventeen beers on tap, including North Carolina and Belgian products. Family-friendly early with excellent food, younger crowd later.

CARY

Fox & Hound

107 Edinburgh S., 919-380-0080

★☆☆☆   Lunch–late (opens at 5 P.M. Sundays)

Food: British pub fare   *Smoking:* Separate sections

Pub was dismantled in the north of England and reassembled here. Mostly British imports among seven beers on tap, but also Carolina Pale Ale on handpump. Ask about the Moriarty legend.

CHAPEL HILL

Carolina Brewery 🅱

460 W. Franklin St., 919-942-1800

★☆☆☆   11 A.M.–closing

Food: Brewpub fare   *Smoking:* Separate sections

A neighborhood spot that incorporates the brewery and beer throughout and attracts a diverse crowd. Names of beers are everywhere, and beer plays a part in food preparation.

TS Elliott's Groundhog Tavern
149 1/2 E. Franklin St., 919-929-4943
★☆☆☆　　Lunch–late
Food: Tavern fare　　*Smoking:* Separate sections

A smoky basement gathering spot for sixty years (though different names and owners). Fourteen taps, one handpump, including imports and microbrewed beers.

Top of the Hill　Ⓑ
100 E. Franklin St., 919-929-8676
★★☆☆　　Lunch–late
Food: Brewpub fare　　*Smoking:* Separate sections

Immaculate pub with a lovely cherrywood bar and stunning views from the terrace. Well-executed traditional English ales from a British brewer and a wide-ranging menu.

CHARLOTTE

Atlantic Beer & Ice
330 N. Tryon St., 704-339-0566
★☆☆☆　　11 A.M.–2 A.M.
Food: Full menu　　*Smoking:* Separate sections

Upstairs a cigar bar, downstairs a jazz club, in between a restaurant that offers a wide range of craft beers and sidewalk seating.

South End Brewery & Smokehouse　Ⓑ
2100 South Blvd., 704-358-4677
★☆☆☆　　11:30 A.M.–10 P.M. (closes at 11 P.M. Thursdays through Saturdays)
Food: Brewpub fare　　*Smoking:* Separate sections

Helped make the South End vastly popular, and still has a line out the door many nights, even though it's immense. Many members of the Carolina Panthers hang out here. Good food, large portions, solid beer.

Also in Charlotte
Rock Bottom Brewery & Restaurant, 401 N. Tynon, 704-334-2739. Brewpub; see Denver, Colorado.

DURHAM

Fishmonger's
806 W. Main St., 919-682-0128
★☆☆☆   Open for dinner, some days earlier
Food: Seafood   *Smoking:* Throughout

Seafood restaurant downstairs, oyster bar upstairs, eighteen taps, with two ciders, craft beers and plenty of imports. We assume the "no swimming/no wading" sign doesn't refer to beer.

Also in Durham
James Joyce Pub, 912 W. Main St., 919-683-3022. Irish pub.

GREENSBORO

Wild Magnolia Cafe
2200 Walker Ave., 336-378-0800
★★½☆   11:30 A.M.–late (opens at 4:30 P.M. weekends, closes at 10 P.M. Sundays)
Food: Southern fare   *Smoking:* Separate sections

Forty-eight beers on tap, everything from mainstream lagers to imports and craft beers. New Orleans-inspired menu and a sign that reads, "Be Nice or Leave."

Also in Greensboro
Chumley's, 2132 Lawndale Drive, 336-691-0960. Brewpub.

HICKORY

Old Hickory Brewery Ⓑ
2828 U.S. Highway 70 SW, 704-327-2743
★★☆☆   Lunch–late
Food: Brewpub fare   *Smoking:* Separate sections

New meaning to "seven-barrel brewery" here, as seven giant 1,000-gallon wine barrels have been turned into unique booths. Nice range of ales, good food. Also operates a taproom in Hickory.

MANTEO

Weeping Radish Brewery Ⓑ
Highway 64, 919-473-1157

★★✬☆   11:30 A.M.–closing

Food: German fare   *Smoking:* Separate sections

German-style beers (mostly lagers) and German food served in a German beer hall decorated with flags and artifacts from Bavaria. Beer garden features a children's playground, decks, walkways, ponds, and fountains. Also operates restaurants in Corolla and Kitty Hawk, though no beer brewed there.

RALEIGH

Greenshield's Pub & Brewery Ⓑ
214 E. Martin, 919-829-0214

★★☆☆   11:30 A.M.–1 A.M.

Food: Brewpub fare   *Smoking:* Separate sections

A spacious pub in Raleigh's historic City Market, with a British-like sitting room (fireplace, bookshelves) but a food and beer lineup that goes beyond British—particularly the excellent German-style beers.

T.S. Elliott's City Market Bistro
205 Wolfe St., 919-839-0405

★★☆☆   Lunch–late (closed Sundays)

Food: Bistro fare   *Smoking:* Separate sections

Also located in City Market and serving a New Orleans-influenced menu, including muffulettas. Twenty-five beers on taps, a mixture of national micros and imports.

Also in Raleigh
Southend Brewery & Smokehouse, 505 W. Jones St., 919-832-4604. Brewpub; see Charlotte.

Tir na nÓg, 218 S. Blount St., 919-833-7795. Irish pub.

Also in North Carolina
Cornelius: Lake Norman Brewing Co., 19707 Liverpool Parkway, 704-892-5622. Brewpub.

Fayetteville: Huske Hardware House Brewing Co., 405 Hay St., 910-437-9905. Brewpub.

Squire's Pub, 482 McPherson Church Road, 910-860-0660. British pub.

Matthews: Hops Grill & Bar, 9950 E. Independence, 704-844-8300. Brewpub.

Wilmington: Front Street Brewery, 9 N. Front St., 919-251-1935. Brewpub.

NORTH DAKOTA

Quite honestly, North Dakota is not particularly specialty beer-friendly. As many brewpubs have closed as opened, and it's not particularly easy to find microbrewery beer. However, Happy Harry's Bottle Shop in Grand Forks does offer hundreds of imports and micros, all stored in coolers.

BISMARCK

The Walrus
1136 N. 3rd St., 701-250-0020
★☆☆☆   10:30 A.M.–1 A.M.
Food: Tavern fare   *Smoking:* Separate sections

A strip mall restaurant with a separate bar area that has eighteen taps, many mainstream lagers plus imports and micro-brewed beers. One hundred twenty bottles, plenty of micros.

DICKINSON

Rattlesnake Creek Brewery & Grill Ⓑ
2 W. Villard, Box 1475, 701-225-9518
★☆☆☆   11 A.M.–1 A.M.
Food: Brewpub fare   *Smoking:* Separate sections

Old West saloon. The story here is that Teddy Roosevelt once drank at the bar, which dates back to the 1800s. As well as an interesting lineup of house beers, offers guest beers from Bud Light to micros.

FARGO

Old Broadway Restaurant & Pub Ⓑ
22 Broadway, 701-237-6161
☆☆☆☆   4 P.M.–1 A.M.
Food: Brewpub fare   *Smoking:* Throughout

A restaurant for twenty-five years that added a brewery in 1995. Beers have received mixed reviews.

Regional beers to look for: Great Lakes Brewing.
Essential stops: Great Lakes Brewing.
Just for fun: Arnold's in Cincinnati. Old-time music on a worn tile floor.
Best city for a pub crawl: Columbus, because of German Village.

AKRON

Liberty Street Brewing ⑬
1238 Weathervane Lane, 216-869-2337
★★☆☆   11:30 A.M.–late
Food: Brewpub fare   *Smoking:* Separate sections

This brewpub has made some excellent beer, some served on handpump, and offers an innovative New Orleans-influenced menu. Very pubby bar area.

BEDFORD HEIGHTS

Winking Lizard Tavern
25380 Miles Road, 216-831-3488
★☆☆☆   11 A.M.–2 A.M.
Food: Tavern fare   *Smoking:* Separate on weekends

The first of six Winking Lizards in the Cleveland area, opened in 1983. Like the others, offers both mainstream and craft beers from twelve taps, plus a large bottle selection (and World Tour of Beers for regulars). Neighborhood tavern.

CANTON

Thirsty Dog Brewing Co. ⑬
5419 Dressler Road NW, 330-479-2739
★☆☆☆   11 A.M.–late (noon–10 P.M. Sundays)
Food: Brewpub fare   *Smoking:* Separate sections

Strip mall outside, friendly pub inside, with ten to twelve beers often on tap and sample tray in the shape of a large bone. Thirsty Dog also operates pubs in Akron and Dayton.

Also in Canton
The Brewhouse Pub & Grille, 4262 Portage St., 330-966-7447. Brewpub.

CINCINNATI

BarrelHouse Brewing Co. Ⓑ
22 E. 12ᵗʰ St., 513-421-2337

★★☆☆   4 P.M.–2:30 A.M. (closed Sundays)

Food: Brewpub fare   *Smoking:* Separate sections

A few blocks from Main Street Brewing in the Over-the-Rhine area, which once was overflowing with saloons and beer gardens. A little more casual, brewing sometimes excellent beer, with some served on handpump.

Rhino's Bar
119 E. 12ᵗʰ St., 513-241-8545

★★☆☆   4 P.M.–2:30 A.M. (opens at 6 P.M. Saturdays, closed Sundays)

Food: No kitchen   *Smoking:* Throughout

Small inviting corner bar in the Over-the-Rhine area with a fine jukebox. Imports, craft beers, and two ciders among the twelve taps. Large list of single-malt whiskies, reasonably priced.

Teller's of Hyde Park Ⓑ
2710 Erie Ave., 513-312-4721

★★☆☆   11 A.M.–late

Food: Brewpub fare   *Smoking:* Separate sections

Set in an old bank building complete with stone-clad pillars, thirty-five-foot cathedral ceilings, a skylight running the entire length of the building, and working bank vault. Has its own small brewhouse, but the primary attraction is thirty taps, serving mostly micros.

Also in Cincinnati
Arnold's, 210 E. 8ᵗʰ St., 513-421-6234. Historic restaurant/bar.

The Dubliner, 6111 Montgomery Road, 513-531-6111. Irish pub.

Heritage Restaurant, 7664 Wooster Pike, 513-561-9300. Restaurant/bar.

Holy Grail Brewery & Grill, 13 W. Charlton, 513-861-7821. Brewpub.

Rock Bottom Brewery & Restaurant, 10 Fountain Circle, 513-621-1588. Brewpub; see Denver, Colorado.

CLEVELAND

Der Braumeister
13046 Lopain Road, 216-671-6220
    ★☆☆☆   11 A.M.–10 P.M. (closed Sundays)
Food: German fare   *Smoking:* Separate sections

Cozy German restaurant serving traditional dishes such as schnitzel and sausages, plus a large selection of German beers on tap and in bottles.

Diamondback Brewery ⓑ
728 Prospect Ave., 216-771-1988
    ★★☆☆   Lunch–late
Food: Tapas/brewpub fare   *Smoking:* Separate sections

Near the baseball stadium, jammed game days. Tapas on restaurant side, less expensive pub fare on pub side. Brewer Bill Morgan, who made interesting and award-winning beers, left shortly before this was written, making rating difficult.

Edison's Pub
2373 Professor, 216-522-0006
    ★☆☆☆   5 P.M.–2:30 A.M. (opens at 9 P.M. Sundays)
Food: No kitchen   *Smoking:* Throughout

Three imports on tap, wide bottle selection. Food available from deli next door. In up-and-coming Tremont neighborhood. Lovely beer garden-style patio.

Great Lakes Brewing ⓑ
2516 Market St., 216-771-4404
    ★★★★   11:30 A.M.–late (opens at 3 P.M. Sundays)
Food: Brewpub fare   *Smoking:* Separate sections

A fine brewpub that grew into a great microbrewery. In the West Side Market area. Upstairs is a taproom with a great back bar, with restaurant seating in another room. Downstairs is a large brick cellar.

Harbor Inn Café
1219 Main Ave., 216-241-3232
    ★☆☆☆   10 A.M.–2:30 A.M.
Food: Tavern fare   *Smoking:* Throughout

Housed in a large brick building dating to 1895, offering no windows and no draft beer but plenty of bottles. Imposing back bar with lighthouses carved into it. Fried fish a specialty.

Wilbert's Bar & Grill
1360 W. 9th St., 216-771-2583
    ★☆☆☆   11:30 A.M.–2:30 A.M.
Food: Full menu   *Smoking:* Throughout

A music venue that books touring national blues acts. Three taps go to Guinness, a Molson beer, and a local microbrewery beer, plus a hundred-plus bottles. Monthly tastings, from vodka to beer.

Also in Cleveland
Cleveland Chophouse & Brewery, 824 W. St. Clair, 216-623-0909. Brewpub; see Denver Chophouse, Denver, Colorado.
Fadó Irish Pub, 1058 Old River Road, 216-771-0066. Irish pub.
Flat Iron Café, 1114 Center, 216-696-6968. Tavern across from Crooked River Brewing.
Heart of the South Side, 2061 W. 10th, 216-861-3220. Tavern.
John Harvard's Brew House, 1087 River Road, 216-623-2739. Brewpub; see Cambridge, Massachusetts.
Rock Bottom Brewery & Restaurant, 2000 Sycamore, #260, 216-623-1555. Brewpub; see Denver, Colorado.
Wallaby's Grill & Brewpub, 503 Prospect Ave., 216-579-7101. Brewpub; see Westlake.

COLUMBUS

Barley's Brewpub Ⓑ
467 N. High St., 614-228-2537
    ★★☆☆   11 A.M.–1 A.M.
Food: Brewpub fare   *Smoking:* Separate sections

Located in an old brick building just across from the new convention center, serving a fine lineup of ales. Comfortable dining in booths or at the bar. A second Barley's is on Dublin Road.

Flaherty's Thirsty Ear Tavern
1200 W. 3rd Ave., 614-299-4987
    ★☆☆☆   11 A.M.–2:30 A.M. (opens at noon Sundays)
Food: Tavern fare   *Smoking:* Throughout

Rock 'n' roll bar, from the posters on the walls to the jukebox. Nineteen taps, mostly micros plus Miller Lite, with some esoteric bottle choices.

Hoster Brewing Ⓑ
550 S. High St., 614-228-6066
★★☆☆   11 A.M.–2 A.M. (opens at 4 P.M. Sundays)
Food: Brewpub fare   *Smoking:* Separate sections

Located in a former streetcar repair shop, with a large island bar near the entrance and large dining area beyond. Named after a defunct Columbus brewery and stocked with breweriana. Fine lineup of both ales and lagers.

Schmidt's Sausage Haus & Restaurant
240 E. Kossuth, 614-444-6808
★☆☆☆   11 A.M.–11 P.M.
Food: German fare   *Smoking:* Separate sections

German Village is a terrific historic area just south of downtown where there are many places you can find German beer on tap. Schmidt's is one, using recipes handed down for five generations. Known for its cream puffs.

Also in Columbus
Columbus Brewing Co. Restaurant, 525 Short St., 614-464-2739. Brewpub.
The Distillery, 1896 N. High, 614-291-3448. Tavern.

MARBLEHEAD

Frontwater Restaurant & Brewing Co.
8660 E. Bayshore Road, 419-798-5914
★☆☆☆   11:30 A.M.–11:30 P.M.
Food: Brewpub fare   *Smoking:* Separate sections

Family-run pub sitting on the bit of land that juts out between Sandusky Bay and Lake Erie. Serves a wide range of beers. No television, riddle nights, beer conversation nights, and board game competitions.

PISGAH

Black Forest Restaurant Lounge
8675 Cincinnati-Columbus Road, 513-777-7600
★☆☆☆   Lunch–late weekdays, dinner–late weekends
Food: German fare   *Smoking:* Separate sections

Menu from the Bavarian Alps served by restaurateur whose family also operates a restaurant in Germany. Forty-foot Bavarian Maibaum (May pole) in front, four German beers on tap, more in bottles.

TOLEDO

Maumee Bay Brewing Co. Ⓑ
27 Broadway, 419-243-1302
★★☆☆   Lunch–late
Food: Brewpub fare plus   *Smoking:* Separate sections

A sprawling, multi-room pub in the renovated Oliver House, a downtown landmark that opened its doors in 1859 as a fine hotel.

Also in Toledo
Ragtime Rick's First Draught, 4733 Glendale Ave., 419-389-0956. Tavern.

WESTLAKE

Wallaby's Grill & Brewpub Ⓑ
3005 Clemens Road, 440-808-1700
★☆☆☆   11 A.M.–late
Food: Brewpub fare   *Smoking:* Separate sections

Inviting family spot with yellow clapboard siding and green-and-white striped awnings. Decorated in Australian theme, with American menu items getting Australian names.

Also in Ohio
Blue Ash: Watson Brothers Brewhouse, 4785 Lake Forest Drive, 513-563-9797. Brewpub operated by Queen City Brewing.
Dayton: McGuffy's House of Draft, 5418 Burkhardt Road, 513-254-0173. Music bar.
Tank's Bar & Grill, 2033 Wayne Ave., 513-252-2249. Tavern.
Garrettsville: Alessis Restaurant/Garretts Mill Brewing Co., 8148 Main St., 216-527-5849. Brewpub.
Kent: Mugs Brew Pub, 211 Franklin Ave., 330-673-7822. Brewpub.
Maumee: Arrowhead Brewing Co., 1500 Holland Road, 419-891-9049. Brewpub.
Newark: Legends Brewing/Bonkey's Brew Pub, 1650 W. Church St., 740-366-1183. Brewpub.
Portsmouth: Mault's Brewpub, 224 2nd St., 614-354-6106. Brewpub.
Put-in-Bay: The Brewery at the Bay, 441 Catawba Ave., 419-285-4677. Brewpub.
Strongsville: Mad Crab Brewery, 12492 Prospect St., 440-238-4877. Brewpub.

Uniontown: Burkhardt Brewing, 3700 Massillon Road, 216-896-9200. Brewpub.

Willoughby: Willoughby Brewing Co., 4057 Erie St., 440-975-0202. Brewpub.

OKLAHOMA

Regional beers to look for: Oklahoma has brewpubs but no microbreweries. A few places, such as TapWerks, sell craft beer from nearby states as well as imports and nationally distributed microbrewery beers.

Essential stop: TapWerks in Oklahoma City.

Just for fun: Pete's in Krebs. Even when Oklahoma was dry, beer was brewed and served at Pete's.

Best city for a pub crawl: Oklahoma City.

Worth noting: In Oklahoma, "strong beer" is anything with more than 3.2 percent alcohol by weight (4 percent by volume). Liquor stores can only sell it at room temperature, but bars and restaurants can sell it cold. Brewpubs, gas stations, convenience stores, and grocery stores sell cold beer, but it must be 3.2 ABW or less. As a result, most of the beer sold in Oklahoma is 3.2, and many large breweries, including Anheuser-Busch and Miller, make 3.2 beer for Oklahoma (and Utah). Also, 3.2 versions of Moosehead, Amstel Light, and others are available and found in gas station coolers.

KREBS

Pete's Place 🅑
420 SW 8th St., Box 66, 918-423-2042

★☆☆☆   4–9 P.M. (closes at 10 P.M. Fridays and Saturdays; noon–9 P.M. Sundays)

Food: Italian fare   *Smoking:* Separate sections

A historic restaurant known for its "choc" beer (named that because it came from the Choctaw Nation) since the 1920s, often brewed outside the law. Today, the sprawling Italian restaurant brews the rather light-tasting beer legally in its brewpub.

MOORE

Royal Bavarian Brauhaus 🅑
3401 S. Sooner Road, 405-799-7666

★☆☆☆   Open late afternoon–after dinner

Food: German fare   *Smoking:* Separate sections

A Bavarian gasthaus, decked out like a chalet and serving Southern German and Bavarian cuisine. The beers, both ales and lagers, are all German-style.

OKLAHOMA CITY

TapWerks Alehouse & Café
5700 N. Western, 405-842-6769
    ★★★☆   10 A.M.–2 A.M. (5 P.M.–2 A.M. Sundays)
Food: Tavern fare   *Smoking:* Throughout

When TapWerks opened in 1996, fifteen of forty-six taps poured mainstream lagers. Now there are more than eighty taps and only two mainstream lagers. Plenty of imports, many Belgian beers, and whatever micros are available in Oklahoma. Casual and comfortable. Opened TapWerks Bricktown with even more taps in late summer 1999.

Also in Oklahoma City
Belle Island Restaurant & Brewery, 50 Penn Mall, 405-840-1911. Brewpub.
Bricktown Brewery, 1 N. Oklahoma Ave., 405-232-2739. Brewpub.
Flip's, 5801 N. Western Ave., 405-843-1527. Restaurant/bar.

TULSA

Slow Duck Saloon
1516 S. Quaker, 918-592-3825
    ☆☆☆☆   3 P.M.–2 A.M.
Food: Limited tavern fare   *Smoking:* Throughout

Moved in where Cherry Street Brewing (a brewpub) failed. Eight taps, with a few micros (Sierra Nevada Pale Ale and a Boulevard beer) and imports.

Also in Tulsa
Steamroller Blues & Brews, 18th & Boston, 918-583-9520. Blues clubs with several micros on tap.
Ursula's Bavarian Inn, 4932 E. 91st St., 918-496-8282. German.

Also in Oklahoma
Choctaw: Old Germany Restaurant, 15920 SE 29th St., 405-390-8647. Restaurant.
Norman: Coaches Brewery & Restaurant, 102 W. Main, 405-360-5726. Brewpub.
    Library, 607 Boyd St., 405-366-7465. Tavern.
Wheatland: The Roadhouse, 6717 Highway 152, 405-745-6639. Tavern.

OREGON

Regional beers to look for: Hair of the Dog Brewing; Deschutes Brewery; Rogue Ales; Widmer; Full Sail Brewing; Saxer Brewing; Portland Brewing; BridgePort Brewing . . . and that's just for starters.

Essential stops: Another list that gets too long, so limiting it to five: Horse Brass Pub and BridgePort Brewery in Portland; Bombs Away Café in Corvallis; Rogue's Bayfront Brewery in Newport; Deschutes in Bend.

Just for fun: Crystal Ballroom in Portland. The "floating" dance floor was great when it was built in 1914, this has been a terrific rock venue and it's just as cool today.

Best city for a pub crawl: Portland (but Corvallis would be our pick in many states).

Worth noting: Oregon is home to the McMenamins brothers' pubs. Many of their pubs carry their name, but others don't. Some are simple neighborhood taverns, while others have involved major overhauls of historic buildings. This is a chain in the loosest sense of the word—we've never heard the adjective "cookie-cutter" used in the same sentence with McMenamins.

ASHLAND

Siskiyou Brewing Co.
31-B Water St., 541-482-7718
  ★☆☆☆   11:30 A.M.–late (opens at 4 P.M. in winter)
  Food: Tavern fare   ***Smoking:*** None

Woody tavern (not a brewpub) that was a Rogue Ales brewery before being swamped by a flood. Offers fifteen beers on tap—Pilsner Urquell, Guinness, and mostly micros. Inviting fireplace.

BEAVERTON

Hall Street Bar & Grill
3775 SW Hall Blvd., 503-641-6161
  ★☆☆☆   Lunch–late (opens at 4 P.M. weekends)
  Food: Full menu   ***Smoking:*** Separate sections

Barbecue grill outside, mesquite grill inside, and ten Northwest craft beers on tap. Halogen spotlights show off an impressive liquor selection.

Also in Beaverton
McMenamins, 6179 SW Murray Road, 503-644-4562. Brewpub.
McMenamins, 2927 SW Cedar Hills Blvd., 503-641-0151. Non-
    brewing chain member.
Old Chicago, 17960 NW Evergreen Parkway, 503-533-4650. See
    Boulder, Colorado.
Riverwood Pub, 8136 SW Hall Blvd., 503-643-7189.
    McMenamins.
Rock Creek Tavern, 10000 NW Old Cornelius Pass, 503-645-
    3822. McMenamins.

BEND

Bend Brewing Co. Ⓑ
1061 NW Brooks St., 541-383-1599
    ★★☆☆   11 A.M.–closing
Food: Brewpub fare   *Smoking:* None

On the banks of the Deschutes River and Mirror Pond, with
fine outdoor seating.

Deschutes Brewery & Public House Ⓑ
1044 NW Bond St., 541-382-9242
    ★★★★   11 A.M.–late
Food: Brewpub fare   *Smoking:* None

Still a restaurant focusing on fresh food and fresh beer, although it opened a stand-alone brewery that sells its excellent
beer throughout the West Coast. Tempting daily specials in
the restaurant, fireplace, beer on handpump.

Also in Bend
MacKenzie's, 1033 NW Bond St., 541-388-3891. Restaur-
    ant/bar.

CORVALLIS

Bombs Away Café
2527 Monroe, 541-757-7221
    ★★★☆   11 A.M.–midnight (opens at 4 P.M. weekends)
Food: Mexican fare   *Smoking:* Separate sections

Excellent Mexican food, twenty-five well-chosen draft selections (mostly West Coast craft beers), extensive tequila and
single-malt whisky lists. Cafeteria in front, bistro in BAC
room.

Squirrel's Tavern

100 SW 2nd St., 541-753-8057

★★☆☆   11:30 A.M.–late (opens at 5 P.M. weekends)
Food: Tavern fare   *Smoking:* Throughout

A woody tavern inside, where you may find a bike parked, benches hewn from wood, a jazz group playing on the landing, and pierogies for seventy-five cents or deviled eggs for a quarter. Fourteen taps, both mainstream beers and West Coast craft products, at very fair prices. Lots of squirrel stuff.

Suds 'n' Suds

1035 NW Kings Blvd., 541-758-5200

★★☆☆   Noon–1 A.M.
Food: No kitchen   *Smoking:* Throughout

A pub/laundromat where you can order pizza from the place next door. Most of the thirty-seven taps are Northwest craft beers, with a few imports and mainstream lagers thrown in.

Also in Corvallis

Fox & Firkin, 202 SW 1st Ave., 541-753-8533. British pub.
Kells Irish Pub, 137 SW 2nd Ave., 541-752-7570. Irish pub.
McMenamins, 420 NW 3rd St., 503-754-7171.
Old World Deli, 341 SW 2nd St., 503-752-8549. Brewpub.

EUGENE

Steelhead Brewery & Café Ⓑ

199 E. 5th Ave., 541-686-2739

★★☆☆   11:30 A.M.–late
Food: Brewpub fare   *Smoking:* Separate sections

A nicely done tavern with stone-and-brick walls and mahogany wainscoting. Easy chairs at some of the tables. The flagship pub for a growing chain, turning out excellent ales.

Wild Duck Brewery Ⓑ

169 W. 6th St., 541-485-3825

★★☆☆   11:30 A.M.–late
Food: Brewpub fare   *Smoking:* Only in the bar

As upscale as Steelhead is laid back. Beautiful and spacious, with an adventurous menu. Wide range of solid beers. Large music hall at the back of the pub.

Also in Eugene
East 19th St. Café, 1485 E. 19th Ave., 541-342-4025. McMenamins
   pub.
Eugene City Brewery, 84 Olive St., 541-345-8489. Brewpub.
High Street Pub, 1234 High St., 541-345-4905. McMenamins
   brewpub.

GOVERNMENT CAMP

Mount Hood Brewing Co. Ⓑ
87304 Government Camp Loop, 503-272-3724
   ★☆☆☆   Noon–late evening
   Food: Brewpub fare   *Smoking:* None

A ski place, right next door to the Timberline Lodge, and decorated with skiing and fly-fishing stuff. Offers a solid lineup of
ales.

HILLSBORO

Cornelius Pass Roadhouse Ⓑ
4045 NW Cornelius Pass Road, 503-640-6174
   ★★☆☆   11 A.M.–1 A.M.
   Food: Brewpub fare   *Smoking:* Separate sections

This is a fine example of a McMenamins reclamation project.
The brewpub is in an old farmhouse that was built in 1866.
The granary on the site was built in 1855 and the octagonal
barn in 1913. Offers the expected lineup of fairly priced food
and beer.

HOOD RIVER

Full Sail Brewing Tasting Room Ⓑ
506 Columbia St., 541-386-2281
   ★★★☆   Limited hours; call
   Food: Limited   *Smoking:* None

A one-room tavern with a very limited menu, but usually eight
of the outstanding Full Sail beers on tap. The outdoor deck offers a panoramic view of the Columbia River Gorge.

Also in Hood River
Big Horse Brewing, 115 State St., 541-386-4411. Brewpub.

JOSEPH

Embers Brew House
204 N. Main, 541-432-2739
★★☆☆ 10 A.M.–11 P.M. (10 A.M.–9 P.M. Sundays)
Food: Pizza, sandwiches *Smoking:* None

A rare find in Eastern Oregon, with all seventeen taps devoted to microbrewed beer. Has both a deck and a yard with a patio.

LAKE OSWEGO

Gemini Bar & Grill
456 N. State St., 503-636-9445
★★☆☆ 11 A.M.–late (opens at 4 P.M. Sundays)
Food: Tavern fare *Smoking:* Throughout

Tavern with separate rooms for live music and pool, with twenty-four beers—mostly Northwest craft offerings—on tap.

Also in Lake Oswego
The Ram/Big Horn Brewing Co., 320 Oswego Pointe Drive, 503-697-8818. Brewpub.

MCMINNVILLE

Golden Valley Brewery & Pub   Ⓑ
980 E. 4ᵗʰ St., 503-472-2739
★☆☆☆ 11:30 A.M.–late
Food: Bistro fare *Smoking:* Separate sections

In the heart of Oregon's wine country, this brewpub also has its own wine label. Those bottles sit on the shelves of a dark classic back bar. Good food, solid beers.

NEWPORT

Bayfront Brewery & Public House   Ⓑ
748 SW Bay Blvd., 541-265-3188
★★★☆ 11 A.M.–late
Food: Brewpub fare *Smoking:* Separate sections

This is where Rogue Ales began. The beer distributed across the country is now made across the bay, where there's also a pub. Both offer the full range of Rogue products. Upstairs rooms are for rent here, where B&B means Bed & Beer, with a six-pack of Rogue beer in the refrigerator. Rogue's other pub, Brewer's on the Bay, is at 2320 OSU Drive.

Uptown Pub

6365 Pine St., 541-265-3369

★★☆☆   7 A.M.–late (opens at 11 A.M. Saturdays and Sundays)

Food: Tavern fare   *Smoking:* Separate sections

The pub's twenty-one taps serve mostly micros and imports, including Belgian beers. Full bar, pool, and music jams twice a week, with an occasional touring blues band stopping by.

NORTH PLAINS

Rogue Pub & Eatery

31500 NW Commercial St., 503-647-5268

★☆☆☆   11 A.M.–late (closed Sundays)

Food: Full menu   *Smoking:* Throughout

Despite the name, not affiliated with the brewery. The pub devotes fifteen of its nineteen taps to microbrewery beer and serves a menu that tends toward upscale.

PORTLAND

Bagdad Theater & Pub

3702 SE Hawthorne, 503-230-0895

★☆☆☆   Lunch–late

Food: Tavern fare   *Smoking:* None inside

A beautifully restored movie theater/pub on one side, complete with tables and chairs, and a second pub on the other. Serves the usual McMenamins beer lineup. The McMenamins also run the Mission Theater & Pub on Glisan, a former Swedish tabernacle.

Barley Mill Pub

1629 SE Hawthorne, 503-231-1492

★★☆☆   11 A.M.–late

Food: Tavern fare   *Smoking:* Separate sections

The original McMenamins pub, set the tone for the rest. Deadhead-friendly—with a chair reserved for Jerry—with lavish murals on the wall. At a typical McMenamins tavern or brewpub you can expect solid pub grub at a reasonable price, a half-dozen or more McMenamins beers made on-premise or at a McMenamins brewing facility, plus several quality Northwest beers.

BJ's Pizza Grille & Brewery Ⓑ
12105 N. Center, 503-289-5566

★★✯☆   Lunch–late

Food: Pizza, pasta   *Smoking:* None

The chain that also has pubs in California and Colorado has staked a solid claim here, with several pub/restaurants in the area. Some brew beer on-premise, and some serve beer from other BJ breweries. A solid lineup of beers, including an excellent pale ale.

BridgePort Brewery Ⓑ
1313 NW Marshall, 503-241-7179

★★★✯   Early afternoon–late

Food: Pizza, calzones   *Smoking:* None

A cavernous brick warehouse with multiple rooms, BridgePort serves tempting pizza and calzones and excellent beer. Usually has several handpumped ales on offer. The warehouse loading dock offers wonderful outdoor seating, with hopvines growing.

Caswell Company
533 SE Grand Ave., 503-232-6512

★★☆☆   Lunch–late (closed weekday afternoons, limited hours weekends)

Food: Bistro fare   *Smoking:* None

Welcomes lawyers in suits and garage band members, serving Italian-inspired fare that pairs well with beer. Fourteen taps, very well chosen. A definite dining value.

Crystal Ballroom/Ringler's Pub Ⓑ
1332 W. Burnside, 503-225-0047

★★★☆   11:30 A.M.–5 A.M.

Food: Tavern fare plus   *Smoking:* Separate sections

Ringler's is downstairs, the Crystal Ballroom is upstairs. The ballroom is a Portland landmark, built in 1914 with a mechanical moving floor that gave dancers the feeling they were "floating." Later a great rock 'n' roll venue. The brewpub downstairs serves the usual McMenamins beer and food, but also more upscale offerings.

Dublin Pub

6821 SW Beaverton Hillsdale Highway, 503-297-2889

★★★☆   2 P.M.–late

Food: Tavern fare   *Smoking:* Separate sections

Sprawling Irish pub with regular live music. The back of the bar area is crammed with rows of taps, 104 in all, serving mainstream beers, imports, and mostly Northwest beers. A beer hangout: You might find beer writer emeritus Fred Eckhardt on the stool next to you.

Goose Hollow Inn

1927 SW Jefferson, 503-228-7010

★☆☆☆   Lunch–late

Food: Tavern fare   *Smoking:* Throughout

A small spot owned by former Portland Mayor Bud Clark. The beer menu is modest, but it is nonetheless fun to drink a locally brewed micro in a bar that once held the distinction of selling more Budweiser per square foot than any other pub in the nation.

Gustav's Bier Stube

5035 NE Sandy Blvd., 503-288-5503

★☆☆☆   11 A.M.–11 P.M.

Food: German fare   *Smoking:* Separate sections

Popular spot for those seeking European imports and beer hall food. Music includes polka on the patio in summer. Sixteen taps also pour Northwest craft beers.

Hawthorne Street Ale House

3632 SE Hawthorne Road, 503-233-6540

★★☆☆   Lunch–late

Food: Brewpub fare   *Smoking:* None

An upscale taproom for BridgePort Brewing Co., with food to match the decor. Only Bridgeport beers served, both on tap and from firkins behind the bar.

Hillsdale Brewery & Pub Ⓑ

1505 SW Sunset Blvd., 503-246-3938

★★☆☆   Lunch–late

Food: Tavern fare   *Smoking:* Separate sections

Nothing special to look at, but the first brewpub in the McMenamins chain, with the trademark sun painted on the ceiling, a beer lineup that includes house beers and guest brews, solid affordable food.

Higgins Restaurant & Bar
1239 SW Broadway, 503-222-9070

★★½☆ Lunch–late (opens at 4 P.M. weekends)

Food: Full menu   *Smoking:* Separate sections

Upscale restaurant, serving Northwest regional cuisine. Nine well-chosen taps and an extensive bottle menu include regional favorites and quality imports. Beer-friendly waitstaff, beer-friendly menu items, and solid dining choices across the price spectrum.

Horse Brass Pub
4534 SE Belmont, 503-232-2202

★★★★ 11 A.M.–2:30 A.M.

Food: British pub fare plus   *Smoking:* Throughout

A beer mecca for more than twenty years that also serves quality food. The forty-eight taps offer a full range of beers and always support small new breweries. Four handpumps. As good as a U.S.-based British pub gets. Adjoining Belmont Station sells beer and beer-related items.

Katie O'Brien's
2809 NE Sandy Blvd., 503-234-8573

★★☆☆ Lunch–late

Food: Tavern fare   *Smoking:* Throughout

Formerly know as Coyote's, with comfortable couches. The thirty taps serve mostly regional favorites, but also include some mainstream offerings.

Kells Irish Pub
112 SW 2nd Ave., 503-227-4057

★★☆☆ 11:30 A.M.–closing

Food: Irish pub fare   *Smoking:* Separate sections

Excellent dining spot with a killer single-malt whisky menu, twelve draft beer choices. Terrific forty-foot-long bar with cast-iron pillars, offers real darts and shows Irish soccer and rugby on the television. Hosts the largest Irish festival on the West Coast.

Kelly's Olympian Co.
426 SW Washington St., 503-228-3669

★☆☆☆ 10 A.M.–late (closes at 5 P.M. Sundays)

Food: Tavern fare   *Smoking:* Separate sections

In business since 1902, this storefront tavern has a standup bar, smokeshop in front, and restaurant in the rear. Nineteen taps feature Northwest craft beers.

Kennedy School ⓑ
5736 NE 33ʳᵈ, 503-249-3938

★★★☆   11 A.M.–late

Food: Full menu   *Smoking:* In Detention Bar only

The McMenamins have put a little of everything in this former school that has neighborhood roots back to 1915. It's the second brewpub-and-breakfast in the chain, has a theater, and the Courtyard Restaurant is a showpiece with a menu that goes beyond the average McMenamins tavern. Home to both the Detention and Honors bars.

Laurelthirst
2958 NE Glisan St., 503-232-1504

★★☆☆   9 A.M.–2 A.M.

Food: Tavern fare   *Smoking:* Throughout

A delightful two-room neighborhood tavern, serving a nice range of twenty-one beers on tap. Live music every night.

Lucky Labrador ⓑ
915 SE Hawthorne, 503-236-3555

★★⯨☆   11 A.M.–11 P.M.

Food: Brewpub fare   *Smoking:* Outside only

Casual warehouse setting—wooden floors, rafters, and skylights inside—has made this a very popular gathering spot. Excellent house beers, some on handpump, and dog-friendly patio in back.

Mount Tabor Theater & Pub
4811 SE Hawthorne, 503-301-8213

★☆☆☆   4 P.M.–2:30 A.M.

Food: Pizza   *Smoking:* In pub, not movie theater

Laid-back plus. Once two theaters, one of which now shows movies while the other is a live music venue. The cafe menu is limited, but the nineteen tap selections include beer from a nice variety of smaller breweries.

Old Market Pub & Brewery ⓑ
6959 SW Multnomah, 503-244-0450

★☆☆☆   9 A.M.–late (opens at noon Saturdays and Sundays)

Food: Brewpub fare   *Smoking:* Separate sections

Large brewpub in a former greengrocer's shop, decorated with old grocery store items. Plenty of room for pool, arcade games, darts, and TVs showing sports. Wide range of ales, including guest beers.

Philadelphia's Steaks & Hoagies Ⓑ
6410 SE Milwaukie Ave., 503-239-8544
★☆☆☆   9 A.M.–late evening (limited hours Sundays)
Food: Sandwiches   *Smoking:* Outdoors only

A small sandwich shop with a tiny brewery, making a surprising variety of ales. Serves hoagies and five versions of Philly cheesesteak sandwiches.

Pilsner Room Ⓑ
307 SW Montgomery, 503-220-1865
★★★☆   11:30 A.M.–late
Food: Full menu   *Smoking:* None

An exquisite, well-appointed pub connected to McCormick and Schmick's, an upscale restaurant, and serving McCormick's food. A Full Sail brewery is next door. Offering a full line of Full Sail beers and several guest products. Looks out onto the river.

Portland Brewing/Brewhouse Taproom Ⓑ
2730 NW 31st St., 503-228-5269
★★½☆   Lunch–after dinner
Food: Brewpub fare   *Smoking:* None

Portland Brewing sold its original brewpub on Flanders Street and now operates this large pub by the expanded brewery. Full range of the widely distributed Portland beers. Stockholders entitled to one free pint daily.

Produce Row Café
204 SE Oak, 503-232-8355
★★½☆   11 A.M.–late
Food: Tavern fare   *Smoking:* Separate sections

Horse Brass Pub owner Don Younger will tell you this is where the Oregon craft beer revolution began nearly twenty-five years ago, when Mike McMenamin started serving quality imports and inexpensive food. McMenamin sold his place before later beginning the pervasive McMenamins chain. The beer prices are still great, the food is still a value, the decor has lots of character, and the outdoor deck seating is way above average.

The Ram's Head

2282 NW Hoyt, 503-221-0098

★☆☆☆   11 A.M.–late (opens at noon Sundays)

Food: Tavern fare   *Smoking:* None

The McMenamins version of a Victorian tavern—it's in a neighborhood of Victorian houses. Vintage carpeting in the bar area and classic area rugs on the wooden floors in the dining room. Carved ram's heads decorate the bar, which offers ten company beers as well as guest products.

Rose & Raindrop

532 SE Grand, 503-238-6996

★★★☆   11 A.M.–midnight

Food: Bistro fare   *Smoking:* Separate sections

American alehouse meets British town-center pub. Uphol-stered chairs, elegant woodwork. Plenty of draft choices offer a mixture of imports and regional craft beers, three handpumps. Innovative cuisine, good spirits menu. No television.

The Twilight Room

5242 N. Lombard, 503-283-5091

★☆☆☆   10 A.M.–2 A.M.

Food: Tavern fare   *Smoking:* Throughout

A longtime fixture in North Portland that broadened its beer menu to twenty-two taps without narrowing its clientele. Popular with students from the University of Portland and working-class regulars.

The White Eagle

836 N. Russell Ave., 503-282-6810

★☆☆☆   Lunch–late (opens at 6 P.M. Saturdays, closed Sundays)

Food: Tavern fare   *Smoking:* Separate sections

Just when you thought the McMenamins had run out of ideas for pubs, they bought one of Portland's best known haunted joints. This has been a tavern since 1905 and has a terrific an-tique wooden bar.

Widmer Brothers Brewing Co. & Gasthaus Ⓑ
929 N. Russell, 503-281-3333

★★★☆   Lunch–late

Food: German fare   *Smoking:* None

Gasthaus meets Northwest—not quite a German beer hall, but big and roomy, featuring German foods prepared with a Northwest bent. Beers are Widmer's widely distributed popular interpretations of German styles.

Also in Portland

Alameda Brewhouse, 4765 NE Fremont, 503-460-9025. Brewpub.

Blue Moon Tavern, 432 NW 21st Ave., 503-223-3184. McMenamins pub.

Captain Ankeny's Well, 50 SW Second Ave., 503-223-1375. Tavern.

Duck & Whistle, 3728 NE Sandy Blvd., 503-281-5464. Irish pub.

Fulton Pub & Brewery, 618 SW Nebraska, 503-249-9530. Brewpub.

Greenway Pub, 12272 SW Schools Ferry Road, 503-620-4699. McMenamins pub.

The Gypsy, 625 NW 21st Ave., 503-769-1859. Trendy tavern.

McMenamins, 9710 SE Washington St., 503-254-5411.

McMenanins on Broadway, 1520 NE Broadway, #900, 503-288-9498.

McMenamins Market Street Pub, 1511 SW Park St., 503-497-0160.

McMenamins St. John's Dublin Pub, 8203 N. Ivanhoe St., 503-283-6880.

McMenamins Tavern, 1716 NW 23rd St., 503-277-0929.

Mickey Finn's Brewpub, 1339 NW Flanders St., 503-222-5910. Tavern located where Portland Brewing's first pub was. One of three Mickey Finn's.

Mission Theater & Pub, 1624 NW Glisan, 503-223-4031. McMenamins pub/theater.

Oak Hills Brew Pub, 14740 SW Cornell, 503-645-0286. Brewpub.

Old Chicago, 1211 SE 82nd Ave., 503-786-5009. See Boulder, Colorado.

Raccoon Roadhouse & Lodge, 7424 SW Beaverton Hillsdale Highway, 503-296-0110. Brewpub.

Raleigh Hills Pub, 4495 SW Schools Ferry Road, 503-292-1723.

Red Star Tavern and Roast House, 509 SW Alder St., 503-222-0005. Restaurant.

Rock Bottom Brewery & Restaurant, 210 SW Morrison, 503-796-2739. Brewpub; see Denver, Colorado.

Snake and Weasel, 1720 SE 12th Ave., 503-232-8338. Restaurant/pub.

Tugboat Annie's, 711 SW Ankeny, 503-226-2508. Brewpub.

SALEM

Cascade Microbrewery & Public Fire House ⓑ
3529 Fairview Industrial Way SE, 503-378-0737

    ★★⯪☆   Lunch–late (closes at 9 P.M. Sundays)

Food: Tavern fare   *Smoking:* None

Most of the forty taps here go to excellent Northwest craft beers, with a section reserved for Cascades' own assertive beers, many of which use solid helpings of Cascade hops. Decorated in firehouse motif.

Also in Salem
McMenamins Boon's Treasury Bar and Grill, 888 Liberty NE, 503-399-9062.

Stonefront Tavern, 5690 Commercial St., 503-364-6835. Tavern.

The Ram/Big Horn Brewing Co., 515 12th St. SE, 503-363-1904. Brewpub.

Thompson Brewery & Public House, 3575 Liberty Road S., 503-363-7286. Brewpub.

SANDY

The Elusive Trout
39333 Proctor Road, 503-668-7884

    ★☆☆☆   Lunch–after dinner

Food: Full menu   *Smoking:* Separate sections

Restaurant with well-chosen selection of twenty-one craft beers. No bar area, so grab a seat.

TROUTDALE

Edgefield Manor
2126 SW Halsey St., 503-492-4686

    ★★★☆   11 A.M.–1 A.M.

Food: Full menu   *Smoking:* None

A poor farm that has been converted into a resort, with lodgings, amazing murals, restaurants, a brewery, winery, golf course, herb farm, movie theater, glass blower, and more. A McMenamins showplace, worth visiting just to take a tour.

Also in Oregon

Albany: Oregon Trader Brewing, 140 Hill St. NE, 503-928-1931. Brewpub.

Astoria: Pacific Rim Brewing, 144 11th St., 503-325-1231. Brewpub.

Cannon Beach: Bill's Tavern & Brewery, 188 N. Hemlock, 503-436-2202. Brewpub.

Cave Junction: Pizza Deli & Brewery, 249 N. Redwood Highway, 503-592-3556. Brewpub.

Clackamas: Gustav's German Pub and Grill, 12605 SE 97th Ave., 503-653-1391. German.

McMenamins, 9757 SE Sunnyside, 503-653-8011.

Coos Bay: Bank Brewing, 201 Central Ave., 541-267-0963. Brewpub.

Enterprise: Terminal Gravity Brewing, 803 SE School St., 541-426-0158. Brewpub.

Grants Pass: Blue Pine Brewing, 422 SW Fifth St., #B, 503-476-0760. Brewpub.

Wild River Brewing & Pizza, 595 NE E St., 503-471-7487. Brewpub.

Gresham: Columbia Gorge Brewing Co., 333 N. Main St., 503-674-2537. Brewpub.

Highland Pub & Brewery, 4225 SW 182nd St., 503-665-3015. Brewpub.

LaGrande: Blue Mountain Brewery & Public House, 1610 Jefferson Ave., 541-963-5227. Brewpub.

Lincoln City: Lighthouse Brewpub, 4157 N. Highway 101, 503-994-7238. Brewpub.

Medford: Osprey Ale Brewery & Public House, 404 E. Main St., 541-734-4808. Brewpub.

Southern Oregon Brewing, 145 N. Front St., 541-858-5723.

Mount Angel: Mount Angel Brewing Co., 210 Monroe St., 503-845-9624. Brewpub.

Oregon City: McMenamins, 102 9th St., 503-655-8032.

Pacific City: Pelican Pub & Brewery, 33180 Cape Kiwanda Drive, 503-965-7007. Brewpub.

Redmond: Seventh Street Alehouse, 855 SW 7th, 541-923-3110. Brewpub.

Roseburg: Umpqua Brewing, 328 SE Jackson, 503-672-0452. Brewpub.

Siletz: Siletz Pizza Pub, 267 Gaither, 541-444-7012. Brewpub.

Springfield: BJ's Pizza Grill & Brewery, 4006 Franklin Blvd., 541-741-6114. See Portland.

Springfield: Spencer's Restaurant & Brewpub, 980 Kruse Way, 503-726-1726. Brewpub.

Tigard: John Barleycorn's Restaurant & Brewery, 1460 SW Sequoia Parkway, 503-684-2688. Brewpub.

West Linn: McMenamins, 2090 SW 8th Ave., 503-656-2970. Brewpub.

Beers to look for: Yuengling & Son; Yards Brewing; Victory Brewing; Stoudt's Brewing; Penn Brewing.

Essential stops: Monk's Café in Philadelphia; Northeast Tap Room in Reading; Victory Brewing in Downingtown; Sharp Edge Beer Emporium in Pittsburgh; and KClingers in Hanover.

Just for fun: Straub Brewery in Saint Marys. Home of the Eternal Tap. You can pour yourself a free beer here, actually two. The brewery only asks that you quit after two and wash your glass when you are done.

Best city for a pub crawl: Pittsburgh; tough call (over Philadelphia), but Bloomfield Bridge Tavern puts the Steel City over the top.

ADAMSTOWN

Stoudt Brewing Co.   Ⓑ
State Route 272, 717-484-4387
   ★★★☆   Dinner nightly, hours seasonal
Food: Full menu, German fare   *Smoking:* Separate sections

An award-winning microbrewery with a fine-dining restaurant (the Black Angus), a bier garten, and a long Victorian bar. Hosts beer festivals, also has an antiques mall and hosts antiques markets.

ALLENTOWN

Cannons Pub
448 N. 9th St., 610-820-9313
   ★★☆☆   3 P.M.–2 A.M. (opens at 8 P.M. Saturdays, closed Sundays)
Food: Tavern fare   *Smoking:* Throughout

A small locals' tavern with simply wonderful food. There's a printed menu, but look at the blackboard first for specials. Eight solid taps, nice bottle selection. Excellent three-part beer mural above the bar.

Sterling Hotel

343 Hamilton Ave., 610-433-3480

★★☆☆   4 P.M.–late (closed Sundays through Tuesdays)

Food: Tavern fare   *Smoking:* Separate sections

Harks back to the days when hotel bars were public gathering places. Built in 1858, now an entertainment complex with a bouncing dance floor. A total of sixty-five taps at the various bars, including six for Guinness and several for micros.

Also in Allentown

J.P. O'Malley's, 1528 Union St., 610-821-5556. Smaller sibling of J.P. McGillicuddy's, with twenty taps.

BETHLEHEM

J.P. McGillicuddy's

25 E. Elizabeth Ave., 610-868-0200

★★⯪☆   11 A.M.–2 A.M.

Food: Tavern fare   *Smoking:* Throughout

Stop in to see the 800-pound carved wooden bear that was fashioned with a chainsaw, stay for the seventy-two beers on tap. Former country-and-western bar now sells samplers in flights of five, with plenty of regional beers available.

Also in Bethlehem

Bethlehem Brew Works, 569 Main St., 610-882-1300. Brewpub.

BLOOMSBURG

Russell's

117 W. Main St., 717-387-1332

★★⯪☆   10 A.M.–2 A.M.

Food: Full menu   *Smoking:* Throughout

Set in the oldest building in town, with dining in one room and a bar in the other. Sixteen beers on tap, 400 in the bottle, frequent beer events. Extensive food and wine menus.

BRISTOL

Newportville Inn
4120 Lower Road, 215-785-6090
★☆☆☆   3 P.M.–midnight (opens at 1 P.M. Sundays)
Food: German-American   *Smoking:* Throughout

A 200-year-old inn, serving German and American food and offering both imports and craft beers from seventeen taps. The barroom is modeled after a British pub.

CARLISLE

Market Cross Pub
113 N. Hanover, 717-258-1234
★☆☆☆   Lunch–late
Food: British pub fare   *Smoking:* Separate sections

The food and atmosphere are intended to re-create a British pub, but the lineup from eleven taps and a hundred-plus bottles includes an equal measure of imports and craft beers.

CONSHOHOCKEN

Flanigan's Boathouse
113 Fayette St., 610-828-2628
★★☆☆   11:30 A.M.–late
Food: Tavern fare   *Smoking:* Separate sections

A long and narrow tavern, decorated in a nautical theme, three floors. Offers thirty-six beers on tap here—plenty of mainstream choices, micros, and imports—and fifty-plus at another Boathouse in Malvern (16 Great Valley Parkway).

DOUGLASSVILLE

Douglassville Hotel
8 Old Swede Road, 215-385-3585
★☆☆☆   11 A.M.–1:45 A.M.
Food: Tavern fare   *Smoking:* Separate sections

Another wonderful old hotel bar, built more than 200 years ago (the hotel is now an apartment building). Big square bar has ten taps, with imports and craft beers, plus an extensive bottle menu of 200-plus.

DOWNINGTOWN

Victory Brewing Co. Ⓑ
420 Acorn Lane, 610-873-0881
★★★★ Lunch–late (closed Mondays)
Food: Brewpub fare *Smoking:* Throughout (well ventilated)

Great ales, great lagers, seasonal beers have a cult following, Excellent food, fine bar for beer chatter, try whatever is on the handpump. OK, the former Pepperidge Farm bakery is a bit cavernous and not easy to find, but it's kid-friendly, and once you've been there, it's easy to find your way back.

EASTON

Pearly Baker's Ale House
11 Centre Square, 610-253-9949
★☆☆☆ 11 A.M.–late (earlier hours Sundays, closed Mondays)
Food: Full menu *Smoking:* Separate sections

In a fine old building from the 1800s. The fifteen draft choices favor craft beers. Bar in front room, restaurant in back.

Porter's Pub
700 Northampton St., 610-250-6561
★☆☆☆ 11 A.M.–2 A.M.
Food: Tavern fare *Smoking:* Throughout

A corner pub with a stone wall in the dining area/music room. Ten taps serving both imports and craft beers. Well-chosen bottle list.

Weyerbacher Brewing Co. Ⓑ
20 S. 6th, 610-559-5561
★★☆☆ 4–11 P.M. or midnight (opens at noon Saturdays; closed Sundays and Mondays)
Food: Brewpub fare *Smoking:* Separate sections

Started as a microbrewery, distributing a full range of interesting beers, and added an intimate pub. Located in charming old livery stables.

EMMAUS

The Farmhouse
1449 Chestnut St., 610-967-6225
    ★★⯪☆   5 P.M.–closing (closed Sundays)
Food: French   *Smoking:* None

Intimate upscale dining in a 200-year-old farmhouse beside a golf course. Six well-chosen taps, wide bottle selection, massive single-malt menu. Small bar in stone-walled cellar. Classic beer dinners.

EPHRATA

Wahtney's Inn
2415 Main St., 717-733-2014
    ★☆☆☆   4 P.M.–closing
Food: Full menu   *Smoking:* Separate sections

A tavern first opened on this spot in 1767, and the original floor and ceiling remain. The walls are made of fieldstones. Six draft choices favor imports and craft beers, and there are seventy-plus choices in bottles.

ERIE

Hoppers Brewpub ⓑ
123 W. 14th St., 841-566-0424
    ★☆☆☆   Lunch–late
Food: Brewpub fare   *Smoking:* Separate sections

Brewpub set in an old train station, with the chandeliers, marble, and old soda fountains still intact. The place rumbles when trains roll by. Solid beers.

Also in Erie
Oscar's Pub & Restaurant, 2147 W. 12th St., 814-454-4324. Tavern.
Plymouth Bar, 1109 State St., 814-453-6454. Bar.

EXTON

Drafting Room/Tap Room & Grill
635 N. Pottstown Pike, 610-363-0521
★☆☆☆   11:30 A.M.–late (opens at 10:30 A.M. Sundays)
Food: Full menu   *Smoking:* Separate sections

New place aimed at an upscale crowd, with nouveau menu, solid beer selection, and massive single-malt menu. The fifteen draft choices (also one handpump) favor imports and nationally known micros over local products. The Drafting Room in Springhouse has seventeen taps.

GETTYSBURG

Gettysbrew Ⓑ
248 Hunterstown Road, 717-337-1001
☆☆☆☆   4 P.M.–closing (opens at noon weekends)
Food: Brewpub fare   *Smoking:* On deck

Located in a brick-end barn that served as a Confederate field hospital during the Battle of Gettysburg. Rustic to this day. Small brewhouse serving beers made from extract.

Also in Gettysburg
Gettysburg Brewing, 15 York St., 717-337-0079. Brewpub.

HANOVER

KClingers Tavern
304 Poplar, 717-633-9197
★★★↯   10 A.M.–late
Food: Tavern fare plus   *Smoking:* Separate sections

Restaurant/English pub/sports bar, with a chainsaw over the fireplace. Family dining early, young crowd later. Thirty-eight draft choices, handpumps, 400 bottles. Place to find esoteric beers, vintage choices.

HARRISBURG

Nick's 1014 Café
1014 N. 3rd, 717-238-8844
★★☆☆   11 A.M.–late (opens at noon weekends)
Food: Tavern fare   *Smoking:* Throughout

A classic long tavern with the bar along the wall, fourteen taps, and one handpump, backed up with a good bottle menu. Real darts and pool in the basement.

Also in Harrisburg
Appalachian Brewing Co., 50 N. Cameron St., 717-221-1080. Microbrewery/restaurant.

HOMESTEAD

Chiodo's Tavern
107 W. 8th Ave., 412-461-3113
★☆☆☆   8:30 A.M.–2 A.M.
Food: Tavern fare   *Smoking:* Throughout

Chiodo's has been around for more than fifty years, and that's the last time some of the bric-a-brac on the walls was dusted. Wide-ranging clientele come for two draft beers, bottled beer at fair prices, and the famous mystery sandwich.

HORSHAM

Otto's Brauhaus
233 Easton Road, 215-675-1864
★☆☆☆   7 A.M.–10 P.M.
Food: German fare   *Smoking:* Separate sections

Otto's has been serving excellent German food since the 1930s. Twenty beers on tap and a hundred in bottles. Excellent Sunday buffet.

HUNTINGDON VALLEY

Bethayres Tavern
22131 Huntingdon Pike, 215-947-9729
★★☆☆   10 A.M.–2 A.M. (opens at noon Sundays)
Food: Tavern fare   *Smoking:* Throughout

The motto here is, "Come as a stranger . . . leave even stranger." The thirty-two taps are split almost equally between imports and craft beers, with the selection always changing. The tavern has been called Bethayres since 1937 and has been around for more than 150 years.

LAFAYETTE HILL

General Lafayette Inn Ⓑ
646 Germantown Pike, 610-941-0600
★★☆☆   11 A.M.–2 A.M. (opens at 10 A.M. weekends)
Food: American colonial   *Smoking:* Separate sections

A lovely restored inn that dates to 1732, with plenty of intimate dining areas. Always interesting house beers, well made.

LANCASTER

Lancaster Malt Brewing Co. Ⓑ
302 N. Plum St., 717-391-6258
★★☆☆   11:30 A.M.–late (opens at 11 A.M. Sundays)
Food: Brewpub fare   *Smoking:* Separate sections

The restaurant and bar is tucked within the microbrewery, serving excellent food and well-made beer in a renovated tobacco warehouse. Busy spot, welcoming staff, kid-friendly.

McFly's Pub
10 S. Prince St., 717-299-3456
★★☆☆   5 P.M.–2 A.M.
Food: Tavern fare   *Smoking:* Separate sections

One of three bars in the Restaurant of Avenues, with thirty-seven taps. Solid mix of quality beers, including fine selection of regional products.

Also in Lancaster
Quips, 457 New Holland Ave., 717-397-3903. British pub.
Rookie's Restaurant & Sports Pub, 40 Rohrerstown Road, 717-291-2034. Multi-tap.

MANAYUNK

Dawson Street Pub
100 Dawson, 215-482-5677

★★⯪☆ Noon–2 a.m.

Food: Tavern fare   *Smoking:* Throughout

Formerly a biker bar, now decorated with breweriana and featuring a carefully chosen beer menu. Most of the eight taps go to craft beers, with some imports included in the rotation. Three handpumps.

NEW JERUSALEM

Alexander's
11 Deysher Road, 610-682-0938

★★☆☆ 11 a.m.–2 a.m. (closed Mondays and Tuesdays)

Food: Tavern fare   *Smoking:* Separate sections

Tucked into a stone building with wood beams and an old stove. No bar area but seven great taps and 200 beers available from the attached deli.

NEWTOWN

Isaac Newton's
18 S. State St., 215-860-5100

★★☆☆ 11:30 a.m.–2 a.m.

Food: Brewpub fare   *Smoking:* Separate sections

Caters to neighborhood folks, families with kids, and an upscale crowd that helps keep the selection of esoteric beers fresh. Seventeen taps, with selections changing often; solid bottle menu, also rotated carefully.

PHILADELPHIA

Artful Dodger
400-402 S. 2nd St., 215-922-7880

★☆☆☆ 11:30 a.m.–2 a.m.

Food: Tavern fare   *Smoking:* Throughout

Housed in a 200-year-old building on Head House Square. One of the eight taps changes every month, with the others favoring imports. House beer by Stoudt's.

Bridgid's
726 N. 24th St., 215-232-3232

★★☆☆   Opens for lunch weekdays, for dinner at 4:30
P.M. nightly
Food: European bistro   *Smoking:* None

Tiny bar with a small, Old World dining room in back. Six excellent beers, cask-conditioned ales, good bottle selection.

Cuvee Notredame
1701 Green St., 215-765-2777

★★☆☆   11 A.M.–late
Food: Belgian   *Smoking:* Separate sections

A cosy restaurant that prides itself on its Belgian cuisine, although there's more. A full menu of Belgian beers designed to complement the food.

Dickens Inn
421 S. 2nd St., 215-928-9307

★★☆☆   11:30 A.M.–2 A.M.
Food: Full menu   *Smoking:* Separate sections

Four bars in this rambling restaurant, one an intimate pub on the first level. Mostly imports from sixteen taps, long single-malt menu. Built where the Old Plough Tavern was located in the 1800s.

Dock Street Brasserie Ⓑ
2 Logan Square, 215-496-0413

★★☆☆   11:30 A.M.–late
Food: Brasserie cuisine   *Smoking:* Separate sections

A classy place, set in a high-rise of recent vintage near the Four Seasons Hotel. A half-dozen or so beers available at any given time, with many seasonals in the repertoire.

The Grey Lodge Pub
6235 Frankford Ave., 215-624-2969

★★☆☆   10 A.M.–late (opens at 11 A.M. Sundays)
Food: Tavern fare   *Smoking:* Throughout

A neighborhood tavern, where the ten taps usually include something for the mainstream drinker and plenty of regional choices for the more adventurous. Conversation-friendly, with an eccentric publican and tomato pies.

London Grill
23rd & Fairmount, 215-978-4545

★☆☆☆   11 A.M.–2 A.M. (opens at 5 P.M. Saturdays)

Food: Full menu   *Smoking:* Separate sections

Lovely turn-of-the-century taproom, offering both casual and more upscale dining, voted best bar menu in Philadelphia. Solid draft lineup.

Ludwig's Garten
1315 Sansom St., 215-985-1525

★★☆☆   11:30 A.M.–late

Food: German fare   *Smoking:* Separate sections

A newer German restaurant that opened early in 1999. Exceptional lineup of seventeen German beers on tap, served in a German tavern as well as the dining room.

McGillin's Old Ale House
1310 Drury Lane, 215-735-5562

★★☆☆   11 A.M.–2 A.M. (closed Sundays)

Food: Tavern fare   *Smoking:* Throughout

The wall behind the bar is decorated with operating licenses that date to 1860, when this was the "Bell in Hand." Sits in what looks like an alley, still serves lunches by the ticket system, and offers twenty-one beers on tap.

Monk's Café
264 S. 16th St., 215-545-7005

★★★★   11:30 A.M.–2 A.M.

Food: Belgian cuisine   *Smoking:* Separate sections

Most of the nineteen taps go to Belgian beers, with the others reserved for regional craft products. The back room has an Old World feel, the menu is Belgian-influenced, and beer is an ingredient in many dishes. Extensive and esoteric bottle menu with many vintage beers. The building used to house a hotel that was a "whisky drop" during Prohibition.

Poor Henry's 🅑
829-51 N. American St., 215-413-2469

★★☆☆   Noon–1 A.M.

Food: Brewpub fare   *Smoking:* Separate sections

Henry Ortlieb's family owned the Ortlieb brewery, where Poor Henry's now operates. It's both a packaging microbrewery and a brewpub, offering good food and venturesome beer.

Sugar Mom's Church Street Lounge
225 Church St., 215-925-8219

★★⯪☆   Noon–2 A.M. (closed Sundays)

Food: Tavern fare   *Smoking:* Throughout

A basement bar in a old sugar refinery, with the entrance tucked back off a side street. It has become a beer destination—what's available from twelve taps is always changing, but includes both imports and hard-to-find craft beers—as well as a spot that gets hipper as the night wears on.

Also in Philadelphia

Bridget Foy's, 200 South St., 215-922-1813. Restaurant/pub.

Cavanaugh's, 119 S. 39th St., 215-386-4889. Restaurant/pub.

City Tavern, 138 2nd, 215-413-1443. Historic tavern.

Fergie's Pub, 1214 Sansom St., 215-928-8118. Great local, fine Guinness.

The Irish Bards, 2013 Walnut St., 215-569-9585. Irish pub.

John Patrick's Ale House, 208 Race St., 215-574-0296. Multi-tap.

McMenamin's, 7170 Germantown Ave., 215-247-9920. Neighborhood tavern (not related to Oregon chain).

Manayunk Brewing Co., 4120 N. Main St., 215-483-4943. Brewpub.

Moriarty's, 1116 Walnut St., 215-627-7676. Irish pub.

Plough & Stars, 123 Chestnut St., 215-733-0300.

Red Bell Brewery & Pub, First Union Center, 215-533-6790. Brewpub.

Tavern on Green, 2047 Green St., 215-235-6767. Tavern.

PHOENIXVILLE

The Epicurean Restaurant & Bar
902-B Village at Eland, 610-933-1336

★★☆☆   11 A.M.–late (closed Sundays)

Food: Full menu   *Smoking:* Separate sections

The six taps here rotate quick enough to make your head spin and almost always feature craft beers. More than 250 bottle choices from thirty-two countries. More than forty single-malt whiskies.

Royal Scot
400 Bridge St., 610-983-3070
★☆☆☆   11 A.M.–2 A.M.
Food: British pub fare   *Smoking:* Separate sections

A lively English pub pouring several imports, most of them British, from seven taps. Serious about darts on Tuesday nights.

Also in Phoenixville
Sly Fox, Route 113, 610-935-4540. Brewpub.

PITTSBURGH

Bloomfield Bridge Tavern
4412 Liberty Ave., 412-682-8611
★★☆☆   11 A.M.–2 A.M. (closed Sundays)
Food: Polish fare   *Smoking:* Separate sections until 9 P.M.

A welcoming tavern with the best Polish food in Pittsburgh. Nine taps favor mainstream beer and imports, with more imports in bottles. A late-night music venue.

Church Brew Works 🅑
3525 Liberty Ave., 412-688-8282
★★☆☆   11:30 A.M.–late (noon–10 P.M. Sundays)
Food: Brewpub fare   *Smoking:* Separate section

Brewpub located in a former Catholic church, with the brewhouse sitting right up on the altar. The pub offers good food and a fine lineup of lagers as well as ales.

Fat Heads South Shore Saloon
1805 E. Carson, 412-431-7433
★★½☆   11 A.M.–2 A.M.
Food: Tavern fare   *Smoking:* Throughout

Excellent twenty-tap lineup and bottle selection, informative printed menu. Good stuff on the handpump. Award-winning wings, "Home of the Headwich" breathtaking sandwiches.

Foundry Ale Works 🅑
2816 Smallman, 412-338-9050
★☆☆☆   11 A.M.–10 P.M. (later Fridays and Saturdays, closed Sundays)
Food: Brewpub fare   *Smoking:* Separate sections

Located in a foundry, a reminder of Pittsburgh's heritage. The beer is quite nice, the food is almost as good. It's kid-friendly.

Kaya
2000 Smallman St., 412-261-6565
★★☆☆   11 A.M.–1 A.M.
Food: Caribbean cuisine   *Smoking:* Separate sections

Caribbean-influenced menu—try the yucca fries served with chipotle aïoli sauce—which works really well with beer. A fine cross-section of beer from eighteen taps.

Mad Mex
370 Atwood St., 412-681-5656
★☆☆☆   11 A.M.–2 A.M.
Food: California/Mexican   *Smoking:* Throughout

One of two Mad Mexes. This one is more of a bar, attracting a student crowd for a fine cross-section of beer. Good food, with salsa made fresh daily. Mad Mex on McKnight Road is more family oriented.

Penn Brewery 🅱
800 Vinial St., 412-237-9402
★★⯪☆   11 A.M.–midnight
Food: German fare   *Smoking:* Separate sections

The first brewery-owned restaurant in Pennsylvania since Prohibition, housed in a former brewery. You can see the old cooling caves in the neighboring hillside. Has a separate beer hall, beer garden, and rathskeller. Excellent German beer and food.

Sharp Edge Beer Emporium
302 S. Saint Clair St., 412-661-3537
★★★⯪   11 A.M.–11 P.M. (noon–7 P.M. Sundays)
Food: Tavern fare   *Smoking:* Throughout

Where real people drink real beer. Fifty taps, an astonishingly large number of which go to Belgian beers. Still a neighborhood bar with bargain food and regulars who argue about what the answer to Final Jeopardy will be and toss ice at each other.

Also in Pittsburgh
John Harvard's Brew House, 3466 William Penn Highway, 412-824-9440. Brewpub; see Cambridge, Massachusetts.
Oregon Bar & Grill, 2310 Babcock Blvd., 412-821-4355. Restaurant/pub.
Squirrel Hill Café, 5802 Forbes Ave., 412-521-3327. Tavern.
Valhalla, 1150 Smallman St., 412-434-0208. Brewpub.

READING

Canal Street Pub & Restaurant Ⓑ
545 Canal St., 610-376-4009

★☆☆☆   11 A.M.–1 A.M. (closed Sundays)

Food: Upscale brewpub fare   *Smoking:* Separate sections

Canal Street is an upscale restaurant, with a more casual pub room in front, serving the beer made at Neversink Brewing Co. in the same building. A solid lineup of lagers, which go well with the white-tablecloth meals, and some ales.

Northeast Tap Room
1101 N. 12th St., 610-372-5284

★★★★   3 P.M.–midnight (closed Mondays and Tuesdays)

Food: Bar food   *Smoking:* Throughout

Everybody may not know your name here but they will know the nickname owner/barkeep Pete Cammarano gives you. The perfect corner bar: good beer (twelve well-chosen taps and a handpump), good bottle selection, good prices, good events (Spam-carving contest), good jukebox, funky decor, regular customers, house dog.

Also in Reading
Jimmy Kramer's Peanut Bar, 322 Penn St., 610-376-7373. Tavern.

Third & Spruce Café, 2385 3rd Ave., 610-376-5254. Multi-tap.

SCRANTON

Cooper's Seafood House
701 N. Washington Ave., 717-346-6883

★★☆☆   11 A.M.–2 A.M.

Food: Seafood   *Smoking:* Separate sections

Beer-and-seafood bliss inside a giant ark topped with sea creatures. Twelve beers on tap—both craft choices and imports—and a long bottle list. You can spend a lot on seafood here, or get a lot at a very reasonable price.

SELINSGROVE

Seling's Grove Brewing Co. ⓑ
119 N. Market St., 570-374-7308
    ★★☆☆   4-11 P.M. Wednesdays and Thursdays,
noon–midnight Fridays and Saturdays (closed other days)
Food: Limited tavern fare   *Smoking:* None

A small basement brewpub turning out excellent beer with a small "Frankenbrew" brewing system owners/brewers Heather McNabb and Steven Leason built themselves.

STATE COLLEGE

Zeno's Pub
100 W. College Ave., 814-237-4350
    ★☆☆☆   11:30 A.M.–2 A.M.
Food: Tavern fare   *Smoking:* Throughout

A basement bar for more than twenty years, attracting an eclectic crowd and a stream of returning alums. The fourteen taps offer both imports and craft beers, with one on handpump.

TANNERSVILLE

Barley Creek Brewing Co. ⓑ
Sullivan Trail and Camelback, 717-629-9399
    ★★☆☆   1:30 A.M.–midnight
Food: Brewpub fare   *Smoking:* Separate sections

Barley Creek used what it could from an 1800s farmhouse that used to stand here—for instance, the forty-foot bar is made from red and white oak salvaged from the house. The pub produces solid beer, some of which is sold elsewhere.

WAYNE

Valley Forge Brewing Co.
267 E. Swedesford Road, 610-687-8700
    ★★☆☆   11 A.M.–late
Food: Brewpub fare   *Smoking:* Separate sections

Luscious darker ales star here. Sprawling brewpub—big enough to easily accommodate a sixty-foot replica of a covered bridge that offers more intimate dining—located in former movie theater.

Also in Wayne

John Harvard's Brew House, 629 W. Lancaster, 617-687-6565.
  Brewpub; see Cambridge, Massachusetts.

WILKES-BARRE

Elmer Suds

475 E. Northampton, 717-825-5286

★☆☆☆   4 P.M.–2 A.M. (closed Sundays)

Food: Tavern fare   *Smoking:* Throughout

A two-room restaurant with a bar that has a history with good
beer, offering mostly craft beers among the eleven taps. Also a
150-plus bottle selection. One room is done in barn wood, the
other in tin and brick.

YORK

Cobblestone's Restaurant & Sports Emporium

205 S. George St., 717-848-3866

★★☆☆   11 A.M.–2 A.M.

Food: Tavern fare   *Smoking:* Separate sections

There are sixty-two beers on tap, so plenty of everything; forty-
five TVs, three ten-foot projection screens, and nine pool tables. It's housed in an old Knights of Columbus building,
occupying the ballroom that still has a silver ball hanging from
the ceiling.

Also in Pennsylvania

Ardmore: McCloskey's Tavern, 17 Cricket Ave., 610-642-9280.
  Tavern.

Doylestown: Mugs on Main Street, 211 S. Main St., 215-489-
  7795. Restaurant/pub.

Greensburg: Red Star Brewery and Grille, Train Station at
  Greensburg, 724-850-7245. Brewpub.

Jenkinstown: Deetrick's Café & Bar, 211 Old York Road, 215-
  576-7690. Beer-friendly restaurant.

King of Prussia: brew moon, 160 North Gulph Road, 610-
  2302739. Brewpub; see Boston, Massachusetts.

Lahaska: Buckingham Mountain Brewery, 5775 U.S. 202, 215-
  794-7302. Brewpub.

Lewistown: Jack's Mountain Restaurant & Brewery, 9074 U.S.
  522 S., 717-242-6483. Brewpub.

Manheim: Prussian Street Brewing Co./Summy House Restaurant, 35 Main St., 717-664-3333. Brewpub.

Pittston: Cooper's Waterfront, 304 Kennedy Blvd., 717-654-
  6883. Restaurant.

Springfield: John Harvard's Brewhouse, 1001 Baltimore Pike, 610-544-4440. Brewpub; see Cambridge, Massachusetts.

Swiftwater: Pocono Brewing Co., Route 611, 570-839-7206. Not a brewery, but offers a wide range of beers.

West Chester: Iron Hill Brewery & Restaurant, 3 W. Gay, 610-738-9600. See Newark, Delaware.

Williamsport: Bullfrog Brewery, 229 W. 4th St., 717-326-4700. Brewpub.

Regional beers to look for: Emerald Isle Brew Works, which made excellent beer, quit brewing in 1999 with plans to re-open as a brewpub.
Essential stop: Mews Taverns in Wakefield.
Best city for a pub crawl: Providence.

BRISTOL

Aidan's Pub & Grub
5 John St., 401-254-1940
★☆☆☆   11:30 A.M.–1 A.M.
Food: Tavern fare   *Smoking:* Throughout

An Irish pub/locals favorite with twelve taps (mostly imports), handpump. There's also an Aidan's in Newport.

NARRAGANSETT

Twin Willows
865 Boston Neck Road, 401-789-8153
★☆☆☆   Lunch–closing
Food: Tavern fare   *Smoking:* Separate sections

Irish pub/tavern with fifteen taps that pour a mix of craft beers, imports, and mainstream products, with two handpumps. Some days, you have a choice of three chowders.

Also in Narragansett
Pancho O'Malley's, 140 Point Judith Road, 401-782-2299. Irish pub with Mexican food.

NEWPORT

Yesterday's
28 Washington St., 401-847-0125
★★☆☆   11:30 A.M.–1 A.M.
Food: Full menu   *Smoking:* Separate sections

Really two restaurants here, Yesterday's Ale House and Yesterday's Wine Bar & Grill, with the wine bar non-smoking and the beer and wine selection available in both. Most of the thirty-four beer taps go to craft beers, with some imports.

Also in Newport
The Red Parrott, 348 Thames St., 401-847-3140. Restaurant/
pub.
Wharf Pub, 37 Bowens Wharf, 401-846-9233. Restaurant/pub.

PROVIDENCE

Goff's
7 Point St., 401-454-5773
★☆☆☆   3 P.M.–late (opens at 5 P.M. weekends)
Food: Tavern fare   *Smoking:* Throughout

Classic pub and reminder of when dockside laborers toiled in
this port town and filled the public houses. Sixteen taps, both
imports and micros.

Union Station Brewing   Ⓑ
36 Exchange Terrace, 401-274-2739
★★☆☆   11:30 A.M.–1 A.M. (closes later Fridays and Saturdays)
Food: Brewpub fare   *Smoking:* Separate sections

Located in the old train station, with classic arched doorways
and windows. Draws a business crowd at day, theatergoers at
night. Under the ownership of the John Harvard's chain; see
Cambridge, Massachusetts.

Also in Providence
Custom House Tavern, 36 Weybosset St., 401-751-3630. Tavern.
Patrick's Pub, 381 Smith St., 401-751-1553. Irish pub.
Trinity Brewhouse, 180 Fountain St., 401-453-2337. Brewpub.

WAKEFIELD

Mews Tavern
456 Main St., 401-783-9370
★★★☆   10 A.M.–1 A.M.
Food: Full menu   *Smoking:* Separate sections

A rambling multi-tap, serving sixty-nine beers on tap, with
New England micros very well represented. The bar also has
forty vodkas, forty rums, thirty tequilas, and fifty-plus single-
malts. Good food, great sweet potato fries. Was a men-only
cocktail lounge when it opened in 1947.

Also in Rhode Island

Block Island: Mohegan Café & Brewery, 213 Water St., 401-466-5911. Brewpub.

Middletown: Coddington Brewing Co., 210 Coddington Highway, 401-847-6690. Brewpub.

Pawtucket: The Celtic Pub, 755 Broadway, 401-726-0990. Irish pub.

Plainville: The Chieftain Pub, Route 1, 508-643-9031. Irish pub.

West Warwick: Cowesett Inn, 226 Cowesett Ave., 401-828-4726. Restaurant/pub.

On the Roch's, 1595 Centerville Road, 401-821-3262. Restaurant/pub.

Essential stops: Hunter-Gatherer in Columbia; Barley's in Greenville

Best city for a pub crawl: Charleston.

CHARLESTON

Horse & Cart Café
347 King St., 843-722-0797
    ★☆☆☆   9 A.M.–2 A.M. (closes at midnight Sundays)
Food: Deli menu   *Smoking:* Throughout

A café in the front of the house, bar in the back. The nine taps include a little of everything, and the 170 bottles offer the widest selection in town. Pub trivia night Sunday.

Mike Calder's Pub
288 King St., 843-577-0123
    ★☆☆☆   11 A.M.–late
Food: British pub fare   *Smoking:* Throughout

Very British, with beer signs, flags, and pictures throughout the building. Tin ceiling, classic standup bar. Of the sixteen taps, thirteen are from the UK.

Also in Charleston
Charleston Battery Sandwich Shoppe & Brewpub, 451 King St., 843-805-7799. Brewpub.

The Griffon, 18 Vendue Range, 843-723-1700. English pub.

Market Street Mill, 99 S. Market St., 843-722-6100. Brewpub.

South End Brewery & Smokehouse, 161 E. Bay St., 843-853-4677. Brewpub; see Charlotte, North Carolina.

Tommy Condon's Irish Pub, 160 Church St., 843-577-3818. Irish pub.

Zebo Restaurant & Brewery, 275 King St., 843-577-7600. Brewpub.

COLUMBIA

Beulah's Bar & Grill
902-C Gervais St., 803-779-4655
    ★☆☆☆   4 P.M.–late
Food: Tavern fare   *Smoking:* Throughout

A blues bar with ten beers—imports and craft—on tap, plus nearly a hundred in the bottle. In an old railroad station; bands play in the baggage claim area to patrons seated in the patio.

Hunter-Gatherer Brewery & Ale House Ⓑ
900 Main St., 803-748-0540
★★☆☆   4 p.m.–closing (Tuesdays through Saturdays only)
Food: Eclectic brewpub fare   *Smoking:* Throughout

Distinctive, British-inspired ales served at an ambient temperature. Striking old brick building with hand-hewn beams. African decor.

Also in Columbia
The Publick House, 2307 Denvine St., 803-256-2207. Restaurant/bar.
Vista Brewing, 936 Gervais St., 803-799-2739. Brewpub.

GREENVILLE

Barley's
25 W. Washington St., 864-232-3706
★★☆☆   11:30 a.m.–late (closed Sundays)
Food: Tavern fare   *Smoking:* Throughout

Offspring of the Barley's in Asheville, North Carolina, with twenty-plus taps, the same excellent pizza. High ceilings, casual atmosphere, regular live music.

Also in Greenville
Big River Grille & Brewing Works, 211 E. Broad St., 864-370-1118. Brewpub; see Chattanooga, Tennessee.
Blue Ridge Brewing, 217 N. Main St., 864-232-4677. Brewpub.
Henni's, 103 N. Main St., 864-370-1090. Brewpub.

Also in South Carolina
Aiken: Aiken Brewing Co. Bar & Grill, 140 Laurens St. SW, 803-502-0707. Brewpub.
Clemson: Nick's Tavern & Deli, 107-2 Sloan St. Restaurant/pub.
Hilton Head: Hilton Head Brewing Co., 7C Greenwood Drive, 803-785-2739. Brewpub.
Mount Pleasant: T-Bonz, 1028 Johnny Dodd's Blvd., 803-971-7777. Brewpub.
Myrtle Beach: Liberty Steak House & Brewery, 1321 Celebrity Circle, 803-626-4677. Brewpub.
North Myrtle Beach: Mad Boar Brewhouse, 4706 State Highway 17, 803-272-7000. Brewpub.
Spartanburg: RJ Rockets Brewing Co., 117 W. Main St., 864-583-3100. Brewpub.

SOUTH DAKOTA

Regional beers to look for: Black Hills Brewing. Sioux Falls was investigating adding a bottling line in the summer of 1999.
Essential stops: Sioux Falls Brewing Co. in Sioux Falls.
Just for fun: Jim's Tap in Brookings. Even if you just want to watch the annual ride through (as opposed to attending on motorcyle) they'll ask you to sign a waiver. Oh yeah, bring earplugs.

BROOKINGS

Jim's Tap
309 Main Ave., 605-692-2833
    ☆☆☆☆   7 P.M.–2 A.M. (opens at 4 P.M. weekends)
Food: No kitchen   *Smoking:* Throughout

A dark tavern with imports and an occasional micro on tap. Noteworthy because once a year motorcyclists come from all over to ride their bikes in the back of the bar and out the front door. Also hosts a Medieval Festival in July, with a big feast in the beer garden. An area is roped off for full-armor combat.

RAPID CITY

Firehouse Brewing Co. ⓑ
610 Main St., 605-348-1915
    ★☆☆☆   11 A.M.–late (opens at 4 P.M. Sundays)
Food: Brewpub fare   *Smoking:* Separate sections

In a red-brick firehouse and decorated with fire equipment. Nightclub above the dining area, nice covered beer garden to the side.

SIOUX FALLS

Sioux Falls Brewing Co. ⓑ
431 N. Phillips Ave., 605-332-4847
    ★★☆☆   11 A.M.–late (opens at 1 P.M. Sundays)
Food: Brewpub fare   *Smoking:* Separate sections

Fine dining on the restaurant side, casual in the pub and a patio just outside the pub. A martini bar in the basement. Interesting, well-made beers.

Also in South Dakota
Spearfish: Sanford Pub & Grub, 546 W. Jackson St., 605-642-3204. Brewpub.

Essential stops: Boscos in Germantown or Nashville; Big River in Chattanooga.

Just for fun: Become a cellarman at Boscos and learn how to tap a British firkin.

Best city for a pub crawl: Nashville.

CHATTANOOGA

Big River Grille & Brewing Works Ⓑ
222 Broad St., 423-267-2739

★★☆☆   11 A.M.–midnight

Food: Brewpub fare   *Smoking:* Separate sections

Located in what was once a trolley barn, very nicely appointed. Offers some well-made house ales, some on handpump, good food.

Stone Lion Tavern
418 High St., 423-266-5466

★☆☆☆   3 P.M.–3 A.M.

Food: No kitchen   *Smoking:* Throughout

A neighborhood beer bar housed in what was once a two-car garage. Fifteen taps pour imports and craft beers, and a hundred more choices are available in bottles.

Also in Chattanooga
Hops Grill & Bar, 2122 Gunbarrel Road, 423-499-9252. Brewpub.

CLARKSVILLE

Black Horse Brewery Ⓑ
134 Franklin St., 931-552-9499

★☆☆☆   11 A.M.–late

Food: Bar food   *Smoking:* Separate sections

A cozy pub in the historic downtown, plenty of exposed brick and wood. Full menu, but the real attraction is a selection of pizzas. Accessible beer with an inviting bar downstairs and separate late-night tap room upstairs. A second Black Horse in Knoxville.

GERMANTOWN

Boscos Pizzeria & Brewery 🅱
7615 W. Farmington Blvd., 901-756-7310
    ★★★☆   11 A.M.–late
Food: Brewpub fare   *Smoking:* Separate sections

Chic suburban mall brewpub with an open kitchen and big brick ovens. By regularly brewing a stone beer and promoting cask-conditioned ales, has raised Tennessee beer awareness.

MEMPHIS

Flying Saucer Draught Emporium
130 Peabody Place, 901-523-7468
    ★★½☆   11 A.M.–late (opens at noon Sundays)
Food: Tavern fare   *Smoking:* Throughout

Offspring of the Flying Saucer in Fort Worth, Texas. Here there are seventy-five taps and there's a whole section of saucers/plates devoted to Elvis. Just up the street from the Elvis Café, near Beale Street, and higher beer prices reflect the neighborhood.

North End
346 N. Main St., 901-526-0319
    ★☆☆☆   11 A.M.–11 P.M. (closes later weekends)
Food: Full menu   *Smoking:* Separate sections

A casual hometown restaurant, serving patty melts to seafood. Particularly famous for its hot fudge pie. Nearly 300 bottled beer choices.

Also in Memphis
Union Jax, 117 Union, 901-525-5258. British pub.

NASHVILLE

Beer Sellar
101 Church St., 615-254-9464
    ★☆☆☆   2 P.M.–3 A.M. (opens at noon weekends)
Food: Sandwiches   *Smoking:* Throughout

Brick and stone, very cellar-like, often rowdy. Fifty beers on tap, mostly mainstream choices and imports. Sells cigars.

Blackstone Restaurant & Brewery Ⓑ
1918 W. End Ave., 615-327-9969

★★☆☆　　11 A.M.–late (noon–10 P.M. Sundays)

Food: Brewpub fare　　*Smoking:* Throughout

Woody with just a touch of elegance, gets crowded around the horseshoe bar after work. Dave Miller, an author of books on brewing, produces a full range of well-made ales and lagers.

Boscos Nashville Brewing Co. Ⓑ
1805 21ˢᵗ Ave. S., 615-385-0050

★★★☆　　11 A.M.–3 A.M.

Food: Brewpub fare　　*Smoking:* Separate sections

Considerably different than its suburban sibling in Germantown, set in a brick building in Hillsboro Village; however, the food and beer are presented just as well. Regular special beer events.

Market Street Brewery & Public House Ⓑ
134 2ⁿᵈ St., 615-259-9611

★★☆☆　　11 A.M.–late

Food: Brewpub fare　　*Smoking:* Separate sections

The oak paneling and stained glass give this brewpub a turn-of-the-century feel. Accessible beer, excellent Cajun-inspired food.

Also in Nashville
Big River Grille & Brewing Works, 111 Broadway, 615-251-4677. Brewpub; see Chattanooga.

Broadway Brewhouse, 1900 Broadway, 615-340-0089. Tavern.

Flying Saucer Draught Emporium, 111 10ᵗʰ Ave. S., 615-259-7468. Multi-tap; see Memphis.

Mulligan's Pub & Restaurant, 117 2ⁿᵈ Ave., 615-242-8010. Irish pub.

Seanachie Irish Pub, 327 Broadway, 615-726-2006. Irish pub.

Sherlock Holmes Pub, 2206 Elliston Place, 615-327-1047. British pub.

SEVIERVILLE

Rocky River Brewery and Grille Ⓑ
1444 Hurley Drive (at Governor's Crossing), 403-908-3686

★★☆☆　　11 A.M.–after dinner (closes later in season)

Food: Brewpub fare　　*Smoking:* Separate sections

A massive microbrewery/restaurant in a developing tourist area, offering everything from pizza to steak. Well-made beers brewed to traditional styles. Spacious decks.

Also in Tennessee

Gatlinburg: Smoky Mountain Brewery, 4001 Parkway, 423-436-4200. Brewpub.

Jackson: Barley's Brewhouse & Eatery, 2254 Highland Ave., 901-668-2038. Brewpub.

Johnson City: Sophisticated Otter, 400 Ash St., 423-928-1705. Brewpub.

Knoxville: Black Horse Pub & Brewery, 4429 Kingston Pike, 423-558-6161. Brewpub; see Clarksville.

Calhoun's Barbecue & Brew, 1655 Kingston Pike, 423-673-3377. Brewpub.

Great Southern Brewing Co., 424 S. Gay St., 423-523-0750. Brewpub.

Hops Grill & Bar, 338 N. Peters Road, 423-692-1430. Brewpub.

Union Jacks English Pub, 124 Northshore Drive, 423-584-5161. British pub.

Regional beers to look for: Celis Brewing; St. Arnold Brewing; Shiner (from Spoetzl Brewery); Yellow Rose Brewing; Live Oak Brewing.

Essential stops: The Ginger Man (Houston, Austin, Dallas); The Flying Saucer in Fort Worth.

Just for fun: Humperdinks in Arlington. Watch the people on the Six Flags rollercoaster scream.

Best city for a pub crawl: Austin.

AMARILLO

The Brewpub 🅑
3705 Olsen, 806-353-2622

☆☆☆☆   11 A.M.–1:30 A.M. (closes at midnight Sundays)
Food: Brewpub fare   *Smoking:* Separate sections

Gone are the jockey's silks and horse-racing decorations from when this was Silks. Now, it's a warehouse sports bar with thirty-one TVs and one big-screen.

ARLINGTON

Humperdinks/Big Horn Brewing Co. 🅑
700 Six Flags Drive, 817-640-8553

★★☆☆   11 A.M.–2 A.M.
Food: Brewpub fare   *Smoking:* Separate sections

This brewpub chain operates under several names from Texas (Big Horn Brewing) to the Northwest (Ram Family Restaurants and Tir na nóg Irish pubs) while passing through the Rockies (C.B. & Potts). The beer here is a cut above the others.

J.R. Bentley's, an English Pub
406 W. Abrams, 817-261-7351

★☆☆☆   11 A.M.–2 A.M. (opens at 4 P.M. Sundays)
Food: Tavern fare   *Smoking:* Throughout

Small, woody, dark and a University of Texas/Arlington institution for both professors and students. Mostly UK beers on tap.

AUSTIN

The Bitter End Ⓑ
311 Colorado, 512-478-2337
    ★★★☆   Lunch–late (opens later weekends)
Food: Bistro fare   *Smoking:* Separate sections

Assertive beers—try the Austin Pale Ale—mix well with an innovative menu. Well-executed wood-roasted fare. The downtown pub is in a renovated warehouse, and the B-Side Bar is a popular nightspot featuring live music. Fine spirits and wine selections.

Copper Tank Brewing Co. Ⓑ
504 Trinity St., 512-478-8444
    ★★☆☆   4 P.M.–2 A.M.
Food: Brewpub fare   *Smoking:* Separate sections

Pub in former livery stable, serving solid ales and good food. Furnishings include a ninety-six-foot mahogany bar and lanterns with sheaves of wheat on them, limestone archways and twenty-foot ceilings. Beautiful outdoor patio with stone fountain.

Crown & Anchor
2911 San Jacinto, 512-322-9168
    ★☆☆☆   11 A.M.–2 A.M.
Food: Tavern fare   *Smoking:* Separate sections

Bar near the University of Texas campus with several mainstream lagers, imports, and micros on twenty-seven taps. Frequent winner of the local paper's "best neighborhood bar" award.

Dog & Duck Pub
406 W. 17th St., 512-479-0598
    ★★½☆   7 A.M.–2 A.M. (opens later weekends)
Food: Tavern fare   *Smoking:* Throughout

An English-style pub, serving twenty-ounce pints, with a pressed-tin ceiling and wood throughout. The twenty-eight taps are well-chosen, with both top-flight imports and local micros.

The Draught Horse Ⓑ
4112 Medical Parkway, 512-452-6258
★★☆☆   3 P.M.–closing
Food: Tavern fare   *Smoking:* Throughout

Brewpub with fifty taps, more than forty of them for guest beers from near and afar. House beers are often more esoteric styles. Two handpumps.

The Elephant Room
315 Congress Ave., 512-473-2279
★☆☆☆   4 P.M.–late (opens at 8 P.M. Saturdays and Sundays)
Food: No kitchen   *Smoking:* Throughout

A jazz bar set in a cozy stone cellar, with jazz seven nights a week. Most of the twenty draft choices are European beers.

The Ginger Man
304 W. 4th, 512-473-8801
★★★⯪   2 P.M.–closing (opens at 1 P.M. weekends)
Food: No kitchen   *Smoking:* Throughout

A stunning wall of taps behind the long bar offers eighty draft selections, so the choices tend to be rather complete. There are sofas in both the lounge and library areas and a nice beer garden.

Lovejoys Ⓑ
604 Neches, 512-477-1268
★★☆☆   4 P.M.–2 A.M.
Food: No kitchen   *Smoking:* Throughout

Beer bar or brewpub? It doesn't really matter. This funky place offers a variety of micros and imports along with its own always-interesting beer. Tables fashioned from objects such as manhole covers, discarded doors, and an old plywood coffin.

Shaggy's Caribbean Grill
1600 S. Congress Ave., 512-447-5375
★☆☆☆   11 A.M.–midnight
Food: Caribbean fare   *Smoking:* Separate sections

Caribbean music and Jamaican jerk-style cooking mixed with the Southwest. The twenty-two beers on tap include local craft selections. Beach bar feel.

Waterloo Brewing Co. Ⓑ
401 Guadalupe St., 512-477-1836
★★☆☆　　11 A.M.–2 A.M.
Food: Brewpub fare　　*Smoking:* Separate sections

The first brewpub in Texas, and delightfully casual, with separate outdoor seating areas and a game room. Good beer, solid food.

Also in Austin
Alamo Drafthouse Cinema, 409 Colorado St., 512-867-1839. Movies/beer.
Fadó Irish Pub, 214 W. 4th St., 512-457-0172. Irish pub.
L'Estro Armonico: The Belgium, 3520 Bee Cave Road, 512-328-0580. Belgian restaurant.
The Library, 407 E. 6th St., 512-236-0662. Bar.
Maggie Mae's, 323-325 E. 6th St., 512-478-8541. Bar.
Scholz Garten, 1607 San Jacinto, 512-477-4171. Restaurant/bar.
Shakespeare's Pub, 314 E. 6th St., 512-472-1666. Pub.
Trudy's Texas Star, 409 W. 30th St., 512-477-2935. Bar.

DALLAS

The Barley House
2916 N. Henderson Ave., 214-824-0306
★☆☆☆　　4 P.M.–2 A.M.
Food: No kitchen　　*Smoking:* Throughout

A neighborhood tavern with twenty-six draft choices, plenty of imports but also Texas craft beers. An excellent music venue, where local bands and up-and-coming national acts often play for free.

The Ginger Man
2718 Boll St., 214-754-8771
★★★⯪　　2 P.M.–2 A.M. (opens at 1 P.M. weekends)
Food: No kitchen　　*Smoking:* Throughout

This member of the chain retains a pub feel despite its size. Offers seventy-one beers on tap, served by a knowledgeable staff. Can be very crowded on weekends.

The Old Monk

2847 N. Henderson Ave., 214-821-1880

★★☆☆   4 P.M.–2 A.M. (opens at noon weekends)

Food: Classic European   *Smoking:* Separate sections

A quiet, European-style pub, with nine well-chosen taps and an excellent bottle selection. Beer-friendly cuisine. The lights over the bar were taken from a monastery in Pennsylvania, while the big wood bar came out of a pharmacy in England.

Routh Street Brewery & Grille Ⓑ

3011 Routh St., 214-353-2661

★★★☆   11:30 A.M.–not particularly late (opens at 5:30 P.M. Saturdays, 11 A.M. Sundays)

Food: Brewpub fare   *Smoking:* Separate sections

The Hill Country comes to Dallas, complete with cut limestone and fireplaces. Located in a hundred-year-old house, featuring a wide menu with German dishes and excellent seafood. The menu includes recommended food-and-beer pairings.

Schooner Brewery Ⓑ

1701 N. Market, 214-651-0808

★☆☆☆   11 A.M.–2 A.M.

Food: Brewpub fare   *Smoking:* Separate sections

Previously knowns as Hubcap Brewing. A large sports bar, with high ceilings, lots of neon, and plenty of TVs. Producing a solid lineup of ales.

Stan's Blue Note

2908 Greenville Ave., 214-824-9653

★★☆☆   11 A.M.–2 A.M.

Food: Tavern fare   *Smoking:* Throughout

A large U-shaped bar focuses on a wall holding fifty taps, serving mainstream beers, imports, and craft beers. Shuffleboard, pool, two fenced-in patios.

Also in Dallas

The Angry Dog, 2726 Commerce St., 214-741-4406. Tavern.

British Rose Pub, 8989 Forest Lane, 972-690-8340. British pub.

Copper Tank, 2600 Main St., 214-744-2739. Brewpub.

The Dubliner, 2858 Greenville Ave., 214-818-0911. Irish pub.

Flying Saucer Draught Emporium, 1520 Greenville Ave., 214-824-7468. Multi-tap; see Fort Worth.

Fox & Hound, 18919 Midway Road, 972-732-0804. British pub.

Henk's European Deli & Black Forest Bakery, 5811 Blackwell St., 214-987-9090. Restaurant.

Hoffbrau Steaks & Brewery, 3205 Knox St., 214-559-2680. Brewpub.

Humperdinks/Big Horn Brewing Co., 6050 Greenville Ave., 214-368-1203. Brewpub.

Humperdinks/Big Horn Brewing Co., 2208 W. Northwest Highway, 214-358-4159. Brewpub.

The Tipperary Inn, 5815 Live Oak, 214-823-7167. Irish pub.

Two Rows Brewing Co., 5500 Greenville Ave., 214-696-2739. Brewpub.

EL PASO

Hemingway's Alehouse
214 Cincinnati Ave., 915-532-7333

★☆☆☆   3 P.M.–2 A.M. (opens at 8 P.M. Sundays)
Food: No kitchen   *Smoking:* Throughout

A student bar, decorated with banners for all varieties of drink. Fourteen taps offer something for everybody. Nightly special favors mainstream beers, but craft beers also promoted.

Jaxons Restaurant & Brewing Co. Ⓑ
1135 Airway, 915-778-9696

★☆☆☆   11 A.M.–late (opens at noon Saturdays)
Food: Brewpub fare   *Smoking:* Separate sections

Popular multi-room restaurant with inviting bar seating (both at the bar and in nearby booths). Good food, sometimes interesting beer.

Also in El Paso
Gunther's Edelweiss, 11055 Gateway West, 915-592-1084. German.

FORT WORTH

Flying Saucer Draught Emporium
111 E. 4th, 817-336-7468

★★★☆   11 A.M.–late (opens at 2 P.M. Sundays)
Food: Tavern fare   *Smoking:* Throughout

This was the first Flying Saucer in a chain that now has six pubs and operates in three states. Located in historic Sundance Square in a hundred-year-old building. This location offers more than sixty beers on tap (there are two others in the D/FW area with even more) and is decorated throughout with saucers and collectible plates.

USA Café at Sundance Square Ⓑ
425 Commerce St., 817-335-5400

★☆☆☆   11 A.M.–2 A.M.

Food: Brewpub fare   *Smoking:* Separate sections

The large Statue of Liberty in relief on the front of this pub assures you won't miss it. Patriotic motif continues inside, where there are four dance floors, dining and a sports bar with three walls of TVs.

Also in Fort Worth

The Blarney Stone, 903 Throckmorton, 817-332-4747. Irish pub.
Pig & Whistle, 5731 Locke Ave., 817-551-1143. British pub.

FREDERICKSBURG

Fredericksburg Brewing Ⓑ
245 E. Main, 830-997-1646

★★☆☆   11 A.M.–after dinner (opens at noon Sundays)

Food: German influenced   *Smoking:* Separate sections

"Bed-and-brew" where customers may opt for a beer sampler instead of breakfast. Rooms are decorated thematically in this century-old building that was once a saloon.

GALVESTON

Foam Depot
215 22nd St., 409-762-8894

★★☆☆   4 P.M.–2 A.M. (opens at 2 P.M. weekends)

Food: Pizza   *Smoking:* Throughout

Guess what they sell here. There are twenty-six beers on tap, plenty of imports, some Texas craft beers, and lots of pizzas.

Also in Galveston

Strand Brewery, 101 23rd St., 409-763-4500. Brewpub.

HOUSTON

The Ale House
2425 W. Alabama, 713-721-2333
★★☆☆   2 P.M.–closing
Food: Tavern fare   *Smoking:* Throughout

Patterned after an English pub and a neighborhood staple for nearly twenty years. Has thirty-three taps, serving plenty of imports but also micros. The second floor is a Gulf Coast music venue. Regulars claim the place is haunted.

The Ginger Man
5607 Morningside, 713-526-2770
★★★☆   2 P.M.–2 A.M.
Food: No kitchen   *Smoking:* Throughout

This was the first pub in the chain that takes its name from J.P. Donleavy's 1958 novel. A professorial/grad student crowd from nearby Rice University gathers in what looks very much like a small house to sample beer from sixty-eight taps.

The Hops House 🅑
2321 S. State Highway 6, 713-496-0623
★★☆☆   11 A.M.–2 A.M. (noon–midnight Sundays)
Food: Tavern fare   *Smoking:* Throughout

A fine beer bar with twenty-four taps that added a small homemade brewhouse to produce more esoteric beers. Still offers a solid mix of imports and micros and serves excellent chicken-fried steak.

Houston Brewery 🅑
6228 Richmond Ave., 713-953-0101
★★☆☆   11 A.M.–late
Food: Tavern fare   *Smoking:* Separate sections

The pub simplified its menu in mid-1999—to emphasize its beer, which won three medals at the 1998 Great American Beer Festival.

McGonigel's Mucky Duck
2425 Norfolk St., 713-528-5999
★★☆☆   Noon–2 A.M. (closed Sundays)
Food: Irish, Texas influenced   *Smoking:* Separate sections

A well-kept pub that manages to be lively without being rowdy. Great live music venue most nights—mixing singer-songwriters from the U.S. with folk music from around the world, including Ireland—but still has an open "sessiun" each Wednesday. Twenty-seven taps, handpump.

Molly Maguire's Pub
15945 Kuykendahl, 713-580-6167
★☆☆☆   11 A.M.–2 A.M.
Food: Irish pub fare   *Smoking:* Throughout

One of seven related Irish pubs—most have "Molly" somewhere in the name—in the Houston area. Most offer dozens of beers on tap.

The Richmond Arms
5920 Richmond Ave., 713-784-7722
★★⅟☆   11 A.M.–2 A.M.
Food: British pub fare   *Smoking:* Separate sections

A Texas-sized English pub with seventy-three taps. Woody and broken up into enough snugs to keep it intimate despite its size.

The Shakespeare Pub
14129 Memorial Drive, 713-497-4625
★☆☆☆   2 P.M.–2 A.M. (opens at 6 P.M. Saturdays and Sundays)
Food: No kitchen   *Smoking:* Throughout

English pub by name, decoration, and beer selection (most of the twelve tap choices are British ales, but there are other imports and craft beers); also a fine zydeco and blues music venue.

Timberwolf Pub
2511 Bissonnet, 713-526-1705
★★★⅟   2 P.M.–2 A.M.
Food: No kitchen   *Smoking:* Throughout

Not quite as big as its Tempe, Arizona, offspring, serving a hundred beers on tap, both imports and micros with plenty of Texas beers. Also built to look like a large log cabin and old Yukon Territory outpost.

Also in Houston
Bank Draft Brewing Co., 2424 Dunstan, 713-522-6258. Brewpub.
Brewery Tap, 717 Franklin St., 713-237-1537. Multi-tap.
Claddagh Irish Pub & Grill, 5757 Westheimer, #105, 713-789-4858. Irish pub.
Huey's Restaurant, 15335 N. I-45, 713-875-2260. Brewpub.
Irish Rover, 10226 Westheimer Road, 713-783-7972. Irish pub.

Old Heidelberg, 1810 Fountainview, 713-781-3581. German restaurant.

Rudyard's British Pub, 2010 Waugh Drive, 713-521-0521. British pub.

Two Rows Restaurant & Brewery, 2400 University, 713-529-2739. Brewpub.

LUBBOCK

Bash Rip Rock
2419 Main, 806-762-2274

★★☆☆   6 P.M.–late (opens at 3 P.M. Fridays)
Food: Tavern fare   *Smoking:* Throughout

Lubbock's first beer bar, offering twenty beers—both mainstream and specialty—plus more than 200 in the bottles.

Cricket's Draft House
2412 Broadway, 806-744-4677

★★☆☆   4 P.M.–late
Food: Sandwiches, pizza   *Smoking:* Throughout

No-frills bar with an unusually large draft selection—the seventy-six drafts include mainstream lagers, imports, and micros.

Hub City Brewing Co. Ⓑ
1805 Ave. G, 806-747-1535

★☆☆☆   11 A.M.–2 A.M.
Food: Brewpub fare   *Smoking:* Separate sections

Airy brewpub with serving tanks on display behind the bar. Wood-fired pizza. Produces lagers as well as ales.

PLANO

Bavarian Grill
221 W. Parker Road, 972-881-0707

★☆☆☆   11 A.M.–late
Food: German fare   *Smoking:* Separate sections

Traditional Bavarian food and more than fifty German beers. Live accordion music nightly, with customers invited to sing along or do the chicken dance.

SAN ANTONIO

Blue Star Brewing Co. Ⓑ
1414 S. Alamo, #105, 210-212-5506
    ★★⯪☆   11 A.M.–late (closed Sundays)
Food: Brewpub fare   *Smoking:* Separate sections

Located in an old warehouse on the banks of the San Antonio River, turning out a surprising range of excellent beer, some served through a beer engine. Southwestern and American cuisine, some Texas wines.

Hills & Dales Ice House
15403 White Fawn Drive, 210-695-2307
    ★★⯪☆   11:30 A.M.–midnight
Food: No kitchen   *Smoking:* Throughout

In an old ice house, offering fifty-four beers on tap, both imports and micros. A package store, so there are 400 bottle choices. Beer is served in plastic cups, but you can bring your own mug.

Houston Street Alehouse
420 E. Houston St., 210-354-4694
    ★☆☆☆   2 P.M.–2 A.M.
Food: Sandwiches   *Smoking:* Throughout

A cigar-friendly bar a block from the river, experimented with forty-eight taps but dropped back to twenty-five when the beer wasn't moving. Plenty of mainstream lagers with some imports and micros.

Also in San Antonio
Fox & Hound English Pub and Grille, 12651 Vance Jackson, 210-696-1356. British pub.

Laboratory Brewing Co., 7310 Jones Maltsberger, 210-824-1997. Brewpub.

Mama's Hofbrau, 9903 San Pedro Ave., 210-342-3219. Restaurant/bar.

O'Neill's Irish House, 302 E. Commerce St., 210-222-8550. Irish pub.

SAN MARCOS

The Tap Room
129 Hopkins, 512-392-9824
★★☆☆   3 P.M.–late (closed Sundays)
Food: Tavern fare   *Smoking:* Throughout

Popular spot for those beyond college age to gather after work and choose from thirty-seven taps—mostly imports and micros. Excellent ribs.

Also in San Marcos
Café & Brewpub on the Square, 126 N. LBJ, 512-353-9289. Brewpub.

SEABROOK

Boondoggles' Pizzeria & Brewery Ⓑ
4106 NASA Road One, 281-326-2739
★★⯪☆   3 P.M.–2 A.M.
Food: Brewpub fare   *Smoking:* Throughout

The brewpub has fifty taps, with all but a few handles going to an outstanding lineup of guest beers. Solid in-house beers, including the hoppy Ruby's Red.

Also in Seabrook
Bay Brewery Steaks & Food, 730 Todville Road, 281-291-0022. Brewpub.

WACO

Cricket's Grill & Draft House
221 Mary Ave., 254-754-4677
★★★☆   11 A.M.–2 A.M.
Food: Tavern fare   *Smoking:* Separate sections

Offspring of the Cricket's in Lubbock and even bigger with ninety-seven taps. Situated in an old train warehouse with high ceilings and nice booths.

Also in Texas
Addison: Flying Saucer Draught Emporium, 14994 Montfort, 214-991-7093. A hundred-plus taps; see Fort Worth.
Hoffbrau Steaks Brewery, 4180 Beltline Road, 214-392-1196. Brewpub.
Humperdinks/Big Horn Brewing Co., 3820 Beltline Road, 972-484-3051. Brewpub.

Old Chicago, 4060 Beltline Road, 214-490-3900. See Boulder, Colorado.

Rock Bottom Brewery & Restaurant, 4050 Beltline Road, 214-404-5456. Brewpub; see Denver, Colorado.

Irving: Humperdink's/Big Horn Brewing Co., 4959 N. O'Connor Blvd., 972-717-5515. Brewpub.

New Braunfels: Faust Brewing Co., 240 South, 830-625-7791. Brewpub.

South Padre Island: Kelly's Irish Pub, 101 Morningside, 956-761-7571. Irish pub.

Padre Island Brewing Co., 3400 Padre Blvd., 210-290-5992. Brewpub.

Webster: Bradley's Restaurant & Brewery, 515 W. Bay Area Blvd., 713-332-8488. Brewpub.

UTAH

Regional beers to look for: Wasatch Brewing; Uinta Brewing.
Essential stops: Red Rock Brewery in Salt Lake; Fiddler's Elbow in Sugarhouse.
Best city for a pub crawl: Salt Lake City.
Worth noting: Because Utah is one of two states that has a statewide 3.2 percent beer law (Oklahoma is the other), some thirsty travelers would rather detour around it. The truth is, Utah brewers consistently prove that it's possible to brew flavorful beer that is 3.2 percent alcohol by weight (equal to 4 percent by volume, about the same as Fuller's London Pride, a British classic).

Utah also has many private clubs, where it's possible to buy stronger beer (plus wine and spirits). Usually, customers simply pay at the door to become a member. Restaurants can hold liquor licenses and sell spirits and stronger beer, but customers there must buy dinner in order to drink.

MOAB

Eddie McStiff's Restaurant & Micro Brewery Ⓑ
57 S. Main, 435-363-2739
> ★☆☆☆   3 P.M.–midnight
> ***Food:*** Brewpub fare   ***Smoking:*** Separate sections

Offers a wide range of ales. Set in the hub of canyonland, just four miles from Arches National Park, making it a popular stop for cyclists.

Also in Moab
Moab Brewery, 686 S. Main, 435-259-6333. Brewpub.

OGDEN

Rooster's 25th Street Brewery Ⓑ
253 25th St., 801-627-6171
> ★☆☆☆   Lunch–after dinner (earlier hours Sundays)
> ***Food:*** Brewpub fare   ***Smoking:*** Separate sections

Beer menu includes Polygamy Ale ("drink one and you'll want another, and another . . ."). Two-story pub in a hundred-year-old building in heart of historic 25th Street. Outdoor barbecues in summer.

Also in Ogden
Ruby River Steakhouse & Brewery, 4286 Riverdale Road, 801-394-0302. Brewpub.

PARK CITY

Park City Brewing Co./Town Lift Pub 🅑
838 Park Ave., 435-649-4323
    ★☆☆☆   11 A.M.–11 P.M.
Food: Brewpub fare   *Smoking:* None

Located just thirty yards from a ski chairlift. Smokehouse menu served in pub area. Five regular beers include distinctive pilsener.

Wasatch Brewpub 🅑
250 Main St., 435-645-9500
    ★★☆☆   11 A.M.–midnight
Food: Brewpub fare   *Smoking:* Separate sections

Wasatch ales have been available throughout the area since 1986, and the pub began operating in 1989. Also serves other alcohol and wine.

Also in Park City
Mulligan's Irish Pub, 804 Lower Main St., 435-658-0717. Irish pub.

SALT LAKE CITY

Brewvies
677 S. 200 West, 801-322-3891
    ★☆☆☆   5 P.M.–1 A.M. (earlier weekends)
Food: Brewpub fare, pizza   *Smoking:* None

A restaurant, movie theater, and tavern rolled into one, with second-run movies, a wide assortment of Utah microbrewed beers on tap. Pool.

Desert Edge Brewery at the Pub 🅑
273 Trolley, 801-521-8917
    ★☆☆☆   Lunch–after dinner
Food: Brewpub fare   *Smoking:* None

Located in Trolley Square, a trolley repair station converted into a mall. Shiny outside, comfortable inside with wood plank floors. Latter Days Stout deserves awards it has won.

Lazy Moon Pub
32 Exchange Place, 801-521-8917
★☆☆☆   Lunch–late (opens later weekends)
Food: Pizza, pasta   *Smoking:* None

Intimate setting in former boiler room of a steam plant. Both Utah and other microbrewed beer on tap, distinctive pizzas and pasta.

Port O' Call Social Club
7½ W. 400 South, 801-521-0589
★☆☆☆   10 A.M.–1:30 A.M.
Food: Tavern fare   *Smoking:* Separate sections

Three floors, plenty of TVs. First floor for those who want to see and be seen, basement for the younger set, and rooftop patio for the mellower. Wide range of beers on tap. Private club.

Red Rock Brewery Ⓑ
254 S. 200 West, 801-521-7446
★★⯪☆   Lunch–late
Food: Brewpub fare   *Smoking:* None

Spacious brewpub located in a former creamery. Distinctive beer, from the best-selling dry-hopped amber to a variety of specialties that win awards in national competitions.

Squatter's Pub Brewery Ⓑ
147 W. Broadway, 801-363-2739
★★☆☆   11:30 A.M.–1 A.M.
Food: Brewpub fare   *Smoking:* None

First brewpub in town, opening in 1989 in carefully refurbished Boston Hotel. Comfortable wood and brick setting. Handpumped ales served at ambient temperature.

SUGARHOUSE

Fiddler's Elbow: An American Roadhouse
1063½ E. 2100 South, 801-463-9393
★★⯪☆   Lunch–late (breakfast Sundays, and closes earlier)
Food: Tavern fare   *Smoking:* None

Thirty-two beers on tap, plenty of microbrewed beer, mostly from Utah. Inviting patio in back. Darts, pool, and six satellite TV feeds for sports fans.

Also in Utah

Brighton: Molly Green's Pub, Mt. Majestic Manor, 435-649-7908. Irish pub.

Helper: Pinnacle Brewing Co., 1653 N. Carbonville Road, 435-637-2924. Brewpub.

Midvale: Avalanche Brewing Co., 94 E. 7200 South, 801-565-3773. Brewpub.

Hoppers Grill & Brewing Co., 890 E. Fort Union Blvd., 801-566-0424. Brewpub.

Regional beers to look for: Catamount; Magic Hat; Otter Creek; Long Trail.

Essential stops: McNeill's in Brattleboro; Vermont Pub & Brewery in Burlington.

Just for fun: Three Needs in Burlington. "Simpsons" Happy Hour six days a week.

Best city for a pub crawl: Burlington.

BRATTLEBORO

McNeill's Brewery ⓑ
90 Elliot St., 802-254-2553
★★★☆   4 P.M.–closing
Food: Tavern fare   *Smoking:* None

Simply a beer place, where customers who like beer leave smiling. Minimalist menu, no TV, conversation-friendly. Broad range of excellent house beers.

Also in Brattleboro
Latchis Grille, 50 Main St., 802-254-4747. Brewpub.

BURLINGTON

Three Needs Brewery & Taproom ⓑ
207 College St., 802-658-0889
★★⯪☆   4 P.M.–2 A.M.
Food: No kitchen   *Smoking:* Separate sections

A popular, conversation-friendly locals' spot that serves eight guest craft beers along with its own well-made brews. "Simpsons" Happy Hour is celebrated Monday through Friday from 5–6 P.M. and Sunday at 8 P.M.

Vermont Pub & Brewery ⓑ
144 College St., 802-865-0500
★★★☆   11:30 A.M.–12:30 A.M.
Food: Full menu   *Smoking:* Separate sections

A multi-room restaurant, with lovely outdoor seating and a very publike bar area. Excellent lineup of beers, good food, the first brewpub in Vermont.

Also in Burlington
Ruben James Restaurant, 159 Main St., 802-864-0744. Brewpub.

NORWICH

Jasper Murdock's Alehouse Ⓑ
225 Maine St., 802-649-1143

    ☆☆☆☆   Call for hours

Food: Tavern fare   *Smoking:* Separate sections

The history of the Norwich Inn, which is said to have a house ghost, dates back more than 200 years to when it was a stage-coach stop. Jasper Murdock's is tucked into the back of the inn, offering casual dining and usually about three ales from a tiny brewhouse.

PLYMOUTH

Salt Ash Inn Ⓑ
Junction Routes 100 & 100A, 800-725-8274

    ★☆☆☆   4-10 P.M. (closed several months a year)

Food: Not in pub   *Smoking:* None

Built in 1830 as a stop on the Woodstock-Ludlow stagecoach line, the Salt Ash Inn is an eighteen-room bed and breakfast. The tiny brewpub (batches are brewed twelve gallons at a time) is intended as "a pleasant surprise" for guests. Eight taps dispense a combination of house ales and other Vermont-brewed beer.

STOWE

Mr. Pickwick's Polo Pub
433 Mountain Road, 802-253-7558

    ★☆☆☆   10:30 A.M.–2 A.M.

Food: Upscale British pub   *Smoking:* Separate sections

Located in Ye Olde English Inne, with twenty tap choices, including UK imports and American craft beers. Two hand-pumps. Huge fireplace, lots of beams, stone, and brass.

The Shed Restaurant Ⓑ
1859 Mountain Road, 802-253-4364

    ★★☆☆   11:30 A.M.–1 A.M. (opens at 9 A.M. Sundays)

Food: Full menu   *Smoking:* Separate sections

A popular restaurant rebuilt after a fire in 1994 and now serving six ales brewed on premise. Foster's Cider Mill was first built on this spot in 1830.

Also in Vermont

Bennington: Madison Brewing Co., 428 Main St., 802-442-7397. Brewpub.

Bridgewater Corners: Trailhead Pub/Long Trail Brewing Co., Junction Routes 4 and 100A, 802-672-5011. Microbrewery tasting room.

Killington: McGrath's Irish Pub, Route 45, 802-775-7181. Irish pub.

Ludlow: Black River Brewing Co., 207 Main St., 802-228-3100. Brewpub.

Shelburne: The Pump House Inn, Falls Road, 802-985-3728. Restaurant/pub.

Waitsfield: Gallagher's Tavern & Brewery, Junction Routes 17 & 100, 802-496-8800. Brewpub.

VIRGINIA

Regional beers to look for: Old Dominion Brewing; Legends Brewing.

Essential stops: Sweetwater Tavern in Centreville; Tuscarora Mill in Leesburg; Bistrot Belgique Gourmande in Occoquan.

Just for fun: Bardo Rodeo in Arlington. Its precise future is up in the air as we write this, but it surely will remain unique.

Best city for a pub crawl: Arlington.

ALEXANDRIA

Bilbo Baggins
208 Queen St., 703-683-0300

    ★☆☆☆   11:30 A.M.–10:30 P.M. (earlier hours Sundays)

Food: Full menu   *Smoking:* Separate sections

Large, filling three historic townhouses, and known first as a restaurant with a major wine menu. Now offering ten draft choices and favoring regional beers.

Union Street Public House
121 S. Union St., 703-548-1785

    ★☆☆☆   Lunch–late

Food: Full menu   *Smoking:* Separate sections

The Tap Room is one of four eating-and-drinking areas in this well-kept but large Old Town fixture. House beer from Old Dominion, wide range of micros on tap.

Virginia Beverage Co. Ⓑ
607 King St., 703-684-5397

    ★★☆☆   Lunch–late

Food: Brewpub fare   *Smoking:* Separate sections

Popular brewpub with long lines many weekend nights. Solid, sometimes excellent beer. Puts a firkin on the bar several times a month.

Also in Alexandria
Bullfeathers, 112 King St., 703-836-8088. Sports bar.

Hard Times Café, 1404 King St., 703-683-5340. Restaurant.

Murphy's Grand Irish Pub, 713 King St., 703-548-1717. Irish pub.

ARLINGTON

Bardo Rodeo
2000 Wilson Blvd., 703-527-9399
☆☆☆☆   11:30 A.M.–2 A.M.
Food: Tavern fare   *Smoking:* None

This one-of-a-kind brewpub downsized, moving its brewing equipment elsewhere in 1999. Legal problems kept it from immediately brewing beer here. Call for status.

Galaxy Hut
2711 Wilson Blvd., 703-525-8646
★★☆☆   5 P.M.–2 A.M. (opens at 7 P.M. Saturdays and Sundays)
Food: Tavern fare   *Smoking:* Throughout

A small pub that offers a solid selection from fifteen taps (a few imports, mostly craft beers) served by a knowledgeable waitstaff.

Hard Times Café
3206 Wilson Blvd., 703-528-2233
★☆☆☆   11:30 A.M.–after dinner (opens at noon weekends)
Food: Chili   *Smoking:* Separate sections

A popular chain of chili parlors serving both Cincinnati-style and Texas-style chili (also vegetarian chili) along with a variety of craft beers.

Rhodeside Bar & Grill
1836 Wilson Blvd., 703-243-0145
★☆☆☆   Lunch–late (opens at 5 P.M. Saturdays)
Food: Full menu   *Smoking:* Separate sections

A one-stop club, with a popular lounge, excellent food, and interesting music. Comfortable basement bar has fourteen solid—though little special—taps, also darts and pool.

Also in Arlington
Capitol City Brewing Co., 2700 S. Quincy St., 703-578-3888. Brewpub.
Champion Billiards Café, 2620 Shirlington Road, 703-521-3800. Pool hall.

ASHBURN

Old Dominion Brewery/Pub 🅑
44633 Guildford Drive, 703-689-1225
★★★☆   11:30 A.M.–9 P.M. (closes at 10 P.M. Fridays and
Saturdays; noon–6 P.M. Sundays)
Food: Tavern fare   *Smoking:* Separate sections

Brewery tap for Old Dominion. Limited menu, but mostly a
place to taste the full line of beers—both excellent ales and
lagers—including Hop Pocket Ale.

BLACKSBURG

Ton 80
215 N. Main St., 540-552-3068
★☆☆☆   Noon–2 am
Food: Tavern fare   *Smoking:* Throughout

Upstairs neighborhood tavern with eight darts lanes, fair tap
selection and wide range in bottles. Excellent North Carolina-
style, hickory-smoked barbecue sandwiches.

CENTREVILLE

Sweetwater Tavern & Brewery
14250 Sweetwater Lane, 703-449-1100
★★★☆   4:30 P.M.–late (opens earlier weekends)
Food: Brewpub fare   *Smoking:* Separate sections

Innovative beers from brewer Nick Funnell, excellent Southwestern fare. Chairs from Taos, New Mexico, and cowboy furniture from Santa Fe. There's also a Sweetwater brewpub in
Merrifield.

CHARLOTTESVILLE

Court Square Tavern
Fifth and East Jefferson, 804-296-6111
★☆☆☆   11:30 A.M.–late (opens at 5 P.M. Sundays)
Food: Tavern fare   *Smoking:* Separate sections

A traditional tavern, with plenty of wood and an emphasis on
conversation. Eight excellent draft choices include imports and
craft beers. Another 120-plus bottles to choose from.

Also in Charlottesville
Blue Ridge Brewing, 709 W. Main St., 804-977-0017. Brewpub.
Monticello Brewing Co., 946 Grady Ave., 804-971-8229. Brew-on-premise with pub.
South Street Brewery, 106 South St., 804-293-6550. Brewpub.

LEESBURG

Tuscarora Mill
203 Harrison St., 703-938-9548
    ★★★☆   Lunch–closing
Food: Full menu   *Smoking:* Separate sections

Set in an old grain mill in a town that was settled in 1758. Up-scale restaurant with a more casual bar area called Tuskies. The selection from twenty-one taps is always changing, lineup is heavy on craft beers.

MANASSAS

Hero's American Restaurant
9412 Main St., 703-330-1534
    ★★🌓☆   Lunch–late
Food: Tavern fare   *Smoking:* Separate sections

An American pub with exposed brick walls and wood floors, plus sixteen taps pouring twenty-ounce pints. Almost all the beer comes from craft breweries, most of them regional.

OCCOQUAN

Bistrot Belgique Gourmande
302 Poplar Alley, 703-494-1180
    ★★★★   Call for hours
Food: Belgian cuisine   *Smoking:* Separate sections

Intimate, conversation-friendly, forty-seat restaurant with excellent Belgian food and beer, losing its reputation as one of the D.C. area's best-kept secrets. Most beers are served with their own glass bearing the brewery's name. Pommes frites beyond compare, special mussels nights, and terrific brunch. No bar area.

RICHMOND

Cobblestone Pub & Brewery
110 N. 18th St., 804-644-2739
★★☆☆ 4 P.M.–2 A.M. (opens earlier weekends)
Food: Tavern fare   *Smoking:* Throughout

One of many bars in the Shockoe Bottom, offering thirty beers on tap, most of them craft products. Not a brewery.

Commercial Tap House & Grill
111 N. Robinson, 804-359-6544
★★☆☆ 4:30 P.M.–1 A.M. (opens at 2 P.M. Sundays)
Food: Tavern fare   *Smoking:* Throughout

Fine stop in the "Fan," one mile from downtown. Neighborhood spot offering twelve draft choices, most of them craft beers, and a solid bottle lineup that includes several Belgian ales.

Richbrau Brewery Co. & Restaurant
1214 E. Cary St., 804-644-3018
★★☆☆ Lunch–late (closes early Sundays)
Food: Brewpub fare   *Smoking:* Separate sections

Copper-topped tables and a fireplace enhance the pub room, where the choicest seats are directly in front of the windows looking onto the street. There's also a dining room, a pool room upstairs, and another with a fish tank with turtles in it. Solid beer and good food.

Also in Richmond
Fox & Hounds, 10455 Midlothian, 804-272-8309. British pub.
Legend Brewing, 321 W. 7th St., 804-232-8871. Brewery taproom.
Penny Lane, 207 N. 7th St., 804-780-1682. British pub.

VIRGINIA BEACH

Jewish Mother
3108 Pacific Ave., 757-422-5430
★☆☆☆ Early morning–late
Food: Deli   *Smoking:* Separate section

Deli known for its desserts, offering national music acts into the wee hours. International bottled beer menu.

Also in Virginia Beach
Taphouse Brewery & Grill, 2865 Lynnhaven Drive, 757-412-0424. Brewpub.

WILLIAMSBURG

Green Leafe Café
765 Scotland St., 757-220-3405
★★⯪☆   11 A.M.–2 A.M.
Food: Tavern fare plus   *Smoking:* Separate sections

An outstanding beer stop where eighteen draft choices are well-handled and the beer dinners are excellent. Some of the tabletops were made from an old bowling alley and the benches are pews out of an old church.

Also in Virginia
Annandale: Main Street USA, 7131 Little River Turnpike, 703-750-0777. Tavern.
Falls Church: The Pawnshop, 5179 Leesburg Pike, 703-998-5306. Restaurant.
Great Falls: Old Brogue, 760-C Walker Road, 703-318-8941. Irish pub.
Herndon: Hard Times Café, 394 Elden St., 703-318-8941. Restaurant.
Newport News: Atlanta BeerGarten, 12644 Jefferson Ave., 757-988-1669. Brewpub.
Norfolk: Commercial Taphouse & Grill, 931 W. 21st St., 757-627-9127. See Richmond.
    Reggie's British Pub, 333 Waterside Drive, 757-627-3575. British pub.

Regional beers to look for: Another state where no list can be complete, but a quick five are Red Hook, Pike, Hale's, Pyramid, and Fish. Pubs in Seattle have made a specialty of tracking down unique beers from small brewers. One example is Diamond Knot, which makes an amazing IPA. Until recently, the brewery operated in 280 square feet in the back of a tavern. It bought the tavern, in Mukilteo, in 1999 and promised to turn it into a brewpub.

Essential stops: Archer Ale House in Bellingham; Fred's Rivertown Ale House in Snohomish; The Swiss in Tacoma; and the Latona Pub in Seattle.

Just for fun: The Brick in Roslyn. The oldest tavern in the state, it will look familiar because it was used in many movies and the TV show "Northern Exposure."

Best city for a pub crawl: Seattle, where you'll never have to leave a neighborhood—Fremont is the best example—to complete a multi-pub crawl.

ANACORTES

Anacortes Brew House 🅑
320 Commercial Ave., 360-293-2444
    ★★☆☆   11:30 A.M.–11 P.M. (opens at 3 P.M. Saturdays and Sundays)
Food: Brewpub fare   *Smoking:* None

Two gold miners built a tavern on this site in 1910, it burned to the ground and was rebuilt as Bogart's Saloon in 1929. Now a bright, airy brewpub with a solid lineup of ales.

BAINBRIDGE ISLAND

The Harbour
231 Parfitt Way SW, 206-842-0969
    ★☆☆☆   11 A.M.–midnight
Food: Tavern fare   *Smoking:* None

A ferry ride from Seattle, this café opened in 1992 in a remodeled home that was built in 1881. A large deck overlooks the harbor, the daily food specials really are, and the twelve taps feature Northwest craft beer.

BELLEVUE

The New Jake O'Shaughnessey's
401 Bellevue Square, 425-455-5559
★★☆☆   11 A.M.–11:30 P.M.
Food: Full menu   *Smoking:* Separate sections

Luxurious steak-and-seafood restaurant with a constantly rotating selection of thirty-six beers on tap. Large single-malt list.

Also in Bellevue
Rock Bottom Brewery & Restaurant, 550 106th Ave. NE, 425-464-9300. Brewpub; see Denver, Colorado.

BELLINGHAM

Archer Ale House
1212 10th St., 360-647-7002
★★★★   3 P.M.–late (opens at 1 P.M. Saturdays)
Food: Tavern fare   *Smoking:* None

Conversation sets this immaculately-kept pub apart as much as the beer, which is terrific and well cared for. The ten taps serve a perfect mix of local craft beer and international classics. Excellent bottle menu includes fifty Belgian beers.

Also in Bellingham
Boundary Bay Brewery, 1107 Railroad Ave., 360-647-5593. Brewpub.
Orchard Street Brewery, 709 W. Orchard Drive, 360-647-1614. Brewpub.

BOTHELL

Canyons
22010 17th Ave. SE, 425-485-3288
★☆☆☆   11 A.M.–2 A.M.
Food: Tavern fare   *Smoking:* Separate sections

Known for its smoked ribs, draws both a sports crowd and families. Most of the twenty-five taps pour Northwest craft beers, with a few imports and mainstream domestics.

CENTRALIA

The Olympic Club Ⓑ
112 N. Tower Ave., 360-736-5164
★★⯪☆   11 A.M.–1 A.M.
Food: Tavern fare   *Smoking:* Separate sections

The McMenamin brothers have reclaimed this magnificent club, which remains much as it did in 1913 when it was built as the "finest upscale establishment" between Tacoma and Portland. Much of the original mahogany paneling, stained glass, and ceramic tile flooring remain. Menu runs on the upscale side for a McMenamins (see Oregon).

COUPEVILLE

Captain's City Brewery Ⓑ
23 Front St., 360-678-9080
★★☆☆   11 A.M.–9 P.M.
Food: Bistro fare   *Smoking:* None

The Front Street Café, a bistro for Christopher's restaurant, is a sort of taproom as well as a coffeehouse with board games. Good food, excellent beer.

Toby's Tavern
8 Front St., 360-678-4222
★☆☆☆   11 A.M.–late
Food: Tavern fare   *Smoking:* Throughout

Toby's actually sits out over the water in Penn Cove (known for its oysters) and is a bit rough-and-tumble, selling plenty of Bud and Rainier as well as craft beer. Its one-piece, carved bar came around Cape Horn in the nineteenth century.

ENUMCLAW

The Mint
1608 Cole St., 360-825-8361
★★⯪☆   11 A.M.–late (closes 9 P.M. Sundays)
Food: Pizza   *Smoking:* None

This small-town tavern is kin to the Milton Tavern in Milton, offering excellent pizza and cheese garlic bread along with a carefully chosen draft list. Almost all the twenty-six taps go to craft beers, many of them from smaller breweries.

EVERETT

Everett Grand Roaster & Ale House
3105 Pine St., 425-339-2000
★★☆☆   11 A.M.–late
Food: Full menu   *Smoking:* Separate sections

Two-room spot, with a casual bar and a dining room serving a nice lineup of grilled and roasted dishes. Good views of Lake Washington. Twenty-six beers on tap, primarily Northwest micros.

Also in Everett
Flying Pig Brewing Co., 2929 Colby Ave., 425-339-1393. Brewpub.
Scuttlebutt Brewing Co., 1524 W. Marine View Drive, 425-257-9414. Brewpub.

FEDERAL WAY

Jake's Ales
2318 SW 336th St., 253-927-1288
★★☆☆   11 A.M.–late (opens at 9 A.M. weekends)
Food: Tavern fare   *Smoking:* None

Tucked away in a strip mall, this looks like a suburban sports bar, but all but a handful of the forty-five taps go to quality beers. The selection of imports is as impressive as the collection of Northwest craft beers.

KIRKLAND

Rose Hill Ale House and Café
12859 NE 85th St., 425-828-9712
★★½☆   11 A.M.–late (opens at 4 P.M. Sundays)
Food: Full menu   *Smoking:* None

A remodeled ale house aggressive about representing smaller breweries, pairing them with excellent food. A few of the twenty-nine taps go to imports, but most to craft beer. Two handpumps.

Also in Kirkland
Kirkland Roaster & Ale House, 111 Central Way, 425-827-4400. Restaurant/pub.

LEAVENWORTH

Leavenworth Brewery 🅑
636 Front St., 509-548-4545
    ★★☆☆   11 A.M.–late (shorter hours in winter)
Food: German fare   *Smoking:* None

Find the sixty-three-foot Bavarian steeple in this town at the edge of the Cascades and you've found the brewery. Usually six or seven beers are available, including both ales and lagers.

MILTON

Milton Tavern
7320 Pacific Highway E., 253-922-3340
    ★★☆☆   11 A.M.–late
Food: Pizza   *Smoking:* None

A terrific lineup of thirty-one taps, with both West Coast stalwarts and smaller local breweries represented. This was a notorious motorcycle bar, but now the large sign out front declares the place non-smoking, and there's parking for bicycles.

OLYMPIA

The Fish Bowl 🅑
515 Jefferson, 360-943-6480
    ★★☆☆   11 A.M.–midnight (closed Sundays)
Food: Brewpub fare   *Smoking:* None

Fish Brewing's hoppy beers are produced here. The fish motif includes an aquarium, fish sculptures, and fish paintings.

Whiskers Tavern
446 Mud Bay Road, 360-753-9964
    ★☆☆☆   10 A.M.–2 A.M.
Food: Tavern fare   *Smoking:* None

A once rural tavern that has been serving interesting beer for more than fifteen years, offering twelve taps and a handpump. Darts and cribbage.

PULLMAN

Rico's
200 E. Main, 509-334-9958

★☆☆☆ 11:30 A.M.–2 A.M. (1 P.M.–2 A.M. Sundays)
Food: Tavern fare   *Smoking:* Separate sections

Locals' spot with a history dating back to 1909, when it was a tobacco shop. Plenty of Northwest beers from fourteen taps.

RENTON

Whistle Stop Ale House
340 Burnett Ave. S., 425-255-9108

★☆☆☆ Lunch–late (closed Sundays)
Food: Tavern fare   *Smoking:* None

The *Spirit of Washington* Dinner Train rolls by on the tracks out front, well-done food is a value, and the sixteen taps represent the Northwest well. Classic back bar came out of the Yukon Territory.

Also in Renton

Foxy's Pub & Eatery, 944 Harrington NE, 425-228-7950. Restaurant/pub.

ROSLYN

The Brick Tavern
1 Pennsylvania St., 509-649-2643

★☆☆☆ 11 A.M.–late
Food: Tavern fare   *Smoking:* Separate sections

Looks much like it did in the television show "Northern Exposure," which used it as a set. It's the oldest bar in Washington, dating to 1889. Both mainstream lagers and Northwest craft beers on tap.

SEATTLE

Belltown Pub
2322 1ˢᵗ Ave., 206-278-4311

★★☆☆ Lunch–late
Food: Bistro fare   *Smoking:* None

Upscale comfortable with brick walls, striking back bar, rowing shell hanging from the ceiling, and classic light fixtures. Great food, eighteen taps, mostly Northwest beers.

Bick's Broadview Grill

10555 Greenwood Ave. N., 206-367-8481

★★☆☆   4 P.M.–11 P.M.

Food: Bistro fare   *Smoking:* Separate sections

House converted into a bistro and more restaurant than bar (though it has a bar area). Eclectic cuisine with plenty of spicy foods. Perfect complement for sixteen draft beers, mostly Northwest craft products.

Big Time Brewing   🅑

4133 University Way NE, 206-545-4509

★★½☆   Lunch–late

Food: Brewpub fare   *Smoking:* Separate sections

A brew-saloon, cousin to Triple Rock and Twenty Tank in the Bay Area. Student hangout jammed with classic breweriana. Excellent beers, some served from handpumps.

Blue Moon Tavern

712 NE 45ᵗʰ St., 206-545-9775

★★☆☆   Noon–late

Food: No kitchen   *Smoking:* Throughout

Novelist Tom Robbins described it as well as anyone can in a phrase, when he called the tavern "a frenzy of distorted joy spinning just outside the reach of bourgeois horrors." Twelve taps, stuff everywhere from when Beatniks hung here in the '50s and the Dead in the '60s.

College Inn Pub

4006 University Way NE, 206-434-2307

★☆☆☆   Lunch–late (opens later weekends)

Food: Tavern fare   *Smoking:* Throughout

A cozy but large basement pub and longtime University of Washington student hangout. Three rooms, including one with tables and chessboards. Rotating selection from fifteen taps, with new stouts regularly available.

Cooper's Alehouse

8065 Lake City Way NE, 206-522-2923

★★☆☆   3 P.M.–late (earlier weekends)

Food: Tavern fare   *Smoking:* Separate sections

One of the first spots in Seattle to feature Northwest beers, now has twenty-six taps that pour both imports and micros. Popular pool and darts bar.

Elysian Brewing Co. & Public House Ⓑ
1221 E. Pike St., 206-860-1920
★★★☆　　11:30 A.M.–late
Food: Brewpub fare　　*Smoking:* Separate sections

Comfortable brewery/restaurant on Capitol Hill. Wide range of fine beers dispensed from unique taps that hang above the bar. Elysian also operates a small brewpub in Gameworks down the hill.

Fabulous Buckaroo Tavern
4201 Fremont Ave. N., 206-634-3161
★☆☆☆　　11 A.M.–late
Food: Tavern fare　　*Smoking:* Throughout

Fabulous neon—a lasso-twirling cowboy on a bucking bronco—and twenty beers on tap, both micros and mainstream beers. Rougher around the edges than many of the remodeled taverns that populate the Fremont neighborhood.

Fiddler's Inn
9219 35th Ave. NE, 206-525-0865
★★½☆　　Lunch–late
Food: Tavern fare　　*Smoking:* None

Inviting cabin setting with pleasant patio in back. Eleven taps favor hoppiest Northwest beers. Regularly features fiddle music. Related to Latona Pub and Hopvine (507 15th Ave. E.).

Grady's Montlake Pub & Eatery
2307 24th Ave. E., 206-726-5968
★☆☆☆　　Lunch–late
Food: Tavern fare　　*Smoking:* Separate sections

Something for everybody: Fourteen taps pour micros, imports, and mainstream beers, and the solid food selection includes a kids' menu until 7 P.M.

Hilltop Ale House
2129 Queen Anne Ave. N., 206-285-3877
★★☆☆　　Lunch–late
Food: Tavern fare　　*Smoking:* None

Could legitimately add "& Grill" to its name. Serving excellent food and eighteen draft choices (two on handpump) in a comfortable setting.

Hopscotch

332 15ᵗʰ Ave., 206-322-4191

   ★★★☆   11 A.M.–late (opens at 8 A.M. weekends)

Food: British pub   *Smoking:* Separate sections

More than a hundred single-malt Scotches, fine lineup of six-teen draft choices (handpump). Mixture of regional beers and quality imports, some special offerings not generally available. Comfortable, family-friendly setting.

Latona Pub

6423 Latona Ave. NE, 206-525-2235

   ★★★☆   3 P.M.–1 A.M.

Food: Tavern fare   *Smoking:* None

Open and airy with a bistro feel, solid food, upstairs room for music. But what sets it apart are twelve taps and a handpump that serve the best and the newest of what's available from the Northwest.

Maple Leaf Bar and Grill

8929 Roosevelt Ave. NE, 206-523-8449

   ★★☆☆   11 A.M.–after dinner (opens later weekends)

Food: Bistro fare   *Smoking:* Separate sections

Moved a few doors down since we visited. A fine neighborhood café that happens to offer innovative menu items, quality wine and excellent craft beer (ten taps).

Murphy's Pub

1928 N. 45ᵗʰ St., 206-634-2110

   ★★☆☆   11:30 A.M.–2 A.M.

Food: Tavern fare   *Smoking:* Throughout

Irish pub. Stuffed chairs face a double-sided fireplace in middle of large room and a small stage that features live Irish music. Plenty of stouts but also a full line of Northwest products from twenty-two taps.

Nickerson Street Saloon

318 Nickerson, 206-284-8819

   ★★☆☆   11:30 A.M.–late

Food: Tavern fare   *Smoking:* None

Just across the Fremont Bridge from Fremont's popular pubs, with eighteen taps leaning toward Northwest beers not served elsewhere and carefully cared for.

Old Town Alehouse
5233 Ballard Ave. NW, 206-782-8323
★★☆☆   4 P.M.–closing
Food: Healthy tavern fare   *Smoking:* None

Ballard neighborhood spot with fast-changing but always fine ten-tap lineup. A hundred-year-old back bar, seventy-year-old wooden cooler. Specialty is "Ballard Wedges," sandwiches served on choice of daily baked breads. Live jazz and blues.

Park Pub
6114 Phinney Ave., 206-789-8187
★★☆☆   3 P.M.–late (closed Sundays)
Food: Tavern fare   *Smoking:* Separate sections

Hard by Woodland Park, basically a place for beer and darts or pool. Devoted to serving distinctive Northwest beers not offered elsewhere, offering eighteen on tap.

Pike Pub & Brewery Ⓑ
1415 1ˢᵗ Ave., 206-720-2218
★★★☆   Lunch–late
Food: Brewpub bistro fare   *Smoking:* In cigar room

Restaurant offers beer-friendly food, beers from the attached microbrewery, and many of the beers that Merchant du Vin imports. Excellent cask ales.

Pyramid Brewery & Alehouse Ⓑ
1201 1ˢᵗ Ave S., 206-682-3377
★★½☆   Lunch–late evening
Food: Brewpub fare   *Smoking:* Separate sections

Warehouse holding both the Pyramid Brewery and restaurant, offering a full line of Pyramid and Thomas Kemper beers. Above-average food, outdoor seating.

Ray's Boathouse
6049 Seaview Ave. NW, 206-789-3770
★★½☆   Lunch–late
Food: Seafood   *Smoking:* Only in bar

Exceptional seafood restaurant with a view of both Puget Sound and the mountains. Set in a rock-solid two-story boathouse, offering more casual dining on second-floor deck. Twenty draft choices, mostly Northwest products, plus excellent wine list.

Reading Gaol
418 NW 65th, 206-783-3002
    ★★☆☆   Mid-afternoon–late (opens earlier weekends)
Food: Tavern fare   *Smoking:* Throughout

Locals' spot, vaguely European, and run by the former owner of the venerable La Bohème. Twenty-plus quality taps, featuring regional beers and often spotlighting one brewery.

Red Door Alehouse
3401 Fremont Ave. N, 206-547-7521
    ★★⯪☆   11 A.M.–late
Food: Tavern fare   *Smoking:* Throughout

A classic tavern, long and narrow with a tall ceiling and a wooden bar along one wall, nice patio in back. Twenty-six taps, one handpump, and fine beer lineup. Crowd gets younger and louder as the evening wears on.

Ridge Pub & Grill
9041 Holmes Road NW, 206-784-7272
    ★★☆☆   3 P.M.–late
Food: Tavern fare   *Smoking:* None

Eighteen-beer draft lineup includes many beers not commonly seen at other spots. The back bar is an old standup piano, and the drip tray is on the keyboard cover. Briefly tried brewing beer in-house, but quickly abandoned the experiment.

74th Street Alehouse
7401 Greenwood Ave. N., 206-784-2955
    ★★☆☆   Lunch–late
Food: Tavern fare   *Smoking:* Throughout

Pictures of British pubs line the walls here, much like family photos. Nineteen beers, mostly Northwest products, and a cider on tap. Handpump. Simple, well-done food.

Six Degrees
790 E. Green Lake Drive N., 206-523-1600
    ★★☆☆   11 A.M.–10 P.M. (closes at 11 P.M. Fridays and Saturdays)
Food: Bistro fare   *Smoking:* None

Has a bar, but in no sense is it a bar. Bright and airy and a popular evening gathering spot. Nouveau pub food with food/beer pairings suggested for many of the innovative dishes. Twenty beers on tap.

Triangle Tavern

3507 Fremont Place N., 206-632-0880

★★½☆   11:30 A.M.–late

Food: Tavern fare   *Smoking:* Separate sections

Two-room pub with excellent food on the dining side and comfortable sofas in the pub room. Sixteen beers on tap, Guinness and microbrewed products.

Trolleyman Pub

3400 Phinney Ave. N., 206-548-8000

★★½☆   Before lunch-late evening (limited hours Sundays)

Food: Limited menu   *Smoking:* None

Although Redhook Brewing no longer brews in Fremont, the intimate taproom remains. Offers Redhook beers, including specials, some on handpump.

Virginia Inn Tavern

1937 1st Ave., 206-728-1937

★★☆☆   11 A.M.–late

Food: Bistro fare   *Smoking:* None

Around since 1903, a classic tavern inside, a sidewalk café outside, with a few tables that offers views of Puget Sound and the Olympic Mountains. A dozen taps, mostly Northwest craft beers.

Wedgewood Alehouse & Café

8515 35th NE, 206-527-2676

★☆☆☆   Lunch–late (opens earlier weekends)

Food: Tavern fare   *Smoking:* Throughout

A tavern forever, with neighborhood regulars who come in for Rainier. The last horseshoe-shaped bar in Seattle. Eighteen beers on tap, mostly regional craft beers.

Also in Seattle

Attic Tavern & Café, 4226 E. Madison, 206-323-3131. Tavern.

Bad Albert's Tap and Grill, 5100 Ballard Ave. NW, 206-782-9623. Restaurant/pub.

Blackthorne Village Pub, 2410 32nd Ave. W., 206-285-9756. Pub.

Central Tavern, 207 1st Ave., 206-622-0209. Tavern.

Comet Tavern, 922 E. Pike St., 206-323-9853. Tavern.

Conor Byrne's Pub, 5140 Ballard, 206-784-3640. Irish pub.

Dad Watson's Brewery & Restaurant, 3601 Fremont Ave. N., 206-632-6205. McMenamins brewpub.

Dexter and Hayes Public House, 1628 Dexter Ave. N., 206-283-7786. Restaurant/pub.

The Dubliner, 3405 Fremont N., 206-634-3161. Irish pub.

Duchess, 2827 NE 55th St., 206-527-0956. Tavern.

Duke's Greenlake Chowder House, 7850 Greenlake Drive N., 206-522-4908. Restaurant/pub.

Elliott Bay Brewery & Pub, 4720 California Ave., 206-932-8695. Brewpub.

Floyd's Place, 521 1st Ave. N., 206-284-3542. Restaurant/pub.

George & Dragon Pub, 206 N. 36th St., 206-545-6864. British pub.

Gordon Biersch, 600 Pine St. (Fourth Floor), 206-405-4204. Brewpub; see San Francisco, California.

The Greenlake Ale House, 7305 Aurora Ave. N., 206-781-8337. Alehouse.

Hale's Brewery and Pub, 4301 Leary Way NW, 206-706-1544. Brewpub.

Hoyt's Pub, 1527 Queen Anne Ave. N., 206-284-2656. Restaurant/pub.

Kells, 1916 Post Alley, 206-682-1397. Irish pub.

McMenamins on Queen Anne, 200 Roy St., Suite 105, 206-285-4722. Brewpub.

The Old Pequliar, 1722 NW Market St., 206-782-8886. Tavern.

Pacific Inn Pub, 3501 Stoney Way N., 206-547-2947. Restaurant/pub.

Pioneer Square Saloon, 77 Yesler, 206-340-1234. Tavern.

Ram Restaurant & Big Horn Brewery, 4730 University Village NE, 206-525-3565. Brewpub.

Roanoke Park Place, 2409 10th Ave. E, 206-324-5882. Sports bar.

Rock Bottom Brewery & Restaurant, 1333 5th Ave., 206-623-3070. Brewpub; see Denver, Colorado.

Rock Pasta, 322 Occidental Ave. S., 206-682-7625. Brewpub.

Romper Room, 106 1st St. N., 206-284-5003. Tavern.

Seattle Brewers Taproom, 580 S. Holden, 206-762-7421. Brewpub.

Six Arms Brewpub, 300 E. Pike St., 206-223-1698. McMenamins brewpub.

T.S. McHugh's Public House, 21 Mercer St., 206-282-1910. Restaurant/pub.

Tir na nÓg, 801 1st Ave., 206-264-2700. Brewpub/Irish pub, operated by Ram/Big Horn group.

Two Bells Tavern, 2313 4th Ave., 206-441-3030. Tavern.

SNOHOMISH

Fred's Rivertown Ale House
1114 1ˢᵗ St., 360-568-5820
★★★★ Lunch–late
Food: Nouvelle tavern fare   *Smoking:* Throughout

Refurbished storefront tavern on a classic small-town street in a popular antiquing town. Thirty-plus well-chosen taps—including ales dispensed from antique beer engines—an innovative menu, and a broad single-malt list. Look for a simple neon sign that reads "Tavern" and points down to the entrance.

SPOKANE

Birkebeiner Brewing ⓑ
35 W. Main, 509-484-0854
★★⅟☆ 10:30 A.M.–late
Food: Brewpub fare   *Smoking:* None

Stylish brewpub that makes a wide range of beers and keeps twelve or more of them on tap. Beers good enough that some Seattle alehouses seek them out, and excellent food.

Fort Spokane Brewery ⓑ
W. 401 Spokane Falls Blvd., 509-838-3809
★☆☆☆ 11 A.M.–closing
Food: Tavern fare   *Smoking:* Separate sections

Blues venue and brewpub in a hundred-year-old brick building with a substantial bar and back bar. Offers guest beers as well as four of its own.

Viking Tavern
1224 N. Stevens, 509-326-2942
★★☆☆ 11 A.M.–closing (closed Sundays)
Food: Tavern fare   *Smoking:* Throughout

Decorated with flags from around the world and old beer posters, with a twenty-five-tap lineup that favors West Coast micros.

Also in Spokane
McQ's Billards & Café, 9164 E. Sprague, 509-891-2622. Pool hall/multi-tap.
The Ram/Big Horn Brewing, 908 N. Howard, 509-326-3745. Brewpub.
Solicitor's Corner/Sweetwater Brewing Co., 6301 N. Division, 509-465-9554. Brewpub.

TACOMA

Ale House Pub & Eatery
2122 Mildred St. W., 253-565-9367

★★☆☆   11 A.M.–late (opens at 9 A.M. weekends)
Food: Tavern fare   *Smoking:* Separate sections

Sports bar with plenty of TVs and sixty-three taps. Plenty of mainstream lagers, but also hard-to-find products from some of the Northwest's smallest craft brewers.

Engine House #9 Ⓑ
611 N. Pine St., 253-272-3435

★★☆☆   11 A.M.–late
Food: Tavern fare   *Smoking:* None

A pub long before it was a brewpub, in a restored brick firehouse built in 1907. Offers a wide range of guest craft beers as well as it own well-made ales. The bar area is separated from the dining room by old horse stall backs, which still have the horses' names on them.

Katie Downs
3211 N. Ruston Way, 253-756-0722

★★☆☆   11 A.M.–closing
Food: Tavern fare   *Smoking:* Separate sections

Tavern built in 1982 on pilings right over the water. The popular argument is, which is better: the pizza or the view of Puget Sound and beyond? Twenty-one taps favor Northwest craft beers.

The Swiss
1904 Jefferson, 253-572-2821

★★★☆   11 A.M.–2 A.M. (opens at 9 A.M. weekends)
Food: Full menu   *Smoking:* Separate sections

Former Swiss meeting hall with a terrific ballroom floor upstairs, now decorated with breweriana and local artwork. Outstanding food, and the beer selection is just as good. Most of the thirty-four taps go to regional craft beers.

Also in Tacoma
Ram Restaurant & Big Horn Brewery, 3017 Reston Way, 253-756-7886. Brewpub.
Rock Pasta, 1920 Jefferson, 253-272-1221. Brewpub.

VANCOUVER

Hazel Dell Brewpub Ⓑ
8513 NE Highway 99, 360-576-0996
★☆☆☆   11 A.M.–late
Food: Brewpub fare   *Smoking:* Separate sections

Comfortable pub with a friendly staff, offering well-made house beers plus a full range of guest beers (mainstream lagers to micros). Good food.

R.P. McMurphey's
400 E. Evergreen, 360-695-9211
★★☆☆   11 A.M.–midnight
Food: Tavern fare   *Smoking:* None

Part multi-tap (thirty, mostly Northwest beers), part Irish pub, and an American literature-themed bar located in a former nineteenth century boarding school for girls. The menu names are those of authors, books, and characters; the banquet room is called the Library.

Also in Vancouver
McMenamins on the Columbia, 1801 SE Columbia River Drive, 360-699-1521. Brewpub.
Salmon Creek Brewing Co., 108 W. Evergreen Blvd., 360-993-1827. Brewpub.

YAKIMA

Grant's Brewery Pub Ⓑ
32 N. Front St., 509-575-2922
★★★☆   11:30 A.M.–after dinner
Food: Brewpub fare   *Smoking:* None

Actually the third location for Grant's, which was the country's first post-Prohibition brewpub. The original brewhouse is here in an old train station. Two beers on handpump, and founder Bert Grant still stops in.

Also in Washington
Chehalis: Market Street Pub, 523 N. Market Blvd., 360-748-7969. Restaurant/pub.
    Red Dawg Brewpub/Onalaska Brewing Co., 429 N. Market, 360-740-8072. Brewpub.
Friday Harbor: Front Street Ale House, 1 Front St., 360-378-2337. Brewpub.

Issaquah: Issaquah Brewhouse, 35 W. Sunset Way, 425-557-1911. Brewpub.

The Roost, 120 NW Gilman Blvd., 425-392-5550. Restaurant/bar.

La Conner: La Conner Brewing, 117 S. 1st St., 360-466-1415. Brewpub.

Lakewood: Ram Family Restaurant/Big Horn Brewing, 10019 59th Ave. SW, 206-584-3191. Brewpub.

Monroe: Sailfish Grill/Twin Rivers Brewery, 104 N. Lewis, 360-794-4056. Brewpub.

Mount Vernon: Skagit River Brewing Taproom, 404 S. 3rd St., 360-336-2884. Brewpub.

Mukilteo: Riley's Pizza/Eagle Brewing Co., 625 Lincoln, 425-348-8088. Brewpub.

Oak Harbor: Oak Harbor Pub & Brewery, 6405 60th St., 360-675-7408. Brewpub.

Port Townsend: Maxwell's Brewery & Pub, 636 Waterfront Place, 360-379-6438. Brewpub.

Public House, 1058 Water St., 206-385-9708. Restaurant.

Puyallup: Powerhouse Brewery & Restaurant, 454 E. Main, 206-845-1370. Brewpub.

Ram Family Restaurant & Big Horn Brewing, 103 35th Ave. SE, 253-841-3317. Brewpub.

Richland: Atomic Ale Brewpub & Eatery, 1015 Lee Blvd., 509-946-5465. Brewpub.

Rattlesnake Mountain Brewery, 1250 Columbia Center Blvd., 509-783-5747. Brewpub.

Seatac: Western Ale & Brewpub, 19224 Des Moines Memorial Drive, 253-870-1746. Brewpub.

Silverdale: Silver City Brewing Co., 2799 NW Myhre Road, 360-698-5879. Brewpub.

Sunnyside: Snipes Mountain Brewery, 905 Yakima Road, 509-837-2739. Brewpub.

Walla Walla: Mill Creek Brewpub/Big House Brewing, 11 N. Palouse, 509-522-2440. Brewpub.

Winthrop: Winthrop Brewing Co., 155 Riverside Drive, 509-996-3183. Brewpub.

Woodinville: Forecasters Public House, 14300 NE 145th St., 425-483-3232. Brewpub.

WEST VIRGINIA

Craft beer has not taken West Virginia by storm. Few breweries have opened and about half of them have closed. We suspect there are pubs serving interesting beer, but we haven't found them yet.

MORGANTOWN

West Virginia Brewing Co. Ⓑ

1291 University Ave., 304-296-2739

★☆☆☆   11:30 A.M.–closing (closed Sundays)

Food: Brewpub fare   *Smoking:* Separate sections

Dining area has a bistro feel and a menu emphasizing fresh pastas, while the bar area is more a pub and a place to hang out. Wide range of house beers.

Also in West Virginia

Davis: Blackwater Brewing Co./Davis Restaurant & Pub, Route 32, 304-259-4221. Brewpub.

Parkersburg: North End Tavern, 3500 Emerson Ave., 304-428-5854. Brewpub.

WISCONSIN

Regional beers to look for: New Glarus Brewing (well known for its cherry beer but brewing all styles well); Sprecher Brewing; Capitol Brewing; Gray Brewing; Green Bay Brewing (Hinterland beers).

Essential stops: Essen Haus in Madison; Baumgartners Cheese Store in Monroe.

Just for fun: Der Rathskeller. It's a student union, it has twenty beers on tap.

Best city for a pub crawl: Madison.

APPLETON

Appleton Brewing Co. Ⓑ
1004 S. Olde Oneida St., 920-731-3322
    ★★☆☆   11 A.M.–10 P.M. (opens at 4 P.M. Sundays)
Food: Mexican fare   *Smoking:* Throughout

Appleton Brewing Co. makes Adler Brau beer on the first floor, and a Mexican restaurant with a particularly cozy bar operates below. Excellent breweriana, good beer.

Also in Appleton
The Clubhouse, at Paper Valley Hotel, 333 W. College Ave., 920-733-8000. Sports bar, twenty taps.
Fox River Brewing Co. and Restaurant, 4301 Wisconsin Ave., 920-991-0000. Brewpub; see Oshkosh.
Pats Tap, 314 E. College Ave., 920-733-9883. Locals' tavern.

EGG HARBOR

Old Stage Station
State Highway 42, 920-868-3247
    ★☆☆☆   8 A.M.–late in season (call in winter)
Food: Tavern fare   *Smoking:* Separate sections

The broadest beer selection in Door County, with twelve beers on tap plus a root beer, two domestics, and the rest imports and craft beers. Also 150 bottle choices.

Also in Egg Harbor
Shipwrecked, 7791 Egg Harbor Road, 920-868-2767. Brewpub.

FOUNTAIN CITY

The Monarch Tavern & Preservation Hall Restaurant
19 N. Main St., 608-687-4231

   ★☆☆☆   11 A.M.–closing (opens at 8 A.M. weekends)
Food: Tavern fare   *Smoking:* Separate sections

The original fifteen-foot-high pressed tin ceilings, hardwood floors, and magnificent handcarved oak back and front bars remain from the Odd Fellows who built this place in 1894. The beer tables have been in daily use for more than a hundred years. House beer from adjoining Fountain City Brewing Co.

FITCHBURG

Quivey's Grove
6161 Nesbitt Road, 608-273-4900

   ★★☆☆   11 A.M.–late
Food: Full menu   *Smoking:* None

There are several lovely dining areas at this excellent restaurant, and the bar is located in the Stable Tap, a mid-nineteenth-century stone building. All but one of the eleven taps go to Wisconsin craft beers, and Quivey's is usually among the first to get a new product from several of the breweries.

GREEN BAY

Kittner's
120 S. Washington St., 920-433-9187

   ★☆☆☆   4 P.M.–late (opens at 4 P.M. weekends)
Food: No kitchen   *Smoking:* Throughout

Moderately hip, with plenty of wood and a gargoyle guarding the place. Twenty taps, mostly imports and micros with a half-dozen Wisconsin beers available.

Microswitch
2105 University Ave., 920-435-0080

   ★☆☆☆   3 P.M.–2:30 A.M. (closed Sundays)
Food: Tavern fare   *Smoking:* Throughout

Nonthing fancy, good beer, good basic food, good conversation. All ten taps are devoted to Wisconsin beers, mostly microbrewed products, and rotated often.

Titletown Brewing Co. Ⓑ
200 Dousman, 920-437-2337
★★⯪☆   11 A.M.–late
Food: Brewpub fare   *Smoking:* Separate sections

Beautifully remodeled historic train depot, nicely divided into dining and drinking areas. A Wynkoop (Denver, Colorado) project that shows the touches with good food, solid beer, and a pool room.

Also in Green Bay

Green Bay Brewing Co., 313 Dousman St., 920-438-8050. Microbrewery tasting room, sells gourmet food.

Legends Brewhouse & Eatery of Green Bay, 2840 Shawano Ave., 920-663-1111. Brewpub.

HUBERTUS

Fox & Hounds Restaurant
1298 Fries Lake Road, 414-628-1111
★☆☆☆   4 P.M.–after dinner (opens at 11 A.M. Sundays; closed Mondays)
Food: Full menu   *Smoking:* Separate sections

A popular seven-room restaurant that has been around since 1933. German beers well-represented among the eleven on tap, but also craft products.

KENOSHA

Brewmasters Pub Ⓑ
4017 80th St., 414-694-9050
★★☆☆   11 A.M.–midnight
Food: Tavern fare   *Smoking:* Separate sections

What was once a stable for show horses is a fine setting for good food and an interesting range of house beers. A second pub, Brewmasters Pub Parkside on 22nd Avenue, also brews.

LA CROSSE

Bodega Brew Pub Ⓑ
122 S. 4th St., 608-782-0677
★☆☆☆   Noon–late
Food: No kitchen   *Smoking:* Throughout

Pleasant storefront tavern that serves primarily Wisconsin craft beers on tap as well as beer from its own small brewhouse. Large bottle selection.

MADISON

Angelic Brewing Ⓑ
322 W. Johnson St., 608-257-2707
★★☆☆   11 A.M.–2 A.M.
Food: Brewpub fare   *Smoking:* Separate sections

Slightly upscale English decor, with blacksmith's puzzles hanging above the bar and patrons playing chess before the nighttime crowds arrive. Fine selection of house beers.

Der Rathskeller
800 Langdon St., 608-262-1234
★★☆☆   11 A.M.–late
Food: Full menu   *Smoking:* Throughout

Located in the University of Wisconsin Student Union, but it looks like a German beer hall. Twenty-seven tap choices include plenty of mainstream lagers, but also imports and Wisconsin craft beers. For Union members only, but one-day passes are available.

Essen Haus German Restaurant
514 E. Wilson St., 608-255-4674
★★★☆   3 P.M.–2 A.M. (closed Mondays)
Food: German fare   *Smoking:* Separate sections

Popular German restaurant and drinking hall, offering fourteen German beers on tap and live music. The low ceiling of the barroom is lined with numbered ceramic mugs belonging to beer club members. In partnership with the Come Back Inn next door, which serves some of the same beers, some different. You can walk between the two with a beer in hand.

Great Dane Pub & Brewing Co. Ⓑ
123 Doty, 608-284-0000
★★⯪☆   11 A.M.–late
Food: Brewpub fare   *Smoking:* Separate sections

Popular brewpub, with seating in a cavelike rathskeller, the first-floor bar and two adjoining rooms, and in the beer garden. Interesting beers, mostly ales with an occasional lager.

Porta Bella
425 N. Frances, 608-256-3186
★☆☆☆   5 P.M.–closing (closed Sundays)
Food: Italian fare   *Smoking:* Separate sections

Italian restaurant upstairs, cavelike wine bar downstairs, with twenty-two beers on tap—including an excellent selection of micros.

Wonders Pub

1980 Atwood, 608-244-8563

★☆☆☆   11 A.M.–closing (closed Sundays)
Food: Tavern fare   *Smoking:* Throughout

A neighborhood bar with a small selection of ever-changing taps showcasing regional craft breweries. Knowledgeable servers and drinkers.

Also in Madison

Dotty Dumplings Dowry, 116 N. Fairchild, 608-255-3175. Tavern with great hamburgers, nineteen taps.

J.T. Whitney's, 674 S. Whitney Way, 608-274-1776. Brewpub.

Old Chicago, 7202 Mineral Point Road, 608-827-0034. See Boulder, Colorado.

MARINETTE

Railhouse Brewery Ⓑ

West 1130 Old Peshtigo Road, 715-732-4646

★☆☆☆   10 A.M.–11 P.M. (sometimes closes earlier)
Food: Pizza, pasta   *Smoking:* Separate sections

Anybody drinking a house beer when a train rumbles by on tracks right outside gets a free beer. A fine new tavern with interesting beer.

MILWAUKEE

Brown Bottle Pub

221 W. Galena St., 414-271-4444

★☆☆☆   11 A.M.–late (opens at 5 P.M. Saturdays, closed Sundays)
Food: Tavern fare   *Smoking:* Separate sections

Any trip to Milwaukee should include a drive to view the architecture in Schlitz Park, where the brewery once was located. This re-creation of a European inn is in one of the artfully crafted buildings and offers more than one hundred bottle choices.

Gasthaus Zur Krone

839 S. 2nd St., 414-647-1910

★☆☆☆   11:30 A.M.–2 A.M.
Food: Tavern fare   *Smoking:* Throughout

Old-fashioned tavern, with large pictures of European royalty hanging above the bar and classical music in the background. Ten taps, large bottle menu.

Karl Ratzsch's
320 E. Mason St., 414-276-2720
★★☆☆ Lunch–after dinner
Food: German fare *Smoking:* Separate sections

Some pick Mader's first, but others call this the best German restaurant in town—with German beer, of course. Inviting stained glass entry, and owned by the same family since 1904.

Kegel's Inn & Fine Dining
5901 National Ave., 414-257-9999
★☆☆☆ Lunch–late (opens at 4:30 P.M. Saturdays, closed Sundays)
Food: German fare plus *Smoking:* Separate sections

Classic dining spot, with inviting bar and German beers at the entry. Stained-glass panels depict drinking scenes. Excellent food.

Landmark 1850 Inn
5905 S. Howell, 414-769-1850
★★☆☆ 3 P.M.–late (opens at 7 P.M. Saturdays and Sundays)
Food: Tavern fare *Smoking:* Throughout

Worn brick building with long wood bar and lots of tables to sit at. More than forty different beers on tap, mostly imports and micros.

Milwaukee Ale House Ⓑ
233 N. Water St., 414-226-2337
★★☆☆ 11 A.M.–closing
Food: Brewpub fare *Smoking:* Separate sections

Located in a former saddlery and sailboat rigging manufacturing plant, the brewpub retains the Cream City brick walls from when the facility was rebuilt following a fire in 1894. Popular ales, upscale dining, deck that overlooks the river.

Port of Hamburg
5937 S. Howell Ave., 414-747-9151
★☆☆☆ 2 P.M.–closing (opens at 11 A.M. weekends)
Food: Fridays and Saturdays only *Smoking:* Throughout

A mecca for German beer drinkers, with twenty-plus taps offering European beers. Full menu served on Friday and Saturday only.

Saz's on State Street
5539 W. State, 414-453-2410
   ★☆☆☆   11 A.M.–midnight (10:30 A.M.–9 P.M. Sundays)
Food: Tavern fare, barbecue   *Smoking:* Separate sections

Fine tavern where the ribs are annually voted best in the city.
The draft lineup includes several Wisconsin craft products, a
few imports, and mainstream beers.

White House Inn (Kneisler's)
2900 S. Kinnickinnic Ave., 414-483-2900
   ★☆☆☆   3 P.M.–late (opens at 11 A.M. weekends)
Food: Tavern fare   *Smoking:* Separate sections

Open since 1891 and was an ice cream shop during Prohibition. The eleven draft choices include imports and craft beers.
Volleyball court outside and darts inside after the kitchen
closes.

Also in Milwaukee
Barrel Riders Pub, 1132 E. Wright, 414-372-2929. Tavern.
Hanley's Irish Pub, 3425 W. State, 414-933-6680. Irish pub.
John Hawk's Pub, 100 E. Wisconsin Ave., 414-272-3199. British
    pub.
Mader's, 1041 N. 3rd St., 414-271-3377. German.
Roman's Pub, 3475 S. Kinnickinnic, 414-481-3396. Tavern.
Rock Bottom Brewery & Restaurant, 740 N. Plankinton, 414-
    276-3030. Brewpub; see Denver, Colorado.
Tony's Tavern, 412 S. 2nd St., 414-273-6321. Tavern.
Von Trier, 2235 N. Farwell, 414-271-9560. Tavern.
Water Street Brewery, 1101 N. Water St., 414-272-1195. Brew-
    pub.

MINERAL POINT

Brewery Creek Inn, Restaurant & Brewery
23 Commerce St., 608-987-3298
   ★★☆☆   11:30 A.M.–9 P.M. (noon–6 P.M. Sundays; closed
Mondays)
Food: Brewpub fare   *Smoking:* None

Brewpub/inn with four guest rooms in a three-story limestone
structure dating to 1854. Beautifully restored with original
oak ceiling joists and pine plank flooring supported by hand-
hewn oak posts and beams. Many of the dishes use beer as a vital ingredient.

MONROE

Baumgartners Cheese Store & Tavern
1023 16th Ave., 608-325-6157
    ★★☆☆   8 A.M.–midnight
Food: Wisconsin fare   *Smoking:* Throughout

Take-out shop in front, irresistible small tavern in back, with most of the four (sometimes five) taps reserved for Joseph Huber Brewing products made just up the street. Micros, imports in bottles. Limburger cheese sandwiches served with a breath mint.

OSHKOSH

Fox River Brewing 🅱
1501 Arboretum Drive, 920-232-2337
    ★★★☆   11 A.M.–10 P.M. (closes 11 P.M. Fridays and Saturdays)
Food: Brewpub fare   *Smoking:* Separate sections

Inviting inside and out, with outstanding food and excellent beer. On the banks of the Fox River, with a large beer garden and docking facilities for forty boats.

Peabody's Ale House
544 N. Main, 920-235-4004
    ★☆☆☆   11 A.M.–late (opens at 3 P.M. weekends)
Food: Tavern fare   *Smoking:* Throughout

Fifteen draft choices here cover the spectrum and usually include at least a half-dozen Wisconsin beers.

Also in Oshkosh
Oblio's, 434 N. Main, 920-426-1063. Nice music tavern with well-handled beer.

PORT WASHINGTON

Smith Brothers Fish Shanty 🅱
100 N. Franklin, 414-284-5592
    ★☆☆☆   11 A.M.–midnight
Food: Full menu   *Smoking:* Only in bar

Midwestern fish such as chub, smelt, and walleye in this longtime seafood restaurant with a brewery in the same building. Fishing theme throughout, including a seven-foot, three-inch marlin. Big picture windows look onto a marina, seawall, and Lake Michigan. Fish market attached.

WHITEWATER

Randy's FunHunters Brewery ⓑ
841 E. Milwaukee St., 414-473-8000
★☆☆☆   Lunch–late (closed Mondays)
Food: Full menu   *Smoking:* Separate sections

Since the 1930s, travelers on the way to Wisconsin Dells have stopped at a supper club in this spot. The brewery was added in 1994, and often features an excellent oatmeal stout.

Also in Wisconsin

Ashland: Railyard Pub/South Shore Brewery, 400 3rd Ave. W., 715-682-4200. Brewpub.

Chilton: Rowland's Calumet Brewery/The Roll Inn, 25 N. Madison St., 414-849-2534. Brewpub.

Cudahy: Gasthaus Nurnberg, 3450 E. Layton Ave., 414-481-9917. German.

DePere: Egan Brewing, 330 Reid St., 920-339-2707. Brewpub.

Eagle River: Loaf & Stein Brewery, 219 N. Railroad St., 715-477-2739. Brewpub.

Eau Claire: Northwoods Brewing, 3560 Oakwood Mall Drive, 715-552-0511. Brewpub.

Hartford: Rothaus Restaurant & Brewery, 4900 Highway 175, 414-644-8181. Brewpub.

Lake Delton: Pumphouse Pizza & Brewing Co., 19 W. Monroe Ave., 608-253-4687. Brewpub.

Mount Horeb: Mount Horeb Pub & Brewery, 105 S. 2nd St., 608-437-4200. Brewpub.

New Glarus: Puempel's Tavern, 18 6th Ave., 608-527-2045. Classic tavern.

Reedsburg: Ende House Brewery & Restaurant, 1020 E. Main St., 608-524-8600. Brewpub.

Rhinelander: Brown Street Brewery/Bugsy's Sports Bar, 16 N. Brown St., 715-369-2100. Brewpub.

Stevens Point: Isadore Street Brewery, 200 Isadore St., 715-341-1199. Brewpub.
    Witz End, 1274 N. 2nd Drive, 715-344-9045. Tavern.

Sturgeon Bay: Sturgeon Bay Brewing Co., 341 N. 3rd St., 414-743-1945. Brewpub.

Superior: Twin Ports Brewing Co./Choo-Choo Pub & Grill, 5002 E. 3rd St., 715-398-5252. Brewpub.

Waukesha: Weissguber's Gasthaus, 2720 N. Grandview Blvd., 414-544-4460. German.

West Allis: Benno's, 7413 W. Greenfield, 414-453-7094. Tavern.

WYOMING

Regional beers to look for: Snake River beers from Jackson Hole; Otto Brothers Brewing.
Just for fun: Humphrey's Bar & Grill in Gillette; anytime, but particularly when the rodeo is in town.

EVANSTON

Kate's
936 Main St., 307-789-7662
☆☆☆☆   2-10 P.M. (closed Sundays)
Food: No kitchen   *Smoking:* Throughout

Six beers on tap, including both imports and craft products, plus an extensive selection in bottles. Tin ceiling in the front room dates to 1910.

GILLETTE

Humphrey's Bar & Grill
408 W. Juniper, 307-682-0100
★★☆☆   11 A.M.–closing
Food: Tavern fare   *Smoking:* Throughout

Party-hard sports bar (there's even a television set in the men's room) with forty-three beers on tap, mostly craft products at excellent prices. Outdoor area includes horseshoe pits with seating for spectators.

JACKSON

Jackson Hole Pub & Brewery ℬ
265 S. Millward St., 307-739-2337
★★☆☆   Lunch–late
Food: Brewpub fare   *Smoking:* None

The windows look out on Snow King, and inside, the pub has an industrial feel, offering the excellent Snake River beers that are also packaged for sale.

LARAMIE

Library Restaurant & Brewing Co. Ⓑ
1622 Grand Ave., 307-742-0500
   ★☆☆☆   Lunch–late
Food: Brewpub fare   *Smoking:* Separate sections

Perhaps the only domed brewpub in the world (the pub re-placed a domed mall). Generally offers four or five beers made on-premise plus two or three guest beers. Dining area done in library motif, while bar is separate, feels like a bar, and backs up to a package liquor store.

Also in Wyoming

Casper: Tommyknockers Brewery & Pub, 256 S. Center, 307-473-2668. Brewpub; see Idaho Springs, Colorado.

Cheyenne: C.B. Potts & Co./Big Horn Brewing, 1650 Del Range Blvd., 307-632-8636. Brewpub.

Sheridan: Sanford's Pub & Grub, 1 E. Alger St., 307-674-1722. Brewpub.

Pinedale: LaVoie Brewery & Grill, 492 Pinedale, 307-367-1337. Brewpub.

Rock Springs: Bitter Creek Brewing Co., 604 Broadway, 307-362-4782. Brewpub.

Four-Star Establishments

Jupiter
Berkeley, California

Anderson Valley Brewing Co.
Boonville, California

North Coast Brewing Co.
Fort Bragg, California

Toronado
San Francisco, California

Brickskeller
Washington, D.C.

Goose Island Brewing
Chicago, Illinois

The Map Room
Chicago, Illinois

The Great Lost Bear
Portland, Maine

Doyle's Café
Boston, Massachusetts

Redbones
Somerville, Massachusetts

d.b.a. 41 1st avenue
New York, New York

Clark's Ale House
Syracuse, New York

Great Lakes Brewing
Cleveland, Ohio

Deschutes Brewery & Public
House
Bend, Oregon

Horse Brass Pub
Portland, Oregon

Victory Brewing Co.
Downingtown, Pennsylvania

Monk's Café
Philadelphia, Pennsylvania

Northeast Tap Room
Reading, Pennsylvania

Bistrot Belgique Gourmande
Occoquan, Virginia

Archer Ale House
Bellingham, Washington

Fred's Rivertown Ale House
Snohomish, Washington

25 Outstanding British Pubs
(English, Scottish, and Welsh)

White Cockade
Boulder Creek, California

The Old Ship Inn
Fullerton, California

Princess Pub & Grille
San Diego, California

Pig & Whistle
San Francisco, California

Frog & Peach Pub
San Luis Obispo, California

Bull & Bush Pub & Brewery
Denver, Colorado

Pint's Pub
Denver, Colorado

Shakespeare's Pub & Grill
Fort Lauderdale, Florida

The English Pub
Naples, Florida

Kings Head British Pub
St. Augustine, Florida

Prince of Wales
Atlanta, Georgia

Duke of Perth
Chicago, Illinois

Broad Ripple Brewpub
Indianapolis, Indiana

Cornwall's
Boston, Massachusetts

The British Beer Co.
Plymouth, Massachusetts

Sherlock's Home
Minnetonka, Minnesota

Dressel's
St. Louis, Missouri

The Ship Inn
Milford, New Jersey

North Star Pub
New York, New York

The Old Toad
Rochester, New York

Rose & Crown
Rochester, New York

Fox & Hound
Cary, North Carolina

Horse Brass Pub
Portland, Oregon

Mike Calder's Pub
Charleston, South Carolina

The Richmond Arms
Houston, Texas

25 Outstanding German Restaurant/Bars

Sudwerk Privatbrauerei Hubsch
Davis, California

Suppenkuche
San Francisco, California

Kaltenberg Castle Royal
Bavarian Brewhouse
Vail, Colorado

Bier Brunnen
Fort Lauderdale, Florida

Chicago Brauhaus
Chicago, Illinois

Resi's Bierstube
Chicago, Illinois

Gardner Haus Inn
Gardner, Illinois

Rathskeller
Indianapolis, Indiana

Student Prince Café
Springfield, Massachusetts

Dakota Inn Rathskeller
Detroit, Michigan

Black Forest Inn
Minneapolis, Minnesota

Gasthof zur Gemutlichkeit
Minneapolis, Minnesota

Gasthaus Bavarian Hunter
Stillwater, Minnesota

Bevo Mill
St. Louis, Missouri

Schneithorst's Hofamberg Inn
St. Louis, Missouri

Helmers'
Hoboken, New Jersey

Kilmeyer's Old Bavarian Inn
Staten Island, New York

Silver Swan
New York, New York

Weeping Radish Brewery
Manteo, North Carolina

Gustav's Bier Stube
Portland, Oregon

Otto's Brauhaus
Horsham, Pennsylvania

Ludwig's Garten
Philadelphia, Pennsylvania

Penn Brewery
Pittsburgh, Pennsylvania

Essen Haus
Madison, Wisconsin

Karl Ratzsch's
Milwaukee, Wisconsin

25 Outstanding Irish Pubs

McCraffey's Irish Pub
Phoenix, Arizona

Plough & Stars
San Francisco, California

Poet & Patriot
Santa Cruz, California

Nallen's Irish Pub & Grill
Denver, Colorado

McGuire's Irish Pub & Brewery
Pensacola, Florida

Four Green Fields
Tampa, Florida

Irish Times
Brookfield, Illinois

Jack Quinn's Irish Ale House
Covington, Kentucky

The Irish Rover
Louisville, Kentucky

O'Flaherty's Irish Channel Pub
New Orleans, Louisiana

Cat's Eye Pub
Baltimore, Maryland

Brendan Behan's Pub
Boston, Massachusetts

Doyle's Cafe
Boston, Massachusetts

John D. McGurks
St. Louis, Missouri

Kinsale Tavern
New York, New York

Swift Hibernian Lounge
New York, New York

The Parting Glass
Saratoga Springs, New York

Coleman's Irish Pub
Syracuse, New York

Kells Irish Pub
Portland, Oregon

The Irish Bards
Philadelphia, Pennsylvania

Aidan's Pub & Grub
Bristol, Rhode Island

McGonigel's Mucky Duck
Houston, Texas

Murphy's Pub
Seattle, Washington

Kelly's Irish Times
Washington, D.C.

The Dubliner
Milwaukee, Wisconsin

21 Mega-Taps

Places with eighty or more taphandles. (Not every handle may pour a different beer.)

The Yard House
Long Beach, California
250

Taco Mac
Cumming, Georgia
224

Taco Mac
Snellville, Georgia
155

Timberwolf Pub
Tempe, Arizona
150

Goat Hill Tavern
Costa Mesa, California
144

TapWerks Bricktown
Oklahoma City, Oklahoma
115

Flying Saucer Draught
Emporium
Addison, Texas
114

Taco Mac
Sandy Springs, Georgia
114

Sunset Grill & Tap
Boston, Massachusetts
112

Dublin Pub
Portland, Oregon
104

Heroes Bar & Grill
Fullerton, California
102

Timberwolf Pub
Houston, Texas
100

Barley's Brewhaus & Restaurant
Overland Park, Kansas
99

Barley's Brewhaus & Restaurant
Shawnee, Kansas
99

Cricket's Grill & Draft House
Waco, Texas
97

Flying Saucer Draught
Emporium
Dallas, Texas
96

Taco Mac
Alpharetta, Georgia
90

TapWerks Alehouse & Cafe
Oklahoma City, Oklahoma
84

Big City
Boston, Massachusetts
82

Jacks at the Cannery
San Francisco, California
80

Ginger Man
Austin, Texas
80

25 Outstanding Microbreweries

Only a few microbreweries make their beer available across the United States. However, many more produce enough beer and are available in a wide enough region that you may look for them well beyond the doors of their brewery. Each state section in this book also includes a list of outstanding micros in that state, and sometimes their beer is available in neighboring states.

Abita Brewing Co.
Louisiana

Alaskan Brewing Co.
Alaska

Anchor Brewing Co.
California

Anderson Valley Brewing Co.
California

Bert Grant's Ales
Washington

Boston Beer Co. (Samuel Adams beers)
Boston

Boulevard Brewing Co.
Missouri

Brooklyn Brewery
New York

Celis Brewery
Texas

Deschutes Brewery
Oregon

Full Sail Brewing Co.
Oregon

Goose Island Brewing Co.
Illinois

Gordon Biersch Brewing Co.
California

Kalamazoo Brewing Co.
Michigan

Mendocino Brewing Co.
California

New Belgium Brewing Co.
Colorado

North Coast Brewing Co.
California

Ommegang Brewery
New York

Pete's Brewing Co.
California

Portland Brewing Co.
Oregon

Pyramid Breweries
Washington/California

Redhook Ale Brewery
Washington/New Hampshire

Rogue Ales
Oregon

Sierra Nevada Brewing Co.
California

Widmer Brothers Brewing Co.
Oregon

Glossary

Breweriana: Antiques and other collectibles related to brewing and beer.

Brewhouse: The area where beer is brewed (a.k.a. the brewery).

Brewpub: By brewpub we mean places in which you may order a glass of beer where it is made. This includes brewpubs and microbreweries with restaurants, as well as some microbrewery tasting rooms.

Cask-conditioned ale: Also known as "real ale." According to Britain's Campaign For Real Ale, it is "a name for draft (or bottle) beer brewed from traditional ingredients, matured by secondary fermentation in the container from which it is dispensed, and served without the use of extraneous carbon dioxide." Generally served via a handpump, although not all beer served by handpump is cask-conditioned.

Craft and microbrewed beers: When we mention craft and/or microbrewed beers, we are referring to U.S. products. Many imports are also craft beer and are produced at small breweries.

Display brewery: A brewpub where the brewhouse is prominently displayed as a part of the decor.

Great American Beer Festival: Held each October in Denver, Colorado, showcasing more than 400 U.S. breweries. A competition is held in conjunction with the festival, and we sometimes refer to GABF awards won by brewpubs and microbreweries.

Guest beers: Beers served at brewpubs that are brewed at other microbreweries.

House beers: In the case of a brewpub, the beer made there. In the case of a bar or restaurant, a draft beer made especially for the bar or restaurant by a microbrewery.

Handpump: See cask-conditioned ale.

Mainstream beers: Sometimes we'll refer to these as domestics, other times as mainstream beers or industrial lagers. These are the beers produced in large quantities and consumed by ninety percent of the beer-drinking population.

Single-malt whisky: Whisky made in Scotland from a single type of malt, as opposed to a whisky made by blending other whiskies. A cousin to beer. Bars with extraordinary selections are duly noted.

Vintage beer: Most beer is best when fresh; however, some beer takes on interesting notes as it ages and may be served several years after it is bottled.

Keeping Up to Date

In the mid-1990s, almost five brewpubs a week opened in the United States. That rate of growth has slowed considerably, but the beer landscape still changes quickly. To keep up to date we suggest:

- The Beer Travelers website (www.beertravelers.com) which we maintain. We keep a variety of lists, including one that details changes that occurred since this book went to press.
- The Real Beer Page (www.realbeer.com), the largest source of beer information on the Internet. Start with the Brew Tour in the Search section and use other search functions liberally. (Disclaimer: Stan is editor at the Real Beer Page.)
- Regional "brewspapers." These free publications, usually published bimonthly, print stories about beer of the region and usually include lists of brewpubs and establishments serving interesting beer. The best place to find one is in a brewpub, a beer bar, or a liquor store that sells craft beer.
- Ask the person on the barstool next to you. We've learned about some of our favorite places this way, but started even more engaging conversations that had little to do with beer.

About the Authors

Stan Hieronymus and Daria Labinsky are longtime newspaper journalists who left their traditional day jobs in 1992 to explore the United States and write about what they found. Over time their writing began to focus more on beer but has not been limited to the subject. Their stories about beer, music festivals, music heritage, and travel have appeared in more than a dozen periodicals and several major metropolitan newspapers.

They are authors of *The Brewpub Cookbook,* the *Beer Travelers Guide, Music Festival Directory,* and a biography of Frank Applegate, a 1920s artist from Santa Fe, to be published in 2001. Stan is editor of the Real Beer Page (www.realbeer.com), and together they write a regular travel column for *All About Beer* magazine. Their stories about beer have won several writing awards.

Much of the research for this book was done when they lived in central Illinois. They now reside in Rio Rancho, New Mexico, with their daughter, Sierra.

Chasing the Thrill

Chasing the Thrill

Obsession, Death, and Glory in America's Most Extraordinary Treasure Hunt

DANIEL BARBARISI

RANDOM HOUSE
LARGE PRINT

Cover images: (left) Cavan Images / Getty Images;
(right) SeanXu / iStock / Getty Images
Spine image: (coins) by joecicak / Getty Images
Cover design by Jenny Carrow

The Library of Congress has established a
Cataloging-in-Publication record for this title.

ISBN: 978-0-593-41446-0

www.penguinrandomhouse.com/large-print-format-books

FIRST LARGE PRINT EDITION

Printed in the United States of America

10 9 8 7 6 5 4 3 2 1

This Large Print edition published in accord
with the standards of the N.A.V.H.

For Elliott and Reid,
who have so many adventures yet to come

Contents

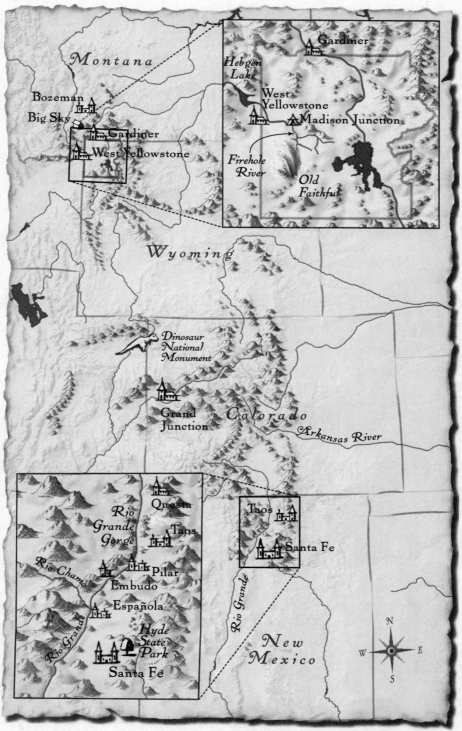

Chasing the Thrill

Prologue

June 7, 2017

"Do you hear that?"

My treasure-hunting partner, Beep, kept his eyes glued to the map. "Hear what?" he asked me without looking up.

"It sounded like thunder," I said, glancing up at the sky, which minutes before had been clear and blue and pristine. Now it was blackening, suddenly ominous.

We were standing on the side of State Road 68 a few miles north of Pilar, New Mexico, several hundred feet up the highway from the Rio Grande Gorge Visitor Center. In front of us stood an impenetrable mass of rock and brush, right where the map said the trail leading to Agua Caliente Falls was supposed to be.

Except it wasn't there. It didn't exist.

A rumble echoed through the canyon, unmistakable this time. Before Beep or I could say another word, the skies opened up and the raindrops began to fall—not a polite, drizzly rain, either. These were big, heavy drops, a cascade of water coming out of the sky with no warning and shocking suddenness.

"Run for the car!" I shouted, and we tore off toward the parking lot, a quarter mile up the road. Eighteen-wheelers rumbled by as we scampered along the shoulder of the highway back to our rented Ford Explorer. Yanking open the doors, we tumbled inside, out of breath, wet, and already defeated. We hadn't even gotten to our search area yet.

"How did we not think to check the weather?" I asked, mostly rhetorically.

"It's the desert. I thought the weather was always the same here," Beep said, looking perplexed. A pasty Canadian, he was shivering in the passenger seat in a gray fantasy sports T-shirt and black gym shorts, fully unprepared for the deluge. At least he was wearing a boonie hat he'd purchased because it seemed like good hunting gear, its floppy brim partially hiding his people-pleaser eyes. Just as well. I figured he'd be looking at me with disappointment for my embarrassing lack of preparation.

Quite the auspicious start to our careers as treasure hunters.

Treasure hunters. It still sounded crazy. A few months before, Beep had discovered the tale of Forrest Fenn, a wealthy New Mexico art dealer who claimed to have hidden a treasure chest worth millions somewhere in the Rocky Mountains north of Santa Fe. In 2010, Fenn published a book and a poem that promised to lead searchers to the treasure—if they could figure out the poem's nine clues. Beep had become completely obsessed with the chase, and I'd followed him down the rabbit hole.

We'd flown into Albuquerque the day before, and made our way up to Santa Fe later that night. Then early the following morning, Beep and I had stowed our newly purchased treasure-hunting gear and jumped into the car for the two-hour drive north through the wilds of New Mexico, the kind of place that isn't really barren but is still sparse enough that you mostly lose cell service. Once outside of 85,000-person Santa Fe, the starkness of the landscape is stunning: flat and broad for miles and miles in every direction, until that land runs into mountains far in the distance on each side. We'd theorized that Fenn's treasure must be somewhere among them—that chest and its cache of gold, diamonds, emeralds.

Driving toward those peaks, the only markers of civilization we saw were the periodic small towns, just hamlets really—a bar, a general store, maybe a school. In between them was nothing—nothing, except crosses at regular intervals along the highway, marking spots where unfortunate drivers had crashed. There were more of them than

I'd ever expected, more than I'd seen along any other stretch of highway anywhere. They were our constant companions as we drove up, pacing the distance between the only true landmarks on this journey: Native American tribal casinos. They rose out of the plains like the palaces of ancient kings, massive and elaborate and blinking with lights and signs and promises of riches. There was so little along this route, and yet one of these strange oases appeared every fifteen miles or so, and the parking lots were all packed. Who were all these people? Where did they come from? They're a bit like us, I figured, hoping to strike it rich—just in the form of plastic chips, not gold coins. And probably just as unlikely to realize their dream.

As we'd made our way to the search spot, I'd found myself growing more confident in our "solve"—our solution to Fenn's poem, our step-by-step route to the treasure. It had actually felt as if the treasure was within reach. The spot we were seeking was barely marked—it didn't even show up on Google Maps, the world's current digital arbiter of what is legitimate and what is not. We'd found the location on a United States Geological Survey map, listing Agua Caliente Canyon and, a few miles' hike away, Agua Caliente Falls. We'd zeroed in on the sites for two reasons. First, Agua Caliente means "hot water" in English. In the first line of Fenn's poem, the all-important verse that is supposed to lead searchers to the treasure, he advises seekers, "Begin it where warm waters halt/And take it in the canyon down."

Many people have taken that instruction literally—seeking out a spot where a river changes in temperature, or where a hot spring hits another body of water. But what if Fenn was just playing with words? What if, instead, he wanted us to start where "warm waters halt" in a different way—to begin where Agua Caliente Canyon ends, and then follow the canyon itself off into the wilderness? From there, we'd make our way to Agua Caliente Falls, which could be the site of "heavy loads and water high," one of the other clues in the poem.

This seemed like a pretty good idea when Beep and I were hashing it out back east, I from my home in Boston and he from his outside Toronto. But now that we were on the ground, hiding in our car, our internet searching seemed remarkably naïve.

"It's a lot easier to do it from your computer," Beep said, giving voice to my thoughts.

As we sat pondering this painfully obvious truth, something started peppering the car. Not rain anymore, but actual physical objects.

Hail.

Hailstones the size of pebbles pelted us by the thousands as we cowered in our rental SUV, still fresh with its new-car smell. I cringed as the little ice balls pinged off the car's exterior with a machine-gun rat-a-tat, desperately hoping they weren't leaving dents. I definitely hadn't paid for the rental insurance.

"Wow" was all Beep could muster. I couldn't even manage that.

"Should we just head back?" I asked, realizing how silly I'd been to think we could find a hidden treasure. We couldn't even get out of the car!

But Beep wasn't ready to go just yet. He had been lukewarm about this spot anyway, noting that Agua Caliente Falls was listed on the map at a higher elevation than the start of Agua Caliente Canyon—so we'd be taking the canyon up, not going "in the canyon down" as Fenn directs. He'd also politely noted the distinction that in English, Agua Caliente technically means "hot water," not "warm water"—which I knew, but, hey, I hadn't heard him offering any bright ideas.

"Let's drive around a little," Beep suggested now. "Let's drive along the river."

Might as well.

The hail was weakening, replaced by a hard rain, which was roiling the Rio Grande. The river looked mean and dangerous now, the water high and running fast as I took our truck down the road that ran alongside it.

Suddenly, Beep pointed at a sign, one marking a side road leading to a small bridge across the river.

"That sign says Agua Caliente Road—is that on the map?" he asked. "Maybe that means something. Maybe that means we're on the right track."

I could hear that glimmer of excitement start to creep into my compatriot's voice, so just to humor him, I drove a little farther down that way, bringing us to the entrance to Rio Grande Gorge. Most of the good maps were back at the Visitor Center, but there was at least a sign here marking the actual entrance and offering some basic geographical info. Beep got out to examine it. The gateway to the Rio Grande Gorge sat at the end of what seemed to be a tiny town, stuck out here on the edge of nowhere. From the car, I could see a few ramshackle houses dotting the sides of the river. One seemed to be guarded by a pair of ferocious-looking dogs. I thought about getting out to help Beep but decided to stay in the car. Hey, I'm a cat person.

Beep returned sooner than I expected, tearing open the car door, panting with excitement. Apparently, there was a Rio Bravo Campground up ahead, which Beep thought might be connected to one of the lines in the poem, "If you are brave and in the wood." His logic was that the word **brave** is **bravo** in Spanish, which keeps with the Agua Caliente/warm waters translation theme, and the campground was in a slightly woodsy area. And on top of that, there was an advisory that this was a brown trout fishing grounds, which could link to another line in the poem that suggests we "Put in below the home of Brown." Maybe that meant finding or using a boat put-in? A place where you'd go fishing for brown trout? Fenn, after all, was a big trout fisherman.

"I didn't expect to find anything there," he said. "But then I saw the Rio Bravo Campground sign, and the map talking about brown trout, so now I think we might really have something."

I was still feeling a bit deflated, but Beep's enthusiasm was contagious. It had always been that way with us; I could be the dour, realistic half of our partnership, and he would be the effervescent, never-cowed, slightly insane side of our coin. It worked well. At least it certainly had in the past. Beep had served as my mentor when, in 2015, I quit my job as a reporter at **The Wall Street Journal** to tell the story of the burgeoning phenomenon of daily fantasy sports from the inside; Beep had guided me on the way to claiming the title of Fantasy Hockey World Champion. Beep—real name Jay Raynor, but widely known by his fantasy sports username, BeepimaJeep, or usually Beep for short—was a legend in that arena, known as one of the top players, certainly, but also as one of the most eccentric. His penchant for wearing a quasi-uniform of a lopsided baseball cap and a T-shirt with an animal of some sort on the front distinguished him on the scene, and his odd talents made him stand out further. He was a former Canadian National board game champion, a self-taught foosball virtuoso, and a wealthy fantasy sports winner despite knowing virtually nothing about sports. I'd once described him as a "Renaissance man of the frivolous," and I think that still held true.

Over time, I'd learned to trust Beep's hunches; even my wife, Amalie, a reporter for NHL.com, had come to believe in them. She was back home, eight months pregnant with our first child, a boy. We had decided to name him Elliott, and I couldn't wait to meet him. Even so, when I'd explained that I needed to fly out to the Rocky Mountains to chase a treasure because Beep thought he had an idea about where it might be, as insane as that seemed, she understood. I married well.

Now Beep was getting enthusiastic again, believing that we were back on the right track. What if, miracle of miracles, we'd started in the right place after all—but had been trying to go the wrong way from there? Maybe Fenn really had wanted us to begin where Agua Caliente Canyon ends, but instead of heading east toward Agua Caliente Falls, he meant we should go west, down into the Rio Grande Gorge. Maybe the gorge itself was his "canyon down." And then maybe we should seek out those brown trout fisheries.

A burst of excitement flared up inside me. The rain was even letting up at last, so we raced ahead toward the Rio Bravo Campground. As we sped along the river, deeper into the canyon, Beep narrated the lines of the poem in Forrest Fenn's lilting Texan drawl. Like any semiserious Fenn hunters, we'd each read the poem so many times, we could recite it from memory. But every time, every read-ing, seemed to offer something new, spark a differ-ent thought. So I didn't really mind hearing it again, Beep's voice the only sound as we drove along.

> As I have gone alone in there
> And with my treasures bold,
> I can keep my secret where,
> And hint of riches new and old.
>
> Begin it where warm waters halt
> And take it in the canyon down,
> Not far, but too far to walk.
> Put in below the home of Brown.
>
> From there it's no place for the meek,
> The end is ever drawing nigh;
> There'll be no paddle up your creek,
> Just heavy loads and water high.
>
> If you've been wise and found the blaze,
> Look quickly down, your quest to cease,
> But tarry scant with marvel gaze,
> Just take the chest and go in peace.
>
> So why is it that I must go
> And leave my trove for all to seek?
> The answers I already know,
> I've done it tired, and now I'm weak.

So hear me all and listen good,
Your effort will be worth the cold.
If you are brave and in the wood
I give you title to the gold.

With the words of the poem ringing in our minds, Beep was now seeing connections everywhere— when he spotted a sign for falling rocks, he started bouncing in his seat.

"That could be the 'heavy loads,'" he said. Not long after, we passed a metal water pipe, about eight feet above the ground, spewing liquid out onto the side of the road. Beep started to suggest that could be the very next clue, but I cut him off.

"If that's his 'water high,'" I said, "this treasure hunt sucks."

Beep seemed to accept that and returned to silence as we sped along the winding road snaking along the basin of the gorge, paralleling the Rio Grande. But "water high" was still throwing us off—the river's waters were certainly high, but it couldn't be quite that simple, and besides, water height changes daily. Then up ahead, we saw a structure along the bank; it looked like a measuring station of some sort.

"That's worth checking out," I told Beep as I pulled off the road. We wandered around, eventually finding a placard telling us that this was a gaging station, one used by the United States Geological

Survey to measure water height. On the back of the station itself, we found a measuring stick, charting the level of the Rio Grande.

"They actually measure water levels here," Beep said, his hand on his chin. "This could be the kind of thing Forrest would think about. Now we just need a blaze."

Ah. The blaze. It is the phrase about the blaze in the poem that causes perhaps the most consternation to Fenn searchers. Right after the part about "heavy loads and water high," Fenn drops his clue about the blaze, that one should find it, and then "Look quickly down, your quest to cease."

So if you've got the blaze, you've got the treasure. The problem? No one, anywhere, can agree on what the heck a blaze is. Some people think it's a place name that references flame. Some think it's a sunset, or a special tree, or a man-made marker of some sort. It could be a rock or a natural formation that looks like an F, or something else that alludes to Fenn and the treasure. A few think it's an actual fire. That's the thing about the blaze—it really could be anything.

I tended to think it was an actual physical marker of some sort—one of Merriam-Webster's definitions for blaze is "a trail marker; **especially:** a mark made on a tree by chipping off a piece of the bark."

Fenn had said he thought his hunt could persist for hundreds of years, so his blaze should persist, as well. To me, it had to be something semipermanent, something that couldn't be moved or washed away or erode easily.

We were walking the site around the gaging station when we found it: a USGS survey marker, noting the siting of this station. The bronze marker was set deep into the rock, the kind of thing that would be there for centuries. This was really something, and Beep and I both realized it, my heart thumping hard.

"If this is the blaze, then we've got to look on the ground around here, maybe in the brush, maybe in the river itself," I told Beep as he scrambled off to look at gaps in the nearby boulders. I looked down again at the marker but didn't dare get too close. The marker was being guarded by a heinously ugly jet black bug, its exoskeleton like tank armor, crawling slowly around our would-be blaze like a wary sentinel. The beast was half the size of my fist. I felt like we were in his territory, so I slowly inched away, not wanting to disturb this guardian of the sacred marker unless absolutely necessary.

I headed for the edge of the Rio Grande, an area right near the gaging station where rocks and trees overhung the water. I wondered if other Fenn hunters had been by this spot before. It was so close to Fenn's home in Santa Fe, it seemed like a logical place to look. Searchers on the message boards often talked about bumping into other hunters canvassing the same ground in popular search areas; I didn't know how popular this was, and we hadn't seen anyone else out here, but that didn't mean there weren't other hunters afoot, vying with us to find the treasure. That coming weekend, hundreds of Fenn hunters would be converging on Santa Fe for the annual Fennboree, a celebration of all things Fenn. They were probably all trying to get a little searching in before the event, just like we were. Feeling a sense of urgency now, I moved forward with purpose toward a cluster of boulders that looked like the perfect place to hide something. Adrenaline started coursing through me as I bought into this, hook, line and sinker. It suddenly seemed so real, all of it. Could something actually be hidden here?

The gaging station hung into the river, so to get around it and to the area with the boulders, I gingerly hopped out onto a few stable rocks perched perilously in the Rio Grande. As water streamed over the bottoms of my shoes, I leaned into the area where the brush projected out over the rocks, pushing aside tree branches and hoping not to fall into the river. My very pregnant wife would not have approved of this behavior.

I craned my neck, looking into the crevices, half expecting a siren to go off and Ed McMahon to show up, telling me what I'd won. Peering in, I squinted my eyes to see something a little less exciting: nothing. Nothing at all, anywhere. There was no treasure chest here. Just a bunch of rocks and running water, the famous river rushing fast and hard, eager to gobble up any who didn't respect its power.

I carefully hopped back to the shore, where Beep reported he'd found much the same. I was suddenly feeling despondent, that adrenaline high fading as quickly as it had arrived, but Beep wanted to head up the road a little bit farther.

We got back into the car.

I wasn't even sure what we were looking for now—a blaze, high waters, heck, a fishing spot with brown trout—any of it. What we found instead was a bridge, a fairly large one, where the main road seemed to end before an offshoot forked up into the mountains.

A sign marked it as the Taos Junction Bridge, and there were a few cars and trucks parked nearby, but no people. We got out again to look around. The trail seemed cold, and the sun was starting to settle low in the sky. The water rushed by us, the bridge spanning the spot where the Rio Grande meets another river, the Rio Pueblo de Taos. I wasn't sure what to do next, so I told Beep I thought we should go home.

Beep was convinced we were on the right track, but he grudgingly accepted. One of his favorite pastimes is predicting outcomes, laying odds on them. Before we'd driven north, he'd put our odds of finding the treasure someday at less than 3 percent. I thought that was wildly generous. But now? Now that we'd started searching the Rio

Grande, Beep was putting us at a whopping 10 to 15 percent.

"I'm just so certain now. I know I shouldn't be. But everything lines up," he said.

I couldn't say I shared his sentiments, but it was hard not to get a little bit excited by our first day of work. We had a long drive back to Santa Fe ahead of us, but we were feeling good; for a few hours, at least, we had felt like real treasure hunters, chasing down hunches. There was an upbeat vibe in the car as we turned the Ford Explorer around and left the Taos Junction Bridge and the handful of parked trucks in our rearview mirror. **Maybe we really are on the right track,** I thought as we raced back to town, feeling like veteran hunters already, capable of tackling anything this chase threw at us.

I couldn't have been more wrong.

One week later, search and rescue personnel would be combing the area around that parking lot in search of a Fenn hunter named Paris Wallace. Wallace had parked his truck there and ventured off to explore the Rio Grande below for the same reason we had: He believed it might hold the key to finding Fenn's treasure.

Wallace would never be seen alive again.

1

YOU CAN'T TAKE
IT WITH YOU

Forrest Fenn had it all.

The Santa Fe art dealer had crafted the perfect life. After spending nearly two decades in the air force and emerging from Vietnam a decorated fighter pilot, the restless Texas boy in him had yearned for something new. So largely on a whim, Fenn had hitched a trailer behind his truck; hauled his wife and his young daughters, Zoe and Kelly, off to New Mexico; and struck out on a career as a dealer of art and antiquities, despite knowing little about either subject.

But he had charm, and he had flair, and he wasn't afraid of hard work, so by the 1980s, Fenn had established himself as one of the Southwest's preeminent art dealers, and a true man-about-town in the rarified, moneyed world of Santa Fe. He hobnobbed with politicians and counted celebrities like

Robert Redford, Suzanne Somers, and Gerald Ford among his clients and friends. He lived in a sprawling walled compound just outside the downtown, and worked out of a palatial gallery right by the State Capitol, whose guesthouse had hosted luminaries from Jacqueline Kennedy Onassis to Steve Martin. When he was feeling real nice, he'd let visitors take a sip from the brandy bottle Jackie O. left behind.

In 1988, he was fifty-eight years old, still in the prime of an exciting and unpredictable life.

And then he learned it was all about to be taken from him.

Cancer. A big, angry tumor embedded in his inferior vena cava, under his right kidney. Doctors weren't optimistic. They gave him a 20 percent chance to live. One-in-five odds? As a man who had stared death in the face repeatedly both over and in the jungles of Vietnam, those numbers didn't sound particularly good to him.

Fenn did what he could to process the blow. For a few weeks, he let it soak in, allowed the reality that he was probably going to die to wash over him. Then he got mad. Indignant, even. Why did he have to go? Who said? Nobody had asked him.

The moment it boiled over, he was in the study of his home with his friend Ralph Lauren, the famed fashion designer. Fenn's study was a magical place, a floor-to-ceiling gallery of artifacts, valuables, tomes, and curiosities from his travels. One piece, a Native American bonnet covered with ermine skins and carved antelope horns, caught Lauren's eye. Believing his friend was not long for this world, Lauren wanted to buy the piece from him, give it a new home. But Fenn wouldn't sell.

Lauren, exasperated, told Fenn he was being crazy. "Your time here is short, and you can't take it with you," Lauren declared.

"Well, then," Fenn shot back, "I'm not going."

Lauren laughed. They moved on.

But later that night, lying in bed, Fenn had a revelation: What if he **could** take it with him? Just a year earlier, his father, Marvin, a school principal, whom Fenn revered, had passed on—had taken his own life, actually. Marvin Fenn had been diagnosed with terminal pancreatic cancer. He'd been given six months to live. Eighteen months later, the resilient Marvin told his son Forrest that it was finally time for him to go. Marvin was going to take fifty sleeping pills that night, he said, and that would be that. Forrest pleaded with his father to wait—he had a plane, he said, and he'd fly up the next morning. The father matter-of-factly told the son that by then, it would be too late. It was.

Rather than being upset, Fenn saw wisdom in his father's controlled exit, saw it as a dignified way to go. Fenn liked the idea of taking charge of his own departure. But he also liked the idea of taking it all with him. What if, he mused, there was a way for him to do both?

An idea started germinating in his head. He would get a chest, fill it with valuables—gold, jewels, artifacts he had collected over his years in the art world—and seal it up tight. It would be a real-life treasure chest.

Then he would write a poem—more of a riddle, really—containing nine distinct clues in consecutive order. If the clues were solved perfectly, they would lead the finder directly to the treasure. But this treasure map in a poem wouldn't just lead to Fenn's treasure chest. It would bring the reader to Fenn himself. Fenn planned to take his chest to the special spot identified in the poem, take pills, as his father had, and quietly leave this world. Eventually, he believed, someone would solve his riddle, and there they would find him, in his eternal rest: his sun-bleached bones, and with them his treasure.

Not long after doctors removed the tumor, and also his right kidney, Fenn began to set his plan into motion. Fenn learned a friend owned a twelfth-century bronze Romanesque lockbox, ten inches by ten inches by five inches, which he believed would make an ideal treasure chest, and he paid $25,000 for it on the spot. He started to fill it with loot. He began writing the poem. His plan was coming along perfectly. There was only one problem.

He got better.

Against all odds, Fenn beat the cancer. He had

his life back. He sold his gallery that same year, and comfortably shifted into a sort of semiretirement.

But the idea stuck with him. It hadn't been merely a moment of desperation, some end-around way of wriggling out of death's grasp. Well, even if it was that, it was also something more. Fenn believed he had hit on something special, and he intended to follow through with some version of his treasure-hunting plan, even if his corpse would no longer be a part of it.

Over the next twenty years, Fenn filled the chest with all manner of valuables. Eventually, it would come to hold a truly magnificent fortune: 265 gold coins; dozens of gold nuggets; a gold dragon bracelet with ruby eyes, studded with diamonds, emeralds, and rubies; 2 gold frogs; a Mayan gold bracelet; a seventeenth-century emerald-and-gold Spanish ring; 2 pre-Columbian gold mirrors; gold dust; 2 gold nose rings; a Tairona fetish necklace thousands of years old; several jade figurines; 2 pre-Columbia wak'as—objects of ritual importance or power—and more, plus a copy of Fenn's as-yet-unseen autobiography, stuffed into an olive jar. There was also a turquoise bracelet that had sentimental value to Fenn, a piece crafted from beads that explorer Richard Wetherill found when he discovered the Mesa Verde complex; Fenn won it playing a game of pool, and he said he would like to buy it back from whoever found the chest. The chest's contents have generally been valued at somewhere between one and two million dollars, though some wildly generous estimates climb as high as four to five million dollars.

Fenn kept the chest in a walk-in vault in his home, occasionally altering its contents, and regularly bringing friends by to see this delightful conversation piece sitting on his shelf. Over time, he tweaked and refined his poem, as well. But perhaps most important, he set to work on the vessel for carrying the poem itself: his memoir.

Originally, when he believed he was dying, Fenn had hoped to have one of his many author friends write the memoir for him. But they all found the idea too morbid. So, long after he had recovered, close to the time when he actually hid the treasure, Fenn wrote it himself, crafting a hokey, folksy telling of his life story. The book, broken into small chapters and conversational vignettes, told of his time growing up in Temple, Texas, as the son of a school principal, and of the misadventures that he and his siblings would get into. It described how they would head to West Yellowstone, Montana, in the summers, and how Fenn fell in love with the place. How he served as a fishing guide, how he'd swum naked in the park's warm pools, ridden his bike through its remarkable environs. It was a Rockwellian yarn of growing up in idyllic fashion, in a world that no longer exists.

But it was also an account of Fenn's later life. How he joined the air force at the outbreak of the Korean War, and eventually found himself stationed in Germany, flying F-100 Super Sabre fighter-bombers with nuclear weapons strapped under their wings. How he made the rank of major, and deployed to Vietnam, where he was shot down twice, the second time in what was to be his final mission, over Laos. How he spent a harrowing night alone in the jungle, cowering from the blasts of B-52 bomb strikes, waiting for rescue helicopters to find him. How he finally got to call his wife, Peggy, after he was rescued, telling her not to worry about the telegram she'd received that his plane had been lost and no parachute was seen, telling her that he was alive.

Fenn's memoir was at times wistful, at times elegiac, as it spoke of days gone by, of the old man's journey into the art world, of the famous people he had known and the close friends he had lost. Of his deep, enduring love for Peggy. Of his joy at the lives of his children. Eventually, it told the story of his cancer. And then, in the final pages of the book, he introduced the poem, the one he had spent two decades fine-tuning, with its "warm waters halt" and "in the canyon down."

By 2010, Fenn was eighty years old. His memoir and his poem were complete. His treasure chest was full. One day—he made sure no one knew exactly when, but it was around that same year—Fenn took the chest from his vault, headed out into the wilderness, and hid it. He did it alone, placing the treasure where "it would be difficult to find but not impossible. It's in the mountains somewhere north of Santa Fe," as he wrote in his book. The chest, he said, took him two trips from his car to hide, because it and its contents weighed an impressive forty-two pounds by then. Hiding it took one afternoon. Then he returned home, and, he said, even his wife was none the wiser.

Fenn printed one thousand copies of his memoir, which he titled **The Thrill of the Chase,** and offered them at wholesale cost to a friend at Santa Fe's Collected Works Bookstore to sell. He stipulated that a percentage of any profits go to a cancer charity, and that the rest go to the store. None would go to him; Fenn wanted to ensure that no one accused him of engineering this hunt in an effort to sell books. The memoir, he said, was sprinkled with subtle clues in its various stories, hints that would help supplement the nine clues of the poem.

Fenn held an event for the release of the book, and the peculiar story of the art dealer giving away a chest full of riches got a bit of press—the local paper, some area television stations. Fenn put it on his website, and that brought in a few searchers from outside the area. He delighted in the small-time coverage, playing the "eccentric millionaire" card for all it was worth as he and his treasure hunt became a southwestern curiosity.

At first, the hunting cohort was small. A few hundred, really, maybe a thousand, mostly people with some connection to Fenn, united by the internet into a loose community. But over time, the story spread—a few pieces in **The Huffington Post,** an item in **Reader's Digest.**

Soon, a few blogs and forums dedicated to discussing the chase sprang up, and a devoted following began to form, arguing over details, discussing possible solutions, trading stories about adventures in Yellowstone or New Mexico or about a chance meeting with Fenn himself. As the community grew, Fenn remained an active part of the hunt; he'd put his email address in the book, so searchers would email him, tell him what they thought, where they were looking, why they loved the experience so much. The chance to correspond with the hunt's creator became one of the most alluring features of entering the search. Fenn would engage with his hunters, countering their questions with cryptic half answers, and seemed tickled that no one could solve his riddle as he gleefully presided over the whole thing.

Still, for those first few years, it remained a minor venture, little known outside its core group of enthusiasts. Word really started to spread with the publication of a story on **Newsweek**'s website, and another in **Hemispheres,** the in-flight magazine of United Airlines. Fliers from around the world learned of this hunt, and took an interest. Sales of Fenn's memoir spiked at the Collected Works Bookstore, and more printings had to be ordered, with the bookstore now paying the production costs, all the way through the current 13th edition.

What truly took it from a curiosity into a full-blown craze, though, was the **Today** show. In early 2013, reporter Janet Shamlian contacted Fenn, hoping to do a full feature on this odd phenomenon taking place in the American West.

And overnight, everything changed.

The piece aired on February 27, 2013. Thousands of copies of Fenn's book were ordered that day. The upstart blogs chronicling the chase crashed from the excess traffic. Other national media outlets followed up with their own stories, creating a frenzy. Before long, there were hundreds of pieces in major media publications around the world, twenty-five-plus documentary films on the subject, and eventually seven more **Today** show segments, as Fenn giddily played media star anytime a reporter arrived with a notebook—or, better, a camera.

Over the next few years, the number of searchers who ventured into the Southwest actively looking for Fenn's treasure went from mere thousands to what Fenn would estimate was well over 100,000. National parks like Yellowstone were suddenly overwhelmed, forced to create special announcements, rules, and cautions specifically for the brazen Fenn hunters as they tramped through protected wildlife zones and even dug up outhouses in search of Fenn's "home of Brown." Search and rescue teams got used to plucking hunters out of areas where they didn't belong after they had tried to venture just one more mile in the cold, or the snow, or too close to a river, certain the treasure was just around the bend.

The state of New Mexico built a tourism campaign around the hunt, and in 2015, the mayor of Santa Fe proclaimed a "Thrill of the Chase" Day, to thank Fenn for bringing so many visitors to his town. An annual gathering, Fennboree, drew aficionados from all over the world to celebrate Fenn and discuss their latest efforts to find his loot. A whole industry grew around the chase, with hunters forming teams, guides selling their services or offering clues and supposed solutions for cash, and others minting coins with Fenn's likeness on them and hawking them across the internet.

Meanwhile, the search community exploded, coalescing into a worldwide society with one thing in common: Fenn. Searchers fell in love and met their spouses on the chase, their shared obsession bringing them together. Factions and cliques developed, all racing to beat one another to the prize. Cautionary tales circulated of regular people who became too obsessed, who blew their life savings seeking the treasure, who went into bankruptcy to fund just one more expedition to the West. Sales of **The Thrill of the Chase** cleared the forty-thousand mark, and Fenn, basking in it all, wrote two more quasi-memoirs about his life (again mostly distributing the profits elsewhere, though profits from some of these subsequent works went into a trust for his grandchildren), each purporting to offer more clues useful in locating the box.

But for all that, no one found the treasure. Though according to Fenn, some at least had come close. Fenn was doing so many interviews that he began to reveal additional information about the location of the chest—sometimes intentionally, sometimes apparently not.

Perhaps most interesting, he said he knew that at least one person had been within two hundred feet of the treasure, setting other hunters on a frantic chase to determine exactly who the two-hundred-foot searcher had been, when it might have occurred, and, of course, where. But Fenn also began releasing new information to narrow down the scope of the chase, partly in order to stop searchers from doing silly things: He had to announce that the treasure was not associated with a "human structure," to stop hunters from digging in those outhouses, for example, and pledged that it was not connected with a graveyard, because at least one man had begun digging up graves, and Fenn feared that his father's was next. He officially narrowed the search area down to the four states of New Mexico, Colorado, Wyoming, and Montana, wiping out the parts of the Rocky Mountains that trickle into Canada, Idaho, and Utah. He revealed that the treasure was at least 8.25 miles north of the northernmost border of Santa Fe—perhaps so that searchers would stay away from his house—and that it was above 5,000 feet and below 10,200 feet, hoping that searchers would stop trying to climb to the tops of mountains. He made it clear that the chest was not "in close proximity to a human trail," warned searchers never to go hunting alone, and advised that they confine their efforts to a search season of spring, summer, and early fall.

But as the chase exploded in popularity, these hints weren't enough to deter hunters from putting themselves in dangerous situations, and it was only a matter of time before tragedy struck.

In February 2016, a Colorado man named Randy Bilyeu ventured out into the Rio Grande River with his dog as his only companion, in search of Fenn's gold. It wasn't long before he was reported missing. Six months later, his badly decomposed remains were found.

For the first time, Fenn and his hunt faced serious opposition. Appeals came from law enforcement, from government, and even from some searchers for Fenn to call the whole thing off. Fenn, defensive and prickly, said Bilyeu hadn't followed his rules, and asserted that he bore no responsibility for the man's death. He dug in his heels and said that his hunt was safe, releasing several new clues intended to keep hunters out of danger.

And for a time, that proved to be enough. Any

controversy died off, and life around the chase returned to normal. By the start of the 2017 search
season, Fenn's quest was bigger than ever, with
what he estimated were 350,000 searchers out on
the hunt. That June, hundreds of them were set to
gather north of Santa Fe for what was expected to
be the biggest Fennboree ever, a true celebration of
Fenn and his wondrous treasure chest.

Beep and I planned to be among them.

2

DETECTIVE WORK

The waiter brought over the beef carpaccio, setting it down in front of us and interrupting our excited dialogue. I didn't really mind. We were at Geronimo, perhaps the finest restaurant in Santa Fe, tucked in among the art galleries and sculpture gardens of Canyon Road, and this meal felt like a just reward for a hard day's hunting.

As I dug in for my first bite, I savored both the taste and the decor—adobe walls, kiva stoves, wood beams everywhere—at a restaurant that would normally be out of my price range. But I was in luck; all my dining on this trip was courtesy of Beep, who was suddenly very rich, thanks to a shrewd stake in the emerging cryptocurrency ether. He'd bought into it when it was around fifty dollars a coin, back in March of 2017. Now that it was June, the token was up over $350 a coin, and Beep had huge amounts.

He joked that thanks to his newfound financial largesse, he'd semiretired at twenty-nine, though I wasn't totally sure if he was joking. Still, he seemed content, and clearly glad to be out of the stressful fantasy gambling world. Now casting about for a new pastime, Beep was dreaming of something a little more stable: being a full-time treasure hunter and cryptocurrency investor.

"Sounds so easy. What could go wrong?" I said, not sure if he exactly sensed the sarcasm.

It was Beep, of course, who had gotten me into this treasure hunt in the first place. It had all started around the end of March, when Beep had suddenly dropped off the map, completely AWOL for about three weeks, impossible to reach by phone or email.

When I finally cornered him, Beep was cagey, which was unusual. We caught up a bit, and finally I asked him where he had been for nearly a month. He took a deep breath and, at last, brought me into his confidence.

"I think I'm onto something big," he said as we spoke over Skype, his words spilling out in his usual rapid-fire patter. "I'm never one hundred percent sure about anything, but I'm about as close as I've ever been. I'm eighty-five percent certain. Maybe even higher. Maybe even ninety percent."

I'd certainly done well trusting in Beep's hunches. And if he really was right about this thing, whatever it was, it would be a life-changing discovery. This was going to be the big one.

"All right, I'm ready," I said, prepared for literally anything, from a drug-smuggling scheme to backing a coup in a small Eastern European nation.

He brought his voice low, as if he had a secret to share.

"Have you ever heard of the treasure of Forrest Fenn?"

Dramatic as it seemed, at the time this meant nothing to me. Beep brought me up to speed about Fenn and his chest in a hurry, admitting that he'd first stumbled upon it via one of those clickbait ads at the bottom of a web page, the ones that say "You won't believe what she's wearing!" or "Top 10 Hollywood feuds," or, apparently, "This ex–fighter pilot hid a $2 million treasure in the Rocky Mountains." I should have stopped him right then and there. But he was so excited that I let him keep going, and I'll admit to feeling my heart skip a beat when he made his next declaration.

"I think I know where the treasure is," he said.

Before I could even fully process what was happening, Beep had moved on to the next order of business, which was retrieving it immediately, somewhere near Yellowstone National Park.

"I'm so, so certain about this, we've got to go get it right away, before someone else figures it out, too," he said. "How soon can you leave? Could you go tomorrow?"

Tomorrow?

This was all insane, as I told him. Still, there was such urgency in his voice as he implored me to look up flights that, against my better judgment, I gamely complied, caught up in his excitement. Beep wanted me along both because he was worried about heading into the great outdoors on his own and because he wanted me there to chronicle his moment of glory, when he retrieved this hidden treasure.

"There's a flight from Toronto to Bozeman, Montana, that takes eight hours, with only one stop, and costs six hundred and fifty Canadian dollars," I told him. "But are you sure it's late enough in the year to do this? There's probably still snow on the ground."

Beep hadn't quite considered that, and it slowed him down briefly. Long enough for me to convince him to walk me through his solution to Fenn's puzzle, to see if I really needed to be booking last-minute flights or if this was just some wild-goose chase.

Beep's big discovery, he explained, was that he believed he had figured out the site of the blaze. He called up a map of Wyoming and Montana and took me through his solve step by step, from its start inside Yellowstone to its detour up into Montana and the Gallatin National Forest, until finally landing upon a spot near a cave. At the spot, Beep linked me a video showing the spot and what he believed he'd found—a marking on a rock formation that looked like the letter **F**.

He was so excited to show it to me that I felt terrible when I squinted hard at what he was showing me and realized I was going to have to tell him that this supposed **F** was just a combination of shadow and the angle of the rocks coming together in the video.

I tried to let him down easy.

Beep was disappointed, crushed, even. But before he went off to stew in his misery, he still had a bit of sage advice to offer.

"You should really write about this hunt," he told me.

How right he was.

I began to research Fenn and the world he had created. Each new revelation reinforced just how crazy all of it was. A treasure hunt simply didn't belong in 2017. To me, treasure hunts live somewhere between the realms of anachronism and imagination, either a vestige of a world long past or a pure fantasy, a kid's story, the kind of thing we grow out of believing.

Yet this hunt was completely real, and that indisputable fact left me with so many questions. I immediately set about answering them. After a few weeks of research, I got back in touch with Beep, telling him that I had a plan, and that he was going to like it.

I was in.

I planned to take a two-pronged approach to exploring and capturing Fenn's world. First, I would do all the things a reporter could and should do. I would interview Fenn and his hunters, tell their stories, and document the growth and spread of this treasure hunt.

But I would also join them in their chase. I told Beep I was hoping to team up with him, forming a quasi-partnership of sorts. He would take the lead, but I hoped to tag along on his adventures, helping where I could, joining him on hunts across the West. He'd be a treasure hunter, and I'd be something of an accessory to hunting as we went through the process of figuring out solves and then testing them in boots-on-the-ground searches. Was it scientific? Somewhat. Profitable? Maybe. Fun? Absolutely.

The real truth was that I wanted this. Maybe needed it. I had spent too long living among fantasy sports gamblers, cooped up inside, staring at computer screens, crunching numbers, laying bets, trying to stay sane even while betting five figures daily like it was nothing. I came out of it with a championship belt, a giant check, a closet full of giveaway fantasy sports T-shirts, and **mayyyyybe** a bit of a gambling problem. This treasure hunt, though, promised a chance to get outside and explore. It felt so innocent, so pure, like such a lark. Maybe it was a way to get back to who I was before the gambling took over.

And besides, what's the point of writing about a treasure hunt if you don't get to at least play at being a treasure hunter?

That's what had brought us to Santa Fe, rampaging around the Rio Grande Gorge earlier that day. As we reminisced about our hunt that night at the restaurant, Beep was bursting with excitement, even after our failure to find anything along the Rio Grande. Now that we'd been on this first boots-on-the-ground search, he just wanted to get back out on the hunt as soon as possible, even if we really had no idea where to look.

Our voices rang out through Geronimo as we ate and discussed the hunt, and what we needed to do next. And in Santa Fe, the subject we were discussing—Forrest Fenn and his treasure—was one that demanded an opinion from every resident.

"I'm sorry," an elderly woman in a sparkly red dinner jacket soon interjected, "but I couldn't resist. Are you here looking for Fenn's treasure?"

We quickly owned up to our pursuit, explaining that we'd spent our day tramping along the edge of the Rio Grande in search of his box of riches. The woman and her two companions all knew Fenn personally, the first woman having hobnobbed with him at parties, a second having sold him a rug in the 1970s for his gallery, their gentleman friend simply bumping into Fenn from time to time in this neighborly city. I guess I shouldn't have been shocked that the locals would guess at our plans so easily—treasure-seeking tourists came from all over just to try their hand at hunting.

What came next was a bit more of a surprise.

"I would be wary of Forrest Fenn," said the first woman, the one with the jeweled jacket, who introduced herself as Lynn. She went on to explain that Fenn had had something of a checkered past even before the treasure hunt, and that now, many in Santa Fe weren't too fond of what he'd brought upon them with his hunt and its fanatical hunters.

"A lot of people have very bad opinions of him for a lot of the negative attention he's brought," she said. "And can anyone really say if his treasure is real or not?"

It was that last thing she said that resonated. She had a point, of course—one that had gnawed at me since Beep first told me of the treasure three months before.

The first step in becoming a treasure hunter is identifying the treasure you want to go after. The second? Determining if that treasure is really there at all.

I hadn't been particularly skeptical of the hunt at

first, so excited by its mere existence that I didn't think to question it. But seemingly every person I told about it would ask almost immediately how we knew it was real, and my initial research had taught me that many of these hunts are either flat-out hoaxes or their legends are inflated over decades or centuries.

Fenn's hunt hadn't had any time to take on mythical properties. But it could surely be a hoax. What did we really know about this guy, anyway? Why did he really do it? What guarantees did we have that this treasure existed before we spent hard-earned dollars (or, in Beep's case, well-invested cryptocurrency) to fly out to New Mexico in search of treasure? We needed to know more.

To answer that question, I had first turned to that ever-ready fount of knowledge, the internet. And fortunately, that's where most of Fenn's hunt lives. Much of the discussion surrounding the treasure takes place on a few main blogs, where hunters hash out solutions, offer their takes on one another's solves, and, more than anything else, get into silly fights and arguments. The internet is, of course, the worst place on Earth, and conflict arises everywhere across it. But it sure seemed like these treasure forums had more than their fair share, accusations flying this way and that about solve stealing, hunters sniping at one another over slightly incorrect references to Fenn talking points, others continuing yearslong online feuds where they probably didn't even remember who had fired the first shot anymore.

The drama was everywhere and the details made little sense to me, to be honest—but what was clear was that there was a small group of hunters whom everyone talked about, who appeared to have a special status inside the hunt. This special group qualified as celebrities within this tiny sphere, the cool kids in high school whom not everyone likes but whom everyone knows and follows, and all of them had reached one-name status: Cynthia, Sacha, Dal, Desertphile, Stephanie. The other posters would talk about them, reference them, praise them, complain about them, grouse over their closeness with Fenn.

These were the people I needed to find. I wanted to meet them, talk to them, get to know them, understand them—and, yes, I'll admit, maybe gawk at them just a little bit. Regardless, they were, unquestionably, the place to start.

For many of those entering the chase, Dal's blog is the first stop, and I was no different. Dal's blog contains the basics of the hunt for the entry-level searcher: the poem, safety warnings, Fenn's collected writings, key clues that have surfaced in interviews with Fenn over the years. It's all presided over by Dal Neitzel, founder of the blog, one of the original Fenn searchers.

Dal is the Paul to Fenn's Jesus, his first apostle, the man responsible for spreading his gospel and, more often than not, doing his PR. This guy has been a true believer almost from the very beginning, and he obviously thinks the treasure is real.

Neitzel is a documentary filmmaker in Washington State, living on a small island out in Puget Sound. The Vietnam vet didn't work full-time anymore, but he still occasionally produced pieces for a local television station—as long as it didn't interfere with his treasure-hunting schedule. When I reached out, Dal was wary of me at first, saying he didn't want to interact with a reporter, necessarily, until he knew my true intentions regarding Fenn and his chase. It wasn't the last time I'd hear that. We'd gone back and forth for a little while, circling each other, until it came out rather accidentally that I was planning to go to New Mexico, to tag along and look for the treasure with Beep. After he heard that I was an active searcher, he opened right up. I immediately filed that away as we began talking about how he'd discovered this hunt.

Dal had actually been a type of treasure hunter even before he found Fenn's chase, spending some time in the 1990s working to salvage old wrecks with a team that ranged all up and down the Americas. One of the men in that squad happened to be Fenn's nephew, Creighton, a well-known salvage specialist.

"When the [space shuttle] **Columbia** blew up over the Pacific Ocean, Creighton was the guy they called," Dal said.

When the chase began, Dal was already familiar with Fenn and learned about the chase through his connection to Creighton. He was immediately hooked. He ordered the book, devoured the poem, and spent the fall and winter of 2010 trying to figure it all out.

"By January [2011], I had it cracked. I mean, I knew exactly where the treasure was. And I couldn't wait to get going. I had already [cashed it in] about ten times over in my head. So in May, I went out there, because I believed it was in New Mexico. I went out to the Rio Grande to look in my spot.

"And, of course, I didn't find it," he said, sighing.

Undeterred, he started the blog that became the clearinghouse for all things Fenn. Along the way, Dal got to know the man himself very well, and became something of a conduit to him—governing access by other searchers, issuing Fenn's proclamations, and declaring his wishes in public. But Dal's prominence in the hunt, and his administering of one of the main forums for searchers to congregate, also made him something of a target. I noted that the Fenn forums seemed particularly combustible, and he said I didn't know the half of it.

"Oh, of course I get death threats." He chuckled. "What, you mean you don't get those?"

I made it clear that I, in fact, did not.

"I probably get three or four a year," he said. "For various reasons. Oftentimes it's because I kick somebody off the blog. They know there's no retaliation. So they say things. Others get kinda creepy about it. They say they know the island I live on, they know where my house is, and they're going to come by in the middle of the night, shoot me dead."

Other times, hunters resented his relationship with Fenn.

"Folks have come after me," Dal said. "I've been to see Forrest many times, I've stayed at his place, I'm close to him, I've talked to him, I've interviewed him. So folks all of a sudden figured out that I must be getting more information than they are. Well, if I know so much, how come I haven't found it?

"They accused me of having too much information, of being too close to Forrest," Dal continued. "And there was a big huge clapback on the blog, that I should stop hunting, because I know too much. And folks were coming down on me. They were really coming down on me. So I said, Okay, I'll stop searching."

But in the end, he didn't stop. He said a groundswell of support arose from some of the more rational hunters, which got him to keep going. Yet he understood that there were always going to be people who hated him, people who begrudged him his relationship with Fenn, people who could never be convinced that this wasn't some giant conspiracy between him and Fenn. Oh, and then there were those who were simply off the deep end to begin with. The chase draws those in by the hundreds, if not thousands, he said.

"Like, let me tell you—and this is not an uncommon point of view: that the treasure chest is filled with evil spirits," Dal said. "That it's important that it not be opened, and these spirits not be able to enter the world, because it will mean the end of the universe. And that Forrest knows this, and he's an evil person."

So Dal banned these crazies, and made enemies in the process. But they still came back under fake names, or went to one of the other blogs and fired back, helping to perpetuate the strangely combative online environment around this treasure hunt.

One of those other blogs, called ChaseChat, seemed to occupy particular importance in Dal's mind. ChaseChat was his clear rival, and he seemed to regard its proprietor, Stephanie Thirtyacre, as something of a peer gone wrong. He volunteered her story, saying that she, too, was one of the early hunters, but that her devotion to the hunt had ruined Stephanie's marriage, caused her to go into debt. There was a hint of sadness in his voice as he told her tale.

"She went over the deep end. What happened was, she went bankrupt. Literally. Not figuratively, literally. She went bankrupt. She way overspent."

As I shook my head at the story, Dal added another out-of-nowhere tidbit.

"I'll tell you something else," he said. "She also accused Forrest of trying to trade sex for clues. C'mon, Stephanie. He's an eighty-five-year-old guy."

That was jarring to hear, and I didn't really understand what it meant; I issued a sort of "Huh," and, as it didn't pertain to what I was focusing on at the time, resolved to deal with that later.

Talking to Dal made me pretty confident that the chase contained its fair share of eccentrics—and perhaps even drove others a little mad—but I still hadn't gotten any confirmation that this thing they were searching for actually existed. I finally posed the question I really wanted answered: How do we know the treasure is real? How did he? How does he still believe, after all these years searching and finding nothing?

"If you get to know Forrest, you'll just know it's real. That's just not the kind of thing he would do," Dal said, the trust evident in his voice.

That was nice to hear, but that wasn't nearly enough for me.

In search of another perspective, I tracked down a different hunter, another of those most famous names in the chase: Cynthia Meachum, considered by most to be the sharpest and best of the lot.

A former engineer working out of Intel's New Mexico facility, now retired and living with her partner, Michelle, outside Albuquerque, Cynthia came to Fenn's world later than Dal, joining the chase in 2013, when it began getting international attention. But she quickly gained Fenn's confidence, and earned a special status within the hunt as a premier searcher, and one with Fenn's imprimatur. She wasn't quite on the inside in the way Dal was—running the blog, filming Fenn's videos and appearances—but was a far more active hunter, going on near-daily searches from her home in Rio Rancho. In that capacity, she was vital to Fenn. As a New Mexico local, she was the searcher he summoned when media members needed someone to tag along with, to observe out in the field—to show that the angry people on the blogs don't represent his hunt. She'd almost made a cottage industry out of it, and one can see why: She's smart, funny, capable, independent, and eminently quotable. She serves as the human face of the hunters to the outside world.

That, she said, had led to Fenn's getting mad at her a few times, when she had said or done something publicly he didn't like, but none of it had seemed to stick. She'd managed to play both sides of the game pretty effectively, fluidly navigating the interesting opportunities her station brought. For instance, regular access to Fenn was obviously a valuable asset to a Fenn hunter—perhaps the most valuable asset of all. I wanted to know how she balanced talking to him like a human being with the reality that anything he said could be a clue.

"I really try to pay attention to everything he says," she said. "When we're in his office, chitchatting, I try to pay attention to every word he says, just in case. He used to talk more about the poem and the actual search than he does anymore. But even then, he was ambiguous, and I think I used to walk away thinking that he might have said something that was a clue, and then it turns out it's not."

Even though none of Fenn's words had proved terribly useful, she tried to maintain a certain distance regardless, both to keep herself in Fenn's good graces and to ensure that other hunters didn't get too angry at her preferential access.

"One thing I don't do, ever, is ask him direct questions about the poem or the chase," she said. "Because I don't want him to think the reason I want to hang out with him is to pump him for information. That's not the reason I hang out with him."

That didn't stop many, many members of the chase community, however, from railing at her for her special access to Fenn. "Fat lot of good it's done me!" she replied, just as Dal had said.

But it made me think—this was something I was going to have to deal with, too, if I ever managed to get Fenn to talk to me. Even if I was letting

Beep do most of the real treasure hunting, I was still a part of this venture, and as a journalist, I was probably going to get access and information that average hunters would never get on their own.

If I overtly helped Beep, would that be ethically proper? Even if I told people I was kinda sorta looking for the treasure, too, and was open about the fact that I was doing it in order to understand the experience of the treasure hunters, did that still make it wrong? That's ambiguous ground, and I wasn't sure how to handle it. But I knew trying to have it both ways was going to cause problems. Splitting the baby never quite works; something gets shortchanged on one end or the other, conflicts of interest arise, people don't understand whether you're really participant or observer. It's complicated. I understood that. After talking to Cynthia, though, I laid out a few ground rules for myself: If I could get to him, I'd never ask Fenn for clues about the treasure, the same way Cynthia made sure not to. And I wouldn't take anything that other hunters told me and pass it along to Beep without their permission. I hoped that would be enough.

In the meantime, Cynthia and I were getting along famously. I could see why she was dispatched to deal with all media—she was a natural at it. And even though she was clearly close to Fenn, she was not afraid to speak her mind about the hunt. We started chatting about whether she believed someone would find it soon, and about how Fenn regularly proclaimed that he didn't care if someone found the treasure while he was still alive or if they found it after he was long gone.

"I think—and he's never said this to me—but I think he'd really like someone to find it while he's still living," she said. "He won't come out and say that. But I think he wants someone to find it.

"He loves media attention," Cynthia continued. "He's a media whore, so what would be better than someone finding it, and him still being alive, to where he can be the star of the show?"

Fenn, however, had pulled back from doing so much media as he'd aged, she said. After years of doing every interview he could, it had become difficult to gain an audience with him. I had to hope I could somehow pull it off; if I couldn't get access to Fenn, then this endeavor would be a failure from the start. Cynthia said she'd put in a good word for me, which I appreciated. Then I asked her the same question I'd asked Dal: Is the treasure real? And she answered just as he had, that Fenn wasn't that kind of trickster, that it didn't add up with his personality, that faith in the chase was part of the fun.

Talking to Dal and Cynthia had been helpful in understanding the world of the chase, but they were both firmly on Team Fenn, and their assurances that Fenn had definitely hidden the chest, because anything else wouldn't be like him—well, that wasn't quite enough. I needed more.

The next person I sought out? She immediately

seemed like someone who could give me the real scoop. How did I know? Because we were both a little bit obsessed with the same thirty-year-old kids' movie.

"Have you ever seen **The Goonies**?" Sacha Johnston asked me the first time we talked about the treasure. "I saw a picture of the treasure map— and it reminded me of the treasure map from **The Goonies.** That was the first vision in my head."

Sacha is a real estate agent based out of Albuquerque, who happened upon the hunt around the same time of the **Today** show boom. Being right around my age, she saw the hunt the way I did—through a treasure-hunting flick from 1985.

The Goonies came out when I was hitting first grade, and from the moment I saw it, I just wanted to find buried treasure, like the cadre of wisecracking kids had in the movie. My childhood friend Robbie and I would draw crude maps littered with clues, leading to caches stocked with Hot Wheels cars or valuable nickels and dimes. We imagined there were others racing us to the treasure, and that we had to use our smarts and the plucky ingenuity of six-year-olds to solve the puzzles and claim the loot first.

Those memories, more than anything, were driving why I wanted to be a part of this hunt; that sense of wonder came flooding back the moment Beep clued me in to Fenn's chase. The whole thing made me feel like a kid again. So I was thrilled when I found that Sacha felt exactly the same way.

Sacha had even thought "warm waters halt" meant the same thing that Beep and I thought it did—that she should look around Agua Caliente, down by the Rio Grande. Again, thanks to **The Goonies,** and a scene featuring a pint-size Corey Feldman in his role as Mouth.

"The kid in the attic, the only one who can speak Spanish, who is like, 'Ye intruders beware.' I thought about that whole scene," Sacha said. "How he had to translate it. What if you had to translate that map into Spanish—would that do you any good? So that's where I started, Agua Caliente. That's the starting point."

With all that in common, I figured Sacha was going to be very useful in determining what to believe about this chase. She knew Fenn personally, and seemed to have a hot-and-cold relationship with the man, saying that sometimes they were close and sometimes they were at loggerheads. Strangely, she joked that she played the role of the "love interest" in his chase, which struck me as odd, but personal, so I didn't press. At the time, I was more interested in how I'd heard she carried a pink handgun on every search, but sadly at our first lunch together, she didn't bring it along.

Regardless, she was definitely a prominent personality in this world, a big figure on the blogs and the subject of some of the same kinds of magazine articles and documentaries that so often featured Cynthia, tailing her exploits out in the wild. The renown she gained from that, coupled with her home in New Mexico, made her a beacon for hunters around the country who wanted her to look for the treasure with them.

"Everyone says they know where it is. And they want me to help them go get it. This is the kind of shit that I deal with every day," she said, sighing, before asking me what felt like a non sequitur.

"Do you remember the story of Lorena Bobbitt?"

I told her of course I did—she was the woman who cut off her husband's penis in the 1990s. Hard to forget that.

"You know who hit me up this morning? John Bobbitt," she said, chuckling at the lunacy of it. "At first, I thought I was being catfished. But it's really him. It's actually that fucking guy.

"John Bobbitt is convinced the treasure's in Colorado, and he wants me to come up there and claim the treasure with him, dressed as pirates," she said and cackled. "This is my life."

"So are all the hunters like that?" I asked her. "A little bit obsessed, a little bit off, perhaps possessing a surgically reattached penis?"

"A lot of these people are coming from the same place," Sacha responded. "It's a chance to redeem themselves. All these people are carrying around all this weight about things they could or should have done in their lives. And they didn't do them. And this is their chance to redeem themselves."

That made sense. It also answered why so many put so much of their faith in Fenn: He and his hunt were their ticket to something great, finally. So they had to believe in him wholeheartedly.

"Perhaps unsurprisingly, then," Sacha continued, "this hunt draws a very specific type.

"I don't know if you've noticed," she said, "but the average treasure hunter is of retirement age, male, Republican, conservative, drives a big truck, devoutly Christian or Catholic, and susceptible to cult mentality."

I was certainly starting to see some of that. Especially the "cult mentality" part. The more I learned about Fenn's hunt, the more it was starting to seem like its hunters treated their leader with a reverence that bordered on the fanatical. Fixating on every minor detail of his life, hanging on his every word in interviews—it wasn't just about the treasure chest. It was about Fenn, the man. You almost had to become obsessed with him, because you never knew when something he said would be valuable, if only you could understand it on a deep-enough level.

I'd felt a little of this myself already when thumbing through **The Thrill of the Chase** for the first time. It was impossible to read it without constantly pondering whether each word was somehow revealing, important, critical. When Fenn and his friend Donnie get lost in the Gallatin Forest outside Yellowstone, is that a clue? When he takes his airplane and flies over Taos Mountain, scattering the ashes of an old woman named Olga, what does that tell us? When he is skillfully relating the harrowing experience of being shot down over Laos that second time, where he waited overnight to be rescued, are there hints in there that speak to something in the poem?

It became clear that Fenn had pulled off something truly impressive. We are all the lead character in our own stories, believing the formative events of our largely mundane pasts are worthy of remembrance. The harsh reality is, of course, that nobody cares all that much. The seminal moments in our own lives just don't matter much to everyone else. Learning that is part of growing up.

But Fenn figured out how to transcend this universal truth: He had managed to mythologize his own past. Solving this treasure hunt meant knowing the details of Fenn's life as well as one knows one's own. It was an ego trip of historic proportions, sure, but also a fascinating move by a man whom I was starting to see as something of an enigma, free with his biographical details but cagey with his true motivations.

"That," Sacha said, "is Fenn's game. He likes to draw people in, and let them think they're seeing the unvarnished truth—when really they're just taking his scraps.

"A lot of people think they know the man," she said. "He likes to mess with you and trick you and send you down rabbit holes. Forrest definitely enjoys the celebrity status he's gotten."

She said that Fenn enjoyed the drama that came with his chase, reveled in it. He liked pitting hunters against one another, and seeing what they'd do, how they'd respond. Or he'd speak to hunters in riddles, stoking their belief that they were on the right track, and then he'd sit back and laugh as they worked themselves into a treasure-addled frenzy. It was all part of the game to him.

"Don't let him fool you," she warned. "He's not some silly little old man. He's very shrewd, very clever. You be very careful with him. He's great at portraying that little-old-man routine. But that's not who Forrest Fenn is. He's very clever. The things I could tell you, man."

I started to ask what those might be, but she quickly changed the subject, leaving me unsure about where I stood with all this. I still hadn't managed to answer the first, and most important, question pinging around my brain: Was this all real? Or was it just an old man's ego trip, his practical joke? If anything, I'd gotten more worried about that—everything Sacha said had made me wonder if he was just playing everyone, crafting a grand game and giggling as he moved the pieces around the board.

So I doubled back to Cynthia. She had mentioned that there was somebody who might be able to give me the kind of proof I was seeking—though this person wasn't actually a hunter. He was a writer. My kind of guy, she said.

The author and journalist Douglas Preston has written more than thirty novels and nonfiction works, many of them national bestsellers, several of them made into movies. Before he turned to writing full-time, he worked at the American Museum of Natural History, in New York. He'd grown up in Wellesley, Massachusetts, next door to the town where my wife, Amalie, and I had just bought a home. So I felt a certain kinship there—author, journalist, Massachusetts guy. He seemed like someone I could trust.

Preston also happened to be a close personal friend of Forrest's, getting to know Fenn after moving to New Mexico in the late 1980s. Preston found Fenn engaging, joining him in the celebrity-filled Santa Fe scene.

"I'd go to parties at his house, and there would be Suzanne Somers, there would be Murray Gell-Mann, the Nobel Laureate—there would be all these famous people. He collected them. And they liked him, because he's so damned interesting," Preston said.

He also delighted in Fenn's mischievous side.

Preston watched as Fenn did some elegantly questionable things to boost his art business—like finding undervalued artists, cornering the market on their work, and then hatching plans to pump their value.

"He'd boost the stock in a very simple way," Preston said. "He'd publish a beautiful, beautiful book about the artist. A gorgeous book, big production value. And then he'd start talking up the artist. And in fact, Forrest had a great eye, so he was able to see that these really were undervalued artists. He made so much money."

Or the time when he came across a warehouse of paintings by the famed art forger Elmyr de Hory. Most art dealers were repulsed by de Hory's actions, and his work. Fenn went the other way, partnering up with John Connally, the former governor of Texas—also, incidentally, one of the people shot and wounded by Lee Harvey Oswald during the Kennedy assassination—to profit from de Hory's work.

"He and John Connally bought an entire warehouse full of Elmyr de Hory's fakes, and they sold them as fakes," Preston said. "Famous fakes! The famous Elmyr de Hory! And they made a fucking fortune. Everyone wanted one of those fakes.

"I've got one of those fakes that they gave to me, a beautiful Matisse ink drawing. It's so smart. He's so smart," Preston marveled.

Fenn related his plan to hide his treasure—and

his body—to Preston early on, and even asked him to write the memoir that would serve as the vessel for the poem. Preston declined, though he borrowed the basics of Fenn's plan for a book of his own, the fictional work **The Codex,** released in 2004—wherein an eccentric New Mexico million- aire, dying of cancer, sends his three sons on a trea- sure hunt to find his tomb, and with it, his fortune.

Fenn kept his friend updated on his progress as he tweaked the poem and filled the chest over al- most two decades. Preston, in fact, has seen the holy grail, and he recalled for me the first time he beheld the actual chest.

"He took me into his walk-in safe and he showed me this chest he'd just purchased, this heavy fifteenth-century or whatever Italian chest, made out of metal, and it was filled with gold. And it had these other things in it, too, like a sheath of one-thousand-dollar bills. A brick. A brick of one- thousand-dollar bills he had in there," Preston said with a hint of wonder.

Over the years, Preston watched the chest fill up with valuables of all sorts, Fenn showing off the new additions every time the author would come over. He even kept Preston updated on his suicide plan, which, apparently, he had not fully aban- doned postcancer, even considering it as an option in the 2000s, close to the time he hid the chest. Preston enjoyed the updates, liked watching the chest and Fenn's plan come together—though he continued to worry about the suicide element.

Then, one day, without warning, the chest simply disappeared from the safe.

"He was eighty, and one day, he just told me, 'Well, I did it. . . . It's gone,'" Preston recalled—which surprised the author, though, of course, he was happy his friend hadn't killed himself.

"After he buried the gold, I asked him, 'Well, why did you change your mind about burying yourself with it?' He said, 'Oh, I didn't want to do that to my family. And I just felt that would be too much on them.'"

Since then, Preston has served as living proof that the chest exists, steadfastly stating that he'd viewed it and the treasures within. If I believed Preston—and I had no reason not to—then from there, only one more leap was required: to believe that Fenn hid it according to the story laid out in **The Thrill of the Chase.** But Preston says that's not a tough jump to make once you know the chest is real, as the author certainly does.

"There are two reasons I think it's real. First, the treasure chest disappeared from the safe, and where did it go? I don't know. And all the artifacts that were in there, the gold nuggets, the gold coins, they're all gone. It all had to go somewhere. And the second thing is that Forrest's personality—it would be impossible for him to pull off a hoax like this. It's just not anything like who he is. I know him well enough to know that that would be impossible."

It was tough for me to rely on the personality argument, again—and all the stuff Preston had told me about boosting art prices and de Hory fakes made a hoax, or at least some sort of trickery, seem more likely, not less. But the other part? That if this chest and all these valuables were real, as Preston swears they are, they had to have gone somewhere—well, that I could buy into. He did something with it, whether it was hiding it in his own backyard or, as Fenn claims, secreting it away in the Rocky Mountains. Maybe it was the fact that someone of Preston's stature was willing to put his own reputation on the line as the guarantor that this is real, but I was sold, and decided to move forward.

But before I was finished talking to Preston, he had a question for me.

"Are you going to tell the full story?" he asked me.

Unsure what he meant, I told him that, yes, I planned to—I was going to try to tell the story of this hunt as completely as I could. Sure, I'd include the zanier doings of some of the hunters, and the story of the man who died searching for it. I'd even heard whispers that Fenn had had some brushes with the law.

He cut me off, as if I clearly didn't know what I was talking about.

"You're going to find out things about Forrest that I'm not going to tell you, but you're going to find them out, things that are very controversial. His family already knew that he—he already put them through a lot. Let me put it that way."

I tried to ask what he meant, but Preston pushed on, starting to laugh now, seemingly finding this all very funny.

"Forrest will sue you," he said through the laughter. "If you write the full story, Forrest will definitely sue you."

What did it all mean? Why were they all warning me against Fenn? I wanted very badly for this hunt to be what I'd first envisioned: a frenzied adventure like that in **The Goonies,** a puzzle and a chase and a pot of gold at the end of one final rainbow, all perfectly crafted by an all-knowing, all-seeing, benevolent creator who had no ulterior motives.

But the reality of treasure hunting is that it's never, ever been as easy as **X** marking the spot.

3

FROM CORONADO
TO OAK ISLAND

Five hundred years before Fenn's hunters began tramping around the hills of New Mexico, another famous treasure seeker was searching those same grounds. Francisco Vásquez de Coronado, a Spanish nobleman, had gone to Mexico in his mid-twenties to seek his fortune in the New World. Coronado was appointed governor of the Kingdom of Nueva Galicia, a state in what is now the northwestern part of Mexico. But his tenure was unremarkable. Rival governors, such as Francisco Pizarro, were conquering vast swaths of territory in other parts of the New World, sending gold and riches back to Spain. In the empire's northern backwater, Coronado was finding little but dust and cows.

In 1536, Coronado saw his chance. Four Spaniards from a doomed expedition to Florida arrived at the edge of his territory, bedraggled and exhausted from having traversed much of what is now the southern United States—the first Europeans to do so. But they spun stories of great cities they had heard about along the way, cities with gold to rival the Inca metropolises Pizarro was conquering in South America. That spurred the government in Mexico City to send out an exploratory mission, led by Friar Marcos de Niza, to recon the area. The monk returned with what seemed like confirmation that cities of gold existed; he called them the Seven Cities of Cíbola, and promised that if Coronado could find them, the riches would be his for the taking.

Coronado was entranced. The lure of treasure overwhelmed him, and soon the Spaniard had organized a fifteen-hundred-man mission to search for the cities—which they were already calling the Seven Cities of Gold.

Coronado and his expedition departed Compostela on Mexico's west coast in 1540, and headed north. This was a conquering army—over three hundred heavily armed Spaniards and more than one thousand native allies, with Coronado envisioning a campaign of pillage and plunder much like that of his predecessor Hernán Cortés against the Aztecs two decades earlier.

Four months after departing, they neared the first of what they believed to be the Seven Cities—the Zuni pueblo town of Hawikuh, near what is now the Arizona–New Mexico border. It had been a long, difficult journey, and Coronado's men were tired and hungry, but the dream that just ahead lay a city teeming with gold spurred them on. When they arrived, they quickly grasped that they had been following a fantasy; they were confronted by a city rich not in gold, but only in stone and earth—and one whose residents were not inclined to be welcoming, meeting Coronado's advance guard with a volley of arrows. The Spaniards attacked, desperate to take the food and water stored inside. It took three hours of battle for the weakened Spaniards to take the pueblo, despite their European technological advantages, and once they were in control, their fears were confirmed—there was little of value to be had. Coronado was forced to reckon with the crushing reality that these cities of gold were probably all just cities of mud.

"The Seven Cities are seven little villages," a crestfallen Coronado wrote in a letter to Antonio de Mendoza, viceroy of New Spain.

Yet rather than turn back, Coronado pushed his men farther in, chasing rumors of richer lands to the east and the north. His men eventually encountered the Grand Canyon, and fought their way across New Mexico toward what would later become Santa Fe. Still, all the disappointed Spaniards found was a series of small pueblos and tiny tribes, no riches or great cities like those of Central and South America.

There was still one more promise out there, though, one more avenue that might lead to gold. An Indian they called "the Turk" said he knew of the site of great riches, in the city of Quivira, to the northeast—and he would guide them. Gold-mad, Coronado drove his forces on, following the path of the Turk up through Texas. Finding nothing, and running short on supplies again, Coronado sent most of his expedition home and soldiered on with a small group of his best men as the Turk led them up into modern-day Kansas. There, with his expedition in shambles, his supplies nearly gone, and his reputation ruined, Coronado finally found Quivira—and it was yet another prairie town, no wealth, no vast riches, nothing the Spanish craved. The Turk—who, it is believed, was intentionally leading Coronado astray to end the conquistador's gold-fueled rampage through New Mexico—was tortured and killed, and in 1542, Coronado and his men limped home to Mexico, where Coronado died in shame in 1554.

Coronado was the first European treasure hunter to explore the American Southwest in search of gold. He would not be the last.

There have always been treasure hunters, of course. They're a part of our culture and our dreams, going all the way back to the legend of Jason and the Argonauts searching for the Golden Fleece, and a part of our reality, dating to the ancient looters who ransacked the mummies in the tombs of the Egyptian pharaohs.

But the European encounter with the New World changed the nature of treasure seeking, bringing it out of the realm of myth and wild exaggeration and turning it into a viable business, where tangible rewards were to be had and common folk could make astounding discoveries. The age of treasure hunting was just getting started.

What makes something treasure?

A twenty-first-century Tiffany diamond pendant created with perfect artistry, care, and precision is extremely valuable. Its craftsmanship far exceeds anything available hundreds of years ago. But unearth a similarly sized diamond in a mummy's hoard, or raise one from a Spanish galleon, and the historic artifact will be worth many times more than the modern piece. Why is one priceless treasure and the other not?

Reasons abound, but to me, one means more than all the rest: Owning a piece of treasure allows you to become a part of history. Forrest Fenn knew this better than most, and it's why his galleries and his antiquities business were so successful. He was able to connect the objects with their time—the way he would offer visitors a sip of the Jackie O.

bottle of brandy, for instance, or let schoolchildren touch a famous painting he owned of George Washington. It's why he filled his chest with more than just gold coins, lining it with artifacts and objects of real meaning and significance.

Treasure hunting is about excitement, about the promise of finding something that will enrich the hunter and make him a part of the treasure's story. It isn't simply about getting rich—there are easier and better ways, including buying a lottery ticket. But hopefuls still hunt for treasure and seek out items of dubious provenance, because they want the drama and the fortune and the fame, the notoriety and the romance. They want to be part of the fairy tale.

The earliest civilizations all had their own treasure-hunting tales, most rooted in their mythology, many of them stories where their warriors used their cunning and guile to claim troves of treasure guarded by fabulous beasts. One of the earliest to be found is the ancient Egyptian treasure-hunting tale of Setnau Khaemweset, supposedly a son of the pharaoh Ramesses II. Setnau went in pursuit of a lost book, the Book of Thoth, which contained several magical spells and was originally contained inside a series of boxes, each one of great value. When Setnau found the location of the book in a wizard's tomb, he had to confront and defeat three ghosts—one of whom he bested in a game of checkers—and eventually won the book. But, as with so many treasure-hunting stories, finding the treasure proved disastrous for Setnau, in this case ultimately leading to the death of his children. He returned the book to the ghosts, glad to be rid of it.

The cultures that developed in subsequent millennia believed less in magic and more in the glory and riches of the people who came before them and what they had left behind. Common people in Europe were weaned on stories that told of treasures buried just beneath them, the leavings of those from long-ago, richer cultures—the Egyptians, the Greeks, the Romans—who had gold and silver to spare and put them in the earth, waiting for them to be found. All in all, it's not so different from buying into a story about a rich old man with gold and silver to spare secreting a chest in the Rocky Mountains.

Most of these hoards were pure fantasy, but there was at least some fact at the heart of these treasure-hunting hopes. The civilizations of medieval and semimodern Europe really were built on top of older, often more prosperous cultures, and while there wasn't usually a Roman, Celtic, or German burial mound underfoot containing ancient valuables, it wasn't completely crazy to think such a thing might exist, either. A hillside cave could hold unknown riches, as could the ruins of an old castle or abbey. There was an attendant myth that at times, particularly during a full moon, treasure became "will-o'-the-wisp," giving off a bluish flame and therefore especially susceptible to recovery. In medieval England, amateur treasure hunters were known as "hill diggers," and laws had to be enacted to prevent them from tearing up graves, crosses, and other important sites. Very little was ever found, but the pull of what might be kept people digging—and hoping.

The years following Coronado's failed expedition to the Southwest were not a great period for treasure hunting. But they were an excellent time for creating what would be, in the future, great treasure hunts. Spain was mining and pillaging vast quantities of lucre from the New World and sending it back to Europe via the best transportation networks of the day: convoys of wooden sailing ships, crossing the treacherous Atlantic Ocean. Vessels were often lost, either to the elements or to pirates and privateers, and tales began to spread of caches secreted away on remote islands by marooned mariners, or of pirates who hid their loot to avoid patrols, or of wrecked galleons lying just beneath the waterline in some inlet or another.

But for the century following the time of the conquistadors, few had retrieved much of anything. Treasure hunting was, at the time, primarily a world of rumor and falsehood.

That is, until one bold captain showed that it could be big business.

In June 1687, Captain William Phips, a burly, fast-talking Bostonian, dropped anchor in the River Thames. When he revealed the cache that was on board his ship, the twenty-two-gun frigate **James and Mary,** the spectacle captivated all of England.

The hold of the **James and Mary** contained thirty-four tons of treasure, worth over 200,000 pounds sterling, a vast fortune in those times. They were the spoils from the discovery of the **Nuestra Señora de la Concepción,** the lead ship of the Spanish silver fleet of 1641, lost at sea that same year, her crew drowned, her vast stores of silver plunged somewhere beneath the waves north of Hispaniola.

The tale of Phips's discovery and salvage of the **Concepción** had all the elements that we have come to associate with classic treasure hunting. There was a map to the treasure: a document known as the Spanish Directions, given to an Englishman who had been imprisoned in Cádiz by a man who was reportedly the original pilot of the ill-fated vessel. There was a race to the treasure between Phips's expedition and that of another captain. There were pirates. There was an attempted mutiny aboard Phips's vessel. And, of course, there was a vast quantity of Spanish silver, lost in a treasure galleon, hidden beneath the waves.

Phips was knighted—he would go on to become

the first governor of the Province of Massachusetts Bay, and preside over the Salem witch trials—and his discovery set off a genuine craze in England, with more than thirty treasure-hunting expeditions organized in the year after the **Concepción** was found. Inventors immediately went to work trying to get men deeper into the water for longer: The number of English patents issued for diving equipment surged in the decade after the discovery, exceeded only by the number of patents for weaponry. And the market for speculation on these treasure-hunting companies was so huge that it was a driving force behind the explosion of joint-stock companies, which eventually morphed into what we now know as the London Stock Exchange. Some historians have argued that the treasure-hunting frenzy was instrumental in the 1694 founding of the Bank of England itself.

This mania wasn't restricted to Europe. In America, treasure hunters fixated on the idea that Captain Edward Teach, the famed Blackbeard, had hidden some of his treasure around the city of Philadelphia, prompting locals to start digging up the shoreline in search of treasure caches. None other than Benjamin Franklin griped that "money digging itself was widespread. You can hardly walk half a mile out of town on any side without observing several pits dug with that design, and perhaps some lately opened. Men, otherwise of very good sense, have been drawn into this practice . . . There seems to be some peculiar charm in the conceit of finding money."

No one found any pirate treasure, of course, but the more famous the story, the more hunters believed they could plumb it for wealth. Take the tale of Captain William Kidd, the noted Scottish privateer turned pirate of the late 1600s. Through the 1680s and into the 1690s, Kidd had worked the Atlantic as both pirate and English privateer—essentially, a government-sponsored pirate, someone who didn't attack his sponsor's ships. In 1698, supposedly protected by an English letter of marque, he and his ship, the **Adventure Galley,** were patrolling off Madagascar when Kidd stumbled upon a grand prize: the five-hundred-ton **Quedagh Merchant,** an Armenian vessel bearing a bounty of silk, gold, and other riches from India. Kidd seized it for his own. But Kidd had plundered the wrong ship, and at the wrong time. In England, opinions regarding privateering and piracy were rapidly shifting, with the leadership and the public suddenly moving against the practice. Even worse, the **Quedagh Merchant** was owned by a wealthy, connected minister at the court of India's Grand Mughal, and with the English wanting to maintain good relations with their budding colony, Kidd was suddenly on the wrong side of the law. When he reached port in Boston, he was arrested and shipped to England for trial.

But before he got to Boston, Kidd took pre-cautions. He buried much of his treasure, putting some on Gardiner's Island, off Long Island, New York, and more elsewhere. Kidd used this trea-sure as his ace in the hole, trying to bargain for clemency by offering to tell the authorities where he'd hidden the rest. It didn't work, and Kidd was hanged in 1701, his body left to rot in a cage over the river Thames as a warning to other pirates. But for hundreds of years, others searched for his treasures, digging holes all along the coast of New England, hoping that Kidd's gold might be wait-ing there. In the early 1800s, **The Constellation,** a New York newspaper, reported that, in the quest for Kidd's lost treasure, "acres of ground have been dug, three fathom deep, for its discovery. In vari-ous places may be seen large pits still yawning as proof of the prevalent belief in this buried treasure, and as mementos of the credulity and the avarice of mankind."

Captain Kidd's treasure proved elusive for cen-turies of searchers, but the methods and practices of treasure hunting evolved, and before long, real treasures were being found as global exploration, archaeology, and treasure hunting all merged. As the nineteenth century wore on, old tales of lost treasures became new again as European adven-turers journeyed into Central and South America, locating the great Mayan temple of Chichén Itzá and other ruins in the 1840s, and into the heart of

Africa, locating the lost city of Great Zimbabwe in 1867. But as much as these explorers were motivated by the thrill of discovery, they and those who came after them also wanted treasure. The explorers of Central and South America hoped that every time they found a temple, it would be the one heralding the entrance to the fabled city of El Dorado, the city of gold. And the explorers who surveyed Great Zimbabwe hoped it might be the legendary city of Ophir, site of King Solomon's mines.

This boom did not come without its problems, however, often leading to some thorny questions. When is one an archaeologist, and when a treasure hunter, or, worse, a grave robber? And did seeking treasure invalidate one's scientific contributions? When the amateur archaeologist Heinrich Schliemann searched for the ancient Greek city-state of Troy in the early 1870s, his aim was to prove the existence of the famed city, thus validating that Homer's **Iliad** was more than a mere fable, a noble pursuit by any standard. But when he discovered treasure at the dig site in western Turkey—treasure that he incorrectly believed was the hoard of King Priam, the legendary king of Troy—he sent away his workers, claimed the loot for himself, and bestowed the "Headdress of Priam" on his young Greek wife, Sophia. (The Turkish government, predictably, did not approve.)

But even in this age of great discoveries, it was a work of fiction that made the biggest impact on the culture of treasure hunting, turning the pursuit into a staple of popular culture with echoes that endure today.

Robert Louis Stevenson was a Scotsman, raised in Edinburgh by a lighthouse engineer. He had no desire to go into the family profession, instead hoping to become a writer, but he studied the law to appease his parents. Sickly as both a child and an adult, Stevenson traveled both for his health—seeking warmer, drier climes—and for his curiosity, spending part of his twenties in France at artist colonies, working on his writing. When in France, he met an older American woman and became infatuated with her, eventually—to the great chagrin of his family—following her back to the United States, and settling in Monterey, south of San Francisco. Still unknown and dirt-poor, Stevenson kept at his writing, and as the 1880s dawned, he hit upon a story that would both create and forever cement the most popular treasure-hunting tropes in the public consciousness.

Treasure Island was first published in 1881–1882 in the magazine **Young Folks,** under a pseudonym. When it was released as a book in 1883, it became a worldwide hit, and one of the most enduring books of all time. It's easy to see why; the book is a magical lark, catnip for bored young dreamers desperate to someday lead a life of journey and excitement. It's **The Goonies** for the 1880s set, and its echoes are heard in virtually every adventure book or movie that followed it.

Drawing from Stevenson's life and his travels, and liberally borrowing from several pirate and adventure books before it, **Treasure Island** tells the story of young Jim Hawkins, the son of an English innkeeper. One night, a mysterious sailor arrives, bearing a small chest, and says another man will be along soon, and he pays Jim a few pennies to keep a lookout for him. But after a fight with another, unknown man, the sailor dies—yet not before telling Jim that he's in danger because others covet his knowledge of a buried treasure, secreted in its hiding place by a pirate captain. Jim and his mother open the chest, finding a journal and a map, an **X** marking the spot where the treasure is hidden.

They contract with a ship's captain and take on a ramshackle crew (including a peg-legged, be-parroted cook, Long John Silver, who is eventually revealed to himself be a pirate captain also seeking the hoard) and head off in search of the treasure. Once they reach the island, Silver leads his coconspirators in a mutiny, and after various misadventures, battles, and deaths, Jim and his compatriots end up coming away with the riches, though Silver escapes with a bag of loot.

Treasure Island was a major hit, and hugely influential. So many of its details became iconic, from the X on the map, to the peg-legged, parrot-toting pirate, to a skeleton pointing the way to the treasure, to pirate phrases like "Shiver me timbers!" **Treasure Island**'s success—and, to a lesser extent, the popularity of the 1885 book **King Solomon's Mines**—stoked interest in treasure hunting, driving regular people in both Europe and North America to dream of finding a map, following it to the X, and claiming a great treasure of their own.

It's perhaps unsurprising, then, that several of the most popular and enduring real-life treasure hunts have their origins in this period. Two of them—the search for the Lost Dutchman Mine and the quest to unravel the Beale ciphers—can both be traced to the end of the nineteenth century, and still vex hunters to this day.

The legend of the Lost Dutchman Mine has changed many times over the years, but at its heart are a few constants: a German immigrant named Jacob Waltz (a "Deutsch man") died in 1891, telling those close to him that he knew the location of a great mine in Arizona's perfectly named Superstition Mountains, near Apache Junction. Waltz had some high-grade ore in his possession when he died, supporting his story. No one has been able to locate the mine since, and a number of people have died seeking it. That much is agreed.

After that, the specifics get fuzzy, with story after

story adding conflicting details and myth over-lapping with fact, including questions surround-ing some of the deaths, and whether they were connected to the Lost Dutchman Mine at all. One particular death does stand out, however: the 1931 demise of treasure hunter Adolph Ruth. Ruth went missing when searching for the mine, and his re-mains were recovered six months later—with (and this, believe it or not, is also up for debate) what seemed to be two holes in his skull. He may not have been shot—the state coroner determined he died either of thirst or of heart failure—but many believed he was, and he had notes on him stat-ing that he had discovered the location of the mine. That stoked theories that he was murdered for the information, and the national wire services and papers ran with it, helping to turn the Lost Dutchman saga into a much bigger story, one that would stand the test of time. Even today, there are those who say that hunters who venture into the Superstitions looking for the mine are watched by gunmen sitting up in the hills, protecting the claim, as they were from Ruth.

There may not be a Lost Dutchman Mine—it is possible that hunters are following only whisper and legend. But one thing that is certain is that the Beale Papers, a series of elaborate codes that claimed to lead to a treasure, are real. Now, whether the treasure promised to the code breaker actually exists? That's another story.

The legend of the Beale Papers is told in a pamphlet, published in 1885, that relates a remarkable tale of buried treasure. It tells the story of Charles Beale, a Virginia man whose traveling party had discovered gold out west, not far from that nexus of all things treasure hunting, the city of Santa Fe. Beale made several trips back to Virginia to stash some of the gold, and on his final one, in 1822, he entrusted a mysterious box to the owner of a Lynchburg hotel, Robert Morriss, promising to come back for it.

He never returned, and decades later, Morriss became curious and opened the box, finding a note written by Beale and three sheets filled with numbers. The note stated that Beale had buried his gold somewhere in Virginia, with the exact location hidden in the accompanying three sheets of numbers. Each sheet contained part of an encrypted code that, when fully deciphered, would reveal the site of the treasure.

According to the 1885 pamphlet, Morriss spent years trying to crack the code, but he never succeeded. Finally, on his deathbed, he told his tale to a friend, who is never identified. That friend, however, is the supposed author of the pamphlet. And this anonymous friend had more success. He managed to decipher one of the three sheets, one that, conveniently, tells that the treasure is worth ten million dollars and is located somewhere in Bedford County, Virginia. What was fascinating, though, was that he said he deciphered it using the Declaration of Independence as the key, matching each number on the sheet to a letter in the famous document. But after twenty years of trying, he, too, gave up on trying to solve the other two segments and apparently decided to tell the world the tale—how altruistic!—so that others could also try to solve the puzzle. The 1885 pamphlet itself was then published by a third man, James B. Ward.

All seems a little too good to be true, right? Besides the obvious hotel/left-behind treasure box parallels with **Treasure Island,** released only a few years earlier, there are a number of anachronisms and inconsistencies in the story that indicate it was probably concocted wholesale in the 1880s, potentially by Ward himself. The pamphlet retailed for almost fifteen dollars in 1880s money, giving its author a compelling reason to tell a tall and engrossing tale, as many believed then and many still do. That's why Fenn, conscious that outsiders would think that he, too, was publishing his treasure-hunting book to make a profit, made sure he got none of the proceeds from the sale of **The Thrill of the Chase** or, beyond the trust for his grandchildren, anything from his subsequent treasure-related books.

I'd never heard of the Beale Papers or the Lost Dutchman Mine before delving into the world of Forrest Fenn. But there was one treasure hunt I absolutely knew of, one that may be the greatest hunt of them all: the Oak Island Money Pit.

The search for treasure at Oak Island goes back to the end of the eighteenth century, when a teenager visiting the tiny island off Nova Scotia found a bit of disturbed dirt in 1795. Believing it meant there was something there—perhaps even the treasure of Captain Kidd—he and two friends dug, and found a shaft that had been previously filled in. The farther down they dug, the more man-made features they found—stone not native to the island, layers of wooden logs, and more. But there was only so deep they could go without resources and backing. Returning almost a decade later with proper tools and funding, they dug deeper, down and down into the shaft, finding man-made barriers or supports every ten feet or so, forty feet down, fifty feet down, sixty feet down. According to their story, a stone was found around eighty or ninety feet, with indecipherable markings on it (the stone has been lost to history, but legend states that the markings were eventually deciphered, and that they read "Forty feet below, two million pounds are buried"). When they got to ninety-three feet, they hit mud, and retired for the night. When they returned the next day, the shaft was filled with water, and their plans for retrieving whatever might have been inside were permanently dashed. But that development only stoked outside interest in the island—the hunters believing that they had been foiled not by natural phenomena, but by pirate booby traps.

The legend grew, the details probably shifting slightly, and in 1849, treasure hunters returned to the island, this time bringing a drill, but running into the same flooding problems as before. An 1861 expedition also failed, and this time cost one hunter his life, when a boiler powering one of the pumps removing water from the pit burst, scalding him to death. It would not be the last life claimed by Oak Island and its Money Pit.

In the 1890s, with interest in treasure hunting spiking, another expedition tried again—with another fatality coming in 1897, and still little to show for over a century of excavations beyond an odd Spanish copper coin, some parchment, and three links of gold chain. Work continued, however, as new hunters and backers entered the project, including, in 1909, none other than future president Franklin Delano Roosevelt, who joined up as a member of the Old Gold Salvage and Wrecking Company. Roosevelt, of course, found nothing, just like the rest, but remained interested in Oak Island his entire life, even planning to return to the site in late August 1939 while visiting nearby Halifax; bad weather and the European crisis that would explode into World War II a week later ruined his plans.

Meanwhile, the legend continued to grow, its cache becoming grander and grander with every new expedition. Stories flew around that Marie Antoinette's jewels were hidden there or that the Knights Templar had secreted the Holy Grail or Ark of the Covenant there. Some claimed that original manuscripts proving that Francis Bacon, not Shakespeare, had written the Bard's plays were the real treasures hidden deep down in the pit.

Over time, myths, curses, and prophecies have arisen around the Oak Island treasure, the most prominent being that seven people will die before the 225-year-old search is complete and the treasure is found. The Money Pit has claimed six lives already.

Yet as we were quickly learning, death doesn't drive people away from treasure hunts. If anything, it only serves to make them more enticing.

4

IN THE DEN OF
FORREST FENN

Beep could hardly contain his excitement as I left the hotel the morning after our dinner at Geronimo. He understood that he couldn't go with me right now—it had been hard enough for me to secure this invite, as he knew—but he just couldn't help himself. Considering where I was going, and whom I was about to meet, he had to ask: Maybe he could join up with us later?

And if that wasn't okay, well, then maybe, just maybe, after I actually got to meet Forrest Fenn, could I ask him what he thought about our solve?

I told Beep I'd think about it, and got in the car to head to Fenn's estate, winding my way through Santa Fe's old town, following the GPS up into the area where the city's wealthier residents ringed their homes with adobe walls. But as I drove, I wasn't concerned with Beep, or the solve, or where the

treasure might be. I was about to meet the man
who had set in motion the greatest treasure hunt
in modern American history, and yet all I could
think about were the words of warning delivered
the night before by those well-meaning locals, layered on top of the cautions from Sacha, Preston,
and the others.

It was a short drive, and almost too quickly the
GPS dinged to alert me that I'd arrived at my destination. There was no longer any time to fret as
I turned off the main road into the driveway of a
magnificent walled compound.

I pressed the buzzer to announce my arrival, and
the heavy metal gate creaked and began to move,
slowly grinding sideways and opening the way into
the courtyard beyond. I put my rental truck into
gear and crept through, gliding under a canopy of
cedar trees, past an ancient covered wagon of the
sort that once traversed the famous Old Santa Fe
Trail. The trail itself, the home's owner would later
tell me, runs through this very yard before it finally
ends in the middle of downtown Santa Fe, just a
few miles away.

As I parked, the front door to the broad adobe
home swung open and Forrest Fenn peeked out,
waving to summon me up the walk. He was decked
out in the standard Fenn uniform I'd seen in countless magazine profiles—blue checked shirt, jeans,
turquoise belt buckle—though he'd gone without
the cowboy hat he sometimes wore, exposing the

long strands of white hair delicately placed across his head.

"You must be Danny," he said, cheerful and friendly.

Before I could say much more than a hello, he launched into a description of his impressive property, how he'd bought it, how it sat on that Old Santa Fe Trail, why it all mattered to him. The covered wagon out front was an old army ammunition hauler from the 1880s, from when the railroad finally arrived in Santa Fe and the trail itself fell into disuse.

He kept it there to remind himself that everything has its time, he said.

Fenn ushered me into a surprisingly simple foyer, eagerly pointing out the copies of **The Wall Street Journal** sitting on a side table.

"That's a darned good newspaper," he informed me, which I took as his way of showing that he remembered who I was and why I was there.

That's how I'd landed this meeting, in fact. Fenn didn't really welcome searchers to his home anymore, and in recent years, as Cynthia Meachum had warned me, he'd finally gotten tired of the media, as well. Yet when I had first gotten in touch with him, fingers crossed that maybe he'd write back, he'd done more than that—he'd said he knew my work from **The Wall Street Journal,** and so he'd be willing to talk to me. That was something of a surprise to me—I'd mostly done sports at the

WSJ, and I didn't guess at Fenn's being a big sports fan. But I didn't question it, happy to get the invite I'd craved.

Getting through that door had been a coup, but now that I was there, I already felt like time was speeding up, like I needed to step back and process each moment for the insight it would give me into both him and this chase. Even mundane things could be clues. What was next to the **WSJ** on his side table? How did he lay out his front hall? Was he clean, messy? Everything mattered. A few family members seemed to be around the house; a younger woman walked by and waved a disinterested hello as I was entering, and someone who seemed to be a housekeeper was moving some laundry and calling out to Fenn's wife, Peggy, who appeared to be home, though in another part of the residence.

But Fenn was already off and away, beckoning me to follow him down a hallway, past a rack of antique firearms and a huge red steel door that looked like it was straight out of a bank. The old man moved fast, descending a staircase, urging me over the threshold and into one of the more magnificent rooms I'd ever seen.

Fenn's office.

I'd heard that his office was part study, part museum: Cynthia Meachum had called it a "mini Smithsonian," and that seemed about right. It was a room telling the story of a complex life, one that had touched and been touched by notable, varied figures, from Tony Hillerman to John Wayne to Cher. But the truth is, the reports didn't do it justice.

Pushing open the long, heavy wooden doors revealed a space covered from floor to cathedral ceiling with antiques, curiosities, books, memorabilia. Anasazi headdresses of inestimable value lined one wall, above a display of fourteenth-century Native American pottery, which sat by a pilot's jacket from Gen. Claire Chennault's Flying Tiger squadron. The jacket was worth half a million, Fenn said; he let me try it on.

There was a curved adobe fireplace, watched over by a fearsome buffalo skull—opposite a gigantic painted buffalo hide looming over the leather couch. The throttle box from an F-100 fighter, just like the ones Fenn was shot down in over the jungles of Vietnam and Laos, rested not far from a case containing his Purple Hearts and other medals. Hardly an inch of the room remained uncovered, curios and masterpieces and mementos simply everywhere—a pair of moccasins here, weapons and shields from various Native American tribes there, a set of dolls farther on. None of it felt haphazard, or thrown together; rather, it appeared curated, like a gallery, one only a select few would ever get a chance to see.

He let me marvel at the scene for a while, standing by proudly, quite familiar with the impact this vista had on any newcomer. Then he motioned me over to the bookshelf in the room's far corner, where he started pulling out books and recounting their pedigrees.

Fenn grabbed a tome by his good friend Donald Rumsfeld, signed personally to him, but then quickly laid that aside in favor of something much more impressive: manuscript pages from a draft of Mark Twain's **A Connecticut Yankee in King Arthur's Court.** Then he put that away, and brought us even further back in history, taking out a box containing a collection of woolly mammoth and saber-toothed tiger hairs and bones.

I gaped at one wonder after another, genuinely overwhelmed by the pace and volume of it all, but something else kept pulling at me, even with all this to gaze at. There was one part of this house that I wanted to explore even more than Fenn's marvelous office, and I had passed it coming down the hall: Fenn's vault, with that red door and bank lock. It was the place where Fenn stored his most prized possessions, but, more important to me, it was the place where Fenn had kept and filled his treasure chest before hiding it out in the Rocky Mountains.

What secrets did it hold? What could it tell me about Forrest Fenn? About the hunt he created? About the treasure itself? If I could figure out how to get in there, I might be able to scrounge up a clue that could help me solve these collected riddles. Now all I had to do was convince him to unlock the door.

—

But first, there was work of another sort to be done. Fenn sat down on his couch, and I took my place on the ottoman of a lounger across from him. Sure, maybe I'd been playing treasure hunter, and maybe it was a ton of fun. But I was still a journalist first, and I was here to interview Fenn, to gain the measure of him, to try to understand what made him tick. I readied myself, and started to ask him my opening question, but he quickly interrupted with a query for me. He wanted to know why I wanted to write about this treasure hunt, why I wanted to live in his world, and among his searchers.

When the interviewee tries to turn things around on the interviewer and gauge his intentions, it's usually a method of taking control—something I could quickly see Fenn was used to having. I was game, though, and started in on my basic pitch, explaining what a unique phenomenon it was, how I wanted to explore why people became so entranced by it—neglecting to tell him just how manically Beep and I had been obsessing over his hunt lately.

He nodded along, seemingly buying my spiel for now.

"And when I say 'unique,' I really don't use that lightly," I continued, starting to get going now. "This absolutely is unique. There have been treasure hunts for hundreds, thousands of years. But the difference between this treasure hunt and pretty much every other one ever is that we aren't left to wonder what the person who hid it, or lost it, really meant—we actually get to talk to the guy who buried the treasure."

He put up a hand and stopped me, looking, for lack of a better word, cross.

"I never said I buried the treasure. When did I say 'buried'? I hid the treasure. That's very important, to get these things right," he said, scowling at me like a disapproving headmaster let down by one of his students once again. He was obviously not won over by any of the high-level bullshit I'd been spouting just moments before.

Fenn was clearly the kind of person who liked these conversations to go one way: his way. I'd read a number of his older interviews, and could see that, as is the case with many frequent interviewees, Fenn had certain questions that he enjoyed being asked, certain places he liked to shift the conversation, certain rote answers he was comfortable giving. He had a role to play, and he knew it well.

So my failing to get the nuance between **buried** and **hid** had me behind the eight ball from the very start. Hell, maybe that kind of a thing was a litmus test he used to see how detail-oriented his interviewer was. To be clear, Fenn had never said he **didn't** bury the treasure—just that using the words **buried** and **hid** interchangeably was a no-no, because it could easily be stashed away somewhere aboveground. Saying "buried" removed that possibility. I understood where he was coming from, so I figured I'd reset things with the most obvious and basic of questions, the most general—but also the most pivotal to understanding this chase.

Why?

Fenn had explained the "what" of his treasure hunt many times. But the tale of his chat with Ralph Lauren in this very office still didn't fully explain what would motivate someone to come up with that kind of idea. What type of a person goes from "I'm going to die" directly to "I should bury a treasure chest and write a poem leading people to it," and then follows through? So I tried to plumb a little deeper, asking what Fenn was trying to say by doing this—what it was really about, beyond his own dislike of death. That seemed to stir something in him, and he launched into what I can only think of as something of a stump speech.

"I think my main reason is that I'm kinda disgusted with America," he told me. "When I was in junior high and high school, nobody was overweight. And I'm not talking about obese; I mean nobody was five pounds overweight. Now everyone's on their devices, and the problem is that you have to do that today if you're going to survive."

So it was about getting people outside, off their butts?

"Look, I had a few reasons; I don't know which was my primary motivation," he said. "But we were just heading into a recession. Despair was written all over the newspapers."

Right—when Fenn was in the final stages of his project, the housing and banking crises were roiling America, and New Mexico was hit particularly hard by what became known as the Great Recession. As Fenn was putting those last baubles in his chest, unemployment was soaring, investment banks were failing, a government bailout was under way, and it seemed like, once again, the little guy had gotten screwed.

"So, I did it to give those people hope," he continued. "My audience is every redneck from Texas who lost his job, has a pickup truck and a bedroll. That's who I hope will read my book and go out and look for my treasure."

There was a ding from the area of his desk, and Fenn excused himself to check something on his computer. As he got up, his breath came more quickly, almost like a dog panting. He was so animated, so high-energy, that until that moment I'd almost forgotten he was a man entering his late eighties, probably more frail than he let on. When he sat back down, I took things in a different direction. Fenn seemed fine talking about death itself, so I asked him if he'd thought about what comes next. Fenn wasn't a religious man, per se. But he admitted that as his body had begun to slow down and his nineties had come into view, he had found himself performing that exercise done by so many before him—wondering what comes after. And if everything he'd done meant anything. He had dealt with his own mortality before, in a more visceral way than most of us have. His response was to bend it to his will, to the extent he could. "Isn't the treasure chest idea," I asked, "a way of living forever—rather than taking it with you, it's a way of leaving part of yourself behind?"

"When you get to my age, Danny, you find that death isn't something to be afraid of," Fenn said, didactic and assured. "I'm at peace with the things I've done. I tried to do what I could for people. I don't know if they understand exactly what I was up to now—maybe they will later—but I tried to do what I could."

I didn't know if I understood it, either, but I found it interesting and telling that Fenn was clearly thinking about how he would be viewed after he was gone, how history would judge him. One of the things that struck me in reading his memoir was a passage about his father, Marvin, a respected school principal, who Forrest Fenn believed had left an impact that would resonate down generations. Yet when Fenn searched for his father on the internet, he noted he found nothing but the site of his grave. Fenn the younger clearly chafed at that and refused to suffer that same fate: This hunt, I believed, was a way of ensuring he did not. But would those who remembered Fenn see him as visionary? Or as egomaniacal cult leader? He'd set up this hunt, and some people loved it, but it had caused others ruin, both financial and personal—for which Fenn had refused to take any responsibility. But when I tried to question him about his legacy and how this treasure chest fit into it, he practically spat the word back at me.

"Legacy? Legacy is something that happens to you after you're dead. If you want to say something about me, say it while I'm alive, so I can rebut it," he said, cutting me off before I could venture further.

"Why do reporters always ask me about legacy?" he said, ruffled. "Danny, lemme tell you something: Everybody who's ever lived, every person ever, has a legacy. It may be that they shot John F. Kennedy, or they stubbed their toe outside a movie theater. But to me, it's nothing. When I die, I'm going to be an asterisk in a book someplace. People will remember what I've done, but I don't know if they'll remember Forrest Fenn. They'll remember a guy from New Mexico, but my name is not an integral part of it anymore."

"Isn't that a type of legacy, though?" I argued. "Nobody remembers the name of the man who invented the internet, but they will all remember and appreciate what he did. Isn't being known as that guy who created the treasure hunt the same thing, and isn't that valuable?"

But Fenn didn't want to play this game, preferring to press on to other subjects—searchers who had wronged him, my own hunting misadventures with Beep. So for the moment, I was willing to let the topic of legacy slide, though I figured Fenn might soon wish I hadn't. Because, instead, I veered into a darker chapter in Fenn's life, some of that checkered past that so many seemed to want me to know about. With the warnings of Sacha and Doug Preston still ringing in my ears, I steeled myself to ask about something I figured would infuriate Fenn, something that might cause him to kick me out right away. Something that was part of that "whole story" Preston had been talking about.

The government raid on Fenn's home.

In 2009, federal agents from the Bureau of Land Management, accompanied by at least one agent from the FBI, burst into this very house, seeking contraband artifacts. It was part of the largest crackdown on Native American artifact trafficking in American history, code-named Operation Cerberus Action, and colloquially known as the Four Corners Raids. Fenn was one of four antiques dealers whose homes were raided, in a sting that led to charges against twenty-six people, and, eventually, three suicides: two of the men charged, and the FBI's lead informant, just weeks before he was set to testify. Seems like a pretty ugly thing to be caught up in, right? The FBI and the BLM don't just raid people's homes without real reason.

Or do they?

On the surface, the mere association of Fenn with any sort of raid or crackdown looked bad. But as I studied up on it, I learned that the Four Corners case had become highly controversial, and over the years, it had been generally accepted that Fenn's involvement with any sort of illegal activity in that case was tangential at worst, virtually nonexistent at best. Fenn was never charged with a crime, and ultimately, he said, he got the government to admit to some wrongdoing.

The Four Corners case was built around the work of one main informant, Ted Gardiner, who was paid $224,000 over several years to acquire $350,000 worth of artifacts using government money, according to the **Santa Fe New Mexican.** But almost since the moment the details of the operation became public, it was widely criticized, both for the methods used and for potentially over-stating how big the black market around these arti-facts really was. In the end, despite all the arrests and the size of the operation, no one served any jail time, and all charges were settled out of court, for probated sentences.

I thought bringing this up would anger Fenn, and I treaded lightly, as talking about it seemed certain to infuriate him.

Yet Fenn's reaction was not at all what I expected. He loved that I'd brought it up. He was positively crowing while talking about the raids—he saw it as a case where he beat the government at its own game, where he proved that they were the crooks, not him.

"They accused me of going in a cave in Arizona, on government property, and taking some things out of it, which was against the law. First of all, it wasn't on government property. Somebody had said something about me, and they bought into it."

That they did, and on June 10, 2009, an army of agents from various government agencies descended on Fenn's compound.

"There were twenty-three agents of the federal government for seven and a half hours searching my property," Fenn said. "It wasn't an FBI raid, though an FBI guy was there. It was BLM. There was Game and Fish, archaeologists, OSHA, even."

They didn't find what they were looking for—not really—but they did find something unexpected: the treasure chest itself.

"They saw the treasure chest. They photographed it. And the last thing they did before they left was call me into my vault, and they wanted me to acknowledge that the thing was still intact. I said, 'It appears to be.' There were two big nuggets. I don't know if anybody stole anything or not. I didn't have the coins counted. But I don't trust anyone."

He was still mad at the government over it, almost a decade later, feeling like he and his name had been unfairly dragged through the mud for little reason. "The search warrant said, 'Look for evidence of anything that would indicate a crime had been committed,'" Fenn said. "Jesus Christ— that's two hundred and seventy–some man hours they spent searching my house, and they didn't find anything."

Well, that's not completely accurate. They did confiscate four items, according to **The Arizona Republic:** "One object, a buffalo skull, was sold to an undercover agent . . . while agents took another buffalo skull, an old basket and an art object he made himself."

But Fenn's larger point stands. Still, though, just where **did** Fenn get a lot of this stuff, the items he built his collection on? That's where it starts to get a little thornier. Whether or not he did anything illegal in this specific case, it has long been contended that Fenn created his collection doing things that those in the archaeological community would consider improper—or that, at the very least, violate the standards they consider normal today.

Fenn's interest in Native American relics dates to his childhood, as he happily details in his books. One of his most prized possessions was the arrowhead he found when he was nine, out walking with his father. Once he joined the air force and was stationed in Europe, he spent his free time flying over, and then visiting, some of the world's most fascinating historic sites. He was kicked out of Pompeii three times. He would fly over the Sahara, land, and then search for millennia-old spearheads in the Libyan Desert.

But the real beginnings of his Native American art collection came in the 1960s, when he was stationed at Arizona's Williams Air Force Base. He would fly over remote Arizona canyons, scanning the ground for possible ruins. Then, on weekends, he'd go exploring, sometimes finding caves that he believed had not been visited since the Native Americans themselves lived there.

Did he take anything from them? A 2012 **Newsweek** article says so. The piece, by reporter Tony Dokoupil, digs into Fenn's past and finds tales of him and a pair of partners adventuring through the Southwest, heading into caves and old ruined pueblos and cliff dwellings, getting into all kinds of high jinks, expecting the law to come bust them at every turn—one time thinking, for instance, that the sound of a helicopter meant rangers coming to nab them, when it turned out to be Arizona senator Barry Goldwater instead, out on an expedition of his own.

"He was a straight up pot-hunter, as they're known, digging for artifacts on the edge of legality," Dokoupil said on Twitter years later.

Dokoupil stops short of explicitly calling Fenn a gravedigger, but says that he interviewed a man who dug with Fenn, and he recalled what the experience of digging back then was like.

"You can't dig out there without digging up some graves," Dokoupil says the man told him.

So Fenn and his friends explored and searched and sometimes dug. But only one of the three adventurers—Fenn—thought to make a profession out of their gatherings, and the group eventually broke up. That was partly because, as one of the trio's daughters told Dokoupil, "Fenn wasn't just taking a treasure or two, but returning to caves and stripping them clean."

On Twitter, Dokoupil said that's where Fenn got the foundation for his art empire.

"As one put it to me on the record: 'He saw something that he could cash in on, and he made his family fortune on it,'" Dokoupil wrote.

Fenn completely disavowed the **Newsweek** article to me, saying it was full of all manner of errors and falsehoods, still furious about it five years later. I later obtained the search warrant application justifying the government's raid, which does detail several recorded conversations between Fenn and informant Bill Schenck wherein Fenn explains how he found many of the items in his collection himself, at old Native American sites. In the warrant application the government alleges that some of these sites were on protected lands. The exact locations and dates of these finds were at the crux of the illegality question. But whether Fenn was acting illegally or not, at least some of his early collection **was** amassed in this fashion, acknowledged his lawyer, Peter Schoenburg. Schoenburg admitted to the **Republic** that some of Fenn's finds were made in this way, but before protective statutes were passed barring much of that kind of searching, thus meaning that he did nothing wrong by the laws of the day. Fenn can also be seen making those types of arguments in the search warrant application—for instance when he says he bought an eagle feather headdress of a type barred from sale today, but that he had bought it in 1948, "one year before the law was passed."

"He certainly was within the parameters of the law," Schoenburg said.

Fenn had also long been in conflict with elements of the southwestern archaeological community because of his ownership and excavation of the San Lazaro Pueblo, a Native American site that many would have preferred to see preserved by historians and archaeologists, not some ex-fighter jock turned art dealer. In the 1980s, Fenn bought San Lazaro—site of a Tano Indian village of thousands of rooms in the Galisteo Basin, occupied from the twelfth century until the early days of Spanish rule in New Mexico—and spent decades exploring it and excavating many of its treasures. He was deeply passionate about the site and believed that he was doing a good deed by bringing these items out so they could be seen and enjoyed.

"I don't violate the rules," Fenn told me. "It's that the archaeologists don't like the rules. The law says that a landowner can excavate on his own land, without a permit. The archaeologists don't like that. Their argument is that if you don't have a Ph.D. in archaeology, you shouldn't be excavating anyplace."

But many archaeologists contend that Fenn's excavations remove these items from their natural context, and thus diminish them and their history. They largely paint a picture of Fenn as cavalier, running roughshod over sites he did not fully understand or appreciate. Yet Fenn wasn't just some lone wolf; when he ran into items he didn't understand or needed assistance on, he'd call in true experts, as he did with the Museum of New Mexico when he found a series of delicate plaster masks requiring special conservation.

For these archaeologists, it was a tricky situation. Any association with Fenn—even when trying to help him conserve these items properly—was controversial for the professionals, Tim Maxwell, the museum's retired director, told the **Santa Fe Reporter.**

"I would say that among my colleagues, it was about 50-50 between those who supported us and who thought we were legitimizing [Fenn's excavations]," Maxwell said.

Those debates rage on today, arising every time an artifact that had passed through Fenn's hands resurfaces. Yet during their raid and their larger operation, the Bureau of Land Management wasn't concerned with any of that. They just wanted to know if Fenn was trafficking in contraband. To me, it seemed pretty clear that Fenn wasn't some sort of big international artifact trafficker, and you have to really stretch the law to suggest that he did anything overtly criminal, even if he did a number of things that would later be declared off-limits and are certainly suspect in any era. But in this particular case of Fenn versus the government, it seemed like a win for Fenn, or at least a solid draw.

He wasn't, however, happy just fighting them off; in fact, Fenn told me that he ultimately got the government to turn tail and run because they had overstepped their bounds in their quest to nail him.

"They falsified the affidavit and the search warrant," Fenn claimed. "We caught them doing it. There's smoking guns in both documents."

Fenn said they agreed to hold him immune from all laws related to the Four Corners case if he agreed not to sue for improprieties in the affidavit for the search warrant.

"My attorney asked me if I wanted to pursue it, to sue them," Fenn said. "I'd spent thirty thousand dollars, I was getting old, and I'd been living under threat of prosecution for four and a half years. What they found out didn't bother me. It was what they were going to make up that worried me."

This sounded a bit overblown, like something that couldn't possibly be true, and Fenn sensed my barely concealed skepticism. He raised himself off the couch, taking those quick, shallow breaths, and

pattered over to his desk, where he brought out
the 2013 non-prosecution agreement with the government offering him immunity in exchange for
dropping his right to sue, signed by all parties. He
didn't stop there, grabbing paper after paper out
of his drawers and handing them to me, each one
illustrating another grievance he had against his
enemy, the government, and supporting his view
that they overreached.

I was drowning in random documents by the
time one of Fenn's daughters came in, bringing
him a piece of mail. She gave me a quick hello.
Fenn hardly paused in his screed to acknowledge
her, but I was certainly curious about her presence,
and her feelings on the hunt: I'd heard whispers
that the family had paid a significant toll as a result
of Fenn's hunt.

"Is all that true?" I asked him. "Have hunters targeted your family?"

Fenn nodded. "What I didn't anticipate is that
seven percent of this country is certifiable. Not
crazy, but mental problems. You wouldn't believe
the emails I get every day."

He sat back down on the couch and raised a finger, pointing in the air as he talked.

"There's a guy who called me on the phone a
couple years ago. He told me, 'If you don't tell me
where the treasure chest is, you son of a bitch, I'm
going to kill you.' I said, 'Listen, if torture and
death are the only things you can threaten me

with, you're in trouble. I'm eighty-four years old."
Fenn chuckled.

Fenn's fighter-pilot bravado seemed real enough,
when the threats were about him. But the danger
to his family clearly terrified him—the prospect of
searchers using his loved ones as ransom, or bait,
to force him to reveal the location of the treasure.
Fenn said he had called the police many times out
of fear of problem searchers threatening his kin,
and several had even invaded his property, trying
to get to him or those close to him. One particular
incident, involving his granddaughter, badly shook
him and his entire family, and had caused major
changes in how he dealt with the public.

"There's a guy in jail out here right now," Fenn
said. "A guy by the name of Francisco Chavez, lived
in Las Vegas, Nevada. His nickname was 'Paco.' He
used to come see me here. I never invited him, but
if they ring my bell at the gate, I can't hear very
well, so they say hello, I let them in.

"He comes in, he brings me cookies, and a cake
he buys downtown. This went on for a couple years.
Strange guy. I never allowed him in my house. I always talked to him out front. Weird, but not crazy.
But all of a sudden, he turned crazy. He decided
that my treasure was my granddaughter, and he
was coming for the treasure."

I'd seen Fenn's granddaughter briefly—she was
the girl in her twenties who had offered me only the
most cursory of greetings when I came in. Now

that Fenn was telling me this tale, I understood her wariness.

"He sent me a package with a big picture of a knife," Fenn said. "He threatened her life, threatened my life. So we got the police involved. They arrested him. Eventually, they let him out of jail, and he went back to Las Vegas, with a tracking device on his ankle. He cut it off of his leg. They traced him coming back to Santa Fe. They found a big knife in his car, and they found him in Gallup, because he was using his cell phone, and using his credit card. They arrested him again. He's been in jail for eight months. It's a crazy thing."

The incident left a lasting scar on Fenn's entire family, prompting his granddaughter—apparently here just to visit now—to move outside of New Mexico.

"My granddaughter left the state because she was so scared. I didn't anticipate that. I anticipated crazy people, but not vicious crazy," he said, slowly shaking his head.

Fenn seemed to have accepted this as the cost of doing business—though I wasn't quite sure his family had, since they never signed up for this kind of danger. It was Fenn's responsibility, but they'd paid the price for his searchers' obsessions. It was hard for me to fathom that some of these searchers would sink to such levels—the treasure wasn't even worth **that** much money, in the grand scheme—and wasn't part of why people wanted to find the

chest just to prove they could? To solve it, to figure
it out, even to gain Fenn's approval and respect? I
guess there's a level of frustration and anger that
enters the minds of those who feel like they aren't
getting what they deserve, or that somehow they've
been cheated out of it. This hunt definitely at-
tracted those who might be in that 7 percent Fenn
was talking about. I found myself wondering how
those people would take it if someone actually did
find the treasure. They might not consider the hunt
over—merely the target altered.

My reverie was broken by a text from Beep, still
back at the hotel. He was going stir-crazy by
now, and still hopeful I'd do something I wasn't
100 percent comfortable with: invite him over to
meet Fenn. Having spent months obsessed with
the chase, Beep was absolutely in awe of Fenn, and
wanted so badly to sit with him, to gauge him—
and especially to tell him about our solve in the
Rio Grande Gorge. But inviting Beep might shat-
ter even the thin veneer of journalistic remove I
still had. I was already trying to walk a very fine
line. Beep's presence might establish me on the
hunter side of things in a way I couldn't fully come
back from.

I did it anyway.

Fenn, surprisingly, was enamored of the idea.

"So he's a searcher, too?" he asked, perking right up when I explained who Beep was and why he wanted to come over. "Absolutely, bring him by; I'd love to meet him."

Extending the Beep invitation turned out to be a good thing. With that ask made, it became clear the interview portion of our meeting was over, and Fenn appeared to visibly relax. He started asking me a bit about myself for the first time, and I showed him pictures of my eight-months-pregnant wife, Amalie, on my phone.

"She's a lot better-looking than you are," he said approvingly. "What's she doing with you?"

I had no idea, and I told him so. We chatted a little bit about Boston, about how long I was staying in Santa Fe, what I'd seen in town. He asked about my past, and seemed to brighten when he learned that I'd been a news reporter for about eight years, then moved over to become a sportswriter for another eight, and then left that job to write books. "It's very important not to do one thing too long," he said with emphasis, "fifteen years at the most, but ideally less than that." He seemed clearly proud of his own varied history as a pilot turned art dealer turned author turned treasure hunt creator.

We talked about my soon-to-arrive son, and how excited I was. "Maybe someday, when he's bigger, I could even take him out treasure hunting with me," I half joked. Fenn appeared to brighten at that idea. He was at ease now, even seemed to like me a bit. I figured this was as good a time as any to make my big ask.

"Forrest, one thing I'd really love to see—the vault. Do you think that'd be all right? Could we take a look in there?"

He looked at me like it was crazy we hadn't done this already.

"Of course!" he said, springing off the couch, still breathing shallowly but moving fast now. "Come on."

This had gone more easily than I'd expected at almost every point. From the vault to the FBI sting to the threats on his family, Fenn had been an open book, eager to talk, eager to put himself out there. Perhaps because I knew he'd been tamping down on the interviews as his hearing and his patience failed, I thought he'd be more difficult to deal with, but he was the opposite—now that he had decided to open himself up again, it was like he had all these thoughts that he'd been itching to get out, and they'd been bottled up, without interviews for him to do.

Fenn led me out of his office and back up the short staircase to the hallway with the large red door and huge, tantalizing lock. This was the home of the chest, the site of its conception and birth. My heart started beating fast as Fenn released the lock and swung the door outward, opening the chamber to reveal the secrets within.

And my first discovery . . . was that it was very, very small.

I admit, I don't know what I expected—something out of a heist movie, maybe? Rows and rows of sleek cages and gold bars and live-in security guards in uniforms, with barking Dobermans? Obviously not quite that, but I'm ashamed to say I was disappointed by what the vault really was. It resembled a closet, maybe even smaller than the walk-in in my bedroom. It had several rows of shelves, but really, it looked like a pantry, yellowed and old.

Fenn didn't catch my surprise, fortunately. He began proudly showing off some of his most prized possessions, the ones that were too important or valuable to leave lying around in his office.

"You're a sportswriter; you'll appreciate this," he said, picking up an old baseball in a stand. The ball was signed by the 1955 Yankee team, that of Hall of Famers Mickey Mantle, Yogi Berra, Whitey Ford, and Phil Rizzuto. Of that group, only Ford was still alive. I can't imagine what it would garner at a memorabilia show today.

Not bad, certainly, but Fenn wasted no more time in going for the pièce de résistance, Sitting Bull's peace pipe, which he'd recently acquired. It was the crown jewel of his collection, a true piece of history.

He offered to let me hold it. Nervously, I declined. But he swung it around, showing it off, and

I could feel the power in it—around the pipe, and really around so much of Fenn's collection, there was a feeling of being close to something important, a proximity to history, to events far larger than ourselves.

But even as impressive as that was, Fenn knew why we were in there, and it was for a piece of much more recent history. "So where was the chest?" I asked him. "Where did it sit?"

"I kept it right here," he said, pointing to a spot on one of the shelves. "And I filled it up over the years, took some things out, put other things in."

The shelf was narrow, speaking to something I'd known but hadn't really weighed in earnest—that in reality, the chest was smaller than the mental image I had of it in my mind. I knew conceptually that it was only ten by ten by five. I'd read that often enough, but still, in my brain there was a picture of a big pirate's chest, several feet long and high and loaded to the brim with treasure. But Fenn's chest wasn't that at all. It was petite, and that was something to remember when out searching for it. It wasn't the kind of thing that you'd see if you weren't certain of where you were looking.

There was something else I'd been meaning to ask him earlier, and I hadn't gotten around to it, but now that we were there, standing right where Fenn had kept his chest, it zipped back into my brain. Doug Preston had told me that when Fenn was putting together the treasure, Fenn had told him he was planning to put some sort of a fail-safe into the chest, a key to a bank account somewhere—Preston said Switzerland—something that would tip Fenn off that the chest had been found, if that money was claimed. I brought it up with him, asking Fenn if he'd ever actually done that. "Is there a fail-safe, a bank account key or code locked away in the chest?"

Fenn seemed startled by the question—this was one he wasn't ready for. He paused before answering, looking off into space for a long moment.

"Lemme tell you what—I don't know whether I did this or not. I don't remember," Fenn said. "But at one time, I wrote out an IOU, and wrote, 'Take this IOU to the First National Bank in Santa Fe, and they will give you one hundred thousand dollars in cash.' But I started telling myself, you know, if somebody finds it eight hundred years from now, that IOU is no good. So, I don't remember whether I left it in there or not. I just don't. But there's something in that treasure chest that no one knows I left in there. And I've never mentioned it to anybody. And it's going to be one of those things that is special just for the person that found it. Nobody else."

Was he bullshitting me? Could he really not remember if he put an IOU in the treasure chest or not? Of course, it seemed like an easy way of avoiding a question he didn't want to answer. But talking to him, watching him as he spoke, it didn't seem that way; it seemed like this was something he hadn't thought about in a while, and that he was actually trying to remember whether he'd done it or not, but he couldn't.

Well, then, if he didn't put something like that in the chest, this IOU or beacon or whatever the heck it was, how did he know for sure it hadn't been found yet?

"If you knew what I know, you'd know the chest was still out there," he said, a sudden twinkle in his eye. That one he'd thought about before, that's for damn sure.

It was hard not to take Fenn at his word. He might redirect or deflect at times, and he certainly had his tropes and well-worn answers that he turned to when needed, but for the most part, Fenn had been approachable, far more so than I'd expected. I was starting to see what Dal and Cynthia had been saying about why, if I got to know Forrest, I'd simply understand that it wasn't a hoax. It was impossible for me to know, of course, but he certainly didn't have the air of someone who was lying, or who had holes in his story. He seemed like someone personally invested in every bit of his chase, who was happy at the good it seemed to be doing, and who really cared how it all turned out. Maybe I'd just been charmed like all the rest, but I couldn't see the upside for him in fabricating this grand, elaborate lie.

Beep texted that he was nearby, but his Uber

driver couldn't find the house. I left Fenn to lock up his vault, and made my way toward the foyer to help guide Beep in. But it wasn't like I could just stick my head out the front door and wave; we were literally in a walled compound. I had to find Fenn's granddaughter, get her to push the button to open the gate, and only then was I able to wander out into the street and flag down Beep and his driver, who were far down the road, in front of another similarly walled compound.

Beep bounded out of the car and practically tore by me on the way to the house.

"Wow, nice place," he marveled as I caught up, and we trotted up the driveway toward the front door. Fenn was standing out front, and I saw Beep straighten up and adjust his Toronto Blue Jays cap as he got ready to meet the man behind the hunt.

"So you're Beeper, is it?" Fenn said, sticking out his hand in greeting.

Beep shot me a look, probably annoyed that I'd referred to him by his fantasy sports nickname in Fenn's presence. For the moment, Jay was Jay.

"Oh, no, I mean, some people call me Beep, but I'm Jay. It's Jay. It's nice to meet you, Forrest," he said.

It didn't seem to matter what he called himself; Beep was enthralled with all things Fenn, grateful simply to be in the old man's presence, and Fenn thrived on hero worship, so they immediately hit it off. The two were soon deep in conversation about the treasure, and Beep's unhealthy obsession with it. Really, that was Fenn's favorite subject—his searchers' all-encompassing lust for his treasure—and Fenn was thrilled to have us stay longer, offering to give us a proper tour of his compound. He led us out of his study, through his airy, sun-drenched kitchen, and out into his lush backyard, the grass well manicured and perfectly green, a stream running through and draining into a koi pond. Yet Beep and I quickly realized we were not alone out there. Hiding behind rocks, next to trees, waiting around the corner of the house were gigantic bronze beasts: animal statues, life-size and terrifying. Tigers, bears, panthers—they lorded menacingly over Fenn's space, their bronze eyes staring right through outsiders like us.

"Wow, Forrest, what do you feed those things?" Beep joked, with his usual hint of childlike wonder. Beep seemed overwhelmed by the grandeur of Fenn's entire complex, all of it a far cry from the bleak environs of his home in frigid Waterloo, Ontario.

I was less taken by the landscaping. The menagerie was so odd, and so lifelike, it brought a chill to my spine. Perhaps it was because I knew that these beasts were merely placeholders for the ferocious creatures Fenn used to keep—live ones. Fenn once owned two full-grown alligators, Elvis and Beowulf, who lived in a pond at his art gallery. He fed them beef liver, going out and handing them the chunks of meat himself. Somehow, he never lost a hand. He seemed to have a real soft spot for the creatures, even though he admitted that they were really there as a marketing gimmick.

"They were not very good pets," he said. "But they were good for the business, and that's why I kept them."

He had to give them up when he sold his art gallery, and now these bronzed versions served as replacements in his backyard. I asked Fenn—mostly kidding—if he was absolutely certain that there weren't any living gators still roaming around that we needed to watch for. He chuckled in reply, and changed the subject, beckoning us over to a thin, wispy tree with a rather unique soil bed. The dirt was littered with shards of Native American pottery, acquired over the years from Fenn's various digs through San Lazaro. He invited us both to choose a piece to keep for our own, but not before handing them over to him so he could tell us what they meant.

We both stooped down and combed over the pile, our eyes scanning for something that looked like it might be important, special, meaningful somehow. The shards were mostly about three to four inches across and high, painted on one side in a variety of colors, everything from bright hues to a deep black. I felt somewhere between a little guilty and slightly uncomfortable sifting through them, but Fenn's whole ethos was that we were supposed to engage with these objects, that this would bring them to life. Look, I understood that these shards were probably of little monetary value, or they wouldn't be piled in his garden, but there was still a large, awkward part of me that felt like I was on the wrong side of the "Do not touch" barrier at a museum, wantonly playing with things I didn't understand.

Ultimately, I went along with it, plucking out a black shard with white lines through it and handing it to Fenn for his perusal. Beep dug through the pile ferociously, eventually choosing a more colorful piece, and handed it to Fenn as we both waited for him to tell us our fortune.

Fenn had honed this routine over time, and he had it down by now. He eyed each piece, one of hundreds we could have opted for, and then coolly explained just what it was, which tribe had created it, how far back it dated. Fenn went into detail on the piece Beep picked, explaining that the markings represented some sort of ancient warrior bird. Beep looked positively thrilled, cradling the piece in his hands as if it were a shard of the Holy Grail.

My turn. Fenn looked at my piece, turned it over a few times, and then handed it back to me.

"This is a piece of a water jug," he said.

I put the shard in my pocket and hid my disappointment as we headed back inside to Fenn's office. As he sat back down at his desk, I figured we'd done enough schmoozing with Fenn that it was finally time to explain to him our solve, and get a chance to read his reaction in person. Other than his favored friends and a few lucky ones at Fennboree, so few searchers ever got this opportunity—even if Fenn's poker face was well practiced by now, I was betting we could read something into his response. Whatever he did and said should give us a hint as to whether we were on the right track—and if we were as close as Beep thought we were.

Beep began detailing our idea, describing our adventures near Agua Caliente Canyon. Fenn was nodding slightly, which I took as a good sign, and I was starting to get the littlest bit excited as Beep recounted how we went down from Agua Caliente Canyon, doubled back, and then headed on into the Rio Grande Gorge—until Fenn suddenly scrunched up his face at those final words and immediately cut Beep off.

"Rio Grande Gorge? But that's not in the Rocky Mountains. I said the treasure's in the Rocky Mountains, not twenty miles south of the mountains," Fenn said with a bemused chuckle.

I watched the blood drain out of Beep's face as he realized the magnitude of our mistake. We were never close to finding the treasure—we hadn't even gotten the most basic of instructions right. We weren't in the search area at all.

I felt incredibly stupid as Fenn sat back, wearing

a grin that I could describe only as satisfied. He had us. We were just like all the rest of his searchers, it turned out—full of vigor, excitement, and hubris, and willing to convince ourselves of anything while in thrall to the chest.

5

A DELIGHTFUL
MASQUERADE

Fenn wasn't the first to craft a treasure hunt around a book.

On August 7, 1979, an artist named Kit Williams set off for Ampthill Park, in the hamlet of Ampthill, in Bedfordshire, England, about ninety minutes north of London. With him was Bamber Gascoigne, a well-known television host. In Williams's possession was a golden hare, one he had molded himself, at the cost of about six thousand English pounds' worth of gold. It was sealed in wax and placed inside a ceramic case to shield it from metal detectors.

Engraved on the case was this message: "I am the keeper of the jewel of the Masquerade, which lies waiting safe inside me for you . . . or eternity."

Williams buried the hare at a precise spot in the park, one he had visited years before. Only

Gascoigne witnessed the moment. But later that same night, Williams stepped in front of a television camera and issued a proclamation.

"Now it has been buried," he said, ensconced in darkness. "And it's up to you to find it."

Those words, and the subsequent publication of Williams's book, **Masquerade,** kicked off a treasure hunt that would come to captivate England for the next three years, changing the world of treasure hunting forever.

Masquerade was the first great armchair treasure hunt, a genre that essentially did not exist until Williams buried his golden hare. Up to that point, treasure hunting had been the realm of professionals, or shot-in-the-dark obsessives seeking lost or haphazardly hidden treasures, uncertain if they would ever find them—because they weren't meant to be found.

Masquerade, however, represented something different; the very point was that the treasure should be found. There had been a few isolated hunts of this sort before, notably the St. Paul Pioneer Press medallion hunts that started in the 1950s, but nothing with this complexity, impact, or reward. There was a guiding hand at work in this hunt, and anyone could find the treasure as long as he or she could decipher the clues.

Williams came to treasure hunting largely by accident. He was a painter, small-time but well regarded on the English art scene. Then a book editor, Tom Maschler, arrived at his door out of the blue one day. He had seen Williams's artwork and believed it would translate well to a children's picture book. Crucially, he wanted the work to be a puzzle book, something that would make people come back and look at it again and again.

Williams was aghast and rejected the idea as one not befitting a serious artist. But then he thought about it, and then thought more about it, and eventually realized that maybe he could get people to view his art in a new way if he tied the paintings to some sort of puzzle—or, even better, a quest.

"I am not interested in puzzles," Williams told the BBC in 2009, on the thirtieth anniversary of his hunt. "Never was interested in puzzles. But I thought what I must do is find a way to make people look, and look, and look again. And if I said, 'This is art, and you must really look at it because this is art,' that turns people off. But if I said, there's some sort of puzzle here that you must figure out, then they'd be looking at art through the back door."

Over the next three years, Williams painted a series of sixteen pictures, all of them telling the story of a rabbit, Jack Hare, tasked with transporting a jewel from the moon to the sun. At the end, Jack Hare realizes he has lost the treasure, and it's up to the reader to discover where it is. Hidden in the paintings were clues that, if taken together, should lead a reader to the exact spot. It was a riddle of Williams's own design.

"If I use a method that's been used before, it's going to be cracked easily by people," Williams said. "I've got to devise a method that's never been used before. It had to be very simple, but it had to be absolutely unique."

And unique it was. **Masquerade** was an absolute sensation from the very start, capturing the imagination of the British population and creating a treasure-hunting frenzy. The quest for the golden hare was featured in print, on radio, and on television, as hunters formed teams and dug up lawns across Britain in search of the treasure. The first edition sold out in two days; **Masquerade** eventually sold roughly two million copies worldwide.

Soon, Williams was receiving two hundred letters a day, and his home was besieged by hunters seeking clues or validation. It drove him into seclusion, hesitant to ever leave the house, fearful of interacting with his obsessed hunters—the very opposite of Fenn's initial welcoming response.

Despite the frenzy, for years no one came to the correct solution. **Masquerade**'s puzzle was difficult: The answer lay in the book's fifteen internal paintings, all of which featured animals of some sort. The key was in recognizing that the eyes and paws of the animals in the pictures pointed in a certain direction; drawing a line from the eyes of each animal, through the paws, and onward would point to a letter somewhere on the page. Take the pointed-out letters throughout the book, put them all together, and they made up this phrase, an instruction of sorts:

"Catherine's Long Finger Over Shadows Earth Buried Yellow Amulet Midday Points The Hour In Light Of Equinox Look You."

That was half the battle. The next stage was to take the first letter of each word and string them together. With an extra step or two, it eventually made up the message "ClosebyAmpthill." Ampthill Park was the site of a cross named for Catherine of Aragon, one of Henry VIII's ill-fated wives. The solution was to go to Ampthill Park at the equinox, wait for midday, and then dig where the shadow fell from Catherine's cross. That's where the treasure would be buried.

For three years, no one figured it out.

In March 1982, however, Williams received a letter in the mail. It contained a drawing, showing the precise spot at Ampthill Park, with the shadow of the cross in the correct location. The letter was sent by a Ken Thomas. Williams called Thomas and told him he had the right spot; he could dig for the hare. Williams and Thomas were filmed together removing the hare from its wax case, though Thomas, according to the BBC, covered his face with a scarf and would agree to be interviewed only from behind a screen. After claiming the treasure,

Thomas largely disappeared from the public eye, stoking years of conspiracy theories among chagrined Masqueraders that something was afoot, that they had all been cheated out of their treasure somehow, the standard stuff that treasure hunters seem to say whenever someone else finds the prize they wanted.

The thing about conspiracy theories, though, is that every once in a while, they're true.

In 1988, **The Sunday Times** published an explosive piece proving that Ken Thomas had colluded with an ex-girlfriend of Kit Williams's to claim the treasure without actually solving the puzzle. The woman, Veronica Robertson, had lived with Williams, and the two of them had spent time at Ampthill Park, at the spot where Williams would later bury his hare. At the time of the hunt, Robertson was dating a man named John Guard—who was business partners with a man named Dugald Thompson: the real name of the secretive "Ken Thomas."

The fraud was discovered when the hare was sold at auction in 1988, after the failure of Thomas/Thompson's treasure hunt company, Haresoft. Haresoft was incorporated to build a treasure-hunting computer game, Hareraiser, which claimed that, if beaten, it would lead to another treasure. That treasure was never found—the game may never have been beatable at all, and merely a cash grab—and when the company was liquidated, reporters looking into it found that the owner's name was Dugald Thompson, not Ken Thomas, setting off the investigation.

It was a massive scandal.

"This tarnishes **Masquerade** and I'm shocked by what has emerged," Williams told the **London Times** in 1988. "I feel a deep sense of responsibility to all those many people who were genuinely looking for it. Although I didn't know it, it was a skeleton in my cupboard and I'm relieved it has come out."

Masquerade may have ultimately ended in scandal, but what it set in motion could not be stopped. By 1982, when the **Masquerade** treasure was claimed, treasure hunting was experiencing another peak moment. Real-world treasure hunters were salvaging wrecks from under the seas, and archaeologists were finding incredible historic sites, like the Terracotta Army, discovered less than a decade earlier. Popular culture was awash in stories of treasure hunting and adventure; **Raiders of the Lost Ark** had exploded into theaters the year before, and its sequel was already in production— soon to be joined by knockoffs like **Romancing the Stone,** kid-focused versions like my old favorite, **The Goonies,** and even a remake of **King Solomon's Mines,** featuring Richard Chamberlain and Sharon Stone. Now that **Masquerade** had made people realize that they didn't just have to read about these adventures or watch them on the big screen, that they could actually participate in them, there was no putting that genie back in the bottle.

"They set a challenge, and they give you an incentive, and they say, 'Can you solve it?'" said Jenny Kile, who has become one of the foremost authorities on armchair treasure hunting, through her website Mysterious Writings, and her book, **Armchair Treasure Hunts: The Quests for Hidden Treasures.**

"It offers a chance for people to explore and learn, and it's an adventure," Kile said. "There's nothing like the hunting moments, and the discovery—it's very satisfying. It's an opportunity to become a kid again and explore. They have the nine-to-five life, and then they can take off and explore."

With armchair hunting—so named because, in theory, you can figure out the solution from your armchair—the appeal of the hunt is doubled by the certainty that the treasure is supposed to be found; that someone is pulling the strings and leading hunters on an adventure.

"With a man-made hunt, you know that it's there," she said.

That made hunters' investment of time and energy seem worthwhile, and these armchair hunts proved intoxicating to so many. But there's another side to all the fantasy and exploration and dreams of riches. Just as with the **Masquerade** hunt, more often than not, these hunts run into trouble—scandal, contention, turmoil of one sort or another.

"It's funny how many treasure hunts actually end in controversy," Kile said. "I have no idea [why]. Some of them . . . get in trouble because their prize was too much for what they can do, and then others, it's—I don't know why. They just are."

In 1982, however, none of that was yet on anyone's minds. The **Masquerade** hunt had just concluded, everything still appeared to be on the up-and-up, and the quest had seemed like an incredible adventure. Hunters wanted more.

The next truly big hunt to capture the popular imagination debuted the same year that **Masquerade** ended, 1982. It was called **The Secret,** and it endures to this day.

The Secret was a direct descendant of **Masquerade,** this time crafted by an American, Byron Preiss. He came up with twelve pictures and twelve matching verses that when properly stitched together would lead to twelve casques, all buried somewhere in North America. If discovered, each of the casques held a ceramic key, redeemable for one of twelve jewels held in a single safe-deposit box. Each jewel was worth roughly one thousand dollars.

The pictures in **The Secret** look like the kind of stuff that would show up on a 1980s metal band's album cover, or on the front of a Tolkien book—gnomes, lions, quasi-religious images, suits of armor; ethereal, astral pictures. But it is genuinely hard; the readers first must figure out which verse matches with which image, and then from there figure out how all of that leads to a treasure. Verse 2, for instance, begins, "At the place where jewels abound, / Fifteen rows down to the ground, / In the middle of twenty-one, / From end to end . . ." and goes on like that. It is believed to be matched with Image 7, which is a picture of a clock, with a withered hand holding up a mask partially obscuring the clock's face. **Secret** aficionados believe that the two halves combine to point to a treasure somewhere in the city of New Orleans, but so far, no one has been able to figure out where exactly it is.

But there have been some successes. The first casque was found in 1984, in Chicago's Grant Park, by a group of teenagers. That confirmed that the treasures are real—and no one has had much reason to doubt that since. But for long after that initial find? Nothing. Two decades passed before the next treasure was found, when an attorney, Brian Zinn, unearthed a casque in a park area in Cleveland in 2004.

The hunt's creator, Preiss, died in a car accident in 2005. Hunters seem to think they have zeroed in on the precise locations of the casques—but then there's nothing at the agreed-upon spots. Still, that hasn't stopped people from searching, either trying new solutions or just hammering at the same old solves, perhaps with their own slight tweak.

Jenny Kile, too, was lured in by **The Secret**'s quest, heading down the eastern seaboard in search of one of the casques. Though with the passage of time, and the very public nature of some of the hiding spots, it's possible the treasure she was seeking wasn't even there anymore.

"There's one in North Carolina at the Elizabeth Gardens at Fort Raleigh. We've looked for that one," she said. "The shoreline has eroded and so it's very possible that that one's been lost to the shoreline. However, people still look for it because, again, you know it's in that area—but you can't confirm that that's where it was without finding the casque. And so until you find the casque, there's still that possibility."

When I learned there was supposedly a casque near me, in Boston, I didn't think much of it; the trail had been cold for so long that it didn't seem worth investigating. But someone else thought differently. In October 2019, a Boston-area dad, Jason Krupat, unearthed the Boston gem underneath home plate of the softball field at Langone Park, in the city's North End.

Krupat had started looking for the Boston casque just a year earlier, after **The Secret** was featured on the Discovery Channel show Expedition Unknown. He figured out that the clues in the so-called Boston Verse were connected to areas of the city's North End that were important to Paul Revere's Midnight Ride to warn the American colonists that the British were coming. It all pointed to home plate, but he wasn't about to go dig it up on a hunch—until one day he ran by and saw crews doing construction work on the site. He told the foreman, and later emailed the construction company, about his belief that there was a treasure buried there. And when one of the construction workers hit something while digging around home plate, the company remembered that kooky guy talking about buried treasure, and called up Krupat.

Not long after, he and the crew from Expedition Unknown unearthed the key, and Krupat took it to New York, where Preiss's widow presented him with the third jewel in a grand ceremony.

"It was emotional," Krupat told **The Boston Globe.** "It was a special event. I told my kids that this was like something out of a novel. We exchanged a buried treasure for a jewel."

Guess I was searching for the wrong treasure.

The Secret may be the most enduring of **Masquerade**'s successors, but it certainly wasn't the only one. As the 1980s went on, armchair treasure hunts sprang up by the dozens to capitalize on **Masquerade**'s popularity.

There was 1984's **Treasure: In Search of the Golden Horse,** a $500,000 hunt issued in both book and film form, leading searchers on a five-year hunt across the United States. (It was not solved by the 1989 completion date, and the prize was ultimately donated to Big Brothers Big Sisters of America.) There was a hunt created by the famed magician David Blaine, which awarded a $100,000 prize to a California woman who figured out the solutions hidden in Blaine's book, **Mysterious Stranger,** itself an odd combination of autobiography, history of magic, and puzzle. Even Kit Williams got back into the game—sort of—issuing an unnamed sequel to **Masquerade** commonly known as "The Bee Book," where readers were tasked with figuring out the book's real title, and rewarded with a golden queen bee statuette. That real title? **The Bee on the Comb,** Williams revealed when the hunt was solved in 1985.

These hunts and many, many others came and went, none of them causing the frenzy that **Masquerade** had. Armchair treasure hunting settled into its niche—a new book coming out to occupy the community every once in a while, but rarely transcending it to make an impact in popular culture.

What took armchair hunting to the next level, however, was the same thing that elevated so many other pursuits: the internet.

The first big online treasure hunters' forum was a UK-based site called Quest4Treasure, which aggregated the hunts and let hunters post their theories and findings. But the online treasure-hunting community really took off with the introduction of **A Treasure's Trove** in 2004.

A Treasure's Trove was another of **Masquerade**'s offspring, a children's book with a treasure hunt inside. But unlike the single quarry that Kit Williams promised, Michael Stadther's book offered up twelve (later found to be fourteen) tokens for readers to find, redeemable for jewels valued at a total of roughly a million dollars. The money was big, yes. But what really set it apart from past armchair hunts was the way it grew—via online forums, with searchers discussing clues, possibilities, theories, their own searches.

At that time, interest in treasure hunting was again cresting. Dan Brown's treasure quest novel, **The Da Vinci Code,** had been published in 2003, stoking interest in mainstays of treasure-hunting folklore like the Knights Templar and the Freemasons, and serving as a gateway into hunting for a new generation. On the heels of **The Da Vinci Code** came the 2004 Nicolas Cage movie **National Treasure,** which incorporated many common treasure hunt tropes, and even sprinkled in a few cribbed from actual American treasure hunts—the Beale Papers' connection to the Declaration of Independence is put to good use in the film, for instance. So when another real-life hunt arrived in the form of **A Treasure's Trove,** the climate was ripe for it.

"**A Treasure's Trove**—that was huge," Kile said. "[Stadther] went on the **Today** show, and he got major publicity, but also, there was the forum at the time, and the internet was around, too. And so it quickly spread, and there were lots of people talking about it."

The biggest **A Treasure's Trove** forum was called Tweleve (misspelling apparently intentional) in honor of the original twelve gems of the hunt. At first, the activity was fairly run-of-the-mill—some users posting thoughts, some responding to others. But once users began to figure out the secret to the book's puzzles—that a code-breaking mechanism called a Polybius square must be used, and that all the tokens were hidden in knotholes of trees—the community really took off, with "trovers" banding together to share information and do their part to help uncover all of the tokens. It became a group race, with the entire hunting community pulling in unison—which surprised Stadther himself.

"I expected internet activity, and I expected clue sharing," Stadther told CNET in 2005. "If I had been a clue solver, I probably would have tried to find two or three more jewels before posting my solution."

What he came to realize was that it wasn't necessarily about the prize; it was about the search, and the communal element to it.

"It almost seems like for the lookers and the finders, the trovers, it was . . . as much fun being in the finding community as it was trying to solve the clues," he said.

Kile got into treasure hunting because of **A Treasure's Trove,** spending time on the forums as she, too, tried to unravel the puzzle.

"Once the method was known, that they were hidden in knotholes, then the whole nation got excited because they were also scattered across the whole United States," she said.

The tokens were all discovered in the space of a few months. The chase had become such a phenomenon that Stadther went on tour with the jewels; his book had sold more than 600,000 copies in just over a year, and his hunt was considered a massive success. Of course, he couldn't stop there—he put out a sequel book and hunt in September 2006, entitled **Secrets of the Alchemist Dar,** with promises that it would lead to two million dollars' worth of rings hidden across the country. And, perhaps predictably, considering how these things seem to go, it ran into problems.

"His illustrations in it infringed on a bit of copyright, so that came into some trouble," Kile said. "So his sequel died and he sort of just went back into the shadows. . . . There was some famous artist['s work] that his illustrations really were almost identical to."

Stadther's publisher, Simon & Schuster, sued for back payment, and Stadther declared bankruptcy. The hunt was canceled, the rings sold off as part of the liquidation, and Stadther disappeared from the hunting scene.

What didn't disappear, however, were the treasure-hunting forums that his hunts spawned. Those remained alive and well, readers puttering away on smaller hunts, all waiting for the next great quest.

Enter Forrest Fenn.

When Fenn first debuted his hunt at New Mexico's Collected Works Bookstore in the fall of 2010, he seemed to think it would be a curiosity, a lark for friends and family to enjoy—maybe a few hundred others, a few thousand at the outside. That's why the first print run of the book was so limited: one thousand copies, nothing like the thousands upon thousands of books initially printed for hunts like **Masquerade** or **A Treasure's Trove.** Fenn's aspirations simply were not on the scale of those other armchair hunts.

For a few years, he was right; only friends, family, and truly devoted armchair treasure hunters tuned in to his quest. Among that final category were many of the people who had searched for the rewards promised in **A Treasure's Trove,** and who kept searching as smaller quests popped up. When these searchers discovered Fenn's quest, they built new online communities at sites like Dal's blog and ChaseChat, many of them bringing over the same familiar usernames—and reputations—from their earlier days hunting and discussing other treasures on other forums.

"When the Forrest Fenn hunt arrived, a lot of those people were still around. And they kind of transitioned over," Kile said. "There had been other hunts presented after **A Treasure's Trove,** but they weren't as powerful, or as legendary, as Forrest Fenn's. When Forrest Fenn's came around, it was like, whoa. This is what they've all been waiting for."

Kile herself wasn't initially taken in by Fenn's hunt.

"I was aware of it when it first came out, and thought, Eh, it's just another million-dollar treasure hunt, because there had been a few others—and on top of that, I was like, Yeah, right," she said, laughing as she warily remembered other hunts that hadn't quite lived up to their promise, or had been outright frauds.

"But then I started looking into it more, and I saw, wow, this is actually for real," she continued. "It's something anyone can do; it wasn't some encrypted, impossible, code and cipher–type puzzle to solve. It was follow the poem, solve the nine clues, and you can find the treasure."

That brought people in, for sure. But what really set Fenn's hunt apart was its creator—and his willingness to interact with his searchers. Kit Williams would sometimes answer letters, but generally he cringed at the attention **Masquerade** brought, and it eventually made him a recluse. Fenn, however, ate it up, responding to nearly every email he got in the early days, especially when his hunting troupe consisted of only a few thousand searchers. It gave the group more of a community feel, with Fenn at its head, making jokes, spitting out dubious words of wisdom, offering validation.

"That's part of what makes Forrest Fenn's so popular, that he's active in the hunt," Kile said. "He's constantly stoking the belief that people can find it, because he's talking to them. The moment that he might pass away, or pulls back, you're going to lose a lot of hunters, because you're not going to have that belief anymore. . . . Actually having the creator there, feeding that belief, is very powerful, and reassuring to the person that they're not wasting their time."

Kile started Mysterious Writings when Fenn's hunt was still nationally unknown. It was the calmer, more relaxed period just before Fenn's **Today** show appearance changed everything, and so she was able to communicate easily with Fenn and earn his trust. She developed a regular series called "Six Questions with Forrest Fenn," offering the growing Fenn hunter community one of the first structured interviews where the queries revolved largely around searcher questions and concerns, hints and clarifications—unlike the larger media articles of the time, which mostly focused on the phenomenon of the hunt and the peculiarities of its creator.

Over time, Fenn came to reveal a fair amount

of new information via these Q&As—with a few answers in particular narrowing down the hunting territory and exposing certain strategies to be nonstarters. One question, when Fenn was asked whether a little girl in India could solve the hunt and remotely locate the treasure, was particularly important: When Fenn said that the little girl could only get as far as the first two clues, it reinforced that the entire hunt could not be solved without getting out into the search area and looking around. The other big addition was Fenn's admission that every clue could be married to a geographic location on a map—meaning that his hunt, unlike so many others, was not about codes, ciphers, or anagrams. It was about words, and locations, and being out in the wild to solve the riddle, which, in some ways, made Fenn's quest not really an "armchair" hunt at all.

Kile had remained, technically, a Fenn hunter herself, though not a particularly active one. But she had her theories about where the treasure might be—ones that happened to line up almost perfectly with how my own thinking had started to evolve, especially when it came to whether Fenn had expanded the boundaries of the hunt.

One line in **The Thrill of the Chase** had always struck me—Fenn's proclamation that the treasure was hidden "somewhere in the mountains north of Santa Fe." Later, as the hunt began to become more popular, in interviews and subsequent books that evolved into "somewhere in the Rocky Mountains." I was starting to understand that at the beginning, Fenn never imagined the hunt would grow as big as it had. He may have believed it would be a local event, something for family and his New Mexico friends to play at. After all, he ordered only one thousand copies of **The Thrill of the Chase** originally. Kile felt the same way. She believed that Fenn didn't want the treasure found too fast, so he did what he could to get hunters out of New Mexico, sending them all over Colorado, Wyoming, and Montana.

"One of my theories is when it got so popular, he expanded it out," she said. "When the book first came out, you did not even know it was in the Rocky Mountains. I'm pretty sure he only said somewhere in the mountains north of Santa Fe . . . and so, I often wonder if, when it got so popular, he was concerned that there would be too many searching in New Mexico."

That's why, she said, the people who think Fenn wanted his treasure found are so, so wrong. Kile didn't agree with Cynthia Meachum, who thought that Fenn would love to see it discovered because he'd revel in all the attention. Kile said it was more important to Fenn that his treasure outlive him.

"I know he says he couldn't care less," Kile said. "But I think he'd be devastated if it was found, because I think his dream is, as he passes away, he'll love the thought that his treasure is out there for someone to find, and for years to come."

At the time, Fenn's hunt was the biggest game in town, and he surely wanted it to stay that way. It was almost certainly the most popular hunt since **Masquerade,** and in some ways, it probably exceeded that phenomenon. What's interesting, though, is that the high profile of Fenn's hunt hadn't really seemed to lead to a second explosion of armchair hunting, the way **Masquerade** had such coattails in the 1980s.

Besides the long-standing hunts like that in **The Secret,** and some newer ones that have resonated, most of the armchair hunts founded around the time of Fenn's have come and gone with little fanfare. Author and self-help guru Pete Bissonette, for instance, created an armchair hunt through his book **Breakfast Tea & Bourbon** in 2017 as a roundabout way to promote his self-help company. He offered up a fifty-thousand-dollar treasure, which was found by a family who had read his book and figured out its puzzle. But the hunt didn't sell nearly enough books to recoup the cost of production and the reward itself, Kile said, and it was soon just another completed challenge.

In general, that was the fate of most of these hunts; Fenn's seemed to block out the sun, and others got little traction—maybe because they were so nakedly profit-oriented. But that doesn't mean there's nothing new or interesting happening. Technology has brought innovation and new types of searches in recent years, turning the idea of what constitutes a treasure hunt on its head.

In Canada, in early 2019, a company called GoldHunt hid three chests, each containing $100,000, in three separate locations—one in Vancouver, one in Edmonton, one in Calgary. The for-profit hunt sold maps via email—a cheaper one without clues, and a more expensive one with clues added—to lead hunters to the treasure. The hunts were chronicled via social media, and hunters compared notes on forums like Reddit. The Edmonton and Calgary prizes were found within a week of the hunt's kickoff, while the Vancouver chest took a bit longer. The success of the hunts had the company debuting a second round only a few months later, and then expanding into the United States with a hunt in Houston.

Then there's the hunting-adjacent practice of geocaching, a sort of diffuse, populist cousin to the more traditional treasure hunts, where searchers follow a set of coordinates to reach a hidden "treasure" of some sort (usually a minor bauble). The practice originated in Oregon in 2000, when computer engineer Dave Ulmer hid a bucket in the woods in order to test the accuracy of GPS tracking equipment. The location was posted on a popular GPS group page, and soon GPS users were hiding caches everywhere for their fellow enthusiasts to find. There are now more than five million geo-cachers, chasing almost two million caches all over the world.

Most geocachers wouldn't call themselves trea-sure hunters; they see it as more of a wilderness activity, and themselves as outdoorsmen. But the basic tenets of it are pure treasure hunting, with a twist: Once you find your quarry, you leave some treasure for the next person. Once geocachers reach the goal, they usually sign a digital logbook, and replace whatever items they find with something of equal value. That makes everyone both the hunters and the hiders, a particularly egalitarian twist on the treasure-hunting story.

There are also games that borrow from some of the core concepts of treasure hunting but adapt them completely for a modern experience. Take the smash hit Pokémon Go, for instance—an aug-mented reality game that lets users "hunt" for fic-tional creatures called Pokémon, visible only on the users' phones if they find them in the right spot at the right time. Users compete to find and "capture" the best and rarest varieties, competing with other users worldwide striving toward the same goal.

And in the spring of 2019, a new hunt debuted that seemed perfect for someone I know quite well. A company announced a bitcoin treasure hunt called Satoshi's Treasure, where its creators hid the keys to one million dollars' worth of bitcoin via a series of logic puzzles and hints spread across both the internet and the real world. Beep called it "Pretty sick!"—but said he'd be interested in diving in only once 80 to 85 percent of the one thousand key fragments were found. Until then, not worth his time.

None of these ventures, though, resonated with the treasure-hunting community the way Fenn's chase did. Armchair hunting certainly has the ability to stir something in all of us, but to really reach beyond its core audience, it needs something more; in the case of Fenn's hunt, its poem, its setting, its prize, and especially the looming presence of its creator combined to make it something special.

"Eventually, Forrest Fenn's treasure will be like those sunken boat treasures and the real hunters will go after it. As of now, it's not. It's an armchair treasure hunt. But eventually it will go into the [ranks of] legendary treasure," Kile said at the time. "It is the ultimate legendary to-be treasure hunt out there right now. And you feel so fortunate that you're at the beginning of it."

I did feel fortunate at that. And even more fortunate that my initiation into the Fenn hunting community was about to begin in earnest.

6

FENNBOREE

The one they call Seattle Sullivan beckoned me away from the campsite. He said he had something to show me, something he normally didn't share with other searchers.

I followed him away from the revelers at Fennboree and over to a wooden staircase snaking up the side of one of the long, sloping hills of New Mexico's Hyde Memorial State Park. We sat down, an odd pair: he in a long, flowing linen shirt open to the navel, his hair in a stringy gray ponytail, I in a slightly too-tight button-down and jeans that I was badly regretting in this June heat.

Seattle Sullivan pulled out a folder, handling it gingerly, clearly confident that what it contained had great value. He placed it in front of us, spreading its contents out across the steps.

Within moments, a five-foot area in front of me

was covered in wrinkled pages, maps, and pictures, all of them festooned with Seattle Sullivan's block-letter printing. This, I realized, was his solve: his formula for finding Fenn's treasure. He looked down at it proudly, grinning with obvious pleasure at the complexity and breadth of his solution.

Then, suddenly, he paused, glancing up. He fixed me with his gaze, eyes narrowing with a mixture of mistrust and sudden, unmistakable fear. He seemed to be realizing that maybe he shouldn't be letting me into his world, showing me his work; maybe I'd use his information to run off and find the treasure before he could.

"Dude, if you go up there and fucking find this, I'll send my friends after you, and they'll kick your ass," he said, halting for a beat. "Okay?"

At first, I thought he was kidding. Then, as his stare bored through me, I understood that he was dead serious. This rambling thesis was his life's work, his ticket to riches, and he was genuinely worried that I was going to swipe it.

Bill "Seattle" Sullivan was a known figure in the Fenn community, his story familiar to many of the other searchers. Before I arrived, several had made sure I knew I should talk to him, because he was not your average searcher—he lived on the streets. He saw Fenn's venture as a way out, a chance to turn his life around. He spent his nights seeking shelter on the streets of Seattle, and his days in libraries, researching the way to Fenn's treasure. Yes, he wanted the money; the fortune in the chest promised an escape from life on the streets. But he also wanted to prove something.

"Let's not beat around the bush," he said. "I'm homeless. But I treat it in a way where, if I find this, I want it to be well known that not all homeless people are heroin addicts."

Unprompted, he pulled up his sleeves to show that his skinny arms were free of the heroin tracks that marred the bodies of so many of his friends.

"See? I'm absolutely a heroin hater. Especially what it's done to my friends' kids up in Washington. I fuckin' hate it. It's an epidemic. So this, solving this is a way to show that not every homeless person is an idiot. Or an addict. That's why I do it. The money is absolutely not even it—it's about solving it."

I was coming to understand that, too. And I wanted to prove as much to Seattle Sullivan, this homeless searcher I had just met, to earn his trust and his respect.

"Hey, man, this seems like a great solve," I stammered, explaining that I was on a totally different track, following Beep and his ideas. "But I've got my own thing going on here; I'm not looking to steal yours. Your solution is safe with me, okay?"

He looked me over, judging my earnestness with an eye honed from a life on the streets. Then Seattle Sullivan leaned back, seemingly mollified. Feeling secure, he proceeded with gusto, explaining his intricate, unlikely solution for finding the treasure. It started with the use of multiple anagrams, made a reference to the Last Supper, and finally veered into a detailed analysis of an octogenarian's alleged obsession with bodily fluids.

"Where he says up the creek with no paddle—it's shit creek," Seattle said, pulling out stanzas from Fenn's poem. "The line about 'heavy loads'—that's shit loads. And the 'home of Brown.' Home of Brown! So, he's a pee talker. Poop, piss. A pee-talker. Pee-taka. Petaca," he said with satisfied finality, pointing on his map to Petaca, a town somewhere deep in the mountains of northern New Mexico.

I didn't know much about how to find Fenn's treasure—yet. But I was pretty sure about one thing: Finding it did not require proving that eighty-six-year-old Forrest Fenn had a secret love of potty humor. Still, I smiled, to show Seattle Sullivan I appreciated his solve, and that he trusted me with it, and he seemed grateful.

He might not have been on the right track with his fecal obsessions, but Seattle Sullivan was right to be wary of sharing his secrets. This was Fennboree, the pinnacle of all things Forrest Fenn. All told, there were more than 150 people here, and it seemed like everybody was trying to pick up treasure-hunting tidbits from everyone else. Most of these searchers were competitive, even cutthroat, in their desire to beat one another to the prize, but get them together, get them talking, and it turned

out that they couldn't help but share information—
everyone wanted to show off how smart they were.

And while I didn't glean anything useful from the
words of Seattle Sullivan, Fennboree had already
yielded several nuggets that had pushed Beep to
consider new avenues, new areas, new ideas in the
quest, now that the Rio Grande Gorge had been
ruled out. His quest? My quest? After our first hunt
a few days before, I was starting to think of it as our
quest. At Fennboree, it was hard not to get pulled
into the excitement of it all.

The event had drawn people from around the
country to this campground at Hyde Memorial
State Park in the mountains north of Santa Fe.
Here, these obsessives could commune with kin-
dred spirits, and feel understood. In their real lives,
when they told people they sought Fenn's treasure
in order to solve the puzzle and not for the loot,
they were laughed at. Here, their words brought
knowing smiles and understanding nods. As Sacha
Johnston had already told me, that's what it was
really about for so many—so I believed Seattle
Sullivan when he said the money wasn't his primary goal. For him and these others, the treasure
granted legitimacy, granted validation that they
were made of more than what they might seem.
For many of these searchers, that was even more
precious than cash.

Even so, I could stomach anagrams about urine
and feces for only so long. Besides, there was one

searcher I was looking for, one man in particular whom I wanted to find.

I bid Seattle Sullivan good-bye and stood up to head back to the main campsite, getting a rush of blood to my head as I rose. Hyde Memorial State Park is up at nine thousand feet, and neither Beep nor I was used to the altitude. The winding road we'd driven here took us far up into these hills, our ears popping as we passed one campground after another, up and up and up, past signs warning of the current level of fire risk (it was low that day), until we found the site of Fennboree.

The park has three public gathering spots, its so-called pavilions, and the pavilion the organizers had reserved was simple enough: just a concrete slab, about fifty feet long by thirty feet wide, with four posts supporting a metal roof. Underneath that roof was a set of six picnic tables, most of them now covered with food. Burgers were on the grill, searchers were downing beers and boxed wine, and the steady buzz of conversation thrummed in the background. It all seemed so pleasantly normal. This could have been any large wilderness gathering, a society of bird-watchers, perhaps, or river-rafting enthusiasts. Many of these searchers had arrived in the Santa Fe area a few days ago, in order to pack in a little pre-event treasure hunting in the mountains of New Mexico. Now everyone's latest hunts—Beep's and mine included—were a prime topic of conversation. Hyde Memorial State

Park itself, however, was neutral territory, as it's less than 8.25 miles from the northernmost border of Santa Fe—and hence outside of Fenn's defined search zone.

That made it possible for these hunters to finally relax and enjoy the area's natural beauty, without turning over every rock in search of treasure. And it **was** beautiful here; the pavilion stood at the base of a steep incline, next to a stream, with a canopy of trees covering the entire area. It was situated next to the main road running through the park but still managed to feel somewhat removed and woodsy. Past the stream was a campsite area where competent outdoorsy types could reserve spots and pitch tents, and about half the Fennboree attendees were, in fact, staying in the park, camping on-site. Beep and I were far less hardy, and would be returning to Santa Fe's Courtyard Marriott once the night was over. I spotted Cynthia Meachum across the pavilion, chatting with Beep, and gave them a wave. Not long after, I bumped into Dal, who was being pulled this way and that by other hunters in need of a word. I said a quick hello, making sure to keep my eyes peeled for my quarry. The searcher I was looking for was hard to pin down, I'd heard, and could be a little flighty in social situations—spending three years living in a cave will do that to you.

My eyes weren't helping. I couldn't spot him anywhere. So I decided to trust my nose instead.

I followed the scent of marijuana, and it wasn't long before I located the founder of Fennboree. As usual, he was outfitted in a well-worn white-striped polo and his rumpled, smelly fisherman's hat. The hat, when paired with his bushy, unkempt white beard, left little room for facial features. When I found the bearded mad hatter, he hopped to and fro, unable to sit still, literally bouncing from one foot to the other in a strange perpetual-motion dance.

Unmistakably, unquestionably, Desertphile.

"Probably the smartest guy looking for the treasure is David Rice," the author Doug Preston had said—using Desertphile's real name—when he urged me to seek him out. "If anyone's going to find it, he will. He's a very smart guy."

Among this group, Desertphile was royalty. One of the very first hunters, he had attained a certain cult status in the treasure-hunting community. Most people thought he was funny and more than a little bit weird. Yet there were many who resented him for his closeness with Fenn, who clearly delighted in Desertphile's high jinks and had made the fellow fisherman into a personal friend. Others believed his antics to be the attention-getting schemes of someone who enjoyed the spotlight a little too much, the same complaints that were often leveled at the other "celebrity hunters," like Cynthia and Dal.

But no matter how they felt about Desertphile, the searchers appreciated that by founding this event, he gave this subculture of scattered treasure hunters a chance to congregate in person. Before Fennboree, the hunters had interacted only via the internet, mostly on Dal's blog and ChaseChat, and those sites could often be cesspools of name-calling, rudeness, and conspiracy theories.

Fennboree, though, had changed some of that. By forcing the hunters to put faces to names, it helped to humanize the warring camps. Having been the peacemaker enhanced Desertphile's special status.

It was instantly hilarious to me that anyone could ever think Desertphile acted the way he did to get attention or media coverage. He was clearly ill at ease around other people, especially groups, and was obviously having a hard time dealing with the mass of hunters at Fennboree.

"Can weeeeee go somewhere else?" he asked after only a few minutes of talking, drawing out the word for reasons I couldn't understand, putting his fingers in his ears. "All of this chattering is starting to get to me."

It was that mentality, that uneasiness with the rest of humanity, that had driven him to abandon society in order to live in the comfort of a cave in the middle of a desert.

Long before he became a treasure hunter, Desertphile worked in Irvine, California, for Baxter Healthcare. He'd taught himself how to operate mainframe computers in the 1970s, and that skill paid off, rewarding him handsomely in the 1980s and 1990s.

"It's a huge health-care conglomerate corporation and they were paying me a shitload of money. So I would work sunup to sundown six or seven days a week for twelve years. And it drove me nuts. I went crazy," he told me, admitting he couldn't handle the corporate world. As the early 2000s arrived, he decided to drop out entirely.

"I had minor problems with schizophrenia now and then, but everybody does that," he said as I nodded gamely. "Everybody goes crazy now and then. But for me, the walls started bending inward; doors started to leer at me. I said, Okay, well, I've had enough of corporate America."

Instead of getting a VW bus and living down by the beach, he went in the other direction: into the desert. The Mojave. He wandered under the hot desert sun, exploring until he found a cave—eighteen feet deep, six feet high, once used by a miner and not far from the U.S. Army's desert warfare center at Fort Irwin, in California. He located a nearby water source. And just like that, he moved in, becoming a full-time cave dweller, free to do whatever he pleased in his little slice of rock.

Mostly, he read books.

"I spent twenty-nine months in that horrible cave, feeling sorry for myself sometimes, feeling like I'm the luckiest person on the planet at other

times because I could do that. I was my own boss.
I could sleep as long as I wanted," Desertphile said.

But the longer he spent out there, the more the
isolation affected him. He started taking less care
of himself, taking more risks. Near his cave was
that army base. Most, even a cave dweller, would
know that's not the kind of place you want to mess
with—especially with the military on high alert in
the immediate aftermath of September 11. Not
Desertphile. The desert had gotten to him. He
began to stalk and track the movements of army
units on their training exercises.

"I would take my binoculars and I would watch
them do their desert battle drills," Desertphile explained. "I was hoping that they would hunt for
me so I could, like, hide from them and it would
be like . . . it would be a way of killing a few [days].
I actually stalked an army squad walking over granite paths late at night—they were making a shitload
of noise, so I just followed behind them quietly
and I tried to see how close I could get to this army
squad without them detecting me. Eventually I figured, This is crazy. They will hurt me."

But he couldn't stop himself. One time, he
sneaked into the middle of an actual war game,
tanks facing off in the desert, using dummy ammunition. Desertphile decided to crash their party,
using a parachute flare, the kind that lights up the
night sky in red, white, and blue. He got as close as
he could, and waited for his moment.

"So, dead of night, I crawled into the battlefield with my parachute flare and I let that puppy go, and then I just ran like hell," he recalled.

Helicopters came flying out, searching for the source. Desertphile evaded them, retreated to the safety of his cave. Once home, he couldn't understand his own actions—why had he put himself in such peril?

"There were times when I did not know what I was doing. It was like I was watching myself behave, like I was externalized. [I told myself,] What you were doing, normal people don't do that," he said.

The breaking point came not long after. He went back to the nearest town, Barstow, California, to buy supplies. He saw his own reflection in the supermarket window. He looked subhuman, caked in filth, wearing rags. He was ashamed to go into the store and buy groceries.

"I said, This is enough. This is crazy."

So he rejoined society, at least partially, finding a job as a caretaker for a New Mexico cattle ranch. It was just him and the animals most of the time. He remained there, largely apart from the world, savoring his independence, connecting with other people mainly for the purposes of treasure hunting, which had become one of his few lifelines. As awkward as he was, he seemed to have found a home of sorts at this gathering, among his peers: those who didn't quite fit into the world, who thought there was another way around life's most basic problems. A legion of earnest misfits built in Fenn's own maverick image.

I wanted to talk more about what first drew him to this, but others were beckoning Desertphile back to the group. Before he went, I made him handicap the hunt for me: Who did he think was going to find the treasure? Who were the best searchers? He started breaking down the odds in a way that would have made Beep proud, saying he had several hundred dollars in his pocket right now, and explaining how he'd divvy up his bets.

"I would place three hundred dollars on Cynthia to win. I would place eighty dollars on Dal and maybe five dollars on Fenn. Because for all we know, he's forgotten where he put it." He giggled.

Making Cynthia the favorite was no surprise. From what I'd seen, I would agree with him. But what of Desertphile himself? What were his own chances? He paused a moment, and then gave himself 30 percent odds of finding it within the next five years.

"At the moment I figure anybody can find it, and if brainpower is going to do it, it should take five years; either I will get it or Cynthia will get [it] or Dal will, because they are the sharp knives in the drawer."

Cynthia, it should be noted, was a New Mexico–only searcher. Desertphile was, too, never bothering to head outside the state. In fact, of all the "name" searchers I'd encountered to that point,

Dal was the only one who searched far outside New Mexico, focusing on Yellowstone.

"Seems like you're pretty sure the treasure is in New Mexico," I said, prodding him.

"I think it is in Rio Arriba County," Desertphile said, nodding slowly. Rio Arriba County is in the north-central part of the state, west of Taos, and the home of Carson National Forest, of Chama, the Ojo Caliente area, and Tierra Amarilla. It was certainly a prime search area, though not the one most New Mexico searchers concentrated on. Why, I asked him, was he so certain that Fenn had hidden the treasure in New Mexico, when there was so much other search territory out there? And when so much of **The Thrill of the Chase** focuses on the Yellowstone area?

"New Mexico has been very good to Forrest and Forrest has been very good to New Mexico, and I'm thinking Forrest would like to have the treasure found in New Mexico because Forrest loves New Mexico—well, he loves the United States' Southwest—but New Mexico has treated him really well," Desertphile said, which lined up with my own thinking on where the treasure might be.

Before I could probe the New Mexico connection further, Desertphile finally scampered off. It was time for one of Fennboree's annual rituals, a contest rewarding the searcher who came from the farthest away. Many of the attendees were from the search area itself—Colorado or New Mexico, particularly—but there were certainly enough who had ventured here from farther afield. Desertphile served as the emcee as searchers yelled out how far they'd journeyed to get here. Texas was shouted out, as was Illinois. I heard there was someone attending from Rhode Island, but that person didn't pipe up. I noted that I had come in from Boston, which seemed to me to be good enough to win, but the judges inexplicably gave the award to a woman who had flown in from Vancouver. If that was the level of geographical knowledge we were dealing with, I could see why none of these people had found the treasure. I shared a chuckle with a couple nearby who seemed to realize the same thing.

James and Mindy had come all the way from Florida, where she worked as an X-ray tech, and he was a postman. As it turned out, they were one of the love stories of this treasure hunt. They met while searching—discussing the treasure on the blogs, emailing about it, and eventually meeting up to look for it together—inadvertently making Fenn into something of a treasure-hiding yenta.

This weekend, everyone had been buzzing around them, saying nice things, because congratulations were in order: They had gotten engaged on the way to Fennboree. In fact, James popped the question while they were searching at his solve spot, the place in Colorado where he believed the treasure was hidden.

"I don't know if the treasure's really there or not, but it'll always be special to us now," he said.

James felt he owed so much to the treasure-hunting community that he was trying to start treasure hunts of his own—not as big or wide-ranging as Fenn's, but smaller and easier to solve, with rewards in the four figures. He pulled out a cylindrical device from his pocket, one dotted with stones of all different colors. It was a cryptex, a Rubik's cube–type object inspired by the portable vault used in **The Da Vinci Code.** Align all the stones in the proper order, the device will unlock, and you'll get your treasure. The genius of the device is in its nearly infinite combinations. Without a very specific series of clues, it's nearly impossible to know how to unlock it. James planned to use the cryptex in his treasure hunt, leading people along and giving them the payoff at the end as they opened his lock at last.

He wasn't alone in wanting to follow in Fenn's footsteps and build his own hunt. Fenn's treasure was the grandest of modern treasure hunts, but it wasn't the only one. Many of these amateur searchers had moved from trying their hand at solving smaller hunts to eventually crafting their own. The night before Fennboree, I'd met a genial, hulking ex-army man from Virginia who went by the moniker "Iron Will." He had planned the annual Fennboree mini treasure hunt, hiding one hundred dollars in cash and an 1884 silver dollar donated by another searcher somewhere near the campsite. He wrote up a series of six clues and spread them across the area. Solve the first, it would lead you to the second, and so on, until you beat these other treasure hunters to the loot. The first clue had been posted right nearby, and I moseyed over, thinking about trying my hand at solving it. I didn't get the chance, though, because suddenly there was a commotion by the front of the pavilion, people jumping up out of their seats, rushing to get close to a Jeep Grand Cherokee that had just pulled up to a reserved parking space—the only reserved spot at the campsite, I realized.

Forrest Fenn had arrived.

At the back of the Fennboree pavilion, near the grill and the coolers of beer, sat a shrine. This place of worship was a tribute to all things Forrest Fenn, curated by his most loyal followers. The shrine was built around the "Golden Fenn," which appeared to be a Captain America action figure painted gold, with a big **F** emblazoned on his chest. From there, others added their offerings. There were maps, personal keepsakes, and a sizable tribute to the fallen searcher, Randy Bilyeu. But most were items of significance to Fenn himself, usually something he mentioned about his childhood in one of his books—a coonskin cap, a map of Taos, a 45 record of Fran Warren's "Sunday Kind of Love."

Each year, the shrine had grown, and at this year's Fennboree, it took up two full picnic tables. In the past, visiting the shrine and leaving an offering was an essential, but bittersweet, part of the event—for those first few Fennborees, the Golden Fenn was as close as most of the attendees would ever get to meeting the man himself. That's why Fenn's impromptu appearance at last year's Fennboree was such huge news inside this community, and there's no doubt that the hope he would return and make one of his now rare public appearances drove attendance at this year's function. But no one was sure if he would really show up—until he did.

As Fenn opened the door to the Jeep Cherokee, the searchers crowded around. A semicircle of twenty or so people formed, most of them with their phones out, snapping pictures as he exited the car. This was their chance to meet a Beatle, to stand before a king, to ask questions of God. And maybe, just maybe, God would let slip a tidbit about where a treasure was buried.

Fenn was in his standard outfit: a checkered blue shirt and blue jeans, this time topping that ensemble with a white cowboy hat. He soaked in the attention, shaking one hand after another and smiling widely as he made his way over to a bench in the front of the pavilion. From there, he spent the next hour communing with his followers, who waited to meet him in a line snaking all around the campsite. Everyone got a few minutes. The old man took all comers graciously, nodding and smiling, using that art dealer charm. When someone told him he'd come in from Memphis, or Denver, or Portland, Fenn would mention an old friend he had in that city, or bring up a restaurant that was once well known. Most of the tidbits were out of date, the friends long dead, the restaurants since closed. But you could see what had made him such an effective salesman in his prime: He forged a fast connection with his customers, giving them more in two minutes than many others would in two hours.

Most of the conversations unfolded the same way: The person would tell Fenn a little about his life, his solve, his search history, his appreciation for what Fenn had done. Fenn would nod and smile gamely. He would offer up a comment or two, usually hopeful and supportive, but never too specific. Then that person's time would be done, and the next searcher would sit down for his turn. Rinse, repeat. Most of the talk was heavily treasurecentric, but there were a few moments where the loot was less important than Fenn's take on other issues.

"Forrest, I have to ask you," Seattle Sullivan began, fixing Fenn with that steely gaze before delivering the payoff: "Do you believe in aliens?"

Fenn didn't miss a beat, pulling Seattle close and

offering his answer sotto voce. "Off the record, yes," Fenn said, conspiratorial and clearly amused.

Seattle was too excited at this answer to respect Fenn's halfhearted attempt to keep his extraterrestrial leanings quiet. Seattle leaped up. "I knew it! I knew he believed in aliens!" he exclaimed, pumping his fist.

It felt like one big family picnic, with Fenn the patriarch at the middle of it all. But as much as he clearly enjoyed being the center of attention, he had become increasingly wary of events like these, especially after the Paco Chavez incident the year before. Now, when Fenn appeared before a crowd, he took every precaution: He had hired private security and had hidden them among the onlookers, plus an armed private detective who happened to be a treasure hunter, and who offered his services for free, Fenn had told me. All of them were packing weapons and ready for trouble—especially since Fenn had had a bad interaction with one particularly aggressive hunter via email only a few days before.

Really, his extra security forces could be most anyone at Fennboree, since so many had attended armed. There were more people than I had expected openly carrying guns; several men had them strapped in holsters around their hips, which for a northeasterner like me was a jarring enough sight. It made me think of the popular image of a Wild West town—everyone with a gun slung at his waist, everyone hailing from somewhere else, no one really sure whether his neighbor in the saloon was his enemy or his friend. The men with guns seemed to carry themselves differently from everyone else, like they were hanging back, expecting a problem, ready for trouble. I didn't know which of these guys were Fenn's security and which were just gun lovers, but the presence of so many firearms was consistent with the overall vibe around the Fenn hunters—antiauthoritarian, survivalist, often right of center. An abnormally high number of the cars and pickup trucks parked around Fenn's Cherokee were festooned with bumper stickers, many of them echoing sentiments like the "resist much, obey little" message on the back of one Chevy Suburban. This was the kind of place where if someone did try to harm Fenn, I was pretty sure we'd end up in an O.K. Corral–level shoot-out within moments, bullets flying everywhere.

Fortunately, no one was causing any sort of trouble so far. As searchers got their face time in and the novelty of having God in their presence started to fade into normalcy, the crowd began to thin out. Yet one tall, bearded man remained perched over Fenn at all times, standing straight as a West Point cadet, eyeing each new arrival with narrowed eyes and watching the movements of everyone who came near. It was Fenn's grandson, Shiloh, vigilantly standing guard, the first line of defense against any who would seek to do the old man harm.

Seemingly around thirty, and sporting a flannel shirt, Shiloh stood out for his youth alone in this crowd. But he would have been notable in any setting for his height and his good looks; he bore a striking resemblance to the movie star Chris Pratt, with his similarly blond, bearded, rugged air. Dorothy Massey, owner of the Collected Works Bookstore and sole retailer of **The Thrill of the Chase,** had known Fenn a long time; she told me that when she looked at Shiloh's face, she saw Fenn himself, reborn.

"Shiloh, to me, is probably what Forrest was forty years ago," she said. "It's not just looks. It's temperament and care and massive intelligence. I think Forrest feels safe when he's with Shiloh."

Shiloh lived on Fenn's compound, in a guesthouse near the front of the property, one with a dirt bike out front and a loyal dog standing guard. He spoke four languages and ran his own wood-flooring business, and when needed, he served as something of a part-time bodyguard for his grandfather.

For some time, a rumor had circulated among the hunters that Fenn took Shiloh with him when he hid the chest, which would make Shiloh the only other person alive who truly knew where the treasure was. Fenn had vehemently denied this, offering up his belief in that old saw that "the only way two people can keep a secret is if one of them is dead."

Assuming Fenn wasn't advocating whacking his

own grandson, I took Fenn at his word that he had hidden the treasure solo and that the secret was his alone. But even if Shiloh wasn't there for the moment of truth, he still knew Fenn as well as anyone—and I guessed it would be Shiloh's responsibility to be caretaker of the hunt once Fenn was gone. The hunters seemed to understand this, and I saw several of them—often the women—approach him gamely, venturing a comment or joke.

Shiloh seemed to have little time for any of them. Perhaps because he was so focused on playing Secret Service agent, he dismissed most of the hunters with icy detachment. Several of them told me that they found Shiloh standoffish and cold, disdainful of their hunt and barely tolerant of the turmoil and danger it had brought into the lives of his grandfather and his extended family. Still, he didn't scare me.

I wandered over and made my introduction, explaining what I was doing there, labeling myself as "the **Wall Street Journal** guy."

Shiloh fixed me with a look I couldn't quite figure out and cocked his head. "I'd heard it was 'former' **Wall Street Journal** guy," he said, putting me in my place right off the bat.

I was happy that he knew who I was and what I was doing, but I was still a little taken aback; I defensively stuttered about how I would have said "former" in the next sentence. As he went back to scanning the crowd for potential threats, I began to think that perhaps that perception of Shiloh as cold and contemptuous of this entire scene surrounding the hunt wasn't far off.

Undaunted, I forged ahead. "Actually, I miss it. But unfortunately, when I did my last book, my bosses said I couldn't be a full-time professional gambler and also a full-time sportswriter, so I kinda had to choose one or the other. I followed the story," I explained.

Then I made a little gamble of my own, hoping that maybe it would get Shiloh to open up. "But with everything that's happening with media and politics and the White House today, I feel like I'm missing out. There's crazy stuff going on, and journalists are on the front lines. Would have been exciting to be in the middle of all that."

It might have been risky, mentioning politics at such a charged time, but something I said seemed to touch something in him.

"It's really too bad," he began, energized all of a sudden, "what's happening with print media today. I like newspapers. I like holding them in my hands. TV news, it's brutal. Newspapers, they're not perfect, but they're important, and we need them."

A fellow true believer! Having found a shared interest, we were soon discussing the larger changes in the media landscape like semi–old pals. I took care to stay far, far away from mentioning anything about the treasure, lest I spook him, and I got the sense he appreciated that. We kept moving around the pavilion, Shiloh following his grandfather as he bounced from one conversation to the next. It was tough to keep up, and eventually we decided to table our conversation until a time when Shiloh wasn't playing rent-a-cop. But I walked away happy, considering it an important foothold in penetrating Fenn's inner circle, and gaining their trust.

Another reason I didn't mind leaving Shiloh was that everywhere I turned at Fennboree, there was someone or something else that was fascinating, weird, different, something screaming out for me to pay it some attention. I came upon two people sitting in folding chairs, a man and a woman, one of them wearing a white cowboy hat that appeared to be festooned with . . . jelly beans. He introduced himself as David but said that he worked in candy, thus explaining the hat, and that most people refer to him by his nickname, earned from years in the field.

"They call me 'the Candyman,' " he said proudly.

The Candyman was born David Klein, and in another life—long before he was a treasure hunter—he had been one of the best at what he did: creating new candies, delighting in giving kids a thrill with a new type of sweet. In 1976, when living in Temple City, California, Klein hit on the candy idea that would change his life—for better and for worse.

Jelly Belly jelly beans.

To that point, jelly beans had been the most

unexciting of candies, just blobs of gummy sugar in one flavor or another, a pleasant but dull experience. But Klein had a brainstorm: What if he jazzed them up, made eating one into a tantalizing surprise? He dreamed up a version that had a hard shell, and gooey insides filled with varied flavors—very cherry, cream soda, root beer, grape—that would burst out when one bit into them. He cooked up a test batch, and rented out a corner of a local ice-cream store to try to hawk his beans, expensive at two dollars a pound.

At first, few were interested in his pricey, weird concoction, and the confectioner was potentially facing a costly failure. But the Candyman has always known how to pique the interest of the media, and this natural showman wasn't going to give up so easily. He managed to get a reporter and photographer from the Associated Press to come down to the store, promising that his candy was a sales phenomenon—and then "arranged for friends and family to form a line snaking out the door" when the media arrived, according to a 2011 profile in the **Los Angeles Times.**

Soon the ruse of having a hit candy made the candy itself into an actual hit: When the article ran, customers began going down to try Klein's creation, and discovered that it was pretty darn good. The word spread, and Jelly Belly became a smash, with Klein serving as "Mr. Jelly Belly" at events, the public face of the candy. They even found a true celebrity patron in a former governor of California, Ronald Reagan, who became a jelly bean devotee as he tried to kick a pipe-smoking habit while governor of California, and enjoyed Jelly Belly jelly beans once they were introduced. When Reagan won the presidency, 3.5 tons of red, white, and blue Jelly Belly jelly beans were shipped to the White House for his inauguration.

But Klein never fully cashed in on the Jelly Belly phenomenon. In 1980, he sold his trademark to candy maker Goelitz for a little more than two million dollars. Goelitz eventually changed its name to Jelly Belly Candy Company, and is today a worldwide candy manufacturer with annual revenue just under $200 million, boasting a Jelly Belly logo seen everywhere from candy stores to pro cycling uniforms. Klein, meanwhile, never made anything beyond his initial payout, and his existence has been virtually erased from the company's version of the candy's origins. He went on to a life of obscurity, ever ruing his decision to sell off his stake for far less than its true value.

Yet not everyone forgot. Klein's son Bert, an animator at Walt Disney Studios, eventually produced the documentary **Candyman: The David Klein Story,** which tells his father's tale. It's an interesting piece of work from a son appraising his father. Rather than stooping to hagiography, it paints him as a bit odd, a bit obsessive, and never the same after he sold off his prized creation—embittered, searching, always looking for a comeback to his glory days.

Sounded like a perfect Fenn hunter.

The Candyman introduced the woman sitting with him as his hunting partner—Stephanie Thirtyacre. I instantly knew who that was, of course. Stephanie was famous in this crowd for being the founder of ChaseChat, for being one of the original Fenn searchers, and for losing her money and her marriage to her obsession with the chase. Word was that she generally stayed away from events like these, and hadn't been around the search much since having some sort of falling-out with Fenn sometime before. I wasn't exactly prepared to get into all of that, though—so I just introduced myself, and let her know I'd certainly heard of her, would love to more formally interview her at some point. She smiled back, said she'd be happy to talk another time, and then other pressing matters beckoned: The Candyman asked if I wanted to try on his jelly bean–bedazzled hat. How could I say no?

Not long after, I was surprised to see Fenn and Stephanie in conversation, the pair walking away from the campground together, looking like they were catching up on old times. Dal appeared next to me as we watched them slowly trudge around, seemingly over whatever had gone wrong between them, perhaps mending fences.

"There's a lot of history there," Dal said in a tone

that imbued that word, **history,** with great weight. I remembered that strange tidbit he had told me the first time we talked on the phone, about Stephanie's public accusation against Fenn, alleging that the octogenarian had sought to trade clues for sex. Watching them walking and talking, I wasn't sure if it seemed more or less outlandish now.

I headed off to find Beep. My Canadian compatriot seemed to be having a good time meeting the other Fenners when last I'd seen him, but Beep can turn cold on events like this in an instant, quickly deciding he's had enough of everyone and everything and wanting to bail, à la Desertphile. More concerning was that Beep has no filter, and little regard for keeping secrets, even in a crowd of his would-be competitors. Not that we'd discovered anything particularly promising so far, but I still felt like I had to keep him on something of a short leash.

I found him near the food area, standing next to an older woman wearing a jean skirt, bedazzled bright red cowboy boots, flaming red lipstick, and a low-cut fire-engine-red blouse to match, all topped off by a cowboy hat. It was like someone had crossed Dolly Parton with Dorothy from **The Wizard of Oz.**

"I like your outfit," Beep was telling her earnestly as I arrived.

"Oh, I'm too old for you boys to be saying that,"

she said, her cheeks turning as red as the rest of her as she shuffled off. I hardly had to ask how he was doing before an ebullient Beep volunteered his take.

"Dan, Fennboree is so, so sweet," he said, using **sweet** in the way others might use **cool.** "Everyone is so nice, and so interesting," he added, gushing about a nurse from Colorado, a doctor from Nashville, and a group of college girls from who knows where. One thing surprised me—it turned out that Beep had met Desertphile, and he was more skeptical of the cave dweller than I would have figured. As a pair of whip-smart eccentrics, I'd assumed the two of them would have been fast friends.

Beep had been on the lookout for bits of useful information, anything he could use to improve his solve. It seemed the biggest revelation was that Beep had met several people who were adherents of the theory that Fenn's books, the actual physical copies of **The Thrill of the Chase,** offered clues to the treasure. His new Colorado nurse friend, Sandy, actually ironed the pages of the book, and put lemon juice on them, looking for invisible ink. It turned out that Mindy, the Florida woman who had met her fiancé on the hunt, did the same thing, using acetone and a magnifying glass to try to unearth hidden symbols on the pages. To me, it sounded like cloud divination. But who was I to judge? All I had learned was Desertphile's hunch that the treasure was likely in New Mexico, not the other states. It wasn't much.

Beep reported that he'd really enjoyed getting to know Cynthia, and it struck me pretty quickly that he had something of a crush on her, despite the generational age difference.

"Cynthia might be my favorite old person ever. If only she was straight. And forty years younger." He paused, deep in thought. "Or maybe if she just had a daughter or something."

The funny thing was, Beep had a surprising number of other options for eligible ladies here at Fennboree. I'd been told that Fenn hunters skewed male, and older. But here at this event, the gender ratio was much closer to fifty-fifty than I'd expected. And unlike the men, many of the women were young, in the thirty-to-forty range.

Nobody seemed to enjoy this more than Fenn. When Beep and I wandered over to where he was holding court, we found him leaning against a wall, surrounded by three attractive younger women, clearly in his element.

"Hey, Danny," he said, a mischievous grin on his face. "I'll introduce you to these three pretty ladies if you give me twenty dollars."

I smiled right back, and made him a counteroffer.

"Well, Forrest, I've already met Amy, Keri, and Shelley—but I'll give you the twenty dollars if you need it so badly," I said, prompting a look of surprise and a bemused chuckle from Fenn. He said something back about not trusting one of my personal checks, but he clearly liked the banter; Fenn was a big fan of needling people, and preferred those who could take it and dish it right back.

One of that trio, Keri, was a repeat visitor to Fennboree, and clearly a Fenn favorite—but her husband, Jerry, was attending for the first time. Jerry had previously been too embarrassed to come to these events. He was one of those who had let the hunt get the better of him, blindly seeking the treasure despite the many dangers of the wild. I asked him about what I'd heard, that he'd gotten into trouble while out searching Yellowstone in wintry conditions.

"I was never lost—I always knew where I was," he said wearily, clearly having done this dance more than once this weekend already. "But my wife didn't know where I was, and I missed my check-in, and so I understand."

At first, Jerry wouldn't talk to me beyond that, expecting that I would not comprehend what he'd gone through. "I don't really like to talk to reporters," he told me, his voice ringing out with a southern twang. "I just don't think y'all understand what it's about."

"But I've been on hunts, too," I responded—"well, one hunt, but I'm a treasure hunter of sorts now, and I understand the obsession. Or, at least, I'm trying to." He brightened up at this. "So you get why it's so important. I respect that," he said, and agreed to tell me his story. We wandered off from the group, toward the back of the pavilion, over by the Fenn shrine.

It turned out Jerry was underselling his misadventures a bit. He may not have been lost, but he had certainly been in danger. Jerry was a maintenance man in Kentucky, but he was also ex-military, so he wasn't afraid of tough conditions. That put him in good company here, where marine and army bumper stickers and tattoos were as prevalent as Trump paraphernalia, and many of the hunters seemed to congregate by wars—the Iraq vets here, the Desert Storm vets there, and, of course, the Vietnam vets closest to Fenn. Still, maybe Jerry should have done a recon mission with some military buddies first, because he didn't know that entering Yellowstone in May basically means walking into the dead of winter. When he arrived, there were still eight feet of snow on the ground, though that didn't stop him from exploring deep into the park on his own. When his truck got stuck, instead of turning back, he abandoned it and pressed even farther in, slogging deeper into the park, a complete cellular dead zone, with insufficient supplies and a poor understanding of the terrain and conditions. The treasure was tempting him, calling out to him, overriding his rational brain.

"I didn't want to stop—part of it is, you spent all this time and money to get out there, and there's this 'what if?' But the snow was very deep," he said. "It was a lot of snow. More than I expected. I went three miles down the road in snowshoes before I even hit a trailhead."

At a certain point, he realized he'd gone much too far, and had lost track of time.

"I trekked in from my truck, probably six miles, in the deep snow, uphill, and I'm from Kentucky, so I wasn't acclimated. The altitude was punching me right in the face—or in the lungs," he said.

Knowing he was stuck, he slung a hammock and, freezing in wet socks—he hadn't thought to bring an extra pair—hunkered down to try to survive the night. When he awoke, his hammock had frozen to the trees, and he had to abandon it.

"I had enough sense about me to know my situation—another night out there? That wouldn't be good," he said.

His best chance at survival was Keri; Jerry figured his wife would be frantically trying to track him down, and he was right. What he didn't realize was that she'd have Fenn's help. In a moment of desperation, she reached out to Fenn, whom she had never met but knew of from her husband's obsession. Fenn quickly sprang into action, contacting Yellowstone Search and Rescue and alerting them to Jerry's predicament. Just what Jerry had been counting on.

"I knew that I'd missed reporting back in. If I was my wife, I'd be calling. So I figured search and rescue was on the way. So I followed the streams, plotting my way out," he said.

In the late afternoon, a helicopter flew overhead, looking for him. Jerry signaled to it with a strobe, and it swung down to pick him up. Jerry was chagrined, Keri was furious, and Fenn was relieved. Jerry had learned his lesson—don't venture out alone; respect the outdoors. But he wasn't driven from the search. Far from it. He'd made perhaps twenty runs out there since.

In fact, Jerry may have come out of his misadventure ahead of the game. Through the rescue process and its aftermath, Keri became close with Fenn, and Fenn brought the couple into his inner circle, to Jerry's delight—he got that valuable access to the creator that every hunter desperately craves, and considers an edge.

"You're always going to try to get to know someone if you're going to try to read their mind," Jerry admitted.

I was starting to understand the degree to which the real currency of the realm in Fenn's world was access to the man himself—authentic, long-lasting interactions with Fenn, offering the chance to observe, interrogate, and understand him. All the best hunters had it. All the others were jealous of it.

In a way, Fennboree actually served to democratize the access game. It was no longer just the VIPs and the people who lived in Santa Fe who could get face time with Fenn; buy a plane ticket to Santa Fe, wait on line at Fennboree, and you'd get your few minutes, too. That's what they were all really here for, and no one was wasting a moment—every person who talked to Fenn at Fennboree seemed to be subtly pumping the old man for information, telling him his or her solve, gauging his reaction. And all of them seemed to believe they had taken something meaningful from the conversation—that Fenn had hinted something to them, said something that they believed meant they were close. I couldn't tell if Fenn was actively trying to egg them on, but he certainly didn't seem to be trying to dissuade any of them about their spots, that was for sure. Almost everyone came away energized. That's just how Fenn wanted it, I started to think.

Jerry and I heard laughter and raised voices from the part of the campsite where Fenn had been sitting, and I craned my neck to see what was going on. It all appeared to be centered on Beep, somehow. Jerry and I left the shrine area behind and went over. To my surprise, Beep looked about as pleased with himself as I'd ever seen him, while James, the mailman, was looking at Beep with nothing less than total awe.

"Oh my God, Dan, I'm so lucky, sometimes I can't believe how lucky I get," Beep said to me, rapid-fire. I'd come to learn with him that **lucky** was his euphemism for **smart,** when he realized that he couldn't go around saying just how sharp he was or he'd sound like a jerk.

As it turned out, James had been telling Beep of his plans to start his own treasure hunt, and about the cryptex he planned to use. Beep, ever curious, asked him if he could try his hand at solving it. People often do that, James explained, treating a cryptex like a Rubik's cube to be casually solved—except because there is only one possible combination that will unlock it, it's virtually impossible to open one offhandedly. The two kept on chatting when Beep offered what seemed like a wild guess: blue blue blue blue blue blue blue. James gasped, and began turning and twisting the device, lining up the colors, until it popped open. Beep had unlocked it, figuring out the secret while the two were standing there.

"I was thinking about James, and what I knew about him, and I figured he would actually want a pretty simple solution—there are so many possibilities, but he wouldn't pick a random one," Beep explained. "I guessed he would use all one color. Which color? He seemed like the kind of person who would pick blue. Like I said, I got so lucky."

Lucky or not, James was stunned. As a crowd gathered, he announced to everyone, "This is the guy who's going to find the treasure."

Suddenly, everyone at Fennboree regarded us a little differently; between my access to all the best hunters and Beep's problem-solving skills, we'd become known as people to watch, maybe even a formidable team. Even Fenn seemed to look over with interest.

The late-afternoon sun was settling in over the park's tall trees. I spotted Fenn saying his good-byes and shuffling over to the Jeep Cherokee on Shiloh's arm, and his exit prompted a steady stream of Fenners to follow suit—some marching off to their campsites, others packing up and heading down the windy mountain road back to Santa Fe.

But not everyone was ready to depart, and a solid core of fifty or so dedicated hunters remained. Someone had drawn a chalk map of the western United States on the concrete floor of the pavilion, encapsulating the search area and labeling important spots like Yellowstone, Santa Fe, and Denver. Beep and I sat back and watched as one searcher after another grabbed a pair of divining rods in their hands and started to walk the map, asking questions as they moved down its perhaps fifteen-foot length.

"Is the treasure in Montana?" asked a woman holding the rods, standing on the makeshift map somewhere near what appeared to be the city of Bozeman. The rods remained steady. That seemed to be a definite no.

Beep's nurse friend, Sandy, grabbed the rods and slowly walked toward a part of Colorado.

"Is the treasure in Brown's Park?" she asked aloud. Amazingly, thanks to the curvature of the Earth or a gust of wind or the firing of minor muscles in Sandy's forearms, the rods began to swing, crossing over one another as spectators cooed and shrieked their excitement. After she gave up the rods, Beep chided Sandy that he now knew her search spot; she seemed so excited by the rods' revelation that she didn't mind.

I would not have been surprised if she'd gone directly to Brown's Park to look for the chest.

By Sunday night, most of Fennboree's attendees had gone back to their corners of Colorado, or New Mexico—or, apparently, faraway Vancouver. Others, like Dal, were getting some hunting in on their way home; he told me he was taking his big white van—nicknamed "Esmerelda"—through Yellowstone once again in order to investigate another lead, one he'd discovered on an out-of-print map made way back in 1912.

But a few hardy hunters remained, still camping up by the pavilion, and Beep and I had apparently made enough inroads with this crew that we were invited to Fennboree's final, semiofficial event.

Now that the hunt was seven years in, Fenn's treasure hunters had begun to exhibit complete life cycles—an excited entry phase, a strong multi-year pursuit, then a gradual disenchantment with the hunt, and finally an exit from it. There were well-known hunters who had arrived with gusto, dazzled their peers with their theories for a year or two, and then dropped off the treasure map, as it were. Beep and I had been invited to witness the end of one man's hunting career as he officially retired from the chase.

Wisconsin Mike was a known and relatively popular character in the Fenn community, a wiry man of around fifty, sporting a head of jet black hair. At Fennboree, he wore a T-shirt that labeled him as simply "Wisconsin Mike," employing that cartoonish **Indiana Jones** lettering for greater effect. He told me how he used to play semipro baseball, how he found the chase a few years back, how he used it as a bonding opportunity for himself and his teenaged daughter, Christine. The two would drive out west and go for long hunts across the search area. Now he'd lost a little faith in the chase. He no longer believed he could find the treasure, and it had simply taken up too much of his time. So this Fennboree would be his last hunting event, as he left this world behind.

But before he departed, Wisconsin Mike wanted to pass on his knowledge, hopeful that whatever inroads he'd made would help someone else find the treasure in the future. So he'd invited a select group—us, Cynthia, Jerry and Keri, Iron Will, Amy, a few others—to his campsite to reveal and explain his solve. Most hunters were extremely protective of their solves, and divulged only the barest details. "It's in Colorado." "It's near a river."

Stuff like that. Now Mike was giving away the whole thing, and he treated it as if he were leaking state secrets.

We were asked to sign in, provide our information, and ink something that had the air of a nondisclosure agreement, if not the binding legal power. More than anything, Mike wanted us all to promise something: that if any of us used his information to find the treasure at or near his spot, we would use the proceeds to send his daughter Christine to college.

"I know once I'm finished, everyone here is going to rush to their cars and head to my spot," he said with not-so-quiet confidence. Across the campfire, I saw Amy roll her eyes.

Once the sun went down, Wisconsin Mike launched into an elaborate presentation, complete with handouts and visual aids that wouldn't have been out of place in a corporate boardroom. Mike believed the treasure was in Colorado, in the area of Dinosaur National Monument and the Green River, he explained as we thumbed through his packet, looking at maps of rivers and valleys spread through western Colorado. He had narrowed his search area using mapping software—eliminating any areas above 10,200 feet or below 5,000, per Fenn's clues, and slicing it down further by using quotes Fenn had offered publicly to knock other zones out of consideration. It was a good methodology, an appropriately scientific approach. As with so many searchers, however, Mike had a good start, and an underwhelming conclusion. Many of Mike's explanations seemed to fit square pegs into round holes—though he did have at least quasi-reasonable arguments for why he thought the way he did on most points. Still, pretty quickly, it became clear that none of these veteran searchers was in any way convinced. Cynthia, in particular, looked skeptical, asking at one point if she could debate his conclusions, before deciding all discussion should wait until the end.

"I don't want to ruin your presentation now," she said, a smile creeping onto her face. "Just wait. I'll ruin it later."

So we all listened attentively and politely—everyone, that is, except Mike's whip-smart daughter Christine, who had been on many of these trips and appeared bored by the whole process. As her father talked, Christine acted as a one-girl peanut gallery, offering snarky commentary and undermining Mike's major points when appropriate. Like when Mike was telling us about his solve for that eternally vexing Fenn line, "Put in beneath the home of Brown." His theory? That it was a geographic area in Dinosaur National Monument called "the basement of time."

"Brown is a proper name. It's somebody's home. A house. What's put in below somebody's home? A basement! It's a basement!" Mike exclaimed, expecting us all to be wowed by his conclusion. He was met with silence, save by his daughter, who looked up from her book to drop in a one-liner.

"Hopefully there aren't any bodies buried there," she said with a roll of her eyes that largely captured all our feelings. Most of her interjections were mere comic relief, but the more I listened, the more I thought she might understand the hunt better than her dad did. At one stage, Mike was going into great detail about why, exactly, the treasure must be in the Dinosaur National Monument area, when Christine brought his whole argument crashing down with a salient point: "It just doesn't seem like a place where Forrest would want to die. It's not special or meaningful."

She was exactly right. The spot had to have personal significance to Forrest. It must relate to his life, or be particularly beautiful, or meaningful to his experience, or, hopefully, all of the above. Forrest literally planned to lie down and die at this spot—it had to be a place where he would be happy to leave this world, and Mike's location wasn't that; it lacked a personal connection to the man. His solve was a little too scientific, not quite emotional enough.

Mike blew right by his daughter's criticism, continuing on with his argument as if Christine had never spoken up. Frankly, he was losing most of us. And, it appeared, he wasn't making any friends, either. At one stage, he described his solve for one of the poem's most confounding lines, "From there it's no place for the meek." That was one that had flummoxed Beep and me; we thought we had a good solution for the lines surrounding it, but we couldn't puzzle out what that specific line meant.

Wisconsin Mike thought he had, though. "So what's the opposite of meek? Manly. Women are meek; men are manly. And it just so happens that the explorer and gold miner William L. Manly traveled through this area, through Echo Park, through the area of the Green River, in the mid-1800s. Manly. Not meek. No place for the meek."

This seemed like a stretch on its face, and the assertion aroused the ire of several of the women in our group, who obviously didn't enjoy being labeled "meek."

"I don't like the sound of that," Keri said, near fury in her face. "Why do women have to be meek? It doesn't even make sense."

Mike tried to defend his position, explaining why the life of William Manly would resonate with Fenn: "I'm just saying what Forrest would have thought back then, growing up, what people thought back then," he stammered as Keri and Amy hammered away at his dubious conclusion.

Cynthia, meanwhile, remained silent for the moment, her brow furrowed, staying out of the gender argument. Wisconsin Mike was still defending his Manly talk, saying something about how it was a hard line to figure out any other way, and maybe he was even gaining the upper hand, when Cynthia dropped in, almost offhandedly, a huge revelation.

" 'No place for the meek' is a fishing term," she said, quietly enough that I wasn't sure everyone had heard. "It means a fly-fishing spot."

Beep and I immediately turned our heads and looked at each other, wide-eyed. That was a tidbit we'd never heard before. If "no place for the meek" was a fly-fishing spot, that would align exactly with our thoughts that Forrest wanted you to be at, near, or in a river at that point in the poem—maybe even to have to cross one. The problem had been that we hadn't known where in a river we should be. Now we knew that the best searcher of all believed it could be a fly-fishing spot, and she made us aware of this by dropping a bit of knowledge that we'd never heard or seen on the internet or from other searchers. She must have just let it slip—or subtly wanted to let all around know that she was anything but meek.

Beep and I could hardly wait for Mike to finish up the rest of his presentation so that we could grill Cynthia about the "meek" tidbit. Finally, he did, and we immediately cornered her, asking where she'd gotten the info.

"I actually heard it from talking to a fly fisherman," she said. "It's not a very well-used term. I don't think anyone's connected it to the hunt, at least not that I've heard. But Forrest, you'd think, would know it."

Exactly. Fenn, the avid fly fisherman, should have been well versed in fisherman's lingo, and it made sense that he would have employed it in his poem. But without context, it didn't mean much—really, the line struck a chord only if you already thought that the treasure had something to do with a river. Which we did.

Maybe it meant something. Maybe it didn't. But I could feel the treasure pulling at me. Being out on the hunt, going to Fennboree, listening to other hunters talk about solves and clues, spurred something, a desire to get out and do more, to really find this thing. And Fennboree had also helped me to understand something bigger about this chase: that it was, in every way, all about Forrest Fenn. The other hunters understood that already—that's why they emailed him, studied him, flew out to meet him. Fennboree had me wanting to get a little more serious about this hunting thing, and being a serious Fenn hunter clearly meant understanding who he was, why he'd really done this, and trying to be as close to him as possible.

I didn't feel like I was pretending at being a treasure hunter quite so much anymore; it kinda felt like they had welcomed me in, that maybe they were starting to think of me as one of them. And I liked it. I liked feeling a part of this grand adventure. A part of this community—bizarre, open, obsessed, and endearing in its innocence.

An innocence that would last only a few more days. As we had been sitting around the fire listening to Wisconsin Mike, one particular hunter had just embarked on a search that would change Fenn's chase forever.

7

DEATH COMES TO
THE HUNT

In a video posted by the Connection Church of
Grand Junction, Colorado, the church's pastor,
Paris Wallace, stands alone on a stage. Behind
him are several guitars on racks, plus a keyboard
and a full drum kit.

Wallace begins the video with his face cast down
toward the ground. He raises his head, his long,
stringy black hair parting to expose a wide, friendly
face, underlined by a goatee. There is no clergy
frock; Wallace sways back and forth in a loose-
fitting, untucked button-down atop a pair of jeans.
Then the pastor begins speaking.

"May we understand that we don't always have
to understand," Wallace says into the camera.
"Because in that point we have to trust. So may
we not only trust but may we trust with all of our
being. Our hearts, our minds, our body."

He delivered that sermon on June 11, 2017.

Wallace was the kind of preacher who drove a motorcycle. The kind who had long hair, who tried his hand at bull riding, who went skydiving for fun.

The kind who searched for treasure.

The fifty-two-year-old Wallace was a Fenn hunter, one who had been in love with the chase since 2014. On that Sunday, June 11, after giving his sermon, Wallace packed up his truck, kissed his wife, Mitzi, good-bye, and began the six-hour drive from Grand Junction down to Española, New Mexico, an hour north of Santa Fe.

Nothing would be the same after that.

Mitzi and Paris met when they were just eighteen, kids going to college in Greenville, South Carolina. Paris was from Palisade, Colorado, outside Grand Junction, and Mitzi hailed from Tennessee. They quickly fell in love, uniting over their devotion to God, their desire to work with kids, and a shared sense of adventure. They were married in 1986, beginning a decades-long journey bouncing together across the country, with numerous stops along the way in places like Georgia or Texas. Often, Paris worked as a youth pastor, and Mitzi taught, but there were stints at other odd jobs: Paris sold Kirby vacuum cleaners; the pair managed an estate together, with Paris as groundskeeper; they ran a home for teens with behavior issues. The one constant thread was that whatever they did, they did it together.

Eventually, in 2005, they moved back to Paris's home state of Colorado, taking their two sons and settling in Grand Junction. It was time for Paris to take the next step in his career—to find a church of his own—and he was named pastor of the non-denominational Connection Church. Over his twelve years at the church, Paris became well known in the community, both inside and outside of his flock.

"He was just a cool guy," Mitzi said. "And a very humble man. He was just Paris. Not Pastor Wallace, just Paris. And that's why people were drawn in to him, because he was just real. He wanted to help people, that's what he was all about."

But he also loved a good adventure. And if there was a little risk involved? Even better.

"Paris was about life, very much so," Mitzi said. "The man has done everything. He rode a bull; he's been on a rattlesnake hunt, he skydived, he cliff-jumped. He just did not have the danger gene in him."

One evening, as Paris was watching television, he called Mitzi in. There was a documentary on, and it referenced Forrest Fenn's treasure. He had found his next adventure, and he wasn't going alone.

"After he explained it to me, I got hooked, too," Mitzi said. "I like puzzles, I like challenges, I like figuring things out. I started understanding it, and

I started studying it for myself to see what I could find, but it's a needle in a haystack."

Over the next three years, treasure hunting became their shared pursuit; they always hunted in northern New Mexico, making the drive down two to three times per summer. Paris would come up with a new solve before each trip, and, like so many hunters, he was always convinced that this would be the one, even if the locations didn't quite make perfect sense.

"Every time we'd go to an area, I would say, 'It can't be here—an eighty-year-old man hid this!'" Mitzi recalled. "And he'd say to me, 'But he was in good shape, Mitzi. He was an eighty-year-old man, but he was in good shape.' We'd be in boulder fields; we'd be on [a] two-hour hike straight up. It was crazy; there was just no way."

On that particular Sunday, Paris had a hunch about an area they had searched before, in the vicinity of the Rio Grande Gorge. It would be the first time that Paris had gone searching alone. But Mitzi had important things to do, and Paris felt so good about his hunch, he had to get moving right away.

He made the drive down to the small town of Española. There isn't much there—a McDonald's, a bunch of gas stations, Walmart, and, of course, a casino—and Mitzi was a little worried, Paris having told her that he was staying in a shady part of town. That first night, maybe to put her mind at ease, he sent a text message, saying, "I found the treasure!" Attached was a picture of a honey bun.

After an unsuccessful search day Monday, Paris and Mitzi talked again that night. The pastor said that on Tuesday, he was going to go back to the first place they had searched: in the Rio Grande Gorge, down by Taos Junction Bridge.

This just happened to be the same area that Beep and I had identified for our very first search. As Paris was making his way down into the gorge on Tuesday, I was getting on a plane, heading back to Boston. The Wallaces liked the area for many of the same reasons we did. While we started at nearby Agua Caliente Falls, and took it down into the gorge itself, they took "warm waters halt" to mean a spot where a tributary of the Rio Grande strikes the larger river. The fallen rocks along the sides of the river might be the "heavy loads," and the same water-gaging station we'd explored made them think of "water high." At points, we'd both thought that the line "Put in below the home of Brown" could refer to a boat put-in near the brown trout fisheries in the area.

But Paris made one crucial, disastrous mental leap that we didn't. One line of Fenn's poem reads "If you are brave and in the wood." **Brave,** Mitzi said, made Paris think that one must be brave, and hence would need to take a risk of some sort—one that might involve crossing the Rio Grande or one of its fast-moving tributaries.

"Tuesday, about eleven-thirty in the morning, I talked to him for the last time, and he told me he had just gone to Walmart and gotten some supplies," Mitzi said. "And I remember thinking in the back of my mind, Okay, what kind of supplies did he get, and what is he going to go do? But I didn't actually ask him anything."

Tuesday evening, Mitzi didn't hear from Paris, and when she tried to call, she couldn't reach him. That was odd, she thought—but not too worrisome. He'd probably dropped his cell phone, or it had simply run out of power. "Anything can happen when you're out there like that," she said.

But when Wednesday morning rolled around, she started to worry. She called his hotel.

"Ah," the desk clerk told her, "we're happy to hear from you, Mrs. Wallace. Mr. Wallace was supposed to check out by now, but he's not in his room, and his belongings are all still there."

"I said, 'Oh, well, is his truck still there?' and they said, 'No.' And I panicked," she recalled. "I said Paris would never do that; he was very frugal, he was very responsible, he wouldn't want to waste his money."

Mitzi immediately called the Española police, gave them a missing person's report, and threw everything she needed into her car for the drive down to New Mexico.

When Beep and I had been in the Rio Grande Gorge, pelted by hail, puttering about blindly, I remember distinctly that the Rio Grande seemed high, its currents fierce and powerful. When I stood leaning over it, by the gaging station, I'd wondered a bit about whether I'd be able to swim out if I fell in. Trying to get in it, let alone cross it, had seemed dangerous in the extreme. From the gaging station, we'd driven up to the Taos Junction Bridge, the spot where both the road and the river twist and turn and the journey farther into the gorge becomes much more difficult. At the time, there were a few trucks parked up by the bridge, though no people that we could see. A week later, Wallace would leave his truck in precisely that spot.

Thursday morning, Mitzi and several companions went to the state police barracks in Española. They gave police the maps and GPS coordinates for where they believed Paris might have been. But at the time, Mitzi didn't tell them that Paris was out treasure hunting; she simply said he was hiking. No one back at the church knew that was why he had headed off into the wilderness, either.

"I tried to keep it quiet," she said. "We weren't telling everybody in the church that he went treasure hunting. It was nobody's business. It was just that he was out of town. That was our private thing that we did, and so I wasn't going to tell anyone that."

Thursday afternoon, state police located Paris's Chevy Tahoe, parked at the Taos Junction Bridge. They began searching the areas around the parking spot, looking up into the hills, because no one thought there was reason to look in the river just yet. That's when Mitzi realized she needed to come clean.

"When the police officers were talking to me on Thursday evening, after we saw Paris's vehicle, I decided, I've got to tell them everything I know to give them our best chance to find him," she said. "And then I did tell one of the officers that he was treasure hunting, that this was what Paris was doing, he was looking for Fenn's treasure."

At some point either Friday or Saturday, Fenn was contacted, but the hunt's creator couldn't offer much help in this instance, as he and Wallace had never corresponded.

But out in the Rio Grande Gorge, a huge manhunt was under way. Horses, helicopters, boats—all manner of police and volunteers were combing the area, looking for Wallace. The on-site search was supplemented by the efforts of friends, family, and coworkers back in Grand Junction. One of them was Michelle Umberger, the financial administrator at his church. She had worked closely with Wallace on the pastor's dream project: a new home for Connection Church. They had recently purchased an old furniture store in Grand Junction and were in the process of turning it into a bigger, grander house of worship. Umberger may have been the last person to speak with him on Tuesday afternoon, discussing an upcoming church event over the phone. Once she and others knew he was missing, the church served as a nexus for friends and family trying to help.

"We kinda had a little command center set up, trying to get information about where he was," Umberger said. "It was just so chaotic around here. We were just trying to figure out what was going on."

Initially, no one at the church had any idea Paris and Mitzi were treasure hunters—"That was his family stuff; we don't need to know about that," Umberger said—but once that revelation came out, the Connection Church staff became amateur Fenn sleuths themselves, combing Dal's blog and trying to figure out anything they could about Fenn's treasure, and how that might lead them to Wallace.

"Once we got tipped off about the Fenn treasure thing, I came across that blog, and maybe it was overkill, but I was like, I'm going to find [a way to help]," she said.

Once all involved understood that Wallace was a hunter, rescue crews, aided by Wallace's friends, started looking in new sections of the gorge—down by the river, in particular, and up by one of its tributaries, the Rio Pueblo de Taos. In that area, one of Wallace's friends found the footpath that leads down to a spot where the rivers intersect. And on one bank, tied to a rock, was a rope.

"Friday morning, we couldn't get in the vehicle

yet because it was locked," Mitzi said. "So we started looking around the area, and within an hour one of us found the footpath. And then we saw the rope and I just went, 'Oh dang.' I just knew at that point. I knew that was Paris."

The rope was broken, indicating that Wallace had tried to use it to cross to the other side but that it had snapped along the way. He had been wearing a heavy backpack, one with several full bottles of water and other equipment inside, and the presumption was that the current took him into the Rio Grande, where he was washed downriver and drowned.

Sunday afternoon, two rafters saw a pair of boots up against a rock in the Rio Grande, seven miles down from where the rope had broken. The body would soon be identified as that of Paris Wallace.

"Until then, he had been on the bottom of the river five days," Mitzi said softly. "It takes five days for the gasses in your body to bring you up, so that's what happened, five days. He popped up."

She was quiet for a moment, and I assumed she was thinking about the final moments of her husband, her partner in life. Then she cracked a smile, looking at me like she didn't want to say something but couldn't stop herself.

"And this is a really morbid story, and I really shouldn't tell it, but I was always really scared about the boys—before they could swim—being around water, and Paris would say to me, 'Oh, don't worry, if they fall in, they'll pop up,'" Mitzi said. "And he would say to me, 'You have air in your lungs and you'll just pop up.' And we would argue back and forth about it. It was this ongoing thing. And that came to me at the time that day. I won. Okay, Paris, you didn't pop up."

With Paris's body located, Mitzi and her children began the grieving process, trying to organize a memorial service, taking the first tentative steps in trying to get on with their lives. But with a body found, the news stories were also starting to spread, people inside and outside the hunt realizing that Paris Wallace was dead, and that Paris Wallace had been a Fenn searcher.

And that was when things really went crazy.

"Boom, it was like wildfire," Mitzi said. "The story just spread everywhere."

Because one dead Fenn searcher is a tragedy, a fluke, and that's all Randy Bilyeu's death in 2016 had been to the outside world. But once there are two?

Well, that's national news.

Randy Bilyeu had joined the chase in 2014, around the same time as so many others in the post–**Today** show mania. But the fifty-three-year-old grandfather took it one step further. He actually moved out to Colorado to be closer to the search area.

On January 5, 2016, Bilyeu set out for the section

of the Rio Grande west of Santa Fe in his Nissan Murano. He had a GPS device, a raft, a wet suit, and waders. And he wasn't alone, not technically: He had brought along his dog, Leo. Bilyeu had been scouting that area for weeks and seemed ready for a grand excursion.

Then more than a week passed, and no one heard from him. Friends and family reached out to his ex-wife, Linda, in Florida, and she filed a missing person's report. On January 15, police found his raft, and they also found Leo, his little white dog, unharmed, about nine miles downriver from where Bilyeu's car was parked.

But they didn't find Bilyeu.

Bilyeu had done something ill-advised, there's no doubt. He was out in early January, searching without a partner, taking a raft into a large river. Those are the kinds of moves that experienced searchers warn against, the ones that are obviously dangerous.

Still, to the Fenn hunters, Bilyeu was one of their own, and one of their own was in real trouble, or worse. So they stepped up.

Sacha Johnston, who lived in Albuquerque, did much of the organizing, banding searchers together via the internet to coordinate their efforts and forming rescue parties, even though she had no experience with anything of the sort. Because the authorities weren't looking, at least not for long enough to satisfy the searchers, the ad hoc, semi-organized effort rose up instead.

"It was batshit crazy when Randy went missing," Sacha said. "The only thing I cared about was helping his family find closure. This happened in my backyard. I thought it was awful that after two days, the police didn't search anymore, the search and rescue didn't search anymore."

Fenners answered the call, coming in from all over New Mexico and Colorado, and were quickly organized into search teams. Even Fenn got into the act, renting a helicopter and flying over the area, touting that he had spent nine thousand dollars looking for Bilyeu. "When we went into it, I knew we weren't going to find a living person," Sacha said. "But I thought there was a slim chance. I got into it because I started seeing all these people saying how they were going to go out looking for Randy. And these people can't find their ass from a hole in the ground."

The searchers found nothing, however, and after close to a month of looking, they eventually abandoned their efforts. For half a year, Bilyeu's story became something between cautionary tale and cause célèbre, his ex-wife and daughter landing a few media interviews, trying to keep the spotlight on Bilyeu, hoping he might be located. When Bilyeu's skeletal remains were finally found six months later by an Army Corps of Engineers crew working along Lake Cochiti, there was sadness, grief, and a feeling of loss—and a recognition that the hunt had forever gone from something whimsical to something that, yes, could be deadly.

But the Fenn hunting community also seemed to come out of it feeling pretty good about itself, like it had done what it could for a man who put himself in a tough spot. After Bilyeu's story was closed, searchers were quick to dismiss it as a one-time incident, a mistake made by someone who wasn't following the rules. He wasn't in the search area. He wasn't out there during the search season. He went out alone. He wasn't really prepared. No one beat that drum harder than Fenn himself.

"The only person responsible for his death was him," Fenn told me. "He wasn't looking in the Rocky Mountains, and he wasn't looking north of Santa Fe. And it was cold. I flew up and down that river in the helicopter; it was frozen over. Snow all over the ground. Everything he did was wrong. He took his little dog out there. He bought a rubber life raft to float that river through the rapids. Paid seventy-nine dollars for it. They call it a two-man raft; it's a one-person. You couldn't get two people in that."

There were, however, a few people who saw Randy Bilyeu's death as something more, as a scathing indictment of everything Fenn had created: that because Fenn had put this carrot out there, all these rabbits would go scurrying out after it, and damn the consequences. No one spoke louder than

Bilyeu's ex-wife, Linda. She lambasted Fenn on the blogs and on her own website, calling for him to end the hunt. Her campaign was noticed in some chase-related media and by a few outlets in the Southwest, but for various reasons, she didn't gain much traction—it didn't help that she repeatedly called the entire thing a hoax, rather than stressing the safety issues—and after a little while, the chase returned to "normal." When Randy Bilyeu was just one man, one easily dismissed outlier, then his death posed no real threat to the existence of the chase.

But now there was Paris Wallace, too. And that meant some new people were beginning to take a critical look at Fenn's chase.

Pete Kassetas had been a cop his entire adult life. He joined the New Mexico State Police immediately upon graduation from New Mexico State University in 1992, and soon took his first posting, as a regular patrol officer in the small city of Grants, west of Albuquerque. He quickly worked his way up the ranks, making patrol sergeant in 1998, joining a regional narcotics task force in 1999, and making lieutenant in 2000.

Kassetas continued to ascend, overseeing investigative units and crime-scene units, until finally, in 2013, he reached the top job: He was made chief of the New Mexico State Police, overseeing one thousand cops and civilian employees, and a budget of more than $116 million.

And in Forrest Fenn's treasure hunt, Kassetas saw a threat to the people of New Mexico.

Paris Wallace's body was found on Sunday, June 18. On June 19, Kassetas conducted interviews with the **Santa Fe New Mexican** and the **Albuquerque Journal,** calling on Fenn to end his hunt in the name of public safety.

"I think it's stupid," Kassetas told the **Journal** that Monday. "If there is indeed a treasure out there, he should pull it. He has the moral obligation at this point to stop this insanity. He's putting lives at risk."

The deaths of Wallace and Bilyeu, Kassetas said, were tragedies that could have been avoided—and he didn't want to put more hunters, or more search and rescue personnel, at risk when the next person went missing.

"I'm not saying he's responsible for their deaths," Kassetas told the **Journal.** "I think his intentions are pure. People are responsible for their own actions. It's about education, and it's about people making good choices. I just think that this treasure has created an environment where people are making poor decisions."

Kassetas's statements marked a pivotal moment in the chase. For the first time, an authority figure was lining up against Fenn, throwing the weight of the state police against the old man and his band of searchers.

Until that point, government entities had largely been supportive of Fenn and his hunters, if they'd weighed in at all. In 2015, the city of Santa Fe had presented Fenn with a proclamation thanking him for all the tourism and goodwill he'd brought to the city. Not long before, the New Mexico Tourism Department had put together a video highlighting Fenn and his hunt as a reason to come to New Mexico. It was all happy-go-lucky stuff. Now, with Kassetas calling for the hunt to end, it galvanized opposition and gave all those opponents a legitimizing bulwark to rally behind.

With the state police suddenly involved, the national media began to descend upon New Mexico, chasing the story. **The New York Times, The Wall Street Journal, The Washington Post,** and all the major television networks ran pieces on the deaths and the controversy. They were looking for anyone who would speak about the chase, positive or negative, and the battle lines were drawn up quickly. Defending Fenn were Cynthia Meachum, Dal Neitzel, and Fenn himself. On the other side were Kassetas and Linda Bilyeu, who used her platform well, speaking to media hungry for the widow's take; she told NBC News that the hunt was "ludicrous, out of control, dangerous, and it should be stopped." Others piled on: The **Santa Fe New Mexican,** until then always a friend to Fenn, ran an editorial pressing him to end the hunt.

Kassetas even contacted Fenn directly to plead with him, setting up a call that was played on **Good Morning America.** (Fenn was unaware the conversation would be broadcast, and was extremely unhappy about it once he figured that out.) The two argued—politely—over what should be done about the hunt, for the benefit of a national audience.

At first, Fenn was his usual obstinate self in response to the criticism, telling **The New York Times** in an email, "If someone drowns in the swimming pool we shouldn't drain the pool. We should teach people to swim."

But as the controversy swirled, even he was taken aback by the intensity of the coverage, and the negative, accusatory tone of so much of it. His enemies had been given an opening, and his friends' supportive words were being overshadowed; deaths have a way of doing that.

Then Fenn did something he had never done in the seven years of his treasure hunt—and something he had rarely done to that point in eighty-six years of life.

He blinked.

In a first, Fenn told the newspapers that he had to respect what Kassetas said, and that he would consider calling off the hunt; he said that Wallace's death touched him deeply, and that he would decide what to do about the chase after a few days of reflection—whether he would alter it to make it safer, or call it off altogether.

On the message boards, all was chaos as searchers picked sides fast. Should Fenn end this shared pursuit? Would it protect people to have this temptation removed? Or would Fenn do his community a true service by staying strong, letting people live their own lives, take their own risks, get out into nature—the very ethos of his treasure hunt?

And underlying it all: Would everyone, in perhaps only a short while, know where the treasure had been all along?

Fenn said that within days, he'd received more than six hundred emails weighing in on what he should do; the vast majority, he said, were in favor of continuing the hunt. As Fenn deliberated, one important voice was heard arguing in favor of the chase, saying it should continue: Mitzi Wallace.

At the time, Mitzi was overwhelmed, coping with the death of the man she had loved for more than thirty years.

"I was angry, I was in shock—you're just in a haze. I'm just trying to stay focused, and put a funeral together, and just make it from day to day, so I didn't expose myself on the outside," she said.

But she gave an interview to the Associated Press, where she weighed in on what Fenn should do. And crucially, she said that the hunt should continue—that the hunt was special to Paris and to herself, and that she hoped to go looking for the treasure in the future.

"Our treasure is that time we spend together," she told the AP.

Mitzi's words gave Fenn some level of cover; he was not facing a unified front of angry widows—it was, as he said, a divided community, grappling with a complex question.

A few days after he had admitted that he was wavering, Fenn made his decision. The hunt would continue, he said, but with additional guidelines in place to prevent hunters from putting themselves in danger. On June 29, he published a warning—some might call it a series of hints—narrowing the search area, and keeping hunters away from the water: "The treasure chest is not under water, nor is it near the Rio Grande River. It is not necessary to move large rocks or climb up or down a steep precipice, and it is not under a man-made object.

"Please remember that I was about 80 when I made two trips from my vehicle to where I hid the treasure. Please be cautious and don't take risks," Fenn wrote.

His warning would not come soon enough to prevent further tragedy.

In 2016, Eric Ashby moved from Tennessee out to Colorado Springs, Colorado, in order to chase Fenn's treasure. The thirty-year-old had fallen in love with the hunt earlier that year, and with little tying him to Tennessee—he was on probation there for an assault charge—he headed west, looking for a fresh start, like so many before him.

Once in Colorado, Ashby waited tables, and in his off-hours became more and more obsessed with the hunt. He gradually drew some friends into his passion, and his devotion reached a high point right around the same time that the controversy surrounding Paris Wallace was playing out.

On June 28, 2017, Ashby convinced a group of friends to head out on the hunt, certain that he knew where Fenn's treasure was this time.

He never returned.

The details of exactly what happened to him remain murky—and were, for some time, the subject of much debate, with friends and family unsure of the truth, and the people who had been with him often unavailable or unhelpful.

The moderators of the public "Find Eric Ashby" Facebook page—later changed to "In memory of Eric Ashby"—described the basic framework of events, in that on June 28, 2017, Ashby ventured out onto the Arkansas River with Becca (Rebecca) Nies, Jimi Booker, Justin Mahone, and Anthony Mahone in search of the treasure. They took a small raft with them, and Ashby decided to use it to cross the river. Ashby, it states, had a rope tied around him, and "yelled to let go of the rope while trying to cross the Arkansas River near Sunshine

Falls (class 5 rapids) in Royal Gorge, Colorado. At that time Eric was swept down the river, the 4 have all said they watched Eric clinging to rocks trying to make it out of the water then lost sight of him, so they packed up their stuff and went home."

The page states that no one in the party reported the disappearance or called for help, and that Ashby's father only learned of his son's death more than a week later, after one of the four companions called him. The only call to emergency services came from a passerby who had witnessed the incident; EMS apparently searched the area but did not find anything.

Ashby's body was eventually found at the end of July, and the remains were positively identified as his six months later. But that didn't end the debate. A lot of unanswered questions still surround Ashby's death, including and especially why the people with him didn't report the incident to police right away. But what struck me the most was how the searcher community reacted.

The same day that Ashby was in the river, I was in the hospital with Amalie, and not long after, with Elliott, too; he decided to come a little bit early, so we got to know him sooner than we expected. Both mom and baby were healthy and happy, and once things settled in a bit, I could revisit what had happened in the chase over those chaotic few weeks following the disappearance of yet another searcher. I started asking around in the Fenn community about Ashby, curious how it would respond to another problem so soon after Wallace's death. To my surprise, all of the major Fenn hunters—and Fenn himself—downplayed any ties between Ashby and the chase, questioning why he'd be out in those kinds of rapids on a Fenn-related search, saying something fishy was going on in that situation, indicating that they weren't sure Ashby was treasure hunting at the time of his death at all. Fenn and several others specifically claimed they had heard that Ashby used drugs, and that was at the real root of this problem.

Apparently, I wasn't alone in getting this treatment. The author of an article in **Wired** magazine on the Ashby incident related much the same experience. Maybe they were worried about what another well-publicized fatality, so closely following on the heels of Wallace's demise, would do to the chase. Maybe they really didn't think the Ashby situation fit the bill of a searcher death. Regardless, there was no all-hands-on-deck search, no help from the community, unlike what there had been for Bilyeu, and little of the widespread sympathy that existed for Wallace. To the large majority of Fenn hunters, Ashby was, and would forever remain, an outsider.

Later that year, with the search season drawing to a close, I sat down with Fenn to talk about all that had happened that summer—the firestorm of attention, the deaths, how it all had almost ended before he wanted it to. A brittle calm had returned to the hunt; it had fallen off the front pages, but the events of the summer still hung heavily over everything.

We had something new to talk about, as well: another fatality. Thanks to Freedom of Information Act requests from a Montana TV station, we in the general public had recently learned that the death toll from that tragic June was even higher than we'd initially believed. Another searcher, Jeff Murphy, fifty-three, of Batavia, Illinois, had fallen five hundred feet down a steep slope while hunting for Fenn's treasure in Yellowstone National Park.

Murphy had been hiking the Rescue Creek Trail, close to Mammoth, on June 8, when he failed to check in and was reported missing by his wife back home in Illinois. His body was found the next day. He had fallen from Turkey Pen Peak, accidentally stepping in a hole, or "chute." The report states that Murphy "stepped or hopped into the chute from the less steep slope above," and fell to his death.

Murphy, according to the park's records, was a Fenn hunter. He had emailed Fenn a few days before departing, and his wife told authorities that Murphy had gone to Yellowstone to seek the treasure.

The park had investigated the death quietly,

and his family had not wanted attention. But records showed that Fenn had been in contact with Yellowstone officials throughout the search for Murphy, and after his body had been discovered.

That meant Fenn knew all about it that June, even before Wallace had died. Cynthia Meachum later told me that the Murphy death had Fenn questioning whether to appear at Fennboree that weekend at all—worried about how it would look if it got out that he was celebrating with his flock when a man had just died. He showed up, of course, smiled and glad-handed with all the hunters, basked in their attention, walked by the shrine to Randy Bilyeu, and never mentioned a thing about another fatality. And when Wallace's death became national news the following week, Fenn certainly didn't cop to the fact that he'd already known about Murphy's demise in Yellowstone or admit during his public hand-wringing over whether to continue the hunt after Wallace's death that he had two bodies weighing on his mind, not just one.

Fenn's hunt already faced so much scrutiny thanks to Wallace's fate and all the attention it received. Had observers known that Wallace had not been the only man to die in such a short period, who knows what might have become of the hunt? That might have ended everything right there.

When I asked him what he knew and when, he said he didn't remember exactly, however. Just that he was informed about Murphy's death at some point. Efforts to press him further on it went nowhere.

Learning all this, I shifted gears and asked if there were any other hunt-related deaths we in the general public didn't know about. What Fenn said surprised me: Sort of, he said. He didn't think it really "counted," but someone else had died in pursuit of the treasure, yes.

"Couple of years ago," Fenn said, "there was a guy—I shouldn't tell you this, but I will—who lived in California and was coming to Santa Fe to look for the treasure. But he climbed up on a silo on a farm in Arizona, fell off and killed himself, and his father blamed me. He sent me a nasty letter, because he was on his way to Santa Fe to look for the treasure, so it's my fault he fell off the silo."

According to the Colorado publication **Westword,** that is believed to be Jeff Schultz, a California resident and Ohio native who died in April 2016 in Arizona.

Fenn shook his head.

"They're looking for somebody to blame for it, to be responsible for what happened to their son," he said, sounding like he was sympathetic, like he understood. I agreed with him that, while tragic, that incident didn't really seem to me to be in the same vein as the other deaths.

But still, those others—Bilyeu, Murphy, Wallace, Ashby. The fact that the death toll was now at four, excluding the man from the silo incident, didn't seem to bother Fenn, not really. Or not in a different way than it did when it stood at one. The deaths were unfortunate, yes. He wished they hadn't happened, certainly. But it seemed little had occurred to change his thinking: that what he'd done was valuable, that it should continue, that people take risks every day, doing anything worth doing.

"I didn't predict people were going to get killed," Fenn said. "But I thought about it for an awful long time, for fifteen years, every day. And I predicted everything that could have happened. I didn't predict that people were gonna die looking for the treasure, but it's predictable that when you go into the mountains and into the rivers, that's what's going to happen. Like I've said before, nine people die at the Grand Canyon every year, but they're not talking about shutting down the Grand Canyon. And I read an article—I think I googled Colorado or something, and something like thirty people a year die in a forest in Colorado."

Fenn was so practiced in his responses that I knew I was getting the same well-worn sound bites that he parceled out when needed, a word or two changed here and there. But what struck me was how unrepentant he was about the individual searchers. When I asked him about whether he'd come around on the Ashby situation—for a long time, Fenn wouldn't even acknowledge Ashby was a searcher—it was clear he hadn't mellowed a bit.

"Eric Ashby, there are so many problems there," Fenn started in. "First of all, he moved to Colorado because he had to get out of Kansas or wherever it was."

He was involved with drugs, Fenn said, "and he was running the river with a bunch of his drug friends. I mean, the cops all knew that. My question was, Why would he get on a little flimsy raft to go through class five rapids to get someplace when a road ran right along the river? Why didn't he get a car and go? I mean, the road was thirty feet away. Why did he get in a boat in class five rapids?"

He paused.

"The argument against my argument is there was a contract and so you just have to throw your hands up." He was referring to the contracts signed by the members of Ashby's group, found in Ashby's car, determining how they would split up Fenn's loot once they'd found it. Pretty hard to argue with those. So Fenn, at the very least, finally acknowledged that Ashby was a searcher. But he still hadn't quite gotten himself to admit that Ashby was actively hunting when he died; he was still insisting something else might have been at play there, though he couldn't put his finger on what.

His words were similar regarding Bilyeu.

"There's so many things he did wrong. First of all, he wasn't searching in the Rocky Mountains. He wasn't searching north of Santa Fe," Fenn said as I, perhaps stupidly, poured gasoline on the fire by noting Bilyeu was searching in the January cold.

"January! I mean, I got in the helicopter up there for four days. Big slabs of ice are floating down the river. The banks are all icy. I mean . . . six or eight miles downriver was frozen solid. I mean, logs were piling up on top of the ice. And he was out there looking. But he had scouted it out, too, for three or four different times before he started; he got up on top, he looked, he had binoculars. Theoretically knew what he was doing. Practically, he didn't."

This way of thinking—that it wasn't the treasure hunt's fault, that the individuals did it wrong, that these people were outliers, that these deaths were freak events—even extended to Paris Wallace, who, of all these dead men, was the one Fenn seemed to hold in the highest esteem.

As we were talking about Wallace then, and, later, I'd come to know his wife, Mitzi—she and Forrest had never spoken—he posited that maybe what Wallace was doing wasn't so dangerous after all, that maybe hunting wasn't the real reason he died, that he was just the victim of lightning-striking bad luck, and that's why he washed away in the Rio Grande.

"The pastor, he may have had a heart attack," Fenn said, largely apropos of nothing.

"The rope broke," I reminded him. "Seems like

the cause of his demise was pretty clear." But Fenn was undeterred.

"He could have had a stroke or an aneurysm. I wonder if they did an autopsy," he mused aloud, starting to question if perhaps Mitzi could answer this.

"Don't ask her," he said suddenly, thinking better of it. "It doesn't matter. But they probably did because the cause of death was unknown."

We went on like this for a while, and honestly, I was surprised at how little sympathy Fenn seemed to have for those who had died in the service of his chest. I didn't directly blame him for those deaths, to be clear, and I didn't agree with the calls to end the hunt—even if, yes, he had created an attractive nuisance, I generally could get behind his Grand Canyon defense, and the larger worthwhileness of the whole endeavor. And to some extent, I understood his prickliness: Fenn was now on the defensive, constantly challenging whether he and his treasure hunt were really at fault before he was even asked.

But even if he wasn't, or didn't consider himself, at fault, didn't he still have a sense of responsibility for the people themselves, the shepherd for his flock? Even with Wallace, he didn't seem to see these as human beings who had lost their lives doing something he had spawned—rather, he was treating them as threats, dangers to his enterprise. And not even immediate dangers—the fear that the hunt would be ended was already in the past.

Were these, then, threats to that which he so hated to discuss, his legacy? Was Fenn fearful that in the end, this whimsical thing he had created would be remembered not for getting people into the outdoors, or for creating hope, but for death, and pain, and loss? It's not that I thought he was being callous, or that he didn't care that they had died. I do believe he cared. But with every word he said, I felt that he cared about how the world, and history, would view him and his hunt a lot more.

And that made me wonder something: How close to ending the treasure hunt had he really come? During those heady days in June, it seemed like the whole adventure hung in the balance, with media flooding Santa Fe and the New Mexico State Police breathing down his neck, all around the very real question of whether this hunt was a danger that should be shut down. But now, knowing how he looked back on those deaths, it struck me that maybe he wasn't seeing it the same way the rest of the world was.

Had he actually thought about ending it? I asked him.

"For that long." Fenn guffawed, holding his thumb and his index finger roughly an inch apart, making it clear that no, he had never really considered ending it.

"I had to say that. I mean, that's—the chief of

the state police asked me," Fenn said. "How can I say, 'Chief, you're full of bull'? I'm not going to say that."

As I told Fenn, I was shocked. I had thought that there was genuine uncertainty in his mind at the time, a real soul-searching moment, where he wasn't sure if what he had created was a force for good, or the opposite.

But it was clear Fenn had never had any intention of calling off his hunt, no matter what he'd said publicly back in June. With four deaths not enough, I asked him just what could happen that would be grounds for him to end the hunt. He sidestepped, insisting he couldn't call it off now even if he wanted to, said the trip to get the treasure would be too taxing—that he could have done it at eighty, but not now at eighty-seven.

"I can't physically go back there," Fenn said. "I can't physically do it. I could have a few years ago, but I can't go get it now."

I asked why he couldn't get someone else to help him, like his grandson Shiloh, and he responded that then Shiloh would know where it was.

But who cared? Why would it matter if Shiloh knew, if the hunt was over? It was obvious from his flimsy excuses that he'd never even considered this as a real possibility, that he didn't want to even consider calling off the hunt. He was giving me the same treatment he gave to the state police; at every turn, Fenn offered unintentional reminders that he didn't care what anyone else thought, that he was never going to listen to anyone's concerns, pleas, or demands. How many deaths would it take for him to really listen? Five? Ten? Twenty? Was there a number, a figure, a person whose loss would be too great? If one of the hunters really harmed a member of his family, would that be too far, disabuse him of his cavalier attitude toward these mounting consequences?

Or perhaps not even then—had he become so dogmatic, so assured of the importance of his creation, that he was willing to sacrifice even those close to him for it to continue?

How far would he take this?

In Grand Junction, Colorado, the Connection Church was struggling. A year after Wallace's death, the renovations intended to turn the former furniture store into a loving, caring religious space were limping along. There were exposed beams, unfinished areas, spots where they hadn't quite figured out what to do. They still hadn't found a new pastor, and Wallace's long shadow hung over everything.

"It was so hard to get back into the swing of things," said Michelle Umberger, who had helped run the church with Paris. "Even now, it's a year later, but we're still like, Oh, I wish Paris was here. This would be so much easier. We're still trying to find a new pastor, and trying to continue the building, and you have people who want to do things a different way, and we say, 'No, Paris would have wanted to do it this way; it has to be like this.'"

The church had lost members, some of them just looking for something different, others unable to deal with the reminders of Paris's loss.

"We've had a lot of people that were superclose to him leave, people who just couldn't handle being here anymore," Umburger said.

"My husband and I got to the point where we thought about going somewhere else, but . . ." She trailed off. "If we take off and leave, then there's nothing left of him."

Wallace was particularly present in one part of the church he had been trying to build. Along one long, otherwise bare stretch of the hallway leading to the restrooms stood a wooden cross and, next to it, a picture of Wallace baptizing one of his flock. On the cross were the words of Paris's last sermon, the one he delivered only days before he went missing.

"May we understand that we don't always have to understand. Because in that point we have to trust," Paris said from beyond. "Even when bad things happen to good people, God is still in control."

Those words gave Mitzi comfort now. She thought of them often, whenever she found herself wondering why—why God took her partner of three decades, why he was lost so senselessly.

"I was asking God, Why this way?" she said. "Why did he have to go this way? I think it's that there's a message in his last prayer that stuck with people. He talks about, that we can't understand everything, and when we don't understand, we have to just trust. And that has stuck with a lot of people. That bad things happen to good people, and we may not understand why, but we just have to trust."

Mitzi had recently begun dating someone else, and her sons were having a hard time with it, not yet understanding that it didn't mean she loved Paris any less, that it didn't mean she wasn't grieving. She thought of Paris every day—how he'd joke in a certain situation, how he'd treat a friend, a word of advice he'd offer.

"It's been hard," she said. "Clay, my youngest, who's twenty, he's still kinda floundering right now. He was his dad's shadow. They even look alike. So there's a huge hole there now. It's hard."

After Paris's death, Mitzi had virtually no contact with the chase community. She'd largely stayed away from them, and they'd stayed away from her. But in the aftermath of it all, once everything had settled, she had gotten a handwritten letter from Fenn. The old man passed along his condolences, said it sounded like Paris had been a wonderful guy.

"He said in the letter, which I'll keep forever, he said that he wished he'd met Paris," Mitzi said.

She still hadn't met Fenn, hadn't talked to him,

but she said she would like to. Would like to tell him in person that she didn't regret a thing, didn't blame him.

"I would tell him, Thank you for doing this. Because it was amazing for us. It got us off the couch, got us outdoors," she said.

She thought that if Paris were here, he'd tell her to go out treasure hunting again.

"I think he would say, 'Eat the cake, buy the shoes, search for the treasure, go on the trip,'" she said. "That's what he would say—live your best life now. Don't wait until your ducks are in a row, because they'll never be fully in a row. Just do it all now."

A few memorials to Wallace had sprung up in Grand Junction, one at the church, one at a local park. But the one that stood out the most, to me, was in New Mexico. It was another of those road-side crosses, erected alongside the Rio Grande on New Mexico State Road 68, seven miles down from where Wallace went into the water. It was put up by another young man who Wallace took under his wing, who became a surrogate son of sorts, one of so many young people Paris Wallace helped along the way.

The memorial reads, "Friend of the broken, father of the lost boy, lion of the faith."

I drove by it every time I went treasure hunting.

8

BACK ON THE HUNT,
OUT WITH THE BEST

I could feel the tree branch start to crack and give way under me as I put my weight on it. I quickly jumped up, landing solidly on the fallen fir that was supposed to serve as my make-shift bridge across the Red River. My jump wasn't perfect, though, and I teetered for a second before finally gaining my footing.

I looked back to the shore and saw Cynthia Meachum laughing at me and gleefully taking pictures.

"You don't want to start your day by falling into the river," she said cheerily.

I offered a halfhearted smile in return and turned my full attention to what I was doing. The fir was stable, and just long enough to get us from the north bank of the Red River to the south if we could get across it—without falling in, of course.

I gingerly stepped forward, grabbing at a protruding branch to steady myself, and inched along the trunk. The water wasn't that deep, but I didn't want to take any chances. Moving slowly, gradually, carefully, I made my way across to where the tree's upended stump remained lodged in the bank. From there, it was a simple matter of grasping at a few roots and pulling myself up onto solid ground.

"It's not so bad," I yelled confidently back to Cynthia, who was beginning her journey across. "Just grab onto the branches along the way; you'll be fine."

It was hilarious that I was even trying to give her any advice at all, sounding so self-assured, a real outdoorsman. Ha! Compared to me, Cynthia Meachum was like a combination of John Muir and Robert Ballard, using logic and technology to narrow down the hunt and then heading out to experience it all in the outdoors. Over the last four years, she'd been on literally hundreds of hunts, ranging all over the hills and forests of New Mexico, in her obsessive search for Fenn's gold.

This time, she'd agreed to partner up with me, lending her expertise in exchange for a cut of the potential profits—and the promise of a new site to explore. I'd flown into Santa Fe a few days before, making my second journey of 2017 to visit Fenn and search for treasure. The intervening months were spent salivating at the chance to get out on the hunt. Ever since our time at Fennboree had ended, and Fenn had popped Beep's Rio Grande balloon, I'd been wanting to get back into the wilderness and try it all again—not because I had any great ideas, mind you, but because the whole thing felt exhilarating, being out there, feeling like you were working on something, seeking this treasure. I was starting to see how these hunters fell so deeply into this so fast.

I'd been hoping to meet up with Cynthia when I was out there, and got lucky when she happened to be over at Fenn's house the day I went to visit him. As we caught up, I explained my plan for checking out a specific spot—Bear Canyon, east of Taos— and to my surprise, she agreed to come along. Maybe I shouldn't have been so shocked—Cynthia was totally obsessed with finding the treasure, and any new leads were like catnip to her.

In fact, Cynthia thinks of the day she was laid off from her job at Nikon Precision Inc. in 2015 as one of the best moments of her life.

"I was so ecstatic," she told me. "The first call I made from work that day, when I left the conference room where I had been laid off, was to my partner, Michelle. The second call was to Forrest Fenn. I told him, 'Oh my God, I am now a fulltime Fenn treasure hunter.'"

Meachum had been a highly trained, highly competent, highly paid engineer, assigned to work on Nikon equipment at the Intel plant in Rio Rancho. But since 2013, she'd had a secret obsession. She was a budding Fenn hunter, a methodical, systematic, logical one. She wasn't fanciful. She attacked it like the sequential logic problem it was.

"Having an engineering background, we really do use logic to solve problems. So the first thing, when I saw this poem, it seemed like a flowchart, things you see at work, fixing things with logic, using it to solve problems. So, yeah, I thought, How hard can this be?"

She just lacked one thing: time. So when she was laid off, she hardly even mourned the job and life she'd lost.

She converted a space in her Rio Rancho home into her "war room," papering the walls with maps of New Mexico, Colorado, Yellowstone, many of them marked up with notes and pins. A rough replica of the treasure chest rested on her table; she built it in order to reference how hard such a small box would be to see in the vast wilderness. Pens, notebooks, a magnifying glass, and more maps lay all about, the signs of a hunter at work. She'd spend most of the winter in there devising new solves, and then hunted near daily during the search season—roughly March to October in New Mexico—covering every bit of ground she could find in the state.

But ever since the deaths of Wallace and Bilyeu, and the increased public scrutiny on the hunt, Cynthia had been forced into a new role. Already serving as the public face of the hunters, the person

the media came calling on when they wanted someone to tell them what life was like inside the hunt,
she now had to answer for the rapidly increasing
death toll. She was on Fenn's side, of course, but
she also tried to paint an accurate picture, saying
that it was dangerous if you let it be, that it could
be hazardous if you were unprepared.

And now, fortunately, she'd let Beep and me into
her sphere. Before she was obsessed with treasure
hunting, Cynthia was obsessed with fantasy sports.
So Beep was almost as exciting a figure for her as
Fenn, and the two immediately hit it off when we
were at Fennboree. We shared some of our ideas,
and she came away impressed—deciding that we
were worthy enough to seriously talk hunting with.
Beep hadn't come on this journey, though; he had
a girlfriend now, Jordan—his first serious relationship ever, really—and he was spending more
time with her, while also trying to create a board
game to sell. So he'd stayed back in Canada, leaving
me to either come up with something on my own
or convince Cynthia to let me tag along with her.

It definitely surprised me when she seemed more
interested in my idea than anything she had going
on. Bear Canyon, the spot I had targeted, was a
rivulet slicing through the Rockies east of Questa,
New Mexico, just south of an old, shuttered molybdenum mine. I'd made some halfhearted arguments as to why this might be a good place—the
mine made the water temperature higher than

normal ("warm waters halt"), and then we could head down into the canyon itself; "too far to walk" could mean crossing the Red River, and after that, there was a brown bat–infested cave near the mouth of the canyon that could be the "home of Brown"—but I didn't really think I had anything. Cynthia, however, felt differently. She'd long focused on the Taos area, but having combed it so thoroughly, she told me that she'd been losing faith in New Mexico's being the home of the treasure at all, and was starting to believe Dal's theories that it was near Yellowstone.

"I was so hooked on Taos," she said. "There were so many things that pointed to Taos. Not anymore."

My idea, however, had rejuvenated her; because my spot was near Questa, not Taos, she hadn't been through it yet, and Cynthia was genuinely excited to attack a new and different zone.

And, truth be told, so was I. This was my first hunt without Beep there, and really the first time that I'd done most of the prep work myself, instead of just piggybacking off what he was doing. I was starting to feel like a real Fenn hunter, studying possibilities on the internet, getting lost in maps, gaining a familiarity with the mountains of northern New Mexico that I'd never, ever expected to have. And rather than being turned off by the deaths, something about them had raised the stakes of this game, made it seem even more pressing that I had to use what I could to get out there and find the treasure. I'd say it was to stop anyone else from getting hurt, but that wasn't really it. It just felt like there was more danger involved now than I'd ever realized before, and something about that made it an even bigger rush, offered more of a thrill. Sitting in my house back east, a (very cute) infant periodically crying, the thought of what could go right—and, yes, even wrong—out in the wilds made me want to get out there and explore.

That's what brought us to that tree trunk lying across the Red River, about three hours' drive north of Santa Fe. Intimidating at first, it was quickly behind us, Cynthia displaying great agility as she scrambled over and across to the south bank.

Safely on the Bear Canyon side of the river, we looked up at the gap in the mountains.

"There's what I guess would be the bat cave," I told her, pointing at a hollowed-out area way up the side of the hill that might or might not have actually contained brown bats—hiking up there to confirm it seemed nearly impossible, or at least ill-advised—but for the moment, seeing the hollow served as reinforcement enough that this solve wasn't awful, and that we should proceed into the canyon.

Remembering my and Beep's hunting excursions earlier that year, I'd prepared better this time—jeans, a hooded sweatshirt, a hat, and a pack that included a bottle of water, a printed eight-by-eleven piece of paper with a map of the area I'd found on Google Maps, hiking boots that dated to college and hence were admittedly almost twenty years old, a couple granola bars, and, yes, a raincoat this time. I was readyish.

Cynthia? She was a lot more prepared. On most every hike, she outfitted herself the same way. She had a pack that she filled with everything she'd need to survive out in the wild for a short time if something went wrong—granola bars, jerky, apples, and lots and lots of water.

"You've got to have something if your truck breaks down in the middle of nowhere and it takes you two days to walk back to the real world," she said.

She traveled with a rock pick for moving earth and rocks as needed, a Leatherman multitool, a spork, and a hunting knife—one plucked from a growing collection, bolstered by friends who bestowed them on her as gifts when they heard she was a treasure hunter. Also in her pack was an emergency bag with standard items like bandages, plus iodine pills for purifying water and metal straws for potentially sipping water in parched desert environments.

She usually brought a raincoat, and for most multiday hunts swapped between two main pairs of hiking pants, doing the same with her two main sets of hiking boots—though on longer excursions, she'd bring extra footwear, and always extra socks, dreading wet feet. On every trip, she brought maps of her search area—not lame little printouts like what I had, but real foldout maps. And she always had a little notepad and pen or pencil, both for taking notes and for making sure to write down the GPS location where she'd parked her truck.

What she didn't have with her now? Bear spray, or her handgun. She generally brought the 9mm Glock only when hunting in Montana or Wyoming, when encounters with bears or other dangerous wildlife were more likely. In New Mexico, they weren't as much of a concern.

So far on this day, our main enemy was thorns. We fought through bramble and brush, absorbing nicks and cuts from the foliage as we went. As I was pushing aside a long, thin branch, I looked back to Cynthia and asked something that had been on my mind.

"When you go out on these hunts—and don't take this the wrong way—do you actually think you're going to find the treasure, like, every time?" I asked.

She chuckled.

"More often than you'd think, which is kind of funny, I guess," she said. "But no, maybe after I spent the winter working on a really good solve, and I'm excited to go out in the spring, then, yeah, I feel it. But not every time. Sometimes it's like checking off a box, that, okay, this area doesn't have it; I can move on."

She quickly added something, seemingly so as not to insult me.

"But I'm excited about this solve. I think it has real potential," she said, cheery as ever.

Not necessary, I assured her as we reached the mouth of the canyon and began to trudge up the slope, a running river to our left, a sheer wall to our right, impossibly high. The canyon narrowed considerably from this point on, and the elevation rose quite quickly as we hiked deeper in. Still, I was feeling good, too. After the deaths, it seemed like Fenn had opened up a bit more, talking more openly, making more public comments, maybe even dropping more of what seemed like hints. Cynthia and I began talking about whether that meant something—that after all this controversy, all the drama of the past year, maybe Fenn wanted to give his chase a happy ending. Maybe, I wondered aloud, he wanted the treasure located, and he was trying to make it happen.

She quickly agreed, saying she first had that thought at a Q&A earlier in the year, following the premiere of a film about the chase, when Fenn had said that if a searcher found the blaze, they'd find the chest.

"He never, ever has said that before. And it's like he wants it found," she said. "And since then two more dead people, or what, now three, the Yellowstone guy, the preacher, and even Eric Ashby. I totally believe he wants it found. And even though he says he doesn't, he does."

That would allow him and his chase to be

redeemed somewhat, I posited—not remembered for the deaths, but for the good it created. Then his legacy wouldn't be as someone who created a controversial, morally murky, attractive nuisance—but for creating something that was tangible, and real, and that ultimately brought good to the world before he passed on.

"He says he doesn't care about his legacy," I said. "That's crazy. Of course he does. And now, with people asking, 'Oh, was this really a good thing?' If somebody finds it, that settles it for all time."

"Right," Cynthia responded. "That's like Linda Bilyeu saying it's a hoax, right? Well, if someone finds it, then he can prove her wrong. You think he wouldn't love to do that? Because she's given him such a hard time . . . it was tough on him."

With Cynthia's affirmation, I found myself fully believing that Fenn was trying to guide searchers toward the chest, potentially for his own ends. And few had more face time with him than Cynthia, right? Maybe something had seeped in through osmosis. It made me suddenly hopeful, like we weren't just walking through the woods up the side of a random hill across from an old mine with an uncertain destination ahead—but that we were walking toward something, with a purpose.

My reverie was broken by a sound I hadn't expected to hear out here—human voices. It had been pretty difficult to even get over to Bear Canyon, and I couldn't imagine other people made this hike just for the heck of it. Cynthia and I began looking around, squinting through the trees to see if, somewhere out there, another person could be spotted—even, maybe, other Fenn hunters. Who else would be out here? I was suddenly nervous, protective of my lousy solve.

But even as the voices echoed through the canyon, we couldn't spot anyone. Until, that is, Cynthia looked up and then pointed her arm to the cliffs above, seemingly miles and miles up. There on the edge were two people walking, peering down at the forest around us, chatting. It made my stomach lurch even to see them up there, that roller-coaster feeling of falling fast overtaking me suddenly as my mind envisioned the drop in front of them. How did they even get up there? This whole area was so remote, I honestly had assumed we'd be the only ones out here. I also felt a little silly for even briefly thinking they might be other Fenn hunters, hot on our trail.

I put my head back down and tried to focus again on the task at hand, trying to bottle up that excitement I'd felt a few moments earlier.

"So," I said, still dreaming big, "what would you do if you actually found it? Found the treasure? Have you thought about that?"

"Ha!" she barked back. "Well, first thing I'd have to do is probably get my gun and hunker down somewhere. Ooh, would people be mad, saying

I cheated or I got clues from Fenn—that's what always gets me: If I'm supposedly getting all this information from him, why haven't I found the treasure yet?

"I guess I'm not sure. I'd definitely bring back that bracelet to Forrest, the one he wants returned," she said, referring to the nineteenth-century Mesa Verde turquoise bracelet that Fenn had offered to buy back from whoever found the chest.

"And there are about half a dozen people who I feel either I owe something to or who helped. And I would have six people come to my kitchen table, and we'd have that treasure chest there. And we would go around picking. It would be like, Okay, I pick first, so I pick what I want; then they'll go. And we will go around until that chest is empty, because I'm not in it for the money."

She sighed.

"But mostly I'd just take a big, deep breath. And then I guess I'd find something else to obsess over."

I said something about its being nice that she'd give pieces to others as we continued our ascent up the canyon, but I had come down from that earlier high as quickly as I'd achieved it; now I couldn't help but fixate on her half joke about getting her gun and hunkering down. Now that I'd met enough of these searchers, I could definitely see that even the rational, normal ones would be furious if they thought something was amiss, that someone had cheated them out of their treasure either through access to "insider" information from Fenn or through some sort of other perceived advantage.

It made me think of a conversation Beep and I had had just before I flew out here, one where he had raised many of the same concerns. I'd told him about my solve, and my hopes of going hunting with Cynthia, and he'd said that we needed to come up with a plan about what we'd do with the chest if we actually found it.

"What do you mean?" I'd asked him, naïve as they come. "We go to Fenn, tell him we found it, and then the treasure's ours."

To that point, it really had not occurred to me that it might be more complicated than that.

"No, Dan, I don't think you understand," he'd warned. "This could be, like, really dangerous."

Beep went on to explain that he worried that once we found the treasure, other hunters—jealous or resentful or angry, or all of the above—could come calling, believing we'd stolen what was rightfully theirs.

"People might come to our houses, wanting to take the treasure from us, thinking that they deserve it. I think we'd need to get rid of it as fast as possible—or just make sure no one ever knew we found it in the first place."

He knew, of course, that I couldn't do that, as I reminded him. I was writing a book on this whole thing. That would be a heck of a thing to leave out.

"Then we need to figure something out, because this could get us killed," Beep had replied.

Was that a bit of an exaggeration? Probably—I hope. Since we were not on the verge of finding the treasure, this was—at least in my mind—more of a conceptual discussion, not an immediate decision to be made, though Beep seemed to feel differently.

But Beep was right to recognize that finding the treasure might not be all plaudits and Scrooge McDuckian laps through our money bin. For the first time, I started to consider that being the one to recover Fenn's chest might actually be a bad thing, that it might come with negative consequences. The realization hit me like a splash of cold water. Even after the deaths, after the questions about Fenn and his intentions, after all the money lost in the service of this hunt, after the nagging questions about whether it was even real at all, I'd still never entertained the idea that finding the treasure might be the worst thing you could do. And once I thought it, it was hard to get the idea out of my head.

It made me think of those stories that pop up every once in a while about lottery winners and how, more often than not, the jackpot ends up ruining the winners' lives. The worst consequences come for those who win reasonably small payouts—one or two million dollars. That's enough money to change your life, yes, but you're certainly not filthy rich; yet everyone treats winners that way, hitting them up for money, favors, real or imagined payback. They are harassed, extorted, blackmailed, robbed—and that's just the extralegal stuff, to say nothing of how it ruins relationships with their supposed friends and family, who now all come calling, expecting handouts and becoming infuriated when they are turned down.

I could only imagine that it would be far, far worse for the person or persons who became known for finding a treasure, what with the expected **Today** show appearances, likely news and magazine stories, all the publicity and fanfare that would come with it.

Then there was the Paco Chavez problem, those truly scary people who might take things too far. If he was emboldened enough to go after Fenn and his granddaughter, what might he do to a normal hunter? It really could be dangerous to find the treasure. The same people who currently went to Fenn's house, believing the treasure was hidden in his backyard or that he or his family was the treasure or whatever—they might just redirect their focus to whoever found it, maybe saying they had been cheated or that we'd gained it improperly, and come to claim it.

I mean, it's not actually crazy to say that Beep and I **did** have unfair access to Fenn, because of my journalist status. How many other searchers got to go to his home, got to have lunch with him whenever they were in town, got to ask him whatever they wanted over hours-long interview sessions?

Who knew what they'd do if they decided to act on that resentment. I now had a four-month-old at home; I couldn't have a community of obsessed, angry treasure hunters coming to confront me over what they wrongly thought I'd stolen from them.

When I'd asked Fenn what might happen to the person who found it, he had largely validated Beep's concerns.

"You're going to be swamped with people," Fenn said. "And half the people who are going to be swamping you are going to be madder than hell, because they've put a hundred and twenty thousand dollars, a hundred and fifty thousand, into finding the thing."

So Beep and I started brainstorming, trying to come up with ideas that were middle-ground ways to claim the treasure without putting giant targets on our backs.

"I think maybe we can set something up through an auction house, maybe, like if nobody knows who found the treasure except the seller—one of those places like Christie's, where people wave the numbers to bid on the item—then we could be safe," he said, pausing. "But what if Fenn tells everyone about us anyway? Do you think we can trust him not to? I think maybe we just don't tell him about it at all."

I had no idea if Fenn was truly trustworthy. But in the end, I knew I couldn't just slip off into the night with the treasure. I had a twofold responsibility:

both to let others know that the hunt was over and to tell the story of how it was found. That little box meant so much to so many people, I'd feel an obligation to relate what had happened to it. And, I admitted, I wanted my due for finding it! As so many others had said, this wasn't just about the monetary value of the treasure—it was about being the one who figured it out. I'd come to feel that as well, and I certainly wasn't above yearning for that.

All that, of course, was the kind of pie-in-the-sky discussion that two hopeful searchers have from the comfort of their homes, a thousand miles away. Now that Cynthia and I were out in the wilderness, I was continually being reminded of just how silly that kind of talk was, and how unlikely we were to ever find anything. Beep and I had been so serious, so concerned about what we'd do when we located the chest. Out here, I was just happy I didn't fall into a river.

Cynthia and I tramped farther into Bear Canyon, the path narrowing even more. In theory, we'd checked off four of the clues so far: "Warm waters halt" was the molybdenum mine. "In the canyon down" was Bear Canyon itself. "Too far to walk" was crossing the Red River. "Below the home of Brown" was passing under the bat cave.

But now that we were at "no place for the meek" and "end is ever drawing nigh," I had no idea either what to think or what to look for. This was a pretty half-assed solve. As the trail disappeared entirely and we came into areas of brush and the occasional clearing, it became obvious that no one ever came up this way. In one sense, that was good—you don't want to be too near a human trail. In another, it was discouraging. Why on earth would Fenn have wanted to come here?

Still, this spot did have one redeeming quality: the river, now more of a stream, trickling down the center of the canyon. It meant this could, just maybe, have been a fishing spot, offering some justification for Fenn's having ventured out this far. I'm not sure it was pretty enough for him to want to sit down, take a bunch of pills, and die here, but it certainly wasn't bad.

As we reached a clearing, we came upon the first sign of civilization I'd yet seen—it looked like a metal pipe, sticking up from the ground, and there were signs of old metal cans flattened into the dirt, with more apparent if we scratched at the ground a little. There were no logos, or wrappers, or anything on any of the metal, and no plastic, either—no telltale signs of mid-to-late-twentieth-century civilization.

"This was probably an old mining camp, a long, long time ago," Cynthia said.

It was all fascinating to ponder, but this was still not the kind of place I could match to any of the clues—I guess, maybe, the presence of a mine could indicate "heavy loads." But that would mean we'd just fully skipped the "no place for the meek" and "end is ever drawing nigh" clues, not to mention having no "water high."

Cynthia and I resolved to follow the river a little farther, reasoning that it offered the best chance of finding something of value, but it was clear our end in these parts was what was ever drawing nigh, to my chagrin.

To keep us focused, I rekindled the conversation from earlier about what she'd do if she found the treasure, beyond splitting it up among her friends. She reminded me that it wasn't quite that simple— there were huge financial and tax implications to claiming Fenn's chest, and, it turned out, there was a ton of debate on what the person who found it should do within the searcher community—much of it having to do with where, exactly, the treasure was actually found.

Fenn, of course, said he spent eight thousand dollars on consulting a lawyer before hiding his chest because he understood that the various categories of land—federal land, state land, private property, tribal land, and a few of their subcategories— meant very different legal outcomes for the person who found his chest.

Even though Fenn put the chest somewhere out in the wilderness, locating it wouldn't quite be the end of the story; it wasn't as simple as just saying "finders keepers," at least as far as the U.S. government was concerned: There are both ownership and taxation issues for any potential finder (it's not clear whether Fenn's chest qualifies as a treasure trove, a legal definition which would bring its own set of rules). Generally speaking, though, Fenn's chest seemed to pretty clearly meet the legal definition of abandoned property—that it was left in a given location intentionally by the owner, who did not plan to return and claim it—but after that, everything got fuzzy, as I learned when I contacted someone at the National Association of Unclaimed Property Administrators, who explained that the rules for dealing with something like a treasure chest would be so varied that there'd be no blanket answer, and it would all depend on jurisdiction among the federal, state, private, and tribal lands.

Tribal land, while plentiful in the Southwest, seemed like an unlikely place to hide a chest—you can't access tribal land without permission, and Fenn wouldn't want searchers routinely trespassing on Native American grounds and sites in the service of his treasure hunt, and getting arrested in the process. Same problem, though a different version, with private property. I didn't think Fenn wanted his hunters shot for searching in someone's backyard.

So that probably left the various types of public land as the best place to hide a chest, with any type of federal land being the trickiest to deal with. That would include the land set aside for national parks, national forests, Fish and Wildlife land, et cetera. In the East, very little land is claimed by federal authorities—but in the West, it's a different story. The federal government administers roughly 30 to 40 percent of the land located in Fenn's four search states, a huge percentage in comparison to anywhere east of the Rockies.

In 2015, **Earth** magazine ran a piece by Mary Caperton Morton, where she examined in detail what would happen if Fenn's chest was found on several major types of land—and talked directly to the agencies involved. The responses, predictably, varied.

The Bureau of Land Management, which administers much of the search area in northern New Mexico, would actually be pretty forgiving to anyone who found the chest, according to the piece. It quotes Allison Sandoval, a BLM representative in Santa Fe, as saying that in New Mexico, if the chest was on BLM land, they could take it—as long as it wasn't buried.

Fenn, of course, had consistently pushed back anytime some joker—myself included—mistakenly used the word **buried** instead of **hidden.** Maybe there was a specific reason for that—a legal reason that "buried" treasure would be a problem on BLM land but "hidden" treasure would not. In any event, BLM land seemed like a pretty good place for him to have hidden it.

Buried or not, however, Fenn hunters would have a problem if Fenn had put it on Forest Service land. The Forest Service is way less forgiving than the BLM, and if someone were to find the chest on Forest Service land and not report it, that would constitute theft of government property.

National park land turned out to be something of a middle ground. Yellowstone, of course, was the primary target of national park–trodding Fenn searchers. I got in touch with the rangers' office at Yellowstone, and learned that, basically, you can't damage or remove any natural features of that or any other national park, and you certainly can't dig. And if the chest was found in a park, it would need to be turned in, and then claimed through an abandoned-property process that could include ensuring the original owner, Fenn, did not want to retain the property.

It was enough to make one's head spin. Beep, ever the pragmatist, suggested the best option was just to take the chest to Fenn, and let him help out with what to do. When I got a chance to ask Fenn, however, he thought that was about as silly an idea as he'd ever heard. Why should someone bring it to him?

"I'm going to say, 'Congratulations. Now go home,'" Fenn had said. "You are under no obligation to bring it to me."

Instead, Fenn had advocated something I hadn't expected—quietly taking the chest back to one's house and sitting on it for thirty days.

When I asked him why he'd specified thirty days,

he launched into a well-thought-out monologue on the ramifications of finding and claiming a treasure chest, and how the various legal thickets surrounding the chest could make actually claiming it very difficult, and certainly costly.

"That's why I say wait thirty days, do nothing, but think about it," he continued.

"If it's on government land, you can end up with it, but you'll spend fifty thousand dollars on legal fees to get it, and then the IRS gets involved, so it's gonna cost you thirty thousand dollars to appraise it. Who's gonna pay for that? Oh, the IRS doesn't like your appraisal, then they'll challenge that, and we're talking about year after year, stretch that out. Everybody wants a piece of it."

There was another way, he suggested, in what I'll choose to take as a hypothetical.

"It would be really easy, if I found the treasure chest, it would be real easy for me to sell the gold coins. One or two at a time," Fenn said, going on to explain further, laying a road map for how one could, theoretically of course, liquidate the chest without having to deal with all those restrictions.

"There's two big gold nuggets in there this big," he said, marking a sizable gap with his hands. "You'd have trouble selling those, but you could do it. But then there are hundreds of other gold nuggets that you can sell in any rock shop or gun show or arrowhead show or any of those things. There's a couple little jade masks in there that are the most beautiful things. They're ancient Chinese, right? But no one has ever seen them. Oh, yeah, can't nobody say that they came out of that treasure chest. There's a couple of things in there that nobody has ever seen that are made out of gold and silver."

That would be the smart way. But realistically, he acknowledged, people weren't going to do that.

"So if you're, on the other hand, you're kind of an egomaniac, you want the notoriety," he said.

But even if you **are** that kind of egomaniac—and really, aren't we all?—you should think about it. Take that pause. Put the chest away for a bit.

"And so you put it under your bed and wait for thirty days."

Then he followed up with a seemingly necessary caveat, considering the plan he had just laid out.

"I would never tell you not to pay your taxes," he said quickly.

While we walked, I explained my findings to Cynthia, and she said that generally lined up with what she understood to be the case, and that Fenn had said the thirty-days thing—though not the rest of it—before in various interviews.

At this point, we were high up in the canyon, fighting through more and more underbrush, and beyond the mining camp, we weren't really feeling like we were getting anywhere for our efforts. We'd probably spent forty-five minutes venturing into the canyon itself, and I had no good clues at this point, no answer for what kind of blaze I should be looking for, no "water high," no nothing. We were essentially just out for a hike. Chagrined and a little embarrassed, I told Cynthia that I was fine with turning back, knowing that I'd wasted her time.

She didn't seem to mind at all.

"This is it; this is hunting. You think on something, you try it, you test it out," she said, chipper as always, her engineer's mind aware that the percentages of success on any search are disturbing low. "I can't tell you the number of times I've done just this. And I've gone hunting on worse solves than this, that's for darn sure."

It made me feel a little better, less guilty. We decided to stick close to the river all the way out of the canyon, both because it was a navigation point and because maybe it would show us something interesting. The descent back down the canyon was slow, gradual, neither of us wanting to twist an ankle or skitter down the slope. I continued to be amazed at Cynthia—she was agile, strong, quick. Half the time I had to be worried about keeping up with her.

She was just ahead of me, clambering down a rock, when she called out to come look at something.

"Here we've got a waterfall," she said. "I always like finding those."

That's not just because they're pretty, she explained. Waterfalls could be the key to the clue "water high." So any waterfall could be promising, could mean you were on the right track after all.

And this waterfall, in particular, was interesting. It was shallow, with a depression behind it, an open space where a person could crawl in if he needed to. The water wasn't coming down particularly hard, and it was perhaps a ten-foot drop from top to bottom in total.

Most intriguing of all? Cynthia thought she could see something in there.

I made my way down to where she was perched on a rock and craned my neck to see what she was pointing at.

Was something glinting there, behind the falling water? I couldn't tell. Maybe. Secreting away a chest behind falling water would certainly count as the chest being hidden but not buried. We hadn't found a blaze, or followed the instruction "Look quickly down, your quest to cease," but so what? There could be something in there, so logical progression of clues be damned.

"I'm going to try to get closer," I volunteered.

For a second, my heart rate picked up as I came close, and there **was** something to see in there, something shiny.

But it was a momentary thrill, hardly even enough to justify the shot of adrenaline. It was a rock. Another rock. A shiny rock, obscured and tantalizing and beautiful, hidden behind a waterfall out in a secluded canyon, but a rock nonetheless.

I reported back to Cynthia, we snapped a few pictures for posterity, and then we moved on, hiking down until we finally cleared the canyon and came out of the trees into daylight and the familiarly heavy brush of this side of the Red River. Now it was just a matter of fighting through all this scrub, climbing back over that tree, and getting to our car. Oh, and then driving hours to Santa Fe. Now that this whole thing was a bust, I just wanted to go home and shower off.

We were gabbing about where to stop on the way—there was a nice burger place in Taos—when Cynthia, leading us through the high, thick brush, put her hand up to halt me. She was staring down at the ground.

I came up behind her and turned my gaze down to where she was looking. In front of us sat a pile of animal dung. Cynthia examined it closely, poking at it.

"That's bear scat. It's real fresh," she said, suddenly alert.

"Its home must be close, maybe through there," she said as she pointed at a thicket near the cliff wall. "I should have brought my gun."

I suddenly realized this was called Bear Canyon for a reason.

I was not a big-enough idiot to think that nature wasn't dangerous, or that we should feel at home out in the wilderness. But I was unfamiliar enough with it—with the nature of the West, at least, the real nature—to have never really felt it as a direct and immediate threat before. On the East

Coast, I'd seen a snake or two out on hikes, but the chances of those being really dangerous were pretty remote. And the occasional coyote I might have seen out in the woods would be more afraid of me than I was of it.

Out here, however? Different story. Just seeing Cynthia suddenly tense was all the reason I needed to be wary, nervous. We were in this brush, with so little visibility around us—the river couldn't be far away, but we had no easy means to get to it. And I didn't think we were exactly where we'd come in— we seemed to be a little ways down, in an unfamiliar area. This was the problem with going where there were so few trails. Should have left some bread crumbs, Hansel and Gretel–style.

"We should talk loudly. There's something about having our voices high and clear that can help keep them away," Cynthia told me.

"So talk about anything. Doesn't matter what. How's Elliott doing?" she said, asking about my four-month-old son.

That was an easy one, fortunately. The kid was so damn cute, I could talk about him all day. Blather on about my kid at high volume? I was a natural for this assignment.

"He's still mostly a little spud," I said, my voice now loud and clear. I was half shouting, half speaking a foreign language. "But he's started to move around a little. The doctors tell you to do this thing called 'tummy time,' where you put them facedown on a towel or something else soft, and they try to pick up their heads. It's good for the neck muscles. And he just loves it! Every time he half-lifts his little head up and moves it around, I'm convinced he's gonna be an Olympic Greco-Roman wrestler."

I felt as if I were Austin Powers, having trouble controlling THE VOLUME OF MY VOICE. But I guess that was the idea. And if I was talking about Elliott, then at least I wasn't thinking about the bear that was about to eat us. We pushed on through the brambles, thick as heck, and I could feel them tear at my sweatshirt and nick at my jeans. We definitely hadn't come in this way, but we couldn't double back now. We just had to push on until we reached the river.

"But the most amazing thing, he rolled over when he was just over a month old," I said, ever the proud papa bear. I mean, proud lion! No bear talk!

"That's something they're not supposed to do until they're like five months old. And he did it at a month. We didn't even have to prompt him; he just kinda did it one day. And at first we thought it was an accident, and then he did it again. So maybe wrestler, maybe gymnast. But very agile. Which is good, because he's tiny. So even if he's small, he can still be a Leo Messi–style soccer player, all quick and mobile."

I had no idea if Cynthia was listening to a word I was saying, but it didn't matter—about eight feet ahead of me, she pushed out through the brush, and we emerged into the clearing near the river, at last. In front of us was the tree trunk we'd climbed in on. Behind us—well, I didn't want to look.

I rubbed my palms along my jeans, trying to dry them off. I was sweaty. So, so sweaty. The thick kind of fear sweat. I hadn't noticed until then. We moved quickly over to the log, and Cynthia started to climb across. I finally looked back, just to make sure there was nothing there, half expecting to see something I really didn't want to see.

But no. There was nothing there. Cynthia was almost all the way across now, and so I tightened the straps on my pack and started to move across the log myself. It was easier this time, whether because of adrenaline or familiarity with it. Didn't much matter which to me. I was just happy when I got to the other side and could exhale at last. I plopped down on the dirt near the tree trunk, letting the tension drain out of me.

Cynthia seemed to slow down and take stock for a moment as well, then issued a chuckle.

"At least we didn't get mauled by a bear," she said. "I was pretty sure we were going to for a while there."

With a brief "Okay, then," she started off toward our car, maybe thirty feet away. I told her I'd be along in a moment, and sat on the near side of the river, tired, spent, having found nothing.

Our drive back home would have been a long one under normal circumstances, about three hours from Taos down through the hills and plains of New Mexico and back into Santa Fe. It got even longer when we hit the worst traffic either Cynthia or I had ever seen, a combination of construction and accidents creating a highway-closing disaster that more than doubled the time of our trip. With all those hours in the car that day, we talked about many, many things, and then nothing, and then other things again. We talked about the treasure, about her past, my past, the landscape, the traffic, whatever.

But one conversation, one short period, stood out. We talked, briefly, obliquely, about something else—something that Fenn searchers mostly all knew at least the basics of but that wasn't considered polite conversation. Something that wasn't mentioned often for various reasons—because searchers felt strongly one way or another about it, didn't know what to think about it, or just didn't want to think about it at all.

The wars on the Fenn blogs, and the accusations against Forrest Fenn.

9

THE BLOGS, AND WHAT THEY SAID ABOUT FORREST FENN

There's a certain irony to the fact that a pursuit created to get people outside and into the wilderness mostly resulted in their spending countless hours hunkered down over a computer screen. But with a few rare exceptions, that was the reality of life for most Fenn hunters, who spent far, far more time researching and discussing the treasure online than they spent out searching for it.

And for many of them, when they were online, they were on the Fenn blogs.

Blog culture was dominant in Fenn's world, providing a place for searchers to study, to learn, to interact, to obsess, and, yes, to quarrel. Accusations about all manner of bad behavior took place on the blogs, with searchers hammering one another and often targeting Fenn himself. For years, Fenn was an integral part of the blog culture, releasing regular "scrapbooks" on Dal's blog to provide additional meat for his searchers to chew on. Sometimes he'd release a video interview, as well. When he would need to make an announcement about the search—a new safety measure, or a clarification about smart searching—he'd do it through one of the blogs, usually Dal's or Jenny Kile's Mysterious Writings. Sometimes he would even respond to comments on a particular story or scrapbook. But as the years went on and the blogs became more and more chaotic, Fenn pulled back entirely, rarely if ever actively participating anymore. It is clear, however, that he either still read them or had someone tell him what was happening on them, as he sometimes engaged with their managers when he saw or was told about something he didn't like.

The Fenn blogosphere was born toward the end of 2011, when Dal first created his site. At that time, the hunt had been under way for about a year, but there was no place for searchers to talk, to gather. Desertphile had posted a few videos of himself searching on YouTube, but otherwise the Fenn world had minimal online presence.

So Dal put together his rudimentary site, offering up some basic information about the chase, a couple of search stories, some interviews with Fenn, a few tips and places to discuss the treasure. The searchers began to trickle in.

"I don't know how the word spread, but it didn't

take long for me to have, say, thirty to forty regular commentators on the blog," Dal said. "People would send me stories and pictures, and I would post them, and it was starting to become a more complicated, complete place.

"But I'm not skilled—the blog was, it was like I had taken a bunch of stories and thrown them into a box. It was just a mess. The only person who could find anything was me, and I couldn't find anything, either. And people were complaining. My excuse was that this was all I knew how to do."

As it began to grow in size and scope, he got help, and the site took on a more professional quality. More visitors arrived, looking for an entrée into the world of Fenn after hearing about it on a local news story or via an internet link. Dal's site offered that, getting searchers started and answering their basic questions. It also became something of a meetinghouse for the growing community. Even if there were only a few thousand real searchers at that time, most of them had at least some connection to the blog, and many were frequent posters.

But, of course, with any enterprise come naysayers, negativity. As the site grew—and especially after Fenn's **Today** show appearance brought thousands of new users flooding in during 2013—the tone of the interactions on it changed. It became less of a family and more of a town meeting, with all the good and bad that such a situation entails. Searchers would challenge one another more, fight with one another more, make accusations, call one another names, all of them sure that they had the best chance of finding the all-important box and unwilling to tolerate anything that got in their way.

Dal would try to police some of the angry talk.

"I don't want that stuff on the blog," he said. "And then, of course, the first reaction is that I'm taking away their freedom of speech. And they forget that I'm the one that pays for the blog and all that. And you're not.

"There's that kind of thing. There's people who just go bozo—they start out normal and then for whatever reason they go on a rant, calling people ridiculous names, fuck this, screw you. I don't need that. The easiest thing to do is just ban them. Thank God WordPress gives me that option."

For a time, there was effectively nowhere else for searchers to go if Dal cut them off. Then Stephanie Thirtyacre founded ChaseChat.

Stephanie first learned of the hunt's existence in 2012, sitting in a hotel room in Michigan, randomly thinking about whether she could start her own treasure hunt for the fun of it. She googled what hunts already existed, and came upon Fenn's first interview on PBS. Not long after, she contacted Fenn, and the two began corresponding regularly as the Illinois-based Stephanie almost immediately became a dedicated, obsessed Fenn hunter. She was soon making numerous trips out west to test her theories, searching up and down the Rockies in pursuit of Fenn's treasure, and fast becoming well known within the community as a mostly friendly rival to Dal.

"It was competitive," Dal said. "It was, Dal or Stephanie, who's going to find this thing first? We had a good time."

For years, many believed Stephanie to be the famed two-hundred-foot searcher, the one who got so close but didn't quite reach the treasure. Many had tried to retrace her steps, and her early hunts, in the hopes of bringing her potential near misses to fruition. She had searched far and wide, willing to go to places other hunters wouldn't in search of the treasure, almost breaking into the Taos airport, for instance, when she believed it might hold the key (she ultimately was persuaded not to, thanks largely to Fenn's intervention). Her fixation with all things Fenn didn't stop there, though. She also wrote a five-hundred-page book dedicated to proving that Fenn, or his brother, was actually the daring aerial robber D. B. Cooper, who hijacked a Northwest Orient Airlines flight in 1971, extorted $200,000 in cash from the company, and then parachuted out the back somewhere over Washington State, never to be seen again. (I've read it—honestly, it's not quite as ridiculous as you would think a book alleging D. B. Cooper was Fenn would be.) She would eventually spend well into six figures on fruitless searches, go bankrupt, and see her marriage crumble as a direct result of her involvement in the chase, and many other hunters held her up to me as an example of how this chase could cause some to go a little too far.

In the early days of 2012, though, she was just another starry-eyed searcher, thrilled to be in touch with Fenn, the two becoming close while discussing the treasure and more via Facebook Messenger.

It was actually Fenn who sent Stephanie down the road to creating ChaseChat. The frequent hunting trips had begun to strain Stephanie's finances; she wanted to continue searching but needed new sources of income. Fenn suggested that she create an app of some sort to try to make money from the search. She did, though initially it didn't amount to much.

But around the same time, Dal was becoming more and more fed up with the tone of the interactions on his blog, and he cut off public messaging on his site. Stephanie saw an opportunity, and she turned ChaseChat into an online forum, hoping to draw in users, and, through them, clicks and ad revenue.

It took off—and did so with a user base populated by many of those jettisoned from Dal's blog. It was a Botany Bay colony of disgruntled Fenn searchers, bitter at Dal for kicking them off, happy to be able to say largely whatever they wanted on Stephanie's site. Dal watched with something between amusement and displeasure.

"Most of the folks we banned are over on

ChaseChat," Dal said. "ChaseChat doesn't usually ban anybody. You can say whatever you want on ChaseChat."

For years, there was a genuine rivalry there, with many searchers staunchly loyal to one site or the other, believing that the rival represented all that was wrong with the chase. Eventually, newer blogs sprang up—Tarry Scant, The Hint of Riches, Harry's Chase forum, a few others. There was some treasure talk, and often more talk about the personalities of the search, much of it veering between catty and outright nasty. The tone of Fenn-related discourse online was not, much of the time, a healthy one.

Yet the blog community could come together for moments of caring and beauty from time to time, unifying to aid another searcher in need. There were the blog-organized efforts to find Randy Bilyeu, but also efforts to help other searchers whose problems were not related to the chase itself.

Take the case of Renelle Jacobson. Jacobson learned about the chase as many others did, in **Hemispheres** magazine around 2013. But she wasn't like so many other searchers: Jacobson, forty-two in 2014, had osteosarcoma, a rare bone cancer. In 2011, her left leg was amputated above the knee. But even with her physical limitations, she became obsessed with the chase and resolved to get out into the wild and start searching.

"I was bouncing off the walls with an overload

of excitement. This adventure is for every little girl and boy who have desperately wanted to look for a hidden treasure. I know I'm silly, but some of us are lucky enough to never completely grow up," Fenn says she told him in one of the stories relayed in his third memoir, **Once Upon a While.**

Jacobson soon became well known inside the chase, and when she needed help with her mounting medical bills, the blog community sprang into action. It organized a raffle and promoted it across the various blogs, the prize a Fenn-crafted bronze jar filled with items from his collection. The raffle ultimately raised $28,000, with Fenn donating $5,000 himself.

Before she passed away in August 2014, Jacobson wrote a note to the Fenn online community, floored by its generosity toward her.

"Many of you promoted the raffle on your respective blogs, and I want to thank you for all your work on my behalf. It would be logical to assume that so many searchers looking for a single prize would be ultra-competitive with each other!" she wrote. "That may be, but you are also community-minded and came together to pull off an event that was successful beyond anyone's imagination. You all have my respect, my admiration, and most of all, my thanks."

Then there was the case of Jamie and Bill Jourdan, Fenn hunters since 2014, who lost their home and their business to California's Mendocino wildfires in 2018. Jamie Jourdan was a regular forum presence, and when she disappeared for a week during the fires, others took notice. When she returned and explained what had happened, the community jumped into action, helping to organize a fund-raiser involving Fenn, where search-related memorabilia would be auctioned off, on top of direct donations to the Jourdans. The event, held in Santa Fe at the Collected Works Bookstore, was a huge success, raising almost sixty thousand dollars, and serves as a real marker of what the Fenn community can be and do at its best.

It was not always that, however.

And since roughly 2015, the Fenn blogsphere had been roiled by one specific online controversy that shook the entire community to its very core, prompting hundreds upon hundreds of threads across the various blogs and sites, and creating rifts and drama that persist to this day.

It started when Stephanie publicly alleged on ChaseChat that Fenn was actively pursuing sexual relationships with women in the chase; that he was asking them for naked pictures, and meeting them at hotels for sexual acts, with the women sometimes believing they might get clues out of the bargain. She said that she had experienced this firsthand, and also that she knew of other women who had had similar experiences.

Unsurprisingly, it created a firestorm.

I had heard about Stephanie's allegations from

Dal the first time we spoke, the first time I'd ever had a conversation with anyone about the chase. He had volunteered them, and then laughed them off because of Fenn's age, making it clear he did not take them seriously. Not knowing or understanding the situation, I had quickly moved past it, not thinking much about it for some time because I rarely delved into the discussions on the message boards myself, especially early on. But on the blogs, talk about this subject was ever-present over a five-year period, and it was hard to spend much time on the non-Dal blogs without running into it at some point. Eventually, I saw and heard enough references to the allegations that I felt it important to look into it in a more serious fashion. Most of the original threads have been taken down by now—ChaseChat seemingly did a significant purge in the past few years, which Stephanie says was due to a server move—but I saw many before they were removed, and also reconstructed the basic chain of events through interviews, reviews of old web pages and threads, and access to screenshots taken by those who witnessed these events at the time.

From the start, Stephanie was attacked for what she said. Most said they did not believe her. Others, even if they seemed open to the possibility that these encounters had occurred, questioned who had initiated them, accusing Stephanie of attempting to manipulate or blackmail Fenn in efforts to find the treasure. It was ugly all around, and it did not go away quickly.

That's where Mindy—of Mindy and James, the couple who got engaged before Fennboree— came in.

Mindy Fausey is a polarizing figure in the chase community, perhaps even more so than Stephanie. She grew up on Florida's Space Coast, where, she said, she watched the **Challenger** disaster from her backyard. After attending the University of Maryland, she joined the air force, eventually rising to the rank of lieutenant. She left the military when she was pregnant in 2000, and became an X-ray tech, which she remains today, living in Florida.

When I'd first encountered Mindy and James at Fennboree, she seemed pleasant enough, though a little distant—she openly admits that she is on the autism spectrum, diagnosed with Asperger's syndrome, and can have a hard time in social situations and with reading the proper cues. She also claims some interesting lineage—saying she is descended from the famed (and potentially apocryphal) Viking Ragnar Lothbrok through his son, Ivar the Boneless.

Mindy got into the chase around 2013, like so many others. An engaging writer, she rose to prominence in the chase after posting a long piece on Dal's blog about her first search trip out to Colorado: "A Florida Girl Heads West."

"That's when Forrest reached out to me and asked

me to contact him," Mindy said. "And that's when the world turned upside down from there."

Once Stephanie had made her allegations about Fenn, and seemingly the whole of the Fenn blogosphere had begun to shout her down, Mindy came to Stephanie's defense. She posted a message saying that she, too, had conducted an extended email correspondence with Fenn and that what began innocently had taken a turn quickly, with Fenn aggressively asking her for naked pictures, and for her to come to Santa Fe to engage in sexual activity with him.

"People should know what's going on behind the scenes," she said about why she posted her allegations. "He is asking females for naked pictures. He is asking females to meet him at hotels. Stephanie had already said this, and people were going after Stephanie. And I couldn't take that—I said, you know what, everything Stephanie said is true. I've seen it. I've experienced it. And all of a sudden they shifted their hate to me."

To back her claims, Mindy posted some of her email exchanges with Fenn from the end of 2014 to the beginning of 2015. They started off routinely, with Mindy first telling Fenn a bit about herself, and offering some non-hunt-related thoughts on some of the more personal passages in **The Thrill of the Chase.** Fenn would respond in kind, and over those first few days in November 2014, they traded emails almost hourly. Mindy posted most of these online in 2015, and shared them again with me more recently in an effort to offer a better sense of their interactions.

From these, it's clear that Mindy was starstruck, overjoyed to be communicating with Fenn, and seemingly connecting with him. They talked about children, about her ambitions, about his past, about her poetry. Throughout, Fenn was always complimentary about her appearance, and decidedly playful.

After a few weeks, Fenn asked that nothing they talked about go beyond them—then they could "come close and be personal." At that point, the emails show Fenn actively turning the conversation in a more sexual direction, layering in innuendos, comments, and questions about her sex life, and repeated requests for her to send him more revealing photos.

Mindy was certainly, as she acknowledged to me, "flirty" in her responses, but she made clear attempts to steer the conversation away from the overtly sexual and back to either general talk about the hunt or about their lives. Not long after, Mindy caved, she said, and sent Fenn a picture of herself in a bikini. Fenn seemed to be emboldened, and in a December 26 email, he became more specific, asking, "If I were there, would you make love with me?" She refused but continued the correspondence.

On New Year's Eve of 2014, they began talking about the coming year, and Fenn said he expected "a really good one, with the promise that you will make love to me when you come here."

Finally, Mindy shut him down, saying that wasn't possible, that wasn't something that was going to happen. At that point, she said, Fenn rescinded the invitation to come see him in Santa Fe.

"He had been insinuating that he didn't want me to bring the kids, and when I finally said no, that that would not happen when I went to visit him, he said, 'Oh—Peggy's sick,'" she said. "I found out later he gives that excuse to a lot of people."

Fenn and Mindy's relationship appeared to chill somewhat from there, though they continued to trade emails periodically for some time. When Stephanie made her public claims against Fenn, and was subsequently vilified and disbelieved, Mindy joined in with a less detailed version of the above tale to say that she believed Stephanie's stories, providing a level of proof to back up both their claims.

Mindy said it was important to share what was going on with the hunting public, because in her mind, Fenn's alleged actions with women involved in the search compromised the chase, destroying the idea of a level playing field.

"I mean, he's a grown man; they're grown adults. It's not that they're hurting their families or whatever," she said. "My whole thing is that this man hid a treasure chest, and is professing to be this hero, this good guy, this man who loves and cherishes his wife and family, but he's doing this with females who are searching for his treasure. In every good thriller, there are female spies who can get information out of any man in that way. So it compromises the chase. It compromises everyone else's chances of finding it."

At this point, with the allegations out there and widely discussed, the Fenn community seemed to divide into a few major camps. There were those who said they believed the women, and believed this compromised or corrupted the chase. Others indicated that they believed the women, but either didn't think it mattered at all to the treasure hunt or dismissed the alleged incidents as unimportant, saying that Fenn's behavior was a case of "boys will be boys," and that certainly in the case of Mindy's emails, there was no actual sexual contact, so really no harm done. Many others didn't cast judgment and said they just wanted to move on with their searching, their greatest concern being that maybe Fenn **had** given out a few hints to these women that the general population didn't get.

And there were those, a great many, who said this was all made up, a ploy by several frustrated, angry women to gain attention and just maybe force Fenn to give them the chest or clues to reach it. They said that Stephanie was lying, that Mindy's emails were doctored or fabricated, and that the whole thing was fake news. (Accurate figures on the prevalence of false claims of sexual misconduct or harassment are difficult to ascertain, but experts say such claims are believed to be rare, akin to their low incidence in sexual violence cases. According to the National Sexual Violence Resource Center, false claims of sexual violence do exist, but the rate is very low, under 10 percent, and as low as 2 percent depending on the type of incident. That obviously drops even lower when there are multiple accusers.) The tone of the dialogue was perpetually vicious. Mindy claims there were threats, many of them.

"It's really grown into this cult, where you can't say anything bad about Forrest, or you will suffer," Mindy said.

Stephanie and Mindy defended themselves in what became a long, protracted battle conducted over many years and many threads, and across many different blogs. The ongoing war led directly to the growth of some of the smaller blogs; ChaseChat was Stephanie's site, and Mindy later became a moderator there, which eventually gave her significant power. When they would get in arguments with detractors, often the opponents would end up banned from ChaseChat, and they would congregate at another site; Harry's Chase forum, in particular, was a hotbed of anti-ChaseChat sentiment, populated by many who had long feuded with the ChaseChat crew over their allegations.

Occasionally, someone would rise to the women's defense, or say they had witnessed or experienced something similar with Fenn. Often these other accounts were written off by doubters as being Mindy or Stephanie posing as someone else in order to falsely buttress their own arguments. Mindy insists that was not the case, and that she has spoken to other women who privately allege much of the same behavior from Fenn but who are afraid to come forward lest they receive the same response Mindy and Stephanie did.

"I've talked to them on the phone; I've seen the emails. They're not aliases; they're all real," Mindy said. "They just figure, you know, hey, I could lose my family. I could get death threats. They see what's happened to me. They don't want that to happen to them."

The boards even developed a name for women who claimed that they had knowledge of Fenn's intimate dealings or who the posters believed had tried to seduce him to gain clues—calling them "Bunnies," and applying it liberally.

Even as all this shook the message boards, Fenn did not engage or acknowledge any of the controversy publicly. Mindy said, however, that she, Stephanie, and a third woman who was involved had a correspondence with him, and that they demanded an apology from him. According to Mindy, he wrote an apology to all three women in late November 2015—which she shared with me—and as a result, Mindy said, she acceded to his requests to remove some of the emails she had publicly posted.

Regardless, the issue didn't seem likely to go away anytime soon—until something even bigger took the searchers' attention. Mindy had posted her emails in November 2015, leading to months of drama. Then in January 2016, when Randy Bilyeu went missing, the boards unified in an effort to locate him, and all of this faded into the background.

There it would mostly remain for years, a bit of static always audible just behind the loud chatter of treasure talk. Mindy, in particular, continued to wage war with her detractors across the various blogs, and from time to time, an incident or issue would arise that would bring the whole subject into the foreground again.

Around the same time that the #MeToo movement exploded into the national consciousness in 2017, the topic lit the boards up anew. Fenn's alleged behavior—a powerful man, aggressively using his position to solicit sexual favors and materials—had much in common with the kinds of things that were suddenly grabbing headlines every day, the kinds of things that powerful men in other industries were being toppled for.

In addition, Mindy says she learned that Fenn was allegedly still engaging in similar activities with other women, prompting her to speak up again. While, at the same time, there was suddenly a national focus on issues of sexual power, Mindy tried to gain media attention for the controversy inside the treasure hunt, tweeting at numerous media outlets and prominent legal minds that she was part of a #MeToo story and that they should get in touch with her to talk about it. This January 2018 tweet, sent to the attorney Gloria Allred, prominent in representing those in #MeToo cases, was typical of the messages: "I'm standing with a few other women against a powerful celebrity who's used/coercively controlled women to fulfill his sexual fantasies. He has a cult following. I get death threats for standing against him. He's convincing some to ruin my reputation. Help."

It did not receive a reply.

Even as all this played out over years, the celebrity hunters mostly did their best to ignore the situation; Dal wielded his banning powers to keep this kind of talk off his blog, and the others rarely engaged with it, though Sacha Johnston would occasionally get into the mix. Cynthia Meachum mostly stayed out of it, but in early 2018, after yet another conflagration, she felt the need to weigh in on the matter on her own blog, in a post she cryptically called "Battle of the B's."

Cynthia made it quite clear that she had little time for the endless wars over Fenn's alleged misdeeds on the blogs, particularly decrying Mindy and the emails she posted.

"Mindy comes along and posts (on ChaseChat) her pathetic, clueless and totally useless private emails from ff," Cynthia wrote, calling Mindy's disclosures "insipid pieces of fecal matter she has shared with us lucky searchers."

Later on, Cynthia told me that it wasn't necessarily that she didn't believe the women; it was that she just didn't care what Fenn had said or written or done—he was an adult, any women allegedly involved were adults, and none of it, in her mind, directly impacted the chase, so to her, it was none of her business.

"I just don't give a shit," she said. "If Forrest had sex with a hundred different searchers, I don't give a shit. I mean, whatever. I don't, I just don't."

As all this dragged on for years, Fenn remained careful about never acknowledging the situation publicly. But privately, we discussed Stephanie and Mindy and the things they said about him, which he said were untrue.

It was clear that he held an affection for Stephanie still, despite all that had happened. He chalked it all up to her being a little too obsessed with the hunt, and the pressures it put on her causing her to "become upset," and do and say the wrong things.

"I think she's okay," Fenn said. "I think basically she's a good human being—she would just become upset. She mortgaged her house. Yeah, lost her husband and everything with it.

"Stephanie is okay. She's grown to hate me since she stopped searching for the treasure. It's my fault that she didn't find the treasure, because I said six years ago that she should have found it by now." Fenn sighed, adding that he had "said that to five hundred people."

"My saying that was carte blanche for her to have a free ticket to the treasure. So it's my fault that she hasn't found it; she thinks she should have."

Mindy, on the other hand, he clearly held in a different regard.

"Don't interview her about me," he hissed. When I said I had talked to her, he went on about how she was not to be believed, and repeatedly pointed out the fact that she had been diagnosed with Asperger's.

"Mindy is not a good human being," Fenn said. "But it may be a medical problem."

At this point, Mindy felt about the same regarding Fenn's status as a good human being. Still, despite all this, all involved made efforts to get along. Stephanie went to Fennboree in 2017, and to a Fenn book signing. Mindy and her fiancé, James, went to Fenn's house a few days before that same Fennboree, sitting with him alongside other searchers. At that juncture, I knew virtually none of this history and backstory and chaos, and would never have guessed at any of it from the way they all spoke politely with one another.

In public, it seemed, it was all just swept under the rug, perhaps for the sake of keeping the chase community strong. And maybe some people didn't know what to think, didn't know what to believe. But I had seen enough email exchanges, and talked to enough people with both primary and second-hand knowledge of these situations—people well beyond just Stephanie and Mindy—that I was pretty sure how I felt about it.

That forced a difficult balancing act. I was here for Fenn's hunt, not for Fenn. But is it truly possible to separate the two? The right thing to do, knowing what I did, is probably to admit that Fenn is Fenn's hunt. The entire exercise is built around him. Compartmentalizing it is nothing more than a rationalization. And maybe a cowardly one.

Still, that's what everyone else seemed to be doing. Stephanie, Mindy, and other women who relayed similar stories were still part of the hunt, and of the community. How did they reconcile what they knew with their continued participation?

I asked Mindy that, and she said I wasn't the first to wonder. Her reasoning for staying in it? She thought that maybe, if she found it, that would mean she'd won.

"People ask me, 'If you think Forrest is such a creep, why would you still go out and search for his treasure?'" she said. "But the truth is, it's a lot of time, and thought, and effort invested in it. I have put a lot of hours into trying to solve the poem. And I feel like if I found it, it would give me some kind of satisfaction, that I beat that guy in the end."

She chuckled.

"Of all the people who he would want to find it, I'd think I'm pretty low on that list. I used to be pretty high on that list. Now I'm real, real low."

10

A FAMOUS FAMILY, A FABULOUS TREASURE

"So, this is actually the oldest elevator in all of Florida," Megan McDowell told me as the ancient device ground its way toward the upper floors of Mel Fisher's treasure-hunting complex in Key West, the headquarters of the most famous family of treasure hunters in the world, the family who had found the lost galleon **Atocha** and its half-billion-dollar hoard.

I guess I shouldn't have been surprised about the elevator. In Key West, everything has a tourist-friendly sign on it, and most of them find some way to trumpet that they're the oldest this in town, the oldest that in the state of Florida. On the way over here, I'd passed the "Oldest Bar in Florida" (Capt. Tony's Saloon), the "Oldest Church in South Florida" (St. Paul's Episcopal), the "Oldest House in Key West," and then finally the "Oldest Schoolhouse in Key West." These people take their history seriously down here, and they sell it hard.

The Oldest Elevator in Florida™ got us to the third floor safely, albeit a little slowly, and Megan stepped out ahead of me to lead the way to the office of her boss, Kim Fisher. The first and second floors of this building—an 1800s U.S. Navy warehouse, probably the oldest on this block or in this time zone, or something—are mostly taken up by the Mel Fisher Maritime Heritage Museum and Mel Fisher's Treasures, the late treasure hunter's outlet for selling gold and silver pieces to the public. But the third floor of the old warehouse is the headquarters of Treasure Salvors, Inc., perhaps the world's most famous treasure-hunting company.

Walking through, it struck me that a treasure-hunting headquarters isn't that different from any other company's offices—there's just a lot more gold and silver lying around. We passed a solid-silver bust of the late family patriarch, Mel Fisher, and framed gold pieces adorning the walls. There were silver bars on tables, and historic weapons and artifacts at seemingly every turn.

As I rounded the corner into Kim Fisher's office, the CEO of Treasure Salvors rose to greet me. The Fishers are famously tall, and Kim is certainly no exception—Mel was six five, and Kim seemed to be somewhere around that height, though age and wear had stooped him somewhat. Mel Fisher died in 1998, but long before that, Kim had begun to take over the operations of Treasure Salvors. One of the three sons of Mel and Deo Fisher, Kim was the studious one. While brothers Dirk and Kane plied the waves in search of treasure, Kim went off to college and then law school, hoping that, in between treasure dives, he could help his family fight the seemingly endless legal battles with the government and others over the jurisdictions and ownership of their finds.

Once they had achieved their greatest successes, Kim settled in to run the business as his father aged, shepherding it into its next phase, gradually bringing up treasure from their older finds and setting out in search of new ventures. But even as he plays the Michael Corleone role as the responsible son, Kim is also a true veteran of hundreds upon hundreds of searches, the former captain of the treasure-hunting vessel **Southwind,** and one of the most famous treasure hunters alive today. On a chain around his neck rested a Spanish gold coin about the size of a Communion wafer, glinting in the light, a constant reminder of exactly who he is and what he does.

Fisher welcomed me with a smile and a friendly greeting, then sat down at a desk that seemed normal enough, save for the enormous silver bar acting as a paperweight of sorts in the corner. A smiling portrait of Mel hung on the wall.

"So you're doing something about that guy in the

Southwest, the one with the treasure chest?" Kim Fisher asked me.

"That's right," I told him. I explained the tale of Fenn in detail, and how—after shadowing amateurs for so long, and feeling the discouragement of wandering aimlessly and finding absolutely nothing—I was looking to see how a real treasure hunter does it, and how a modern treasure-hunting company operates today.

But first I wanted to get his thoughts on Fenn, his chase, all of it. Kim Fisher has spent his entire life treasure hunting, finding his first silver coin when he was nine years old, searching alongside his dad on land and sea for the most famous treasures in history. Did he consider the Fenn searchers to be real treasure hunters like he is?

Fisher smiled broadly.

"Sure they are," he said. "People walking down the beach with a metal detector, finding stuff that tourists drop, rings and gold coins—to me, they're all treasure hunters, absolutely."

He leaned his large frame back against his office chair. He doesn't go out on many actual hunts anymore—at sixty-three, he is more the administrator now, less the digger. But something about talking treasure brought out the little boy in him.

"It's the search," Fisher said. "Once you've seen one hole with treasure in it, you're never the same. You always think that next hole you dig, it'll be the one."

And the Fenn hunters? I asked again. Even though they were searching for a man-made treasure, a manufactured hunt, did he think it all came from the same place?

"For these guys, they're out there looking for this treasure, swinging a metal detector, and they think it's right over this next hill. And they believe that. And you do." Fisher smiled and paused, seemingly lost in his own memories for a moment.

"Oh man, I'm getting goose bumps just talking about it." He grinned. "It's the thrill of that search, the anticipation about what you're going to find."

The thrill of the search—sounds familiar, I thought. Maybe Fisher should go out looking for Fenn's treasure, I joked.

Fisher chuckled at that. He had enough on his plate right now, he said. Besides, once you've been to the top of the treasure-hunting world, and made perhaps the greatest find of all time, everything else is a letdown. But in those goose bumps, in the way his eyes lit up, I could see that the treasure-hunting bug never really leaves a hunter—especially one like Kim Fisher, who can hardly remember a time when he wasn't hunting, watching his father, Mel, and fellow pioneers like Kip Wagner become the most famous modern treasure hunters in the world.

Without Kip Wagner, it's possible no one would have ever heard of Mel Fisher. Wagner grew up in landlocked Ohio, far from the sandy shores of Florida. But as a child, he'd visit the Sunshine State on family vacations, and he fell in love with its waters and its beaches. Not long after World War II, he moved his family to Florida's east coast, settling near Vero Beach.

Wagner, a contractor, made friends with the locals, and they told him that sometimes Spanish silver coins would wash up on the beaches, the result of shipwrecks hundreds of years ago. Most were said to come from one great treasure fleet, destroyed in a mammoth hurricane somewhere off Cape Canaveral in 1715. Eleven of the twelve galleons were lost, wrecked at sea or slammed upon reefs or the beach itself. At the time, the Spanish salvaged what they could of the treasure, but well more than half was said to remain under the sea. In the 250 years since, no one had claimed the vast haul, and over time, even the general location of the wrecked fleet had been lost to history.

One day after a storm in the late 1950s, Wagner was walking the beach when he came upon a silver coin. He cleaned it off and saw a date: 1714. He realized that if a coin of that vintage could wash up here, the wrecked fleet must be somewhere nearby. He partnered with a treasure-hunting aficionado, Dr. Kip Kelso, and the two began researching the Spanish salvage efforts from the 1700s, reasoning that if they could find the camp the Spanish had set up to manage the recovery, it might lead them to the treasure. They began by looking through historical records, and at the Library of Congress, they struck document gold: a 1775 almanac listing the rough location of salvage efforts on the wrecked fleet. From there, they contacted Spain's national archives and, translating archaic Spanish, found a specific reference to the site of the Spanish camp. The salvage efforts had lasted four years, and while the Spanish worked, they had to fend off attacks from pirates, British privateers, and other fortune seekers intent on recovering some of the fleet's haul for themselves. Their camp had been a fortified site, significant enough that remnants should still be buried somewhere under the sand, waiting for Wagner and Kelso to zero in on them.

Technology had come a long way since the early 1700s, and improvements to search and salvage methods in World War II gave Wagner options unlike any available to those who had searched for this fleet before. Even a rudimentary metal detector gave him a huge leg up, so, accompanied by an old hound, Wagner began combing the beaches in search of the campsite. After months of searching, his metal detector lit up, and he dug to find the remains of the camp on a sandy bluff above the beach.

Now that he knew that location, he scouted the seas directly beyond the camp, first diving in the area, then eventually hiring a plane and flying over the water, seeking dark spots that might hide a ship. He found several, and, believing he had found the fleet, he managed to lease out a fifty-mile area of the coast from the state of Florida for salvage operations. He was finally ready to hit the search locations—but Wagner was coming up against his own limitations. He was a contractor, not an explorer or a salvage expert. He realized he needed help.

Wagner and Kelso began seeking out people with special talents, building a team of engineers, expert divers, and boatsmen familiar with the local waters. Each of the eight team members had a role to play, and the group quickly jelled to become more than the sum of its parts. They believed they were on a grand adventure, and even gave themselves a name, one that would go down in treasure-hunting lore: the Real Eight Company, named for the Spanish reales, the empire's coins. The group leased and converted an old Liberty ship into a rudimentary treasure-hunting vessel, naming it the **Sampan,** and began diving at the purported wreck sites.

Almost immediately, they found signs of the lost ships, including hunks of coins fused together with rust, and over the next few years, they would gradually bring up small amounts in coins, bars, and jewelry from the scattered wrecks of the 1715 fleet.

But Wagner and his group still hadn't found the main cache. They knew they were close, but they needed help.

That arrived in the form of Mel Fisher.

Fisher was a complicated figure. Born in Indiana, he attended Purdue University before joining the U.S. Army in World War II, serving in the Army Corps of Engineers in Europe. Afterward, he cast about, veering from farming to music to scuba diving and salvage. He met his wife, Deo, and the two formed a lifelong partnership, learning scuba and salvage basics from their home in Redondo Beach, California, and then founding the state's first dive shop to teach the emerging discipline to others. Yet Mel remained restless; he still didn't know what he wanted to do with his life. But he'd grown up reading **Treasure Island,** thumbed through a few other books on real lost treasure, and when he heard about what Kip Wagner was doing in Florida, he decided he had to be a part of it. He moved his family—sons Dirk, Kane, and Kim from his marriage to Deo, son Terry from a previous marriage, and daughter Taffi—to Florida in 1963, where he convinced Wagner and the Real Eight crew to let him salvage the 1715 fleet for free for one year— paying his own expenses—in exchange for giving Wagner half of whatever he found.

Mel was charismatic, but in a roundabout way. He was talkative, but just as prone to mumble and lose his train of thought mid-sentence as he was to make grand speeches inspiring those around him. He developed a reputation as a consummate showman: To close business deals, he was known to stir the drinks of potential investors with a tiny gold bar, or to serve them food on golden trays pulled up from under the sea. He was also accused of being a charlatan, of routinely exaggerating his finds and his prospects for future scores, and late in his life his company was fined for selling counterfeit coins. A heavy drinker, he ran an operation that was as disorganized as it was ambitious, with boats often in dock without fuel or funding, the atmosphere described as a hippie commune of sorts, the employees sleeping on the boat decks for lack of other accommodations.

Yet he was also brilliant and inventive, and, perhaps more important, single-minded in the pursuit of what he wanted.

At first, Fisher's partnership with Wagner yielded nothing. In fact, for nearly the entire year of their permitted search, he and his crew found squat. But they tried, and failed, and learned, and just as the yearlong deal was expiring, they found a few tidbits that let them know they were on the right track. Then, with the deadline looming, everything came together. One day, Fisher put on his gear, dived underwater, and saw a "carpet of gold" lying along the ocean floor, more than one thousand gold doubloons in all—the mother lode of the 1715 fleet.

As Fisher related in Jedwin Smith's book on his exploits, **Fatal Treasure,** the sight was mind-blowing, and truly life-changing. "The ocean's bottom was literally paved with gold," Fisher said. "When you've seen something like that, everything else pales by comparison. As far as I could see, there was nothing but gold coins."

The discovery made Wagner and Fisher solvent, if not quite rich, and immediately famous. **National Geographic** published a huge piece on their adventures, and the pair were soon treasure-hunting celebrities, the first men to bring up significant amounts of sunken Spanish treasure in modern memory. Wagner would stay in the central Florida area, salvaging the rest of the 1715 fleet. Fisher, however, was already moving on. He was in search of an even greater haul, perhaps the grandest sunken treasure of all, and he believed he knew where to find it.

In 1622, Spain was the world's preeminent power. The riches it had stripped from its New World colonies, chief among them silver and gold, allowed the Spanish empire to dominate in Europe and to expand its reach across the globe, with outposts in North and South America, Africa, and Asia. Spain operated a huge and interconnected network of mines, bases, missions, and trading ports as far-flung as the Philippines on down to Tierra del Fuego, with all roads eventually leading back to Madrid.

Yet by the 1620s, cracks were beginning to show as Spain's perch at the top became more precarious. The Thirty Years' War was sapping Spanish resources and manpower, and the annual infusion of New World gold and silver had become essential in allowing Spain to fund and provision its military. A new king, Philip IV, ascended to the throne in 1621, and with the war not going well for Spain, the riches of the 1622 treasure fleet were badly needed to restore imperial coffers—and pay back the bankers who were funding so much of the war effort.

The Spanish treasure fleets were usually comprised of between eight and twelve main ships, the famed galleons—huge, heavily armed, ornately decorated—that would ferry the precious gold and silver across the Atlantic and back to Spain, escorted by a flotilla of smaller vessels. In the spring, the galleons would depart from Europe, then make stops in the Spanish ports of the Caribbean and South America to pick up gold, silver, and valuable stones before reuniting in July in Cuba to make the trip back home. In 1622, the fleet was already running late by the time all the ships assembled in Havana, increasing the risk that it would run into one of the hurricanes that ravaged the Atlantic in late August and early September. And Dutch ships were nearby, ready to threaten the fleet once it set sail. But they could not afford to wait longer; Spanish authorities demanded the gold. So, in early September, much of the treasure was loaded onto two great galleons: the **Santa Margarita** and the recently completed **Nuestra Señora de Atocha.**

The very day after they set sail, disaster struck. A

fast-moving hurricane swept up the mid-Atlantic, immediately endangering the entire fleet. Smaller ships were swamped right away, and the large, slow, heavily armed galleons struggled to stay afloat as the seas lashed at them. The **Santa Margarita** and the **Atocha** were driven into the Florida Keys, where shallow waters and ship-wrecking reefs loomed. The **Santa Margarita** was the first to crash, grounding on a reef but remaining mostly intact. From their damaged ship, the crew of the **Santa Margarita** watched the demise of the **Atocha,** which would not be nearly as fortunate. Lifted by a wave, the galleon came down hard, smashing upon a coral reef. Her main mast snapped as the broken ship began to go under, sinking below the surface in roughly fifty-five feet of water. Only the stump of the mast could be seen above the waves. All but 5 of the 265 souls on board drowned.

After the hurricane cleared, Spanish authorities came to terms with what was suddenly a national emergency. The ships had to be located quickly in order to keep the entire Spanish economy running. Salvage efforts began immediately, and soon, the **Santa Margarita** was found, and much of her gold recovered. But the **Atocha**—while briefly located— was ultimately never salvaged, the ship having been moved by subsequent storms before the Spanish could establish any kind of recovery operation, its precise location lost beneath the waves.

So for 350 years, the **Atocha** remained a mystery,

its riches scattered somewhere on the bottom of the ocean floor, its legend growing over time.

Mel Fisher wanted to find it.

By 1967, some of the luster of their score with the 1715 fleet had worn off. There were millions of dollars' worth of treasure down there, certainly, but the costs of salvage were high—despite bringing up gold regularly, Fisher and his group were living hand to mouth as early investors were paid back, and much of the treasure was tied up in court battles. Those battles came courtesy of the state of Florida, which had jumped into the treasure-hunting craze by claiming much of what Wagner and Fisher had discovered as its own. The men soon found themselves in protracted legal tussles over ownership, ones that would eventually wind their way to the United States Supreme Court. The incidents soured Fisher on the spoils of the 1715 fleet, and on treasure hunting so close to land in general; he wanted to search in international waters, outside of the three-mile boundary where the state of Florida could reasonably think to claim some of their loot.

More than that, though, what called to him was the promise of making the ultimate score, the biggest find ever. And that's just what the **Atocha** was. The 1715 fleet was worth, perhaps, tens of millions. The **Atocha**'s treasure? That was believed to be hundreds of millions, perhaps even half a billion dollars' worth of gold, silver, and emeralds.

So over the late 1960s, Fisher transitioned his operation from central Florida, where the 1715 fleet was located, down to the Florida Keys, the assumed site of the 1622 fleet's wreck. By now, he was a salvage veteran, one who brought several of his own inventions to the job. Chief among these was the "mailbox," a modification placed on the back end of his boats, near their engines, enabling salvors to use the boats' propellers as a kind of fan. Fisher's boats would redirect the thrust of the propellers to fire plumes of water toward the ocean floor, blasting away sand from areas they thought might be promising. Divers would then head down and explore the "holes" created, hoping to find something of value.

Innovations like these helped. But the reality is that nautical treasure hunting is long, boring, slow, laborious work. Most of the time, it involves dragging a proton magnetometer—another Fisher-adjacent invention, crafted by a friend of his, Fay Feild—through the ocean behind the boat, "magging" the area, as it was called, in the hope that it notices a bit of iron. Where there's iron, in the form of old nails or struts, there might—stress on **might**—be something more valuable nearby. Or it could be a piece of ocean junk, or one of the many, many bombs dropped in the Florida Keys when the area was a military testing ground in the World War II era.

From the time he started searching for the **Atocha**

in earnest, in 1969, through 1980, Fisher found relatively little. Occasional pieces, yes, but scarcely enough to keep investors at bay and keep his boats fueled and on the hunt. He stayed barely one step ahead of creditors, selling "points" in the future profits from the **Atocha** at fifty thousand dollars a point.

It was never enough. The Fishers lived on a houseboat moored to an embankment, Kim Fisher told me, and couldn't afford to pay salaries to many of the divers and crew. They stayed on anyway, catching fish to eat, sleeping atop the decks of the houseboat because there was nowhere else to stay.

"Foam rubber mattresses," Kim Fisher recalled. "We'd have money for fuel. We'd fuel the boat up and we'd go out and spear fish to eat, catch lobsters. I was so sick of fish, and lobsters. I don't even like lobster still."

It was only Mel Fisher's persistence and drive that kept the entire operation going.

"He got people to believe in his dream," his son recalled. "He was a great salesman. And he just managed. I mean, we ran out of money several times. He never filed for bankruptcy or anything, but we ran out of money and just had to stop working."

The elder Fisher did what he could to keep his crew members' spirits high. His favorite saying was "Today's the day!" and he would cheerily impart that bit of wisdom to whoever would listen.

They did make some progress. In 1970, Mel

Fisher had made a breakthrough in the **Atocha** case; a second look at some old Spanish records by a man named Eugene Lyon caused Fisher to re-focus the search from the Matecumbe Keys to the Marquesas Keys, and soon Fisher realized he was on the right track. Over the next few years, Fisher and company would determine that the **Atocha** was in the Marquesas for sure, pulling up gold bars with markings identifying them as part of the ship's hoard.

But even he would eventually find himself laid low, struck by tragedies, as what hunters had come to call "the curse of the **Atocha**" took its toll.

The curse of the **Atocha** was established in the seventeenth century, when Spanish authorities tried to find and raise the sunken ship. Lore says that all who searched for her perished, most of them Caribbean divers; others were Spaniards using a diving bell to try to comb the ocean floor. There is no telling exactly how many died in those early searches, but it was enough that the ill-fated ship's macabre reputation grew.

Then in 1973, Nicholas Littlehales, the eleven-year-old son of **National Geographic** photographer Bates Littlehales, was killed when he was swept into the propellers of one of Fisher's treasure boats as they scanned the seas for the ship.

Two years later, another tragic event struck, one so terrible that it poisoned this treasure hunt for-ever for the Fishers.

Dirk Fisher was Mel and Deo's eldest son, twenty-one years old in 1975. In the summer of that year, he made perhaps the most significant find to date, pulling up nine of the **Atocha**'s bronze cannons from the ocean's depths—guaranteeing that the ship and her treasure hoard were close and fully legitimizing Fisher's pursuit in the eyes of outsiders.

The Fisher family was riding high when, a week later, Dirk and his ten-person crew were aboard **Northwind,** out on the waters chasing the **Atocha** again. They had just turned in for the night when a bilge pump malfunctioned, and as they slept, the boat began to fill with water, listing badly before anyone woke up and realized anything was amiss. When one crew member finally recognized what was wrong, it was too late. The **Northwind** capsized, trapping Dirk; his wife, Angel; and diver Rick Gage in its hull. The other seven crew members managed to find a raft, and clung to it until they were rescued. But they came ashore knowing that they had to tell Mel and Deo Fisher what had become of their firstborn son, his wife, and his friend.

"That telephone call was every mother's worst nightmare," Deo Fisher said in Jedwin Smith's **Fatal Treasure.** "After almost six years of frustration, we truly believed that our prayers had finally been answered, that Dirk had finally found the **Atocha.** Instead . . ." She paused, then said, "Dirk was my baby."

The death of the three treasure hunters devastated the entire group and cast a pall over Fisher's enterprise.

"The only time we ever thought about giving up was when my brother died," Kim Fisher said. "For a couple months there, we were all pretty much done—we didn't even think about going out and finding treasure. But then, then we talked about it and we figured that Dirk would want us to continue, and so it actually kind of increased our determination. We were going to find it for him."

So they went out to their boats and labored on, heading back to sea and once again magging the ocean floor in their endless search for iron and its cousins, gold and silver.

The search proceeded slowly, but it received a boost when, in 1980, Fisher's crew members rediscovered the wreck of the **Santa Margarita**—partially but never fully salvaged by the Spanish—and began pulling up treasure from the **Atocha**'s doomed sister ship. The **Margarita**—a total of perhaps twenty million dollars in loot—was not nearly as rich a find, but its discovery kept the investors satisfied, everyone fed and housed, and buoyed the team's collective spirits, reinforcing that finding treasure in this area really was possible.

Still, by 1985, Fisher's crews and backers were running out of patience, and once again Fisher was running out of money. It had been sixteen years since they'd focused their efforts on the **Atocha,** and all they had to show for it was some stopgap treasure from another ship, some cannons, and a painful history of death and woe.

Until another of Mel's sons stepped up.

Kane Fisher—brash, tall, and still angry over the death of his brother—was searching what would become known as "Kane's Trail." It was July 20, 1985, ten years to the day that Dirk, Angel, and Rick Gage had died aboard the **Northwind.** Kane was searching the area because he believed that Dirk had the right idea when he found the **Atocha**'s cannons a decade earlier.

"Everyone had their theory where the **Atocha** was, and I had mine—Dirk's theory," Kane said in **Fatal Treasure.** "I knew those cannon he'd found just didn't drop there from out of the sky."

That July day, Kane and his boat, the **Dauntless,** were magging and blowing the ocean floors in a promising area along Kane's—he would argue, Dirk's—Trail. Kane sent two divers, Andy Matroci and Greg Wareham, down into the water, where they quickly realized they were in a good diving spot. Coins, pottery, and barrel hoops abounded. Promising, yes, but they had found spots like this before. It wasn't until the pair swam a bit from their dive site, somewhat on a whim, that everything changed.

"I see this huge clump materialize up ahead

from out of the shadows, and the closer I got all I could think was **holy shit,**" Wareham said in **Fatal Treasure.**

What he saw ahead of him was "[a]n honest-to-goodness treasure chest—just like you read about in those pirate books."

And then there it was, just beyond the chest, all of it resplendent before them: the **Atocha's** treasure. Stacks upon stacks of silver bars, four feet high, twenty feet wide, seventy-five feet long. Silver coins everywhere the eye could see, covering the ocean floor. They sped for the surface, bursting to tell Kane what they'd found.

At 1:05 p.m., Kane Fisher radioed to his father's headquarters on land.

"WZG9605. Unit 1, this is Unit 11," Kane said. "Put away the charts. We've got the 'Mother Lode'!"

That they had, as great a find as they had all hoped—hundreds of millions of dollars' worth of gold and silver bars and coins, and a cache of emeralds even grander than what the hunters had anticipated. It was more than Kim Fisher could process when he dived down there, just stacks of silver as far as he could see.

"It was amazing," Fisher told me. "There were stacks; they were all tipped over and everything was infested with silver sulfide and most of it was still buried in the mud—but the piles of silver bars were just sticking up out of that mud."

Mel Fisher rushed to the dive site, and his team

began bringing up treasure immediately—too quickly, in their excitement, at first failing to preserve the site and follow proper procedures—as the discovery of the galleon and her hoard became a worldwide phenomenon.

More than four hundred reporters from media outlets all around the world descended upon Key West to tell the story. Jimmy Buffett went out to the recovery site and played a mini-concert from the deck of one of Fisher's boats, sitting atop a pile of silver bars. A TV movie was made about the search, **Dreams of Gold: The Mel Fisher Story,** with Cliff Robertson as Mel and Loretta Swit as Deo (and **Karate Kid** star Billy Zabka, leader of the Cobra Kai, playing Kim Fisher!). Fisher went from being a local curiosity to something of a Key West icon. In the 1980s, when Key West briefly "seceded" from the United States in the midst of a dispute over aggressive border checks, Fisher was voted king of the upstart "Conch Republic"— a role he would hold for life.

And yes, finding the **Atocha** made Mel Fisher truly rich at last, though it wasn't quite the windfall for his crew and investors that all had expected. The treasure was so vast that even the tiny, sub–1 percent shares that many hands were owed were still worth hundreds of thousands, paid in actual treasure—gold and silver bars, emeralds and the like. But that type of lucre isn't easily liquidated into cash, and when an incredible amount is thrust onto the market at once, all of it is devalued. That wouldn't have been a problem if most of the treasure hunters hadn't needed to convert their treasure into U.S. dollars immediately—but they did. The federal government wanted its cut, demanding up to 50 percent of the value of each share in taxes, and swiftly. Many of the hunters ended up having to take out loans just to pay their taxes, and remained cash-poor until they could eventually unload some of their gold and silver at a nondepressed price.

Fisher would spend the next fifteen years bringing up loot from the **Atocha** and seeking out other treasures. Tourists would delight in seeing the famous treasure hunter perched atop a bar stool at the Schooner Wharf Bar, armed with his rum and Diet Coke, telling stories of the treasures he'd found and those still to come. He remained a beloved local institution, and the world's most famous treasure hunter, until his death in 1998. He died having been proved right: Eventually, today really was the day.

Kim Fisher leaned back in his chair and exhaled. The goose bumps might not have been visible, but the gleam in his eye surely was; he clearly loved to talk about the past, when his dad was around, the glory days. But it's not like they stopped searching for treasure once the **Atocha** was found. Really, they wouldn't even have known how to stop. They were and are treasure hunters, and that meant it was on to the next search.

"At first it was like, now what?" Fisher said of life after the **Atocha** find. "But it didn't last long. There's lots more shipwrecks."

That there were.

The Fishers' successes finding the **Santa Margarita** and especially the **Atocha** spurred interest and investment in treasure-hunting projects worldwide. And the methods and technologies they and their contemporaries developed in their searches spread across the oceans as hunters and salvors dived deep to locate and recover famous wrecks.

After the **Atocha,** perhaps none of the great gold ships loomed larger in the minds of treasure hunters than the SS **Central America.** Unlike most of the others, the **Central America** was a relatively modern wreck. She was a steamship, one that went down off South Carolina in 1857, carrying gold worth about $300 million today, all mined and panned from the California gold rush. Unstable and overloaded, the **Central America** sank in a hurricane during her journey, taking more than four hundred passengers along with her to the ocean's depths. The **Central America** was long considered too far out to be salvageable—she sank in deep ocean waters, and dragging and magging techniques wouldn't be effective out there. But a new technology was quickly making the ocean floors accessible: remote-controlled submersibles.

In 1988, the **Central America** was located, approximately eight thousand feet down, by a group led by Columbus, Ohio, marine engineer Tommy G. Thompson. A year later, Thompson piloted a specially designed ROV (remotely operated vehicle) down to the site of the wreck and began pulling up gold bars, eventually three tons in all. The saga of the **Central America** then moved to the courts, where the original insurance companies who had vouchsafed the 1857 journey insisted they were entitled to the gold, not the treasure hunters. Ultimately, Thompson and his group won claim to 92 percent of the treasure, and Thompson himself sold his stake for roughly fifty million dollars—which, in the end, was mostly money he owed investors, whom he left largely high and dry. Like so many other treasure hunters, Thompson proved to be a little bit brilliant, and a little bit of a rogue—he ended up on the lam, leading his creditors on a multiyear, multistate chase that concluded in 2015, when he and his partner were finally tracked down and arrested in Florida. Thompson was sent to jail for years, until he admitted where he was hiding some of the gold he owed his backers.

And then in 2015, a treasure even greater than the **Atocha**'s was located: that of the **San José.** The Spanish galleon had gone down off the coast of Colombia in 1708, her powder stores exploding during a firefight with four English ships. Researchers from the Woods Hole Oceanographic Institute, the Colombian navy, Maritime Archaeology Consultants, and Switzerland AG combined to find the ship, but its discovery wasn't made public for a few years because of the complex ownership questions surrounding its treasure—which is valued at well over a billion dollars. Some estimates give it a truly exorbitant value, placing it as high as seventeen billion; so it's little surprise that Spain, Colombia, and the actual treasure finders are all locked in a dispute over who gets the rights to the spoils.

These nautical hunts gained their fair share of attention, but there were efforts made to locate some of the great treasures on land, as well.

At Oak Island, the legend of the Money Pit had not faded. Expeditions were mounted in earnest in the 1930s and the 1960s, bringing with them new methods and far, far more elaborate digging equipment. These ventures were able to secure backing from luminaries like the actors Errol Flynn and John Wayne. The searchers sank shafts parallel to the Money Pit, tried to change the island's water table to stop the pit from flooding, and used such technology as remote cameras to go where explorers before them could not. But still they found no treasure—only tragedy again, as in 1965, when four men of that expedition were killed by hydrogen sulfide fumes in one of the shafts, bringing the death total of the various expeditions to six—just one short of the prophesied seven who would die before the treasure was found. Interest in Oak Island, incidentally, has spiked in the past few years as a pair of brothers, Rick and Marty Lagina, bought much of the island, began a major and well-funded expedition there, and landed a History Channel show, **The Curse of Oak Island,** documenting their as-yet-unsuccessful efforts.

More would die seeking the Lost Dutchman Mine, as well. In 1947, a prospector named James Carvey ventured into the mountains via helicopter on a well-publicized voyage to find the mine. Once he was dropped off, however, he lost contact with his team—and was never seen alive again. His head-less skeleton was found the following February. Several other hikers, searchers, and prospectors died seeking the mine over the next two years, some of them bearing bullet wounds when their bodies were discovered, bolstering the theories of those who believe something sinister is at work in the Superstition Mountains. The death toll has kept rising in the present day—one in 2009, and three in 2010, all from the elements or accidents—but that hasn't stopped searchers from trying.

And some impressive minds went to work try-ing to unravel the Beale cipher, bringing in new methods of code breaking and even rudimentary computing technology to solve the puzzle. Herbert Yardley, founder of the U.S. Cipher Bureau—the forerunner to the NSA—became deeply interested in cracking the code, as did Col. William Friedman, a famed World War II code breaker and chief of the Signal Intelligence Service. Friedman actually added the Beale cipher to his SIS training programs, believing it a formidable code and one worthy of teaching to his charges. In the 1960s, new weapons were brought to bear: supercomputers. Dr. Carl Hammer, the head of computing services at Sperry Rand UNIVAC—at the time a leading maker of government supercomputers—employed all the technology at his disposal to try to break the codes, to no avail.

The Fisher clan sought all three of these famous treasures, and as we know with them, nothing was ever done halfway. When they went hunting for the treasure of the Beale Papers in Virginia, they bought a property, brought in heavy equipment, and created a huge stir.

"This guy thought he had deciphered it and we went and dug this big empty hole," Kim Fisher said. "It kept getting bigger and bigger. We started out with shovels, you know? Brought in a backhoe. By this time the news media is like, 'They're going to find something here.'"

I leaned forward, eager for whatever might come next.

"But then it started snowing, and Dad said, 'Time to go back to Key West.'" Fisher laughed.

In fact, the "value" in treasure hunting may come in focusing on some lesser-known land hunts, ones where fewer people are searching; those are still long shots, though, at best. In that vein, Kim Fisher sought the Tears of the Sun treasure, a cache of Spanish gold buried up in the foothills near San Francisco. As is often the case, another treasure hunter came to him, promising that he had good research, hoping to benefit from Fisher's resources and technology. They ventured up to California and started wandering the wilderness in search of buried treasure.

"This guy Casey came to me—he had some research on it," Fisher said. "We came up with the term **the Casey mile** because we'd be hiking out there and [I'd say], 'How far is it, Casey?' 'About a mile.' Every time, it seemed like ten miles. It was probably two miles. But yeah, we got permission to drill some holes. This lady wouldn't let us dig holes, but we got permission to do some holes, and used ground-penetrating radar and looked for that one."

Those kinds of proposals—long on excitement, short on facts—still come in all the time, but after so many years of fruitless searches, Fisher now commits his company's resources only when something feels concrete.

"I've got a file on my computer called 'Wild Geese,'" he said. "And basically, I'm over going after the wild geese. If there's some research, and some location data, then I'll consider it. But 'My uncle told me he saw this guy bury this treasure here in the swamp . . .'" He trailed off, waving his hand to signify that those kinds of "tips" are largely worthless.

"So yeah, we've gotten to the point where if there's no documentation, we don't go after it."

The Fenn treasure, incidentally, may not have qualified as a wild-goose chase by those standards—but the value of the chest was too low for the professionals to devote serious time and energy to it. They were looking for bigger scores.

Kim Fisher now has a staff of more than thirty, three vessels, and numerous part-time helpers and contractors combing through records, working on technology, cataloging artifacts, and, of course, searching the seas for treasure ships. He has a growing list of investors, many of them owning a tiny sliver of the company—but his father taught him never to turn away backing, no matter how small.

For the last few years, they've been seeking two ships in particular: the 1622 fleet galleon **Consolación,** and a ship they've code-named the **Lost Merchant,** sunk in deep water. It should be no surprise that they're still seeking the treasures of the sea, in the areas they know best—Treasure Salvors has an admiralty claim to search certain protected areas that other companies couldn't get today, and it's probably their most valuable asset.

The process of investigating a treasure claim is relatively straightforward. First, gather all the information you can, especially solid documentation. In the case of both land- and sea-based treasure, hearsay is worst, and government documents are best.

"You go to the Spanish archives, or other archives," Fisher said. "There's Spanish documents still in Mexico City and other cities in Mexico. Cuba."

Fisher hires professional researchers to comb through these archives, seeking tiny tidbits of data hidden in near-indecipherable texts from hundreds of years ago—ship manifests, personal letters, navigation charts. Often pages are missing, or pieces are ripped out—something that became a particular problem in the search for the **Atocha,** where the researchers got to a key section in one document detailing the Spanish salvage attempts and then found that they were stymied at exactly the pivotal point.

"Right where it told which direction to go, there was a wormhole in the document," Fisher said. "So we didn't know which direction to go."

That type of hiccup is fairly standard. So they get what they can, and then give it their best guess. Armed with some sort of location information, the next step is renavigation: literally, trying to trace the last steps of those who hid or lost the treasure. Find their route, find their trajectory, and rebuild it.

If that's on land, walk their path, accepting that things now may not look as they did then. If it's at sea, try to re-create their journey, understanding that the patterns of the winds and seas are largely unknowable.

Whether on land or on water, the key is to create a search zone. Once that zone is established, it's time to get out there and seek the quarry. On land, that means digging. At sea, that means sweeping the ocean floor, back and forth, zone by zone, for as long as it takes.

The technology used to conduct the actual searches hasn't changed all that much since the 1960s, when Mel Fisher and his compatriots developed many of the basic tools of the trade. Iterations of the magnetometer—the device used to detect underwater metals—and the side-scan sonar are used to let hunters know when they might have a bead on something down below.

Then it's a matter of sweeping, looking, seeking, pushing aside mountains of sand with the "mailbox," sending an ROV on trip after trip—just going over each bit of ground until you're certain there's nothing there. Even with all the improvements in technology, at a certain point, the most important ingredients in treasure hunting remain time, persistence, and patience.

If they're lucky enough to find something of value, the work isn't over. Fisher walked me down the hallway—past another mural of a smiling Mel Fisher, in dive gear, painted on the wall—into Treasure Salvors' lab, where senior conservator John Corcoran was busily working over several vats containing relics dredged up from the wrecks of the **Atocha** and the **Santa Margarita.**

"I'm sorry there isn't more in here right now; you're catching me at an off time," Corcoran said cheerily as he motioned me over to look at an arquebus—an early type of firearm—pulled up from one of the vessels. The piece was submerged in an electrolysis tank, which slowly worked to desalinate it after its centuries in salt water.

Corcoran took me around the lab, showing off various pieces—a dagger, several more early firearms, kitchen equipment—all in various stages of the conservation process. Maps of the search sites adorned the walls, with markers indicating where various pieces and piles had been found. In his office, there was a beautifully preserved wooden post to a four-post bed sitting in a drying tank, slowly returning to some semblance of normalcy after centuries at sea.

"It's not all gold and silver and weapons," Corcoran explained. "The wealthier passengers on these boats, they'd have homes in the New World, and when they'd go back to Spain, they'd need to send their belongings back with them."

Kim Fisher said that preserving items like this is part of the treasure-hunting business, and they're happy to do it—many of these objects are displayed in the museum on the building's first floor, or loaned out to other exhibits around the country; they believe they're doing a service for the public by locating and displaying these artifacts, and that they do a good and responsible job of preservation—while acknowledging that in the early days, that wasn't always the case. But times have changed; there are standards now: state oversight, archaeologists on staff and on call, a consistent push to ensure that treasure hunting is a responsible and historically beneficial process.

Still, not everyone sees it that way.

If anything has changed over his lifetime as a treasure hunter, Fisher said, it's the sway of the archaeology community, and in particular one wing of it—what Fisher called the "in situ" archaeologists.

"There's a group of purist archaeologists that are anti–private sector," Fisher said. "They don't think the private sector should be out salvaging shipwrecks. So they do whatever they can to harass us, slow us down."

Fisher looked ticked off for the first time in our conversation as he started to grouse about his opponents.

"That in situ preservation is ridiculous because nobody's ever going to see it, if you leave it buried," Fisher said. "And even more so in the ocean because of the corrosive effects of the salt water and the teredo worm. The wood is gone. I mean, and the metal, every day it's out there, it corrodes more. Except gold. Gold, nothing affects gold."

These complaints sounded familiar to me—they were similar to the gripes Fenn had when he railed against the archaeologists who didn't want him disrupting the finds at San Lazaro Pueblo. Fenn wanted to bring the relics out, display them. His argument was similar to Fisher's—that people should be able to experience these ancient objects, be close to them, smell them, touch them.

That battle rages on land in the Southwest, and at sea, as well—and according to Fisher, the preservationists are winning. Right now, he's in a permitting battle over how much preservation, cataloging, and reporting work he has to do while out hunting, and he said the latest regulations will cripple his business.

Fisher will be all right, of course. His operation will survive, both because of the **Atocha** money and because of the grandfathered-in claims they have to work certain areas, claims issued long before the standards were as strict as they are now.

But theirs is a uniquely successful operation, and other would-be treasure hunters don't have that luxury. Treasure hunting's golden age is long over, many of the biggest treasures found, many of the hunters' cavalier ways now blunted by a bureaucracy that stifles these hopeful efforts before they can get off the ground.

"They've pretty much put everybody else out of business," Fisher said, shaking his head. "I'm the only one with a marine salvage permit in any marine sanctuary in the United States. Because there's so many rules and regulations, and they keep making it more and more onerous."

Those fights are suddenly cutting into the heart

of the treasure hunt. What was once a romantic—if financially motivated—search for the secrets of the ocean has become, in some ways, both far more controversial and far more mundane. Because finding a treasure in the twenty-first century isn't as simple as opening the chest and taking home the gold.

There are tax collectors to satisfy. There are lawyers to argue against. There are court proceedings and insurance companies and legal thickets that threaten the great adventure that Kip Wagner and Mel Fisher set out on fifty-plus years ago. Then it was a quest, even if investors eventually cut into the profits. It makes it all a little bit harder to dream on—the hope that one could move to Florida, set up operations, and come up with a life-changing, world-famous score is now quite a bit dimmer than it once was.

Still, even with the regulatory oversight, even with the archaeological supervision, even with the legal morass that treasure hunters might anticipate encountering at the end of their search, the hunts continue.

Because as Kim Fisher knows as well as anyone, there is nothing in the world like finding a treasure.

11

THE RISE OF THE FENNTUBERS

Sacha Johnston was not happy.

To start with, she was upset with her estranged boyfriend, Jason—a fellow Fenn searcher whom she had met through the hunt, the pair quickly becoming one of its best-known couples.

But now Sacha and Jason were on the outs, and Sacha was doubting everything about their courtship.

"I don't think he ever loved me," she spat. "I think he just used me for YouTube hits and access to Forrest Fenn."

Sacha and Jason had been dating for months, but recently they'd had a fight over money, and now Jason was gone, their relationship issues prompting the army man to leave early for his deployment to another part of the country.

"I wish I wasn't still in love with him," she said and moaned.

Next, she was pretty displeased with me.

We were on New Mexico State Road 68, once again passing through the dreary town of Española on our way up to the Pilar area, the place where Beep and I first searched and where Paris Wallace drowned. I'd convinced Sacha to let me tag along to her search spot, but she was clearly already regretting it, because she thought she was onto something, like really onto something this time—and that there was a very real chance we were going to find the treasure that day. That made my presence a problem.

Sacha had gone on more than three hundred boots-on-the-ground hunts, and now she believed that, finally, she was closing in.

That was great, I thought, and I told her so, but she didn't see it that way. She knew I was going to tell the story of all this, and to her, that was unacceptable. If—when—she found the treasure, she said, people were going to come out of the woodwork, searching for her, looking to exploit her, and she couldn't have that. She wasn't going to put her kids—a daughter in college at the University of New Mexico, and a young son—in that position. Which meant she insisted that when she found it, I had to promise not to tell a soul for ten years— which, this being 2018, meant 2028.

"I can already tell that you can't keep a secret," she said as we stopped for lunch at Burger King in Española on the way up to her search spot.

The problem was, of course, she was right: I couldn't keep that kind of secret—and I had no intention of doing so, as I repeatedly explained to her as we drove through this now familiar territory north of Santa Fe, haggling over whom I could and couldn't tell and when, in the extraordinarily un-likely event that we did find the treasure that day. I was literally telling the story of this hunt! Of course I couldn't keep it secret if she found it. And Sacha didn't like that one bit.

But fortunately for me (and Jason), it wasn't the two of us whom Sacha was really, **really** mad at right now. Believe it or not, we were lesser problems.

At the moment, Sacha was especially furious at the FennTubers.

The introductory video on Facebook and YouTube for the channel A Gypsy's Kiss hums with the mel-low, pleasantly atmospheric music you'd hear in a hotel spa, the kind that urges you to get that cu-cumber facial treatment and accompanying two-hundred-dollar massage. Over the placid tones, a woman's voice begins to speak, equally warm and welcoming, as the mood transitions into that of a late-night infomercial.

"Are you one of the thousands searching for the treasure Forrest Fenn hid someplace in the mountains north of Santa Fe?" the woman, Shelley Carney, asks. "No need to spend hours, days, or weeks thoroughly researching every blog article, video, and forum post. Watch A Gypsy's Kiss, where my partner, Toby Younis, and I will give you current research and accurate, logical information to help you find that magic box at the end of Fenn's rainbow. Save yourself some time and subscribe to our YouTube channel today."

It was always inevitable that people were going to try to make money off Forrest Fenn's search. It was natural, really. The phenomenon had grown so far and so wide, and drawn from such a varied population, that the key question for many wasn't whether people would try to monetize it, but how.

The bloggers, like Dal and Stephanie, had been making a little money from the chase all along, through the operation of the blogs themselves and the things they sometimes sold on them. Sacha had also given it a shot, operating a website selling Fenn-related items—shirts, maps, that kind of stuff—for obsessed hunters a few years back. She never really made any money from it, and eventually gave it up.

But the most recent movement, the latest and best attempt to cash in on this thing, was the rise of the FennTubers.

FennTubers are exactly what they sound like: searchers who post videos on YouTube about hunting for Fenn's treasure.

They take viewers along on their searches, host prominent guests for Q&As, and often just talk about the latest issues in the chase, sometimes in roundtable format. It's another way to discuss a shared passion, and an avenue for some searchers to become quasi-famous within this community. And it's a way of making money.

The most prominent of the FennTubers in 2018 was the partnership of Younis and Carney, who operated what was by far the biggest YouTube Fenn vlog, A Gypsy's Kiss, named for an actual smooch Younis got from a Gypsy when he was a much younger man.

Younis is a Santa Fe native who joined the U.S. Army in 1969 and served a two-year tour in Vietnam with the Special Operations Detachment of the Army Security Agency. He said he moved over to the NSA as an intelligence analyst when his five years of active-duty army service ended, using his photography skills on assignment around the world while deployed to faraway sites like "Nairobi, Kenya, to stalk the Russian embassy there," as Younis put it.

Younis said he left the NSA in 1979 but maintained his security clearance, and he spent the following decades as an independent contractor working with the intelligence community, doing all kinds of film and photography work as the Cold War led into the war on terror and beyond.

He moved back to New Mexico in 2010 to retire, but he discovered he couldn't sit still for long. He felt too idle when not working, and the urge to have new adventures pulled at him. He was among the legions of 2013 adopters, seeing a news report about the budding phenomenon and figuring he'd try his hand at it. He spent years researching and searching, without success, but enjoyed the sport too much to give it up.

Younis and Carney were already business partners, working on video-related projects in New Mexico, when Younis introduced Carney to his hobby. If Forrest Fenn's bold claims that there were 350,000 searchers out there were even close to reality, Younis figured, then there was a market for them to tap by bringing YouTube-based content to the searcher community. Younis was a devoted, committed, longtime Fenn searcher, but he made it clear from the start that this was a business venture, not some labor of love.

"I have something of a mercenary mentality about it, which some people don't like," Younis said.

Starting in the spring of 2017, the pair began broadcasting regularly on their YouTube channel, putting out new content—book analyses, interviews with Fenn and other searchers, roundtables, Q&As—four to five days a week. It quickly became a full-time, forty-hour-a-week job; they started small, but soon they had more than one thousand subscribers and counting.

"We were doing a lot of work on this, but that's how you build a subscriber base," Younis said.

YouTubers make money in three primary ways. First, once you reach one thousand subscribers to your channel, YouTube pays you per view.

"Pennies on the dollar, but you do get paid for that," Younis explained.

Then there's the advertising that YouTube puts on successful channels—reach a certain threshold, and YouTube thinks you're useful and sends ads your way. Again, more subscribers and views mean better ads and more revenue.

Finally, subscribers themselves can pay extra for a premium experience. Some call them "donations," but really it's paying for extra access or preferential treatment in the chat that accompanies each live YouTube video.

"You offer premiums, like Super Chat. If we're going live, and in chat, people can contribute up to five hundred dollars for special chat status," Younis said. "If they like what you have to say, or if they want to ask a question, they can put in a Super Chat, and the question comes in, and it's highlighted based on the amount they've contributed."

Chasing these tripartite goals, Younis and Carney gradually grew their audience, and with the amount of content they were putting out, A Gypsy's Kiss became required viewing for the truly devoted Fenn searcher.

A few competitors emerged, and though they were smaller, a budding FennTuber community began to develop, all of them trying to become the biggest and best, all of them looking for something to set them apart in the suddenly crowded Fenn space, everyone fighting for slices of the viewership pie.

At the peak of A Gypsy's Kiss's popularity, the channel was getting seventy thousand views a month on its videos, reaching close to four thousand subscribers, and Younis and Carney were making about one thousand dollars a month between views and advertising. But that, obviously, wasn't the level of return they were looking for, and both the following and the cash were minuscule compared to successful YouTubers in other fields. The biggest names have millions of subscribers and tens of millions of views per month; even much, much more pedestrian YouTubers who have zero name recognition outside of their target area can build six-figure subscriber bases and gain over a million views on good posts.

Still, A Gypsy's Kiss had been the most successful Fenn-related operation, and while it wasn't going gangbusters, it wasn't nothing, either. Seeing their reach, others began trying to find different ways of making more money off it, tapping Fenn's name

in the hopes of resonating with his faithful. One
FennTuber, Mike Cowling, known as Cowlazars,
came up with the idea of creating a series of Fenn-
related coins and selling them on his channel. The
idea took off—Cowlazars paid about $3.50 per
coin and was able to sell each for more than ten
times that. Younis was impressed—but not everybody liked that level of entrepreneurship.

"He made up one thousand of them, and made
a big profit on it, and I don't think Fenn thought
he was going to make a real profit on them, and he
immediately got mad," Younis said.

Fenn began to chafe at the naked profiteering
of the FennTubers, and started to distance himself
from their operations, Younis said.

"It does irritate him when people try to lever-
age his name to make money," Younis said. "But
honestly, he made a career out of making money
off artists he didn't know, but he was smart enough
to buy their work and profit from it. So I don't
think he has any complaints about people using
his name to make money, because he used other
people's names to make money for himself and
his family."

Yet Fenn wasn't the only one irritated by these
new developments. The Fenn community has always been filled with drama, but the FennTubers
putting their faces out there, making themselves so
prominent, and, yes, trying to make money off the
chase, made them into especially obvious targets.

Cowlazars also ran into criticism from the community over a plan he and another YouTuber, Kpro, hatched to buy and resell a series of old topographical maps that Fenn had once owned. The maps were being sold by Shiloh, who saw a way to make money on otherwise near-worthless paper. But the plan wasn't a big moneymaker, and it brought more criticism that they were profiteering. Soon, Cowlazars posted a video defending all his practices, from the map project to selling coins to the concept of FennTubing altogether.

"Anybody with a camera and a Google account can make a YouTube account and upload their videos," Cowlazars argued. "It just so happens that [A Gypsy's Kiss's] videos and my videos are monetized.

"If you don't like it, you don't have to," he told his viewers. "I'm not telling you to like it. I just don't understand why it's any of your business—if you don't like it, don't watch. If you don't want a coin, don't watch."

His argument was that the coins and other Fenn-related paraphernalia weren't just profiteering—they added something to the chase.

"You know why I made the coins?" Cowlazars said on a stream explaining the move. "Because this is good for the chase. This'll be around generations from now. . . . When I'm gone, and the two coins my boys have, [when the boys are] long gone, they'll be given to their children and their grandchildren and so on—this keeps the chase going for hundreds of years, because this coin is always going to be here. I don't see how that's a bad thing."

Many didn't find that convincing. And some of the loudest opposition has been led by none other than Sacha, who pilloried the FennTubers to me, and online.

Sacha's boyfriend, Jason, was a FennTuber himself—and Sacha, an important figure in the search and one of the most connected, best-known hunters, happily appeared on his channel, helping to boost his profile in the community.

But now Sacha and Jason were quarreling, and Sacha was taking aim at the entire FennTuber phenomenon, saying their money-hungry ways had corrupted the search.

A week before I met her for this hunt, she posted a long, impassioned diatribe against the FennTubers on several of the most popular Fenn blog sites. Entitled "Sacha wakes up," it purported to tell the common Fenner about the secret world of the FennTubers, and what they were really after.

"To some of the FennTubers, you are not people," she wrote. "You are subscribers and viewers. You are a nameless hash mark, only counted towards the ultimate goal of 1000 (or whatever goal) subscribers, and monetization."

She railed against the moneymaking tendencies of the FennTubers, accused some of trying to snake clues and insight about the treasure out of their viewers, said they passed on incorrect information, and hammered them again for their demands for donations and their unabashed desire to grow and pick up subscribers. Then she went into how they dealt with Fenn himself.

"Some of the Fenntubers have outright harassed Forrest for words and information, just so that their shows can get more views," Sacha wrote. "He had to institute a 'No YouTubers' rule because these people were relentless in their efforts. They want Forrest to be on their show, answer questions, and give tidbits of info. Sometimes, it isn't for money, but because they want to rub it in the face of other YouTubers. There is a lot of manipulation, back-stabbing, and rumor spreading that goes on between the Fenntubers themselves. There are cliques, factions, bullies, and megalomaniacs (a person who is obsessed with his or her own power). I have seen at least one budding YouTuber be run off by another, more experienced set."

There was much, much more—the whole screed was over thirteen hundred words—and the piece had set tongues wagging within the Fenn community.

As we neared our search zone, I asked her what response she'd been getting to her missive. It had actually been pretty positive, she said—many long-time searchers had reached out to offer some version of "glad somebody finally said it." Others, who had left the chase, told her they hoped it would make a difference.

But she doubted that it would. Now that some had figured out how to effectively monetize the community, she suspected there would only be more of this kind of profiteering.

We were nearing the Rio Grande Gorge area, and even though Fenn had already said—to Beep and me privately, and then to everyone in the aftermath of Paris Wallace's death—that the treasure wasn't in or around the Gorge, Sacha believed that her spot was far enough away from the Gorge that Fenn's words of warning didn't apply. And, man, was she ever sure about this spot.

Since she entered the hunt in 2013, Sacha had searched only in New Mexico—and for the most part, she'd searched in only a very, very small area of the state, tracing and retracing her steps, going over the same pieces of ground, moving incrementally through each zone until she was convinced she'd exhausted the sliver.

That day, we were heading up State Road 68 past Embudo, and then veering off the main road toward the town of Dixon. Sacha had first started looking into the exact same location Beep and I had— Agua Caliente Falls and Canyon. She loved Agua Caliente as a starting point, and then she hit upon what she considered her brainstorm: Without giving too much away, she used comments Fenn had made about distances—specifically, his comments about the treasure's being at least 8.25 miles north of Santa Fe—and the old fighter pilot method of triangulation to settle in on a spot near Dixon.

She'd been searching that area for literally years, driving up for the day several times a week, testing new areas and theories, investigating the next patch of land, and then heading home. Then, a few days later, she'd try again.

Now, however, she thought that she'd finally zeroed in on a specific location within her chosen zone, a place where she felt it just **had** to be. So we were heading back to investigate it further, to poke around in parts where she hadn't quite been yet. This was why this day's hunt was so important to her, and why she was so insistent that I not jeopardize the results—not threaten the future that she wanted so badly for her children, or let the past she'd left behind come crawling back to fuck it all up.

"I don't know who my father is," she told me, explaining that she'd had a very tough childhood. At times, she said, she had wondered who her real father might be, and so she tracked down several possibilities, and administered DNA tests to them, without a positive result. But there were others out there, others who knew they might be options.

"If I found the chest, twenty men would come out of the woodwork, claiming to be my dad. I don't need that shit," she said.

We had entered a zone where cell phones didn't

work and GPS was largely useless, but Sacha knew this area by heart. She instructed me to pull off the road near an old mine and then follow a weathered dirt path that snaked up into the hills. We drove into a clearing, one she had been to many, many times before, and she quickly hopped out of my rental car to have a smoke and get ready for the path ahead. She pointed to the hills around us, waving her hand across the landscape.

"I've searched all up and down that hill, up and down that one, been over there, I've been through this whole area," she said. "But that was before I really knew what to look for."

I pulled out my light black jacket, grabbed my Brown University cap, and slung on my backpack as Sacha finished her cigarette. She dragged her gear out of the back, donning a blue fleece and a white Spartan Race hat, and then took out something else, something I'd known to expect but had forgotten about: her trademark pink handgun. The 9mm Ruger pistol wasn't all pink—the barrel was black, but the rest was pink, and it was distinctive and fierce in its own way.

She looked at me as she checked it, then strapped it on. Was it for protection against bears? Against other travelers we might meet along the way? Against me?

I didn't bother asking as she smiled and began walking off down the path toward her spot, about a mile away. We were hardly under way when she stopped, jumping back slightly, pointing at something just off the path.

"Holy shit, this wasn't here the last time I was here; this is new," she said.

It was the spine and rib cage of a sizable animal—a deer or something similar—picked clean, down to the white bone. A pair of legs and a pelvis were strewn nearby, not quite as well chewed yet.

Remembering my and Cynthia's encounter with the bear scat the year before, I was suddenly happy Sacha had that pink handgun.

We hiked down and up and down again, a constant back-and-forth of inclines and declines interrupted by a few meandering trails. Sacha regularly pointed out every slight difference between now and the last time she'd been here, which was only recently. She examined boot prints, making sure that she saw only her own, constantly seeking reinforcement that no one else was zeroing in on her solve. At one spot where our trail met up with another, she spied the prints of unfamiliar boots, and was only assuaged when she saw that they led off in another direction.

We'd gotten lucky, with the weather cool yet sunny, perfect for wandering around New Mexico's rolling hills at this time of year. It was pretty here, and I was just starting to hear the rush of water as we neared her target area: Embudo Creek.

"So what's special about this area? What would make it mean something to Forrest?" I asked her, wondering if she had the answer that so many seemed to lack about their chosen locations.

"This is a spot where Forrest went fly fishing," she said, which didn't do much for me, since everyone used that reasoning about any river in their search zones. We came out onto the creek—a spit of running water pocked with boulders, flanked by high trees and rock walls on each side—and as we emerged, she added something interesting.

Sacha pointed up to the higher part of the river, where two bluffs overlooked the water below. Then she mentioned a name that made my ears perk up: Eric Sloane.

"Eric Sloane and Forrest were going to build a bridge over the river near here," she said, referring to Fenn's close friend. "This area meant something to both of them."

I wasn't sure how she could know that, but any connection that involved Sloane was attractive— Beep had mentioned numerous times that he believed the late Taos-based artist was a key to understanding the hunt. Sloane and Fenn had been great friends, meeting later in life, once Fenn was established in the art world. Sloane—married seven times—was a true bon vivant, an established landscape painter, a vaunted wit, and, seemingly, something of an inspiration to Fenn. During one of our lunches together, Fenn had waxed nostalgic about Sloane, saying he wished I'd met him.

Then, unsolicited, he'd given me a book he'd written about Sloane's work, **Seventeen Dollars a Square Inch: A Personal Tribute to Eric Sloane,** and signed it, "To Dan, You would have loved my Eric." So Sloane clearly had significant meaning to Fenn, and I mentioned to Sacha that I thought it was really promising that she thought there was a connection between Sloane and this spot. She didn't seem to need my approval, though, quickly going on to point out other features of her solve, explaining why this area just had to be the spot.

First, she said she knew the treasure was along the opposite side of the bank, because there was a literal rainbow along the wall, ending at a certain point, roughly where she believed the treasure to be. As we stood on the near side of the bank, Sacha pointed to the opposite wall, her arm arcing to demonstrate where I should see the rainbow.

"That's where we start," she said. "See the rainbow?"

"Wow," I responded gamely, not sure exactly what I was looking at. I saw a discoloring in some of the rock, maybe. But a rainbow?

Then she narrowed down the area in front of us, focusing in on a cluster of trees, because the formation of the trees itself visually represented the periodic table of the elements—something that Fenn hunters sometimes connected to him for reasons I wasn't 100 percent sure about. Regardless, if one looked at the trees and rocks on the opposite bank from the side we were on, the left side was supposed to represent the top left portion of the table—the hydrogen, lithium, magnesium area of the chart, if I was remembering high school science correctly—and then it swung down before arching up again toward a tree and rock formation that she believed resembled the helium, boron, carbon, nitrogen area on the other side of the chart. Were those the noble gases, on the far right? Or was that on the left? I mostly doodled jet planes while stuck in high school chemistry, so I had no idea.

But Sacha did—she knew the periodic table inside and out now. And she said that she'd found a picture of a group of schoolchildren in Fenn's book that had the exact same number of children in the picture as there are elements in the periodic table, something that reinforced that she was on the right track. So, working from that picture, and superimposing it upon the landscape in front of us, she teased out two big rocks across the bank as representing elements 79 and 80—gold and mercury—in the periodic table. Gold seemed obvious enough as a connection, and she thought the rocks, side by side, might also represent Fenn's parents' graves.

It was funny: Maybe a year ago, I would have thought that all sounded crazy. Graves, periodic tables, rainbows—maybe I'd been in this a little too long, but it no longer shocked me. I could see how her mind worked to justify these conclusions, and while it was almost certainly wrong, it wasn't such a bad piece of logic. Over time, seeing some of the things that Beep had come up with, some of the ideas that I had bought into, most of the weird conclusions I now came across just didn't seem quite so weird anymore. Well, some of them, maybe. But most of them, I'd come to accept—if you were going to find this thing, you had to get a little bit crazy yourself.

She quickly scampered off toward an archipelago of rocks that served as a makeshift bridge across the river, hopping like a mountain goat from one to the next, and telling me to follow her footsteps exactly; her boyfriend, she said, never liked this part, uncertain about the footing of her route.

"He would always get nervous that he was going to fall in—it's really not that tough," she said confidently, springing from one boulder to the next.

With my pack on my back, I was a little uncertain as well, but it turned out to be a relatively easy crossing—and one where, if I'd fallen in, the water was shallow enough that it wouldn't have been that dangerous anyway.

When we reached the other side, Sacha pointed backward, up at the rock face we'd just left behind, drawing my attention to three stones on the opposite wall.

"See those? Remember **The Goonies**?"

Of course—Sacha and I had bonded over **The Goonies,** with its hidden treasure and pirate ships, from the start.

"That's the three masts of a pirate ship, up there," she said.

As usual, I mostly just saw three rocks, though I got this sign a little more than the others.

Sacha started up the incline on the far side of the bank, heading into the trees that composed the middle sections of the periodic table in her mind's eye. I followed, stepping over roots and small boulders until we both reached a tiny clearing, where two enormous slabs of rock sat horizontally, accessible, before the cliff wall shot upward and became largely impassable.

Sacha stood in front of them, hands on hips, looking at the two rocks.

"This, on the right, is mercury," she said, pointing to the smaller of the two rocks before setting her gaze on the larger one. "And that's gold."

These rocks, she believed, had significance to Fenn. Since, in her mind, this was his old fishing spot, he'd brought others here. To this very rock.

"I think this place is special to Forrest because he made love here, to a woman who was not his wife," she said. "On this rock."

Then she paused.

"So Jason and I made love on this rock," she said matter-of-factly.

Oh. Okay.

After they had done the deed, she carved their names into the rock, so that they would be part of it and its story for all time. Until she and her boyfriend started having trouble. Then she came back and scratched his out.

As I was looking at the carved "Sacha" in the rock—and the accompanying #%@!%—she did something that shocked me: She reached under the "gold" rock, into a small, hollow area beneath it, and pulled out a shovel that had been hidden there. Then, shovel in hand, she went over to another rock and from behind it she pulled up a bundle of small pink lawn flags, the kind used for marking territory. She seemed satisfied.

"Good. No one's been here," she said, happy to see her cache undisturbed.

"You just leave this stuff here, and use it every time you come?" I asked, bewildered, and a bit impressed.

She explained that, yeah, she'd been here a number of times so far, trying different approaches. She used the flags to mark out certain areas, and the shovel, well, that was self-explanatory—and, now, important.

This time, with me here, her specific purpose was to burrow into the area below the "gold" rock. The slab of rock was perhaps twelve feet long by eight feet wide, with the cutout beneath it maybe a foot and a half deep—and she wanted to get all the way underneath, use the shovel to dig away at the dirt under the rock, and make sure nothing was secreted below. There was that whole Fenn **buried/ hidden** distinction to account for, but she wouldn't actually be digging underground, just moving dirt aside to get deeper into the crawl space under the rock. Besides, who knew that the thing actually wasn't buried anyway? So many of Fenn's "clues" and pronouncements were so opaque as to make them questionable, depending on the situation.

"You're just here to tell the authorities what happened to me if this falls, and make sure my kids get the life insurance," she said as she started crawling under the rock.

I thought she was kidding. But as she started to inch underneath, beginning to disappear under this enormous slab of stone, I began to recognize how truly dangerous this was. She was going to be fully under this thing, actively displacing the dirt that was holding it in place—and if it moved, it would absolutely crush her to death.

"Are you sure you want to be, like, digging away at that? It really could move," I said.

"No, no, it's safe; it's sturdy. I've been on this rock before." Man, had she ever! "Shine your flashlight here, will ya?"

She dug away, tossing dirt, pebbles, and sometimes even small rocks in my direction as I tried to shine my phone's beam into the crevice to give her some light.

"Shine it right up by the top," she said, a sudden urgency in her voice. "You see that? That shiny area?"

I kinda did, a little, maybe, a rock that looked different from the rest, deep under the larger rock. Sacha was grinding herself deep underneath, trying to get closer. She was fully covered by the rock now, dead for sure if the mammoth stone moved even a few inches.

I drew closer and directed the flashlight where she was digging, getting a faceful of dirt tossed my way for my trouble. She was reaching for something, pulling more earth out from under the rock, more pebbles, more support. I was about to say something else, when suddenly she stopped and released a deep breath, and for a moment there was silence.

"It's nothing. There's nothing under there," she said.

Sacha began to shimmy her way out from beneath the rock, emerging one limb at a time. She stood up, her blue fleece covered in dirt and muck, looking defeated. The treasure hunter brushed some undergrowth out of her hair, then sat down on the leaf-covered ground, arms across her knees, and hung her head.

"I just keep looking and looking, and I don't know what I'm doing wrong," she said quietly.

Then she yelled out, loudly enough to be heard all the way to Santa Fe, "I'm in the right place.

So where is the fucking box? Where is the fucking box, Forrest?"

As we wound our way back down south toward Española, and eventually on to Santa Fe, Sacha didn't seem discouraged by yet another failed search. She seemed invigorated, actually: happy to have gotten out and crossed off another possibility and already moving on to other concepts, other spots to try within her area. More than that, though, what was really pushing her was her crusade against the FennTubers. As I drove, she sat in the passenger seat and regaled me with things they'd done wrong, ways they've ticked off Fenn or damaged the hunt. At one point, she took a phone call from another Fenn hunter, and the conversation with him went much along those same lines.

In many ways, she seemed to be pining for more innocent days within the search, circa 2015, when no one had yet died, the community was smaller, and no one had really figured out how to profit from the whole enterprise.

"The hunt is all about making money now," she said as we came upon Española. "Where have all the good searchers gone?"

But maybe that wasn't the right question. Maybe the right question was whether there were ever that many good searchers to begin with.

In my conversations with Toby Younis, of A

Gypsy's Kiss, I began to realize that he had a better handle than pretty much anyone on the actual size of the Fenn community—if anyone had any real data on this, it was the people trying to make money off it, using metrics and the internet to track Fenn-related traffic.

Fenn's world existed in two places: the random wilds of the Rocky Mountains and on the internet. Other than the annual Fennboree, there were no meetups, no clubhouses, no get-togethers, really. There were just the message boards, the vlogs, the chat rooms. If you were into hunting Forrest Fenn's treasure, you were doing it via the internet.

That was why Younis and Carney figured they could tap that community as they started on their project. And what they'd found was that every estimate, at every point, had likely vastly overstated the number of searchers who were really out there.

It was in everyone's interest, starting with Fenn himself, and moving on to the television stations, magazine writers, and, yes, authors who were fascinated by this chase, to be able to tout as large a number of searchers as possible looking for this thing.

So when Fenn routinely said he believed there were from 300,000 to 350,000 interested, active searchers worldwide, those numbers were repeated and passed on and took on a life of their own. But what were they based on, really? Anything?

I contacted a few governmental agencies—the

New Mexico Tourism Department, Tourism Santa
Fe, the Yellowstone National Park administration—
but none of them had any idea how many visitors were Fenn-related. The closest I got to any
sort of answer about whether it was a lot or a little
was from the New Mexico Tourism Department,
which said very few, if any, requests or queries from
out-of-state Fenn hunters were received, even after
it released the video relating to his chase in 2014.

When I asked Fenn where he got that number
from, he said it was an extrapolation based on the
number of emails he got per day—another figure
to take with a grain of salt, but one that I at least
gave him the benefit of the doubt on when he said
he received more than one hundred daily. But how
many of those were from the same people? How
many repeats? And how, based on that, could one
get a number upward of 300,000 anyway? It obviously was not exactly rigorous statistical analysis.

"So the three hundred and fifty thousand number is just impossibly big. I don't even know how
he came [to] that," Younis said. "He says it's based
on his emails, but based on the activity that we see,
it's really just not that big a number."

But even once Younis realized that Fenn's figures were cartoonish, he still assumed there was
a sizable community out there—if not 350,000,
then at least big enough to support a viable online
enterprise—something in the six figures, at least.

Over time, however, he had come to believe he was wrong.

"We picked this market—what we didn't know at the time is that it's a very limited market. There's not 350,000 people out there searching for it; it's much, much smaller than that. I'm going to estimate that it's an order of magnitude less than Fenn thinks it is. Maybe thirty to fifty thousand interested searchers," Younis said.

Younis was basing his numbers on the traffic to his and other blogs, to the YouTube channels and chat rooms, and the total downloads of Fenn-related videos. Using a website called Social Blade, he had rigorously tracked the growth of his following, analyzing the normal subscribers, the onetime viewers, the people who visited and didn't watch a video, the obsessives who watched ten videos per day—all of it. A Gypsy's Kiss, undisputedly the most popular Fenn channel, was getting 70,000 views a month, and went over a total of 1.3 million views in the winter of 2018.

Sounds like a lot, right? It's not. Much—most—of that was repeat traffic, and growth was incredibly slow. Once the core, devoted followers were in, there just wasn't a lot of market to tap, Younis said. The audience wasn't there.

"If there are, they're not using the internet, because you can't get on the internet, search Forrest Fenn, and not find us."

"We only had three thousand subscribers, we were making one thousand dollars a month, and I don't think any other FennTuber was even close to that," Younis said. "It was straightforward, until we realized the market couldn't grow. If we had stayed doing thirty to forty hours a week, two hundred and fifty–plus original programs, in five years we'd have twenty thousand subscribers. So you had to ask yourself, Is this just the wrong market for us?"

Younis looked at the traffic that the other Fenn blogs brought in, tried to identify how many searchers were really out there. He found an echo chamber.

"Dal Neitzel's site has about three thousand," Younis said. "ChaseChat, which has been around as long as Dal, has about three thousand, and about ten percent of them are active. It's very low traffic. It's the same guys talking about the same stuff."

But as a result of trying to gauge the market, Younis had also collected some of the best data—the only data, really—available on the Fenn searcher community. A Gypsy's Kiss ran searcher surveys in 2018 and 2019, asking questions about who the searchers were, where they got their information, where they liked to search, and so on. Over three hundred searchers responded each time, and the responses are illuminating.

For instance, the 2019 survey, with its 343

respondents, seems to bear out the assumption that most searchers were male; 75 percent of those who responded said they were. The most common age group was comprised of those between fifty-five and sixty-four, with 30 percent of respondents, followed close behind by those between forty-five and fifty-four, with 26 percent.

Close to 60 percent of the 2019 respondents were recent arrivals to the chase, starting in 2017 or later. Still, 10 percent came from the first big year, 2013, and so many of the most prominent searchers still claimed 2013 as their start date. Whatever their vintage, they all spent a fair amount of time researching: Forty-two percent said they spent between four and ten hours a week studying the hunt, and 16 percent said they spent a whopping twenty-plus hours weekly on the chase.

But that doesn't mean they were out searching all that often. Of this group, 34 percent had never gone boots-on-the-ground, and another 23 percent had ventured out only once or twice. Two percent said they'd been on more than one hundred hunts.

The biggest chunk, 39 percent, believed that the treasure was somewhere in New Mexico, and 11 percent thought it was in Yellowstone. The non-Yellowstone parts of Montana were surprisingly attractive, with 21 percent of respondents picking that as the spot, followed by non-Yellowstone Wyoming at 16 percent, and Colorado at 12.5 percent. And they thought it would be found soon—75 percent believed it would be found by 2022 or earlier.

Who would find it? Well, they would, of course. Of this group, 17 percent believed they were 100 percent certain to find the treasure, and another 15 percent thought they were upward of 75 percent likely to find it. Beep was probably down with the 36 percent who thought they had a less than 25 percent chance of finding it, while on all but my best days, I'd slot myself in with the 18 percent who believed they had a 0.0 percent chance of finding the treasure.

The data mostly confirmed the commonly held assumptions about Fenn hunters, and Younis considered it heartening that most of the hunters had come to the chase more recently.

But as time wore on, Younis started to have second thoughts about continuing with the channel, for reasons both personal and financial.

First, his experiences in the eye of the Fenn storm, with all its associated drama, made him unsure that he'd ever want to actually find the chest. He thought Fenn was understating it when he opined that 7 percent of the people out there were crazy, and Younis had come to believe the treasure might just be more trouble than it was worth.

"The people who are looking for it are at the stage where they're looking for it in order to solve their problems," Younis said, giving voice to the thoughts that had been plaguing me of late. "A part of me says to myself, Considering the seven-percenters, would it really be wise to own that treasure? And I'm not so sure it would be."

The other reason was financial. Seeing so little growth, and understanding that the market was more limited than they'd initially believed, Younis and Carney came to a decision: They would give up A Gypsy's Kiss in favor of something more lucrative.

"We've spent thousands of hours and thousands of dollars looking for the treasure, and we still have no idea where the treasure could be hidden, and we're not getting any younger, and we have other, more productive things we want to do with that time and money," Younis told their followers in a farewell message delivered toward the end of 2018.

"So we are off to a new project with a bigger market," he said.

For a time, his working hours were increasingly devoted to the pair's next venture: crafting courses for the online learning platform Udemy. The other FennTubers tried to fill the gap, hoping that their streams would benefit from the absence of A Gypsy's Kiss; it began working, slowly. Not long after A Gypsy's Kiss retreated, Cowlazars went over two thousand subscribers.

But the pull of the treasure was strong. Fans in the community clamored for the return of the program, and Younis and Carney admitted they missed being involved. So only a few months later, A Gypsy's Kiss made its return. They cut down on their schedule of shows, and those they did offer included a few more pitches that viewers check out Younis's other, potentially more lucrative projects— but they were there, once again a part of the chase's ongoing dialogue.

Really, how could they stay away? Even for someone like Younis, who had described his own efforts as mercenary, the allure of the box and all that had grown up around it continued to prove hard to resist.

Unfortunately, someone else I knew was grappling with that very same problem.

12

BEEP'S REVELATION

The tears started trickling down Beep's cheeks as he finally broke down, admitting what both Tyler and I had already guessed to be true.

"This treasure hunt has cost me my relationship with Jordan," Beep said. "And I just don't understand why you don't respect how much I've put into this."

There it was. Beep had told me a little while ago, almost offhandedly, that he and his girlfriend, Jordan, had broken up, but he hadn't divulged the cause. Only now, when we were sitting in a cabin in West Yellowstone, Montana, hours from actually going hunting for the treasure, was he willing to admit what had really happened—that his hunting mania was what had driven them apart. And he had acknowledged that ugly truth only because our friend and now hunting partner Tyler wouldn't back down and accept the percentage of the spoils that Beep wanted him to take.

When it had been just Beep and I partnered up, it had always been relatively easy to work this stuff out. We were just going to divide the treasure evenly. But this time, Beep, inexplicably, decided to invite a third party on this hunt—a friend from the daily fantasy sports world, Tyler—and offered him an actual percentage of the spoils. I thought it was an immediate mistake. Why add another mouth to feed, especially when Tyler knew virtually nothing about the hunt? What did he bring to the table?

He may have known nothing about treasure hunting, but Tyler sure did know about betting, and gambling, and how to drive a hard bargain. Shortly before they flew from Toronto to Montana, Tyler let Beep know that he wanted 17 percent of the potential payout, and no less. Beep, flabbergasted, couldn't fathom that Tyler was trying to take what Beep believed to be rightfully his, and the issue strained their interactions all the way to the present moment. Now crammed into this little cabin on the edge of West Yellowstone, voices were rising, emotions were running hot, and our makeshift triumvirate was on the verge of falling apart before we even got out on the hunt.

"I've put in literally thousands of hours in the past few months, basically ruined my whole life,"

Beep said as the tears flared into anger. "I just want what's fair for what I put into it."

Over the last few months, Beep had become truly obsessed with the chase, to an extent that I started to think was legitimately unhealthy. As the 2018 search season began and hunters began getting boots on the ground, Beep had spent hundreds of hours hunkered down in front of his computer instead, trying out new solves, spending entire nights wide awake, diving down internet rabbit holes. He suddenly seemed to have time for little else in his life.

Beep always needed something to fixate on, and now the hunt was filling that need for him. For a while after he had left the world of fantasy sports behind, Beep had scratched that itch with a few different things: cryptocurrency investing, hanging out with Jordan, treasure hunting, and, primarily, building his board game.

But now that the game was proving frustrating, and the value of cryptocurrency had been taking a big plunge over the past few months, Beep had gotten more and more into the treasure hunt, spending long nights prowling the internet, poring over Fenn's books and scrutinizing maps of the Rocky Mountains, finally going to bed when the sun came up. And he'd started to drag Jordan into it with him.

Beep can be convincing when he believes he's

figured something out, and so Jordan had trusted him when he said he was on the verge of finding the elusive chest. Even, to her credit, when that meant jetting out to Yellowstone on hardly a moment's notice.

Beep had always been much more focused on the Yellowstone area than I was, but around the same time he really became obsessed, he'd started to zero in on the park and its surrounding areas in earnest, believing that he was coming up with solutions no one else had yet devised.

Never one simply to ruminate on a good idea, Beep would be seized by a compulsion to act once he had one of his brainstorms. That meant searching for the treasure immediately—like right that moment. After spending days incommunicado, fervently studying the treasure, he'd suddenly surface. And then at 11:00 p.m. on a weeknight, I'd get text messages like this one, which arrived in late spring: "Dan! What are your plans for this weekend? I'm heading out to grab the treasure, flight leaves at 6:40 a.m. tomorrow."

Yeesh.

With Amalie away covering the NHL play-offs, and our son, Elliott, only around a year old, I wasn't going to join him on these last-minute expeditions west. Instead, Beep took Jordan along, promising adventure and excitement and, of course, that they would find a treasure.

Jordan gamely agreed, even though Beep was

hijacking her birthday weekend, as it happened, with that particular trip. That expedition was a near-total disaster, with Beep searching for a ground well that wasn't there, getting lost in Idaho (hardly realizing that he wasn't even in the same state as Yellowstone), and royally pissing off the first real girlfriend he'd ever had.

Less than two weeks later, Beep believed he was on the verge of discovery yet again. He puzzled out a much better solve, and dragged Jordan along again, as well as his dad. He was so certain of his spot, in fact, that he wanted additional reinforcements, and with my being unable to go, he did something smart and contacted a veteran searcher for help: Cynthia.

Knowing that he was a pretty terrible explorer, Beep had offered to hire her out for the trip—offering $600 for her time, plus $150,000 if they actually found the treasure through his solve (Beep, in an uncharacteristic moment of frugality, promised his dad and girlfriend only $25,000 each). Cynthia, frustrated with New Mexico and looking to branch out, had already hoped to be searching the Yellowstone area around June, so she quickly agreed. They set out into the wilderness, trekking around Imperial Geyser in Yellowstone, a three-mile walk from the main trail. Beep believed the chest might be around the sagebrush near the geyser itself—sagebrush being a key link to the line "If you've been **wise** and found the blaze," but once they were on-site, Cynthia quickly figured out why Fenn's treasure couldn't be there: "It's too far for Forrest to walk from the road," she'd said. "An eighty-year-old man wouldn't do two of these trips in one afternoon."

They headed back home unfulfilled. What's worse, these trips were costing Beep in more than just travel expenses. Every time he went, he'd make a five-figure bet with his friend Mike McDonald, a well-known poker pro who goes by the nickname "Timex," that he would find the treasure. Every time he came back empty-handed, he'd owe Timex another $10,000, or more.

Still, after his two failed attempts, Beep came back to me once again with something new, saying he'd discovered something so perfect, so incredible, so revolutionary, that he was 100 percent certain the treasure was there. He was guarding his revelation so carefully that he wouldn't tell me what it was over the phone or on Skype or text, too nervous that our calls were being monitored by the government. I tried to explain how crazy that was—that government employees would be actively bugging a pair of idiots like us, first, and then that they would use the information to swipe Fenn's treasure ahead of us. But he refused to take the chance. And he didn't want to just fly out overnight this time; he wanted me there with him to claim it.

"Dan, you're not going to believe this," he told me. "It all fits, everything. It's so, so sick. It's one hundred percent. We just have to go out there and pick it up."

How could I say no to that? With a few weeks' lead time, I agreed to join him, and was excited about finally hearing the details of this epic break-through once we reached Yellowstone. But then Beep threw a wrench into all of it with his surprise decision to invite Tyler, and he now seemed to be in genuine distress about his breakup with Jordan.

I was sympathetic to Beep, wanted to be there for him, wanted to acknowledge both his exten-sive work and what it all had cost him. And with tempers rising, I knew this situation needed to be defused, and fast. Sensing that Beep was at the end of his rope, I tried to offer a compromise before this devolved even further.

"Okay, how about this? I'll take thirty percent, and if Tyler keeps seventeen, then you still get more than half," I suggested.

That didn't solve the real problem, however, which in Beep's mind was Tyler's unfair desire for such a big share in the first place. We seemed des-tined to sink deeper into this mess, screaming at one another over slices of something as real and tangible as the holy grail.

For a fleeting second, I started to think this thing might get physical. But somehow, Tyler blinked before Beep did.

"You know what, fuck it. I'm going home. I'm getting the first flight out tomorrow. I just don't want to be involved in this anymore. I thought it was going to be fun, like an adventure, and that's not what it is at all," Tyler said. "I don't even want a percentage. I don't want any part of this anymore. I just want to leave."

His words came as welcome relief, the only real solution at this point. I started to protest a little, but halfheartedly—I liked Tyler, but I, too, wanted him gone. Tyler hadn't been a part of this whole journey, and now that we might be nearing something great, why did he get to latch on at the very end? The treasure had to be earned. And he hadn't put in the time like we had. Even if I hadn't spent the hours Beep had on it, I'd brought something to the table—access, knowledge, insight that had helped Beep form his conclusions. I'd been on boots-on-the-ground hunts. I'd shared in the risks. I deserved it, Beep deserved it, but Tyler? No.

I could be territorial, too.

With Tyler's retreat, at last the tension began to ebb as we all came to terms with the fact that Tyler would be flying back to Canada barely twenty-four hours after traveling all the way out here, having never even seen Yellowstone—and yet somehow this treasure hunt had made us all feel it was for the best.

"Should get some dinner, walk around a little maybe, eh?" Beep suggested, suddenly bouncy and ebullient again.

Desperate for some fresh air—in every sense—we

agreed that was a good idea, and after a brief rest, we headed out into town. We'd all flown into Bozeman, Montana, earlier that day, and made the two-hour drive down to West Yellowstone immediately, arguing about percentages much of the way. It was a beautiful drive, one long, winding road through tree-lined canyons, with little to no civilization along the way except for the tiny town of Big Sky. When we reached West Yellowstone at last, we were all too wound up to appreciate it, but now that things seemed settled—for better or worse—I could get my bearings a little, and recognize what an alien place we had landed in.

Even after spending years as a traveling baseball writer, crisscrossing the country, heading from one big city to the next, this trip to Montana marked my first time in that vast expanse of nothingness stretching from Seattle to Minneapolis. It was like nowhere I'd been before—even the people on the plane coming into Bozeman looked different. They weren't western, nor southern, they were something close but altogether different. They were tough. Like if you slapped some period clothes on them, they could all seamlessly become extras in **Lonesome Dove.**

The town of West Yellowstone is a 0.8-square-mile rectangle, a tiny oasis of civilization plopped in the middle of nowhere, next to the west entrance of Yellowstone National Park. The moment you reach the edge of that rectangle, the town stops abruptly;

there are no random houses, or service roads, or suburbs, or anything—just the forest leading to the park in one direction, and little but dirt in the others.

West Yellowstone exists solely to serve the park. The town was founded when E. H. Harriman—president of the Union Pacific Railroad—took a trip to Yellowstone in 1905, was mesmerized by its charms, and decided that the Old Faithful area toward the western edge of the park needed dedicated rail service. He built a line from St. Anthony, Idaho, to the park's entrance. Once the rail line arrived in 1908, the railroad terminus instantly became a tiny town, populated by only three families at first, but one that grew steadily over the years, until it became West Yellowstone, the thriving, sweet little summer village that Fenn chronicled with such affection in his books.

Walking around West Yellowstone brought memories flooding in—someone else's memories. Fenn's memories. All these place names were so familiar, each one harkening back to something from one of Fenn's hokey stories, the ones he told in his books, stories that might have offered clues to the treasure, or might have just been an old man reminiscing. I'd studied those tales so carefully that Fenn's landmarks now seemed like my own—the Gallatin River, Eagle's Store, the place names so familiar that it gave a thrill to actually see them in person. It was akin to how everyone knows the names of parts of Los Angeles, because they're used as locations in so many movies. We searchers knew West Yellowstone in that same way, because it was part of Fenn's lore, the home base for the tales of his youthful frolicking in the great outdoors.

But the truth was, West Yellowstone wasn't how I'd imagined it. Well, a bit of it was—the skeleton of the town that had existed here long ago, with its old rustic-architecture general stores and its long-shuttered train depot, now a museum. But most of the town that was there now? I couldn't imagine that Fenn would even recognize it. As Beep, Tyler, and I walked down one of the two main streets, past the IMAX theater and the indoor shooting range offering to let us fire machine guns, we were struck by how commercial it all seemed, how processed.

"This place feels like Niagara Falls," Tyler said, and for someone from Toronto, that wasn't a compliment. As anyone who has ever gone to see the beautiful falls soon finds, the city of Niagara Falls is a complete tourist trap. West Yellowstone isn't quite there, but it's not that far off, either.

The streets were lined with stores selling merchandise, so many Yellowstone-related knickknacks and generic T-shirts, more than could clothe twenty seasons' worth of park-going tourists. How could so many of these stores possibly exist? I must have counted ten or twelve at least.

A surprisingly eclectic collection of ethnic restaurants serving visitors from all over the world were scattered through the town, often flanked by miniature casinos, the storefront kind with slot machines and a few tables, giving the town the feel of a kind of rural, extremely low-rent Vegas strip. Unsurprisingly, since my party consisted of two professional gamblers, we were soon heading inside one, Beep saying he'd like to check it out, maybe play some slots. As soon as we opened the door, however, we realized that this establishment might be more than just a few rungs down from the Bellagio. The dimly lit space was even more depressing than you'd think a rural Montana storefront casino would be. A general pall of death hung over the entire room.

"Yeah, I don't think this is my kind of place," Beep said as he turned around and led us right back out the front door again. "I really only like the old-timey slot machines where I can pull the arm, anyway. Pressing the button just isn't the same."

Fenn, his brother, and a friend had actually built a motel in West Yellowstone, the Dude Motel, in the early 1960s, and it was still there; we passed it while walking around the town. But curiously, Fenn said on a 2017 podcast that he hadn't been back to the town of West Yellowstone in over fifty years—something that sent the Fenn community aflutter. Fenn later clarified that wasn't what he had meant, and Dal argued on Fenn's behalf that the old man was referring to the last time he'd spent a full summer there, in 1950. Regardless, he clearly hadn't spent much time there lately, and I don't think he would have loved what the town had become. I'd certainly imagined something purer, more natural, less commercialized, though maybe I was guilty of seeing it through Fenn's mind's eye, those seventy-five-year-old rose-colored memories of an impressionable young boy.

Still, there were redeeming elements here, vestiges of the Americana that Fenn loved and espoused so well. We walked by one fishing shop after another, entering a few, and all the guides and employees were friendly as can be. When we passed Eagle's Store, the sign proudly noted that not only had it been founded the same year as the town, 1908, but that it was still being run by the same family who'd created it. There was a live theater, the Playmill, which put on performances near nightly, doing **The Little Mermaid** and **Annie Get Your Gun** when we were in town.

There was even a rodeo being held outside the town that night, and a car festooned with rodeo ads drove by promoting it. The driver, armed with a car-mounted loudspeaker system, cruised down the streets, barking out the times of the main events just like Jake and Elwood Blues did to promote their concert in **The Blues Brothers**— something I never thought really happened outside of the movies.

We settled into a dinner at the Three Bears Lodge, and, thankfully, we all seemed to have reached a sort of détente. Tyler was still intent on going home, but he didn't seem angry about it—a little relieved, even. He wasn't alone.

Beep, now assured of a larger percentage, was manic, thinking and talking only of the treasure and how he couldn't wait to get out into the field the next day and find it. Incredibly, he still wouldn't tell me his solve, so I didn't even know where we were supposed to be going, just that we'd be heading somewhere inside Yellowstone. Beep said we wouldn't need to walk too far off the trail; that we should be able to park our car, walk away from the tourist areas, and go pick the treasure right up. Could it really be that easy? I wondered.

We were supposed to meet Cynthia Meachum in the morning, to say hello and grab some bear spray from her; we had plans to go hunting with her as well, later in the week, and to attend an event she was planning for Fenn hunters in the Yellowstone area, a kind of pseudo-Fennboree for anyone searching up in Wyoming or Montana. But with Beep so sure we were going to find the treasure, I couldn't get my mind off the hunt to come the following day. My partner was generally a bit excitable, sure. But I'd never seen him this protective of his stake in something, fully willing to sacrifice his longtime friendship with Tyler over a few more percentage points of this find. Did that mean he was right? Or that Fenn's hunt had taken him, and he was its latest casualty—just another hunter who had gone too far, sacrificed too much, for a box we would never find?

The first reports depicting the wonders that would become Yellowstone National Park date to the 1860s, and what they described was considered so fantastical that it could not be believed. Holes venting hot steam from the ground? Mud pots? Rainbow-colored pools dotting the landscape? Geysers spewing water one hundred feet in the air, hourly, like clockwork? Such a place couldn't exist. One report, sent to a reputable East Coast magazine, was denied with a reply of "Thank you, but we do not print fiction."

It was, of course, no mere fiction. Yellowstone was real, and it was spectacular. In 1871, an organized expedition brought a survey team and a photographer to the area, and when the photos and illustrations were sent back east to confirm the earlier written reports, it created a sensation. Congress got involved, as did the railroads, which believed that the lure of this so-called wonderland would spur tourists to head west on the newly completed transcontinental railroad.

In 1872, President Ulysses S. Grant signed legislation creating Yellowstone as the world's first national park. Six years later, roads were cut through the wilderness, and by 1883, the Northern Pacific Railroad built the first spur line to serve the area, allowing guests to travel through the north entrance by stagecoach and tour the park. Hotels began springing up inside Yellowstone, largely sponsored by the railroads—gorgeous oases in the wilderness, like the Mammoth Hotel, and the Old Faithful Inn, which still stands today and may be the largest log building in the world. Soon, other rail lines followed, like the western entrance spur, which brought West Yellowstone into being, and then, finally, the advent of the automobile truly made Yellowstone accessible to all.

Today, more than four million visitors enter the park annually, roughly a million more visitors per year than toured it just ten years ago, Fenn hunters comprising a tiny but consistent slice of those in the 2010s.

I'd contacted the Yellowstone press office just before my journey, wanting to talk about the toll the Fenn hunters had taken on the park. I knew from my own conversations that they wandered off trails, damaged irreplaceable natural phenomena, and strayed too far in pursuit of a treasure they were so sure was just around the bend. Documents I later obtained showed that Yellowstone officials had responded to twenty-one incidents of various degrees of seriousness involving Fenn hunters from 2013 through the summer of 2020. There had undoubtedly been more, situations caused by those who wouldn't admit to being on the hunt when they got themselves in trouble or in danger.

I talked to an employee of the West Yellowstone Fire Department, who was fed up with the wanton recklessness of the Fenn searchers; West Yellowstone was often called in to help on these rescue operations in and around the park, or to back up other stations when park search and rescue was deployed. The hunters drove them crazy.

"It's the same people, over and over," the person said. "They go out once, they get in trouble, have to get rescued, and then they go right back out again. They get a little farther this time. They have to get rescued again. They don't learn."

And why would they? the person stressed. It wasn't their money used on the searches.

"It doesn't matter to them; it's not costing them anything. What do they care that it costs two thousand, ten thousand dollars, whatever. They're not paying for it. They just want to get back out. Then it happens again."

One of those hunters was Darrell Seyler, a former cop living in Seattle. Like so many others, Seyler became obsessed with the treasure, eventually leading a group of adventurers into Yellowstone to find it. Things quickly went wrong, according to a gripping story by Peter Frick-Wright in **Outside** magazine, detailing Seyler's April 2014 trip to Yellowstone, where he entered the park and quickly flipped his raft while attempting to cross the Lamar River.

"He was washed 1.5 miles downstream, nearly

drowned, and spent a 26-degree night soaking wet on the river's snowy banks before search and rescue got there. But then, instead of waiting to see which of the 16 misdemeanors and park violations local prosecutors were going to pursue, Darrell drove back to Yellowstone in May, crossed the Lamar on foot, lost track of time, spent another night on the riverbank, and was again picked up by search and rescue," according to the account in **Outside.**

Yellowstone officials charged Seyler with reckless endangerment, illegal camping, and possession of a metal detector in the backcountry, Frick-Wright wrote. Seyler spent six days in Montana's Bighorn County Jail, and was ordered to pay a six-thousand-dollar fine in monthly installments. The repercussions didn't end there. Seyler lost his job, was kicked out of his apartment, and was forced to live in his car. Eventually, he fell behind on the fine payments, and a warrant was issued for the ex-cop's arrest. None of this stopped him from hunting for the treasure. He would go to McDonald's and use their Wi-Fi to keep looking.

At that moment, I could understand how he felt.

Beep and I were finally heading into this beautiful, historic, dangerous park, having spent two hours driving Tyler all the way up to Bozeman to take his plane, and then hauling the two hours back. The ride up to the airport was frosty, strained. Beep clearly wanted to talk about the treasure, but he refused to reveal his solve with Tyler still in the car. Tyler just wanted out of the entire situation. I mostly wanted everyone to get along. It was a weird vibe. But with Tyler gone, and with us now heading directly for the park, Beep was at last comfortable enough to explain his solve, the brilliant revelation he'd had that was going to lead us to the treasure. And now that he had his chance, he couldn't keep the words from coming out—he was burbling over, like someone had finally popped the cork.

"Oh my God, Dan, you're not going to believe how sick this solve is. It's like, it's so perfect, I can't believe that nobody else has figured it out," he began.

"Okay, okay," I said, prodding him, trying to keep one eye on the long, winding roads. "What is it? Where are we going?"

"We're going to the Upper Geyser Basin," he said. "To Old Faithful."

Old Faithful? That took me by surprise.

"So after my last solve, at the Imperial Geyser, I went back to the books, all three of them," Beep said, referring to Fenn's memoir trilogy.

"Fenn says that a good hunter will go read the poem, and then read the books again, and then read the poem, back and forth. I did. And that's when I found it," Beep said, pausing for effect.

"The geyser map. It's a key. The key to unlocking the puzzle."

Yellowstone's most famous feature is, of course,
Old Faithful, the geyser that erupts roughly every
ninety minutes, spewing superheated water more
than one hundred feet in the air. Crowds gather and
watch, and an entire visitor center has been built
around the geyser zone. But what I didn't know—
and what Beep believed very few others had considered—is that there are hundreds and hundreds
of geysers in Yellowstone, big, small, and tiny, dotting the landscape. And they all have names.

I listened, rapt, as Beep explained that something sparked in his brain when he saw the word
faithful used in a strange context in **The Thrill of
the Chase.** It was something about having a faithful car—a strange, almost forced way to use the
word. Beep couldn't help but notice it. It made
him wonder, What about the other geyser names?
He started looking up some of the bigger, better-
known ones—and realized they had connections to
the book. Teapot Geyser could reference "Tea with
Olga," a cryptic story in this memoir, where Fenn
sips tea with an acquaintance named Olga, and
then later scatters her ashes atop Taos Mountain.
Fan Geyser might reference another tale in the
book, one where Fenn crashes his car, and pays
particular attention to the image of the radiator
fan spinning around. Beep started listing off one
after another, and referencing the spots in Fenn's
books where touchstone words would appear, then
making the connection to one geyser after another.

Fenn had always said that a child with a map could solve his riddle—that it was actually really simple. And what could be simpler than just looking at the geyser names and then using the key to unlock the poem? A child really could do it. You just had to figure out the key.

And the key, Beep said, would lead us directly to the Upper Geyser Basin, the home of Old Faithful. There are more than five hundred geysers in the park, spread across hundreds of miles of land. But when Beep tried applying the names of geysers from other areas, there were no connections. Only the 150 geysers in the Upper Geyser Basin correlated to words and stories from Fenn's book. So the key was a geyser map, but a specific geyser map— telling us to search the Old Faithful area.

"Nobody goes to the Old Faithful area, because it's so crowded with tourists. But what if Fenn knew that, and expected that, and it's been under everyone's nose this whole time?" Beep said. "He played all around these geysers as a kid, when there weren't so many tourists around them. They're all special to him."

That was brilliant—but also flawed, I pointed out. Beep just stated the crux of the problem with his own solve: all the people. How can a treasure chest be hidden in what is essentially plain sight? Fenn had said the chest wasn't in "close proximity to a human trail." That seemed impossible here.

"Are any of these spots secluded enough to

really fit?" I asked as we crossed the state line from Montana into Wyoming, drawing ever closer to our goal. "Like, you've got to be a couple of hundred feet away from the trail, at least. And if these are so close to the tourist spots, wouldn't somebody have found it almost by accident already?"

"So that's the thing, Dan. For most of the geysers, yes, they're too close. But look at this," he said, pulling up a map on his phone. I craned my head over to see it, trying not to veer off the road and into the trees.

It was a map, one I'd never seen before—a map that showed all the names of the geysers in Yellowstone. Not just the big ones but all the smaller ones, too. They all have names, many of them ridiculous, seemingly random—Baby Daisy Geyser, Catfish Geyser, Radiator Geyser, Bijou Geyser—and most are concentrated close to Old Faithful, which we knew was overrun by tourists. But Beep zoomed in on an area north of the main section, near Biscuit Basin, a few miles from the tourist zones. There sat a pocket of about fifteen geysers, running along the Firehole River, near a trail, but not too near. The kind of area that an old man could walk to from his car, but one that was secluded enough that tourists didn't really frequent it.

"And the geysers in there—the names are perfect. Slide Geyser—the story of him sliding down the pole. Atomizer Geyser—Fenn flew planes armed with atomic bombs in Vietnam. Iron Spring—when his pants got stained like iron," Beep said. "They're all around one giant geyser, Artemisia Geyser."

Artemisia, he explained, is the root genus of sagebrush. Sage, as in wise—"If you've been wise and found the blaze." It actually sparked something else for me—that **Artemisia** comes from the name Artemis: the Greek goddess of the hunt. Beep's key felt like a revelation, maybe the first real one we'd had. Suddenly, I was seeing connections all over the place, and so many of Fenn's seemingly nonsensical stories and anecdotes now seemed to make sense: They were vessels for him to use all these weird words, directing us to follow the clues. His rambling tale about sliding down an iron fire escape? Slide Geyser and Iron Spring, just like Beep had said. When he goes on what seems like a non sequitur tangent about spanking? Well, there's Spanker Geyser. So many things fell into place when seen in this context. Hell, it even made me think of that movie **National Treasure,** where the key to a complex puzzle is hidden in plain sight, on the back of the Declaration of Independence. My heart started to race, and I pressed harder on the accelerator.

"I am so happy I know you, you beautiful, beautiful genius," I told Beep, who was positively beaming. "Okay, so now how did you apply the key? Where do we actually find the treasure?"

And that was when it all began to fall apart.

"So I started to apply the poem twice, so that

we start at Madison Junction, as where 'warm waters halt,' and continue down the Firehole canyon, until it takes you to Old Faithful," Beep said.

"And then once you reach Old Faithful, you run the poem again, and use the key to apply the geyser names to parts of the poem," he continued.

Running the poem twice? I'd never heard of anyone doing that.

"Cynthia mentioned it once, like, you run the poem until it takes you to an area, and then you run it again, and it brings you to a more specific spot," Beep said.

Hmm.

I started pressing Beep to get more details, and it was suddenly disturbingly clear that my partner didn't have answers for how many of the original parts of the poem were supposed to correspond to specific points on the map; he had a few—the Nez Perce Creek as "the home of Brown," for instance, because it was where brown trout were first introduced to the park—but other pieces, he had no answer for. He just wanted to have a reason to get us down to Old Faithful, and to allow him to start rerunning the poem from there. I kept my reservations in check, and asked about where the second run starts.

"So what's 'warm waters halt' on the second run, then?"

"That's Old Faithful," Beep said, as if that should be obvious to anyone with half a brain, though I couldn't quite see how a geyser spouting hot water could constitute the water halting. "Or it could start even earlier, at Solitary Geyser, above Old Faithful—that could be Fenn's 'I have gone alone in there.'"

"And what's 'the canyon down'?"

"Well, it's a different elevation here," he said, "so that's down, but that's not that important."

Not that important? I thought. One of the two main original clues? Still, I let Beep continue.

"'The home of Brown' could be the Brown Spouters, and when he's talking about 'no paddle up your creek,' that's Spanker Geyser, because it's that kind of paddling, paddling like spanking. 'Heavy loads' is Bulger Geyser. Or maybe Rift Geyser. I'm not sure," Beep said, and I think my silence gave away my skepticism.

"But it doesn't matter, because I know the end," he said with assured finality. "I know where the treasure is, where it's supposed to lead you."

He pointed to a spot on the map, far, far from all the main touristy geysers, that original cluster he had pointed out when he began his explanation. Right along the Firehole River: Restless Geyser.

"So Restless Geyser is like, Fenn is a restless guy; he's done a lot of things in his life. Maybe that works. But that's not its real name. I bought a book on all the Yellowstone geysers, and look what it says the original name for Restless Geyser is."

Beep swiped his phone to a different screen,

showing a screenshot of a page describing Restless Geyser in detail. And there, below it, was a sentence detailing the original name of Restless Geyser: Owl Mask Spring.

"Owl Mask Spring. Owls are wise. So that's where it has to be. It makes too much sense. 'If you've been wise and found the blaze'—and I don't think the blaze matters that much, or, like, we'll know it when we see it."

My heart sank. Having discovered something potentially game-changing, Beep rushed to apply it, and his solve had huge, Yellowstone-size holes in it. And he didn't even have a blaze.

Why, I asked my friend, would Owl Mask Spring, or Restless Geyser, or whatever it's really called, be a special spot for Fenn, the place where he would want to go and die?

"I don't know; maybe he proposed to his wife there or something," Beep said, dismissing the problem.

Beep finally stopped talking, and I realized he was waiting for my opinion on his solve. I try not to lie to Beep—he's so earnest, in all things, and he runs so hot—but I wanted to let him down easy here. I basically didn't think there was any chance it was at this spot. I thought the key he'd discovered was incredible, a remarkable find. Everything after that seemed fairly haphazard. I didn't really want to offer up a white lie, tell him I was more excited than I was, but I knew I had to tread carefully. If I was too harsh, I'd lose him—he'd get mad, petulant, like he'd been the night before with Tyler. And I needed him fully engaged and happily using that nimble brain if we were going to make the most out of the rest of this search, whether or not the treasure was at Beep's original spot—which it was almost certainly not.

"Earlier, you'd said you're one hundred percent certain we're gonna find it here," I said, starting in gingerly. "I can't say I'm one hundred percent. The key is amazing, totally. But some of the applications—I just don't know if it's a contiguous solve, the way Fenn says it should be. Where we can go from one clue to the next. I'm just not sure it's there yet."

I could feel him immediately retreat, withdrawing into his seat. He was clearly annoyed, bitter that I didn't see what he did, that I wasn't over the moon about his hard work, and his quasi-discovery. I tried to keep him with me.

"I'm still so psyched about this. What you've done represents just so much effort, and it's going to change everything for us. But just hear me out, okay? In case—just in case—we don't find it here, I don't want you to lose faith in the key. It just means you may need to apply it differently—and I'm not saying we won't find it today! But just if. If we don't. Don't lose hope. Does that make sense?"

Beep grudgingly said it did, and a silence came over us, the first one in a while. I leaned back into my seat. The lull allowed me to really look around, taking in the scenery. We'd been driving through Yellowstone proper for about a half hour now, and I had to admit, so far it didn't look all that different from other scenic parkscapes I'd seen in the East, or the North. Heavy tree coverage, some mountains—so far, it could have been a nice stretch of Vermont. The Madison River had run along our right much of the drive, and we were finally approaching Madison Junction, which was where, in Beep's mind, "warm waters halt."

From Madison Junction, we'd enter the Grand Loop, the giant circular road that guides visitors through the main areas of the park. Laid out in the 1870s and 1880s by the park's original superintendent, it's still the same basic roadway system that took the first tourists on stagecoach rides through the park, though obviously paved for cars now. If we took it north, we could wind our way to Mammoth Hot Springs, by the park's north entrance. If we followed it far enough east, it would eventually bring us down to the enormous Yellowstone Lake, so big that it looks like an ocean from the shore.

Fortunately, we only needed to take the loop south, making another hour's drive down the Firehole canyon and toward Old Faithful and the Upper Geyser Basin. This is the most popular section of the park, and it was already beginning to show as we passed through Madison Junction; we were in a line of cars ahead and behind, and the single-lane road jammed up from time to time as drivers slowed down to snap photos of bison, or elk, or pronghorns congregating along the side of the roads, largely oblivious to their human observers. They probably shouldn't be; we passed a sign that said WATCH OUT FOR ANIMALS: 12 BISON HIT IN 2018. I tightened my grip on the wheel.

The animals were cool and all, but I'll admit I was still waiting to see what all the fuss with Yellowstone was about, what differentiated it from another forest or nature preserve.

I didn't have long to wait.

Continuing south, we emerged from the early sections of the Firehole canyon out into a plain. Suddenly, in front of us was a sight like nothing I'd ever seen before.

Giant plumes of steam rose up out of mounds spread across the landscape, clouds of white rising twenty, thirty, forty feet in the air. There were four or five of them in total, each one constantly emptying into the sky. Beyond them we could see a pool, perfectly blue at the center, a multicolored rainbow along its rim, wispy white steam rising from it, reminding me of a gigantic hot tub on a cold day. These were the Fountain Paint Pots, the first of the geyser formations encountered along the road to Old Faithful. As we got closer, we saw there were signs for something called a Red Spouter, promises of bubbling mud pots, and the way down to the Morning Geyser itself, which, if we were lucky enough to see it erupt, would have spouted up to 150 feet high. As we kept driving, similar features appeared to our left and right, each more magnificent than the next. I don't know what I was expecting at Yellowstone—maybe something like this, at the climactic and famous Old Faithful area—but I certainly hadn't thought that these kinds of things just appeared along the side of the road, commonplace, regular, and yet wholly alien.

The beauty of the landscape dissolved any lingering tension between Beep and me. This was Beep's third Yellowstone trip, and the grandeur of the place had captured him, just as it had Fenn so many years ago.

"Isn't it amazing?" he said. "Once you see it all, like really see it all, you're going to get it, that Fenn just couldn't hide it anywhere else. It has to be here."

I'd been so focused on the treasure hunt that I'd hardly looked at any Yellowstone guides, or maps, or pictures, ignored the fact that we were heading to one of the most famed and universally beloved places in the world.

The only problem with all this splendor was that everyone else was here to see it, too. As we passed over the Nez Perce Creek and came nearer to the famous multicolored Chromatic Spring, our progress slowed to a crawl. The park's roadways were never intended to handle this level of traffic, and with so many more people coming now than even a decade ago, at the high times—like now, in mid-June—the park becomes clogged with tourists, interfering with those who have legitimate business to conduct, like, ahem, we treasure hunters.

With so many tourists passing through each day, Yellowstone's major attractions have had to be rebuilt to accommodate the constant influx of people shuffling by, posing for photos, wanting to dip a finger into the heated pools or stand in the sulfuric smoke rising up from the geysers. So the more popular tourist areas, like Biscuit Basin or Chromatic Spring, have boardwalks built along and through them, allowing onlookers to leave their cars, walk the area, and move on to the next attraction down the road. That's just what Beep and I did at Biscuit Basin, which was crowded, overrun with tourists trying not to knock one another off the narrow boardwalks as they lined up their iPhone pics. With so many people around us, all of us shuffling along the boardwalks in near single-file order, I couldn't escape the feeling that we were on line at a theme park, slowly moving from one "ride" to the next.

"It's like Disney's Yellowstone adventure," I said to Beep. He didn't disagree.

We got back in our car and continued on down the road, finally nearing the complex surrounding Old Faithful, where the roadways out here in the middle of nowhere briefly became like big-city highways, complete with overpasses and on-ramps to direct all the traffic. Old Faithful is, and always has been, the park's main attraction, and there'd been significant development here even before the Old Faithful Inn was built in 1904. But pulling into one of the gigantic parking lots, the scale of what had been constructed was astounding.

I quickly understood why no Fenn hunters thought the treasure was anywhere near here; it was simply too crowded an area, far too developed. The setting was almost like a college campus—one giant building after another, some of them lodges or hotels, some visitors' centers, cafeterias, some park administration buildings. People and cars were everywhere as far as the eye could see, and even finding parking was no small feat.

Our spot was up the road from here, but since we were by Old Faithful anyway, Beep and I decided to check out the famous geyser. The geyser was surrounded by a semicircular viewing area filled with benches, and hundreds upon hundreds of people had already staked out their seats, awaiting the next show. Old Faithful erupts roughly every sixty to ninety minutes, and apparently it's getting to be longer between eruptions as the geyser's water supply seemingly starts to dwindle. The crowds standing around looking at this hole in the ground were four or five deep. It had to happen pretty soon, we figured, with this many people waiting around.

Nearby, we saw a Yellowstone ranger giving a talk, and wandered over to listen. "Officer Phil," as his name tag said, was explaining why geysers exist, and what causes Yellowstone's unique geologic features. Yellowstone, he said, rests atop an active volcano, which is eventually going to blow up and wipe the place out.

"Right now, we're sitting on a magma field the size of Idaho," he said.

Now, **eventually** means something very different to regular people than it does to geologists. In geologic time, the eruption is going to happen "soon." But soon, to geologists, is probably thousands of years. So chances were, we were not all going to be imminently killed by a volcanic explosion. That's a long-term problem. In the short term, all that magma and pressure underneath the surface make for some pretty cool effects. The magma heats the groundwater lying just under the Earth's surface, and when the pressure from the hot water builds up, it needs a place to go. That's how we get geysers; they're literally the Earth blowing off steam. The United States is one of only five countries in the world with an active geyser field. (The others are Chile, Iceland, Russia, and New Zealand, in case that comes up at the next bar trivia session.) And the centerpiece of it all is, of course, Old Faithful.

Old Faithful isn't the biggest geyser in the world—that's Steamboat Geyser, also at Yellowstone—but it's the most consistent. Whereas Steamboat erupts once every few years, Old Faithful goes off many times per day. Officer Phil was busy explaining how to calculate how often it erupted, when he was distracted by more pressing business. Hardly missing a beat, he stopped his speech, turned his head, and barked in a practiced park ranger shout at some woman who had decided to wander out into the geyser field.

"Ma'am. Ma'am! Do not go there. Do not!" he said, shaking his head. "Thank you."

The woman slunk back into the crowd, but Officer Phil saw this as a teaching moment, a chance to ensure that we Neanderthals stopped destroying his park.

"These features are very impressive. They are awe-inspiring. They are why we are here. But they are not people-proof," Officer Phil said.

"We know this from studying these features. There was a thermal pool one-point-five miles down the path named Morning Glory. Morning Glory is named after the morning glory flower, which is blue and purple. That comes from micro-fracture of the superheated water, in excess of one hundred and ninety degrees Fahrenheit.

"But if you go to Morning Glory Pool today, it is green and yellow, a little bit of orange, and some red. That comes from bacteria that grow in cooler water. Morning Glory Pool has cooled down."

He had to stop again to yell at another interloper. "Ma'am! Ma'am! Do not! Thank you."

"It has cooled down because the road used to go

right past there," Officer Phil said as he resumed his lesson, "and people would treat Morning Glory like a wishing well. In the nineties, we partially drained Morning Glory, and removed eighty-nine dollars in pennies. There were various auto parts, and other currencies.

"These features are impressive," he repeated as he solemnly walked off. "They are not people-proof."

We waited around about ten more minutes, contemplating what we'd just heard, until finally there were yelps from members of the audience, who noticed a little burbling. Water started to crest over Old Faithful's surface, little belches of liquid, each one a bit bigger than the last, as the crowd oohed and aahed.

All of a sudden, the water flow became consistent, gushing up from the ground, ten, fifteen feet in the air. There was a lot of it. And within seconds, it rose higher, going from fifteen feet to fifty feet to one hundred feet in the blink of an eye. It was a constant flow, as if somebody were pointing a hose straight up, and what struck me most was the sheer volume of what Old Faithful was putting out. All that water flying up and crashing down gives it a bit of a Niagara Falls effect—the actual falls this time, not the chintzy shops—where the water hitting the earth creates huge amounts of steam and mist all around.

After about a minute at full strength, the flow began to peter out; it just seemed to lose strength, the water no longer soaring as high, the whole thing appearing to lose its oomph, until it faded to nothing.

The crowd applauded, but we didn't wait for the performer to take a bow. There were thousands of people here, and we wanted to get out ahead of them, and on to the hunt, so we rushed our way toward the exit that leads to the road north, toward the rest of Upper Geyser Basin, thanking Officer Phil for his presentation as we passed by him. We were like dads at the ballpark, trying to hurry the kids out in the middle of the ninth inning to beat traffic, unmoved by the drama that might unfold on the field below.

It was only a few miles' drive from here back toward Biscuit Basin, where we would head onto the trail that would take us to Restless Geyser. Thanks to our dad-maneuver early exit, we cleared the Old Faithful area with relative ease, and followed a roadway route that roughly mirrored Beep's solve; from Old Faithful, we headed north, past the geysers that he believed represented clues in the poem: Solitary Geyser as his "alone in there," Spanker Geyser for the "no paddle up your creek," Mortar Geyser and Fan Geyser as his "heavy loads and water high" (corresponding to stories in the book), and more. It didn't take long before we were parked near Biscuit Basin again, strapping on our gear as we prepared to head off into the woods, up toward the Artemisia Geyser formation.

We each had a backpack, a raincoat, long warm-up pants, and hiking boots; our bags were filled with lots and lots of bug spray, a decent supply of energy bars and nonperishables like beef jerky, flashlights, water bottles, and finally a change of clothes in case we got too soaked, either from bad weather or from having to descend into the water in search of treasure. Beep was going hatless for the moment; I was wearing a Boston Bruins hat, so hopefully any bears we met would know I was on their side.

"It shouldn't be that far ahead," Beep said as we hiked up the path. "It looks on the map like we get to Artemisia Geyser, and from there, we go off the road and right down to Restless Geyser. And then I guess we just pick it up."

I smiled at my friend, not sure if he was kidding or serious. I knew he was positive we were about to find the treasure, but I thought my measured uncertainty might have brought him back to earth somewhat. If it had, it wasn't apparent. I paused by a sign at the trailhead, one whose warning was so matter-of-fact, it gave me a momentary flutter in my stomach.

DANGEROUS GROUND, it read. An explanation followed: "There is no way to guess a safe path. New hazards can pop up overnight, and some pools are acidic enough to burn through boots. More than a dozen people have been scalded to death and hundreds badly burned and scarred. Leaving the boardwalk or trail, or taking pets past this point, is unlawful and potentially fatal."

The sign drove home its point with a sketch of a tourist child having his feet burned in the acid of one of the pools as his mother looked on, her camera in hand.

We padded our way up the trail, a well-groomed spit in the middle of Yellowstone's tall trees. At one point, we passed a family of five coming in the other direction, and gave a friendly wave, but otherwise we seemed to be alone. It was only a few miles up from Old Faithful, but the masses crowding that part of the park were nowhere to be found.

We walked for another half mile, past Gem Pool, Pinto and Sprite Springs, and up toward Iron Spring Creek. Finally, we came up into a clearing, overlooking a large, steaming, multicolored pool, perhaps fifty feet by fifty feet. The sign identified it as Artemisia Geyser. We were here.

"Oh my God, Dan, it's so close," Beep said, positively giddy, bouncing on the balls of his feet. "I don't see any sagebrush from here, but that's okay. Maybe it's down by the river."

From here, we could see the road—far, but not too far away—and we could spot the Firehole River below us. But we couldn't see Restless Geyser, or the one next to it, Slide Geyser, which on the map appeared to be right along the river itself. That was good; we wanted them to be by the river, and secluded. Even better, Restless Geyser was clearly more than a few hundred feet off the trail, thus satisfying one of Fenn's qualifications. The problem was, we couldn't get down to it. There was a sheer drop of perhaps twenty-five or thirty feet down to Artemisia Geyser, and that whole area was a mess of bubbling, dangerous hot springs and geysers. We couldn't try to go there—on both the danger and illegality scales, that was a ten out of ten. Even though we were not supposed to leave the trail at all, the reality was, we were going to need to in order to reach our spot. We just needed to do it at a place that was a more palatable four or five on the risk-o-meter.

"Maybe if we head up a little farther, we can find a way to cut down, and double back to Restless from along the river," I suggested. Beep agreed, and we marched up a ways, soon finding a cutout in the tree line for some power lines, one that led right down to the river. It was a straight shot, and it didn't seem like we'd be entering particularly sensitive territory when leaving the trail, or damaging anything fragile. It was mostly just scrub brush. Even so, I could hear Officer Phil's voice in my head, telling me, "Do not! This park is not people-proof!" But at this point, what else could I do? We'd come this far; how could we turn back now?

We were preparing to head off the trail, when we spotted another hiker coming up the path, an older man with long, flowing gray hair, tremendously fit. He looked like the apotheosis of the cool, outdoorsy hippie. He slowed down as he saw us, and gave us a greeting, and a warning.

"Hey, you guys, be careful out here—on this trail, this morning, Rangers say a bear and her cub were spotted. Pass it along if you see others out here."

We thanked him, and he headed on down the trail. As he did, something flickered in my brain, and I tore off my pack and started to dig through it. Did we leave the bear spray that Cynthia gave us in the car?

"Oh Jesus, I definitely don't have mine," I said, checking the outside compartments and coming up empty-handed. "Did you bring yours?"

"No," Beep replied. We were both unarmed. All the more reason to get after this treasure quick and get the hell out of here, I thought.

We hiked off the path, under the power lines, down toward the river. It was a steep descent, through rocks and downed trees, but we had a commanding view of the area, and I couldn't see another person for what must have been a mile around. The Firehole River drew near, familiar from so many references in **The Thrill of the Chase.** I could picture it in many of Fenn's scenes—him fishing along it, frolicking in it. I'd always thought that if the treasure was actually hidden in Yellowstone, it would be somewhere right along the Firehole itself; something in me believed that Fenn could have hidden the treasure by his old fishing spot along the river. It was a place that meant something to him, that factored into so many of his stories, a spot that he would have considered a meaningful, beautiful, important place for him to sit down and die. Against my better judgment, I was starting to let myself get a little bit excited again.

We reached the bank of the Firehole and turned north; Restless Geyser would be about a quarter mile up, along the river. Beep took out his phone, videotaping everything, convinced we were about to make history. At first, all his camera recorded was a boring march through more downed trees and brush. But when we got closer to the area of Artemisia Geyser, the landscape changed completely.

Artemisia Geyser was several hundred feet up an incline from us, not visible over the crest of the hill. But right in our path was a huge, wet field of gray and white, runoff from the geyser, the hot water coming out of the Artemisia pool and trickling down toward the river.

The ground itself was a chalk white, the liquid shimmering on it like mercury. Up close, the water running over the ground gave it a look like a shucked oyster, quivering before you slip it down your throat. Panning out, the whole area looked a little like the pictures I'd seen of the Bonneville Salt Flats, where they set those land-speed records; on its own, it might not be beautiful, merely stark;

but here, against the river—that chalky white surrounded by the lush green of the forests—it was striking.

The problem was, we had to cross that beautiful, striking, vulnerable area to get where we were going.

"Look, up ahead, there's some steam past that hill; that's got to be Owl Mask Spring," Beep said, pointing frantically.

I was a little less enthused; when we were just wandering through scrub brush, I hadn't really cared that we were off the path. But now that we needed to cross this natural formation, something that looked like nothing I'd ever seen before, I was no longer sure if I wanted to go any farther. The last thing I wanted to do was damage Yellowstone.

I expressed my reservation to Beep, whom I expected to dismiss it outright. Instead, he offered a reasonable response—that Fenn wanted us to be in, and see, places like this.

"Forrest wants people to get off the trails. We never would have seen this if we had stayed up top. He doesn't like the rules; he wants searchers to be places where they maybe technically shouldn't be, as long as they don't mess anything up," Beep insisted.

He wasn't wrong. Fenn did want that. But did that make it right? We were not experts. We shouldn't be the ones deciding where we should or shouldn't go. And treasure-addled as we were, it seemed to me that we were exactly the kind of excited amateurs most likely to do irreversible damage.

"I can get behind that conceptually," I told Beep. "But what I'm worried about is that we **are** going to mess something up." But I knew what he meant. I didn't want to stop here, either; I wanted to find a pretext for going forward. I looked down at the ground, trying to see if there was a route through the field on the parts that appeared to be solid, dry stone.

"If we walk on the harder, dry parts, and try to stay away from the water, I think it's mostly okay. I don't think any of that is too breakable," I said, trying hard to convince myself, wanting so badly to be both right and justified.

The instant I gave my tacit approval, Beep was off and scampering ahead, jumping from dry spot to dry spot, weaving back and forth and over the rivulets of shimmery water. I took a deep breath and followed, fingers crossed.

With the Firehole on our left and Artemisia Geyser up the hill on our right, we moved forward, Frogger-style, terrified of stepping where we shouldn't. We could see that plume of smoke behind a small hill drawing ever closer, with a second plume rising from perhaps twenty feet behind it. According to the map, that should be Restless in the foreground, and Slide Geyser in the back.

We were in the right place.

Beep cleared the runoff field first, reaching a rocky outcrop, and I joined him a few moments later. Somehow, we had managed to avoid stepping in anything sensitive.

"See?" he said proudly. His eyes were wide, and he brought out his phone again to document the moment of triumph. Restless Geyser was just over the next hill, maybe twenty feet away now.

"Oh, man, my heart is beating like so fast," Beep said as he strode ahead.

Mine wasn't, actually, something I thought about for a few seconds as we walked up and crested the hill leading to Restless Geyser. I wondered why I didn't trust in Beep more—this area seemed so good, he'd clearly put so much time into this solution, he'd learned from his mistakes, and he really was pretty damn brilliant. So why was I not believing? Why was I still not that excited?

And then my heart did start to race. Because right in front of us, there it was, unmistakable, perfect, incredible.

The blaze.

As we came over the hill, Restless Geyser was right where it was supposed to be, a small hole, steaming on the ground. And right behind it was something I didn't even know could possibly exist.

A stream the color of fire ran from the forest to our right, just past Restless Geyser, down into the Firehole. It was maybe five feet wide, the water a shade of orange so bright it seemed unnatural, impossible. A hidden treasure that you would never see from the trail, something visible only to someone who ventured down here. It sat alone and spectacular, waiting for someone to find it.

"It's the blaze. Holy shit, this is really the blaze," I said to Beep, who was standing next to me, equally dumbfounded.

The fiery orange color, I'd learn later, is a function of what's called Cyanobacteria, tiny organisms living in the water running off from Atomizer Geyser up above. Three billion years ago, cyanobacteria were the first photosynthesizers, helping to create the oxygen-rich atmosphere that allows us to survive. The bacterial mats of these tiny organisms come in various colors—brown, green, yellow . . . and sometimes, when the water is roughly 150 degrees Fahrenheit, orange. Orange like fire. Orange like a blaze.

We stood there for a moment, silently taking it in. Then I nodded once.

"Okay."

Wordlessly, we began searching the area around Restless Geyser. The geyser itself is small, just a hole in the ground, really, perhaps two feet wide, emitting a light but steady plume of steam, reeking like sulfur. There was no real place to hide a treasure chest in it, but I leaned over it and peered in anyway—not the best idea, perhaps, but these were extenuating circumstances.

Nothing.

Beep was ten feet up the hill from me, looking at a ridge in the orange river, where an overhang created a little waterfall. He shook his head.

Nothing.

I moved on to poke around at a tree, about five feet high, sitting at a bend in the orange river.

Nothing.

I saw Beep walking farther up the hill, exploring a group of pine trees, looking at their bases and pushing aside their branches.

Nothing.

I started to skitter down the hill, the incline somewhat steep, and moved closer to the Firehole River itself, scanning the reeds along the riverbank.

Nothing.

From there, though, I could see into the water, where it was about a foot or two deep along the bank. There was something in there, something square, looking about a foot wide. I put my hand on the ground to steady myself as I clambered down farther, walking in the reeds along the riverbank. I saw a tiny water snake about five feet away, and decided I'd gotten close enough. I squinted my eyes to get a better look at whatever this square object was. Fenn had always said the chest wasn't submerged in water, but maybe it had gotten moved; maybe it had originally been a few feet closer to land, just on the shoreline . . . maybe . . .

It was a rock. A stupid rock.

Nothing.

I looked up and saw Beep coming down toward me. His once-hopeful eyes now looked pained.

"Do you see something down there?" he asked, yearning.

"No—I thought—maybe, I thought I did, but it's a rock."

He perked up at that shred of possibility.

"Are you sure?" he asked. "Maybe we should go in the river and see."

"Jay, it's a rock," I said with finality.

I trudged back up the hill and stood next to him. He reported he'd looked all through the trees, and of course found nothing. I looked around. The orange river was flowing in front of us. The geyser was here. We were definitely far enough away from the trail that we weren't in "close proximity," were secluded enough that no one knew we were here, and this place was remote enough that no one was going to show up here by accident. It was near enough to the road that Fenn could have easily made his two trips here in one afternoon. It would have all been accessible to an eighty-year-old man. It was beautiful, and right next to the river where he'd fished as a child, and I could certainly see him lying down next to this tree, taking his pills, and quietly ending his life.

There was just one problem: There was no place here to hide a treasure chest.

There were no caves, or piles of rocks, or over-hangs. Everything was out in the open. If he had wanted to hide it here, there would have been no-where to put it where it wouldn't be lying around on the ground, for some random passerby or park ranger to just grab it eventually.

"It isn't here," I said, feeling it necessary to state the obvious.

"Maybe we're just not looking in exactly the right place," Beep said. "Maybe we need to just spread out a little more."

Fenn had said that if a hunter got to within twelve feet of the chest, he was going to find it. So it was supposed to be obvious if you were in the right location. There was nothing obvious here. Hence, we couldn't be in the right location. But I was will-ing to humor Beep; he deserved that much, cer-tainly. We walked along the riverbank a bit more, and found a second orange river, just as bright as the first, also leading into the Firehole. This one lay near a rocky outcrop, one that hid a small cave, perhaps three or four feet deep, shaded, hidden from view until one was close, its interior not vis-ible from the river itself. My pulse quickened again as we came upon it; this was definitely the kind of spot that could house a treasure, even if it was per-haps fifty feet from Restless Geyser.

We scrambled over to the outcrop and peered down into the cave area. Nothing. Again, nothing.

Beep started pushing around some of the rocks on the tiny cave's floor, as if perhaps so many pebbles had accumulated over the past eight years that they might now obscure a treasure chest.

I just stared inside, at so much nothing, and then sat down for the first time in what seemed like hours, the ground rocky and uncomfortable and sharp. I leaned over, my arms atop my knees. It wasn't here, either.

Beep was still looking around, prodding at things, checking and rechecking the same places. He spoke for the first time since we'd come to this second spot.

"Maybe it was here, and somebody already found it, or moved it," he said.

I felt anger surge up in me, hot like magma. Anger at the whole Fenn chase, at the silliness of it, at all these stupid hunters, at ourselves for getting sucked into it, at Beep for trying to fool himself into thinking he was still right. He was sounding just like those hunters who had had it all figured out, the ones who thought that if they couldn't find it, the whole hunt must be a fraud, a hoax. That everything was about them. That it was all one big conspiracy. I was seized with fury at the hubris of the whole thing, to think that no, we **had** to be right, that it was the rest of the world that was wrong, rather than realizing that we were looking for the ultimate needle in a four-state-wide haystack and finding this thing was fucking impossible. And I couldn't help myself—I lashed out at him.

"Don't be like them," I spat. "Don't be like those idiots, always so sure they've got it right, 'but, but, but, except for this, except for that, somebody found it, Fenn moved it,' whatever. If it's not here, it's not here. It's not some fucking conspiracy against you. It's not all about you. We had it wrong."

Beep looked hurt, almost physically retreating into himself, and I immediately felt awful. This idea was his baby, his big brainstorm, and he had put so much into it. Sacrificed his relationship. Made all these trips. Spent all this time and money. And, again, nothing. And what the hell did I have to offer? It wasn't like I had a better solve.

I immediately pulled back, my anger dissipating into frustration, defeat.

"I'm sorry," I said. "I'm sorry. I'm disappointed, too."

We picked up our things and gingerly recrossed the white runoff zone, hugging the Firehole all the way back to the clearing, where we could rejoin the trail. We walked mostly in silence, save for warnings to watch out for this hole or that branch.

Linking up with the trail, we headed on back to where our car was parked, spotting an elk but, fortunately, no bears. Exhausted, we piled in, doffed our gear, and prepared for the hour-long drive to town.

The early part of the trip back was spent in quiet stillness, watching the gorgeous scenery pass us by, thinking about what might have been. Beep was staring out the window, and I couldn't know what was in his head, but I thought I had a pretty good idea. He was disappointed, deflated, worse than the times before. He had been, as he said, "one hundred percent certain." And now we were back to square one, he was thinking. All that for nothing. I couldn't let him think that way.

"I don't want you to get discouraged," I told him. "You came up with a hell of an idea, a brilliant breakthrough. Now we just have to find the right way to apply it. This is big progress. I feel so, so good about where we are. We just need to apply the key, figure out how it fits the geyser field, and follow that path from point A to B to the treasure. We're gonna do this. I promise."

He seemed buoyed ever so slightly by my speech, which made me feel a little better about snapping at him before.

If only I believed anything I'd said.

13

THE CANDYMAN'S
CONSPIRACY

The hunters had been trickling into West Yellowstone for a few days now. We'd bumped into them at dinners, wandering the streets, shopping in stores. Even if we hadn't recognized some of them from last year's Fennboree, they'd be easy to spot anyway. Older, sometimes wearing Fenn-related paraphernalia, maybe a little ragged or wide-eyed.

This year, the mania around finding Fenn's treasure had reached a new high, and as usual, it was Forrest Fenn's fault. In his annual "Six Questions" interview with Jenny Kile, published in February 2018, before this hunting season started, Fenn had made a proclamation.

"My gut feeling is that someone will find it this summer," he'd said.

He hadn't laid out his reasoning, but my hypothesis

was that he'd given out so many clues over the past year that he'd narrowed down the search area quite a bit, making the hunt easier than ever. Fenn's bombshell lit a fire under the hunting community, giving us all the feeling that we were racing against the clock to get to the treasure before someone else did. So every time Beep and I saw another hunter over our week out in West Yellowstone, I could only think of that person as competition, another foe to be wary of.

We were supposed to play nice with this bunch, though; most of these hunters were here for Cynthia Meachum's event, which she was calling "the Function in the Junction," in honor of Madison Junction, so important in Fenn lore. Cynthia had invited anyone expected to be in the Yellowstone area to come out for a few nights of treasure-hunting talk, drinks, and maybe some group searching. About thirty hunters had said they'd show up at some point over this week.

In theory, this was what Fennboree was supposed to be. But Fennboree was a shadow of itself this year. Even as the hysteria of the individual hunters was peaking, they were becoming more fragmented, and it seemed that last year's Fennboree was something of a high-water mark for the community, in terms of its cohesiveness.

That event, with its 150 people and its all-together-now vibe, took place before Paris Wallace had died, before Jeff Murphy was known to have died, before Eric Ashby had died. It was just a year ago, but it felt like a totally different world; there was so much more controversy, more negativity, more antipathy toward Fenn, and nearly as much toward those close to him, his favored hunters. And I'll admit, the way I'd come to view him, and them, had changed a great deal since then, as well.

I thought back to how Fenn had so quickly and casually dismissed the deaths of Murphy and Wallace so close to each another. How he had, according to Cynthia, attended Fennboree and had a grand old time, knowing that at that very moment one hunter had just been found dead directly because of his hunt. Even if only a select few hunters knew that, it left a bad taste in my mouth about future Fennborees or the like.

Still, a core group of hunters wanted to gather, and initially, they were still going forward with the 2018 Fennboree at the same site in Hyde State Park where we'd attended the year before. Then a particularly bad fire season dealt the event a deathblow—the U.S. Forest Service temporarily banned events in the park because of the fire risk. So the traditional Fennboree didn't quite happen, replaced to some degree by a Fenn book signing at the Collected Works Bookstore and a get-together at a room in a Santa Fe hotel—but to me, that wasn't the same, and it certainly wasn't on the same scale. This year, the Function in the Junction would have to do.

Over a few nights, the crowd had gradually built up, Cynthia hosting get-togethers every evening. The hunters were mostly new to me, though there were a few repeats, like Colorado-based Sandy, the divining rod–wielding nurse from last year's Fennboree, and a mailman named Gene.

Beep had flown home not long after our failed search at Restless Geyser, needing to attend a wedding somewhere up in Canada. His departure made me the youngest adult searcher at this gathering, which was mostly comprised of people over fifty. The meetups took place at the Buffalo Bar, the best spot in a town with a surprising number of drinking establishments for a place so small. The Buffalo Bar was sandwiched between a gas station and a row of houses on one of the town's two main roads, and it was a lively place at nearly all hours of the day. In one corner were about fifteen slot machines, the area usually at least half full, and at the other end of the bar was a crowded casino-style poker table, complete with a professional dealer several nights a week. The jukebox played rock 'n' roll at all times, and over a few nights under its vaulted ceilings, I witnessed a parade of regulars come through the doors, all familiar to one another, all seemingly friends or enemies forever, all with the histories and beefs and crushes that come with life in a town of twelve hundred.

The nights at the Buffalo Bar seemed a welcome respite from all these days wandering the trails—Beep and I had made two follow-up hunts before he left, both clearly unsuccessful—though the truth was, the more veteran a hunter I became, the more some of the talk at these hunter events began to grate on me—specifically, the ironclad certainty that everyone had about their solves could be tough to take. Initially, it was fun to hear people share solves, their reasons for taking up the hunt, their search stories. In my early days in the hunt, I'd even thought I was getting gold-plated tidbits from these interactions. And maybe sometimes I was, at least from the Cynthias and Desertphiles and Dals of the community. But after more than a year at this, I'd studied up enough on prominent theories to know that the rank and file were mostly offering derivative ideas; people cribbing other solves off the web, ones I'd heard about or read before. Or ones so outlandish, or so clearly contravening some of Fenn's laid-out conditions, that it was hard to listen without interrupting. After what had happened with Beep and me the other day—how close it had felt like we'd come—the truth was, I was weary, weary of the whole thing. Still, most of these were genuinely nice people, and I tried to be polite and play along. Pretty much all the hunters remained eager to show off what they'd come up with, always stopping short of the full reveal for fear someone else would rush over there first—and always armed with a good excuse as to why they hadn't grabbed it yet, even though they **clearly** knew precisely where the treasure was.

Gene, the mailman, at least offered a novel spin on that motif. He explained his solve, an approach that incorporated a lot of Native American imagery and connections, and ended around the Buffalo Bill History Center of the West, in Cody, Wyoming. (Gene has Native American ancestry; I'd found that nearly everyone's solves related directly to the hunter's own past experience or background.) Anyway, by the end, Gene dropped on me that he knew exactly where the treasure was, was certain of it, believed Fenn had tacitly confirmed that for him.

Then why hadn't he gone and picked it up?

"I don't want to take it away from other people. They deserve to have it in their lives, too, so they can chase it," he said.

That, at least, was an excuse I could get behind.

Even if none of them was about to claim the treasure for whatever reason, the hunters all seemed to be having a grand old time, grateful for the chance to discuss their passion in person with real, live, actual people.

One of the loudest voices was that of a big, gregarious man in his fifties or early sixties named Doug. Doug seemed the picture of the southwestern good ol' boy, with his big, droopy mustache, a cowboy hat festooned with a turquoise stone, even a southern accent. Doug had been on hundreds of hunts; he was one of the original hunters, and his loud, infectious personality took over the room.

Doug hunted with a fifty-year-old woman named Brooke, from Texas, a massage therapist who was training to be a pro pool player on the side. Brooke had a rather unique method for finding the treasure. She saw clues in her dreams, she said—full, complete solves, sometimes—and when those visions would come to her, she'd search where the dreams took her. So far, it had been just as successful as every other method, I suppose, so I didn't crap on it unduly, though some of the others at the table raised their eyebrows a bit.

I asked Doug if he was a Texan, too—that would have made it easier for them to hunt together.

Instead, he revealed that he was from Michigan, to my great surprise. I told him that wasn't exactly what I'd been expecting, based on his dress and his affect.

"Yeah, everybody thinks that," he admitted. "I guess I'm just a northern cowboy."

I headed over to the bar to grab another beer, and while I was waiting, two local guys asked me what the gathering was. I told them it was a group of Fenn hunters, which prompted eye rolls from both men. I wasn't sure whether I understood or was offended. I think it was the latter.

We, the hunters, were regarded as the weirdest of

the weird by the West Yellowstone regulars, all of whom seemingly had a story to share about some crazy thing they'd heard a Fenn hunter had done— and about some buddy of theirs who was crazy for the Fenn treasure, too, and who had ventured into Yellowstone in search of it.

When I returned to the table, the talk turned to how much hunting would be going on in Yellowstone that weekend; a few groups were going out together, but I wasn't terribly interested in joining them. Beep was gone, and my best chance of finding the treasure had departed with him.

Or had it?

I guess it depended on whether you believed in conspiracy theories.

Only a few days before I was set to leave for the trip out to Yellowstone, something odd had popped up in my in-box. It was a warning, from the Candyman.

I'd last seen the Candyman at Fennboree the year before. Now he was reaching out because he needed to alert me that I was about to play a role in Fenn's great game. I was to be a lamb sacrificed to a secret partnership between Fenn and Cynthia Meachum, one designed to keep the treasure out of the hands of hunters Fenn didn't like and to direct it to those he supported. My role, the Candyman informed me, was to give the entire thing a veneer of legitimacy—to be the unwitting enabler of their grand con. When Cynthia and I went hunting in Yellowstone the next week, he told me, she was going to "find" the treasure, with me there to document it.

"We believe he gave it to Cynthia, whom we assume you are going to follow in the Yellowstone area and we have a gut feeling she will 'discover' it while with you so it can be a verified find," the Candyman said. He went on to imply that Fenn and Cynthia were specifically conspiring against him and his hunting partner, Stephanie, because of the allegations of sexual misconduct she'd made against Fenn.

"I believe there is the possibility that this treasure hunt is tainted. I believe we did know where the chest was and I believe he's moved it in order for Stephanie not to find it, because he was angry with her for speaking out against him. I believe he's chosen someone he wants to find it and has possibly set you or someone else from the media to give this person credibility upon its discovery," the Candyman wrote.

I wasn't sure what to make of this at all. But he was right about one thing—that I had been planning to go hunting with Cynthia the next week. Beyond the creepiness of his knowing my schedule, it would have been easy to dismiss this email as a bit paranoid, at the very least. But at the same time, his words had ticked something deep in the recesses of my brain.

These warnings took me back to my first encounters with Fenn and his treasure, and my own nagging skepticism concerning all of it. Could Fenn be trusted? I'd never quite settled that question. There were so many little things that gave me pause about him, from his reaction to the deaths, to the accusations from Stephanie and Mindy, to the warnings against Fenn that came even from his supporters and friends, those stray comments that the old man wasn't some gentle grandpa, that he was clever and calculated always. When looking at this search critically, most doubters focused on whether the whole thing was a hoax; I'd managed to shove down any concerns about that through discussions with Fenn and those around him—Dal, Shiloh, Doug Preston—and I still believed it was real.

But what if whether it was real or not was never the issue? What if, as the Candyman suggested, it wasn't about whether the box was out there, but about what, exactly, Fenn was going to do with it? Could it be that Fenn had just been waiting for the right time to deliver it to someone he liked, to get the neat, happy ending he craved? Could his comment about his gut feeling that someone will find it this summer be more than just a feeling—could it be a bit of foreshadowing from the ultimate puppet master?

So as outlandish as this all sounded, something about it made me willing to at least listen. As part of their theory, Stephanie and the Candyman said they had already figured out just where the chest was, and that it was later moved from that spot by Fenn specifically to foil their efforts—and, subsequently, to allow Cynthia to find it. And, more so, that this was all part of a convoluted scheme to pay the taxes on the San Lazaro Pueblo, the old Native American archaeological site that Fenn himself had long owned.

It was not the first time I'd heard of San Lazaro, which held a prominent place in Fenn's life.

San Lazaro was a city of the Tano people, a four-hundred-plus-acre site featuring thousands of rooms that may have once housed as many as eighteen hundred residents. It reached its heights before contact with the Spanish in the late 1500s, and was one of the most important pueblos to take part in a great revolt against Spanish rule in the late 1600s, when the native people rose up, pushed the Spanish out of Santa Fe, and took back that area of the Southwest for a decade.

The thing about the Spanish, though, was that they didn't give up easily. And they had cannons. Eventually they came back, with greater firepower, and snuffed out the power of the pueblos for good. San Lazaro was abandoned, and its people resettled elsewhere.

Fenn had bought the San Lazaro Pueblo in the

1980s, and excavated it for its many artifacts—
a move that did not sit well with many archaeologists and preservationists, who resented that
he removed these treasures, depriving them of
their historical context. But the site had always
held great importance for Fenn—both emotional
and financial. And that was the key to the whole
hunt, Stephanie and the Candyman believed. They
thought the treasure had been in San Lazaro all
along, and Stephanie had told Fenn of her hypothesis in a series of emails. They believed he'd
essentially confirmed this through a series of implications and later balder statements to them—but
he'd also told her not to go to San Lazaro, that she
would be arrested if she tried.

And now, they believed, Fenn was in a bind—if
the treasure was found in San Lazaro, then Fenn
would be in trouble for not allowing Stephanie to
search there years before. They said he didn't want
Stephanie to be the one to find it.

"It couldn't be found in San Lazaro because
Stephanie would be able to prove he wouldn't give
her permission and she told him the location years
ago," the Candyman said.

I quickly had questions. How the chest could be
at the pueblo at all; it had been reported that Fenn
had sold the pueblo, and beyond that, the pueblo
sits south of Santa Fe, outside the marked search
area. It seemed that those two facts should have
ended the discussion right there. But in the world

of Fenn hunting, nothing was taken at face value, ever. In a community where the name of every hill or mountain was parsed for hidden meanings, where every bend in a river was examined to see if it looked like a Greek letter, the drive to seek out the real "truth" behind otherwise pedestrian words, phrases, or ideas could overwhelm hunters.

So neither Fenn's sale of the pueblo nor its being outside the search area deterred Stephanie or the Candyman, who believed that Fenn was simply toying with them, and everyone else—and that the treasure really had been at San Lazaro regardless, hidden in an old altar at a place called Medicine Rock.

"San Lazaro wouldn't seem to be in the search area as it's supposed to be north of Santa Fe, but Stephanie realized early on that north doesn't stop, and goes all the way around the Earth, and the medicine rock is a rocky mountain," the Candyman replied.

Oh. Uh, well, okay, then.

The Candyman went on to explain that despite reports of the sale, Fenn was still listed as the principal owner of the pueblo, and he added, "There's no way to find out if any shares have been sold or given. He has said he sold it but still has access."

They also offered up a motive, which was that Fenn wanted to pay off back taxes on his pueblo with moneys from the treasure. Whether or not he could even do this was questionable—and Fenn's needing money to pay taxes on the property seemed to run counter to the idea of hiding a chest of valuables at all—if he was hard up for cash, why wouldn't he just sell off all those gold nuggets and jewels instead of setting up this treasure hunt?—but they offered up one tiny bit of evidence to back up their claims, which was that Fenn had created and registered a San Lazaro Holding Company with the state of New Mexico in 2010, right around the time he'd hidden the treasure. That, I was able to verify independently. So if they were right about that, at least, what else might they be right about?

As Fenn-related conspiracy theories go, this one was, at least, better than most. It had bits and pieces that lent it a little more credibility than others I'd encountered. Did I believe it? No. But what if there was even a grain of truth in it, somewhere, as there was with **Masquerade**? I certainly didn't completely trust Fenn, and I wouldn't have put it past him to have tried to organize some sort of benefit for himself when he initially hid the chest, before the whole thing blew up and became an international sensation. Their San Lazaro "north doesn't stop" theory was pretty weak, but maybe there was some other trickery afoot that would put San Lazaro in play despite its being south of Santa Fe. And maybe after all the deaths, all the drama, there was part of Fenn that did want the whole thing over, and would prefer if one of his chosen hunters, like Cynthia, found it so all could end happily. That, I could see.

Beyond their feelings that Cynthia was his favorite, his "pet," they were suspicious that Cynthia was the one in cahoots with Fenn because it was known she'd been hunting Yellowstone a few weeks back—a surprise to them, with Cynthia known primarily as a New Mexico hunter—and that she would be going again soon. Two trips in such a short period of time? To them, it was a red flag.

Of course, I knew a few things the conspiracy theorists didn't: that Cynthia had been out with Beep when she was in Yellowstone those few weeks back, and now she was going to be heading out again, with me. I didn't know what to make of it all, but I knew enough by now to be on high alert—this treasure hunt was full of surprises, and maybe I was in for the biggest one of all.

Cynthia picked me up early in the morning— well, early for me, late for her—in order to beat the crowds as we made our way into Yellowstone. After five days there, I felt like I was starting to get the rhythms of the park. I knew my way around the major roads, hardly turned my head to gawk at the big tourist spots, had seen a bald eagle, dodged a grazing elk, spent hours stuck in a bison jam (yes, just what it sounds like), and had gotten so many mosquito bites that it looked like I had chicken pox.

But I was no closer to finding Fenn's treasure. Beep and I had visited our search area three times before he left, and by now we were only sure of one thing: It wasn't there.

Cynthia, however, wasn't so easily convinced. Beep and I had taken her into our confidence the night before he left, and explained the geyser key. She was blown away, saying it made so many things clearer.

"Once I heard what you guys had, I said, Oh man, my shit sucks," she admitted that morning.

The upshot was that she didn't want to go search any of her old spots at all—she just wanted to head to our search area, over by Artemisia Geyser, and get a feel for what we were looking at.

While I was happy she thought we had something, this was problematic for me, because what I wanted was for her to take me to **her** spot. If there really was anything to this conspiracy—that I was to be used to verify the historic find—then that had to happen on her terms, not mine.

Still, there was at least a little bit of potential left in the Artemisia area; Beep had emailed along one more location to search, a pair of small hot pools not far from Artemisia Geyser. I didn't think the treasure was there—Beep's logic in directing us toward this one was hard for me to even follow, honestly—but Cynthia was amped up, excited for any possibility, and so I went along with it.

As we drove these now familiar roads, Cynthia admitted something that took me by surprise: that she'd started to lose faith she'd ever find the treasure. Or, really, that anyone would. It had now been eight years—five for her—and she'd gone on hundreds of individual searches and shared clues and solves with all the best hunters out there, and she couldn't really say that anyone was any closer than he or she had been at the start. That dragged her down.

"I just don't think anyone is going to find it," she said. "The more I search, the more disillusioned I am that I, or anyone, is going to find it."

Dal, she said, was also a little burned-out on the whole thing, weary of the endless questing. But Cynthia said she was going to stick with it, even though she didn't believe she was going to come away with the treasure anymore. This hunt had a place in her life now; she had status within it, was known as a hunter outside of it. She approached it like a professional, and that meant sticking to it, even when emotionally down, much like a pro athlete would—like Tom Brady would, she said, referencing my New England home.

"That's how I feel about the treasure," she said. "Go until the whistle."

But her devotion to this treasure hunt was about

more than professionalism, or status. Even when it was frustrating, it was still her getaway, her chance to leave all the trappings of the real world behind for a bit.

"This is a total escape for me," she said.

Cynthia was usually so relentlessly positive that her admitting that this treasure-hunting life could grind one down took me a bit by surprise. I hadn't heard her talk like that before; usually, she was Fenn's number-one cheerleader. But maybe all this was a ploy, a diversion, to throw me off the scent of what was going to happen, to make sure I didn't suspect any collusion between her and Forrest. Maybe it was the result of spending too many days out in the wilderness, or maybe it was because my hunts with Beep hadn't panned out, but something about this conspiracy was starting to resonate with me. Not all the "go around the world upside down to find it at San Lazaro Pueblo to pay some tax" junk—that was still outlandish—but the idea that maybe Fenn wasn't as detached as he seemed, that maybe he could be plotting to direct the treasure to the people he liked. That, at least, didn't seem beyond the man I'd come to know and follow. Fenn liked letting the chips fall where they might, but he liked a good tale, with a good ending, even more—and by his own admission, he'd never been afraid of jazzing it up a little to get the best final result.

Before I could plumb the thought any further, Cynthia snapped back into total positivity, throwing aside that negative chatter and saying that she had a newfound verve now. Beep's key, she said, had given her a reason to be excited once again. We took a right at Madison Junction and headed south along the Firehole on the way back to our spot, about fifteen miles away, down by Biscuit Basin. Cynthia had been searching this general area by herself all week, and had ranged a little farther to the south and west during her trip a few weeks back, the one where she and Beep went hunting together (when she'd supposedly hidden the treasure for us to later "find," according to the Candyman).

She was not nearly as familiar with this area as she was with the New Mexico search zones, but Cynthia had a keen eye for detail, and kept pointing out interesting sights as we passed them. When we reached Nez Perce Creek—known to me and other Fenners as the spot where brown trout were first introduced to the park—Cynthia informed me that there was a lot more to the history of that spot than just a trout drop.

"I stopped yesterday and got out and read this sign about Chief Joseph and the Nez Perce," she said. "God, it's really depressing."

It should come as no surprise that Fenn hunters weren't the first to encounter tragedy, and even death, in Yellowstone. Fifteen years after Yellowstone was founded, the Nez Perce raced through the area on a dramatic fighting retreat that careened across four states and captivated the recently reunified nation. But it is remembered now only as a tragic episode, one that went down as perhaps the darkest chapter in the park's history.

The Nez Perce were a tribe of the Pacific Northwest who were first forced onto a reservation and then ejected from it when gold was discovered there. They resisted, beating back U.S. Army forces long enough for their ragtag column to attempt to flee to the relative safety of either the Great Plains or Canada. In 1877, the tribe passed through the park, where it encountered groups of early Yellowstone tourists, and two of these were killed by Nez Perce warriors as the situation deteriorated and the pursuing army closed in.

The Nez Perce were partly led by Chief Joseph, who would become famous during this war, largely for the poetic, solemn words he spoke to end it. As the army caught up with the Nez Perce near the Canadian border at Bear Paw Creek, the Nez Perce fought a dramatic but doomed last stand before Joseph and the remaining chiefs laid down their arms. The surrender message attributed to Chief Joseph is eloquent and sad, and has become widely known, particularly its poignant last line: "Hear me, my chiefs! I am tired; my heart is sick and sad. From where the sun now stands, I will fight no more forever."

At one time, there were numerous markers around the park signifying the various stages of the Nez Perce journey, from the encounters with the tourists to their routes of escape. But for some reason, those have been removed over the years, and now virtually all that remains is the placard Cynthia saw on the side of the road, with its "Chief Joseph Story."

We left it and Nez Perce Creek behind us as we came upon Biscuit Basin, got out of her truck—always unmistakable for its TTOTC (**The Thrill of the Chase**) license plate—and geared up for the walk to Artemisia Geyser. Cynthia kept telling me how excited she was to see our spot. But still, something nagged at her.

"You know, the more I read from Forrest, I'm just not sure it's in the park at all," she said as we began our hike up the path. "There's so many legal complications with it being on national park land, and I just don't think he'd want to deal with all of that."

I noted that I'd pondered the same question, had kept trying to steer Beep in the direction of Hebgen Lake—prominent in Fenn's stories, near West Yellowstone but outside the park itself—and how he'd refused to consider it.

I filed the tidbit away, and pulled out the geyser map, trying to figure out exactly where Beep wanted us to go. He had directed us to locate a trio of hydrothermal spots—Pinto Spring, Gem Pool, and Sprite Spring—and then head down a hill to the area around two geysers, Hillside and Seismic, along the bank of the Firehole.

We were off the path now, again slinking around in areas where we weren't supposed to be, and we were both quite aware of it. We ran from shrubs to clumps of trees to try to avoid being seen out in the open, staying low the way soldiers do in war movies when shuffling from one position to the next. Cynthia seemed to be even more concerned about getting caught than I was—knowing that if she was publicly sanctioned or, worse, arrested for wandering in prohibited areas, her status as a Fenn hunter would make the whole thing into a humiliating news story for her, Fenn, and everyone involved in the chase.

"Can you imagine how embarrassing, how damaging, that would be for me, in particular?" she said. "My name and everything out there?"

We soon found the areas Beep had wanted us to search, and after about thirty minutes of poking around, we concluded there was nothing there. We were pretty close, though, to Restless Geyser, just a few hundred feet up the riverbank, and Cynthia was curious to see this spot we'd talked so much about.

"I've got to see this blaze; the way you've described it doesn't sound real," she said in her southwestern lilt. I didn't think she was saying she doubted me, just noting that it sounded like it couldn't be true—a river of fire. Never one to turn down even a casual challenge, within minutes I was guiding her up along the bank, pushing aside tree branches as we wound our way toward the spot, coming from the direction opposite to the one taken during my earlier visits with Beep. It wasn't long before we cleared the brush, and I didn't even have to say anything—Cynthia gasped as it appeared before her.

"Oh my Gawd," she said, that lilt kicking in again. "That might be the best blaze I've ever seen."

She paused for just a minute, then started glancing around.

"I see what you mean, that there's nowhere really to hide it—you've gone through those trees up there?"

Then, acting on what I imagined was instinct at this point, Cynthia started searching the entire area, studiously peering into all the overhangs and crevices Beep and I had canvassed over our last few days here, scanning the riverbank, the trees, anywhere there might be a few feet of cover to hide a treasure chest.

"And you're sure it's not here?" she asked.

"There's nothing here," I said with a hint of weariness in my voice—I was frustrated with this area, and feeling a little exposed. "We should probably get back to the trail."

Cynthia agreed, and we made our way back toward the path. Except there was something I hadn't factored in. When I'd been here with Beep before, we'd simply leaped across the river of fire in order to get back to the trail. It was probably four feet wide, maybe five, but that hadn't been such a big deal for us. Cynthia, even though she was in great shape for her age, was still in her mid-sixties, and short—not exactly the perfect combination for jumping across rivers, fiery or otherwise. We stared at the orange river for a minute, looked all around for an alternative, and, seeing none, prepared to do what was both foolish and unavoidable. It wasn't like there was any danger—the river was maybe a few inches deep, at most—but we wanted to do everything possible not to disturb this beautiful environment, where, by the way, we were clearly not supposed to be.

I took a few steps back, got a running start, and vaulted over the river. Safely across, I extended my hand and got ready to try to help Cynthia over. She retreated a few paces, then started to run forward, leaving her feet awkwardly as she cleared the bank. Her right foot came down straight into the river, leaving a deep, ugly, shoe-shaped brown scar on its orange floor. I pulled her the rest of the way, and we stared in silence at the damage we'd just done to this special place.

We trudged silently back up to the trail, meeting it soon after and turning toward the parking lot.

"Well, I guess that now that I've helped disrupt a millennia-old ecosystem, I'm a true Fenn hunter," I said, expressing what I hoped was dark humor.

Cynthia hardly looked up as she shot back a response.

"At least we didn't dig."

—

Back at her truck, we stowed our gear and pulled out of the parking lot at Biscuit Basin. Our day seemed set to end there, another unsuccessful search to add to the growing list. There had been nothing suspicious, nothing out of the ordinary, nothing to validate the fears of the conspiracy theorists.

Until, as we were turning onto the main road, Cynthia made a suggestion that piqued my interest immediately.

"I've got a spot I'd like to show you," she said. "Have you been to Ojo Caliente?"

Ojo Caliente. It was perhaps the original "where warm waters halt" spot in Yellowstone, ground zero for Fenn hunters looking for a starting point inside the park. In an early scrapbook, Fenn had written about the Ojo Caliente hot spring, which sits along the Firehole River, as his favorite bathing spot when he was young. So many had quite logically looked at where the spring hits the cooler water of the Firehole as the spot "where warm waters halt."

I had not been there, and I was excited at the prospect of seeing it. Inside, of course, my senses were suddenly afire. Ojo Caliente and its surroundings had been picked over by hundreds, if not thousands, of Fenn hunters over the eight years of the search. The chest couldn't possibly be near there—unless it had been placed there recently.

Cynthia, of course, knew just how searched-out the Ojo Caliente area was. She shouldn't have wanted anything to do with it. So why, then, did she want to take me there? Was this the moment I had been warned of?

"Sure," I told her. "I'd love to see it. All the blogs always talk so much about it. Do you actually have a solve somewhere around there?"

She told me that she had a thought or two, maybe something a little bit nearby. I was half listening, pondering whether I was about to be part of a grand plot.

The rational angel on one shoulder kept saying that Cynthia was a responsible, kind, reasonably sane human being who had been nothing but open and trustworthy to me so far—while the people fingering her as in cahoots with Fenn had, at best, unclear intentions, and seemed to cling to any piece of information that would support the point they wanted to make, while excluding anything that didn't jibe with their preconceived notions. Classic conspiracy theorists, in other words.

But the chaotic devil on my other shoulder kept whispering something else—that Fenn was not to be trusted, that this damn chest should have been found already, that I really didn't know Cynthia, or Fenn, nearly as well as I might have thought, that I was still a novice in this unfamiliar world, one who could easily be played for a patsy, used for his connections. I decided to start probing the issue.

"So, how often do you talk to Forrest?" I asked innocently, good-naturedly.

"We email most every day," Cynthia responded.

"Email, right. How often do you see him, like go over to the Fenn compound or whatever?"

"Oh, not very much at all," she said. "I last saw him for lunch on May first. He was looking healthy, which is good, because I'd heard some not-so-great things about that a while back."

That was more than I'd expected they talked, but if she hadn't seen him in six weeks . . . hmm. I hadn't talked to Fenn in a while, and he shouldn't have known I was here, unless Cynthia had told him. I asked how much he knew about my role here, my presence.

"He knows I'm here with you and Jay. He knows you were going to be up here searching and talking with the other hunters at the meetup."

That gave me a start. I hadn't really considered that Forrest would be kept abreast of my whereabouts, though it did jibe with what the conspiracy theorists thought.

Perhaps against my better judgment, I started probing a little further to see if there was something there. I asked her about her relationship with Stephanie, the Candyman's search partner. Cynthia responded that she and Stephanie didn't talk anymore—they used to be reasonably close, sharing information about the hunt in 2014, but then they'd had a falling-out.

Cynthia said that back then, Fenn had told her that Stephanie had come within two hundred feet of the treasure—which would be an absolutely enormous clue, a game-changing bit of knowledge. Just go retrace your steps near all the areas you'd told Fenn you'd searched, and eventually you have to find the treasure, right? Cynthia promptly went and told Stephanie, and Stephanie, shocked, doubled back and asked Fenn about it, seeking more information. Fenn didn't like that, and he, completing the game of telephone, went back and barked at Cynthia for betraying his trust—while also disavowing having ever said it in the first place.

" 'I told you that?' " Cynthia recalled him saying. " 'I don't know why I would have said that, because she wasn't within two hundred feet. Never. She never was.' "

But Cynthia was certain of what she'd heard, and she thought she knew why Fenn had said what he had. He told people what they wanted to hear—what they needed to hear, so that they stayed obsessed with his hunt, even if it seemingly contradicted other things he'd said before.

"Fenn likes to toy with people," Cynthia said as she headed toward Ojo Caliente. "Tell them whatever they need to hear so they keep searching. So he can keep getting the publicity."

The upshot was that no one had been happy with anyone else in that situation—Fenn with either woman, Cynthia with Stephanie for going right to

Forrest, Stephanie with Cynthia for indirectly getting Forrest mad at her. They hadn't spoken much
since. (Fenn later stated that the two-hundred-foot
searcher had no idea how close he was, and had
hinted that the person was male, and not a well-
known, regular searcher.)

As we again crossed Nez Perce Creek and reached
the turnoff for Ojo Caliente, a Yellowstone patrol
truck raced the other way, sirens flashing. We both
tensed up, irrationally thinking that maybe they
were after us for walking on prohibited land.

The truck sped by, and we pulled into a lot
crowded with pickup trucks and SUVs.

"We're safe now," Cynthia said, smiling. "No
rangers waiting for us with handcuffs."

This was another popular spot for sightseers and
hikers, a sprawling plain split by the Firehole River.
There was a bike path leading to the Ojo Caliente
Spring, and cyclists cruised by us, reminding me of
something, almost a non sequitur, but not quite.

"Beep was telling me this crazy story, that they
actually don't like cyclists in most of Yellowstone,
because bears think they're fast-moving prey—
like a gazelle or something—and they chase them
down," I told Cynthia, though I wasn't sure how
that squared with the fact that this was clearly a
bike-friendly trail, one of many in the park.

Cynthia pointed ahead of us to the bridge over
the Firehole.

"That's Ojo Caliente there on the right, and you

can see over there"—she gestured to her left—"all the fishermen down by the river."

Indeed, there were at least five men in waders, casting into the water. This was clearly prime fishing ground. With the Ojo Caliente Spring right here, it seemed like the perfect spot for a 1940s teenager to ride his bike, fish, bathe, and generally frolic around for hours: an ideal place for "where warm waters halt," really. The whole area would be special to Fenn, I realized.

"I've been searching around this area these last few days," Cynthia told me, "up and down the riverbank here. But it's not over here. What I really want to do is head out that way, over toward Boulder Spring. I've got the GPS coordinates for it, and it looks really promising. Or at least as promising as these things get."

Boulder Spring wasn't a spot that was familiar to me and wasn't a prime Fenn hunting location. From where she was pointing, it looked to be about five hundred feet off the path, sitting at the bottom of a geographical feature that I think is called a drumlin, a hump-shaped hill rising out of a plain, left over from glacial movement—but really, don't take my word for it; I got a C+ in my college geology class.

Cynthia liked the idea of Boulder Spring because she subscribed to a theory that the entire hunt might take place within a surprisingly small area— that, if one started at Ojo Caliente, for instance, everything might really be at the outside edge of walking distance, despite Fenn's "too far to walk" line. But that could apply in other ways, like needing to cross the bridge over the Firehole, for instance, or to ford a smaller river. And she liked that Boulder Spring was essentially at the end of Fairy Creek, a tributary off Fairy Falls. Fairies show up in the Fenn lore quite frequently, and that might be a play on the line "no paddle up your creek," perhaps hinting that a fairy might simply fly up it. It was certainly not in close proximity to a human trail, Fenn could have easily made the trip twice, and it would have been accessible for an eighty-year-old man—it checked a lot of Fenn-related boxes. And even though it was near all these popular Fenn hunting spots, it didn't seem like anyone ventured over this way much. It was not quite protected territory in the way Artemisia Geyser was, but they probably didn't want you tromping over the wetlands to get out to it, the way Cynthia and I were about to do, and it required fording Fairy Creek at some point, which was enough to deter most casual hikers.

A buffalo was wandering along the side of the road as Cynthia and I passed Ojo Caliente and crossed the Firehole River, heading toward Boulder Spring. In only a few days here, I'd already gotten used to seeing sights like that, so much so that they'd become quasi-routine. We trudged a few hundred feet farther on, leaving the path and marching west. There was no question in my mind that if this conspiracy was real, if Cynthia was really going to "discover" the treasure in my presence, this was where it was going to happen.

We came upon Fairy Creek, about six or seven feet across, rushing a little faster than either of us would have liked. We scouted around for a way across that didn't involve jumping into the water; we'd done enough of that already. About one hundred feet down, we found an uprooted tree trunk and gingerly walked across, reaching the other side without incident.

There in front of us was Boulder Spring, steaming, surrounded by ten-foot-high boulders, all sitting at the base of that drumlin, or whatever type of hill it is. Large rocks in the water separated the spring into what made it seem like multiple pools and obscured parts of it from view. It appeared to be the perfect place to take a quiet, solitary dip, which got Cynthia excited. She started scurrying from one end of the spring to the other, snapping pictures, all charged up.

"It could be here," Cynthia said, her words coming quickly, sharply. "It could really be here. Forrest liked to bathe naked, and this could have been a spring where he did that."

Could it be? A bathing spring, near his old fishing hole, hidden from view but not far from the main trails? It made some sense. We spread out and began to search among the rocks and in any covered areas near the boulders themselves. There was no blaze to speak of, but I didn't care—if this thing was here, I was convinced it was going to be because Cynthia had put it here, and so I just needed to find a box, not puzzle out an actual solution. I was watching her as much as I was looking for a treasure chest, wondering when she was going to break out in her "Eureka" moment.

She ambled around the rocks, poking this way and that, looking for something, possessed of the same energy that she had displayed back by the Artemisia area. If this was all for my benefit, she was certainly putting on a good show. I started to climb up the hill above Boulder Spring myself, figuring that maybe I was supposed to be the one who actually discovered it. That would add a wrinkle, I supposed. If it was her spot but I laid eyes on it first, I'd probably be entitled to some share of the total—wait, was that how they wanted to co-opt me? Shit.

I looked down the slope, and Cynthia was still poking around the smaller rocks near the hot spring itself. She didn't appear to be finding anything. Which I guess meant this was up to me, preordained or not.

There was one more gigantic boulder along the hillside, and that was probably the last place around here that one could hide a treasure. The hillside was dangerously steep, and it was hard to keep my footing as I skittered along the side of the hill toward it.

The boulder must've been ten or twelve feet high, just as wide, and its entire rear was shielded from view. No reason to climb up behind it unless you really, really wanted to be there. If I were going to plop down a treasure near this spring, that's probably where I'd do it.

I slipped once as I finally neared the boulder, my feet sending dozens of pebbles cascading down the hillside. Could eighty-year-old Fenn have reasonably reached this? Maybe. Maybe not. Didn't matter now. I clasped my hands to the boulder for stability and inched around toward the back, the place where a treasure might be hidden, concealed from public view but crying out for someone to find it. Someone like me.

I took a deep breath and turned the corner. And there it was, just what I always found, every time.

Nothing.

I thrust a breath out of my nostrils, fired up, annoyed again. Mad at Cynthia for leading me here, and then for not pointing me straight to the treasure, mad at Beep for leaving early, mad at myself for paying to spend a week out here and getting nothing, as usual. I looked down and saw Cynthia, standing over one of the springs. She played her hand in the water, dipping her fingertips in. She didn't look like she was part of some grand conspiracy, a plotter trying to deceive all these other, legitimate hunters. She just looked . . . disappointed, really. Just like me. Her time in Yellowstone was almost up, too, I realized. She'd have to go home to New Mexico, a place she believed to be totally searched-out after her hundreds of expeditions there over the past four years. And here, another chance, lost. She'd gotten nothing out of her hunt with Beep and me, or her hunts with him earlier in the summer. She'd gotten nothing out of her week here. After five years in the hunt, she was no further along than when she'd started, really. And every one of these near misses had taken something out of her.

Cynthia wasn't part of some grand conspiracy— she was just another wanderer, a searcher, seeking a box, yes, but also an escape.

That recognition forced me to focus on what I was actually mad about—at my own gullibility for even considering that this woman was part of some plot. Had I fallen into the trap of wanting to believe? Was that my problem? Did I want to think that this was just one big sham, that it wasn't on the level, and that because I couldn't find it, the game must be rigged? I had told Beep to watch out for those kinds of feelings, but maybe I'd fallen victim to them myself.

I trudged down to where Cynthia was still standing and dipped my hand in the spring, as I'd seen her doing in a different pool moments before. I immediately yanked my hand back—the water was hot, damn hot, scalding hot. Idiot. Served me right.

"So, nothing here, I assume?" I asked her as I shook off my burning hand.

She shook her head no, lips pursed in frustration.

"But you know," she said, perking up a bit, "maybe we should check up the hill. I doubt many people have searched up there before. While we're here . . ."

There was nothing up there. I knew that. She knew that. But that was what this was all about, wasn't it? Searching far and wide? And I bet there was a helluva view up there, of the Firehole River, and the steaming geysers, and Fairy Falls, not that far away to the south. Yellowstone laid out in all its beauty, the pristine, sacred place of Forrest Fenn's memories.

"Sure," I told her, smiling now, too. "Let's go look up there."

14

IN THE CROSSHAIRS

Over the next year in the chase, things only seemed to get crazier. The message boards overflowed with fights, the FennTubers kept up their frequent sparring, and the rank-and-file searchers seemed to be taking more risks, too often going a little too far in seeking the treasure.

Or in the case of Scott Conway, a little too deep. Many, many searchers had gone to great lengths to find Forrest Fenn's gold. But it's fair to say that none had dug deeper in pursuit of it than Conway.

Conway, a veteran of the 1990s Gulf War, believes that during his time in the Middle East, he was exposed to a nerve agent, one that has led to constant health problems over the last thirty years. When he discovered the chase in 2013, he quickly believed he'd cracked the code—tying the treasure to Heron Lake State Park, in northern New

Mexico. He visited the site with his son that same year. When walking around a creek in the park, he said, he came upon fire-scorched logs arranged in the shape of an **X.** That, he thought, had to be the blaze.

But Conway didn't listen to—or outright ignored—some of Fenn's rules, tips, and hints, such as those about not doing what an eighty-year-old man couldn't do, or that Fenn had hidden the treasure over two trips from his car in one afternoon, or that it wasn't necessarily buried. He became fixated on the spot, certain the chest was hidden beneath the ground there, and started digging in order to retrieve what he was sure was secreted below.

"What do you do when you think you've found an **X** that marks the spot of a treasure? You dig," Conway told me.

And then he kept digging. And digging. And digging.

In the course of seventeen trips over five years, Conway and a host of friends and family dug for the treasure at his spot, using water pumps and other gear to eventually carve out a series of holes, some of them sizable—the final hole measuring double-digit feet deep and wide, perpetually filled with rainwater—in the New Mexico landscape, undetected by park rangers. All this work cost him more than thirty thousand dollars.

But on his last trip to the site, in 2018, things got out of hand. Conway was working on his hole when he heard the sound of trucks rumbling up on the road near his search spot.

They shouldn't be here, he thought.

He went to get a closer look and spotted what he feared most—park rangers disembarking and heading his way. Out this deep in Heron Lake State Park, there was no question about their purpose: They were here to stop him from digging his hole.

Conway panicked. Believing that one of the men previously helping him had sold him out to the rangers, he knew he had to escape, and fast.

"I'm like, He fucking ratted on us; we've got to get out of here," Conway said.

As the rangers descended upon his spot, Conway and a friend scrambled to get away. They careened toward their vehicle, looking back briefly and realizing with a shock that the situation was more dire than they'd realized—the rangers were carrying assault rifles, treating Conway as a grave threat.

"On our way up the mountain, thirty feet away, there's a park ranger with an M-16, and he was serious," Conway said. "He was trying to sneak up through that arroyo to get at us."

Conway managed to slip away from the authorities, eventually returning to the lodge where he was staying and preparing to alight for what he believed was safety in Colorado. But the rangers and accompanying state troopers tracked him down there, and Conway had no choice: He gave himself up.

Yet even as he did, he begged the troopers for the

chance to go just a little farther, certain that he was on the brink of finding the treasure, desperate for one more go—the state, he said, could even keep digging at his spot if they wanted. He just needed to be proven right.

"At that point, I'm caught," Conway said. "I'm like, Why not just go farther? I'm only two, three feet away from it."

Unsurprisingly, the state did not take him up on his offer.

Conway was issued three misdemeanor citations: one for destroying public land, one for using a metal detector in a state park, and one for littering. A month later, he went to a Fenn book signing, where he briefly met Fenn, and the two shared a joke about whether Conway was going to jail. It was a quick meeting, an instant during a much larger event. But Conway believed that in that moment, and in things he said and did during that book signing, Fenn was intentionally sending him subtle hints, ones that suggested and reinforced he was on the right track.

When I asked about his interactions with Conway, Fenn seemed bewildered by Conway's view of it; Fenn said he didn't even recall meeting the man, and knew about the hole incident only through what he'd read of it. That said, he was sympathetic to Conway's predicament.

"I don't remember the guy," Fenn said. "But his sister said there's something off with him, mentally.

I don't know. But that case is pending. They're going to charge him. It shouldn't be so serious to dig a hole. It's in the middle of no place—there's no victim."

If only all of them were as harmless as Conway, Fenn commented as we spoke in June of 2019. Because since Conway's arrest, Fenn had had two major scares—both at his very doorstep, both threatening his and his family's safety.

In November 2018, Fenn was out with one of his daughters, and the pair came home and found that they couldn't get back into his walled compound— the main gate wouldn't work—but that somebody else seemed to be inside, having entered via a tiny side door.

"We were at the dentist. I'd had a tooth pulled," Fenn said. "We came back and the gate wouldn't open. This guy had kicked my wooden door, the emergency door. He had kicked right through the thing."

According to the report I got from the Santa Fe Police Department, Robert Miller, forty-one, of Pennsylvania, had broken into Fenn's compound that afternoon in search of the treasure. According to officer Jared R. Loesing, "Mr. Miller stated he flew out to Santa Fe because, according to the poem, the treasure is at this location. Mr. Miller stated to me he read in the poem something to the effect of 'put in the hole [sic] of brown.' Mr. Miller told me he thought that was referencing the small wooden gate next to the main driveway gate. . . . Mr. Miller told me he broke the window to the front door of the building to the right. Mr. Miller told me he searched the house and found a wooden treasure box."

Miller had actually broken not into Fenn's house, but into the guesthouse on the property, where Shiloh lived. And he had found, admittedly, a chest of sorts—a wooden seventeenth-century Spanish trunk. Of course, this was no treasure chest: Shiloh used it for holding linens and towels. But that didn't stop Miller from trying to abscond with it; which is when Fenn and his daughter, who had finally gotten inside, came upon him. Fenn immediately called for backup as they waited for the police.

"My other daughter, who lives a couple blocks from here, she ran down with a gun," Fenn said. "She held this guy there with a pistol, and I went and got another pistol. When's the last time you pointed a loaded gun at somebody?"

A little surprised by the question, I responded that I had not done that, ever.

"Well, we never had, either." Fenn smiled. "But the guy started crying. He was sorry."

Body-camera footage from the incident shows Miller looking confused, uncertain, terrified.

"I thought the poem directed me into here," Miller tells the officer in the video.

"Poem?" the bewildered officer responds.

"Yeah, the treasure map, the treasure hunt, you know?" Miller says.

"So you came on the property because of a poem? Are you serious?" responds the officer.

"Yeah."

"You weren't here to break in [or] anything?" the officer says, still stunned.

"I was taking that box of clothes right there, like the poem said," Miller replies.

"Here's the thing, man. That's burglary, dude."

"I know. I thought I had it figured out," Miller says, looking so sad that it's hard not to have some sympathy for him.

Fenn didn't press charges. He told Miller that if he'd pay the expenses for fixing everything— sixteen hundred dollars—then it would be forgotten. Miller did.

Like so many other close calls, that one ended without incident. And Fenn seemed content to treat Miller as just another misguided soul, another of his flock who went a little too far, instead of as a dangerous criminal who broke into his home. I wondered if that served his interests—portraying most of them as just a little overzealous, instead of as dangers to themselves and others? That maintained the idea of a treasure hunt as a lark, rather than as a community hazard. Fenn continued to insist that Miller was not a problem—in fact, that the experience had been good for him, in a way, and that Fenn was staying connected to him, working to rehabilitate him, ever the good, caring shepherd.

"He didn't seem like a criminal. He was just a treasure hunter. He emails me now. I'll email him back," Fenn said, seemingly used to this kind of thing.

In a sense, Fenn **was** used to all this by now. He'd even been taken to court over his treasure chest, with a Colorado man, David Hanson, filing a $1.5 million lawsuit in 2019 against Fenn, claiming he had misled his hunters. Fenn filed a counterclaim, saying Hanson was just trying to extort money from him or gain the location of the chest, and Hanson's lawsuit eventually went away.

But there was one incident, one man, Fenn couldn't just brush off.

Paco Chavez had returned.

"The guy that was stalking my granddaughter, he did it again," Fenn said, bristling at any mention of Chavez. On April 20, 2019, Chavez—having just finished a previous sentence for his earlier attempts to get at Fenn and his family—returned to Santa Fe and rang the bell at Fenn's compound, announcing that he wanted to talk to Fenn. Fenn, of course, was alarmed.

"I grabbed a gun and went out to the gate," Fenn said. "I didn't want him coming over my wall."

When Fenn got out there, Chavez was gone. But police tracked Chavez down and arrested him for violating a restraining order.

"So the police caught him, and my daughter and I testified before a grand jury last week, and they indicted him. He's already served three and a half years, and he's looking at another three to four in prison, here. They extradited him to New Mexico.

"He told the police officer, 'As long as I'm out of jail, I'm coming back.' He's scary," Fenn said, agitated throughout the conversation, disliking any talk of Chavez, and, really, most chatter about the dangers of his hunt. Yes, it had been two years since anybody had died, all those fatalities concentrated around that ugly time in 2017, but it wasn't like the hunters weren't trying. Not long after we spoke, the Gallatin County Sheriff's Office issued a public warning, specifically calling out Fenn hunters for their recklessness and urging them to be safe, after another searcher was injured that June while seeking Fenn's loot in Montana.

With all this in mind, I asked Fenn if things really were getting worse in the chase, a little more out of hand? The regular hunters getting bolder, the obsessives just a little more reckless, the truly crazy a little more unhinged?

"Ostensibly, you would think that," Fenn admitted. "But with more people getting involved, that brings new problems. I've been widely quoted [as saying] that seven percent of the people in the country have certifiable mental issues. I'm starting to think it's more like ten or twelve percent. They're not all bad people; they're just crazy."

So was this all worth it? I asked him. Did he still believe his chase to be ultimately a force for good, despite all of this, despite everything that had happened?

Fenn took a deep breath and looked down toward his couch.

"Knowing everything I know now, I wouldn't do it again," Fenn said. "It cost four lives."

That took me by surprise. It was an unusual admission from Fenn, normally so unerring, so infallible. If even he was starting to see that the bad had perhaps outweighed the good, what were the rest of us to think?

And did that mean, perhaps, that he would consider ending it? Had it gotten so bad that he would consider calling all of this off? I'd asked him this two years before, amid all the Paris Wallace tumult, and Fenn had said absolutely not; back then, he wouldn't consider it under any circumstances, couldn't do it, wouldn't do it.

This time, I got a different answer.

"Murder. If someone was murdered because of the chase, I think I would have to consider it," Fenn said.

So it turned out that he did have limits after all.

Things hadn't gotten **that** bad in the chase—yet. But all of this was adding up for me. I hadn't tried to come up with a single solve that whole winter of 2018–2019; after hunts in all four search states (even a particularly flimsy Colorado one near the

Continental Divide), about twenty-five boots-on-the-ground days in total, the fire just wasn't burning bright anymore. I had Elliott at home, and another son scheduled to arrive in late spring or early summer, and this treasure hunt was starting to feel less like a distraction and more like an imposition, or worse. Beep, I think, mostly felt the same. We talked more about some of the drama in the search, and the dangers, and the problems that would arise even if we were lucky enough to find the chest. But then one day that spring, he'd come up with one last idea, and he felt good about it, talking the way he used to, full of confidence, buzzing with anticipation again, assuring me he'd learned from our previous attempts.

And so we'd made our reservations for another trip out to New Mexico, one final hunt for the treasure—this one surprisingly close to Santa Fe, actually. Beep was now focusing on an area near Los Alamos and Bandelier National Monument—and with Beep excited again about a solve, texting and emailing me repeatedly in the days before the hunt, I started to get a little bit excited, too. He had wanted to check out Bandelier primarily because the lowest and highest elevations of the park corresponded exactly with what Fenn said the low and high boundaries of his search zone were: 5,000 feet low and 10,200 feet high, which seemed too precise to be mere coincidence. He built up a somewhat compelling case from there, promising me, as always, that there was more to come when next we met.

Instead, there was only disappointment. When we convened at the Denver airport for our connecting flights into Albuquerque, Beep dropped some devastating news. He realized on his first flight that he had gotten his bearings wrong, and the spot and area he wanted to search wouldn't qualify as 8.25 miles north of Santa Fe, violating one of Fenn's cardinal rules. So it was out. Just as we were flying into New Mexico, we were confronted with the reality that we suddenly had nowhere to look.

We puttered around on a few backup ideas, but Beep was losing his lust for the chest, I could tell. His solves were becoming increasingly ragged, the specifics lacking, the conclusions merely reaches, his energy waning.

Disenchanted, Beep changed his flight and headed home to Canada earlier than he'd originally planned, leaving our hunting trip without having gone out searching even once.

But I stayed. Not so much to go hunting again—it had been almost a year since I'd been out on a real hunt of my own, I had no ideas, and really very little drive to come up with new ones. But I still liked a lot of the hunters I'd met over the past few years, and so I stuck around and headed over to Toby Younis's house to meet up with him, Shelley Carney, and Cynthia for a nice home-cooked meal.

Everything was going pleasantly until Toby gave

me some news I didn't quite expect, something that shocked me to my core.

"Did you see the video Sacha posted about you?" Toby asked, a bit of a Cheshire cat smile on his face.

The world of Fenn internet drama had come for me at last.

Sacha leaned down into the camera, preparing to deliver an important message to her fellow searchers, the ones following along on her YouTube channel. Then she got right to it: There was someone out there in the search who couldn't be trusted, who wanted to steal her solve, she said. That was his secret agenda, and the chase community needed to watch out for him, avoid him, be wary of him.

I felt my stomach drop as she delivered the coup de grâce.

"His name is Dan, and he's writing a book."

I was flabbergasted. As she went on to rip into me in the video, I could scarcely believe it—much less understand what had put me in her crosshairs, and why. I didn't want her solve! The last time I had seen Sacha was during the previous search season, almost a year earlier—when we had wandered into Embudo Creek and she'd shown me the rock she believed Fenn had used as a makeshift love nest. I had smiled, nodded—but come on, I wasn't there to plumb her for ideas; I was trying to understand

and capture her experience as a hunter, an interesting and entertaining one at that.

But that didn't matter; Sacha had made her accusation, there were message-board posts about it, and the damage had been done. It was certainly not the first time Sacha had gone after someone in the search—not even the first time she'd made accusations against a reporter. This was actually the second video of this type; she had previously made another video, accusing another reporter of trying to take her solve, but now she was apologizing for that one, saying that guy wasn't the real offender, and redirecting to her actual target, me. It was a lot to take in.

But still, she was important, and influential, and people would listen to her. It may sound silly to outsiders (especially when Sacha had willingly taken multiple reporters to her search spot), but solve stealing was a serious accusation in the Fenn community. Searchers treated their solutions like copyrighted intellectual property. So now others might not trust me, might be angry—and what might that lead to? My mind started to race with the possibilities, none of them good.

But more than all that? Honestly, I was actually a little hurt, and certainly surprised. I liked Sacha, and I'd thought she understood what I was doing better than that.

So I needed to talk to her about it, clear the air,

get all this out into the open. Licking my wounds, I contacted her and pushed for a meeting. I was friendly as could be, not mentioning I had seen the video.

Sacha agreed, and invited me to a taping of her TV show.

Sacha had managed to parlay her treasure-hunting celebrity and real estate gig into a local television show, highlighting quirky events and people in the Albuquerque area on a weekly basis. She'd offered to let me join her for a segment she was filming on "505 Food Fights," a **Top Chef**–style competition held to pick some of the best chefs in the region, pitting them against one another as they whipped up challenging dishes with surprise ingredients. I drove down to Albuquerque to meet her at the High Point Grill, site of the competition, and found Sacha running around with her cameraman, interviewing the finalists.

I bided my time as the contestants got their dishes ready for cooking, and soon the chef-on-chef combat came to a lull, allowing us to make some small talk and catch up a bit. I told her about those recent conversations with Fenn about the hole digger, and Paco Chavez, and about the home invasion, and how I'd asked him if things were getting worse in the chase. To her, there was no question; things had gone from weird to frightening.

"No doubt, absolutely no doubt," Sacha said. "There's so many of them now; they're batshit.

There's so much that doesn't even get reported, stuff that I know about, other people coming to Fenn's house. People are getting so much crazier with this shit; it's scary. I worry about posting things because I don't want these people coming after me, my kids."

Kids. That subject was starting to loom ever larger in my mind. Elliott was about to turn two, and it was now a matter of weeks before our second would arrive. Being out here in the desert once again with Amalie so close to giving birth seemed far, far crazier than it had in 2017. Now, it felt juvenile, selfish, maybe even dangerous. I had a family now. And just like Sacha, I was starting to worry that this treasure hunt might put them in danger.

Which got me back to why I was here.

"Hey, do you want to go sit down?" I asked her as the dishes continued to simmer. We grabbed some Caesar salad and lasagna from a pair of aluminum pans, then settled at a table in one of the few non-bustling corners of the restaurant, away from the (surprisingly good) house band.

"So, Sacha," I said as we sat down, "I need to talk to you about that video you posted."

She immediately turned white, drew a deep breath, and put her head in her hands.

"Ohhhhhhh, God, you saw that. I was so hoping you hadn't seen that," she said. "I'm so, so sorry. I screwed up. It's my fault. I got you confused with someone else."

Well, she had and she hadn't—she had, and then she'd apologized for attacking the other reporter and inexplicably blamed me anyway—but I let it slide. She went on to explain that she had gone out hunting with several reporters around the same time, and had confused and overlapped them with one another, though she still couldn't quite account for where the "stealing solves!" thing had come from.

"I get paranoid. You know my background, my history—I just find it very hard to trust," she said.

And I did get that. But to me, that wasn't even the point, and I told her so.

"Sacha, look, I don't want your solve," I said, explaining that I wasn't looking for an apology. I had come to a new understanding about this treasure hunt, a new recognition of my place in it. Through this episode with her video, through the conspiracy theories of the Candyman and Stephanie, through the women's accusations against Fenn on the message boards, through the latest tales of searchers who had gone a bit too far, I'd come to see it all in a very different light.

And that meant making sure I would never ever be the one to find that damned treasure chest.

"Honestly—and I know this may sound crazy—but I don't want to find the treasure, at all," I told her. "I can't, really. That, to me, would be the ultimate nightmare. It's the worst and most dangerous thing I could do to my world. And ultimately, you're the one who first helped me to understand that."

She looked at me quizzically.

"This chase," I continued, "has gotten a little crazier than I expected. Like we were talking about before—the seven-percenters are growing, or they're getting bolder, or both. And before we went out hunting together that last time, at the Burger King in Española, you told me how the only way you'd go hunting with me was if I agreed to keep it quiet if you found it—and I told you I couldn't really do that, and you said I couldn't be trusted to keep a secret.

"Well, you were one hundred percent right," I said. Sacha seemed to soften as she came to realize that I really wasn't there to berate her.

"The problem for me is, I can't keep a secret for me any more than I can for you. I have an obligation to tell the story, contractually, ethically, journalistically. I couldn't just sit on the treasure even if I did find it. People would need to know that I'd done it.

"And as soon as I acknowledged that I'd found it," I told her, "I'd be putting a giant target on my back."

The more time I spent in the hunt, the more I'd come to believe that those fringe elements could be genuinely dangerous to whoever finally found the box. It's something I'd started worrying about when, two years earlier, Beep began to raise questions about what we'd do if we found it, and those whispers in my head grew after I'd talked to Sacha. Over this past year, with the hole digger, and the home invader, and the return of Paco Chavez, I couldn't drown them out anymore. I had become scared of the hunt, and wary of what some hunters might do.

I explained to Sacha that anyone and everyone would assume I'd found it only because I had special access to Fenn, via my reporting on him. Even though he never said a damn thing that was useful to me, they'd think I was cheating somehow.

Sacha had driven all of this home for me with her video—the way that these things could take on a life of their own, with accusations of solve stealing and the like, how fast they could get out of hand, especially for someone in my position, who **was** gaining special access to the big-name hunters and to Fenn. After I saw that video, I couldn't stop thinking about Elliott at home, and our second son, about to be born, and someone coming to do me or them harm because of a treasure hunt. A treasure hunt!

I told Sacha all this, and I think she understood—maybe more than I'd expected her to, agreeing and saying she'd had her own doubts of late, too.

"Sometimes it feels like it's too much. All the drama. The forums. I just don't know when it's not worth it anymore," she said as we picked at what was left of the lasagna.

Perhaps she had changed a bit, too.

With her local television show and her increasingly non-treasure-related YouTube channel, Sacha seemed to be trying to parlay her treasure-hunting renown into other areas. And she was considering an even bigger escape—she and Jason were happily back together, and she was weighing moving to Kansas to be with him, which would certainly mean the end of her days as a regular treasure hunter.

Maybe it would be a chance for her to make a clean break after so many years of searching. Maybe that would be a good thing, I suggested.

But then her eyes went to the side, like she was remembering something.

"But then I feel like, I'm just so close," she said, a smile creeping onto her face. "I couldn't take it if somebody found the treasure and I almost knew where it was. I just think I'm really, finally getting there on it."

I understood that feeling now. I could relate to it. But I no longer felt it burning inside me. At its best moments, seeking this chest had felt like a grand adventure, but it was one I couldn't justify anymore. I'd made my decision, and I was at peace with it.

A few days later, I flew back to Boston, happy to be back home.

I'd never go hunting for Fenn's treasure again.

15

FORTUNE AND GLORY

Cynthia Meachum was in her so-called war room when the email arrived.

She and another searcher, a guy named Matt DeMoss, from Texas, were comparing their thoughts on the Gardiner, Montana, area. Cynthia had been searching up near Gardiner just a few weeks back, and shortly after she'd been there, Matt had explored roughly that same territory. So on his way back to Texas, Cynthia invited him to her home outside Albuquerque to compare notes.

"We were actually in my war room at my maps going over each of our solves," she said. "I mean, drawing the lines with our fingers. I'm saying, 'This is mine'; he was saying, 'Mine started at the same place, but then I went this direction.' And we were doing this when that email came across."

The email was from Forrest Fenn. That in itself

wasn't unusual. But when Cynthia opened it, her heart nearly stopped.

The chase was over, it said. The chest had been found.

At first, she didn't believe it. The email must not have been from Fenn. It couldn't be.

"I immediately thought, Oh my god, someone hacked his account," she recalled. "I mean, I immediately reached out to Forrest, and said, 'Is this real?' And he wrote back, 'Yes, it is.'"

For Fenn hunters, the moment they heard the chest was found was akin to learning about the Kennedy assassination, or the **Challenger** explosion, or the 9/11 attacks—they remember exactly where they were and what they were doing when they heard the news.

And for the top hunters, those memories all date to Saturday, June 6, 2020. Sacha Johnston—now Sacha Dent—was sitting on the couch watching Netflix with her husband, Jason, when she learned of the discovery. Sacha had moved to Kansas to be near Jason in the fall of 2019, and the pair had gotten married the following March, just before the COVID-19 pandemic hit America and everything went crazy. Despite that, life in Kansas was going well, and she hadn't been able to get back to the Rockies to do much searching, though the hunt was still often on her mind.

When the email came in, Sacha thought the exact same thing Cynthia had: It couldn't be true.

"I get this email, I look at it and I show it to my husband, and neither one of us believe it," she said. "So I call Forrest immediately. I called him and I said, 'Forrest, I just got an email from you. This email, that's real? It's true?' He said, 'Yes, it is. Yes, the chase is over.'

"And then he said, 'I hope you at least got something out of it,'" Sacha continued. "And I said, 'Well, you know, Jason and I got married because of it. So he goes, 'Well, that's something.'"

Sacha told Fenn she wouldn't take up too much of his time, and she let him go as she tried to process the moment.

"Saturday night was shock. Just shock. Just like, did that really happen? It doesn't impact you until the next day. The next day, it was real. So, of course, I was very sad, and very disappointed."

Up in Washington State, it was much the same for Dal Neitzel. He lives on an island, removed from the rest of the world, and with the pandemic roiling the nation, getting out and treasure hunting was far from his mind. By early June, the hunting season would normally have been in full swing, and preparations for Fennboree would have been well under way. Instead, talk on his blog was muted, everyone's attention elsewhere. In that environment, Fenn's email arrived like a thunderbolt.

"It was a huge surprise to me when Forrest sent that note saying that the chest had been found,"

Dal said. "I mean, I wasn't expecting it. I wasn't ready for it. I hadn't even been thinking about it."

He reacted just like the others had.

"I think I initially looked for some kind of a way out. I think initially, I was, Okay, this isn't from Forrest. This is from somebody else. So I had to check with Forrest to make sure that he actually sent it. And then he said, 'Yes, I really sent that.' And at that point, I decided to go ahead and get pouty about it."

Dal, however, couldn't be pouty for long. He had a job to do. He was instructed to put a message from Fenn up on his blog, informing the rest of the chase community that the hunt was over, that the chest had been found.

Fenn's message, initially posted on his own website, the Old Santa Fe Trading Company, was written with the same evocative flair so evident in his original poem. It did not name a finder, nor disclose a location, but it made it perfectly clear: The chase was over.

"It was under a canopy of stars in the lush, forested vegetation of the Rocky Mountains and had not moved from the spot where I hid it more than 10 years ago," Fenn's message said. "I do not know the person who found it, but the poem in my book led him to the precise spot. I congratulate the thousands of people who participated in the search and hope they will continue to be drawn by the promise of other discoveries. So the search is over. Look for more information and photos in the coming days."

And with that, the decade-long hunt for Forrest Fenn's treasure chest came to an end.

The controversy around it? That was just beginning.

I wasn't high-status enough to get one of the personalized Fenn emails declaring the chase was over, so I first heard that it had ended the next day. We had lost power in a storm the night before, and I was rushing around trying to get nonrefrigerated lunches ready for Elliott and little brother Reid, when a coworker (I'd taken a job as a senior editor at the sports website **The Athletic** in 2018) who knew about my involvement forwarded me an article from the **Santa Fe New Mexican** on the conclusion of the search. She also asked, somewhat seriously, if I was the one who'd found it—which seemed ludicrously comical to me until I read some of Fenn's quotes in the piece.

"The guy who found it does not want his name mentioned. He's from back east," Fenn had told the newspaper, adding he had confirmation of the finding via a photograph the man had sent him.

Having not been on a real hunt in almost two years, I was most definitely not that guy from back east—but that didn't stop dozens of people from reaching out and inquiring if I was. When I went online to see how the community was responding, I was impressed and heartened by what I found. On the blogs, there was an air of resignation, yes, but perhaps also one of relief, and of respect for the searcher who had finally cracked the code. Comment after comment wished the finder well, most of them with an "Aw shucks, I wish it'd been me, but cheers to this smart person" air to them.

Of course, the messages weren't only about sending best wishes; as always, the searchers' collective certainty in their own solves shone through even now. Countless hunters claimed online and on FennTuber shows that they had actually figured out the riddle, too, and had been going to go pick it up the following weekend, or that they had been out right near it only a week or two before and had had to turn back because of weather or some other external factor, just before they claimed the chest. The usual pie-in-the-sky searcher claims, making the veterans roll their eyes.

"It's so absurd. I just can't get over how many people there are thinking that," Cynthia said, cackling with laughter. "Everybody calling in, thinking that they have it solved and someone just beat them to it. Yeah. Thank you. It's like, You stupid bastards, you haven't been right for all these years."

One unexpected development, though, came from those same searchers and others publicly sharing their solves—because they all wanted to prove how close they had been when Fenn did finally reveal the location. Even Beep couldn't help himself, sending Cynthia, Fenn, and me an incredibly detailed version of his own most recent solve, just to make sure it was recorded with the proper authorities.

Still, with everyone finally putting their cards on the table, it seemed as if at the final moment the chase community had set aside all its grievances, packed away its vitriol, and decided to celebrate the end of this shared pursuit.

That lasted about twenty-four hours.

When it became clear in the following days' rounds of newspaper articles that Fenn was not going to be releasing the name of the finder or, seemingly, the location of the treasure, and that he was quickly cutting off contact with the media—on Monday, June 8, he told the **Santa Fe New Mexican** he was not "going to talk about it anymore"—the mood in the hunting community shifted instantly.

"It was pretty sad on Sunday," Sacha said. "But then on Monday, the world started becoming unhinged. Three lawsuits are dropped. The chase community absolutely started to turn on Forrest, demanding information, calling it a hoax, not believing the announcement—like, all the conspiracy theories abounded."

Searchers immediately felt cheated. They demanded more information. For the most part, they understood the desire to keep the finder anonymous. From potential tax issues to fears about jealousy or dangerous actions from some in the Fenn community, most searchers seemed to have come to the same conclusion I had—that anonymity was a valid, necessary armor for the finder.

But almost to a person, they were upset that Fenn wasn't releasing the location of the solve—even a generalized location, or a state—or, seemingly, providing any proof that the chest had been found, just assuming instead that people would take his word for it.

"I don't think he realized the stink it would cause," Cynthia said. "I think he thought everyone would just believe him. And no, it works the opposite way. None of us believed him."

The blogs exploded in anger and doubt, and those in the mainstream media began to write negative pieces, as well. Doubters came from all sides: Old Fenn nemesis Linda Bilyeu weighed in, reiterating her belief that the whole thing had been a hoax all along. She had new ammunition to pepper Fenn with, as well—there had been a fifth death in the chase, a searcher named Michael Wayne Sexson, fifty-three, of Deer Trail, Colorado, who had died while searching for the treasure out in Dinosaur National Monument in March 2020. Sexson had been hunting with a sixty-five-year-old friend, and the pair, unprepared for the conditions, became stranded in the park with little food or water. After several days out in the cold, Sexson perished. It had prompted Bilyeu to do another round of interviews slamming Fenn and his chase. Now, with it simply declared over and little evidence to be seen, she was raising the volume of her opposition.

"I believe he never hid the treasure," Bilyeu said in an interview in the Colorado publication **Westword.** "He needed attention and this is how he got it. Fenn needed more attention, which is why he said the treasure has been found, with 'no proof.'"

Another name from Fenn's past, former Newsweek reporter turned **CBS This Morning** anchor Tony Dokoupil—who back in 2012 had written the first article to deeply examine Fenn's mixed history—weighed in via a Twitter thread and subsequent interview on **Inside Edition** with a unique theory of his own: that this was all just another Fenn twist. The treasure was still out there, he said, and this was another stage in Fenn's game.

"So why don't I think that anyone really found Fenn's treasure? Because Fenn is a salesman first and always, a 'hustler,' as he told me. And this whole gambit is about Fenn's pursuit of immortality," Dokoupil tweeted, going on to state his belief that Fenn might be engineering a way of completing his original plan, to bury himself next to his chest.

"The real reason why I don't think the treasure has really been found is because Forrest told me that his plan was to entomb himself along with the treasure," Dokoupil further explained on **Inside**

Edition. "I think the treasure is in a location where an older man can still get to it and crawl or insert himself in and alongside the chest. I mean, that's how it was explained to me.

"You have a guy who's been collecting archaeology his whole life, is so in love with it he's hatched a plan to make himself part of that record for all time and invite the public in to try to find it and his bones," he continued, doubling down on his belief that the treasure was real, and was still waiting to be found. "I am confident it is not a hoax. Forrest wants to be remembered for thousands of years, and this is his way of doing so."

Beep's friend Mike McDonald, the poker pro, even got in the game, putting out a bounty on the chest via Twitter. McDonald, saying he was skeptical the chest ever existed, offered up $10,000 for anyone who could prove they found it, plus another $10,000 as a fee for whoever connected McDonald with the finder.

The cynics, hoaxers, and conspiracy theorists were one thing. They had always been a part of the chase. But those lawsuits Sacha had referred to? They added another layer to the drama in the days after the announcement.

One of them was a revival of the suit filed the year before, by David Hanson of Colorado—who had sued because he believed that Fenn had intentionally sent him false clues that directed him away from the treasure. Early in 2020, Hanson had apologized to Fenn and offered to settle the suit for one dollar, seemingly ending the matter. Now Hanson was attempting to bring it back to life. Another came from an Arizona lawyer named Brian Erskine, who alleged that Fenn owed him the treasure because the poem and book constituted a written contract to deliver the chest to whoever solved the poem, and that he, Erskine, of course, had solved it.

The most, er, interesting came from Chicago lawyer Barbara Andersen, who claimed in her suit that she had figured out the solution but that that solve was subsequently stolen by another person, who used it to find the chest, and then sent her harassing texts about it. Having reviewed the texts in the filing, she was clearly having an unpleasant text exchange with another person, but to suggest that those harassing texts had even the slightest bit to do with the treasure hunt at all, let alone to think they were from the finder, was an enormous stretch.

As all of this swirled around, it left Dal in a difficult position. With Fenn suddenly clamming up, no longer speaking in public and not responding to emails, everyone saw Dal as the last remaining avenue for getting additional information. Dal, ever loyal, had to defend Fenn with limited info, asking everyone to hold off, to calm down, to give Fenn some time to work everything out. But Dal had little to give. He didn't want to badger Fenn, and in what interactions they did have, he saw a man stunned by the level of pushback he was receiving.

"For him, I think one of the expectations would be that some of this nonsense in his life would fizzle away," Dal said. "And it only got worse. There was no instant relief from the burden of the crazies out there."

So Dal did what he could to keep everyone at bay, telling searchers that "Forrest may have changed his mind about additional info."

That went over about as well as you'd expect.

On June 9, recognizing the level of fury, Fenn sent Dal a message to be posted on his blog.

It read: "Please folks, give me a little time. I'll be back." It was signed "f."

That surgical application of Fenn's humanity helped a little. Searchers recognized that there might be issues Fenn needed to sort out between himself and the finder, or the finder and his bank, or the finder and the IRS—something.

But there was a growing din, and with each passing day that no new information came, it got louder. Why couldn't Fenn release more information? Some sort of proof? Why this delay, and what did it mean? Was this all everyone was going to get? Hadn't Fenn planned all along for just this moment? It was unsatisfying, it hardly made sense, and it was just plain strange. The doubters, the conspiracists, the skeptics—their voices all rose louder in the vacuum. Was the chase actually over? Had the chest really been found? So many treasure hunts ended in a muddled, unsatisfying fashion. Would this be just another added to that long list?

Everyone waited to see what Fenn had up his sleeve.

What does a treasure chest look like when it's been out in the elements for ten years? Is it perfectly intact, a gleaming, golden prize to be claimed? Is it worn and battered like the man who hid it, weathered but unbowed by time? Or is it broken and failing, like the chests the Fisher family found beneath the sea, prizes bursting out of it, yearning to be found?

On June 16, Forrest Fenn gave the world its answer.

That day, Dal posted a series of pictures on his blog, direct from Fenn. There were three main shots: a picture of the treasure chest, opened, out in the wild, and two shots of Fenn going through the treasure, presumably after the finder had returned the chest to him. It was all there for the eye to see: the treasure, the proof, the conclusion.

I hadn't been on a real boots-on-the-ground hunt in years. I considered myself well cured of the Fenn hunting bug. And still, seeing the chest and the treasure piled inside it took my breath away.

Fenn had shown us the treasure before, yes. But

the pictures in **The Thrill of the Chase** were a little like viewing treasure in a museum—it was pristine, removed, almost theoretical. This felt undeniably real.

The first picture was shot from a top-down view, taken by somebody standing over the chest somewhere outdoors, presumably close to the location where it was found. The chest looked worn, with the lining at the front, in particular, damaged and warped. There was a rusty metal key sitting atop the loot, along with a twig of some sort. The coins and gold nuggets were strewn and piled about the chest, while other valuables were contained in baggies.

Beneath it, Fenn had written a caption: "The treasure chest was found by a man I did not know and had not communicated with since 2018."

Looking closely at the photo reveals fascinating details. The dates on some of the gold coins are visible—1903, 1900. There are plastic baggies filled with gold dust, necklaces, the pre-Columbian gold mirrors, a golden frog, gold hoops, the golden dragon bracelet—it's all there as Fenn promised, glorious and tangible, even if it wasn't exactly what some had built it up to be in their minds.

"I felt like I dreamed about finding the treasure so many times," Beep said when we connected to talk about the photos. "It was probably one hundred times as cool, seeing what it actually looks like.

"Though it wasn't at all like how I'd envisioned it,"

he said, a little sheepish, admitting that there was a part of him that expected it to be grander. "I kind of thought it would look like it did in **Aladdin.**"

The next picture is of Fenn himself, depicting him wearing the turquoise bracelet that he had asked to have returned, the one with sentimental value. It is captioned, "The bracelet on my arm was wet when found. The silver tarnished black."

The final photo is a shot of Fenn in what looks to be an office of some sort—a lawyer's office, perhaps—with the chest on the table, and the treasure spread around, as Fenn goes through it piece by piece.

"Removing objects from the chest. It is darker than it was ten years ago when I left it on the ground and walked away," the caption reads.

A second caption followed that, seemingly a final proclamation from Fenn: "The finder wants me to remain silent, and I always said the finder gets to make those two calls. Who and where. f"

Had he? I certainly didn't recall the finder getting to dictate if everyone else would know the location of the find. But that was clearly how Fenn was playing it.

Either way, it was now clear. Forrest Fenn's chest had been retrieved, and the hunt was truly over. All the Linda Bilyeu talk of hoaxes, of the chest never really having been hidden, seemed a bit silly now. It had been out there all that time, waiting to be found. And finally, it had been.

If that was to be it, though, it still left a bit of mystery to this chase. Where had it been hidden? These pictures of the chest offered a trove of new information, and searchers went to great lengths to analyze the shots and learn what they could about the chest and its whereabouts over the past ten years.

One searcher, Cynthia's friend Matt, who goes by the name "Smell the Sunshine" on his YouTube channel, did a Zapruder-style forensic analysis of the three pictures, breaking them down in incredible detail. For the first, outdoor picture, he surmised from the shade and reflections of the sky that it was taken around 9:30 or 10:00 in the morning, and was likely taken with a cell phone camera, judging by the shape of the photo and the distortion in the lens.

He went on to explain that the pictures tell us much about how and where the chest was hidden. The rusty key and the wearing away of the chest's lining could be tremendously revealing in answering the question of where it might have spent the last ten years.

"There was water in the chest, to be sure, thus the rusty key," Matt said. "But everything looks dry here. This might suggest the chest was sitting on the ground."

Rain splashing in front of it, but not on it, might account for that moisture and dirt accumulating inside over time, he suggested—meaning it might have been secreted away in or around a cluster of rocks.

"I think some kind of rock formation, with a crevice near the bottom, seems like a good candidate," he said. "The chest is tucked inside, somewhat hidden and protected, especially if you have trees and scrub and rocks here and there. The back of the chest is largely untouched by the elements, but rain splashes within a few inches of the front of the chest, causing debris to enter the chest, little by little, over time.

"This also explains why the wood lining at the back of the chest looks pristine, while at the front, we can detect severe warping and separation. The front of this chest was somewhat exposed, while the back of the chest was not," he concluded.

The pictures themselves were scrubbed of metadata, so there is no way to know when they were taken, something that some searchers found significant.

All this amateur detective work on the pictures also turned up a few other interesting tidbits, including a tantalizing glimpse at who might have taken them. There was a slight reflection in the outdoors shot of the treasure chest, making it possible to see, just barely, a person—presumably the finder. He appears to be wearing a hat, perhaps yellow in color, Matt said. But no one could figure out much about the identity of the picture taker beyond that.

Searchers did their best to divine what they could, but ultimately we were all taking Fenn's scraps. And if that was to be it, then what an unsatisfying ending. No idea where the chest had been. Not even the state where it was found. No idea who found it. Never knowing where "warm waters halt," or what "the home of Brown" might be. No certainty about the blaze. Nothing.

"I understand not releasing the exact location, because either people will turn it into a shrine or they will desecrate it, because they will go and they will take a souvenir," Cynthia said. "But both Dal and I were so mad that he didn't at least release the state it was found in—he could even say, within a fifty-mile radius of Gardiner, or a twenty-five-mile radius of West Yellowstone, or something. I wanted to know if I was ever close."

Yes, even Dal was unhappy. Always patient and understanding, always publicly supportive of whatever Fenn did, even Dal believed this result was not good enough.

"When the second announcement came in, it was very unfulfilling," Dal groused. "We didn't find out a freakin' thing. That was what was disturbing to most people, because at that point, we expected it to unfold differently. And so folks were upset, you know, and I can sort of understand that.

"I don't think Forrest owes anybody anything, but we did play his game for a long time," Dal continued. "And, you know, when you play the game, to have somebody suddenly change the rules at the very end is, is, you know, it's disheartening and makes you not want to play the game with them anymore."

The game was over now. Everyone agreed on that. Fenn wasn't speaking anymore in public, to the media or anyone else, and it was pretty clear that what the searchers had was what they were going to get when it came to the treasure chest, its finder, and its location. There wasn't much else left to be said.

They all responded to this new reality in different ways.

Dal seemed happy—relieved, he told me—to be done with the whole thing, especially the constant maintenance of the blog, which he said took between eight and ten hours a day most of the time. He said he didn't plan to get involved in any more treasure hunts. He sounded like a man who had just had enough of the whole thing.

"I'm quite relieved that it's winding down, that it's been found, and that I can move on to something else. I think nine years is plenty long enough to do one thing," he said.

Barely a month after Fenn announced the chest had been found, Dal announced that he would soon be taking his site down entirely, along with all the years and years of Fenn comments, scrapbooks, controversies—all of it, scrubbed from the internet (though he did archive it privately for posterity).

He didn't leave, though, before issuing a long, impassioned good-bye, one that lauded Fenn, and slammed all who had come up against him over the years.

"To all those wanna-be poachers, trolls, spammers and woofers . . . I say 'fuck you.' We made it work in spite of you," Dal wrote.

"It is now a bitter, bitter end to witness greed in the shape of pernicious litigation and malevolent spite that has accumulated against Forrest," he continued. "I know that most humans are wonderful people, but I have also learned that some are despicable and have no more function in the world than to spread hatred and create a malicious environment in a place that was intended to be joyful and playful. I don't know what makes them tick and I don't care."

The other blogs kept churning on; Stephanie Thirtyacre kept ChaseChat up and running, constantly making it known that she found the entire end of the chase suspect, and relaying her hopes that scathing truths about Fenn would come out in the court documents related to the various lawsuits now flying around.

Mindy Fausey and James Gulden left Florida and moved to the Blue Ridge Mountains in Virginia. Mindy started her own YouTube channel, which, while not explicitly treasure-related— it featured segments on Bonnie and Clyde, the Vikings, and more—still delved into Fenn's treasure from time to time.

Toby Younis and his FennTube partner, Shelly Carney, "went through the five stages of grief in about a half hour," Younis said.

"Fenn fumbled the proverbial football on this rollout, and left us with more questions than answers," Younis added. But in his estimation, either way, the Fenn treasure hunt was over. Which meant it was time for something new. He and Carney were starting their own treasure hunt and were in the process of writing a **Thrill of the Chase**–type book to lead searchers to their treasure. Paying it all forward, as it were.

They weren't the only ones inspired to create new hunts. The Candyman returned, selling tickets for $49.99 to a hunt that he said would end in his giving away a candy factory in Florida. And even Sacha got into the hunt-creating business. Sacha was happily ensconced in Kansas with Jason, having moved on to a career working for the local school department, doing public relations. Despite how deeply she'd been into Fenn's hunt, she seemed remarkably at peace with the outcome, saying she actually hadn't even wanted to know if she'd been close—no reason to know if you're the "first loser," she said—and instead spent her time on her newest pursuit. That was as part of a group digging into the story behind the Netflix documentary **Tiger**

King, and, more specifically, trying to unearth information to prove that **Tiger King** character and CEO of Big Cat Rescue Carole Baskin killed her second husband, Don Lewis, in 2002.

"We do nothing but investigate Carole," Sacha said. "We've talked to volunteers who used to work there at the time, you know; we investigate different theories and go down the rabbit holes and try to figure all this stuff out."

That takes up much of her spare time, but Sacha couldn't let treasure hunting go entirely. Like Younis, she just decided to go at it from the other side. She and Jason started their own venture, Kansas Treasure Hunts, hiding small treasures of their own and encouraging others to stash treasures away, trying to provide a little hope in the difficult times of COVID.

"We're never gonna be able to hide a million-dollar chest holding jewels," Sacha said. "But getting other people to be able to have a little adventure, solve a puzzle, get out of their house and have some fun and win some money in the process is just a way to, you know, bring up the morale of people right now."

That's what Fenn's chase had originally been about, he'd said, giving people something to boost their morale. But since the chest was found, so many searchers remained unhappy with the outcome, and with how little news and information Fenn had released. In a difficult time of illness and political strife, Fenn's chest was proving to be just one more disappointment.

Finally, almost two months after the initial announcement, Fenn gave in. He offered the yearning crowd a concession, one meant to appease, and to satisfy: the state where the treasure had been hidden those ten years.

"The finder understands how important some closure is for many searchers, so today he agreed that we should reveal that the treasure was found in Wyoming," Fenn wrote in a final message posted on Dal's blog. "Until he found the treasure, the treasure had not moved in the 10 years since I left it there on the ground, and walked away.

"Perhaps today's announcement will bring some closure to those whose solves were in New Mexico, Colorado, or Montana," Fenn wrote.

Unsurprisingly, the number of people who said they were sure it had been in Wyoming seemed to suddenly skyrocket—though it also brought out more doubters. Some pointed out that if the chest was found in the mountains of Wyoming in early June, why was it, and the ground below it, so dry in the pictures we had seen? In most Wyoming locations around that time, snow melt should have altered the conditions. Still, Beep, who had believed it was in Wyoming for some time, felt a sense of vindication. He'd had a hard time once he heard the treasure had been found, still holding out a little hope that maybe it was still out there, until, finally, all the evidence made it clear that it was well and truly over.

"Emotionally, I think I went through minor stages of grief, where at first I was like, Ah, nice for the finder, and then after a few days I kind of felt like there's a little piece of my life that was missing, and then kind of wanting closure," Beep said.

At least now he could feel assured that he'd been in the right area. Me? I just felt ever dumber—my one semioriginal thought was that the way he'd first described hiding his treasure in the book, those "mountains north of Santa Fe," meant it was likely in New Mexico. Wrong from beginning to end—at least I was consistent.

For most searchers, though, that was finally enough. We now knew that, yes, the chest had been found, and we all had some general idea where it was. This latest announcement did seem to offer the resolution so many needed.

But not everyone was ready to move on.

Not too long after Fenn released his pictures and it seemed like everything was wrapped up, I got a call from Cynthia. We'd corresponded a bit as it was all unfolding but hadn't really caught up in earnest. Cynthia had a lot going on in her life; she and her partner, Michelle, were no longer living together, and Cynthia was selling her house and moving to Las Vegas to start a new chapter in her life.

Yet something about the end of Fenn's hunt didn't sit right with her.

Besides Dal, perhaps no one had been a stauncher public supporter of Fenn. Cynthia had always been on his side, believing in the goodness of his hunt, and steadfastly saying she didn't care about any of the other stuff, the problems with women, the deaths, any of it. To her, the greater good outweighed anything else, and this treasure hunt represented a greater good.

Which made what she had to tell me all the more shocking.

"I don't believe there was a finder," Cynthia said. "I think Forrest ended the hunt."

Fenn had realized that if he passed on with the chest still out there, it would have been a disaster for his family, Cynthia believed. The incidents with those like the stalker Paco Chavez, or the home invader Robert Miller, would only transfer to his children and his grandchildren, perhaps indefinitely. He would be cursing those he loved most to a lifetime of persecution. No treasure hunt was worth that.

"I think that he finally recognized what kind of hell would continue if it was still out there after he died," Cynthia said. "What it would do to his family, his grandkids, the chase community."

So, she believed, he agreed to put an end to this, for their sake. His family, especially his daughters, Zoe and Kelly, had always hated the hunt, she said, and that had only gotten worse in the past few years. The pressure from them to end it had been significant, and Fenn finally either caved in or came to agree with them. So he invented this nebulous tale of a finder from "back east," and figured that would be that.

But then there was so much backlash, so much anger, such a refusal to take Fenn at his word, that Fenn needed the chest itself as proof.

"I think what happened was there was so much disbelief that there was a finder that he actually had to then go tap someone to retrieve it and bring it home," she said, fingering Shiloh as the likeliest candidate to have gotten it, and saying that accounted for the ten-day delay between the time he announced the ending and the release of the pictures.

Coming from Cynthia, that alone would have been meaningful. But this was no run-of-the-mill conjecture, no message-board conspiracy theory. No, Cynthia had information. She knew something everyone else didn't, about a specific episode, the day Fenn told those closest to him that the hunt was ending. Something that afternoon that she believes led directly to Fenn's decision to call it off.

That Saturday, June 6, there had been another incident at Fenn's house, she said.

"That day, there was just some family stuff, some slightly negative stuff that happened at the Fenn house around one o'clock in the afternoon, which I know exactly what it was."

That afternoon, she said, a searcher arrived at Fenn's home. Shiloh intercepted the person and questioned him, asking what he was doing there, telling him no one was allowed in, especially in the age of COVID-19. The person began to leave, she said, but at that point Shiloh learned that Fenn had actually invited the searcher to his house. So they called the person back and grudgingly allowed him to come in.

"The family is so pissed off," she said, "but they allow the guy in the house. And then it ends up that the family catches Forrest and this guy in the house without masks on in the house. And the shit hits the fan."

Fenn had always thought himself invincible. After all, he'd twice crashed his jet in the jungles of Vietnam, and lived to tell of it. So some virus? Something he couldn't see? Well, that wasn't going to stop him. But his wife, Peggy, had respiratory issues, and, as Cynthia explained, if the virus entered their house, Peggy would die. Likely Forrest, too. His family understood that. Fenn seemed not to. That led to a significant confrontation between Fenn and his family, Cynthia said, one that felt like just the latest in a long string of problems related to the treasure hunt, big and small.

"The incident that took place on that Saturday was another unfortunate moment—not a crazy searcher thing, just something that had to do with COVID. And them not having a mask on and Forrest not seeming to give a shit about it," Cynthia said.

Fenn's family had put up with a great deal over the years, from basic searcher intrusions to the truly scary Paco Chavez–type incidents. They didn't ask for this hunt to take over their lives. Who could blame them for wanting it to be over?

"So all this takes place. One o'clock in the afternoon on Saturday. Isn't it funny how there's a finder at eight o'clock that night?" Cynthia said. "What if his family made him end it that day? What if his family said, 'This is the straw that broke the camel's back'? That 'Today is the day you're gonna announce it was found'?"

Cynthia added what she saw as proof, pointing me to quotes and interviews dating back to 2018 and 2019 that showed that the family was clearly putting pressure on Fenn to end it, and that perhaps, just maybe, his public statements indicated he was heading in that direction. There was that fifth death, too, of Michael Wayne Sexson in Colorado in March. Fenn could no longer say that all those deaths in 2017 had been from another time, before he had given additional tips and warnings intended to keep his hunters safe. Instead, here was macabre evidence that the deaths would keep coming, likely indefinitely, as long as the chest was out there. The loss of another life was a weight and a pressure of a different sort, something else pushing down on the scale, neither he nor his family wanting to see more death.

It all made sense; I certainly had to admit that much. If Fenn were to die unexpectedly, the burden would fall right on his family, until . . . forever? The Fenn treasure was tantalizing now, and with Fenn gone, it would eventually take on the status of legend. His children, his grandchildren, and their grandchildren might be harassed because some searcher down the line believed they might know something. It was a scary idea.

"I think that this was in the works since last year," Cynthia said. "I think the ending was in the works since last year, because the family had put so much pressure on him. And I just think that Forrest was starting to understand that something needed to happen before he died."

Okay, I said, but what if the person who visited his house that day was the finder? That would make sense and explain a great deal.

No, she said emphatically. She knew who the person who visited the house that day was, and even though she wouldn't reveal his identity, for fear he would face harassment, he was absolutely not the finder, she said.

I next queried her on why he needed a finder at all. Couldn't he have just retrieved the chest and explained that the hunt was over?

"Everyone would have said it was a hoax," Cynthia

said. "He would have been accused of never having hid it by a lot of people, even the people that believe. . . . Everyone would have said yep, everyone who thought it was a hoax was right. He never hid it. He had to have a finder."

Cynthia even said she had challenged Fenn about it. The very night he had emailed her to announce the treasure had been found, she said, she had ultimately written him back to tell him she didn't believe him.

"After he said 'Yes. Yes, it was me that wrote [the email announcing the find].' My reply was, 'I know this is bullshit.' And then I went on to say, 'Because I know what took place at your house today.'"

Fenn did not respond.

Cynthia didn't seem agitated or upset. She seemed sympathetic to Fenn's predicament, actually. She knew the burden this had put on Fenn and his family. It's all just a shame, Cynthia said, that it had to end this way.

"I feel bad for him about the way it ended," she said. "I don't want him to think that I'm going to be mad at him forever. Or I want him to know that I understand that this, you know, was what he had to do."

It wasn't that crazy, was it? It made sense. I was painfully aware that I'd been drawn into a conspiracy theory or two already on this hunt, and that I needed to guard against that again. But, man, this added up. I kept thinking about how the

Masquerade hunt had ended, and how its conclusion had been shrouded in controversy. Why couldn't that be the case here? Cynthia knew more about this hunt than practically anyone else, and she believed this was true. On top of that, Cynthia knew about something important, something that no one else did: the 1:00 p.m. searcher visit, and the fight with Fenn's family that followed.

At a loss for what to believe, I tried to find out what I could. Fenn wasn't returning my emails right then, so I contacted Shiloh, hopeful he could clear some things up, and also heard nothing.

I also asked around, questioning other searchers as to whether they believed it possible that Fenn had just ended the hunt himself. Sacha said she didn't believe it and wanted to move on entirely, not think about the what ifs.

Dal, however, surprised me with his reaction.

"It's a possibility that you can't rule out, but I'm not a believer in that theory," Dal said, before wavering. "But, yeah, how can you not consider that? . . . I do understand that, you know, the pressure on his family has been tremendous. And they put a lot of pressure on him. I mean, it could be that, you know, he finally folded."

Then he stopped.

"But I don't—I'm not ready to go there yet."

I wasn't, either. Not completely. Cynthia's theory made a lot of sense to me, but I wasn't convinced. I talked to Beep about it, probably the most conspiracy-fluent person I knew, someone who had been down every rabbit hole the internet had to offer, and he wanted no part of it. He believed the finder was real, and encouraged me to think the same.

I wasn't sure. How could we know? With Fenn keeping silent and no finder to be had, it seemed like Fenn's hunt might remain a mystery forever, even after the chest had been retrieved, an outcome that left me somewhere between frustrated and unsatisfied.

And then everything changed one final time as the founder left the stage and the finder entered the scene.

16

THE NEXT BEST THING
TO FINDING A TREASURE

For a decade, Forrest Fenn had lived as creator, promoter, steward, and defender of perhaps the most extraordinary treasure hunt America had ever known. He lived to see its conclusion. And then, barely three months after the hunt he had brought into the world had ended, Fenn was gone.

On the morning of September 7, 2020, Fenn was found unconscious in his study, having fallen, according to the police report. He was taken to CHRISTUS St. Vincent Regional Medical Center, then released to the care of his family, who returned him to his home. There he died later that same day, never having regained consciousness. The first responders who arrived on the scene that morning were initially responding to a cardiac arrest call, indicating Fenn may have had a heart attack that precipitated his fall.

His funeral arrangements were private, and searchers were kept at arm's length. The family did eventually post a message on Fenn's website, thanking the search community: "To the many searchers who joined us in the thrill of the chase over the last decade, your stories, emails, and tales of the hunt sparked joy in his life and we are forever grateful for your enthusiasm." It was up for only a few weeks, though, before it and all of Fenn's writings were taken down.

After an initial outpouring of grief, there were conflicting reports on the various message boards about Fenn's condition leading up to his death. Some said that Fenn had been fine until the day he passed, while others claimed that he had been in decline for the last few months, or even longer. I'd spoken to Cynthia, who had visited with Fenn that summer, and she said he seemed to be in both good health and good spirits.

The author Doug Preston said much the same; he hadn't been able to be there for Fenn's ninetieth birthday in late August—due to COVID-19, the Fenn family held a car parade for friends to drive by and say hello—but Preston called soon after, and found his friend well.

"Whatever happened to him happened to him pretty quickly. I spoke to him ten days after his birthday, maybe a week," Preston said. "He sounded great. He didn't sound like he was in any kind of decline at all. Now there may have been something going on that I didn't know about. But his mind was there. He was cheerful. His vigor was still there, in terms of his intellectual capabilities. I did not notice any decline.

"And then not long after, he passed," Preston said. "So whatever happened was pretty sudden."

When they connected, Preston said they didn't talk much about the end of the treasure hunt—he could tell that Fenn was tired of discussing it. They did chat a bit about the finder's wish to remain anonymous, though, and Fenn shared his belief that eventually the identity of the finder and the location where the treasure was hidden would both come out.

" 'Things like this can't be kept secret,' " Preston recalled Fenn's telling him. " 'It isn't going to come from me,' he'd said, 'but it's going to come out; these things always do.' "

Then they moved on. But Preston said he could sense a sadness in his friend—a melancholy that the treasure hunt that had defined the final stage of his life had ended.

"He just seemed disappointed that the treasure had been found. A little bit disappointed."

After Fenn's death, an outpouring of sadness, grief, and love came from the searcher community, with tributes to Fenn on all the prominent blogs and message boards. Many searchers told stories of their interactions with Fenn, or of what the hunt had meant to them, or just publicly thanked Fenn for what he had brought into their lives.

But not everything written after Fenn's passing was mere remembrance. One article, published by **The Guardian** a week after Fenn's death, took things in a new direction. It was a story about the end of Fenn's hunt, but it ventured into one area that no major media outlet had yet touched: Fenn's dealings with the women of the chase. The article quoted several women, Mindy Fausey among them, who had spoken on the record, making allegations that Fenn had solicited nude photos and made advances toward women who had contacted him about the hunt. Before he died, Fenn denied the allegations—as he had to me—in an email, saying, "I am aware of several fake emails that say I did" ask for nude photos and more. He said that they were from searchers "angry with me because I would not help them find the treasure."

The claims made in the article were consistent with what I had heard from numerous women involved in the search, and there was a sense of vindication among some of the women who had shared these stories in the past, publicly and privately. (With all of this now finally public, I asked Preston if this had been what he had been warning me about with Fenn some three years earlier; he said no, that he had no knowledge of any of these allegations—and that he had been referring to the legal issues in Fenn's past, like his run-in with the FBI.)

Fenn's passing had made all the major papers, and while the airing of the allegations against him were certainly noted by the search community and a segment of the greater public, with Fenn gone, the story seemed to end there. Indeed, most of the pieces about him in the days after his death treated the moment with a general sense of finality. The hunt was over, and now its architect was gone. The anonymous finder was nowhere to be found, and while that left many—myself included—with countless questions, I thought perhaps this might bring the story of this treasure hunt to a close, at last.

I should have known better.

On September 23, just over two weeks after Fenn died, a post surfaced on the website Medium, a self-publishing platform that allows users to distribute essays and other written works anonymously if they choose. Entitled "A Remembrance of Forrest Fenn," it was written by "The Finder," who described himself thusly: "The author is the finder and owner of the Forrest Fenn treasure."

In three thousand well-crafted words, the finder penned an ode to Fenn, whom he described as his friend.

"I am the person who found Forrest's famed

treasure," he wrote. "The moment it happened was not the triumphant Hollywood ending some surely envisioned; it just felt like I had just survived something and was fortunate to come out the other end."

In his essay, the finder revealed a great deal about the circumstances under which he had found the treasure—but crucially, he would not divulge exactly where he had located it, and said he did not plan to. He was also careful not to let any details about his own identity slip, indicating only that he was a millennial and had student loans to pay off. Beyond that, he was an enigma.

He explained that in 2018 he had figured out the location where Fenn wished to die, matching locations in that area to clues in the poem, and then spent a combined twenty-five days over the next two years searching that general area until he finally located the treasure.

He said that to find the solution, he'd paid close attention to things Forrest had said in interviews and managed to pick up a few crucial crumbs which informed his thinking.

"[Fenn] never made more than a couple of subtle slipups in front of all the dogged reporters who came to his house, and even those apparently haven't been caught by anyone besides me," the finder wrote.

The finder said that he planned to sell the treasure and that he would try to honor a "final wish" for where Fenn hoped the treasure would end up, without elaborating further. He did say, as well, that he had sold the turquoise bracelet back to Fenn, as Fenn had always hoped the finder would.

"The way his face lit up was indescribable," the finder wrote of Fenn's reaction to putting the bracelet back on.

It was, all in all, a highly unusual piece of writing. Rather than some gloating "I found the treasure!" victory lap, the finder's post was vulnerable, uncertain. He recounted how he'd cried—and not for the first time on this hunt—after he'd found the treasure; how his self-confidence had been at a dramatic low; how his emotions on finding the treasure had not been those of celebration, but of relief.

His ode to Fenn featured a lengthy biography section, revisiting some of the highlights of Fenn's life. It recounted the finder's post-find visit with Fenn in Santa Fe in June 2020, and the kinship he'd felt with Fenn, discussing things only the two of them could understand. As he called Fenn his friend, he indicated Fenn had felt the same—Fenn, he said, had asked him to move to Santa Fe so that they could continue their relationship more easily.

And perhaps most important, he included pictures. These were pictures never before seen. Some of them were taken in the wilderness, shortly after the finder retrieved the treasure. The others were taken at what was assumed to be a lawyer's office, a continuation of the series posted by Fenn in June, showing Fenn examining the treasure, and wearing the bracelet. They were the ultimate proof that this essay was legitimate—having pictures of the chest in both locations would be possible only for the finder, or for Fenn, and now Fenn was gone.

That, of course, didn't stop the doubters.

It was clear that the essay had been written by someone with a connection to the treasure—the pictures made that impossible to deny, and beyond that, the essay was linked to from Dal's site, and on Fenn's Old Santa Fe Trading Company site, showing that it had the stamp of approval from Fenn's family and associates. But many, many searchers refused to believe that it had been written by the finder himself. Instead, conspiracy theories flew: that Doug Preston had written it; that Shiloh had written it; that Fenn had penned it before his death, with the intention that it be published after he was gone, to cover his tracks and throw searchers off the scent of the real truth—that he had ended the hunt himself.

But I didn't think that.

To me, the Medium post immediately seemed authentic. Beyond the pictures, the emotions of the finder were so nakedly on display, and so relatable; this person understood what it was like to seek the treasure, to obsess over it, to yearn for it, to feel it just out of one's grasp.

All those questions I'd had about whether Fenn had ended the hunt himself, the ones inspired by

Cynthia's information—well, they faded further with every word I read. The interactions he related with Fenn seemed consistent with the ones I'd had myself. And as for Fenn, or Shiloh, or Preston writing it? No way. Fenn didn't think or write like this, and neither did Preston. A writer's work is like a fingerprint—read enough words by someone, and consistencies emerge. This had none of the marks of either Preston's or Fenn's writing. Could it be Shiloh's handiwork? I guess. But nothing I knew of him indicated it would or should be. This was the product of someone who had genuinely sought the chest, and had really lived that life. This person had simply done what no one else could.

After finishing the essay, I no longer had any doubt that there was a finder.

Much else, though, remained unresolved. The finder had teased so many things in his essay, left me and everyone else wanting more. He'd said he'd answer more questions at some point, but I didn't particularly want to wait, or leave what he answered up to him alone.

So I contacted him.

Medium doesn't generally allow readers to contact the author of a piece directly, which is one reason it's good for anonymous posting. It does allow users to post public comments on a piece, and more than one hundred people quickly had, most of them supportive, some of them skeptical, a few of them angry and aggressive. But I wasn't going to just post my email in the comments where anyone could read it; that left me no guarantee that the person I might end up in contact with would be the finder.

I had one trick up my sleeve, though. There's a little-known way to send a direct message to the author of a Medium piece: You have to flag a section of text, indicating that it contains an error or a typo. That notifies the author of the piece that something needs to be corrected in his or her work. The system doesn't give you a lot of space, just enough to describe the problem. So I flagged a section of the essay, barely squeezed in who I was and how to contact me via email, and hoped for the best. I had no guarantee that the finder would look at the message, or that he would understand exactly why he should get in touch. But it was worth a shot.

Less than a day later, an email popped into my in-box. It was from an address whose name referred to Fenn's treasure. The finder had replied.

He'd heard of my project, he said, and he might be willing to talk to me. But he insisted that we'd have to keep things off the record for now. And so began a month of back-and-forth correspondence, sometimes several emails a day.

I soon had absolutely no doubt that the finder was legitimate. We discussed things other than the treasure, sometimes talking baseball—he was interested in why I voted the way I did on my Hall of Fame ballot, and not a fan of my leaving off Barry Bonds and Roger Clemens—or, after he'd read my last book, gambling. That led things in an unexpected direction when he realized that Beep's friend Mike McDonald, who had put out the $10,000 bounty for proof of the existence of the chest, was a minor character in my last book—and hence that I knew him. The finder, who seemed to have a mind for numbers and betting and an interest in poker, asked me if I would put him in touch with McDonald, serving as a go-between of sorts so the finder could claim the bounty. I agreed, but McDonald wouldn't accept the find as legitimate if the finder wouldn't reveal his identity, and with the finder unwilling to do that at the time, the discussions fizzled.

For me, all of this was fascinating stuff, and I was glad the finder seemed to trust me, but it all got me only so far; I still had no idea who the finder was, and he still hadn't agreed to an actual interview.

Two months after our initial correspondence, though, all that changed. After a lull in our on-going conversation, an email from the finder appeared in my in-box.

"The lawsuit against me took a weird turn," he wrote. "Looks like you'll have my name within a week."

Fenn had been dealing with lawsuits before the chest was found, but they hadn't gone anywhere. After the chest was located, though, another lawsuit had dropped, this one leveled against both Fenn and the unknown finder as defendant. This was the suit brought by Chicago lawyer Barbara Andersen, claiming that the finder had stolen Andersen's solve via text and email hacking and used it to find the chest, despite her belief that the chest was in New Mexico, and his contention that he located it in Wyoming.

To this point, I hadn't given the lawsuits much thought. I'd read them, and though I am most certainly not a lawyer, I showed them to one; neither of us expected much to come of them.

Clearly, I should have paid them a little more attention, because this suit was likely about to answer one of the major outstanding questions about the chase. While the lawsuits seemed likely to be dismissed eventually, the Andersen suit had at least progressed to the point where the finder's name would be revealed. The finder seemed resigned to that fate, so even as he remained guarded about the solve and the location of the treasure, he now didn't mind telling me his true identity.

And that's when I learned that a thirty-two-year-old Michigan native and medical student was the person who had finally solved Fenn's poem.

His name was Jack Stuef.

Stuef first heard about Fenn's chase on Twitter in early 2018, and couldn't believe it had escaped his notice for eight whole years. He was instantly hooked.

"I've probably thought about it for at least a couple hours a day, every day, since I learned about it," Stuef said. "Every day."

The treasure hunt immediately brought him back to his youth, when he was obsessed with a 2002 TV series called **Push, Nevada,** which allowed viewers to try to solve a real-life mystery that carried a million-dollar prize. Stuef also got caught up in magician David Blaine's book **Mysterious Stranger,** which combined autobiography with a treasure hunt and offered a $100,000 prize.

Over time, those teenage dreams of adventure receded, and Stuef went on to attend Georgetown University, where he served as editor in chief of **The Georgetown Heckler,** a campus humor magazine. He graduated in December 2009 and began a career as a writer, both in humor—he worked for **The Onion**—and in more traditional media. He became embroiled in a few controversies early in his career, both at **Wonkette,** which he left after he made what **Poynter** describes as "a tasteless joke about one of Sarah Palin's children having Down Syndrome," and while freelancing for **Buzzfeed,** which had to apologize after an article Stuef wrote incorrectly painted a popular internet cartoonist as a hard-line Republican. He left the media business soon after.

"I don't think those were giant incidents," Stuef said. "I regret them, but I don't think about them very often. It was a long time ago now."

Looking for a fresh start, he entered a post-baccalaureate program, and then enrolled in medical school. But he disliked most everything about medicine beyond treating patients, he said, and something else captured his attention: Fenn's chase. As the hunt took up more and more of his time, Stuef mostly kept the extent of his pursuit hidden from friends and family. He didn't think they would understand.

"I think I got a little embarrassed by how obsessed I was with it," Stuef says. "If I didn't find it, I would look kind of like an idiot. And maybe I didn't want to admit to myself what a hold it had on me."

Finally knowing who Stuef was after months of just reading his emails was a little mind-bending for me. I'm not sure I could say quite what I expected him to be like, but I can say it's not exactly what he turned out to be. I had some inkling he had something to do with media, just from the way he wrote, and the familiarity he had with the particular rules—things like what was off the record, what was on background, and so on. He had been so cognizant of how to navigate all that, and so committed to protecting the chest's location, that even after a few months of speaking to him anonymously, I still didn't know much about the subject that had brought us together in the first place: how he had located the chest.

With his identity now known to me, though, all that changed. In one single afternoon, Stuef told me the long story of how he found Fenn's treasure.

Many searchers start in the chase with great confidence, figuring they can read the poem, match the clues to some place-names on a map, and brain it all out. Stuef was no different.

"I did the stupid thing and tried to figure it out without reading the book first," he said.

Initially, he spent a little time on the blogs, learning what the community thought of the chase, seeing some of the most popular hypotheses. But he quickly moved away from that.

"I finally bought the book after a few weeks," Stuef said. "And I was like, 'oh.' He had totally different motivations than what I was expecting, just based on reading the internet. Once I got the book it completely changed my research approach."

Stuef soon came to the conclusion that the key to the hunt was in truly understanding Fenn, and his motivations for hiding the chest. There was no need to use anagrams, or break codes, or find GPS coordinates hidden in the words, as so many searchers were trying to do. One needed only to understand what the poem's author wanted to convey, Stuef recognized.

"I don't want to ruin this treasure hunt by saying it was made for an English major, but it's based on a close read of a text. I mean, that's what it is. It's having the correct interpretation of the poem," Stuef said.

So he stayed far away from the blogs, and began devouring every bit of primary source material he could find from Fenn, particularly any media interviews Fenn had done since hiding the chest.

While poring over those, Stuef caught what he called a slipup from Fenn, one that got him to see the poem, and the problem itself, in a different way: that one must understand the part of Fenn's psyche that wants to go to this one specific place, this place that is so special to him that he wanted to die there.

"That got my mind on the right track for seeing the structure of the poem, the story of the journey that he's presenting: It's not a bunch of random, different elements, 'something pulled from history, something pulled from art' or some random interest of his—it is really how he sees the journey, getting to the place where he wanted to die," Stuef said.

"And understanding the context of that journey, the emotional undercurrent in that, I think is very important to seeing it out in front of you and being able to see it through his eyes," he continued. "So I think that that slipup helped me with that. And the second time through the material, I noticed the other slipup."

These two "slipups" sent him in a certain direction, narrowing both his understanding and the search area. After about two months of trying to marry physical locations both to segments of the poem and to places where he believed Fenn would want to die, he hit on an area that felt right, with a journey to reach it that seemed to line up with the clues in the poem.

"I did have, like, a moment of epiphany. And everything kind of slipped together at once, that there is good evidence that this is the place, and that this is the journey that he sees of getting there," Stuef said. He had not yet solved every clue in the poem. But he believed he understood the general area where Fenn wanted to be, and had matched enough locations to clues that he had a search zone, if not a search spot, exactly.

His epiphany came late one night. He immediately booked the first flight out the very next morning, and headed west to seek the treasure.

That was the first of three trips Stuef would make to Wyoming in 2018, searching the same general spot each time. His initial guess was less than two hundred feet from the place where, two years later, he would eventually retrieve the chest.

But at first, he had no success. He tromped

around his search area on trip after trip, exhausted. He even had a strange encounter with what he describes as a "fake blaze," something he is sure was put there by another Fenn hunter, intended either to tease or to confuse other hunters searching this zone.

"I was not long out of my car, making my way through some difficult terrain, and suddenly I saw something in the distance, and it was this blaze," Stuef said. "Someone put some real thought into this thing. I mean, it wasn't just like, you know, an **f** on a tree, or like a funny message. Someone had considered things that he had said over the years and incorporated it into this fake blaze, in which there was clear human intervention."

When he saw it, Stuef believed he was about to find the treasure.

"It immediately struck me that it was right," he said. "Time slowed down, I felt I got punched in the stomach. I felt like, even though it was difficult terrain, I glided over there, and I looked below that blaze and there was nothing there. And I spent a few minutes, you know, like, Well, I'm at the correct location. Where is it?"

After much searching—including follow-up visits to that spot, just to be certain—Stuef concluded that the fake blaze was just that: a fake, one he still can't fully explain. But that experience colored his hunting going forward. He would be a little more paranoid after that, and a little warier at getting excited about anything, trying to keep himself measured and steady no matter whether his hunts were bringing him good news, or ill.

As 2018 ended, he had gone through his initial search area in great detail, and, having found nothing, was actively trying to find another area to test.

"I really didn't want to get stuck on that place. I didn't want to be one of those people who get stuck on one spot. I'd put in the days on the ground there. I didn't find what I was looking for. I'm going to become psychotic if I keep coming back to the same place."

He toyed with a few new ideas, but nothing struck him as having much potential. And then, going through Fenn's interviews and book, he found something he considered crucial, something that sent him back to that first spot, and kept him focused on it long-term.

And perhaps more important? He figured out the mystery of the blaze.

"December of 2018," he recalled. "I figured out that I definitely needed to try and figure out what the blaze is, if I can. And there was a hint in the book. So I figured out what the blaze was supposed to be. So I knew what I was looking for."

But that got him only so far. Once he understood what the blaze was, he also understood just how difficult it would be to find.

"I had to figure out the process for finding it,

because I realized it was probably going to be akin to finding a needle in the haystack," Stuef said.

As 2019 dawned, he planned his most extensive search yet. A ten-day hunt in June, and this time nothing would be left to chance.

"I finally got a GPS device, and I tracked myself, so that I covered every square foot of the possible search area. Within those parameters, considering the two-hundred- and five-hundred-foot comments, the total **possible** search area, which is, you know, much bigger than the total **probable** search area," Stuef said.

He would stay out all day, listening to podcasts—Dan Carlin's **Hardcore History** is a mutual favorite of ours, and Stuef plowed through parts of the hours-long "Supernova in the East" series while searching—and walking methodically over the ground, checking every place. He'd nap in the afternoons, under the pines, and then continue forward, checking, looking, searching.

And yet he found nothing. It was dispiriting, of course. But his confidence in his solution was so extreme that he didn't wonder whether he was wrong—he wondered whether the chase was on the level to begin with.

"I didn't question if I was in the right place at all," Stuef said. "I questioned, for the first time, Did he not really put this out there?"

Perhaps, he pondered, Fenn had only gone to the

place in his mind's eye, that it was all theoretical, that he didn't really hide the chest? But all his research into Fenn as a person screamed the opposite. That he **had** to have put the chest out there. He said he did it, so he did. Stuef didn't know Fenn, not really. He'd communicated with Fenn from time to time, calling him once in 2018, a brief conversation where he said Fenn couldn't hear him well and just wanted to get off the phone with this random searcher, and then—despite Fenn's statement that they had not communicated since 2018—in a few emails over the next two years, never receiving more than cursory responses from Fenn. But Stuef had done so much research on Fenn, lived inside his head to such a degree, that he still felt like he understood him, and what he would and would not have done.

So he kept searching. And when that trip ended in failure, Stuef was at a loss. He thought he was in the right spot. He thought he knew what the blaze was. He had searched the area. And yet, no chest. If all those things were true, as he believed they were, then something else didn't add up.

"So the only explanation was, something happened to the blaze, it got damaged in nature," Stuef said.

Once he had settled on that, the situation seemed even bleaker. If some natural phenomenon had damaged the blaze, it could have damaged the chest as well, or obscured it such that it would be beyond a reasonable effort to locate. Stuef began grasping at straws—thinking of bringing out a metal detector, or some form of ground-penetrating radar.

"And I really didn't come up with a good solution, to be honest with you, to figure out how to find it. I thought I might be looking for this for the rest of my life. Knowing it's there," he said.

For a while, these feelings consumed him. That he might never really know. That it would hound him forever. That he could believe he was right, and not be able to prove it.

But there was no turning back now, so as any true Fenn hunter would, he returned to his search area. He won't say exactly when he departed on this trip—Stuef is almost as protective of the "when" of his treasure hunting as he is of the "where"—but this time, he was committed to searching for a damaged blaze, and he would go over some of the ground from his ten-day search, with the pursuit of the blaze foremost in his mind.

He walked through the forest, out amongst the pines, retracing his steps. He was in a spot he'd been through before, the GPS confirmed that. This time, though, he knew what to look for. As he searched, something on the ground caught his eye, a bit of disturbed earth, something unusual protruding from the forest's floor. But it wasn't the first time that had happened. He didn't get too excited yet. It was when he looked up a moment later that everything fell into place.

Because suddenly, there it was; the blaze.

"I was looking for a damaged blaze in the hopes that it was damaged, but still recognizable, not totally destroyed. And I found it," he said.

He immediately turned his attention back to the object on the ground. Something was there, that was certain. But it was hard to be sure of what.

"I could tell that there was something on the ground, or something that was just above the ground that had debris on it," Stuef said. "And you could tell that it was roughly the shape of the square top of the treasure chest."

Fenn hadn't buried his chest; he'd hidden it in what Stuef calls a nook, a depression in uneven ground in the middle of a Wyoming forest. But over the ten years that the chest sat out in the wild, a decade's worth of dirt and pine needles and other debris had layered on top of it to the point that nature had done the job of burying it anyway, such that unless a searcher knew to look for it in exactly that spot, they would likely never find it.

Stuef knelt down, took his glove, and started brushing it off. At first he was not particularly excited, he recalled. After his experience with the fake blaze, he was wary, uncertain. Even as he began clearing off the chest, he remained skeptical.

"I got all those pine needles off there, and the

dirt that was on the lid, and I started to see the shape of those figures going up the ladders that are on the top of the treasure chest," he said.

And yet even that wasn't enough for him.

"Going through that awful experience of the fake blaze, I didn't want to be tricked again. And my thoughts immediately went to that people have made reproductions of this treasure chest, that doesn't mean it's the real one," he said.

He started trying to dig out this chest, scooping aside debris so that he could get to the latch on the front. Finally, he exposed it. He undid the latch and opened up the chest.

In his mind, perhaps irrationally, he was expecting something that mirrored those beautiful pictures Fenn had put in his book, of a gleaming mountain of gold, the coins and nuggets all piled atop one another.

What he found was altogether different.

"It was very dirty, very dirty," Stuef said. "There were spiderwebs around the perimeter, and inside, a bunch of coin-shaped objects that I could tell were gold colored. It wasn't so dirty that I couldn't tell what they were, and I started to get more excited that this could be the real treasure chest. I picked up a gold nugget, and it was really heavy. I realized, I think, the only time I'd ever held gold before in my hand was probably picking my dad's wedding ring up off his dresser when I was a kid."

He saw the dragon bracelet, in a plastic bag, filled with water. The other important items were in bags as well, brimming with water.

Then he saw the key to the treasure chest, badly rusted up against one of the gold coins, covered in spiderwebs. It had all clearly been here a long time. He saw the olive jar, said to contain Fenn's autobiography. He took it out, read the few words he could. They were about things related to Fenn's life. He put it back, amid the waterlogged bags and grime-covered coins and web-filled chest.

It was real.

And yet he did not feel anything triumphant, no sense of victory.

"My immediate feeling at that point went from skepticism to paranoia," he said.

Even though he'd been searching out there alone for so long, he was suddenly terrified that someone would come upon him and find him together with the chest. And he was overwhelmed by the potential problems finding the chest would cause, legal and otherwise. So he did something unusual, unexpected: After he took a few photos, he put the chest back, and covered it up as best he could. Then he left the forest, seeking a place where he could be sure he could make a phone call, send an email. He wanted to contact Fenn before he removed the chest from its hiding spot.

"I always thought when I found it, I would not move it without his explicit permission. But I knew this could become a legal hot potato really quickly. And I didn't want to make any moves without his explicit permission. So I left it exactly where it was, exactly how I found it, and made my way back to my car."

When Stuef reached his car, he broke down in tears, as he described in the Medium piece. And then, incredibly, he left the chest where it lay and drove off, confident that no one else would find it until he returned.

Stuef remains cagey about times and dates on his searches, but he is clear that on June 5, 2020, he was at the search spot, left the treasure there, and headed for his hotel, where he set up his laptop and prepared to compose just the right email to Fenn, informing him the treasure had been found. Even though he'd envisioned this moment in his head for years, the message came out stilted, formal.

"It's like, you know, 'I believe I have found the treasure chest that is depicted in the 2010 book **The Thrill of the Chase,**' " Stuef said, laughing at himself. " 'And I would like to send photos for you to tell me yes or no, if it is truly your actual treasure chest. And then we can discuss our next steps. And if it is yours, if you will give me permission to retrieve it from the place where I found it where I left it.' I gave him my phone number in that email."

He sent the email that Friday evening and then settled in to wait, having no idea how long it would take for Fenn to respond. Within minutes, he got an email back. It was Fenn, congratulating him and asking for pictures. Stuef sent Fenn his photos as evidence.

"I sent him the photos and he called me," Stuef said, appearing to tear up slightly. "It was a big life moment for me. He congratulated me over and over and over. I think we talked a little bit about the place and what it meant to him, and then he said it was his treasure and that I had permission to retrieve it. And then we would figure out the next steps from there, but he did want me to bring it to Santa Fe."

The next day, Saturday, June 6, he returned to the hiding spot and took the treasure from its home for good, placing the dirty, heavy chest into a sturdy blue Ikea bag, putting that in his backpack, and hauling it out of the forest.

"The next day I went back out there, pushed away the debris that was on it, put it in my backpack, and took it to my car.

"All at once, in one trip," he joked, a reference to the then-eighty-year-old Fenn initially making two trips to bring the treasure to the spot.

Then he called Fenn to confirm he had possession of the chest, and set off for Santa Fe, embarking on something of a surreal journey with the treasure chest as his companion.

"It was a very new experience to have an object with a million-dollar value on the floor of the seat next to me," he said.

He ended up talking to the chest at times, treating it a little bit like Tom Hanks's companion Wilson the volleyball in the film **Castaway,** discussing searchers' reactions to his finding the chest as he drove. Word of the find was beginning to trickle out; Fenn had insisted that they begin to let searchers know immediately, so that no one got in a bad spot searching for a chest that was no longer there.

"His thought was that as soon as it's out of place, we need to let people know. People have died, there could be issues," Stuef said.

So as news of the find started to spread, Stuef played some of the responses on YouTube, chatting it up with the chest about all the things people were saying.

He was, of course, terrified to let it out of his sight. But there were a few times when it could not be avoided. He stopped at a Walmart along the way in order to get food, and raced through the store, making eye contact with no one, desperate to get back to the car.

When Stuef got to the hotel he was staying at for the night, he brought the chest inside, and decided he couldn't bring it to Fenn in its current condition: filled with dirt and water, pine needles, spiderwebs, covered in ten years' worth of grime. So he laid it out and cleaned it off as best he could.

"I went through all the towels in that hotel room. They were all full of dirt." He paused. "I left a nice tip when I left."

He got back on the road to Santa Fe in the morning, even making a quick stop at a national park he'd always wanted to visit, taking a perverse joy in making such a carefree detour with such a valuable item in tow.

But as he resumed his journey, he learned that finding a treasure chest isn't all congratulatory phone calls and road trips with your new million-dollar best friend.

"I didn't even get to Santa Fe before I was being sued," he said.

Finally getting a chance to actually talk to Stuef, and seeing his face in Zoom interviews we conducted, opened a new dimension in my understanding of him and the story of the chest. And it also gave me an opportunity. If, I figured, his name was going to be made public anyway via the courts, did he mind if I wrote a story about it? If I was the one to break the news of his identity?

After a little discussion, he agreed; he didn't want to do more than one major interview, and wanted it done with someone who knew a lot about the hunt. In theory, no media member knew more than me! So after we had talked more formally, I pitched a story to **Outside** magazine, which had done good work on Fenn's chase in the past. In it, we revealed who Stuef was, and explained the basics of how he had retrieved the chest, talked about his plan to sell the chest to someone who would display it for the searcher community to see, and delved deeper into his—and, he said, Fenn's—reasoning for wanting to keep the location of the find secret.

"He didn't want to see it turned into a tourist attraction," I quoted Stuef saying in the piece. "We thought it was not appropriate for that to happen. He was willing to go to great lengths, very great lengths to avoid ever having to tell the location."

When it published in early December of 2020, the story went viral.

Shiloh posted his own statement an hour after the piece was released, confirming on behalf of the family that Stuef was the finder. Initially, Stuef mostly stayed out of the public eye, not wanting to do any more interviews, intending at first only to write a follow-up post on Medium explaining his concerns about having to go public, and his hopes that he could still lead something of a normal life despite being the finder of the chest.

"I thought that whoever found the chest would be absolutely hated, because it ends everyone's dream," he said. "That's something of a burden. I realize I put an end to something that meant so much to so many people."

But the reaction to his unmasking surprised him—it was, he said, a bit more positive, not as nasty as he had feared.

Many searchers cheered him, and tried to learn about him, the one who had done what they could not. He remained something of an enigma. Stuef had decided he didn't want to become a doctor despite expecting to complete his master's degree, and intended to use the proceeds from the sale of the chest to pay off his medical school bills. But he was not rushing to sell it, wanting to ensure that the lawsuits were no threat before he dealt with a sale, though that was less of a concern once the suits were dismissed in early 2021. He'd tried to fulfill Fenn's final wish for where the chest would end up, but that didn't appear to be going anywhere, and in March 2021 he began preparations to sell it at auction.

The finer points of the chest's ownership weren't really public knowledge, either. Fenn had officially given the chest to Stuef so that he had legal ownership of it, when they met in Santa Fe a few days after Stuef had retrieved the chest from Wyoming. I pressed the finder on how that worked, and how the taxes were being handled, but he would not go into detail, speaking only in generalities.

"Everything has been done legally, under the advice of tax lawyers," he said. "So that there is not an issue down the line. And I'm very confident there will not be an issue down the line. This is not something I would ever hide from the IRS. I have paid my taxes that are due every year since I was a teenager, I would not use this experience to create a crime."

With his name out there, Stuef finally managed

to claim that $10,000 bounty from Beep's friend Mike McDonald, who now felt secure enough that the find was real to pay out the money. McDonald also offered me the $10,000 he had earmarked as the fee for whoever put him and the finder in touch, but I declined, feeling that to profit in that fashion would be an absolute journalistic no-go, not a gray area like so much of the other stuff I'd done in this chase. So McDonald decided to give the other $10,000 to Stuef as well.

Everything seemed to be going well for Stuef, better than he'd expected, and so, heartened by the reaction he'd received, he opened up a bit. He still refused all media interviews, but he proved surprisingly willing to answer specific searcher queries via email—as long as his answers revealed nothing about where the chest was actually found.

Even if they appreciated Stuef's answering some questions, many, many, many searchers still took issue with his stand on holding back the search spot. They wanted that closure, and many felt Stuef was denying it to them by keeping the location to himself.

And perhaps because of that, conspiracy theories still floated around the community, a constant drumbeat that something wasn't right. Searchers sought to pick out holes in his story, trying to find inconsistencies in his public comments, in the **Outside** piece, in emails he had sent to hunters that were subsequently posted on the various forums.

There were charges that he hadn't really found it in Wyoming, but in another state; that he was in cahoots with the family to deceive the searchers in some fashion; even that Stuef wasn't, somehow, the real finder, or that he didn't really have the treasure.

Having written the **Outside** article, my in-box was suddenly flooded with searchers claiming this or that about Stuef or his solve was fraudulent, and asking me to prove it or use my knowledge to validate their own competing solves. I still had no idea where the treasure was, and I truly didn't want to know, but that didn't stop searchers from FedEx-ing their theories to my home, or others from claiming that I was somehow involved in some of these conspiracies. I know we live in a post-truth world now, but even as conspiracies around the 2020 election dominated life outside the hunt, the level of disbelief I encountered within the chase still shocked me.

Should I have been so surprised? Conspiracy theories have plagued this hunt from the start. I'd fallen for them myself. The truth was that there were definitely many, many things I didn't know about Stuef, gaps in my knowledge of his story, things he had done that struck me as odd or difficult to explain, things he would tell me only off the record about the chest and how he had found it. I was able to dismiss most of the conspiracies out of hand based on things I knew, but in other cases I couldn't be positive about everything, and even when I pressed him there were things he was clearly holding back.

I had to come to terms with the fact that there were things we were likely never going to know, and others that I couldn't write, even if I did know them. But even if there were some details I couldn't quite square, I remained sure that Stuef was the finder, and that no grand conspiracy was at play here.

How could I be so certain? Part of it was confidence in the facts we all did know. Part of it was, as Paris Wallace had said in his fateful, final sermon, understanding that at a certain point, "we have to trust."

And part of it was that I had experienced something the other searchers had not. A few months earlier, I had flown to Santa Fe one last time, and opened Forrest Fenn's treasure chest myself.

I tightened my mask as I stepped off the plane, out onto the tarmac at Santa Fe Regional Airport, and into the cool October air. I'd flown sitting in the copilot's seat of a small single-engine turboprop, making a harrowing night landing amid the mountains that surround the city. Originally, I'd planned to fly commercial into Albuquerque, as I had all those times I'd come to Santa Fe to see Fenn in the past. But these were the days of COVID-19, and Amalie, who is on immunosuppressant medication, was justifiably nervous about my going through a crowded airport, getting on a plane, connecting through another crowded airport, eventually de-planing in yet another crowded airport, and then repeating it all on the way back.

So my mom convinced her husband, a recre-ational pilot with his own plane—a TBM 850—to fly me across the country, all the way to Santa Fe. We'd stopped for fuel in the tiny town of Macon, Missouri, but otherwise made it straight through to New Mexico, and it had been a fascinating ex-perience sitting in the cockpit as we crossed the country, being passed from one air-traffic-control center to the next, adjusting flight routes to save fuel, changing elevations, dodging weather.

This trip had come together quickly, out of no-where, really. One day, back when I still didn't know who Stuef was—when he was still just "the finder" to me—he'd sent me a particularly un-expected email, offering something I hadn't really asked for, but had absolutely craved.

"Hey," it read. "Do you want to come see the treasure?"

I pounced on the offer, quickly commandeered my plane and pilot, and got to Santa Fe as fast as I could, thrilled at the chance to be so close to some-thing I'd dreamt about for so long.

As I left my hotel the morning after flying in and made my way toward the finder's lawyer's of-fices, the streets of Santa Fe were barren, devoid of the traffic that normally choked Cerrillos Road. It was October, usually one of the busiest times of the year in Santa Fe. In normal years, October brings Albuquerque's famed balloon festival, featuring hundreds of hot-air balloons and a carnival atmosphere, and enthusiasts come from around the world to experience it. My trips to see Fenn and the other searchers in 2017 and 2018 had overlapped with the festival, and so I can attest both that it's great, and that it jams Albuquerque and Santa Fe with tourists.

Not this year, I thought as I cruised down the near-empty road, my face mask sitting on the console between the two front seats. But it wasn't just the pandemic that made Santa Fe feel strangely empty. For me, Fenn's absence loomed larger than the lack of tourists, or people driving to work.

This was the first time since learning of this hunt that I had come to Santa Fe for a reason other than to see Fenn; I still had much I wanted to ask him, and now I'd never get the chance. It was impossible not to think of him as I drove along, passing a restaurant in the Santa Fe Railyard where we'd had lunch, going by the turnoff to get to his gallery. The reality was that I couldn't imagine Santa Fe without him. For better or worse, he and the city he called home had become synonymous in my mind.

It had been a month now since his death. His wife, Peggy, had herself passed the week before I arrived, living just four weeks beyond her husband. Peggy and Forrest Fenn had been married almost sixty-seven years.

How would Fenn be remembered? He had been so concerned that his father had left no mark, that Marvin Fenn had no imprint on history until his son brought him back via his words and books. Forrest Fenn clearly would not suffer that same fate. His treasure hunt had made a greater impact than Fenn could have ever imagined. Still, his passing so soon after the end of the hunt—a hunt that I believe he'd hoped would outlive him—did end the story of Fenn's life in the eyes of the outside world. His chapter in history was interesting, compelling, complicated, flawed. A moment in time, an amazing tale. But now over. Fenn had wanted to live on through his treasure hunt, through his chest. With the chest found, I don't know if he'll truly do that.

The chest. Now that I was mere minutes away from actually holding it in my hands, I was brimming with anticipation, feeling that little tremble that comes from adrenaline coursing through my body. Was just seeing it as good as finding the treasure? Well, no, you're a couple million poorer, but in some ways, I don't know, maybe it was better. A chance to experience and understand this treasure, without the burden of having to own it. At least that's what I was telling myself.

What did I really know about it? It was small,

deceptively so. Cynthia had built a replica and placed it out in the wilderness to underscore how near impossible it would be to identify the chest at distance if you didn't know precisely where it was. It was ten by ten by five inches, and that's just not very big. And it was heavy. The chest itself weighed twenty pounds, the contents weighed twenty-two pounds, and Fenn had needed his famed two trips to get it all to his spot.

There had been a few attempts at chronicling what was in it—some of the best work done by Cynthia's pal Matt DeMoss. DeMoss's efforts had been aided by the release of both sets of conference room pictures, which I now understood had been taken at the finder's lawyer's office, the one I was about to visit. Nobody except for Fenn and the finder, however, had been able to really go through the chest, pull everything out, and document the contents—until now. The actual chest, I knew, was the bronze Romanesque lockbox, dating from roughly 1150, with carvings along its sides and top depicting the "Castle of Love," a well-known Gothic art motif where maidens sit atop the castle, and knights at the base try to scale it and reach them. It was not locked, but it did include a key, and it was latched with a gargoyle of some sort. There was some type of wood, perhaps oak, serving as a lining.

Based on what he believed to be in the chest, DeMoss had compared each item to similar examples currently on sale, and guessed the low-end sale value of all the items inside at $555,487, with the high-end sale value at $1,327,450. Even if we split the difference, chances are it would sell for more than that, because these items are part of the Fenn Treasure, a factor DeMoss said he did not incorporate into his analysis.

Included in his estimates were the 265 gold coins of varying types, the gold nuggets and dust, the golden frogs, the golden mirrors, the gold nose rings, the gold necklace—gold, gold, gold. There was the ancient Tairona/Sinu necklace, the Chinese carved jade faces, the turquoise bracelet that Fenn had wanted to buy back, and Fenn's twenty-thousand-word autobiography, in addition to a few other, smaller items of note. Then there were the "emeralds, rubies, diamonds" that were often mentioned as being in the chest. Were those merely included in what was perhaps the chest's most impressive single item, the golden dragon bracelet, which itself contained hundreds of precious stones? Or were there additional jewels to be found beyond that? Nobody knew, except for Fenn, the finder, and whoever had been there when the chest was examined. There could still be curiosities waiting, surprises to be found, answers to be had. Now I was going to be privy to them.

I'd agreed to a few conditions when the finder had offered to let me view the chest. First, we'd agreed that I would pay his attorneys' hourly rates for their time, such that my seeing the chest wouldn't actually cost the finder money—pretty standard journalistic practice.

He'd also stipulated that he didn't want me to identify his attorneys—there were three representing him, two men and a woman—in any meaningful way, so that they couldn't be tracked down by overaggressive searchers. I agreed. And then one more: The finder wanted to make sure I didn't open the vial containing Fenn's autobiography, which remained sealed, and that if I could read any of what was inside through the glass, I wouldn't relay any of that information. I agreed to that, as well.

The conditions weren't onerous, and I was eager to make this happen. As far as I knew, examining the chest was not a privilege that had been extended to anyone else—and in that, it was not lost on me that I was getting to do something that others might not like. I hadn't searched for a few years now, and even if it hadn't been found, I hadn't planned on searching again. But still, there were people far more deserving than I who would have killed to see what I was about to see. Even if the finder managed to give the chest some sort of public exhibition at some point, I assumed no one would get to go through it, touch it, experience it the way I was about to. As I parked the car, I could feel a certain weight to what I was about to do, a responsibility to do it all right, whatever that meant. That, and maybe a few pangs of guilt, for getting to enjoy what other, better searchers couldn't.

I parked near the offices, put on my mask, and walked along the sunny, empty streets toward the front door. There were COVID-related signs posted about not entering without an appointment. I was pretty sure I had one of those—though even at that late moment, there was still the tiniest sliver of doubt in my mind. At the time, I still had never heard the name Jack Stuef, and hence had flown out here on a tiny plane on the offer of someone whose name I didn't know, based on a cold-call email and little more than that. I was pretty sure, as close to certain as I could be, that this was the finder and that everything was legit, but until I was actually opening that chest myself, nothing was truly guaranteed.

So it was heartening when I swung open the large, heavy door, went into what seemed to be an impressive professional suite of law offices, gave my name at the front desk, and waited only moments before the finder's attorney came out and introduced herself.

"We'll just go right in here," she said, pointing to a set of doors leading into a conference room, "and then we'll bring the chest right in."

That simple, huh?

I pushed open the doors and entered a reasonably

sized room with an oblong wooden conference table covered by glass. It was instantly familiar from the two sets of pictures posted to validate the find.

"Is this where you showed Fenn the chest?" I asked.

"It is," she replied. "He sat right there," she said, indicating a chair at one end of the table. "You can sit right where he sat if you want."

I wasn't sure if that was a little too fanboyish. But it seemed like a good place to sit anyway, so I threw my backpack down near where she'd gestured. This was perhaps the only time on the hunt when I was absolutely, definitely, unquestionably following in Fenn's footsteps, instead of puttering around in the wilderness two states away from where he'd left his treasure. Here, I was really and truly doing just what he had done, only a few months before, when he'd gone through this chest for the first time in a decade.

From the moment I'd entered this chase, the chest had been the goal. In some ways, it was a MacGuffin, like the Maltese Falcon or the Death Star plans—it was what this chase was about, yes, but it wasn't **really** what this chase was about, y'know? Still, it mattered. Up until this moment, the chest had been purely theoretical to me. I'd never expected to find it, so I wasn't one of those searchers who had already spent the money in it ten times over. For me, it was more about figuring out the clues, getting the answer.

Yet now that I was going to be laying eyes on it, touching it, it moved from the realm of the theoretical to the actual in a hurry.

That understanding fundamentally altered my entire view of the chase. It meant that despite whatever else he'd done, Fenn had been telling the truth about this box and what was in it: that he had hidden it somewhere out there, and the finder really and truly had obtained it, and was now letting me see and touch it. That most basic set of facts was real, and that gave me a sense of certainty about this chase, of a kind I had never really had until now. Did that improve Fenn's standing a bit in my mind? It was a complicated question. To this point, I'd managed somewhat to separate the man from the hunt, even though it was hard to do. And knowing that he was telling the truth did mean something for the man, somewhat. It didn't excuse what had likely gone on with the women. It didn't mean all the deaths hadn't happened, or that he hadn't always responded and reacted the wrong way when they did. It didn't mean he hadn't played favorites, messed with searchers, lived a gigantic ego trip—all of it. But he **had** done this, just the way he'd said he had. And that, in my mind, counted for something.

I started to ask if they needed me to sign anything before we began, as I stretched on the latex gloves that I'd brought for the examination. Then, just like that, the conference room door opened and a man walked in bearing a bronze box, ten by ten by five, worn and weathered and perfect. He hurried quickly over to my side of the table as I, in true surprise, stammered something out about not expecting it all to be quite so easy.

He chuckled in reply as he walked up and casually handed me Forrest Fenn's treasure chest.

I took it, my fingers curling around the base, my hands closing around the raised nine-hundred-year-old designs carved into the chest's sides. I looked down at the intricate figures on the lid, taking in their beauty, just standing there for a moment with this apparition made real.

Holding Fenn's chest in my hands gave me one brief thought, and one thought only: that I wished Beep were here. I felt unworthy to be the one doing this, when there were people I knew who cared so much more. Cynthia, Sacha, people like that, sure—but really Beep, who was the one who had truly felt the pull of this, and obsessed so deeply over it that for a time it cost him a part of who he was.

Okay, yes, I did have one more thought: The chest was heavy. Dense, weighty metal, that bronze filled with all those coins. I wanted to put it down, but I had to be careful—you can't just drop a forty-two-pound bronze treasure chest onto a glass table. It has to be placed down gently, carefully, and so I did just that, resting it near the edge, probably right around where Fenn had gone through it months before.

I stood over it, and with little hesitation I pulled up on the gargoyle latch and opened the lid, revealing Fenn's treasure piled inside. It looked just as I had imagined, and how it had in the pictures I'd seen—gold coins heaped throughout, interspersed with hunks of gold and with dirty, worn Ziploc bags containing greater, more valuable treasures. The tube containing the autobiography was there; I could see the golden frog, the Alaskan gold nugget, the case containing the Chinese jade faces—tiny, carved, staring back up at me.

I wish I could say I treated the moment with the reverence it deserved. That I stood back for a while, gazing at the huge gold nuggets and gleaming golden coins and the sumptuous jewelry and thought deeply about what it all meant, the long road this took from Fenn to the finder and eventually to me.

But I didn't do that. Instead, I almost immediately dived in, ravenous, pulling items out and placing them on the glass-topped table. Quickly—perhaps more quickly than I should have—I grabbed one after another, fingers greedily handling each nugget as I tried to put similar types of items into makeshift piles. There was an undeniable hunger, a ferocity to what I was doing. And there **were** time constraints: My reason—excuse?—for being here was that I was the chronicler of this hunt, my job was to document what was in this thing, and I had an hour to do it.

But that wasn't it, not really. Pulling the items out was like a kid ripping the wrapping paper off his birthday presents: I just wanted to see what the next thing was, and the next thing, and what was after that, digging deeper and deeper into the chest until I'd uncovered all of its secrets.

I started making stacks of the single eagle gold coins, and the more valuable double eagle ones. I pulled out the baggies, first the one containing the Tairona/Sinu necklace, and placed that gently off to the side. Ditto the baggie holding the dragon bracelet, which I couldn't wait to examine, but I wasn't ready to remove those big-ticket items from the bags yet, saving that for later.

"It's so funny to see all these valuable items sitting in Ziploc bags," the finder's lawyer said.

And it was! So wildly incongruent. Here was this brilliant dragon bracelet with its diamonds and emeralds and rubies, sitting in a weathered baggie, next to a badly rusted key, shoved into a chest piled with all this gleaming gold. It was a strange scene as I extracted nugget after nugget, coin after coin, giving a running commentary to the lawyers of what I saw at each point.

"This is a coin from . . . the Austro-Hungarian Empire, it looks like. Eighteen ninety-one? Emperor Franz Joseph is on the back. And here's one from the

Russian Empire, with the tsar on it—like, **the** tsar, the Romanov tsar, the one who was killed," I said, grasping for the name. "Nicholas, Tsar Nicholas."

There were coins from Mexico, marked in Spanish, spanning various centuries; coins from Victorian England; coins from Canada. The vast majority, though, were American, the single and double eagles. I counted forty of the more valuable double variety. Each one was worth thousands.

The lawyers actually seemed as interested in all this as I was. Even though they'd done this before, when Fenn had come to examine the chest and meet the finder, they seemed to pay close attention as I evaluated each coin and piece. I asked the finder's lawyer what Fenn had been like when he got a chance to go through the chest after all those years.

"He was a little bit like you—giddy," she said.

I guess I was that. So much for those efforts at appearing measured and detached.

"He was nostalgic, too," she said. "He picked up every piece, looked it over."

"Everything he put in here meant something to him," I told them, even though they probably knew that already. "He didn't just throw gold in here; he really tried to curate the best treasure chest possible. He put things in, took others out, changed it all over the years."

And that meant the record of what was actually in this chest was a little uncertain. Eventually, as expected, I got to a few items I didn't recognize.

There was a chain made of what looked like golden lug nuts that I wasn't familiar with, along with a number of unanticipated rings and hoops. And I extracted a pair of inch-long pieces of gold jewelry shaped a little like thimbles and looked on them with curiosity, having no knowledge of them. It struck me that they looked like the stacks from nuclear power plants, except golden. The finder later told me he didn't know what they were, either, and that he was a little taken aback when he asked Fenn about it and Fenn wasn't sure himself.

One piece, the lawyers told me, had been added to the chest after it was found. Fenn realized after he had hidden the chest that he had left out one of the two golden frogs, the smaller one attached to a necklace. The finder confirmed that when I asked him about it later.

"Forrest told me he found that in his vault sometime after hiding the treasure chest and said, 'Oops,'" Stuef told me when we discussed it later. "He showed it to me when I went to his house. It was in a little drawer on the right side of the vault in one of those Whitman's Sampler boxes that hold four chocolates. It was given to my lawyer later."

Another thing I sought out, and didn't find, was some sort of item that would have let Fenn know the chest had been found. He'd always teased hunters, and me, with the cryptic statements that something in the chest, or something about the chest, would tip him off when it had been retrieved. But no such thing was apparent here. I asked Stuef later what that had been, and he said he is not sure, either—it was not ultimately a physical item, he believed, but the need to contact Fenn to take legal possession of the chest.

"I thought about that for a long time," Stuef said, after his identity had been revealed. "And I couldn't think of any logical explanation for something that would survive that long other than a legal mechanism. And that's what it ended up being. If I wanted to own it legally, then I need to tell him. I mean, if I didn't want to own it legally, I could have tried to hide it, and sell it off piecemeal and hope nobody noticed . . . but I wasn't going to do that."

As I went through the chest, I pulled out the pre-Columbian nose rings, the millennia-old Mayan gold necklace, a seven-hundred-year-old turquoise disk bead Fenn had excavated from San Lazaro and had attached to a gold nugget, and a series of golden hoops and other rings. I dug out the autobiography, still sealed in its glass vial, with strands of Fenn's hair attached in case there was any need to do a DNA test on it years from now—and, yes, I tried to peer in and read what was inside, with limited success.

Finally, I got to the bottom, where three pre-Columbian gold mirrors lay along the floor of the chest—one more than I had expected. Removing them left an empty box in front of me, a treasure chest without any treasure. A wave of disappointment washed over me, both in that the exhilarating process of emptying the chest was over and that there hadn't been any great surprises, no astonishing secrets to be revealed inside. A few things I hadn't expected, yes, but nothing that really blew one's mind. I'm not sure what my irrational brain was hoping for—what hidden truth would there even be to reveal this late in the game?—but I felt a sense of disappointment nonetheless.

I quickly banished that sensation and got back to work. I had my laptop out, and I began documenting everything I'd removed from the chest, trying to count the coins and their types, snapping photo after photo of each item. I spent particular time on the dragon bracelet, which was the one item that truly astounded with its beauty. And the only one I didn't touch? The Tairona/Sinu necklace. It was so old and seemed so delicate that I left it in its bag, defying Fenn's edict that items like these are meant to be handled and explored and appreciated.

Time was flying by quickly, and so with the treasure spread out into my various piles, I forced myself to pause for a moment and take it all in. Fenn's treasure covered a corner of the table, coins piled high, nuggets in groups, necklaces and mirrors and beads all sitting in clumps around the empty chest, its lid open. It was a magnificent sight, at once more than I had expected—and also less.

Before I departed for Santa Fe, the finder had

expressed some concern that I might not feel the trip was worth it, that perhaps, once I saw the treasure, it wouldn't live up to my expectations, however I'd built it up in my head. I'd assured him that wouldn't be the case. And it wasn't. Seeing and touching the treasure was an electric thrill. It made me want to go seek more. It harkened back to when I went to Key West to visit with Kim Fisher, the head of that family of treasure hunters, and how he'd said that once you find that first little piece of treasure, the feeling of wanting more never leaves you, ever. How he still got goose bumps just thinking of pulling up real treasure from beneath the ocean. I hadn't found anything myself, but I could feel that sensation at play here, the pull and magic of the treasure. And this was a real treasure—having transcended its gimmicky origins—and seeking it had been a real adventure. This treasure hunt deserved its weird, but authentic, place in the history of treasure hunting.

But I think I understood what the finder had been hinting at when he talked about disappointment. In that larger context, that of "real" treasure hunts, one imagines piles of Spanish silver like the kind Kim Fisher saw at the bottom of the ocean. Or a chest two feet wide and three feet high, filled with the queen's jewels, or, like Beep had said, something fanciful straight out of **Aladdin.** This wasn't that. The chest was small. Beyond the dragon bracelet, none of the items in it really took one's breath away. It felt almost unfair—ungrateful?—even to think it, but, no, Fenn's treasure could never, and would never, measure up to those great hoards. It barely covered the corner of an oblong table in a Santa Fe conference room.

Still, this treasure mattered. It meant something. Every item in it had had value to Fenn, and, by extension, it had value to us. This wasn't just a pile of gold. It was Forrest Fenn's treasure, and in that sense it wildly exceeded my expectations.

As I stood over it, though, I also recognized that because this was Forrest Fenn's treasure, nobody would believe a word about any of this if there weren't extensive documented proof—and even then, they'd probably come up with reasons to dis-believe. A segment of the chase community would always have its doubts about all of this, even if, in this hour, my feelings had gone entirely in the other direction, probably permanently. Could it still be possible that I was being used as a patsy, just as Stephanie and the Candyman had warned before I went to Yellowstone years ago—that I was having a shiny, beautiful treasure chest dangled in front of my eyes so that I could help legitimize a con, perhaps to throw people off the scent that the family had ended the hunt themselves, designated a finder on their own? I suppose anything's pos-sible. But I couldn't figure out a logical way that would even viably work, and every single interaction I'd had after contacting Stuef had told me that wasn't at all the case here. Sometimes the simplest explanation is the right one, and that's how I felt about this. The treasure was real, even if there were things I still didn't know, or couldn't fully square, and any real conspiracy at this stage would be more complicated and unlikely than I could reasonably believe in, knowing what I knew. So I asked one of the lawyers to take some pictures with me and the loot, documenting my connection to it for all time, and moved forward, feeling assured.

At that point, though, my time was winding down, and I found myself needing to deal with a question I'd never once considered for a single moment of my life, and probably never will again.

How does one repack a treasure chest?

Very few people in human history have had to address this issue. But it isn't easy, and you can't screw it up. I didn't want to put something heavy on top of something delicate and thus ruin some ancient object. And besides that, there's a presentation element. I had no idea who would next open this chest. I wanted whoever opened the chest to have the same moment of awe and wonder that I'd had. That person couldn't just see a pair of clouded Ziploc bags when he or she opened it up. Whoever it was, he or she needed to have that instant of amazement, of seeing all the coins and nuggets and jewels and trinkets and, yes, baggies, all of it together.

Even if it was the finder who opened it next, I wanted him to have that feeling every single time.

First, I placed the gold mirrors on the bottom, as I'd found them. Then I rested the glass cases filled with coins atop those. I started to fill in the bottom with some of the smaller gold nuggets, then layered some of the smaller gold coins on top of those. I put the tubes and bags of gold dust along the edges—they were by far the least impressive-looking items—and then put the Chinese jade faces in, placing them inside their case. I placed a few of the gold hoops and rings in the middle, but didn't think I was quite ready to put the two delicate items in baggies—the Tairona necklace and the dragon bracelet—in yet.

The finder's lawyer could see me puzzling over the best way to do it all, painstakingly considering what should go where.

"Fenn actually did it really quickly," she said. "He just kinda put everything back in."

"Well, he knew where and how everything was supposed to go," I said. "Or maybe he just didn't care?"

I placed the delicate items inside, put the larger gold nuggets strategically around them, and then started layering gold single and double eagle coins in and around all these other valuables. It was really starting to look like a treasure chest again, and I was a little bit proud of my handiwork.

Until, that is, I realized I hadn't accounted for

the size of Fenn's autobiography, placed as it was inside its glass jar. I tried putting it in, and it was too high; the lid of the box wouldn't close. The lawyers saw me sheepishly recognize what I'd done, and they began to playfully needle me a bit about it. I didn't mind.

I stripped out many of the valuables, made sure there was room for the glass tube, and tried again. This time, everything fit, and it looked right. Gold piled on top of artifacts piled on top of gold, all of it valuable and meaningful and important. It looked beautiful.

One of the lawyers came over, and I handed him back the chest. He put a piece of paper on top of it and whisked it away to some back room, its presence disappearing from my life, back into the realm of imagination. I couldn't help but think of the scene in **Raiders of the Lost Ark** when the ark is boxed up and put inside a warehouse containing multitudes of similarly important, powerful objects. Where would the chest live until it was next called for? Who would be the next one to see it and hold it?

That was out of my hands.

I left the lawyers' office, returned to my car, and then ventured into downtown Santa Fe, seeing reminders of Fenn's chase everywhere. I walked by the Blue Corn Café, where I had lunched with Fenn once as he told me stories of test-flying the newest air force jets, and how he'd always manage to convince the right colonels and generals to let him get into their cockpits before nearly anyone else. It occurred to me that I might come back to Santa Fe again someday, but it would never again be because of Forrest Fenn, never again to chase or dream about or even see his magical chest.

I found myself suddenly nostalgic for it all, and for the feeling of these remote locations mattering. None of these places would hold the same allure anymore. The Rio Grande would be just a roaring, racing river. The mountains around Taos would still be gorgeous and captivating as they scraped the sky, but they would lack the promise of something greater. Even majestic Yellowstone, geysers and all, was just Yellowstone now. Beautiful, special, but not necessarily containing riches. All of it felt a little duller, more muted.

I wandered down Galisteo Street, and there I came across the Collected Works Bookstore, the spot where this treasure hunt had officially begun, almost exactly a decade before. It was partially open, offering curbside pickup during the pandemic. I peered inside. Could Fenn have ever really imagined what he had set in motion that day he secreted away his chest? Had he understood all along what it would make people think, believe, do? Had all of it been part of his grand plan? Or had he just liked to play games with the world, roll the dice and see what happened?

Ultimately, did it matter? We all got a chance to play. And we were all a little richer for it.

I started back down the street, heading back to the airport, and to real life, once again.

Acknowledgments

For about a million very good reasons, the publishing industry is wary of book ideas that don't have a nice, clean ending. So when I explained that I wanted to invest years in doing a book on a treasure hunt where, in all likelihood, the ending would be unsatisfying—because, really, what were the odds someone was going to find the treasure in exactly the time frame I needed—it required a whole lot of trust from a whole lot of people.

First among those was my agent, Jane Von Mehren of Aevitas Creative Management, who understood what a great story this was and committed to go on this journey, ending or no. Next was Tim O'Connell, my fantastic editor at Knopf, who believed in and understood this project from the very start. From my first conversation with Tim, I could see he simply **got** what this book was supposed to be, and he proved to be an indispensable, ever-reliable counsel through all the (many) twists and turns of this project. Everyone at Knopf proved to be both immensely supportive and also absolutely first-class professionals, and it made this process a breeze, with Rob Shapiro and Jessica Purcell in particular really helping me along.

Thanks to my coworkers and superiors at **The Athletic**—in particular Sean Leahy and Emma Span—who were understanding when I would need to take a few weeks off at a time to go gallivanting around the southwest in search of treasure, or really, in pursuit of a great story.

I'm tremendously appreciative to all the hunters who shared their time and thoughts with me, including—but certainly not limited to— Dal Neitzel, Sacha (Johnston) Dent, Toby Younis, Mindy Fausey, Bill Sullivan, David Rice, and especially Cynthia Meachum. I was also very thankful to Mitzi Wallace for letting me sit down with her and tell her husband's story. And, of course, to Jack Stuef, for deciding to talk to me.

My mom, Barbara Goodstein, has always been awesome, but she also proved incredibly helpful when she volunteered her husband, Dennis Wolf, to fly me to Santa Fe to play with a treasure chest. Thanks, Mom! And Dennis!

A special thanks to Jay Raynor, who clearly hadn't had enough of our adventures in the last book, and so was smart enough to think of me when he happened into this one. I couldn't have asked for a better treasure hunting partner, and friend.

An extra-special, can't-even-quantify-the-level-of-appreciation thanks to my wife, Amalie, who not only let me head off on all these crazy book trips, not only delivered two kids during the narrative of this book, and not only then watched those two kids every time I took off on another trip, but also read and edited every chapter of this book, through its seemingly countless rewrites. I really could not have done this without her.

And a final thank-you to Elliott and Reid, who make the whole thing worth it. Truly, my little dudes, the treasure is you.

Notes

Forrest Fenn's treasure hunt existed for almost seven full years before I ever even heard of it. In that time, it matured and evolved, and it was the subject of much inquiry. I was lucky in that way. By the time I decided to involve myself, a parade of skilled writers had already made the trip to Fenn's study, and their work provided a strong foundation to build on. As I sought to chronicle the hunt and what it meant, I did so benefiting from what they had already learned, and I happily acknowledge the debt I owe them and all the other sources I used here.

Tony Dokoupil's **Newsweek** piece ("Forrest Fenn Wants You to Find His Treasure—and His Bones," August 20, 2012) was the first to shine any sort of critical eye on Fenn or the hunt, deepening the mystery around it (and royally pissing off Fenn).

To my mind, it's the first real journalism in this space, and one of the best examples to date.

I learned about the roughly 2014–2015 period of the hunt, and the story of lost-in-Yellowstone ex-cop Darrell Seyler, from Peter Frick-Wright's gripping work ("On the Hunt for America's Last Great Treasure," **Outside,** August 11, 2015), perhaps my favorite piece of this type.

The sad tale of Eric Ashby was followed ably by David Kushner ("A Deadly Hunt for Hidden Treasure Spawns an Online Mystery," **Wired,** July 26, 2018).

I first read in detail about the story of Scott Conway through the work of Chris D'Angelo ("A Chest of Gold Hidden in the Rockies Is the Ultimate Social Experiment," **HuffPost,** November 23, 2018) and Miranda Collinge ("Lost in America: The Man Who Buried a Treasure in the Rocky Mountains and the Thousands Searching for It," **Esquire,** January 11, 2018), and both stories also offered additional smart color.

The work of Julia Glum at Money.com ("There's a Treasure Chest Worth Millions Hidden Somewhere in the Rocky Mountains. These Searchers Are Dedicating Their Lives and Savings to Finding It," June 17, 2019, and "Thousands Are Searching for Forrest Fenn's Treasure in the Rocky Mountains. And Many Are Making Serious Cash Off the Hunt," June 21, 2019) was helpful in giving additional context to the FennTuber efforts to cash in on the chase.

Mary Caperton-Morton's article in **Earth** magazine gave me a direct framework for understanding the differences among the various kinds of land where Fenn might have hidden his chest ("On the Trail of Treasure in the Rocky Mountains," February 18, 2015).

An article by Geoff Williams in **U.S. News & World Report** ("How to Be a Modern Day Treasure Hunter," October 11, 2013), one by Samuel Gilbert in **The Guardian** ("The Treasure Hunters on a Deadly Quest for an Eccentric's $2 m Bounty," July 2, 2018), and one by Zachary Crockett on Vox.com ("In Search of Forrest Fenn's Treasure," June 30, 2017) were all helpful in gaining perspective on Fenn's world.

Part of the fun of this project was digging through the history of treasure hunting itself, of the ruffians and pirates and fortune seekers who sought great riches. I knew the most basic tales of treasure hunting, but Jane McIntosh's **Treasure Seekers: The World's Great Fortunes Lost and Found** (Carlton Books, 2000) really served as a fantastic ten-thousand-foot view over that landscape, getting me familiar with most of the better-known hoards and hunts in history. From there, I went in search of more specifics. Peter Earle's **Treasure Hunt: Shipwreck, Diving, and the Quest for Treasure**

in an Age of Heroes (St. Martin's Press, 2008) tells the tale of Captain William Phips in excellent detail. C. W. Ceram's **Gods, Graves, and Scholars: The Story of Archaeology** (Vintage, 1986) brought me up to speed on the ancient history of treasure hunting and how it intersects with archaeology. J. Frank Dobie's **Coronado's Children: Tales of Lost Mines and Buried Treasures of the Southwest** (University of Texas Press, 1978) related exactly what the title implies.

When I needed to get into more granular detail on the modern-day exploits of Kip Wagner and Mel Fisher, I turned first to the primary accounts of R. Duncan Mathewson, and his **Treasure of the Atocha: A Four Hundred Million Dollar Archaeological Adventure** (Dutton, 1986). Much of the additional detail came from Jedwin Smith's page-turner **Fatal Treasure: Greed and Death, Emeralds and Gold, and the Obsessive Search for the Ghost Galleon Atocha** (Wiley, 2005), which I really enjoyed.

Jenny Kile's **Armchair Treasure Hunts: The Quests for Hidden Treasures** (CreateSpace Independent Publishing Platform, 2018) was the gold standard in that subgenre of treasure hunting.

Robert Underbrick's **Treasure Trove: An Annotated Bibliography of Books Concerning Sunken Gold, Lost Mines, and Buried Treasure** (Lamplighter, 1974) also led me to some older, more obscure source material.

Some of the most interesting research was done in person at various museums where I could actually see some of the items that had inspired great hunts or check out primary source material related to some of history's more famous hunters.

I learned much of the history of Coronado and his time in New Mexico—and many tidbits about New Mexico in general—at the New Mexico History Museum, the Palace of the Governors, and many thanks to the staffers who were generous with their time there. I also visited the Robert Louis Stevenson House State Historical Monument in Monterey, California, where the staff was gracious and helped me to understand the man and his work in a way that just reading through his works or biographies never could. The Mel Fisher Maritime Museum in Key West told not only the story of Fisher but of treasure hunting, piracy, and settlement in the Florida Keys area, and I very much enjoyed the chance to go through it and to speak with the staff.

A shout-out to the librarians at the Needham, Massachusetts, library for helping me to figure out how to get books from other libraries, pointing me in several right directions, and having an excellent children's room to occupy my frenetic sons.

Cheers to the many newspaper reporters who have done quality quick-hit and long-form work on the Fenn subject, in particular Robert Nott of the **Santa Fe New Mexican,** Michael Roberts of

Denver's **Westword,** and numerous staffers from the **Albuquerque Journal.**

Fenn's chest has also inspired creators in film, and those projects informed my work, as well. Director Tomas Leach's **The Lure** (2016) is a solid primer on the world of Fenn, while Matt Maisano's enjoyable **Fenn's Searchers** (2017) gives one a feeling of personal connection to many of the "names" of the hunt. The story of **Masquerade** was ably told in the perfectly titled BBC documentary **The Man Behind the Masquerade** (2009), which gave me much of the background on that fascinating phenomenon.

Oh, and I rewatched **The Goonies** (Richard Donner, 1985), of course. It mostly held up! So that was nice.

A NOTE ABOUT THE AUTHOR

DANIEL BARBARISI is the author of **Dueling with Kings.** He is a senior editor at **The Athletic,** after years as a reporter at **The Wall Street Journal** and **The Providence Journal.** He lives with his wife and two sons outside Boston, Massachusetts.